Fractional Order Complex Systems: Advanced Control, Intelligent Estimation and Reinforcement Learning Image Processing Algorithms

Fractional Order Complex Systems: Advanced Control, Intelligent Estimation and Reinforcement Learning Image Processing Algorithms

Guest Editors

Jin-Xi Zhang
Xuefeng Zhang
Driss Boutat
Da-Yan Liu

Basel • Beijing • Wuhan • Barcelona • Belgrade • Novi Sad • Cluj • Manchester

Guest Editors

Jin-Xi Zhang
State Key Laboratory of
Synthetical Automation for
Process Industries
Northeastern University
Shenyang
China

Xuefeng Zhang
College of Sciences
Northeastern University
Shenyang
China

Driss Boutat
INSA Centre Val de Loire
Bourges
France

Da-Yan Liu
INSA Centre Val de Loire
Bourges
France

Editorial Office
MDPI AG
Grosspeteranlage 5
4052 Basel, Switzerland

This is a reprint of the Special Issue, published open access by the journal *Fractal and Fractional* (ISSN 2504-3110), freely accessible at: https://www.mdpi.com/journal/fractalfract/special_issues/fractional_image2.

For citation purposes, cite each article independently as indicated on the article page online and as indicated below:

Lastname, A.A.; Lastname, B.B. Article Title. *Journal Name* **Year**, *Volume Number*, Page Range.

ISBN 978-3-7258-3403-7 (Hbk)
ISBN 978-3-7258-3404-4 (PDF)
https://doi.org/10.3390/books978-3-7258-3404-4

© 2025 by the authors. Articles in this book are Open Access and distributed under the Creative Commons Attribution (CC BY) license. The book as a whole is distributed by MDPI under the terms and conditions of the Creative Commons Attribution-NonCommercial-NoDerivs (CC BY-NC-ND) license (https://creativecommons.org/licenses/by-nc-nd/4.0/).

Contents

About the Editors vii

Jin-Xi Zhang, Xuefeng Zhang, Driss Boutat and Da-Yan Liu
Fractional-Order Complex Systems: Advanced Control, Intelligent Estimation and Reinforcement Learning Image-Processing Algorithms
Reprinted from: *Fractal Fract.* **2025**, *9*, 67, https://doi.org/10.3390/fractalfract9020067 1

Longxin Zhang, Jin-Xi Zhang and Xuefeng Zhang
Generalized Criteria for Stability and Admissibility of Fractional Order Systems
Reprinted from: *Fractal Fract.* **2023**, *7*, 363, https://doi.org/10.3390/fractalfract7050363 6

Tingsheng Huang, Xinjian Wang, Da Xie, Chunyang Wang and Xuelian Liu
Depth Image Enhancement Algorithm Based on Fractional Differentiation
Reprinted from: *Fractal Fract.* **2023**, *7*, 394, https://doi.org/10.3390/fractalfract7050394 26

Ying Zou, Xinyao Li, Chao Deng and Xiaowen Wu
A Finite-Dimensional Control Scheme for Fractional-Order Systems under Denial-of-Service Attacks
Reprinted from: *Fractal Fract.* **2023**, *7*, 562, https://doi.org/10.3390/fractalfract7070562 47

Ying Di, Jin-Xi Zhang and Xuefeng Zhang
Alternate Admissibility LMI Criteria for Descriptor Fractional Order Systems with $0 < \alpha < 2$
Reprinted from: *Fractal Fract.* **2023**, *7*, 577, https://doi.org/10.3390/fractalfract7080577 61

Kai-Di Xu and Jin-Xi Zhang
Prescribed Performance Tracking Control of Lower-Triangular Systems with Unknown Fractional Powers
Reprinted from: *Fractal Fract.* **2023**, *7*, 594, https://doi.org/10.3390/fractalfract7080594 74

Runan Ma, Jian Chen, Chengxing Lv, Zhibo Yang and Xiangyu Hu
Backstepping Control with a Fractional-Order Command Filter and Disturbance Observer for Unmanned Surface Vehicles
Reprinted from: *Fractal Fract.* **2024**, *8*, 23, https://doi.org/10.3390/fractalfract8010023 90

Qi Yang, Yilu Wang, Lu Liu and Xiaomeng Zhang
Adaptive Fractional-Order Multi-Scale Optimization TV-L1 Optical Flow Algorithm
Reprinted from: *Fractal Fract.* **2024**, *8*, 179, https://doi.org/10.3390/fractalfract8040179 115

Rehan Akram, Jin Seong Hong, Seung Gu Kim, Haseeb Sultan, Muhammad Usman, Hafiz Ali Hamza Gondal, et al.
Crop and Weed Segmentation and Fractal Dimension Estimation Using Small Training Data in Heterogeneous Data Environment
Reprinted from: *Fractal Fract.* **2024**, *8*, 285, https://doi.org/10.3390/fractalfract8050285 132

Wei Ai, Xinlei Lin, Ying Luo and Xiaowei Wang
Fractional-Order Modeling and Identification for an SCR Denitrification Process
Reprinted from: *Fractal Fract.* **2024**, *8*, 524, https://doi.org/10.3390/fractalfract8090524 162

Dong Chan Lee, Min Su Jeong, Seong In Jeong, Seung Yong Jung and Kang Ryoung Park
Estimation of Fractal Dimension and Segmentation of Body Regions for Deep Learning-Based Gender Recognition
Reprinted from: *Fractal Fract.* **2024**, *8*, 551, https://doi.org/10.3390/fractalfract8100551 181

Liangliang Li, Xiaobin Zhao, Huayi Hou, Xueyu Zhang, Ming Lv, Zhenhong Jia and Hongbing Ma
Fractal Dimension-Based Multi-Focus Image Fusion via Coupled Neural P Systems in NSCT Domain
Reprinted from: *Fractal Fract.* **2024**, *8*, 554, https://doi.org/10.3390/fractalfract8100554 213

Ganbayar Batchuluun, Seung Gu Kim, Jung Soo Kim, Tahir Mahmood and Kang Ryoung Park
Artificial Intelligence-Based Segmentation and Classification of Plant Images with Missing Parts and Fractal Dimension Estimation
Reprinted from: *Fractal Fract.* **2024**, *8*, 633, https://doi.org/10.3390/fractalfract8110633 239

Seung Gu Kim, Jin Seong Hong, Jung Soo Kim and Kang Ryoung Park
Estimation of Fractal Dimension and Detection of Fake Finger-Vein Images for Finger-Vein Recognition
Reprinted from: *Fractal Fract.* **2024**, *8*, 646, https://doi.org/10.3390/fractalfract8110646 273

Bin Yan and Xiameng Li
RGB-D Camera and Fractal-Geometry-Based Maximum Diameter Estimation Method of Apples for Robot Intelligent Selective Graded Harvesting
Reprinted from: *Fractal Fract.* **2024**, *8*, 649, https://doi.org/10.3390/fractalfract8110649 305

About the Editors

Jin-Xi Zhang

Jin-Xi Zhang currently works as a Distinguished Associate Professor (First-level Associate Professor) and Doctoral Supervisor at the State Key Laboratory of Synthetical Automation for Process Industries, Northeastern University, China. He received a bachelor's degree in automation and a doctorate in control theory and control engineering from Northeastern University. He was a postdoctoral fellow at the University of Johannesburg. He was selected as one of the top 2% of scientists in the world in 2024. His main research directions include intelligent control, high-performance control, fault diagnosis, fault-tolerant control, nonlinear control, multi-agent, unmanned systems, and image processing.

Xuefeng Zhang

Xuefeng Zhang received a B.Sc. degree in Applied Mathematics, an M.S. degree in Control Theory and Control Engineering, and a Ph.D. in Control Theory and Control Engineering from Northeastern University, Shenyang, China. Currently, he is a long-term Full Professor at the College of Sciences, Northeastern University. He has published more than 200 journal and conference papers and three books. His research interests include fractional order control systems and singular systems. He is also an Associate Editor of *Information Sciences*, *IJCAS*, *JCIE* and *Fractal Fract*, and is a committee member of the Technical Committee on Fractional and Control of the Chinese Association of Automation. He is an expert in the *Science and Technology Review* of China Association for Science and Technology and a reviewer of *American Mathematical Review*.

Driss Boutat

Driss Boutat received a Ph.D. degree in differential geometry from the University of Claude Bernard, Lyon I, France, in 1993. Then, he obtained his aggregation in mathematics in 1996. He joined ENSIB, Bourges, France, in 1997, as the Head of the Department of Mathematics, where he earned the Accreditation to Supervise Research (HDR) in 2007. Since 2008, he has been a Full Professor with ENSIB, which developed into the INSA (French National Institute of Applied Sciences) Centre Val de Loire, Université d'Orléans, Bourges, in 2014. From 2011 to 2017, he was the Leader of the Control Team, PRISME Laboratory. Since then, he has been the Head of the Observer and Estimation Team, PRISME Laboratory. His research interests mainly focus on developing observer normal forms for nonlinear dynamical systems.

Da-Yan Liu

Da-Yan Liu received his Ph.D. degree in Applied Mathematics from the University of Lille 1 & INRIA Lille-Nord Europe in October 2011. Since then, he has held postdoctoral positions in Arts et M'etiers ParisTech, France, and at the King Abdullah University of Science and Technology (KAUST) in Saudi Arabia. Currently, he is an Associate Professor at INSA (French National Institute of Applied Sciences) Centre Val de Loire, where he belongs to the Control Team in PRISME Laboratory, and he earned the Accreditation to Supervise Research (HDR) in January 2022. His main research interests concern non-asymptotic estimation and identification for integer-order and fractional-order systems. He has published over 100 journal and conference papers. Currently, he is a member of the IFAC's Technical Committee on Linear Control Systems and the CAA's Technical Committee on Fractional Order Systems and Control. He serves as a Subject Editor for the *International Journal of Robust and Nonlinear Control* and as an Editorial Board Member for *Fractal and Fractional*, *AIMS Mathematics*, and *Intelligent Control and Systems Engineering*.

Editorial

Fractional-Order Complex Systems: Advanced Control, Intelligent Estimation and Reinforcement Learning Image-Processing Algorithms

Jin-Xi Zhang [1], Xuefeng Zhang [2,*], Driss Boutat [3] and Da-Yan Liu [3]

[1] State Key Laboratory of Synthetical Automation for Process Industries, Northeastern University, Shenyang 110819, China; zhangjx@mail.neu.edu.cn
[2] College of Sciences, Northeastern University, Shengyang 110819, China
[3] INSA Centre Val de Loire, Universite d'Orléans, PRISME EA 4229, 18022 Bourges, France; driss.boutat@insa-cvl.fr (D.B.); dayan.liu@insa-cvl.fr (D.-Y.L.)
* Correspondence: zhangxuefeng@mail.neu.edu.cn

In this Special Issue on "Applications of Fractional Operators in Image Processing and Stability of Control Systems", more than 20 high-quality papers have been published. An escalating body of research across various scientific and engineering disciplines has concentrated on dynamical systems, which are distinguished by the interplay between artificial intelligence theory and fractional differential equations. As a result, a multitude of computational fractional intelligent systems have emerged, each accompanied by a stability analysis and potential applications in image processing.

This current Special Issue builds upon and extends the work presented in the preceding edition, with the aim of compiling articles that reflect the most recent advancements in applied mathematics and advanced intelligent control engineering. The contributions encompass interdisciplinary topics such as control theory, fractional calculus, and their applications in image processing, in addition to practical implications within the realm of engineering science. This collection not only underscores the depth of research in these areas, but also signifies the broadening scope and theoretical underpinnings of fractional intelligent systems.

This Special Issue compiles cutting-edge research in applied mathematics and advanced intelligent control engineering, focusing on interdisciplinary topics such as control theory, fractional calculus, and image processing. The articles highlight the significant attention that fractional calculus has received, particularly its applications in control systems and image processing. Fractional-order systems extend classical integer-order models, providing a more accurate description of real-world physical phenomena. In image processing, critical techniques like noise suppression and image fusion in medical imaging are essential for clinical diagnosis and treatment. The increasing diversity of image acquisition models has further emphasized the importance of these techniques. Recent advancements have seen fractional operators play a pivotal role in image processing, serving as powerful tools for noise reduction and feature enhancement. Additionally, new fractional operating tools have been developed, enhancing the analysis and design of nonlinear control systems. Singular systems, characterized by singular differential equations, exhibit unique properties distinct from classical systems. Methodologies for fractional-order control systems, inspired by integer-order approaches, are gaining traction within the control community due to their enhanced capabilities. Overall, this Special Issue showcases the latest developments in fractional calculus and its transformative impact on multiple disciplines, setting the stage for future innovations in applied mathematics and engineering.

Received: 11 January 2025
Accepted: 20 January 2025
Published: 23 January 2025

Citation: Zhang, J.-X.; Zhang, X.; Boutat, D.; Liu, D.-Y. Fractional-Order Complex Systems: Advanced Control, Intelligent Estimation and Reinforcement Learning Image-Processing Algorithms. *Fractal Fract.* 2025, 9, 67. https://doi.org/10.3390/fractalfract9020067

Copyright: © 2025 by the authors. Licensee MDPI, Basel, Switzerland. This article is an open access article distributed under the terms and conditions of the Creative Commons Attribution (CC BY) license (https://creativecommons.org/licenses/by/4.0/).

Seventeen high-quality papers were accepted for publication in this Special Issue. The papers were written by different authors, showcasing the wide scope of the Special Issue. The published papers will be briefly summarized.

In the work of [1], a unified framework based on the linear matrix inequality region was proposed to analyze the stability and tolerability of fractional-order systems and singular fractional-order systems in the range of $0 < \alpha < 2$, and to solve the related stability analysis and controller design problems, making the analysis and design process simpler and more unified.

The study in [2] proposed a fractional differentiation-based depth image enhancement method, which solved the problems of blurring, aliasing, and other issues that were prone to occur during the processing of depth images. The paper enhanced the textural details and clarity of the images using fractional differential operations, effectively improving the quality of the depth images and providing a new and effective means for processing and analyzing depth images.

The study in [3] proposed a hierarchical security control framework for non-linear cyber-physical systems under denial-of-service attacks. Using fractional-order calculus theory and incorporating system state feedback and attack information, the method ensured system stability and security, effectively mitigating the disruptions and damage caused by DoS attacks. The framework allowed for the precise control and adjustment of system states, enhancing the system's resistance to interference and providing new insights and methodologies to ensure the security of cyber-physical systems.

In [4], a novel admissibility criteria was proposed for descriptor fractional-order systems (DFOSs) with the order of (0,2) without separating the order into (0,1) and [1,2). The methods included the use of alternate admissibility criteria based on non-strict and strict linear matrix inequalities, with a focus on reducing the decision variables. These criteria ensured the stability and admissibility of DFOSs, enriching the theoretical research and allowing for its wider application, particularly in handling systems with uncertain derivative matrices.

In [5], a performance control approach is proposed for lower-triangular systems with unknown fractional powers and uncertainties. This method uses barrier functions to limit tracking errors and remove previous restrictions, enhancing its applicability. The control law ensures accurate and fast tracking without the need for function approximation, parameter identification, or additional techniques. Overall, this paper contributed a robust and flexible solution to the tracking control problem for lower-triangular systems with unknown fractional powers and uncertainties.

The article in [6] introduced a backstepping control strategy for unmanned surface vehicle trajectory tracking, incorporating a fractional-order finite-time command filter to estimate the derivatives of intermediate controls and reduce chatter, as well as a fractional-order finite-time disturbance observer to approximate and compensate for model uncertainties and external disturbances. The proposed method ensured the global asymptotic stability of the closed-loop system.

The study in [7] proposed an adaptive fractional multi-scale optimization optical flow algorithm that balances global features and local textures to mitigate over-smoothing in total variation models. By constructing a fractional-order discrete L1-regularization total variational optical flow model and utilizing the ant lion algorithm for iterative calculation, the algorithm dynamically adjusted the fractional order to ensure convergence and efficiency. This enhanced the flexibility of optical flow estimations using weak gradient textures and significantly improved the multi-scale feature extraction rates.

The paper in [8] focused on crop and weed segmentation in heterogeneous data environments for smart farming. By minimizing pixel variability and using just one training sample, it achieved real-world applicability. It also integrated fractal dimension estimation for distributional characteristics, pioneering the use of heterogeneous data to address the reductions in accuracy following segmentation.

In [9], the authors present numerical simulations of anti-symmetric matrices in the stability criteria for fractional-order systems. They then studied the admissibility criteria for descriptor fractional-order systems with orders of (0,2), focusing on systems without boundary axis eigenvalues. A unified admissibility criterion using minimal linear matrix inequalities was also provided.

The authors in paper [10] proposed a T-S fuzzy modeling approach for fuzzy fractional-order, singular perturbation, and multi-agent systems of the orders (0,2). A fuzzy observer-based controller was designed to achieve consensus and decompose the error system into fuzzy singular fractional-order systems. Consensus conditions were derived using linear matrix inequalities without equality constraints, addressing issues of uncertainty and nonlinearity. The effectiveness of the approach was verified through an RLC circuit model and numerical example.

The study in [11] applied a fractional-order system to model an industrial process with inertia and a large time delay, extending the traditional integer-order model. An output-error identification algorithm was used to determine the fractional-order model's parameters. Compared to integer-order models, the fractional-order model provided a better fit for selective catalytic reduction denitrification process data. A PI controller was designed based on both models, and validation tests showed the fractional-order model's advantages in such industrial processes.

In [12], a rough body segmentation-based gender recognition network was proposed to address the challenges regarding the low recognition performance obtained in long-distance gender recognition using only IR cameras. The method emphasizes the silhouette of a person through a body segmentation network, integrating anthropometric loss, and uses an adaptive body attention module to effectively combine segmentation and classification. Fractal dimension estimation was introduced to analyze the complexity and irregularity of the body region, enhancing the framework's analytic capabilities.

The authors in paper [13] presented a novel approach to multi-focus image fusion by integrating fractal dimension and coupled neural P (CNP) systems within a nonsubsampled contourlet transform framework. Addressing the limitations of camera lenses and depth-of-field effects, this method used a local topology-based CNP model to merge low-frequency components and a spatial frequency and fractal dimension-based focus measure to merge high-frequency components. This multi-focus image-fusion method significantly improved image clarity throughout the entire scene.

The study in [14] addressed the limitations of limited camera viewing angles in image-based plant classification by introducing a method that incorporates both shallow segmentation and classification networks. The proposed shallow plant segmentation network used adversarial learning with a discriminator network, while the shallow plant classification network applied residual connections. Additionally, fractal dimension estimation was utilized to analyze the segmentation results, aiming to improve the overall classification performance.

The work in [15] addressed the emerging threat that generator adversarial networks (GANs) pose to finger-vein recognition systems by developing a new, densely updated, contrastive learning-based self-attention GAN to create elaborate fake finger-vein images for training spoof detectors. Additionally, an enhanced ConvNeXt-Small model with a large kernel attention module was proposed as a new spoof detector. To improve spoof detection performance, fractal dimension estimation was introduced to analyze the complexity and irregularity of class activation maps from real and fake finger-vein images, facilitating the generation of more realistic and sophisticated fake finger-vein images.

The authors of [16] proposed an maximum apple diameter estimation model for smart agriculture and precision agriculture using RGB-D camera fusion depth information. The model was developed by collecting and statistically analyzing the diameter of a Red Fuji apple, obtaining depth and two-dimensional size information of apple images using an Intel RealSense D435 RGB-D camera and LabelImg software, and exploring the relationship between these variables and the maximum apple diameter. Multiple regression analyses and nonlinear surface fitting were used to construct the model. The proposed model can provide a theoretical basis and technical support for selective apple-picking operations using intelligent robots based on apple size grading.

The paper in [17] examined the leader-following H_∞ consensus of fractional-order multi-agent systems (FOMASs) under conditions of input saturation using output feedback. The study provided sufficient conditions for a H_∞ consensus for FOMASs with α in the ranges (0,1) and [1,2). It used iterative linear matrix inequalities to solve the quadratic matrix inequalities and transformed the input saturation issue into optimal solutions of linear matrix inequalities to estimate stable regions. The approach avoided disassembling the entire multi-agent system and reduced conservatism.

Funding: This work was supported by the fundamental research funds for the central universities (N2224005-3) and national key research and development program topic (2020YFB1710003).

Acknowledgments: The Guest Editors of this Special Issue would like to thank the anonymous reviewers and the editorial office for their hard work during the review and publication process.

Conflicts of Interest: The authors declare no conflicts of interest.

References

1. Zhang, L.; Zhang, J.; Zhang, X. Generalized criteria for admissibility of singular fractional order systems. *Fractal Fract.* **2023**, *7*, 363. [CrossRef]
2. Huang, T.; Wang, X.; Xie, D.; Wang, C.; Liu, X. Depth image enhancement algorithm based on fractional differentiation. *Fractal Fract.* **2023**, *7*, 394. [CrossRef]
3. Zou, Y.; Li, X.; Deng, C.; Wu, X. A finite-dimensional control scheme for fractional-order systems under denial-of-service attacks. *Fractal Fract.* **2023**, *7*, 562. [CrossRef]
4. Di, Y.; Zhang, J.; Zhang, X. Alternate admissibility LMI criteria for descriptor fractional order systems with $0 < \alpha < 2$. *Fractal Fract.* **2023**, *7*, 577. [CrossRef]
5. Xu, K.; Zhang, J. Prescribed performance tracking control of lower-triangular systems with unknown fractional powers. *Fractal Fract.* **2023**, *7*, 594. [CrossRef]
6. Ma, R.; Chen, J.; Lv, C.; Yang, Z.; Hu, X. Backstepping control with a fractional-order command filter and disturbance observer for unmanned surface vehicles. *Fractal Fract.* **2024**, *8*, 23. [CrossRef]
7. Yang, Q.; Wang, Y.; Liu, L.; Zhang, X. Adaptive fractional-order multi-scale optimization TV-L1 optical flow algorithm. *Fractal Fract.* **2024**, *8*, 179. [CrossRef]
8. Akram, R.; Hong, J.; Kim, S.; Sultan, H.; Usman, M.; Gondal, H.; Tariq, M.; Ullah, N.; Park, K. Crop and weed segmentation and fractal dimension estimation using small training data in heterogeneous data environment. *Fractal Fract.* **2024**, *8*, 285. [CrossRef]
9. Wang, X.; Zhang, J.X. Novel admissibility criteria and multiple simulations for descriptor fractional order systems with minimal LMI variables. *Fractal Fract.* **2024**, *8*, 373. [CrossRef]
10. Wang, X.; Zhang, X.; Pedrycz, W.; Yang, S.H.; Boutat, D. Consensus of T-S fuzzy fractional-order, singular perturbation, multi-agent systems. *Fractal Fract.* **2024**, *8*, 523. [CrossRef]
11. Ai, W.; Lin, X.; Luo, Y.; Wang, X. Fractional-order modeling and identification for an SCR denitrification process. *Fractal Fract.* **2024**, *8*, 524. [CrossRef]
12. Lee, D.; Jeong, M.; Jeong, S.; Jung, S.; Park, K. Estimation of fractal dimension and segmentation of body regions for deep learning-based gender recognition. *Fractal Fract.* **2024**, *8*, 551. [CrossRef]
13. Li, L.; Zhao, X.; Hou, H.; Zhang, X.; Lv, M.; Jia, Z.; Ma, H. Fractal dimension-based multi-focus image fusion via coupled neural P systems in NSCT domain. *Fractal Fract.* **2024**, *8*, 554. [CrossRef]

14. Batchuluun, G.; Kim, S.; Kim, J.; Mahmood, T.; Park, K. Artificial intelligence-based segmentation and classification of plant images with missing parts and fractal dimension estimation. *Fractal Fract.* **2024**, *8*, 633. [CrossRef]
15. Kim, S.; Hong, J.; Kim, J.; Park, K. Estimation of fractal dimension and detection of fake finger-vein images for finger-vein recognition. *Fractal Fract.* **2024**, *8*, 646. [CrossRef]
16. Yan, B.; Li, X. RGB-D camera and fractal-geometry-based maximum diameter estimation method of apples for robot intelligent selective graded harvesting. *Fractal Fract.* **2024**, *8*, 649. [CrossRef]
17. Xing, H.S.; Boutat, D.; Wang, Q.G. Leader-following output feedback H_∞ consensus of fractional-order multi-agent systems with input saturation. *Fractal Fract.* **2024**, *8*, 667. [CrossRef]

Disclaimer/Publisher's Note: The statements, opinions and data contained in all publications are solely those of the individual author(s) and contributor(s) and not of MDPI and/or the editor(s). MDPI and/or the editor(s) disclaim responsibility for any injury to people or property resulting from any ideas, methods, instructions or products referred to in the content.

Article

Generalized Criteria for Admissibility of Singular Fractional Order Systems

Longxin Zhang [1], Jin-Xi Zhang [2,*] and Xuefeng Zhang [1,*]

[1] College of Sciences, Northeastern University, Shenyang 110819, China
[2] State Key Laboratory of Synthetical Automation for Process Industries, Northeastern University, Shenyang 110819, China
* Correspondence: zhangjx@mail.neu.edu.cn (J.-X.Z.); zhangxuefeng@mail.neu.edu.cn (X.Z.)

Abstract: Unified frameworks for fractional order systems with fractional order $0 < \alpha < 2$ are worth investigating. The aim of this paper is to provide a unified framework for stability and admissibility for fractional order systems and singular fractional order systems with $0 < \alpha < 2$, respectively. By virtue of the LMI region and GLMI region, five stability theorems are presented. Two admissibility theorems for singular fractional order systems are extended from Theorem 5, and, in particular, a strict LMI stability criterion involving the least real decision variables without equality constraint by isomorphic mapping and congruent transform. The equivalence between the admissibility Theorems 6 and 7 is derived. The proposed framework contains some other existing results in the case of $1 \leq \alpha < 2$ or $0 < \alpha < 1$. Compared with published unified frameworks, the proposed framework is truly unified and does not require additional conditional assignment. Finally, without loss of generality, a unified control law is designed to make the singular feedback system admissible based on the criterion in a strict LMI framework and demonstrated by two numerical examples.

Keywords: admissibility; generalized criteria; stability; singular fractional order systems

Citation: Zhang, L.; Zhang, J.; Zhang, X. Generalized Criteria for Stability and Admissibility of Fractional Order Systems. *Fractal Fract.* **2023**, *7*, 363. https://doi.org/10.3390/fractalfract7050363

Academic Editor: David Kubanek

Received: 5 April 2023
Revised: 25 April 2023
Accepted: 25 April 2023
Published: 28 April 2023

Copyright: © 2023 by the authors. Licensee MDPI, Basel, Switzerland. This article is an open access article distributed under the terms and conditions of the Creative Commons Attribution (CC BY) license (https://creativecommons.org/licenses/by/4.0/).

1. Introduction

In the development of fractional calculus theory [1] and computer technology, the study of fractional order systems (FOSs) has become an important research topic. Since fractional derivatives can be used to study the behavior of materials and systems with power-law, nonlocal, long-term memory, or fractal properties, FOSs described by fractional order differential equations have better modeling and analysis capabilities in describing complex systems [2,3] and nonlinear phenomena [4–6].

The stability analysis of FOSs is an important aspect of fractional order control theory. With further research, it has been found that the stability of fractional order systems is quite different from that of integer order systems. Therefore, new methods for analyzing stability need to be developed to accommodate the special properties of FOSs. Many basic concepts and results of traditional state-space systems have been successfully extended to FOSs. Matignon's fractional order stability theorem [7] proposed that the stability of fractional order linear time-invariant systems can be checked by the eigenvalues of the system matrix, while it is inconvenient to calculate all the eigenvalues of the matrix to control the system. In the 1990s, with the introduction of the interior point method for solving convex optimization problems [8–10], the LMI problem was well solved, and the LMI toolbox was also launched in MATLAB, which greatly promoted the application of LMI in the control field. Based on the importance of LMI in the control theory of integer order systems, many scholars aimed to apply LMI to the control theory of FOSs. Furthermore, many scholars began to explore more effective and LMI-based stability criteria [11–13]. The robust stability problem of FOSs with interval uncertainties was studied in [14,15], and an algorithm code in MATLAB was proposed.

The key point in dealing with LMIs is convexity. However, the stability domain of FOSs with fractional order $0 < \alpha < 1$ is nonconvex. Therefore, the classical stability conditions cannot be directly extended to FOSs. The stability in the case of $1 \leq \alpha < 2$ is studied in [12] and a criterion in the form of LMI is given. Another LMI-based criterion in the case of $1 \leq \alpha < 2$ is given in [13]. These two criteria are consistent with the results of pole placement in convex subregions of integer order systems in the left complex plane given in [16,17]. In addition, Ref. [13] also gives the stability criteria of FOSs with multiple differential orders in the interval of $(0,1)$. However, these criteria are given in the form of matrix inequalities including the terms of $A^{\frac{1}{\alpha}}P$, $(-(-A))^{\frac{1}{2-\alpha}}P$ and $e^{j(1-\alpha)\frac{\pi}{2}}AP$, which make it difficult to solve by using the LMI toolbox when designing the controller for the associated closed-loop system, because of the existing powers of $\frac{1}{\alpha}$, $\frac{1}{2-\alpha}$ at $A + BK$ and complex variable in $e^{j(1-\alpha)\frac{\pi}{2}}(A + BK)P$. Another criterion for the stability in the case of $0 < \alpha < 1$ is studied in [15] and the result is in the form of LMI, which requires additional conditions when designing the controller. Ref. [18] first proposed the conditions guaranteeing the admissibility of singular fractional order systems (SFOSs) when the fractional order α belongs to the interval $(0,2)$. The unified LMI criterion of $0 < \alpha < 2$ is first proposed in [19]. However, the criterion is unified only in the form of mathematical expression, that is, it needs to add a conditional assignment statement associated with the fractional order α when using the LMI toolbox to solve the problem.

Corresponding to the fact that FOSs have attracted extensive attention in the control community, SFOSs have also become an important research object. Singular systems [20] have a more general form than normal systems. Singular systems are described by both differential and algebraic equations, so they are also called differential-algebraic systems, generalized systems, etc. Singular systems, due to the consideration of admissibility, including regularity, impulse-freeness and stability, are more complex to study than normal systems. In [21], the robust stabilization of SFOSs is studied in two cases of $1 \leq \alpha < 2$ and $0 < \alpha < 1$.

Ref. [22] extended the concept of singular systems from integer order to fractional order and proposed a criterion for the admissibility of SFOSs on the basis of the stability results given in [15]. However, this result requires additional conditions when designing controllers. Another criterion for the admissibility in the case of $0 < \alpha < 1$ is proposed in [23], which is in the form of complex LMI. Ref. [24] gave three different criteria for the admissibility and stabilization of SFOSs when the differential order is in the interval $0 < \alpha < 1$, which promoted the research [25,26] on related problems of SFOSs to some extent. The admissibility of SFOSs is still a hot topic in the field of control. Refs. [27–29] give LMI-based criteria with complex matrices in the case of $0 < \alpha < 1$. The criteria for the admissibility with differential order $1 \leq \alpha < 2$ are given in [27], and the scheme for designing the controller is given in the form of bilinear matrix inequality. Based on the result in [19], the necessary and sufficient condition for admissibility and quadratic admissibility of SFOSs with fractional order $0 < \alpha < 2$ are given in [26,30], respectively.

At present, the stability of FOSs is still a hot topic [31–35]. Although there have been a lot of papers in the field of stability for FOSs, most of the existing results focus on the stability analysis of FOSs separately when the fractional order α belongs to the interval $[1,2)$ and $(0,1)$, and thus can only give different forms of criteria. This means other related studies based on the premise of stability can only be divided into two cases, which makes the research results relatively fragmented. The stability and admissibility problems of FOSs with $0 < \alpha < 2$ have been studied in [26,30], but their results are still in the form of a piece-based function, that is, it is still divided into two criteria rather than a unified form. In view of the above observation, this paper is concerned with the stability and admissibility in terms of fractional order $0 < \alpha < 2$ and provides several unified frameworks, respectively, for stability and admissibility regardless of the fractional order interval. Here is the contribution of our work:

- An LMI region and a GLMI region are appiled to study the stability region of FOSs in the case of $0 < \alpha < 2$, leading to a unified criterion for the stability of FOSs, which

can only be discussed and studied separately in most existing results because of the different convexity in the case of $0 < \alpha < 1$ and $1 \leq \alpha < 2$. Furthermore, since this method is applicable to larger fractional intervals, it is more advantageous than the existing results when investigating systems with varying fractional orders.
- Based on isomorphic mapping and congruent transform to deal with the unified criteria for stability with complex decision variables, the new approach to stability analysis of FOSs with $0 < \alpha < 2$ is derived, which contains the least decision variables and does not involve a complex matrix. This avoids the problem that the existing results need to solve the complex variables directly, which is difficult to solve by using the LMI toolbox.
- The new way to analyze the admissibility for FOSs with $0 < \alpha < 2$ eliminates the equality constraints, avoids the non-strict LMIs and has the form of strict LMIs, so it offers an easier method to solve the decision variables than the existing literature. In addition, this method only involves a few real decision variables, so it can be directly used to design the controller without additional conditions and has no conservatism.

Notation 1. *In the paper, $A < 0$ and $A \leq 0$ denote that the matrix A is negative definite and negative semi-definite, respectively. We denote by A^T the transpose of matrix A, by A^* the transpose conjugate of A and by $\mathcal{H}\{A\}$ the Hermitian expression $A + A^*$. We denote by $\Re(A)$ the real part of A and by $\Im(A)$ the imaginary of A. For $0 < \alpha < 2$, $a = \sin(\alpha\frac{\pi}{2})$ and $b = \cos(\alpha\frac{\pi}{2})$. We denote $\begin{bmatrix} a & b \\ -b & a \end{bmatrix}$ by Θ. I_t represents the t-dimension identity matrix. The zero matrix with appropriate dimensions is represented by 0. The symbol $*$ is used to represent the matrices irrelevant in the later analysis. $\lceil \cdot \rceil$ is the ceiling function to increase $\cdot$ to the next highest whole number and $\lfloor \cdot \rfloor$ is the floor function to reduce $\cdot$ to the next nearest whole number. Given two arbitrary matrices $F = (f_{ij})_{m \times n}$ and $G = (g_{ij})_{t \times r}$, the Kronecker product is defined as $F \otimes G = (f_{ij}G)$.*

2. Problem Statement and Preliminaries

In this section, the purpose of this paper is given and some definitions and lemmas are recalled as mathmatical preliminaries.

2.1. System Description

Consider a singular fractional electrical circuit with resistors, supercapacitances, superinductors and voltage sources. There are the following relationships:

$$i_C(t) = CD^\alpha u_C(t),$$

$$u_L(t) = LD^\alpha i_L(t),$$

where α is the fractional order. C and L are the capacity and the inductance, respectively. $i_C(t)$ and $i_L(t)$ are in turn the currents in a supercondensator and a superinductor. $u_C(t)$ and $u_L(t)$ are the voltage on the supercondensator and the superinductor. Due to the above physical expression, a singular fractional electrical circuit is essentially an SFOS described by

$$ED^\alpha x(t) = Ax(t) + Bu(t), \tag{1}$$

where $A \in \mathbb{R}^{n \times n}$, $B \in \mathbb{R}^{n \times l}$, $E \in \mathbb{R}^{n \times n}$ is supposed to satisfy $0 < \text{rank}(E) = m < n$. $x(t)$ and $u(t)$ are n-dimensions system state and l-dimensions control input. The symbol $D^\alpha x(t)$ is used for the Caputo fractional order derivative of $x(t)$, which is defined in [1]. When $u(t) = 0$, system (1) becomes an unforced SFOS described by

$$ED^\alpha x(t) = Ax(t). \tag{2}$$

We can always find two matrices L, R such that

$$LER = \begin{bmatrix} I_m & 0 \\ 0 & 0 \end{bmatrix}, \quad LAR = \begin{bmatrix} A_1 & A_2 \\ A_3 & A_4 \end{bmatrix}.$$

System (2) is regular if $\det(s^\alpha E - A) \neq 0$ and is impulse-free if A_4 is invertible. Then we denote by $\mathrm{spec}(E, A) = \mathrm{spec}(I_m, A_1 - A_2 A_4^{-1} A_3)$ the spectrum of matrix $A_1 - A_2 A_4^{-1} A_3$, where A_1 is a square matrix in m-dimensions. If $E = I$, system (2) comes down to a normal FOS with the following form:

$$D^\alpha x(t) = Ax(t), \tag{3}$$

and then we abbreviate $\mathrm{spec}(I, A)$ to $\mathrm{spec}(A)$ for ease of expression. The stability of (3) and the admissibility of system (2) both with the fractional order $0 < \alpha < 2$ are studied in the sequel. For the stability of system (3), Matignon's fractional order stability theorem presented in [7] states that system (3) with $0 < \alpha < 2$ is stable iff

$$|\arg(\mathrm{spec}(A))| > \alpha \frac{\pi}{2}. \tag{4}$$

However, it is inconvenient to control the system by computing all eigenvalues of the matrix A, so a more suitable unified framework needs to be found. As shown in Figure 1, from the criterion (4), the stability domain for the system (3) is $D_1 \cap D_2$ when $1 \leq \alpha < 2$ ($\varphi_1 = -\varphi_2 = (\alpha - 1)\frac{\pi}{2}$) and $D_1 \cup D_2$ when $0 < \alpha < 1$ ($\varphi_1 = -\varphi_2 = (1 - \alpha)\frac{\pi}{2}$). In addition, system (2) is called admissible if it is regular, impulse-free and stable. Thus, this paper aims to provide a unified framework for stability and admissibility.

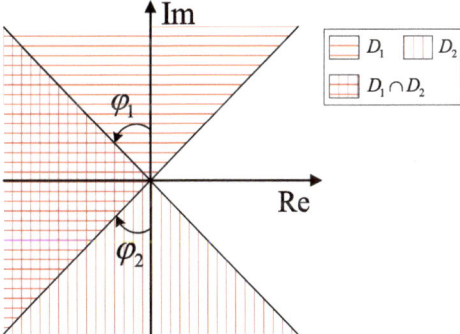

Figure 1. Stability domain of FOSs with the fractional order $0 < \alpha < 2$.

2.2. Definitions and Lemmas

In this subsection, we introduced the definitions of the LMI region, generalized LMI region in the complex plane and their associated lemmas. Note that the stability domain of the FOS (3) is a subregion of the complex plane according to the criterion (4), so these definitions and lemmas are useful tools for the analysis of stability and admissibility of FOSs in this paper.

Definition 1 ([16]). *A convex LMI region is a convex subset D_R of the complex plane defined by*

$$D = \{s \in \mathbb{C} : f_{D_R}(s) < 0\}, \tag{5}$$

where $f_{D_R}(s) = L + sM + \bar{s}M^T$, L is a symmetric matrix and $L \in \mathbb{R}^{q \times q}$, $M \in \mathbb{R}^{q \times q}$.

Lemma 1 ([16]). *All the eigenvalues of A are in the region described by (5) iff there exists $P \in \mathbb{R}^{n \times n} > 0$ such that $L \otimes P + M \otimes (AP) + M^T \otimes (PA^T) < 0$.*

It can be seen that the LMI region defined in Definition 1 is limited to a convex subregion in the complex plane, so it can only be used to study the stability for FOSs with $1 \leq \alpha < 2$. To solve the stability problem in the case of $0 < \alpha < 1$, the following definition is introduced, which generalizes the region in Definition 1 to regions including but not limited to convexity.

Definition 2 ([36]). *Let $\mathcal{M}$ be a set of n_M Hermitian matrices M_k, $k = 1, 2, \ldots, n_M$, $M_k \in \mathbb{C}^{2d \times 2d}$. A generalized LMI region D_U of degree d is defined by*

$$D_U = \{s \in \mathbb{C} : \exists \eta = \begin{bmatrix} \eta_1 & \eta_2 & \cdots & \eta_{n_M} \end{bmatrix}^T, \eta_k \in \mathbb{R}^{+*}, f_{D_U} < 0\},$$

where $f_{D_U} = \sum_{k=1}^{n_M} f_{D_k}$, $f_{D_k} = \eta_k \begin{bmatrix} I_d & sI_d \end{bmatrix} M_k \begin{bmatrix} I_d & \bar{s}I_d \end{bmatrix}^T$. When $d = 2$, f_{D_U} is an available description deduced from a scalar inequality. In addition, D_U is the union of n_M subregions D_k, $k = 1, 2, \ldots, n_M$.

Lemma 2 ([36]). *Let D_U be a generalized LMI region described in Definition 2. All eigenvalues of the matrix $A \in \mathbb{C}^{n \times n}$ are in the region D_U iff there exists a set of Hermitian positive definite matrices $P_k \in \mathbb{C}^{n \times n}$, $k = 1, 2, \ldots, n_M$ such that*

$$\begin{bmatrix} I_{dn} & I_d \otimes A \end{bmatrix} \left(\sum_{k=1}^{n_M} M_k \otimes P_k \right) \begin{bmatrix} I_{dn} & I_d \otimes A \end{bmatrix}^* < 0.$$

An LMI in complex variables can be converted to an LMI of larger dimension in real variables through an equivalence. Before giving the framework, it remains to give the following lemma to solve the solution problem caused by complex linear matrix inequalities.

Lemma 3 ([37,38]). *Given $X \in \mathbb{R}^{n \times n}$ and $Y \in \mathbb{R}^{n \times n}$,*

$$X + jY > 0,$$

iff

$$\begin{bmatrix} X & -Y \\ Y & X \end{bmatrix} > 0,$$

or

$$\begin{bmatrix} X & Y \\ -Y & X \end{bmatrix} > 0.$$

Proof. First, we aim to demonstrate the equivalence of $X + jY > 0$ and $X - jY > 0$. By the definition of a Hermitian positive definite matrix, $X + jY > 0$ is equivalent to $z^*(X + jY)z > 0$ for all non-zero vectors $z \in \mathbb{C}^n$. Since z is arbitrary, we also have $\bar{z}^*(X + jY)\bar{z} > 0$. By the property that the conjugate of a positive real number is itself, it follows that $\overline{\bar{z}^*(X + jY)\bar{z}} > 0$, which implies $z^*(X - jY)z > 0$ for all non-zero vectors $z \in \mathbb{C}^n$, and hence $X - jY > 0$. Similarly, it can be shown that $X - jY > 0$ implies $X + jY > 0$. Thus, we have

$$\begin{bmatrix} X - jY & 0 \\ 0 & X + jY \end{bmatrix} > 0. \tag{6}$$

Pre- and post- multiplying (6) by

$$\begin{bmatrix} 1 & 1 \\ j & -j \end{bmatrix} \otimes \left(\frac{I_n}{\sqrt{2}} \right),$$

and its conjugate transpose, respectively, from the congruence transformation property, (6) turns to

$$\begin{bmatrix} X & -Y \\ Y & X \end{bmatrix} > 0. \tag{7}$$

Using the Schur complement on (6), the following inequality

$$\begin{bmatrix} X & Y \\ -Y & X \end{bmatrix} > 0,$$

is derived. And vice versa, (6) can be derived from (7) in the same way. This completes the proof. □

3. Main Results

The unified criteria for stability and admissibility of FOSs are sequentially introduced in this section.

3.1. Stability of FOSs

This subsection provides five criteria for the stability of FOSs with $0 < \alpha < 2$ in a unified framework.

Theorem 1. *System (3) with $0 < \alpha < 2$ is stable iff there exist $X_1, X_2 \in \mathbb{C}^{n \times n}$ satisfying $X_1 > 0$, $X_2 > 0$ and*

$$\mathcal{H}\{(a+jb)AX_1 + \lceil 1-\alpha \rceil (a-jb)AX_2\} < 0. \tag{8}$$

Proof. Note that the convexity of the stability domain of $0 < \alpha < 2$ changes with different value ranges of α. Therefore, it is appropriate to discuss two cases: $1 \leq \alpha < 2$ (its stability region is convex) and $0 < \alpha < 1$ (whose stability region is nonconvex).

Case $1 \leq \alpha < 2$: In this case, the stable region is $D_1 \cap D_2$, shown in Figure 1. Note that the stability region is an intersection of D_1 and D_2, where

$$D_1 = \{s \in \mathbb{C} : f_{D_1} < 0\},$$

$$D_2 = \{s \in \mathbb{C} : f_{D_2} < 0\},$$

where f_{D_1}, f_{D_2} are defined in Definition 2, $n_M = 1$ both in f_{D_1} and f_{D_2}, and the matrix M_1, M_2 in f_{D_1}, f_{D_2} in turn are

$$\begin{bmatrix} 0 & a+jb \\ a-jb & 0 \end{bmatrix}, \begin{bmatrix} 0 & a-jb \\ a+jb & 0 \end{bmatrix}. \tag{9}$$

As for some $s \in \text{spec}(A)$, $\bar{s} \in \text{spec}(A)$, and note that D_1 and D_2 are symmetric with respect to the real axis, either one of f_{D_1} and f_{D_2} is equivalent to the stability region of A. From Lemma 2, all eigenvalues of the matrix A are in the region D_1 iff there exists a Hermitian positive definite matrix X_1 satisfying

$$(a+jb)AX_1 + (a-jb)X_1A^T < 0,$$

which is identical to (8) with $\lceil 1-\alpha \rceil = 0$. This completes the proof for the case of $1 \leq \alpha < 2$.

Case $0 < \alpha < 1$: In this case, the stability region becomes $D_1 \cup D_2$, where D_1 and D_2 are defined in Definition 2 with M_1, M_2 in f_{D_1}, f_{D_2} defined by (9). From Lemma 2, all eigenvalues of the matrix A are in the region $D_U = D_1 \cup D_2$ iff there exist two Hermitian positive definite matrices X_1, X_2 satisfying

$$(a+jb)AX_1 + (a-jb)X_1A^T + (a-jb)AX_2 + (a+jb)X_2A^T < 0, \tag{10}$$

which is identical to (8) with $\lceil 1-\alpha \rceil = 1$. This completes the proof for the case of $0 < \alpha < 1$. Combining the above two cases, this completes the proof. □

Theorem 2. *System (3) with $0 < \alpha < 2$ is stable iff there exist matrices $X_1, X_2 \in \mathbb{C}^{n \times n}$ satisfying $X_1 > 0, X_2 > 0$ and*

$$\mathcal{H}\{\Theta \otimes (AX_1) + \lceil 1 - \alpha \rceil (\Theta^T \otimes (AX_2))\} < 0. \tag{11}$$

Proof. Along the same lines as in the proof of Theorem 1 with M_1 defined as

$$\begin{bmatrix} 0 & \Theta \\ \Theta^T & 0 \end{bmatrix},$$

in the case of $1 \le \alpha < 2$ and

$$M_1 = \begin{bmatrix} 0 & \Theta \\ \Theta^T & 0 \end{bmatrix}, \quad M_2 = \begin{bmatrix} 0 & \Theta^T \\ \Theta & 0 \end{bmatrix},$$

in the case of $0 < \alpha < 1$. Now it only remains to show that the region D_1 described by f_{D_1} and D_2 described by f_{D_2} is identical to the region D_1, D_2 shown in Figure 1, with M_k, $k = 1, 2$ in f_{D_1}, f_{D_2} defined as above. Note that the equation $f_{D_1} < 0$ with M_1 is

$$\begin{bmatrix} 2a\Re(s) & 2b\Im(s) \\ -2b\Im(s) & 2a\Re(s) \end{bmatrix} < 0. \tag{12}$$

Then the following region can be equivalently derived by Lemma 3

$$\{s \in \mathbb{C} : a\Re(s) + jb\Im(s) < 0\}. \tag{13}$$

Clearly the region described by expression (12) is the region D_1. Similarly, the region characterized by $f_{D_{U_2}} < 0$ can be equivalently rewritten as

$$\{s \in \mathbb{C} : a\Re(s) - jb\Im(s) < 0\}, \tag{14}$$

which is identical to the region D_2. This completes the proof. □

The two LMI-based criteria stated in Theorems 1 and 2 involve complex variables that are untoward when solved with the LMI toolbox. In order to avoid using complex matrices, the following theorems are presented.

Theorem 3. *System (3) with $0 < \alpha < 2$ is stable iff there exist matrices $X_1, X_2, Y_1, Y_2 \in \mathbb{R}^{n \times n}$ satisfying*

$$\begin{bmatrix} X_1 & Y_1 \\ -Y_1 & X_1 \end{bmatrix} > 0, \quad \begin{bmatrix} X_2 & Y_2 \\ -Y_2 & X_2 \end{bmatrix} > 0, \tag{15}$$

$$\mathcal{H}\{(\Theta \otimes A) \begin{bmatrix} X_1 & Y_1 \\ -Y_1 & X_1 \end{bmatrix} + \lceil 1 - \alpha \rceil (\Theta^T \otimes A) \begin{bmatrix} X_2 & Y_2 \\ -Y_2 & X_2 \end{bmatrix}\} < 0. \tag{16}$$

Proof. We divide the discussion of α values in the interval $0 < \alpha < 2$ into two cases: $1 \le \alpha < 2$ and $0 < \alpha < 1$.

Case $1 \le \alpha < 2$: Following the proof of Theorem 1, the stability domain can be described by $f_{D_{U_1}}$ with

$$M_1 = \begin{bmatrix} 0 & a + jb \\ a - jb & 0 \end{bmatrix}.$$

From (15), we obtain $P := X + jY > 0$. It follows from Lemma 2 that system (3) is stable iff there exists a feasible solution $P = X + jY \in \mathbb{C}^{n \times n}$ such that (15) and

$$(a + jb) \otimes (A(X + jY)) + (a - jb) \otimes ((X - jY)A^T) < 0. \tag{17}$$

From Lemma 3, the inequality (17) is equivalent to

$$\begin{bmatrix} aAX + aXA^T - bAY + bYA^T & aAY + bAX + aXA^T - bXA^T \\ -(aAY + bAX + aXA^T - bXA^T) & aAX + aXA^T - bAY + bYA^T \end{bmatrix} < 0, \quad (18)$$

which can be arranged as

$$\mathcal{H}\left\{(\Theta \otimes A)\begin{bmatrix} X & Y \\ -Y & X \end{bmatrix}\right\} < 0. \quad (19)$$

Note that the inequality (19) is identical to (16) when $1 \leq \alpha < 2$.
Case $0 < \alpha < 1$: From (15) and Lemma 3, we obtain

$$P_1 := X_1 + jY_1 > 0, \quad P_2 := X_2 + jY_2 > 0. \quad (20)$$

Following the proof of Theorem 1, substituting (20) into (10) and merging the real and imaginary part terms separately, we obtain (10) is identical to

$$\mathcal{H}\{aAX_1 - bAY_1 + aAX_2 + bAY_2 + j(aAY_1 + bAX_1 + aAY_2 - bAX_2)\} < 0. \quad (21)$$

Using Lemma 3 on (21), it is derived that

$$\mathcal{H}\left\{\begin{bmatrix} aAX_1 - bAY_1 + aAX_2 + bAY_2 & aAY_1 + bAX_1 + aAY_2 - bAX_2 \\ -aAY_1 - bAX_1 - aAY_2 + bAX_2 & aAX_1 - bAY_1 + aAX_2 + bAY_2 \end{bmatrix}\right\} < 0,$$

which can be rewritten as

$$\mathcal{H}\left\{(\Theta \otimes A)\begin{bmatrix} X_1 & Y_1 \\ -Y_1 & X_1 \end{bmatrix} + (\Theta^T \otimes A)\begin{bmatrix} X_2 & Y_2 \\ -Y_2 & X_2 \end{bmatrix}\right\} < 0. \quad (22)$$

Both of these cases cover all situations where $0 < \alpha < 2$. This completes the proof. □

It is noted that the criterion in Theorem 3 requires additional conditions when it is used to design a controller, which is conservative. Therefore, by reducing the matrix variables, the following theorems are presented.

Theorem 4. *System (3) with $0 < \alpha < 2$ is stable iff there exist $X, Y \in \mathbb{R}^{n \times n}$ satisfying*

$$\begin{bmatrix} X & Y \\ -Y & X \end{bmatrix} > 0, \quad (23)$$

$$\mathcal{H}\left\{(\Theta \otimes A)\begin{bmatrix} X & Y \\ -Y & X \end{bmatrix} + \lceil 1 - \alpha \rceil (\Theta^T \otimes A)\begin{bmatrix} X & -Y \\ Y & X \end{bmatrix}\right\} < 0. \quad (24)$$

Proof. It only remains to prove that the criterion in Theorem 4 is equivalent to the one in Theorem 3.

(Necessity). Pre- and post- multiplying (16) by $\begin{bmatrix} 0 & I \\ I & 0 \end{bmatrix}$ and using congruent transformation, we obtain

$$\mathcal{H}\left\{(\Theta^T \otimes A)\begin{bmatrix} X_1 & -Y_1 \\ Y_1 & X_1 \end{bmatrix} + \lceil 1 - \alpha \rceil (\Theta \otimes A)\begin{bmatrix} X_2 & -Y_2 \\ Y_2 & X_2 \end{bmatrix}\right\} < 0. \quad (25)$$

Summing Equations (16) and (25) yields

$$\mathcal{H}\left\{(\Theta \otimes A)\begin{bmatrix} X_1 + X_2 & Y_1 - Y_2 \\ Y_2 - Y_1 & X_1 + X_2 \end{bmatrix} + \lceil 1 - \alpha \rceil (\Theta^T \otimes A)\begin{bmatrix} X_1 + X_2 & Y_2 - Y_1 \\ Y_1 - Y_2 & X_1 + X_2 \end{bmatrix}\right\} < 0. \quad (26)$$

Let $X = X_1 + X_2$ and $Y = Y_1 - Y_2$; Equation (26) becomes Equation (24). From Lemma 3, Equation (15) is equivalent to

$$\begin{bmatrix} X_1 & Y_1 \\ -Y_1 & X_1 \end{bmatrix} > 0, \begin{bmatrix} X_2 & -Y_2 \\ Y_2 & X_2 \end{bmatrix} > 0.$$

Equation (23) is derived by summing

$$\begin{bmatrix} X_1 & Y_1 \\ -Y_1 & X_1 \end{bmatrix}, \begin{bmatrix} X_2 & -Y_2 \\ Y_2 & X_2 \end{bmatrix}.$$

(Sufficiency). Suppose there exist X, Y satisfying (23) and (24). Letting $X_1 = X_2 = \frac{1}{2}X$, $Y_1 = Y_2 = \frac{1}{2}Y$, it is easy to obtain (15) and

$$\mathcal{H}\{(\Theta^T \otimes A)\begin{bmatrix} 2X_1 & -2Y_1 \\ 2Y_1 & 2X_1 \end{bmatrix} + \lceil 1-\alpha \rceil (\Theta \otimes A)\begin{bmatrix} 2X_2 & 2Y_2 \\ -2Y_2 & 2X_2 \end{bmatrix}\} < 0,$$

which is equivalent to Equation (16). This completes the proof. □

It is noted that the above unified form criteria are useful tools for testing stability, but when designing and solving the controller gain using them, additional conditions are required, which is conservative to a certain extent. Therefore, the following theorem for stability is presented to reduce the conservatism in controller design.

Theorem 5. *System (3) with $0 < \alpha < 2$ is stable iff there exist matrices $X, Y \in \mathbb{R}^{n \times n}$ satisfying*

$$\begin{bmatrix} X & Y \\ \lfloor \alpha - 1 \rfloor Y & X \end{bmatrix} > 0, \tag{27}$$

$$\mathcal{H}\{(\Theta \otimes A)\begin{bmatrix} X & Y \\ \lfloor \alpha - 1 \rfloor Y & X \end{bmatrix} + \lceil 1-\alpha \rceil (\Theta^T \otimes A)\begin{bmatrix} X & \lfloor \alpha - 1 \rfloor Y \\ Y & X \end{bmatrix}\} < 0. \tag{28}$$

Proof. Similar to the proof of Theorems 1 and 3, the proof also proceeds by two cases.

Case $0 < \alpha < 1$: In this case, Equations (27) and (28) become Equations (23) and (24) in Theorem 4, respectively.

Case $1 \leq \alpha < 2$: As presented in [16], the stability domain is an LMI region that can be characterised by

$$\{s \in \mathbb{C} : s\Theta + s^*\Theta^T < 0\}. \tag{29}$$

From Lemma 2, it can be derived that system (3) is stable iff there exists $X \in \mathbb{R}^{n \times n}$ satisfying

$$\Theta \otimes (AX) + \Theta^T \otimes (XA^T) < 0,$$

which is obviously equivalent to (28) with $1 \leq \alpha < 2$.

This completes the proof. □

Clearly the criterion provided in Theorem 5 is in the form of real LMIs, which is suitable to be solved using the LMI toolbox in MATLAB.

3.2. Admissibility of SFOSs

A similar unified approach can be used to construct unified criteria for the admissibility of SFOSs in the following theorems. Since the criterion in Theorem 5 is most suitable for designing controllers for normal FOSs in the proposed framework, only the result in Theorem 5 is extended to admissibility and stabilization for SFOSs in this subsection.

Theorem 6. *System (2) with $0 < \alpha < 2$ is admissible iff there exist matrices $X, Y \in \mathbb{R}^{n \times n}$ and $Q \in \mathbb{R}^{(n-m) \times n}$ satisfying (28) and*

$$\begin{bmatrix} EX & EY \\ \lfloor \alpha - 1 \rfloor EY & EX \end{bmatrix} = \begin{bmatrix} X^T E^T & \lfloor \alpha - 1 \rfloor Y^T E^T \\ Y^T E^T & X^T E^T \end{bmatrix} \geq 0, \quad (30)$$

Proof. (Sufficiency). For system (2), choose two invertible matrices L, R such that

$$LER = \begin{bmatrix} I_m & 0 \\ 0 & 0 \end{bmatrix}, \quad LAR = \begin{bmatrix} A_1 & A_2 \\ A_3 & A_4 \end{bmatrix}. \quad (31)$$

Let

$$R^{-1} X L^T = \begin{bmatrix} X_{11} & X_{12} \\ X_{13} & X_{14} \end{bmatrix}, \quad R^{-1} Y L^T = \begin{bmatrix} Y_{11} & Y_{12} \\ Y_{13} & Y_{14} \end{bmatrix}. \quad (32)$$

Considering (32), pre- and post-multiplying (28), (30), respectively, by

$$\begin{bmatrix} L & 0 \\ 0 & L \end{bmatrix},$$

and its transpose, using contract transformation gives that the following two equations hold:

$$\mathcal{H}\{(\Theta \otimes \begin{bmatrix} A_1 & A_2 \\ A_3 & A_4 \end{bmatrix})(\begin{bmatrix} R^{-1} & 0 \\ 0 & R^{-1} \end{bmatrix}\begin{bmatrix} X & Y \\ \lfloor \alpha - 1 \rfloor Y & X \end{bmatrix}\begin{bmatrix} L^T & 0 \\ 0 & L^T \end{bmatrix})$$
$$+ \lceil 1 - \alpha \rceil (\Theta^T \otimes \begin{bmatrix} A_1 & A_2 \\ A_3 & A_4 \end{bmatrix})(\begin{bmatrix} R & 0 \\ 0 & R \end{bmatrix}^{-1}\begin{bmatrix} X & \lfloor \alpha - 1 \rfloor Y \\ Y & X \end{bmatrix}\begin{bmatrix} L^T & 0 \\ 0 & L^T \end{bmatrix})\} < 0, \quad (33)$$

$$\begin{bmatrix} X_{11} & X_{12} & Y_{11} & Y_{12} \\ 0 & 0 & 0 & 0 \\ \lfloor \alpha - 1 \rfloor Y_{11} & \lfloor \alpha - 1 \rfloor Y_{12} & X_{11} & X_{12} \\ 0 & 0 & 0 & 0 \end{bmatrix} = \begin{bmatrix} X_{11}^T & 0 & \lfloor \alpha - 1 \rfloor Y_{11}^T & 0 \\ X_{12}^T & 0 & \lfloor \alpha - 1 \rfloor Y_{12}^T & 0 \\ Y_{11}^T & 0 & X_{11}^T & 0 \\ Y_{12}^T & 0 & X_{12}^T & 0 \end{bmatrix} \geq 0. \quad (34)$$

Letting

$$V = \begin{bmatrix} I & -A_2 A_4^{-1} & 0 & 0 \\ 0 & I & 0 & 0 \\ 0 & 0 & I & -A_2 A_4^{-1} \\ 0 & 0 & 0 & I \end{bmatrix}, \quad (35)$$

considering (32) and the constraints among the relevant variables in (34), pre- and post-multiplying (33) by V and V^T and using contract transformation, we have

$$\mathcal{H}\{\begin{bmatrix} \tilde{A}(aX_{11} + \lfloor \alpha - 1 \rfloor bY_{11}) & 0 & \tilde{A}(aY_{11} + bX_{11}) & 0 \\ * & A_4(aX_{14} + \lfloor \alpha - 1 \rfloor bY_{14}) & * & A_4(aY_{14} + bX_{14}) \\ \tilde{A}(-bX_{11} + \lfloor \alpha - 1 \rfloor aY_{11}) & 0 & \tilde{A}(-bY_{11} + aX_{11}) & 0 \\ * & A_4(-bX_{14} + \lfloor \alpha - 1 \rfloor aY_{14}) & * & A_4(-bY_{14} + aX_{14}) \end{bmatrix}$$
$$+ \lceil 1 - \alpha \rceil \begin{bmatrix} \tilde{A}(aX_{11} - bY_{11}) & 0 & \tilde{A}(\lfloor \alpha - 1 \rfloor aY_{11} + bX_{11}) & 0 \\ * & A_4(aX_{14} - bY_{14}) & * & A_4(\lfloor \alpha - 1 \rfloor aY_{14} + bX_{14}) \\ \tilde{A}(bX_{11} + aY_{11}) & 0 & \tilde{A}(\lfloor \alpha - 1 \rfloor bY_{11} + aX_{11}) & 0 \\ * & A_4(bX_{14} + aY_{14}) & * & A_4(\lfloor \alpha - 1 \rfloor bY_{14} + aX_{14}) \end{bmatrix}\} < 0, \quad (36)$$

where $\tilde{A} = A_1 - A_2 A_4^{-1} A_3$. Two results can be obviously obtained from (36):
(i) $\mathcal{H}\{A_4(\lfloor \alpha - 2 \rfloor bY_{14} + 2aX_{14})\} < 0$, which implies A_4 is nonsingular.

(ii) The following inequality holds.

$$\mathcal{H}\begin{bmatrix} \tilde{A}(aX_{11} + \lfloor\alpha-1\rfloor bY_{11}) & \tilde{A}(aY_{11} + bX_{11}) \\ \tilde{A}(-bX_{11} + \lfloor\alpha-1\rfloor aY_{11}) & \tilde{A}(-bY_{11} + aX_{11}) \end{bmatrix}$$
$$+ \lceil 1-\alpha\rceil \begin{bmatrix} \tilde{A}(aX_{11} - bY_{11}) & \tilde{A}(\lfloor\alpha-1\rfloor aY_{11} + bX_{11}) \\ \tilde{A}(bX_{11} + aY_{11}) & \tilde{A}(\lfloor\alpha-1\rfloor bY_{11} + aX_{11}) \end{bmatrix} < 0. \qquad (37)$$

It is easy to see that the inequality (37) is identical to

$$\mathcal{H}\{(\Theta \otimes (A_1 - A_2 A_4^{-1} A_3)) \times \begin{bmatrix} X_{11} & Y_{11} \\ \lfloor\alpha-1\rfloor Y_{11} & X_{11} \end{bmatrix}$$
$$+ \lceil 1-\alpha\rceil (\Theta^T \otimes (A_1 - A_2 A_4^{-1} A_3)) \times \begin{bmatrix} X_{11} & \lfloor\alpha-1\rfloor Y_{11} \\ Y_{11} & X_{11} \end{bmatrix}\} < 0. \qquad (38)$$

From Theorem 5, the inequality (38) means

$$|\arg(\mathrm{spec}(A_1 - A_2 A_4^{-1} A_3))| > \alpha \frac{\pi}{2}.$$

From (i), (ii), it follows that system (2) is admissible.

(Necessity). Supposing that system (2) is admissible, for two arbitrarily selected invertible matrices L_1, R_1 given by

$$L_1 E R_1 = \begin{bmatrix} I_m & 0 \\ 0 & J_{n-m} \end{bmatrix}, \quad L_1 A R_1 = \begin{bmatrix} \tilde{A}_1 & 0 \\ 0 & I_{n-m} \end{bmatrix},$$

it is implied that $J_{n-m} = 0$ and $|\arg(\mathrm{spec}(\tilde{A}_1))| > \alpha\frac{\pi}{2}$ hold. From Theorem 5, there exist $X_{11}, Y_{11} \in \mathbb{R}^{m \times m}$, such that

$$\begin{bmatrix} X_{11} & Y_{11} \\ \lfloor\alpha-1\rfloor Y_{11} & X_{11} \end{bmatrix} > 0,$$

$$\mathcal{H}\{(\Theta \otimes \tilde{A}_1)\begin{bmatrix} X_{11} & Y_{11} \\ \lfloor\alpha-1\rfloor Y_{11} & X_{11} \end{bmatrix} + \lceil 1-\alpha\rceil (\Theta^T \otimes \tilde{A}_1)\begin{bmatrix} X_{11} & \lfloor\alpha-1\rfloor Y_{11} \\ Y_{11} & X_{11} \end{bmatrix}\} < 0.$$

Letting

$$X = R_1 \begin{bmatrix} X_{11} & 0 \\ 0 & -I_{n-m} \end{bmatrix} L_1^{-T}, \quad Y = R_1 \begin{bmatrix} Y_{11} & 0 \\ 0 & 0 \end{bmatrix} L_1^{-T},$$

denoting by Ω the left side of (28), to verify the matrix variables constructed above satisfy (28) and (30), pre- and post- multiplying Ω and

$$\begin{bmatrix} E & 0 \\ 0 & E \end{bmatrix}\begin{bmatrix} X & Y \\ \lfloor\alpha-1\rfloor Y & X \end{bmatrix},$$

respectively by

$$\begin{bmatrix} L_1 & 0 \\ 0 & L_1 \end{bmatrix},$$

and its transpose, the following two equations hold:

$$\begin{bmatrix} L_1 & 0 \\ 0 & L_1 \end{bmatrix} \Omega \begin{bmatrix} L_1 & 0 \\ 0 & L_1 \end{bmatrix}^T = \mathcal{H}\left\{ \begin{bmatrix} \bar{A}_1(aX_{11} + \lfloor\alpha-1\rfloor bY_{11}) & 0 & \bar{A}_1(aY_{11} + bX_{11}) & 0 \\ 0 & -aI_{n-m} & 0 & -bI_{n-m} \\ \bar{A}_1(-bX_{11} + \lfloor\alpha-1\rfloor aY_{11}) & 0 & \bar{A}_1(-bY_{11} + aX_{11}) & 0 \\ 0 & bI_{n-m} & 0 & -aI_{n-m} \end{bmatrix} \right\}$$
$$+ \lceil 1-\alpha \rceil \begin{bmatrix} \bar{A}_1(aX_{11} + \lfloor\alpha-1\rfloor bY_{11}) & 0 & \bar{A}_1(aY_{11} + bX_{11}) & 0 \\ 0 & -aI_{n-m} & 0 & -bI_{n-m} \\ \bar{A}_1(-bX_{11} + \lfloor\alpha-1\rfloor aY_{11}) & 0 & \bar{A}_1(-bY_{11} + aX_{11}) & 0 \\ 0 & bI_{n-m} & 0 & -aI_{n-m} \end{bmatrix} \} < 0, \tag{39}$$

$$\begin{bmatrix} L_1 & 0 \\ 0 & L_1 \end{bmatrix} \begin{bmatrix} E & 0 \\ 0 & E \end{bmatrix} \begin{bmatrix} X & Y \\ -Y & X \end{bmatrix} \begin{bmatrix} L_1^T & 0 \\ 0 & L_1^T \end{bmatrix} = \begin{bmatrix} X_{11} & 0 & Y_{11} & 0 \\ 0 & 0 & 0 & 0 \\ \lfloor\alpha-1\rfloor Y_{11} & 0 & X_{11} & 0 \\ 0 & 0 & 0 & 0 \end{bmatrix} \geq 0. \tag{40}$$

From (39) and (40), it can be easily deduced that X, Y satisfy (28) and (30). This completes the proof. □

The criterion provided in Theorem 6 contains equality constraints, which are troublesome when solved using the LMI toolbox. Therefore, the following theorem provides a criterion that does not contain equality constraints and is in a form of strict LMI.

Theorem 7. *System (2) with $0 < \alpha < 2$ is admissible iff there exist matrices $X, Y \in \mathbb{R}^{n \times n}$ and $Q \in \mathbb{R}^{(n-m) \times n}$ satisfying (27) and*

$$\mathcal{H}\{(\Theta \otimes A)\begin{bmatrix} XE^T + SQ & YE^T \\ \lfloor\alpha-1\rfloor YE^T & XE^T + SQ \end{bmatrix} + \lceil 1-\alpha \rceil (\Theta^T \otimes A)\begin{bmatrix} XE^T + SQ & \lfloor\alpha-1\rfloor YE^T \\ YE^T & XE^T + SQ \end{bmatrix}\} < 0, \tag{41}$$

where $S \in \mathbb{R}^{n \times (n-m)}$ is any matrix satisfying full column rank and $ES = 0$.

Proof. (Sufficiency). Suppose that there exist matrices $X, Y \in \mathbb{R}^{n \times n}$ and $Q \in \mathbb{R}^{(n-m) \times n}$ satisfying (27) and (41). Denoting $XE^T + \frac{1}{2}SQ$ by $\tilde{X}$ and YE^T by $\tilde{Y}$, Equations (27) and (41) show that $\tilde{X}, \tilde{Y}$ satisfy (28), (30). From Theorem 6, it can be concluded that the system (2) is admissible.

(Necessity). Supposing that the system (2) is admissible, there exist arbitrarily chosen invertible L_1, R_1 satisfying (31) and

$$|\arg(\mathrm{spec}(\bar{A}_1))| > \alpha \frac{\pi}{2}.$$

That is, there exist $X_1, Y_1 \in \mathbb{R}^{m \times m}$, satisfying the two following inequalities:

$$\begin{bmatrix} X_1 & Y_1 \\ \lfloor\alpha-1\rfloor Y_1 & X_1 \end{bmatrix} > 0,$$

$$\mathcal{H}\{(\Theta \otimes \bar{A}_1)\begin{bmatrix} X_1 & Y_1 \\ \lfloor\alpha-1\rfloor Y_1 & X_1 \end{bmatrix} + \lceil 1-\alpha \rceil (\Theta^T \otimes \bar{A})\begin{bmatrix} X_1 & \lfloor\alpha-1\rfloor Y_1 \\ Y_1 & X_1 \end{bmatrix}\} < 0.$$

Let

$$X = R_1 \begin{bmatrix} X_1 & 0 \\ 0 & I_{n-m} \end{bmatrix} R_1^T, \quad Y = R_1 \begin{bmatrix} Y_1 & 0 \\ 0 & 0_{n-m} \end{bmatrix} R_1^T,$$

$$S = R_1 \begin{bmatrix} 0 \\ I_{n-m} \end{bmatrix} H, \quad Q = H^{-1} \begin{bmatrix} 0 & -I_{n-m} \end{bmatrix} L_1^{-T},$$

where H is any invertible matrix. Then it is derived that (27) and the following inequality

$$\mathcal{H}\{(I_2 \otimes L_1^{-1})((\Theta \otimes \begin{bmatrix} \bar{A}_1 & 0 \\ 0 & I_{n-m} \end{bmatrix}) \times \begin{bmatrix} X_1 & 0 & Y_1 & 0 \\ 0 & -\frac{1}{2}I_{n-m} & 0 & 0 \\ \lfloor \alpha - 1 \rfloor Y_1 & 0 & X_1 & 0 \\ 0 & 0 & 0 & -\frac{1}{2}I_{n-m} \end{bmatrix}$$
$$+ \lceil 1 - \alpha \rceil (\Theta^T \otimes \begin{bmatrix} \bar{A}_1 & 0 \\ 0 & I_{n-m} \end{bmatrix}) \times \begin{bmatrix} X_1 & 0 & \lfloor \alpha - 1 \rfloor Y_1 & 0 \\ 0 & -\frac{1}{2}I_{n-m} & 0 & 0 \\ Y_1 & 0 & X_1 & 0 \\ 0 & 0 & 0 & -\frac{1}{2}I_{n-m} \end{bmatrix})(I_2 \otimes L_1^{-T})\} < 0, \tag{42}$$

hold. Note that Equation (42) is identical to (41). This completes the proof. □

Without loss of generality, consider the SFOS (1) and the following state feedback controller:
$$u(t) = Kx(t), \; K \in \mathbb{R}^{l \times n}. \tag{43}$$

Using this controller (43) on system (1), the following system can be obtained:
$$ED^{\alpha}x(t) = (A + BK)x(t). \tag{44}$$

Then the controller can be designed by the following theorem.

Theorem 8. *There exists a state feedback controller (43) such that the closed-loop SFOS (44) is admissible iff there exist $X, Y \in \mathbb{R}^{n \times n}, Q \in \mathbb{R}^{(n-m) \times n}$ and $Z \in \mathbb{R}^{l \times n}$ satisfying (27) and*

$$\mathcal{H}\{(\Theta \otimes A)(\begin{bmatrix} X & Y \\ \lfloor \alpha - 1 \rfloor Y & X \end{bmatrix} \bar{E}^T + \bar{S}\bar{Q}) + \lceil 1 - \alpha \rceil (\Theta^T \otimes A)(\begin{bmatrix} X & \lfloor \alpha - 1 \rfloor Y \\ Y & X \end{bmatrix} \bar{E}^T + \bar{S}\bar{Q})$$
$$+ \lceil \alpha - 1 \rceil (\Theta \otimes B)(I_2 \otimes Z) \lceil 1 - \alpha \rceil (I_2 \otimes BZ)\} < 0, \tag{45}$$

where $\bar{E} = I_2 \otimes E, \bar{S} = I_2 \otimes S, S \in \mathbb{R}^{n \times (n-m)}, ES = 0, \bar{Q} = I_2 \otimes Q$. Then, one can choose a stabilizing state feedback controller with gain matrix

$$K = Z(\lceil \alpha - 1 \rceil (XE^T + SQ) + 2\lceil 1 - \alpha \rceil (aXE^T - bYE^T + aSQ))^{-1}. \tag{46}$$

The practical code for solving the LMIs (27) and (45) using the LMI toolbox in MATLAB is presented in Appendix A, and it can be seen that the proposed framework does not require additional conditional statements such as: if $1 \leq \alpha < 2$, execute statement 1; elif $0 < \alpha < 1$, execute statement 2. Thus, it is a truly unified framework. According to Table 1, the proposed framework in this paper has advantages in the unity of the structure, the generality of the criteria, the non-conservatism of the controller design and the ease for solving.

Table 1. Comparison of existing methods and ours.

Ref.	α Range	Var. Kind	FOS or SFOS	Nonconservative Stabilization	As a Special Case of Ours	Unified
[11]	(0,1)	Complex	FOS	No	Th. 1	N/A
[12]	[1,2)	Real	FOS	No	N/A	N/A
[11]	[1,2)	Real	FOS	Yes	Th. 5	N/A
[15]	(0,1)	Real	FOS	No	Th. 3	N/A
[19]	(0,2)	Real	FOS	Yes	N/A	No
[27]	[1,2)	Real	SFOS	Yes	Th. 5	N/A
[24]	(0,1)	Real	SFOS	Yes	Th. 7	N/A
[26]	(0,2)	Real	SFOS	Yes	N/A	No
[30]	(0,2)	Real	SFOS	Yes	N/A	No
Ours (Th. 5)	(0,2)	Real	FOS	Yes	N/A	Yes
Ours (Th. 7)	(0,2)	Real	SFOS	Yes	N/A	Yes

4. Numerical Examples

Two numerical examples are used to verify the effectiveness of the proposed scheme.

Example 1. *Consider the FOS (3) with the parameters $\alpha = 0.5$ and*

$$A = \begin{bmatrix} 1 & -1.5 & 0 & 0 \\ 1.5 & 1 & 0 & 0 \\ 1 & 0 & 0.6 & -1 \\ 0 & 1 & 1 & 0.6 \end{bmatrix}. \tag{47}$$

It is easy to see that system (3) is stable because all eigenvalues $\lambda_i (i = 1, 2, 3, 4)$ of the system matrix A satisfy

$$|\arg(\lambda_i)| > \frac{\pi}{4}.$$

Using the LMI toolbox to solve (27) and (28) in Theorem 5, the following feasible solutions can be obtained:

$$X = \begin{bmatrix} 25.0228 & 0 & 14.666 & -11.5702 \\ 0 & 25.0228 & 11.5702 & 14.666 \\ 14.666 & 11.5702 & 94.5643 & 0 \\ -11.5702 & 14.666 & 0 & 94.5643 \end{bmatrix},$$

$$Y = \begin{bmatrix} 0 & 21.2230 & 7.0284 & 15.6533 \\ -21.2230 & 0 & -15.6533 & 7.0284 \\ -7.0284 & 15.6533 & 0 & 76.8874 \\ -15.6533 & -7.0284 & -76.8874 & 0 \end{bmatrix}.$$

Further, for system (3) with system matrix A given in (47) and the fractional order $\alpha = 0.7$, it is unstable because there exists an eigenvalue λ_i of system matrix A that does not satisfy

$$|\arg(\lambda_i)| > 0.35\pi.$$

According to Theorem 5, a state feedback controller $u = Kx(t)$ can be designed to make the closed-loop system (1) with $E = I$ stable, where the control matrix can be arbitrarily chosen as

$$B = \begin{bmatrix} 1 & 1 & 1 & 1 \end{bmatrix}^T.$$

Using the LMI toolbox to solve the LMIs (27) and

$$\mathcal{H}\{(\Theta \otimes A)(\begin{bmatrix} X & Y \\ \lfloor \alpha - 1 \rfloor Y & X \end{bmatrix}) + \lceil 1 - \alpha \rceil (\Theta^T \otimes A)(\begin{bmatrix} X & \lfloor \alpha - 1 \rfloor Y \\ Y & X \end{bmatrix}) + \lceil \alpha - 1 \rceil (\Theta \otimes B)(I_2 \otimes Z) + \lceil 1 - \alpha \rceil (I_2 \otimes BZ)\} < 0,$$

the following feasible solutions can be obtained:

$$X = \begin{bmatrix} 80.1117 & 6.5456 & 13.5362 & 14.6681 \\ 6.5456 & 31.3419 & 12.4094 & -16.9618 \\ 13.5362 & 12.4094 & 42.7925 & 15.3142 \\ 14.6681 & -16.9618 & 15.3142 & 47.8344 \end{bmatrix},$$

$$Y = \begin{bmatrix} 0 & 28.0858 & 1.8549 & -23.5956 \\ -28.0858 & 0 & 0.9793 & -0.9894 \\ -1.8549 & -0.9793 & 0 & 14.5734 \\ 23.5956 & 0.9894 & -14.5734 & 0 \end{bmatrix},$$

$$Z = \begin{bmatrix} -105.2726 & -50.9853 & -42.4700 & -53.9358 \end{bmatrix}.$$

Then, the controller gain K can be designed by

$$K = Z(\lceil \alpha - 1 \rceil X + 2\lceil 1 - \alpha \rceil (aX - bY))^{-1} = \begin{bmatrix} -0.3080 & -2.0298 & 0.7833 & -1.2884 \end{bmatrix}.$$

Using the LMI toolbox to solve the LMIs provided by Theorem 3 in [15], the following feasible solutions are obtained:

$$X = \begin{bmatrix} -3.4790 & -2.1393 & -2.3830 & -1.8168 \end{bmatrix},$$

$$Q = \begin{bmatrix} 4.0730 & 0.5549 & 2.2858 & 1.5569 \\ 0.5549 & 1.0757 & 0.3187 & 0.05248 \\ 2.2858 & 0.3187 & 1.6994 & 1.0874 \\ 1.5569 & 0.05248 & 1.0874 & 0.80109 \end{bmatrix},$$

$$K = XQ^{-1} = \begin{bmatrix} 0.8217 & -2.9167 & 2.9709 & -7.7067 \end{bmatrix}.$$

The positions where the eigenvalues of the system matrix $A + BK$, where K is obtained by the above two methods, fall on the complex plane are shown in Figure 2. It can be seen that the controller designed by Theorem 5 can configure the eigenvalues $\lambda_i(A + BK)$ in the right stability region, while the method presented in [15] can only configure the eigenvalues $\lambda_i(A + BK)$ in the left semi-complex plane.

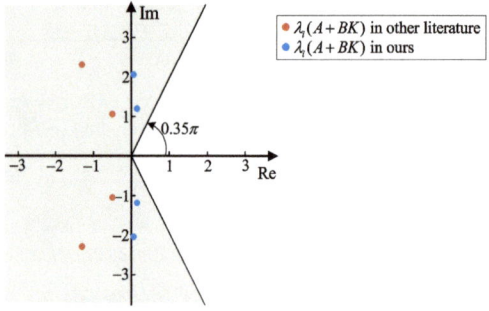

Figure 2. The positions of the eigenvalues $\lambda_i(A + BK)$ ($i = 1, 2, 3, 4$) on the complex plane where K is designed by Theorem 5 in ours and Theorem 3 in [15] with $\alpha = 0.7$.

Remark 1. *When using the stability analysis method provided by Theorem 1 in [15], four decision variables need to be solved, so the solution calculation speed is slow. In addition, the LMI provided in Theorem 12 of Ref. [13] involves complex decision variables, so it is difficult when solving with the LMI toolbox.*

Remark 2. *The LMIs provided in Theorems 9 and 10 of [13] involve the terms $\mathcal{H}\{(A + BK)^{\frac{1}{\alpha}}X\}$ and $\mathcal{H}\{-(-A - BK)^{\frac{1}{2-\alpha}}X\}$, respectively, so both of them cannot be used directly to design controllers. The stabilization analysis method presented in [15] provides a sufficient but unnecessary criterion, which is conservative to a certain extent. Using the LMI toolbox to solve the LMIs of Theorem 3 in [15] with $A = \begin{bmatrix} 1 & 2 & 0; -2 & 1 & 0; 1 & 0 & 1 \end{bmatrix}$ and $B = \begin{bmatrix} 0; 0; 1 \end{bmatrix}$, one obtains the following information, which means Theorem 3 in [15] is invalid.*

Result: best value of t: 6.205424×10^{13}
f-radius saturation: 0.000% of $R = 10^9$
Marginal infeasibility: these LMI constraints may be feasible but are not strictly feasible.

Example 2. *Consider the SFOS (1) with the fractional order $\alpha = 0.7$ and 1.5, respectively, and other parameters as*

$$E = \begin{bmatrix} 1.2 & 0.2 & 0.2 & -0.8 \\ 0.2 & 1.2 & 0.2 & -0.8 \\ 0.2 & 0.2 & 1.2 & -0.8 \\ 0.4 & 0.4 & 0.4 & -0.6 \end{bmatrix}, A = \begin{bmatrix} -0.6 & -2.6 & 2.4 & 0.4 \\ 1 & -3 & 2 & 0 \\ 0 & -2 & 3 & -1 \\ -0.4 & -2.4 & 2.6 & 0.6 \end{bmatrix},$$

$$B = \begin{bmatrix} 1 & 1 & 1 & 1 \end{bmatrix}^T.$$

It is easy to determine

$$\det(s^{0.7}E - A) = 2s^{0.7} - s^{0.21} + 4 \neq 0,$$

$$\det(s^{1.5}E - A) = 2s^{1.5} - s^{4.5} + 4 \neq 0,$$

$$\deg(\det(sE - A)) = \mathrm{rank}(E) = 3,$$

$$\mathrm{spec}(E, A) = \{-1+j, -1-j, 2\}.$$

Thus, the system (1) is regular and impulse-free but unstable in the case of $\alpha = 0.7$ and 1.5. That is, the system (1) is not admissible. By solving (45), we obtain the following feasible solutions:
Case $\alpha = 0.7$:

$$X = \begin{bmatrix} 14.6934 & 6.8766 & 5.0576 & -1.0284 \\ 6.8766 & 25.8541 & -2.6300 & -2.7650 \\ 5.0576 & -2.6300 & 18.0273 & 2.0579 \\ -1.0284 & -2.7650 & 2.0579 & 25.4384 \end{bmatrix},$$

$$Y = \begin{bmatrix} 0 & 0.2877 & 1.2145 & -0.7511 \\ -0.2877 & 0 & 1.9940 & -0.8532 \\ -1.2145 & -1.9940 & 0 & 1.6042 \\ 0.7511 & 0.8532 & -1.6042 & 0 \end{bmatrix},$$

$$Q = \begin{bmatrix} -377.0389 & -380.1311 & -376.0045 & -351.8424 \end{bmatrix},$$

$$Z = \begin{bmatrix} 55.2985 & 138.0754 & 110.3800 & -204.6825 \end{bmatrix},$$

$$K = \begin{bmatrix} 3.5125 & 10.7956 & 21.8878 & -21.1369 \end{bmatrix}.$$

Case $\alpha = 1.5$:

$$X = \begin{bmatrix} 0.9927 & -0.1731 & 0.5139 & 0.2102 \\ -0.1731 & 2.1292 & -0.9060 & 0.3519 \\ 0.5139 & -0.9060 & 1.2105 & 0.4678 \\ 0.2102 & 0.3519 & 0.4678 & 1.2390 \end{bmatrix},$$

$$Y = 0,$$

$$Q = \begin{bmatrix} -2.2345 & -1.4041 & -2.8467 & 0.4759 \end{bmatrix},$$

$$Z = \begin{bmatrix} -1.8134 & 6.6435 & -5.4609 & -0.26022 \end{bmatrix},$$

$$K = \begin{bmatrix} 0.4144 & 1.1978 & -4.2450 & 1.3810 \end{bmatrix}.$$

As shown in Figures 3 and 4, the system (1) is admissible under the designed control law.

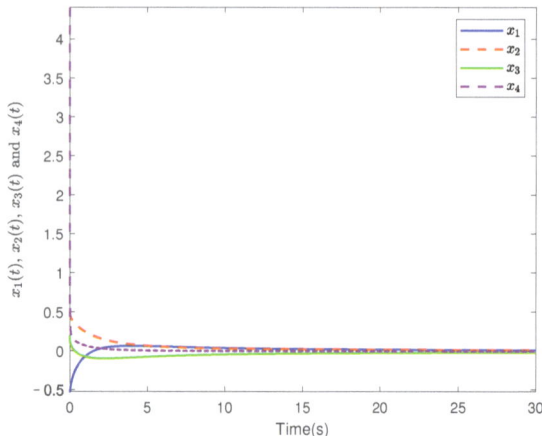

Figure 3. The closed-loop SFOS (1) state in Example 2 for $\alpha = 0.7$.

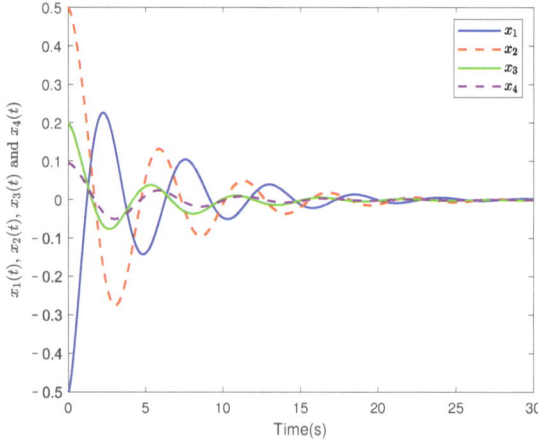

Figure 4. The closed-loop SFOS (1) state in Example 2 for $\alpha = 1.5$.

5. Conclusions

In this paper, necessary and sufficient conditions for stability and admissibility are presented for fractional order systems and singular fractional order systems with $0 < \alpha < 2$, respectively. Theorems 1–4 provide LMI-based criteria containing complex matrices and real matrices, respectively. In particular, in Theorem 5, a real LMI-based framework, is proposed, which can be easily used to design controllers. Theorem 6 provides a unified critera for testing admissibility, but it contains an equality constraint. A unified criterion for admissibility without equality constraints and non-strictness is presented in Theorem 7, and is used to design a controller for an SFOS. Compared with the unified framework for stability in [19] and admissibility in [26,30], the proposed framework does not need to design the form of elements in linear matrix inequalities in different cases ($1 \leq \alpha < 2$ or $0 < \alpha < 1$) and is thus a truly unified framework. Strict linear matrix inequalities with few real variables are developed to test the stability and admissibility of the system. The analytical framework is more applicable than other results, and can be directly used to design the controller. In the future work, the control and stabilization problems of H_∞ control and robust control problems for singular fractional order systems with the fractional order $0 < \alpha < 2$ can be extended based on this result, so that the control synthesis problems of fractional order systems can be unified.

Author Contributions: Conceptualization, L.Z.; methodology, L.Z. and X.Z.; writing—original draft preparation, L.Z. and J.-X.Z.; writing—review and editing, J.-X.Z. and X.Z. All authors have read and agreed to the published version of the manuscript.

Funding: This work was supported in part by the National Natural Science Foundation of China under Grant 62103093 and the Fundamental Research Funds for the Central Universities of China under Grant N2108003.

Data Availability Statement: Not applicable.

Conflicts of Interest: The authors declare no conflict of interest.

Appendix A

Listing 1: The partial code for solving LMIs in Theorem 8

```
n = size(A,1);
nK = size(B,2);
m = rank(E);
setlmis([]);
[X,m1,sX]=lmivar(1,[n 1]);
[Y,m2,sY]=lmivar(3,skewdec(size(A),m1));
[Z,~,sZ]=lmivar(2,[nK n]);
[Q,~,sQ]=lmivar(2,[m,n]);
[P1,~,sP1]=lmivar(3,[sX -floor(alpha-1)*sY;floor(alpha-1)*sY
    sX]);
[P2,~,sP2]=lmivar(3,[sX floor(alpha-1)*sY;-floor(alpha-1)*sY
    sX]);
[barQ,~,sbarQ]=lmivar(3,[sQ zeros(m,n);zeros(m,n) sQ]);
[barZ,~,sbarZ]=lmivar(3,[sZ zeros(nK,n);zeros(nK,n) sZ]);
lmiterm([-1 1 1 P1],1,1)
lmiterm([-2 1 1 P2],1,1)
lmiterm([3 1 1 P1],kron(theta,A),barE','s')
lmiterm([3 1 1 barQ],kron(theta,A)*barS1,1,'s')
lmiterm([3 1 1 P2],ceil(1-alpha)*kron(theta',A),barE','s')
lmiterm([3 1 1 barQ],ceil(1-alpha)*kron(theta',A)*barS,1,'s')
lmiterm([3 1 1 barZ],ceil(alpha-1)*kron(theta,B),1,'s')
lmiterm([3 1 1 barZ],ceil(1-alpha)*kron(eye(2),B),1,'s')
```

References

1. Podlubny, I. *Fractional Differential Equations*; Academic Press: New York, NY, USA, 1999.
2. Moghadam, R.A.; Ebrahimi, S. Design and analysis of a trsional mode MEMS disk resonator for RF applications. *J. Multidiscip. Eng. Sci. Technol.* **2021**, *8*, 14300–14303.
3. Montazeri-Gh, M.; Mahmoodi-K, M. Optimized predictive energy management of plug-in hybrid electric vehicle based on traffic condition. *J. Clean. Prod.* **2016**, *139*, 935–948. [CrossRef]
4. Özköse, F.; Yavuz, M.; Şenel, M.T.; Habbireeh, R. Fractional order modelling of omicron SARS-CoV-2 variant containing heart attack effect using real data from the United Kingdom. *Chaos Soliton. Fract.* **2022**, *157*, 111954. [CrossRef]
5. Zeb, A.; Kumar, P.; Erturk, V.S.; Sitthiwirattham, T. A new study on two different vaccinated fractional-order COVID-19 models via numerical algorithms. *J. King Saud. Univ. Sci.* **2022**, *34*, 101914. [CrossRef]
6. Yan, H.; Zhang, J.X.; Zhang, X. Injected infrared and visible image fusion via L_1 decomposition model and guided filtering. *IEEE Trans. Comput. Imaging.* **2022**, *8*, 162–173. [CrossRef]

7. Matignon, D. Stability results on fractional differential equations with applications to control processing. *Comput. Eng. Syst. Appl.* **1996**, *2*, 963–968.
8. Boyd, S.; Vandenberghe, L. *Convex Optimization*; Cambridge University Press: Cambridge, UK, 2004. [CrossRef]
9. Jin, W. Cognitive radio spectrum allocation based on IOT and genetic algorithm. *J. Commerc. Biotechnol.* **2022**, *27*. [CrossRef]
10. Norouzi, A.; Golmohammadi, A. Developing a framework for analytical hierarchy process in the hesitant fuzzy environment for group decision making (case study: Business process prioritization in Markazi electricity power distribution company). *Fuzzy Syst. Appl.* **2022**, *5*, 231–267.
11. Farges, C.; Moze, M.; Sabatier, J. Pseudo-state feedback stabilisation of commensurate fractional order systems. *Automatica* **2010**, *46*, 1730–1734. [CrossRef]
12. Tavazoei, M.S.; Haeri, M. A note on the stability of fractional order systems. *Math. Comput. Simulat.* **2009**, *79*, 1566–1576. [CrossRef]
13. Sabatier, J.; Moze, M.; Farges, C. LMI stability conditions for fractional order systems. *Comupt. Math. Appl.* **2010**, *59*, 1594–1609. [CrossRef]
14. Chen, Y.Q.; Ahn, H.; Podlubny, I. Robust stability check of fractional order linear time invariant systems with interval uncertainties. *Signal. Proc.* **2006**, *86*, 2611–2618. [CrossRef]
15. Lu, J.G.; Chen, Y.Q. Robust stability and stabilization of fractional order interval systems with the fractional order α: the $0 < \alpha < 1$ case. *IEEE Trans. Automat. Control* **2010**, *55*, 152–158. [CrossRef]
16. Chilali, M.; Gahinet, P. H_∞ design with pole placement constraints: An LMI approach. *IEEE Trans. Automat. Control* **1996**, *41*, 358–367. [CrossRef]
17. Anderson, B.; Bose, N.; Jury, E. A simple test for zeros of a complex polynomial in a sector. *IEEE Trans. Automat. Control* **1974**, *19*, 437–438. [CrossRef]
18. Xu, J. Study on Some Problems in Analysis and Control of Fractional-Order Systems. Master's Thesis, Shanghai JiaoTong University, Shanghai, China, 2009.
19. Zhang, X.F.; Lin, C.; Chen, Y.Q.; Boutat, D. A unified framework of stability theorems for LTI fractional order systems with $0 < \alpha < 2$. *IEEE Trans. Circuits Syst. II Express Briefs* **2020**, *67*, 3237–3241. [CrossRef]
20. Xu, S.; Lam, J. *Control and Filtering of Singular Systems*; Springer: Berlin, Germany, 2006. [CrossRef]
21. N'Doye, I.; Darouach, M.; Zasadzinski, M.; Radhy, N.E. Robust stabilization of uncertain descriptor fractional-order systems. *Automatica* **2013**, *49*, 1907–1913. [CrossRef]
22. Yu, Y.; Jiao, Z.; Sun, C.Y. Sufficient and necessary condition of admissibility for fractional-order singular system. *Acta Autom. Sin.* **2013**, *39*, 2160–2164. [CrossRef]
23. Marir, S.; Chadli, M.; Bouagada, D. A novel approach of admissibility for singular linear continuous-time fractional-order systems. *Int. J. Control Autom.* **2017**, *15*, 959–964. [CrossRef]
24. Zhang, X.F.; Chen, Y.Q. Admissibility and robust stabilization of continuous linear singular fractional order systems with the fractional order α: The $0 < \alpha < 1$ case. *ISA Trans.* **2018**, *82*, 42–50. [CrossRef] [PubMed]
25. Song, S.; Meng, B.; Wang, Z. On sliding mode control for singular fractional-order systems with matched external disturbances. *Fractal Fract.* **2022**, *6*, 366. [CrossRef]
26. Zhang, X.F.; Zhang, J.X.; Huang, W.K.; Shi, P. Non-fragile sliding mode observer based fault estimation for interval type-2 fuzzy singular fractional order systems. *Int. J. Sysi. Sci.* **2023**, 1–20. [CrossRef]
27. Marir, S.; Chadli, M.D.; Bouagada, D. New admissibility conditions for singular linear continuous-time fractional-order systems. *J. Franklin Inst.* **2017**, *354*, 752–766. [CrossRef]
28. Zhang, Q.H.; Lu, J.G.; Ma, Y.D. Time domain solution analysis and novel admissibility conditions of singular fractional-order systems. *IEEE Trans. Circuits Syst. I-Regul. Pap.* **2020**, *68*, 842–855. [CrossRef]
29. Zhang, X.F.; Yan, Y.Q. Admissibility of fractional order descriptor systems based on complex variables: An LMI approach. *Fractal Fract.* **2020**, *4*, 8. [CrossRef]
30. Wang, Y.Y.; Zhang, X.F.; Boutat, D.; Shi, P. Quadratic admissibility for a class of LTI uncertain singular fractional-order systems with $0 < \alpha < 2$. *Fractal Fract.* **2022**, *7*, 1. [CrossRef]
31. Danca, M.F. On the stability domain of a class of linear systems of fractional order. *Fractal Fract.* **2022**, *7*, 49. [CrossRef]
32. Zhang, J.X.; Yang, G.H. Low-complexity tracking control of strict-feedback systems with unknown control directions. *IEEE Trans. Automat. Contr.* **2019**, *64*, 5175–5182. [CrossRef]
33. Zhang, J.X.; Yang, G.H. Fuzzy adaptive output feedback control of uncertain nonlinear systems with prescribed performance. *IEEE Trans. Cybern.* **2018**, *48*, 1342–1354. [CrossRef]
34. Zhang, J.X.; Yang, G.H. Fault-tolerant output-constrained control of unknown Euler-Lagrange systems with prescribed tracking accuracy. *Automatica* **2020**, *111*, 108606. [CrossRef]
35. Ahmad, M.; Zada, A.; Ghaderi, M.; George, R.; Rezapour, S. On the existence and stability of a neutral stochastic fractional differential system. *Fractal Fract.* **2022**, *6*, 203. [CrossRef]
36. Bosche, J.; Bachelier, O.; Mehdi, D. An approach for robust matrix root-clustering analysis in a union of regions. *IMA J. Math. Control Inf.* **2005**, *22*, 227–239. [CrossRef]

37. Lu, J.G.; Chen, G.Y. Robust stability and stabilization of fractional order interval systems: An LMI approach. *IEEE Trans. Automat. Control* **2009**, *54*, 1294–1299. [CrossRef]
38. Iwasaki, T.; Hara, S. Generalized KYP lemma: Unified frequency domain inequalities with design applications. *IEEE Trans. Automat. Control* **2005**, *50*, 41–59. [CrossRef]

Disclaimer/Publisher's Note: The statements, opinions and data contained in all publications are solely those of the individual author(s) and contributor(s) and not of MDPI and/or the editor(s). MDPI and/or the editor(s) disclaim responsibility for any injury to people or property resulting from any ideas, methods, instructions or products referred to in the content.

Article

Depth Image Enhancement Algorithm Based on Fractional Differentiation

Tingsheng Huang [1,2], Xinjian Wang [1,2], Da Xie [1,2], Chunyang Wang [1,2,*] and Xuelian Liu [2,*]

1. School of Electronic and Information Engineering, Changchun University of Science and Technology, Changchun 130022, China
2. Xi'an Key Laboratory of Active Photoelectric Imaging Detection Technology, Xi'an Technological University, Xi'an 710021, China
* Correspondence: wangchunyang19@163.com (C.W.); tearlxl@126.com (X.L.)

Abstract: Depth image enhancement techniques can help to improve image quality and facilitate computer vision tasks. Traditional image-enhancement methods, which are typically based on integer-order calculus, cannot exploit the textural information of an image, and their enhancement effect is limited. To solve this problem, fractional differentiation has been introduced as an innovative image-processing tool. It enables the flexible use of local and non-local information by taking into account the continuous changes between orders, thereby improving the enhancement effect. In this study, a fractional differential is applied in depth image enhancement and used to establish a novel algorithm, named the fractional differential-inverse-distance-weighted depth image enhancement method. Experiments are performed to verify the effectiveness and universality of the algorithm, revealing that it can effectively solve edge and hole interference and significantly enhance textural details. The effects of the order of fractional differentiation and number of iterations on the enhancement performance are examined, and the optimal parameters are obtained. The process data of depth image enhancement associated with the optimal number of iterations and fractional order are expected to facilitate depth image enhancement in actual scenarios.

Keywords: deep image enhancement; edges; fractional differentiation; fractional differential inverse distance weighted

Citation: Huang, T.; Wang, X.; Xie, D.; Wang, C.; Liu, X. Depth Image Enhancement Algorithm Based on Fractional Differentiation. *Fractal Fract.* **2023**, *7*, 394. https://doi.org/10.3390/fractalfract7050394

Academic Editor: António Lopes

Received: 31 March 2023
Revised: 29 April 2023
Accepted: 10 May 2023
Published: 11 May 2023

Copyright: © 2023 by the authors. Licensee MDPI, Basel, Switzerland. This article is an open access article distributed under the terms and conditions of the Creative Commons Attribution (CC BY) license (https://creativecommons.org/licenses/by/4.0/).

1. Introduction

In recent years, with the growing popularity of artificial intelligence and autonomous driving technologies, depth image processing algorithms have attracted increasing attention. A depth image is an image that contains depth information in each pixel, which can be used in three-dimensional (3D) reconstruction, object detection, face recognition, and in other fields. Depth image processing involves several problems, such as low contrast, high noise, and blurring problems. To address the problem of insufficient textural information in a depth image, mainstream processing methods focus on enhancing the edge of a depth image. However, only a few methods can effectively enhance the textural information of depth images without introducing fuzzy information. Consequently, depth image enhancement is a research hotspot at present, especially as enhancing the texture of a depth image can enable the obtainment of additional textural information from an image.

Various depth image processing algorithms have been developed. Masahiro devised a method to reduce the noise and number of voids in a depth image pixel by pixel and thereby improve the resolution [1]. Specifically, by reducing the depth image random noise, the coordinates of the correct object surface are obtained; missing values are thus identified and then inserted between the existing pixels. Subsequently, new pixels are inserted between them to enhance the depth image. Zhang et al. developed an image enhancement algorithm based on an adaptive median filter and fractional-order differential [2]. Wang et al. devised an image-denoising method based on fractional quaternion wavelet analysis [3]. Zhou et al.

used the fractal dimension method to enhance a depth image [4]. Moreover, Zhou et al. established an edge-guided method for the super-resolution of depth images to obtain high-quality edge information. The edge-guided method can maintain edge sharpness, thereby avoiding blurry and jagged edges during depth image processing [5]. Researchers have also used a variety of image processing techniques, such as histogram matching, edge-preserving filtering, and local contrast enhancement, to improve the quality and clarity of depth images [6–8].

The above-described studies have provided strong support and useful references for depth image processing. However, the existing algorithms have several limitations, such as high complexity, low processing efficiency, and an inability to adapt to different scenarios. Thus, there is a need for efficient, stable, and reliable algorithms capable of depth image enhancement. Fractional differentiation is an emerging differential method that has wider applicability and stronger expressive power than existing methods. Moreover, fractional differentiation has been widely applied in the field of image processing with promising results. Fractional calculus is a mathematical tool that extends traditional integer-order calculus to non-integer orders and can be used to analyse complex systems with long memory and non-local dependencies. By incorporating fractional calculus into image processing techniques, researchers have improved these techniques' image enhancement, restoration, and segmentation performances.

For example, Gupta et al. devised an adaptive image-denoising algorithm based on generalised fractional integration and fractional differentiation [9]. They combined this algorithm with an innovative noise-detection method to detect salt-and-pepper noise in images. Moreover, they used an adaptive mask based on generalised fractional integration to update noise-free pixels to enhance the details of images. This framework served as a flexible tool for image enhancement and image denoising. Zhang et al. designed an image fusion method based on fractional difference, which enables better visual perception and more objective evaluation and retains more image details than traditional methods [10]. Harjule et al. compared the traditional method with a fractional-order-based method for texture enhancement in medical images. To minimise the mean square error, the fractional-order operator for all images was optimised using the grey wolf optimiser. The results indicated that score-based operators with a differential order outperformed traditional integer order operators in the textural enhancement of medical images [11]. Zhang constructed a new image-enhancement algorithm based on a rough set and a fractional-order differentiator. An image enhanced by this algorithm has a clear edge and rich textural details, and it can retain information from the smooth areas in an image [12,13].

Despite these promising results, several limitations remain to be addressed. First, most existing methods consider only the local features of images and ignore the non-local dependencies between different regions. Second, these methods may not be effective for images containing complex textures or structures. Finally, only a few researchers have focused on depth image enhancement processing and the application of fractional differentials in depth image processing. Therefore, the introduction of fractional calculus in depth image applications must be further explored.

This study aims to apply a fractional differential for depth image enhancement. This application involves several challenges, such as avoiding the introduction of fuzzy information and inconsistency with an actual scene. To address these problems, an improved algorithm, named the fractional differential-inverse-distance-weighted depth image enhancement method, is developed. The results of experiments show that the algorithm can effectively integrate local and non-local information into the enhancement process and effectively enhance depth images with complex textures and structures.

The remainder of this paper is organised as follows. Section 2 describes the application of a fractional differential in image enhancement and the result, and discusses the problems in a depth image subjected to fractional differential enhancement. Section 3 describes the inverse distance weighting technique and the development of the fractional differential-inverse-distance-weighting depth image enhancement method. The method is used to enhance depth images of different orders, and the fractional differential order is optimised. The results indicate that the algorithm is effective. Section 4 presents the experimental results. The algorithm is applied to the depth image of a dataset, and the effect of the fractional differential small order and number of iterations on the algorithm's performance is verified. The results show that the algorithm is universal, can effectively solve the interference of edges and voids in depth images, and can enhance textural details. Section 5 presents the concluding remarks and recommendations for future research.

2. Fractional-Differential-Based Depth Image Enhancement

As an important branch of digital image processing, image enhancement has broad application aspects. The visual effect of image shooting may not be satisfactory owing to environmental conditions, and thus, image enhancement methods must be used (i.e., certain features of the target object in an image must be improved). Acquiring the typical characteristic parameters of a target in an image enables the effective recognition and detection of the target in the image [14,15]. The objective of image enhancement processing is to strengthen the valuable areas in an image and weaken or remove the non-essential information in the image. By enhancing the useful information, the image obtained in an actual scene can be transformed into an image that can be analysed and processed by humans or other systems. The features of an image (that is, the main information contained in the image) are typically present in the edge and textural details. Enhancing textural feature information can provide a valuable basis for further processing, such as image segmentation, recognition, or super-resolution. Fractional differentiation can help to improve the high-frequency and instantaneous-frequency (IF) parts of a signal, thereby nonlinearly strengthening the IF component while preserving the low-frequency and direct current parts. That is, fractional differentiation can enhance the edge and contour information and weak textural areas of an image. Thus, fractional differentiation is a valuable tool in image processing [16–20].

According to fractional calculus theory, a fractional differential operator has a weak reciprocal, which can enhance the high-frequency components of a signal while retaining the low-frequency components [21]. Therefore, by applying fractional calculus theory to image processing, the prominence of the edges of an image can be increased while retaining the textural information of the smooth areas of the image. It is generally believed that the value of fractional calculus theory and algorithms in image processing lies in their ability to add an additional degree of freedom. By selecting the appropriate fractional order and constructing a convolutional mask operator to select the fractional order v ($0 < v < 1$), satisfactory results for image signal enhancement ($v > 0$) and image signal denoising ($v < 0$) can be achieved. Guo et al. derived the formula of a fractional differential operator, realised the enhancement of a two-dimensional (2D) image based on the Grumwald–Letnikov (G–L) definition and a fractional calculus model, and discussed its application in image processing [21–23].

2.1. Construction Based on a Fractional Differential Operator

Based on the G–L definition, a v-order differential can be expressed as follows (Equation (1)):

$$_a^G D_x^v = \lim_{h \to 0} h^{-v} \sum_{n=0}^{\frac{t-a}{h}} (-1)^i \binom{v}{i} f(x - ih), v \in R \quad (1)$$

where v is the fractional differential order; h is the calculus step size; a and t are the lower and upper bounds for fractional calculus, respectively; Γ is the gamma function; and $\binom{v}{i}$ is the binomial coefficient.

$$\binom{v}{i} = \frac{\Gamma(v+1)}{\Gamma(i+1)\Gamma(v-i+1)} \quad (2)$$

The continuous interval of the one-dimensional signal $f(t)$ is defined as $[a,t]$ and divided equally into units specified by $h = 1, m = \left[\frac{t-a}{h}\right] = [t-a]$. Then, the equivalent expression of the v $(v \geq 0)$-order fractional differential of the unary signal is

$$\frac{d^v f(t)}{dt^v} \approx f(t) + (-1)^1(v)f(t-1) + (-1)^2\left(\frac{v(v-1)}{2}\right)f(t-2) + \cdots + (-1)^i \frac{\Gamma(v+1)}{\Gamma(i+1)\Gamma(v-i+1)} f(t-i) \quad (3)$$

The 2D signal $I(x,y)$ is defined by assuming that the fractional differential of $I(x,y)$ for the two directions (x- and y-axes) are separable in certain conditions. Given the separability of the Fourier transform, it can be used to extend the fractional calculus from one-dimensional space to two-dimensional space. The 2D image signal $I(x,y)$ is equally divided by $h = 1$ (unit time) to realise the fractional differentiation of the x- and y-axes.

From the equivalent expression of Equation (3), the approximate solution of the fractional calculus of the x- and y-axes can be obtained as follows:

$$\frac{d^v I(x,y)}{dx^v} \approx I(x,y) + (-1)^1(v)I(x-1,y) + (-1)^2\left(\frac{v(v-1)}{2}\right)I(x-2,y) + \cdots + (-1)^i \frac{\Gamma(v+1)}{\Gamma(i+1)\Gamma(v-i+1)} I(x-i,y) \quad (4)$$

$$\frac{d^v I(x,y)}{dy^v} \approx I(x,y) + (-1)^1(v)I(x,y-1) + (-1)^2\left(\frac{v(v-1)}{2}\right)I(x,y-2) + \cdots + (-1)^j \frac{\Gamma(v+1)}{\Gamma(j+1)\Gamma(v-j+1)} I(x,y-j) \quad (5)$$

Using the limit form, the numerical expressions of the fractional differential in the x- and y-axis directions are as follows:

$$\frac{d^v I(x,y)}{dx^v} = \lim_{N \to \infty} \left[\sum_{m=0}^{N-1} (-1)^i \frac{\Gamma(v+1)}{\Gamma(i+1)\Gamma(v-i+1)} I(x-i,y) \right] \quad (6)$$

$$\frac{d^v I(x,y)}{dy^v} = \lim_{N \to \infty} \left[\sum_{m=0}^{N-1} (-1)^j \frac{\Gamma(v+1)}{\Gamma(j+1)\Gamma(v-j+1)} I(x,y-j) \right] \quad (7)$$

Equations (6) and (7) can be used to obtain the v $(v \geq 0)$ order fractional differential operator coefficient R:

$$R = (-1)^m \binom{v}{m} = (-1)^m \frac{\Gamma(v+1)}{\Gamma(m+1)\Gamma(v-m+1)} \quad (8)$$

Assuming that the mask size is 3×3, i.e., if $N = 3$, the approximate solutions for the two axis directions can be obtained using Equations (7) and (8):

$$\frac{d^v I(x,y)}{dx^v} \approx I(x,y) + (-1)^1(v)I(x-1,y) + (-1)^2\left(\frac{v(v-1)}{2}\right)I(x-2,y)\# \quad (9)$$

$$\frac{d^v I(x,y)}{dy^v} \approx I(x,y) + (-1)^1(v)I(x,y-1) + (-1)^2\left(\frac{v(v-1)}{2}\right)I(x,y-2)\# \quad (10)$$

2.2. Fractional Differential Enhancement Operator and Convolution Template

By extending the formula of fractional differentiation to the other six directions, the approximate solutions of fractional differentiation in these six directions can be obtained. The eight directions are rotationally invariant; thus, the approximate solutions of fractional differentiation in these eight directions are used to construct the fractional differential operator.

Thus, the eight-directional mask template is established as shown in Figure 1. The coefficients for the positive and negative directions of the x-axis are defined as a_0^v and a_{180}^v, respectively, with a_{45}^v, a_{135}^v, a_{225}^v, and a_{315}^v in the counterclockwise direction. The coefficients for the positive and negative directions of the y-axis are a_{90}^v and a_{270}^v, respectively.

a_2^v	0	a_2^v	0	a_2^v
0	a_1^v	a_1^v	a_1^v	0
a_2^v	a_1^v	$8a_0^v$	a_1^v	a_2^v
0	a_1^v	a_1^v	a_1^v	0
a_2^v	0	a_2^v	0	a_2^v

Figure 1. Fractional differential mask.

The coefficients are defined as follows:

$$a_0^v = 1 \tag{11}$$

$$a_1^v = -v \tag{12}$$

$$a_2^v = \frac{v(v-1)}{2} \tag{13}$$

In an image, adjacent pixels have a certain similarity, and the closer the pixels are to the central target, the greater their similarity. Thus, the presence of too many adjacent pixels introduces unnecessary spatial and time complexities. Therefore, image processing should be aimed at exploiting the local neighbourhood pixel information of the target pixel. The 3×3 mask a_*^v in eight directions is used to perform convolution calculations on the image point $I(x,y)$, which is 5×5 in size, as follows:

$$I(x,y)_*^V = I(x,y) \times a_*^V \tag{14}$$

The convolution of each direction is calculated and weighted linearly to obtain the mask calculation results, as shown in Equation (15):

$$
\begin{aligned}
I(x,y)_*^V = \frac{I(x,y)_0^V}{sum(x,y)} &\times I(x,y)_0^{-V} + \frac{I(x,y)_{45}^V}{sum(x,y)} \times I(x,y)_{45}^V \\
&+ \frac{I(x,y)_{90}^V}{sum(x,y)} \times I(x,y)_{90}^V + \frac{I(x,y)_{135}^V}{sum(x,y)} \times I(x,y)_{135}^V \\
&+ \frac{I(x,y)_{180}^V}{sum(x,y)} \times I(x,y)_{180}^V + \frac{I(x,y)_{225}^V}{sum(x,y)} \times I(x,y)_{225}^V \\
&+ \frac{I(x,y)_{270}^V}{sum(x,y)} \times I(x,y)_{270}^V + \frac{I(x,y)_{315}^V}{sum(x,y)} \times I(x,y)_{315}^V
\end{aligned}
\tag{15}
$$

where

$$
\begin{aligned}
sum(x,y) = &\, I(x,y)_0^V + I(x,y)_{45}^V + I(x,y)_{90}^V + I(x,y)_{135}^V + I(x,y)_{180}^V \\
&+ I(x,y)_{225}^V + I(x,y)_{270}^V + I(x,y)_{315}^V
\end{aligned}
\tag{16}
$$

The image data are computed through the fractional differential mask convolution, and the convolution result is continuously enlarged or reduced. The results of convolution calculation can be normalised by defining the normalisation factor q as

$$
q = \sum_{\theta=0}^{360} I(x,y)_\theta^v \quad (\theta = 0, 45, 90, 135, 180, 215, 270, 315)
\tag{17}
$$

Then, q is substituted into Equation (18), and a 5×5 mask template is used to obtain filtered data $I(x,y)_*^V$:

$$
I(x,y)_*^V = \frac{I(x,y) \times a_*^V}{q}
\tag{18}
$$

2.3. Effect of the Fractional Differential Enhancement Algorithm on the Depth Image

In a 2D image, noise and edges are discontinuities of the local features. The pixel values of noise and edges are considerably different from those of neighbouring areas. Thus, noise and edges correspond to high-frequency signals, which are enhanced by fractional differential pairs. Therefore, fractional differential filtering is performed on a depth image, and the filtered depth image and corresponding point cloud image are obtained.

Figure 2 shows a depth image after fractional difference enhancement. The edge and noise points are enhanced to varying degrees. The point cloud image clearly shows the edges and several high-frequency noise spots. The objective of depth image enhancement is to enhance the textural information. However, as shown in Figure 2, edge noise is introduced into the depth image after fractional differential enhancement. Because the presence of such noise can limit the application of depth images in practical applications, such as 3D reconstruction, the enhancement method must be modified to effectively enhance the textural information.

As shown in Figure 2, the differential mask enhances high-frequency points or edge noise in the case of drastic changes in the edge information. However, the enhanced depth image cannot be used for 3D reconstruction. Moreover, according to experiments, gradient judgement-based methods cannot effectively distinguish weak noise from textural information.

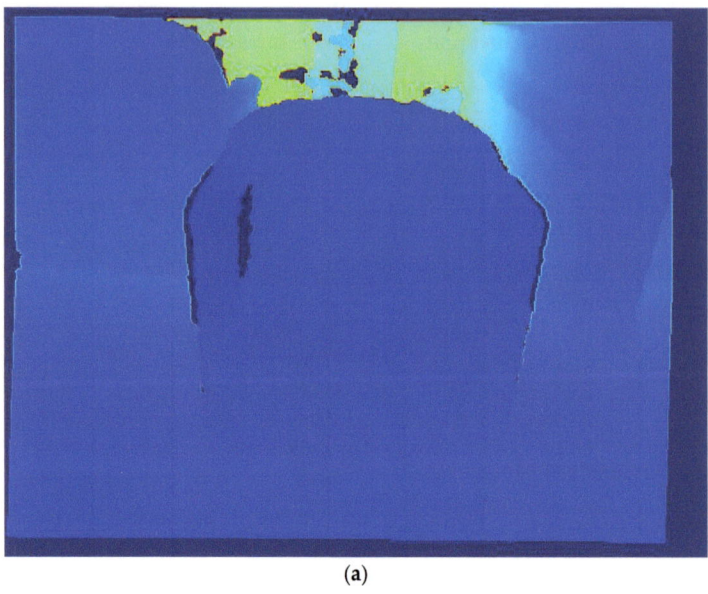

(a)

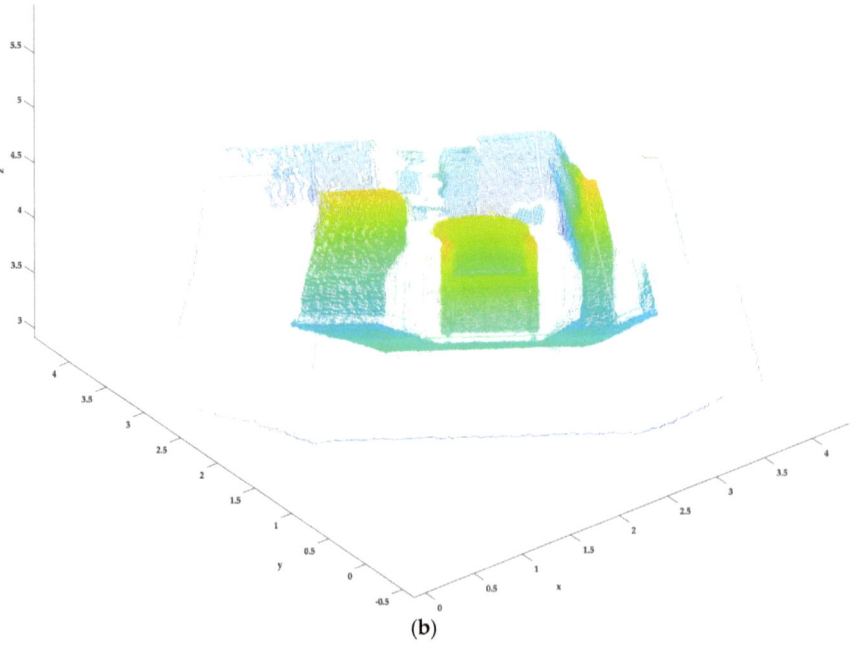

(b)

Figure 2. *Cont.*

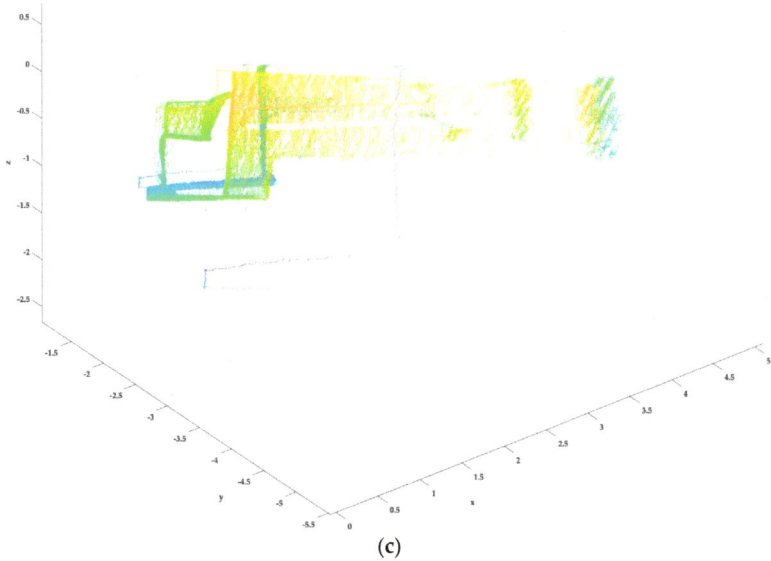

(c)

Figure 2. Fractional differential image enhancement. (a) Pseudo-colour image of the depth image. (b) Front view and (c) side view of the point clouds.

3. Fractional differential-Inverse-Distance-Weighted Enhancement Algorithm

A depth image, also known as a range image, takes the distance (depth) from an image collector to each point in a scene as the pixel value, which directly reflects the geometric shape of the visible surface of the scene. Such images are also termed spatial distance images. Based on the principle of similarity, the depth value is used as a weight, and this is used to estimate a reasonable value for a point to be interpolated. Assuming that each adjacent point has a local influence, an inverse-distance-weighted model is constructed. The distance between the point to be interpolated and a sample point is used as the weighting factor for weighted summation. A sample point at a smaller distance corresponds to a higher weight, so the weight decreases as a function of the distance.

3.1. Design of the Fractional differential-Inverse-Distance-Weighting Algorithm

The point to be inserted into a space is defined as $P(x_p, y_p, z_p)$, and known scattered points $Q_i(x_i, y_i, z_i), i = 1, 2, \cdots, n$ exist in the neighbourhood of point $P(x_p, y_p, z_p)$. The attribute value z_p of point $P(x_p, y_p, z_p)$ is interpolated using the distance-weighted inverse ratio method. The inverse distance interpolation principle states that in calculating the attribute value of the point to be inserted, the attribute value of the known point in the neighbourhood of this point must be considered. The attribute value of the point to be inserted is obtained from the inverse distance weighted average. The weight is related to the distance between the point to be inserted and point in the neighbourhood, where κ $(0 \leq \kappa \leq 2)$ is the power factor (κ is generally set to 2).

$$z_p = \frac{\sum_{i=1}^{n} \frac{z_i}{d_i^2}}{\sum_{i=1}^{n} \frac{1}{d_i^2}} \qquad (19)$$

where d_i is defined as the unit of distance from the point to be inserted to the i-th point in its neighbourhood.

$d_n(x,y)$ is defined as the distance from the point $d(x,y)$ to be interpolated to the adjacent point $d(x_n, y_n)$, as follows:

$$d_n(x,y) = \sqrt{(x-x_n)^2 + (y-y_n)^2} \tag{20}$$

The interpolation function $F(x,y)$ represents the weighted average of the function value $f_i(x,y)$ at each point, and $W_i(x,y)$ is the function of the reciprocal of the interpolation, as follows:

$$F(x,y) = \sum_{i=1}^{n} f_i(x,y) W_i(x,y) \tag{21}$$

$$W_i(x,y) = \frac{\frac{1}{d_i(x,y)}}{\sum_{i=1}^{n} \frac{1}{d_i(x,y)}} \tag{22}$$

The interpolation function is introduced into the data weighting process after fractional filtering, and the equalisation parameter φ is introduced considering that the function value may be zero.

Overall, $d(x,y)$ is the depth value of the image point $I(x,y)$ to be filtered, $d_i(x,y)$ is one of the convolution sums of eight fractional operators, and $\hat{d}(x,y)$ is the new depth value after filtering.

The weighting calculation formula is modified, and the linear weighting formula presented in Equation (19) is used—based on the inverse distance weighting method—to derive a new inverse distance weighting formula, as follows:

$$d(x,y) = I(x,y) \tag{23}$$

$$d_i(x,y) = I(x,y) * a_\theta^v, (\theta = 0, 45, 90, 135, 180, 215, 270, 315) \tag{24}$$

$$\hat{d}(x,y) = F(x,y) = \sum_{i=1}^{8} f_i(x,y) W_i(x,y) \tag{25}$$

$$f_i(x,y) = \sqrt{(d(x,y) - d_i(x,y))^2 + (\varphi)^2} \tag{26}$$

Q, obtained using Equation (17), is added into Equation (27), and the new $I(x,y)_*^v$ is obtained after applying the v-order fractional differential filter with a 3 × 3 mask, as follows:

$$I(x,y)_*^v = \frac{\hat{d}(x,y)}{q} \tag{27}$$

3.2. Depth Image Enhancement Effect of the Improved Algorithm

Equation (27) is applied to perform fractional differential enhancement of the depth image. The fractional order ranges from 0.1 to 0.9, and five iterations are performed. Figure 3 and Table 1 present the fractional differential enhancement effect associated with different orders.

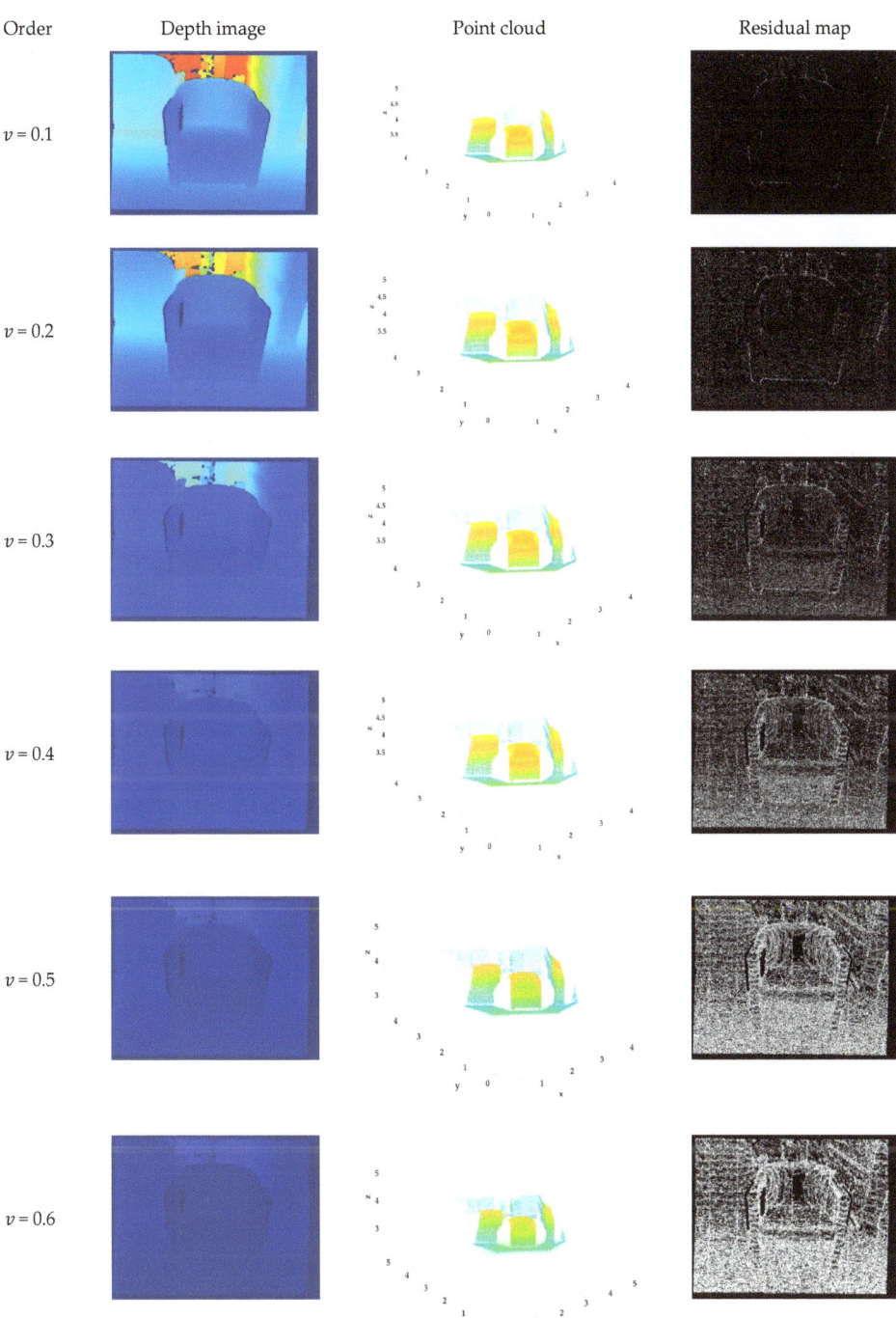

Figure 3. *Cont.*

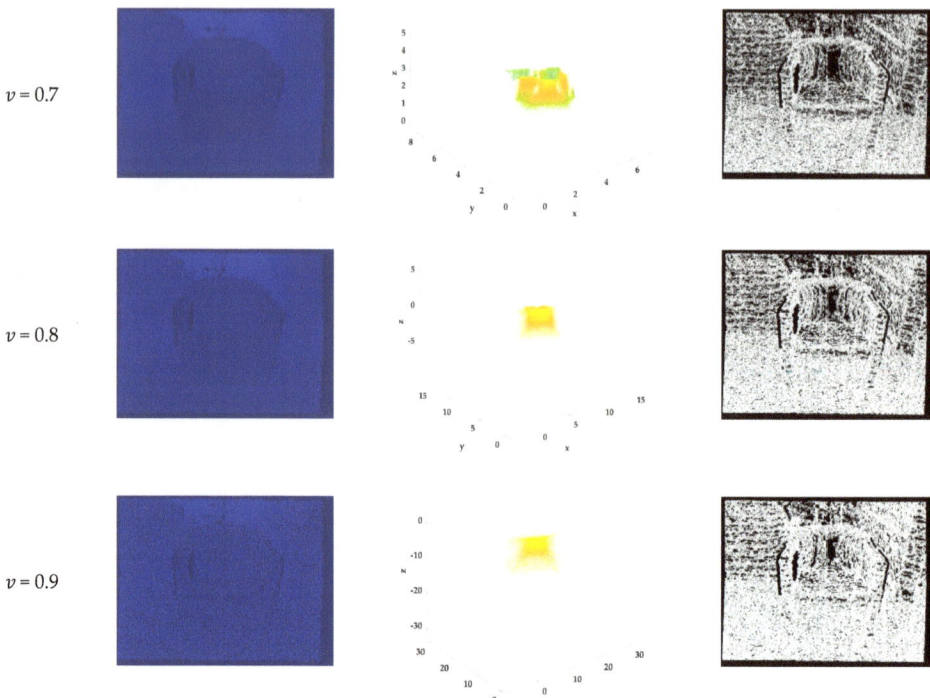

Figure 3. Fractional differential enhancement effect.

Table 1. Enhancement effect of fractional differential of different orders.

Fractional Order	Enhancement Effect (PSNR)
$v = 0.1$	61.872 dB
$v = 0.2$	54.026 dB
$v = 0.2$	44.996 dB
$v = 0.4$	35.875 dB
$v = 0.5$	26.832 dB
$v = 0.6$	19.698 dB
$v = 0.7$	13.143 dB
$v = 0.8$	3.532 dB
$v = 0.9$	0.135 dB

Figure 3 shows that when the fractional differential order is greater than 0.5, excessive enhancement occurs. In contrast, when the fractional differential order is less than 0.5, the enhanced texture details are insufficiently rich. Therefore, v is set to 0.5 as the optimal enhancement order, based on subjective evaluation.

4. Experimental Results and Analysis

4.1. Influence of the Number of Fractional Differential Iterations

The characteristic of the fractional order is that multiple iterations of a small order can be performed to realise refined processing. Therefore, the fractional-order differential-inverse-distance-weighted enhancement model is used to enhance the depth image for 1 to 5 iterations. Dataset [24] number 00333 is used. The continuous iteration results presented in Figures 4–8 indicate that the enhancement model using inverse distance weighting has the most realistic enhancement effect. Similarly, a comparison of Tables 1 and 2 shows that the effect of one iteration of order $v = 0.5$ is similar to that of five iterations of order $v = 0.1$, indicating that the performance obtained from multiple iterations of a small order is similar to that obtained from fewer iterations of a large order. Moreover, multiple iterations of the fractional differential-inverse-distance-weighting model have a uniform enhancement effect, which shows that this model can effectively enhance the texture and solve the enhancement problem of drastic changes in an edge. Thus, this enhancement model is practical for use in scenarios involving similar textural information.

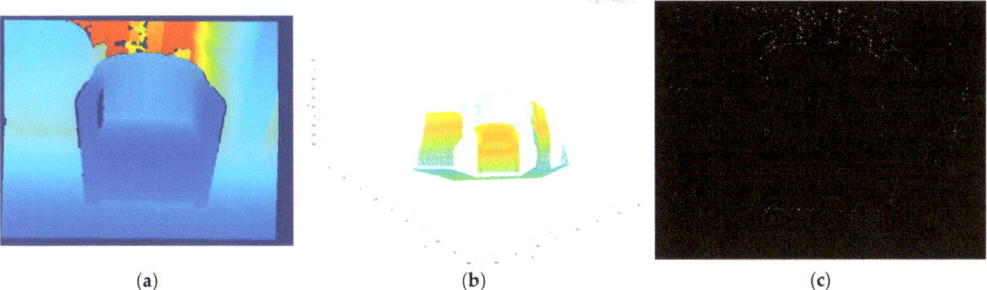

Figure 4. Results of one iteration of fractional differential enhancement ($v = 0.5$, PSNR = 64.680 dB). (**a**) Pseudo-colour image; (**b**) front view of the point cloud (after one-iteration enhancement); (**c**) residual image of the enhanced result.

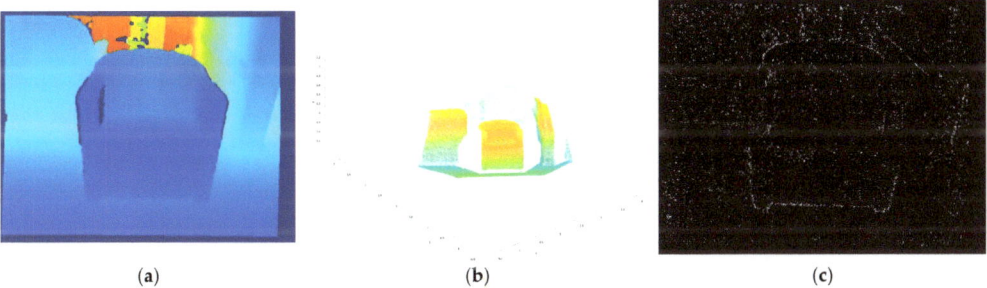

Figure 5. Results of two iterations of fractional differential enhancement ($v = 0.5$, PSNR = 53.476 dB). (**a**) Pseudo-colour image; (**b**) front view of the point cloud (after one-iteration enhancement); (**c**) residual image of the enhanced result.

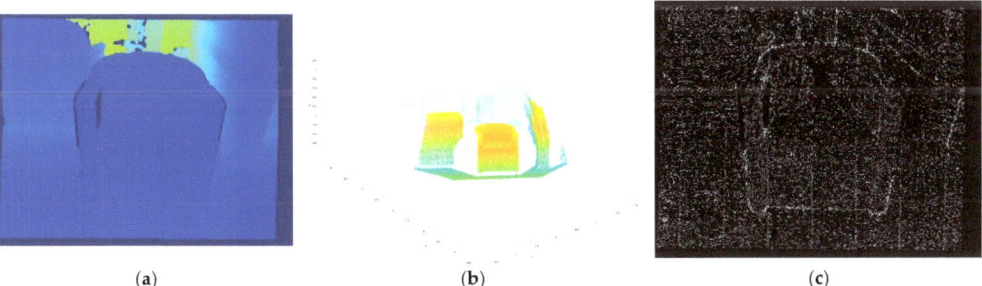

Figure 6. Results of three iterations of fractional differential enhancement ($v = 0.5$, PSNR = 43.639 dB). (**a**) Pseudo-colour image; (**b**) front view of the point cloud (after one-iteration enhancement); (**c**) residual image of the enhanced result.

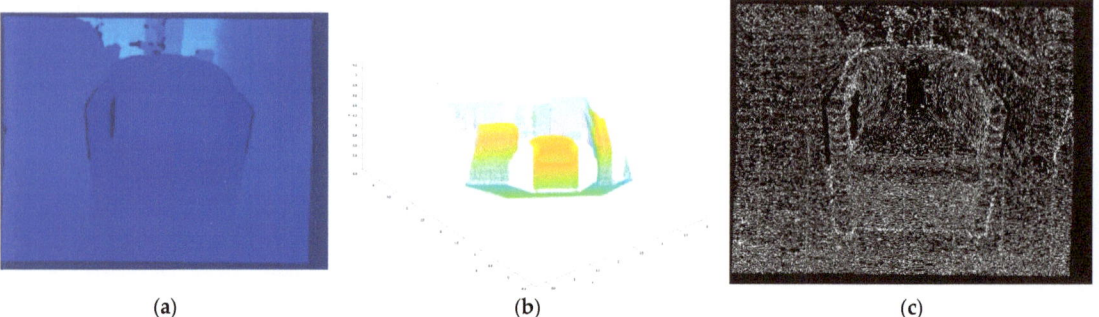

(a) (b) (c)

Figure 7. Results of four iterations of fractional differential enhancement ($v = 0.5$, PSNR = 34.621 dB). (a) Pseudo-colour image; (b) front view of the point cloud (after one-iteration enhancement); (c) residual image of the enhanced result.

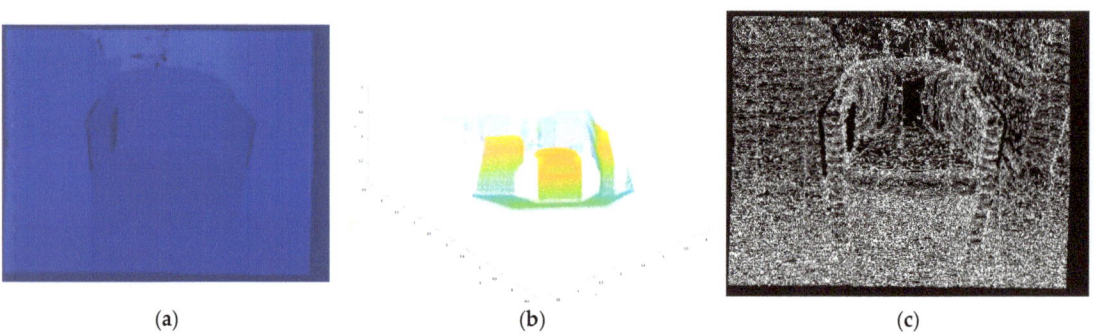

(a) (b) (c)

Figure 8. Results of five iterations of fractional differential enhancement ($v = 0.5$, PSNR = 26.832 dB). (a) Pseudo-colour image; (b) front view of the point cloud (after one-iteration enhancement); (c) residual image of the enhanced result.

Table 2. Enhancement effect of fractional differential with various numbers of iterations.

Iterations	Enhancement Effect (PNSR)
1	64.680 dB
2	53.476 dB
3	43.649 dB
4	34.621 dB
5	26.832 dB

4.2. Experimental Analysis and Verification of Depth Image Enhancement

To verify the universality of the fractional differential-inverse-distance-weighted enhancement model, it is used to enhance depth images with different levels of textural information. Figures 9–16 show the enhancement results for the depth images. These confirm that the model is universal, can achieve excellent textural enhancement effects even after many iterations, and exhibits high robustness.

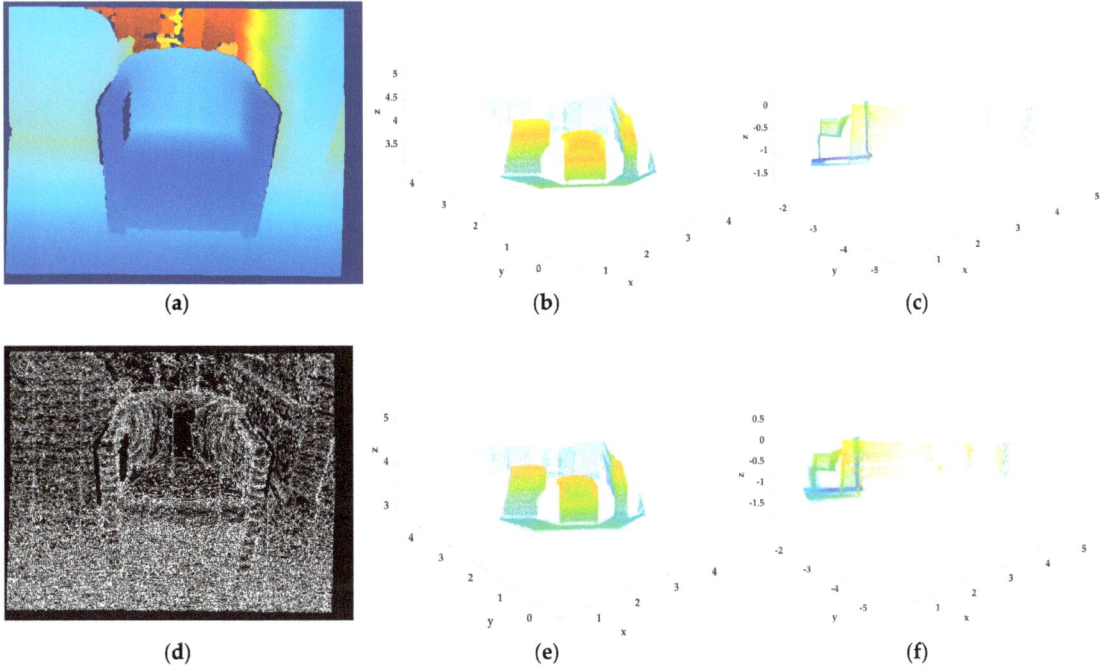

Figure 9. Results of five iterations of the fractional differential enhancement model (with dataset number 00333) ($v = 0.5$, PSNR = 26.832 dB). (**a**) Pseudo-colour image; (**b**) front view and (**c**) side view of point clouds (unenhanced image); (**d**) residual image of the enhancement result; (**e**) front view and (**f**) side view after five-iteration enhancement.

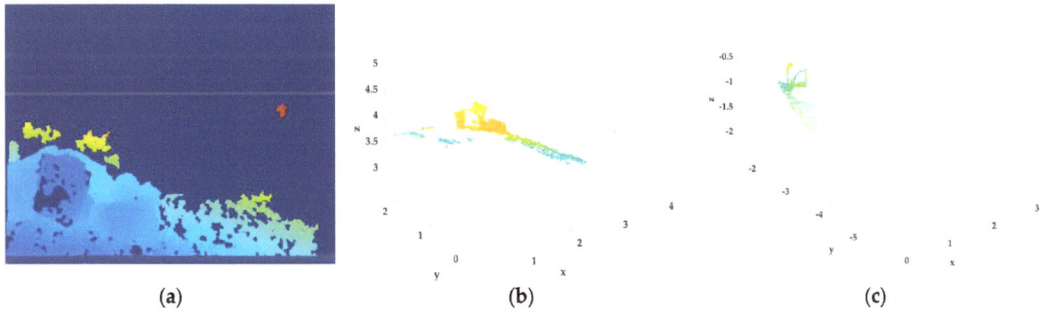

Figure 10. *Cont.*

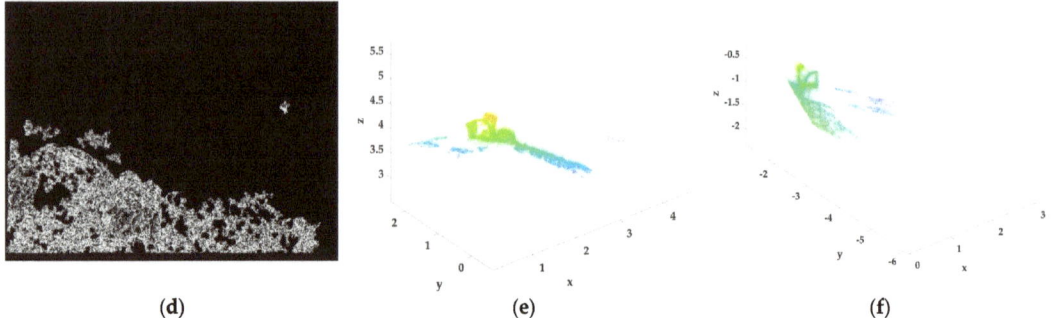

Figure 10. Results of five iterations of the fractional differential enhancement model (with dataset number 02350) ($\nu = 0.5$, PSNR = 35.606 dB). (**a**) Pseudo-colour image; (**b**) front view and (**c**) side view of point clouds (unenhanced image); (**d**) residual image of the enhancement result; (**e**) front view and (**f**) side view after five-iteration enhancement.

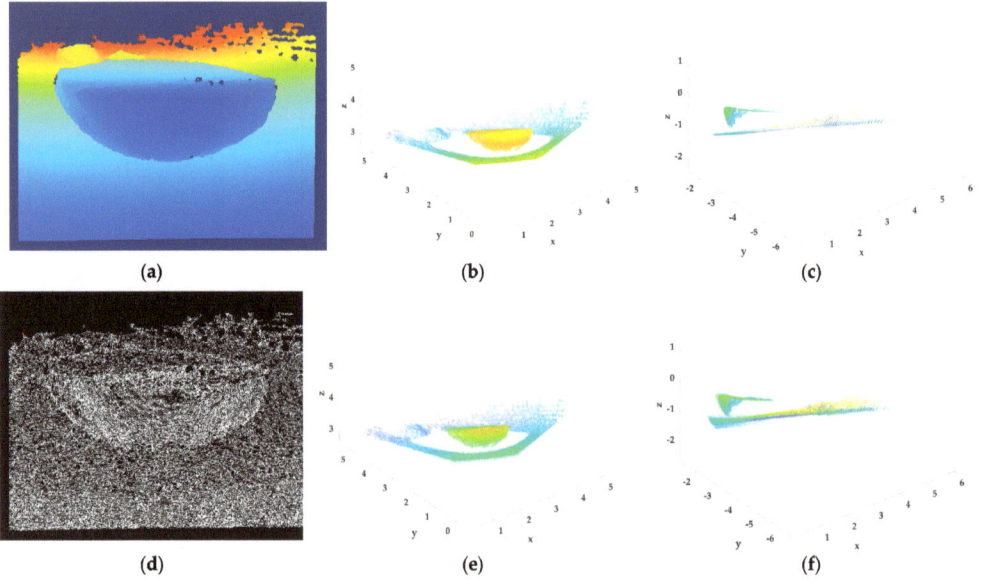

Figure 11. Results of five iterations of the fractional differential enhancement model (with dataset number 03236) ($\nu = 0.5$, PSNR = 29.931 dB). (**a**) Pseudo-colour image; (**b**) front view and (**c**) side view of point clouds (unenhanced image); (**d**) residual image of the enhancement result; (**e**) front view and (**f**) side view after five-iteration enhancement.

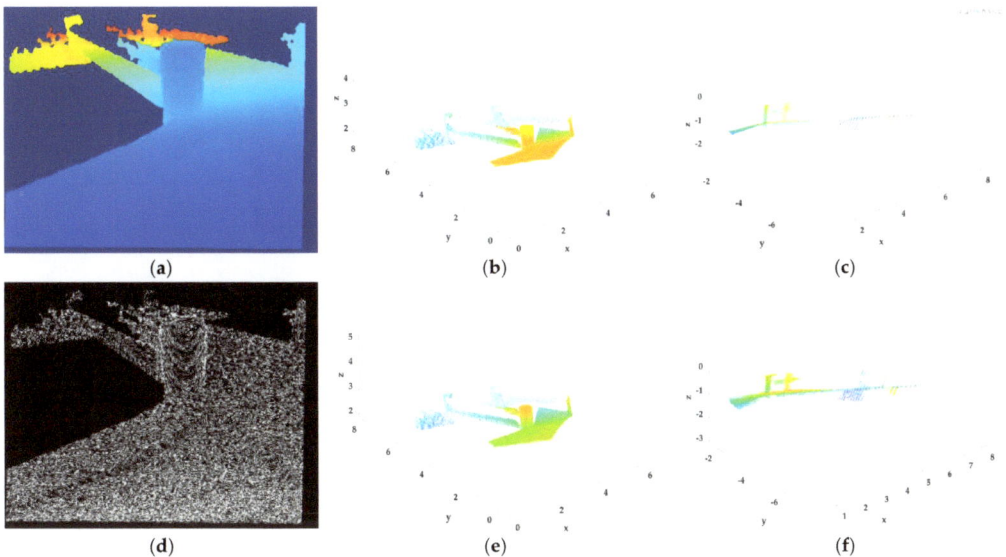

Figure 12. Results of five iterations of the fractional differential enhancement model (with dataset number 03528) ($\nu = 0.5$, PSNR = 31.189 dB). (**a**) Pseudo-colour image; (**b**) front view and (**c**) side view of point clouds (unenhanced image); (**d**) residual image of the enhancement result; (**e**) front view and (**f**) side view after five-iteration enhancement.

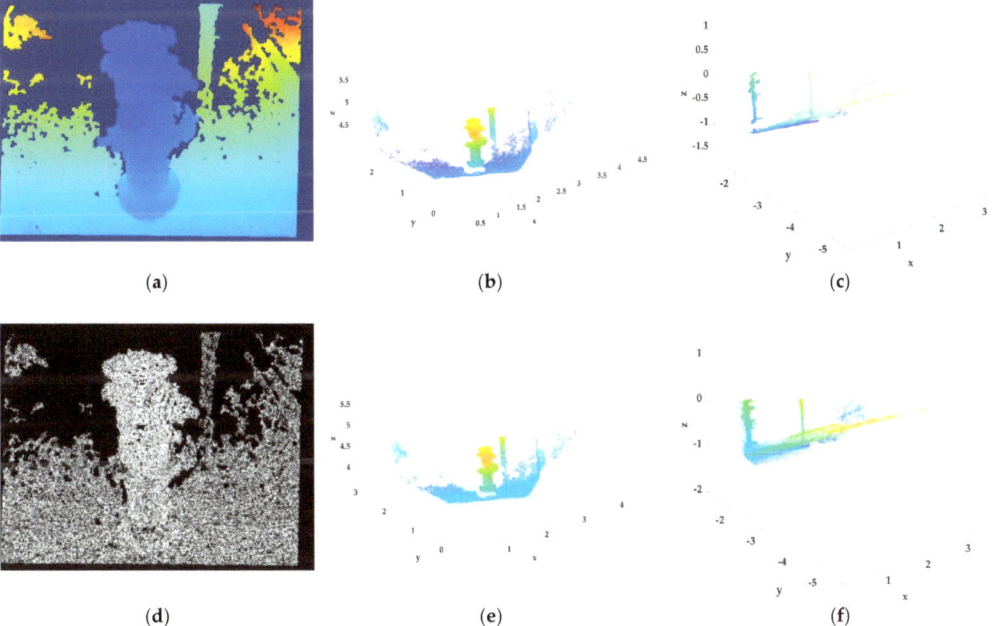

Figure 13. Results of five iterations of the fractional differential enhancement model (with dataset number 04797) ($\nu = 0.5$, PSNR = 32.671 dB). (**a**) Pseudo-colour image; (**b**) front view and (**c**) side view of point clouds (unenhanced image); (**d**) residual image of the enhancement result; (**e**) front view and (**f**) side view after five-iteration enhancement.

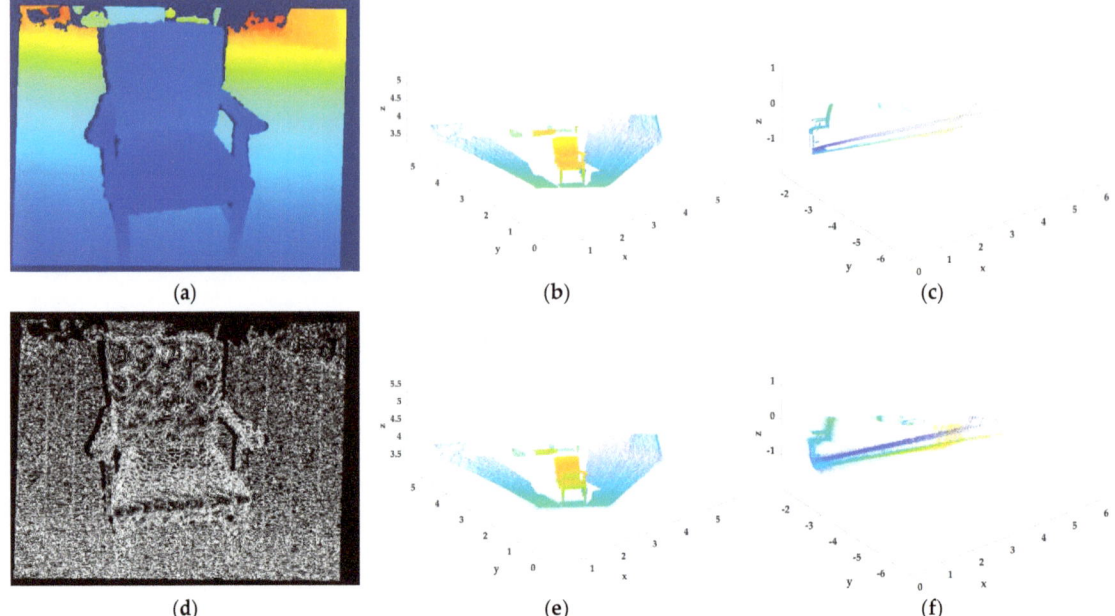

Figure 14. Results of five iterations of the fractional differential enhancement model (with dataset number 05989) (ν = 0.5, PSNR = 34.016 dB). (**a**) Pseudo-colour image; (**b**) front view and (**c**) side view of point clouds (unenhanced image); (**d**) residual image of the enhancement result; (**e**) front view and (**f**) side view after five-iteration enhancement.

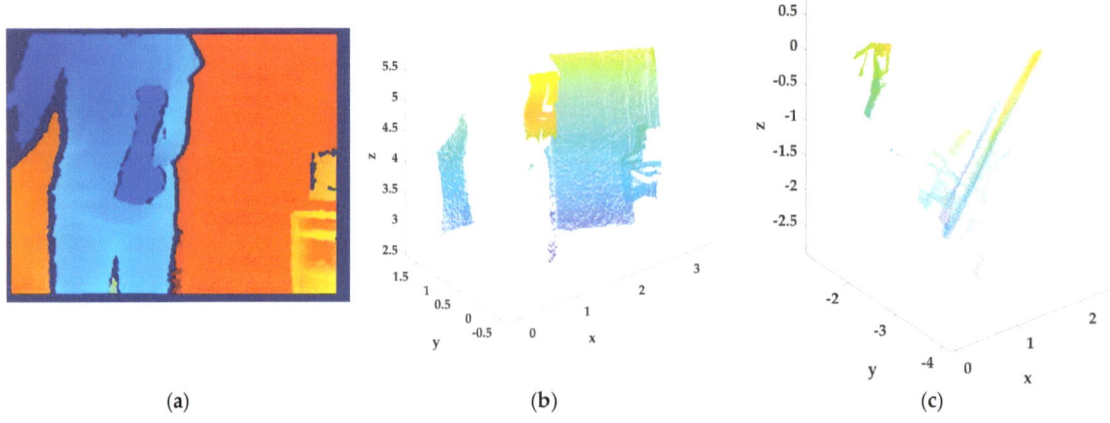

Figure 15. *Cont.*

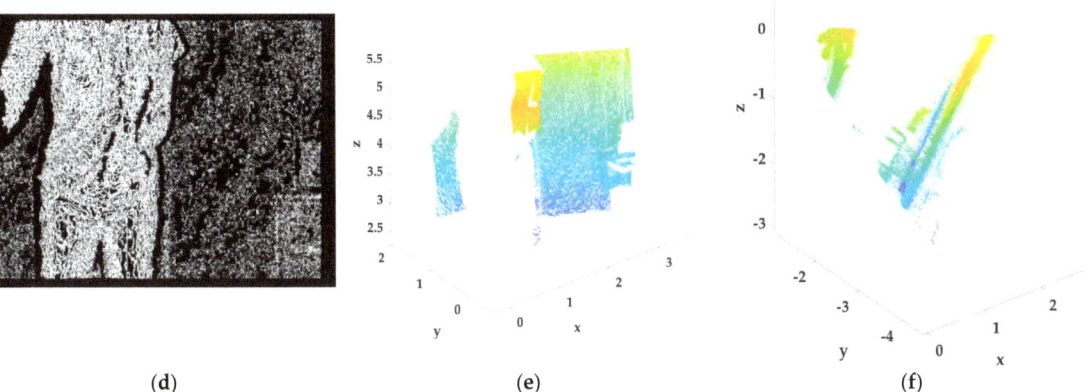

Figure 15. Results of five iterations of the fractional differential enhancement model (with dataset number 09860) (ν = 0.5, PSNR = 28.462 B). (**a**) Pseudo-colour image; (**b**) front view and (**c**) side view of point clouds (unenhanced image); (**d**) residual image of the enhancement result; (**e**) front view and (**f**) side view after five-iteration enhancement.

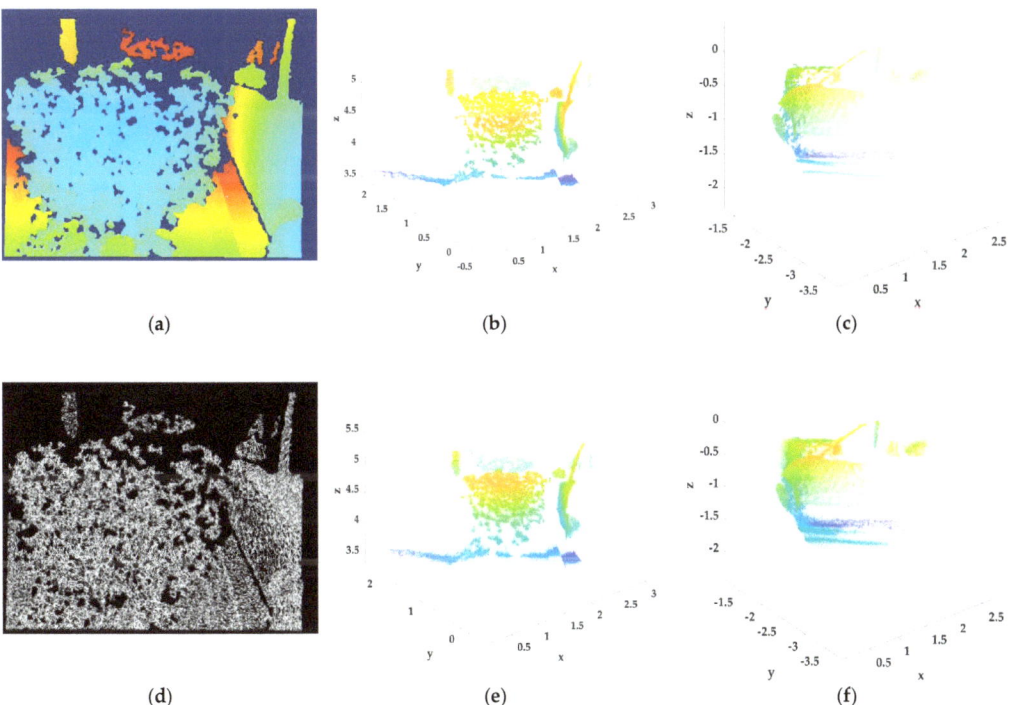

Figure 16. Results of five iterations of the fractional differential enhancement model (with dataset number 08343) (ν = 0.5, PSNR = 29.913 dB). (**a**) Pseudo-colour image; (**b**) front view and (**c**) side view of point clouds (unenhanced image); (**d**) residual image of the enhancement result; (**e**) front view and (**f**) side view after five-iteration enhancement.

In different environments, the textural information can be effectively enhanced through multiple iterations, and the enhancement amplitude of the textural information can be adjusted by modifying the number of iterations. The experimental results verify that the model selectively enhances textural information by optimising the order and the number of iterations. Moreover, the edge information of a depth image is retained after the enhancement process, which indicates that the model can effectively distinguish edge information from textural information and thereby achieve selective enhancement.

5. Discussion

Based on an examination of the existing depth image enhancement methods, a novel depth image enhancement algorithm based on a fractional differential is devised. The fractional differential-inverse-distance-weighted enhancement method is developed to solve the problem associated with high-frequency noise in fractional differential enhancement. First, image enhancement is performed based on fractional differentiation to effectively enhance the quality of a depth image. The contouring and high-frequency details of a depth image are enhanced by constructing a fractional differential mask for convolution. However, point cloud observation shows that this method introduces certain high-frequency noise at an edge. Thus, the image directly enhanced by fractional differentiation cannot be used for 3D reconstruction. Second, inverse distance weighting is applied to improve the weighted calculation of the convolution result of fractional differentiation. The improved fractional-order differential-inverse-distance-weighting algorithm can alleviate the high-frequency noise problem while maintaining the edge features of an enhanced depth image. The distance between the interpolation point and sample point is used as the weight factor to calculate the convolution result. The distance of the sample points is inversely proportional to the weight assigned in the inverse distance weighting process. The accuracy and smoothness of the resulting data are increased by the introduction of fractional filtering through the interpolation function. The experimental results show that the enhancement effect of the fractional differential-inverse-distance-weighting model is realistic and that uniform enhancement can be achieved, even after multiple iterations.

In summary, the effectiveness and superiority of depth image enhancement based on a fractional differential are demonstrated through theoretical and experimental studies, and a fractional differential-inverse-distance-weighted enhancement method is developed to solve the problems associated with fractional differential enhancement. This novel approach represents the first attempt at integrating a fractional differential into depth image enhancement and is an effective solution for depth image enhancement. For example, in the fields of medical image processing, machine vision, and autonomous driving, and compared with current methods, this algorithm could provide clearer depth images for more accurate recognition of objects and scenes.

Depth images have a wide range of practical applications, such as in 3D modelling, robot navigation, and virtual reality. Therefore, future research directions could include and verify the utility of the fractional differential enhancement algorithm in practical application scenarios and explore more efficient algorithms. First, depth image enhancement should be further combined with the depth image data required for an actual scene, and the algorithm should be applied to a scene requiring additional textural information for its depth image. Second, as the algorithm is not efficient enough to achieve real-time depth image enhancement, further research on the computational speed of the algorithm is an important future research direction. The algorithm can be implemented using a graphics processor or neural network processing unit to enable real-time depth image enhancement. Finally, the effect of the algorithm on 3D reconstruction after depth image enhancement and the 3D reconstruction of depth images with more abundant textural information than those in this study must be explored in future studies.

Author Contributions: Conceptualization, T.H., X.L. and C.W.; methodology, T.H. and X.W.; software, T.H. and D.X.; formal analysis, T.H. and X.W.; data curation, X.W. and D.X.; writing—original draft preparation, T.H. and X.W.; writing—review and editing, T.H., X.L. and C.W.; funding acquisition, X.L. and C.W. All authors have read and agreed to the published version of the manuscript.

Funding: This research was funded by National Key R&D Program of China, grant number 2022YFC3803702.

Data Availability Statement: Not applicable.

Conflicts of Interest: The authors declare no conflict of interest.

References

1. Murayama, M.; Higashiyama, T.; Harazono, Y.; Ishii, H.; Shimoda, H.; Okido, S.; Taruta, Y. Depth Image Noise Reduction and Super-Resolution by Pixel-Wise Multi-Frame Fusion. *IEICE Trans. Inf. Syst.* **2022**, *E105-D*, 1211–1224. [CrossRef]
2. Zhang, X.-F.; Yan, H. Image Denoising and Enhancement Algorithm Based on Median Filtering and Fractional-order Filtering. *J. Northeast. Univ. Nat. Sci.* **2020**, *41*, 482–487.
3. Nandal, S.; Kumar, S. Image Denoising Using Fractional Quaternion Wavelet Transform. In *Proceedings of the 2nd International Conference on Computer Vision & Image Processing: CVIP 2017*; Springer: Singapore, 2018; Volume 2. [CrossRef]
4. Shanmugavadivu, P.; Sivakumar, V. Fractal Dimension Based Texture Analysis of Digital Images. *Procedia Eng.* **2012**, *38*, 2981–2986. [CrossRef]
5. Zhou, D.; Wang, R.; Lu, J.; Zhang, Q. Depth Image Super Resolution Based on Edge-Guided Method. *Appl. Sci.* **2018**, *8*, 298. [CrossRef]
6. Hui, T.-W.; Ngan, K.N. Depth enhancement using RGB-D guided filtering. In Proceedings of the 2014 IEEE International Conference on Image Processing (ICIP), Paris, France, 27–30 October 2014; pp. 3832–3836.
7. Senthilkumaran, N.; Thimmiaraja, J. Histogram Equalization for Image Enhancement Using MRI Brain Images. In Proceedings of the 2014 World Congress on Computing and Communication Technologies, Trichirappalli, India, 27 February–1 March 2014; pp. 80–83.
8. Wang, Z.; Lv, G.Q.; Feng, Q.B.; Wang, A.T.; Ming, H. Resolution priority holographic stereogram based on integral imaging with enhanced depth range. *Opt. Express* **2019**, *27*, 2689–2702. [CrossRef] [PubMed]
9. Gupta, A.; Kumar, S. Generalized framework for the design of adaptive fractional-order masks for image denoising. *Digit. Signal Process.* **2022**, *121*, 103305. [CrossRef]
10. Zhang, X.; He, H.; Zhang, J.-X. Multi-focus image fusion based on fractional-order differentiation and closed image matting. *ISA Trans.* **2022**, *129*, 703–714. [CrossRef] [PubMed]
11. Harjule, P.; Tokir, M.M.; Mehta, T.; Gurjar, S.; Kumar, A.; Agarwal, B. Texture Enhancement of Medical Images for Efficient Disease Diagnosis with Optimized Fractional Derivative Masks. *J. Comput. Biol.* **2022**, *29*, 545–564. [CrossRef] [PubMed]
12. Zhang, X.; Liu, R.; Ren, J.; Gui, Q. Adaptive fractional image enhancement algorithm based on rough set and particle swarm optimization. *Fractal Fract.* **2022**, *6*, 100. [CrossRef]
13. Zhang, X.; Dai, L. Image enhancement based on rough set and fractional-order differentiator. *Fractal Fract.* **2022**, *6*, 214. [CrossRef]
14. Zhang, L.; Jia, Z.; Koefoed, L.; Yang, J.; Kasabov, N. Remote sensing image enhancement based on the combination of adaptive nonlinear gain and the PLIP model in the NSST domain. *Multimed. Tools Appl.* **2020**, *79*, 13647–13665. [CrossRef]
15. Liu, X.; Pedersen, M.; Wang, R. Survey of natural image enhancement techniques: Classification, evaluation, challenges, and perspectives. *Digit. Signal Process.* **2022**, *127*, 103547. [CrossRef]
16. Hacini, M.; Hachouf, F.; Charef, A. A bi-directional fractional-order derivative mask for image processing applications. *IET Image Process.* **2020**, *14*, 2512–2524. [CrossRef]
17. Li, M.M.; Li, B.Z. A Novel Active Contour Model for Noisy Image Segmentation Based on Adaptive Fractional-order Differentiation. *IEEE Trans. Image Process.* **2020**, *29*, 9520–9531. [CrossRef]
18. Balochian, S.; Baloochian, H. Edge detection on noisy images using Prewitt operator and fractional-order differentiation. *Multimed. Tools Appl.* **2020**, *81*, 9759–9770. [CrossRef]
19. Yu, L.; Zeng, Z.; Wang, H.; Pedrycz, W. Fractional-order differentiation based sparse representation for multi-focus image fusion. *Multimed. Tools Appl.* **2022**, *81*, 4387–4411. [CrossRef]
20. Pan, X.; Zhu, J.; Yu, H.; Chen, L.; Liu, Y.; Li, L. Robust corner detection with fractional calculus for magnetic resonance imaging. *Biomed. Signal Process. Control* **2021**, *63*, 102112. [CrossRef]
21. Xu, L.; Huang, G.; Chen, Q. -L.; Qin, H.-Y.; Men, T.; Pu, Y.-F. An improved method for image denoising based on fractional-order integration. *Front. Inf. Technol. Electron. Eng.* **2020**, *21*, 1485–1493. [CrossRef]
22. Huang, G.; Xu, L.; Chen, Q. -L.; Pu, Y.-F. Research on image denoising based on time-space fractional partial differential equations. *Xi Tong Gong Cheng Yu Dian Zi Ji Shu/Syst. Eng. Electron.* **2012**, *34*, 1741–1752.

23. Pu, Y. -F.; Wang, W.X. Fractional differential masks of digital image and their numerical implementation algorithms. *Acta Autom. Sin.* **2007**, *33*, 1128–1135.
24. Choi, S.; Zhou, Q.Y.; Miller, S.; Koltun, V. A Large Dataset of Object Scans. *arXiv* **2016**, arXiv:1602.02481.

Disclaimer/Publisher's Note: The statements, opinions and data contained in all publications are solely those of the individual author(s) and contributor(s) and not of MDPI and/or the editor(s). MDPI and/or the editor(s) disclaim responsibility for any injury to people or property resulting from any ideas, methods, instructions or products referred to in the content.

 *fractal and fractional*

Article

A Finite-Dimensional Control Scheme for Fractional-Order Systems under Denial-of-Service Attacks

Ying Zou [1,†], Xinyao Li [2,*,†], Chao Deng [3] and Xiaowen Wu [1]

1. School of Information and Electrical Engineering, Hunan University of Science and Technology, Xiangtan 411201, China; yingz_2020@126.com (Y.Z.); xwu@hnust.edu.cn (X.W.)
2. School of Automation, Guangdong Polytechnic Normal University, Guangzhou 510450, China
3. Institute of Advanced Technology, Nanjing University of Posts and Telecommunications, Nanjing 210023, China; dengchao_neu@126.com
* Correspondence: lixinyao@gpnu.edu.cn or E180209@e.ntu.edu.sg
† These authors are co-first authors.

Abstract: In this article, the security control problem of discrete-time fractional-order networked systems under denial-of-service (DoS) attacks is considered. A practically applicable finite-dimensional control strategy will be developed for fractional-order systems that possess nonlocal characteristics. By employing the Lyapunov method, it is theoretically proved that under the proposed controller, the obtained closed-loop fractional system is globally input-to-state stable (ISS), even in the presence of DoS attacks. Finally, the effectiveness of the designed control method is demonstrated by the numerical example.

Keywords: security control; discrete-time networked systems; denial-of-service (DoS) attacks; fractional-order

1. Introduction

The utilization of fractional-order calculus, due to its distinctive nonlocal features, is highly advantageous in precisely representing the dynamic characteristics of a multitude of real-world phenomena or systems that have infinite memory; see, for instance, [1–3].

The research and development of fractional-order systems and their associated controls have recently been garnering increased interest [4–6]. It has been proposed that fractional-order differential equations can more accurately capture the rheological constitutive equation (RCE) for the viscoelasticity of polymer materials, as evidenced in [1,5]. In [7], a full-cell model of fractional order with a distinct physical interpretation was developed. Two studies [8,9], utilize fractional-order methods to simulate lithium-ion batteries. Several recent works regarding the application of fractional systems can be found in, for example, [10–13]. For the continuous-time case, the concept of a proportional integral derivative (PID) controller of fractional order was initially presented in [14]. The linear fractional-order systems' stability is discussed in [15]. Sampled-data control schemes for linear fractional-order systems that take the unique properties of fractional-order calculus into account are investigated in [16–18]. The fractional-order Lyapunov direct stability analysis method employed in [19] yields Mittag–Leffler stable conditions for nonlinear fractional-order systems. In [20–23], the development of adaptive backstepping-based controllers for fractional-order uncertain nonlinear systems subject to unknown disturbances is reported. An adaptive fractional controller is developed for high-order nonlinear integer uncertain systems in [24]. By truncating the fractional operator, which is infinite-dimensional, refs. [25–28] propose the finite-dimensional control approaches for fractional-order systems in the discrete-time domain based on the truncated approximated finite-dimensional systems. Further improvement was then made in [29–31], where the finite-dimensional approximation errors were considered in designing a controller by treating them as the additive uncertainty terms, thus ensuring practical asymptotic stability of the actual fractional-order systems.

Attacks on communication links in a networked control system can be divided into two categories: denial-of-service (DoS) attacks and deception attacks. An interruption of communication between networks leads to a DoS attack [32], whereas deception attacks usually involve altering the data that are sent [33]. This article focuses on DoS attacks. Nowadays, some controllers have been created to mitigate the impact of DoS attacks on integer-order systems [34–38]. In [37,38], event-triggered resilient cooperative control schemes are proposed for continuous-time multiagent systems under DoS attacks, such that the controlled multiagent systems can achieve secure consensus exponentially. As for discrete-time multiagent systems in the presence of aperiodic sampling and random DoS attacks, a distributed output-feedback control scheme is developed to reach output consensus by assuming that the sampling process is nonuniform and the consecutive attack duration is upper-bounded [36]. Despite this, there are a limited number of published security control studies for fractional-order systems in the literature. References [39,40] analyze the control problem for continuous-time fractional-order multiagent systems and complex networks that are vulnerable to DoS attacks, respectively. Reference [41] studies the control of discrete-time fractional-order multiagent systems under DoS attacks, disregarding the nonlocal characteristics of fractional-order calculus when designing the control scheme. As of yet, the topic of DoS attacks and their effects on discrete-time fractional-order networked systems has not been explored in depth, which provides the impetus for this work.

In spite of the aforementioned discussion, in this work, we analyze the discrete-time fractional-order systems in which the plant and controller are connected via the network, while the attacker attempts to disrupt the control system's stability by hindering communication between the sensors and controller (measurement channel). The main contributions of this work are outlined in the following:

1. The development of a safety control protocol for discrete-time fractional-order systems subject to external disturbance and DoS attacks is investigated in this article, with the unique properties of fractional-order calculus being taken into account.
2. The controller proposed is finite-dimensional, which makes it possible to calculate the control input with only a limited number of prior system states, making it suitable for practical use.
3. A sufficient condition is provided to guarantee the global stability of the closed-loop system, resulting in the system output eventually settling at an ultimate bound around the origin.

This article is organized as follows: Section 2 presents the problem statement. The controller design procedure is given in Section 3. In Section 4, the proposed control strategy will be examined by simulation example, and finally, Section 5 provides the conclusions of this work.

2. Problem Formulation

Consider a discrete-time linear fractional system described as follows:

$$\begin{cases} {}_0\Delta_{k+1}^\alpha z(k+1) = Az(k) + Bu(k) + B_\omega \omega(k) \\ y(k) = C_2 z(k), \ z(0) = z_0 \end{cases} \quad (1)$$

where $z(k) \in \mathbb{R}^n$ is the state vector at time step $k \in \mathbb{N}_0$, ${}_0\Delta_{k+1}^\alpha z(k+1) = [{}_0\Delta_{k+1}^{\alpha_1} z_1(k+1), \cdots, {}_0\Delta_{k+1}^{\alpha_n} z_n(k+1)]^T$, $u(k) \in \mathbb{R}^m$ is the control input, $y(k) \in \mathbb{R}^p$ is the measurement output, $\omega(k) \in \mathbb{R}^r$ is the exogenous disturbance signal bounded as $\|\omega(k)\| \leq q_\omega$ with $q_\omega > 0$ and A, B, B_ω and C_2 are known real matrices with appropriate dimensions. In accordance with Remark 4 in [18], the state, control signal, and disturbance before the initial time are considered to be all equal to zero in this work, i.e., $z(q) = 0$, $u(q) = 0$ and $\omega(q) = 0$, $\forall q < 0$.

Remark 1. *For discrete-time fractional systems, several existing works [25–31] focus on the control problem. Nevertheless, none of these present studies concern the influence of attacks when designing control schemes, which highlights the advantages of our work where a safety control strategy is proposed for discrete-time fractional systems.*

According to [42], the Grünwald–Letnikov (GL) fractional-order difference of a discrete-variable bounded function $f(k) : \mathbb{N}_0 \to \mathbb{R}$ is defined as

$${}_0\Delta_k^\alpha f(k) = \sum_{j=0}^k (-1)^j \binom{\alpha}{j} f(k-j), \; \alpha \in \mathbb{R}^+, k \in \mathbb{N}_0, \tag{2}$$

where

$$\binom{\alpha}{j} = \begin{cases} 1 & j = 0 \\ \frac{\alpha(\alpha-1)\cdots(\alpha-j+1)}{j!} & j > 0 \end{cases} \text{ for all } j \in \mathbb{N}_0. \tag{3}$$

Define $c_j(\alpha) = (-1)^j \binom{\alpha}{j}$, and due to the fact that $|c_j(\alpha)| \leq \frac{\alpha^j}{j!}$, for any $\alpha \in \mathbb{R}^+$, the sequence $\{c_j(\alpha)\}_{j \in \mathbb{N}_0}$ is absolutely summable.

For the i-th state ($i = 1, 2, \cdots, n$), we have

$${}_0\Delta_{k+1}^{\alpha_i} z_i(k+1) = \sum_{j=0}^{k+1} c_j(\alpha_i) z_i(k+1-j), \tag{4}$$

in which α_i is the fractional-order corresponding to z_i. Equation (4) can be rewritten as

$$z_i(k+1) = {}_0\Delta_{k+1}^{\alpha_i} z_i(k+1) - \sum_{j=1}^{k+1} c_j(\alpha_i) z_i(k+1-j), \tag{5}$$

and hence, the evolution of $z(k+1)$ can be expressed as

$$z(k+1) = Az(k) + Bu(k) + B_\omega \omega(k) - \sum_{j=1}^{k+1} F_j(\alpha) z(k+1-j) \tag{6}$$

where $F_j(\alpha) = \text{diag}(c_j(\alpha_1), c_j(\alpha_2), \cdots, c_j(\alpha_n)) \in \mathbb{R}^n$. Alternatively, (6) can be presented as

$$z(k+1) = \sum_{j=0}^k A_j z(k-j) + Bu(k) + B_\omega \omega(k) \tag{7}$$

in which $A_0 = A - F_1(\alpha)$ and $A_j = -F_{j+1}(\alpha)$ for $j \geq 1$. As a result, the linear discrete-time fractional-order system (1) can be described as

$$\begin{cases} z(k+1) = \sum_{j=0}^k A_j z(k-j) + Bu(k) + B_\omega \omega(k) \\ y(k) = C_2 z(k), \; z(0) = z_0. \end{cases} \tag{8}$$

Notation. I_n indicates an identity matrix with a dimension equal to n. $\mathbb{R}^+$, $\mathbb{R}$, $\mathbb{N}_0$, $\mathbb{N}$, and $\mathbb{Z}$, respectively, represent the set of non-negative reals, reals, non-negative integers, positive integers, and integer numbers. The identity function is denoted by Id, i.e., $Id(z) = z$. $\|z\|_\infty = \sup_{j \in \mathbb{Z}} \|z(j)\|$ and $\|z\|_{-[j_1, j_2]}$ is defined as:

$$\|z\|_{-[j_1, j_2]} = \begin{cases} \max_{j_1 \leq j \leq j_2} \|z(j)\|, & \text{if } j_1 \leq j_2 \\ 0, & \text{if } j_1 > j_2. \end{cases}$$

It can be seen from the expression of the GL fractional-order difference of function $f(k)$ given in (2) that the cumulative term used to implement the fractional-order difference will increase as k increases. Different from the controller proposed in [43], which is a linear weighted combination of all the past states of the observer, which will consequently result in the computational explosion as time goes by, a finite-dimensional controller that contains finite steps of recent states is considered in this work.

Reformulate (8) as

$$\begin{cases} \hat{z}(k+1) = \hat{A}_L \hat{z}(k) + \hat{B} u(k) + \hat{B}_\omega \hat{\omega}(k) \\ y(k) = \hat{C}_2 \hat{z}(k), \end{cases} \quad (9)$$

where $L \in \mathbb{N}_0$, $\hat{z}(k) = [z^T(k), z^T(k-1), \cdots, z^T(k-L)]^T \in \mathbb{R}^{(L+1)n}$ is the recent-finite-steps state vector, $\hat{\omega}(k) = [\omega^T(k), z^T(k-L-1), \cdots, z^T(0)]^T \in \mathbb{R}^{r+(k-L)n}$, and $\hat{A}_L, \hat{B}, \hat{B}_\omega$ and $\hat{C}_2$ are defined as

$$\hat{A}_L = \begin{bmatrix} A_0 & A_1 & \cdots & A_{L-1} & A_L \\ I_n & 0 & \cdots & 0 & 0 \\ \vdots & \vdots & \ddots & \vdots & \vdots \\ 0 & 0 & \cdots & I_n & 0 \end{bmatrix}, \hat{B} = \begin{bmatrix} B \\ 0 \\ \vdots \\ 0 \end{bmatrix},$$

$$\hat{B}_\omega = \begin{bmatrix} B_\omega & A_{L+1} & \cdots & A_{k-1} & A_k \\ 0 & 0 & \cdots & 0 & 0 \\ \vdots & \vdots & \ddots & \vdots & \vdots \\ 0 & 0 & \cdots & 0 & 0 \end{bmatrix}, \hat{C}_2^T = \begin{bmatrix} C_2 \\ 0 \\ \vdots \\ 0 \end{bmatrix}.$$

Assumption 1. *The pair $(\hat{A}_L, \hat{B})$ is stabilizable.*

Assumption 2. *No DoS attacks occur at initial time $k = 0$.*

Remark 2. *Assumption 1 is needed for the existence of the positive matrices P and Q that will be applied during the controller design in Section 3. As will be mentioned in Section 3, under the influence of DoS attacks, in this paper, the latest received state will be utilized for control until receiving the next successfully transmitted state, and thus, Assumption 2 is required for avoiding the whole control system becoming open-loop at the beginning of the control stage.*

The openness of network communication in networked control makes it susceptible to cyberattacks. This study investigates the effects of aperiodic DoS attacks on the measurement channel. A graphical illustration of the total networked fractional-order system under our proposed control law is depicted in Figure 1.

Suppose that a DoS attack occurs in the measurement channel at the instant $a_i \in [k-L, k)$, where i denotes the i-th attack event. The control objective of this work is to design a finite-dimensional controller that the corresponding closed-loop fractional-order system (1) is globally input-to-state stable (ISS) under DoS attacks, i.e., for arbitrary initial condition $z_0 \in \mathbb{R}^n$, the closed-loop state satisfies

$$\|z(k)\| \leq \beta_a(\|z_0\|, k) + \gamma_a(q_\omega), \ k \in \mathbb{N}_0, \quad (10)$$

where function β_a is a $\mathcal{KL}$-function and γ_a is a $\mathcal{K}$-function. Detailed definitions of the $\mathcal{KL}$-function, $\mathcal{K}_\infty$-function, and $\mathcal{K}$-function [44] are given below.

A continuous function $\gamma: \mathbb{R}^+ \to \mathbb{R}^+$ is a $\mathcal{K}$-function if it is strictly increasing and $\gamma(0) = 0$. A continuous function $\beta: \mathbb{R}^+ \times \mathbb{R}^+ \to \mathbb{R}^+$ is a $\mathcal{KL}$-function if for each fixed $t \geq 0$, function $\beta(\cdot, t)$ is a $\mathcal{K}$-function, and for each fixed $s \geq 0$, function $\beta(s, \cdot)$ is decreasing and $\beta(s, t) \to 0$ as $t \to \infty$.

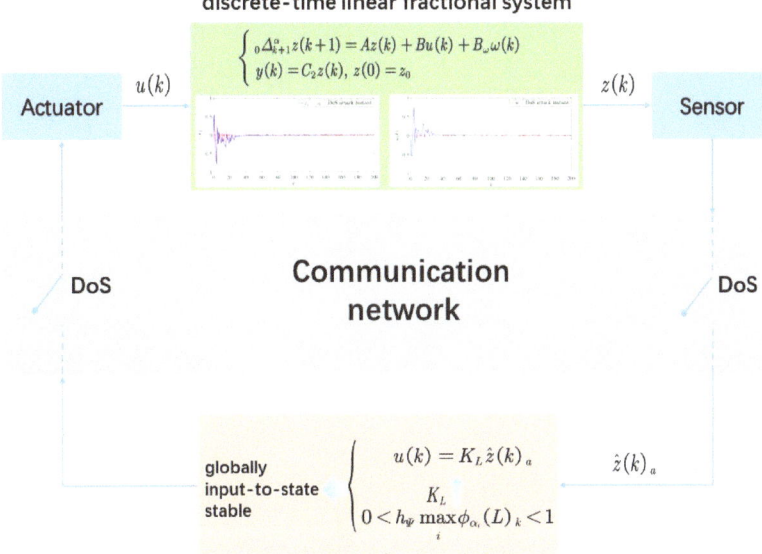

Figure 1. Framework of closed-loop fractional-order networked systems under DoS attacks.

3. Controller Design

Define the difference vector as

$$\hat{e}(k) = \hat{z}(k)_a - \hat{z}(k) \tag{11}$$

where $\hat{z}(k)_a$ stands for the recent-finite-steps state vector under DoS attacks that is utilized for controller design. In this work, if a DoS attack occurs at the current time instant, or in other words, no information is available for the controller currently, then the latest received state will be used for controlling until the next successful state information transmission. The controller is designed as

$$u(k) = K_L \hat{z}(k)_a \tag{12}$$

with control matrix $K_L \in \mathbb{R}^{m \times (L+1)n}$.

Theorem 1. *Consider the closed-loop discrete-time fractional-order system consisting of the system (1) and controller (12). Under Assumptions 1 and 2, for $L \in \mathbb{N}_0$ that satisfies $0 < h_\Psi \max_i \phi_{\alpha_i}(L)_k < 1$ $(i = 1, \cdots, n)$, where h_Ψ and $\phi_{\alpha_i}(L)_k$ will be defined later, then the obtained closed-loop fractional system under DoS attacks is ensured to be globally ISS, with (10) being satisfied.*

Proof. With the controller designed in (12), the evolution of the recent-finite-steps state in the closed-loop system can be expressed as

$$\begin{aligned}\hat{z}(k+1) &= \hat{A}_L \hat{z}(k) + \hat{B} K_L \hat{z}(k)_a + \hat{B}_\omega \hat{\omega}(k)_a \\ &= \hat{A}_L \hat{z}(k) + \hat{B} K_L \hat{z}(k) + \hat{B} K_L \hat{e}(k) + \bar{\omega}(k)_a\end{aligned}$$

$$=\Phi\hat{z}(k)+\hat{B}K_L\hat{e}(k)+\bar{\omega}(k)_a \tag{13}$$

where $\hat{\omega}(k)_a$ is the $\hat{\omega}(k)$ under DoS attacks, $\bar{\omega}(k)_a = \hat{B}_\omega\hat{\omega}(k)_a$ and $\Phi = \hat{A}_L + \hat{B}K_L$. According to Assumption 1, for any positive definite matrix Q, $\Phi^T P\Phi - P + Q = 0$ holds for a positive definite matrix P.

Let the Lyapunov function be $W(k) = \hat{z}^T(k)P\hat{z}(k)$, then

$$\begin{aligned}W(k+1) =& \hat{z}^T(k+1)P\hat{z}(k+1)\\ =& \hat{z}^T(k)(P-Q)\hat{z}(k) + 2\hat{z}^T(k)\Phi^T P\hat{B}K_L\hat{e}(k)\\ &+ 2\hat{z}^T(k)\Phi^T P\bar{\omega}(k)_a + \hat{e}^T(k)K_L^T\hat{B}^T P\hat{B}K_L\hat{e}(k)\\ &+ 2\hat{e}^T(k)K_L^T\hat{B}^T P\bar{\omega}(k)_a + \bar{\omega}(k)_a^T P\bar{\omega}(k)_a\\ =& W(k) - \hat{z}^T(k)Q\hat{z}(k) + 2\hat{z}^T(k)\Phi^T P\hat{B}K_L\hat{e}(k)\\ &+ 2\hat{z}^T(k)\Phi^T P\bar{\omega}(k)_a + \hat{e}^T(k)K_L^T\hat{B}^T P\hat{B}K_L\hat{e}(k)\\ &+ 2\hat{e}^T(k)K_L^T\hat{B}^T P\bar{\omega}(k)_a + \bar{\omega}(k)_a^T P\bar{\omega}(k)_a.\end{aligned} \tag{14}$$

From (14), we obtain

$$\begin{aligned}W(k+1) - W(k) \leq& -\lambda_{\min}(Q)\|\hat{z}(k)\|^2 + \|2\Phi^T P\hat{B}K_L\|\|\hat{z}(k)\|\|\hat{e}(k)\|\\ &+ \|2\Phi^T P\|\|\hat{z}(k)\|\|\bar{\omega}(k)_a\| + [K_L^T\hat{B}^T P\hat{B}K_L]\|\hat{e}(k)\|^2\\ &+ \|2P\hat{B}K_L\|\|\hat{e}(k)\|\|\bar{\omega}(k)_a\| + P\|\bar{\omega}(k)_a\|^2.\end{aligned} \tag{15}$$

The following inequality should be guaranteed to ensure closed-loop system stability:

$$\|\hat{e}(k)\| \leq \sigma\|\hat{z}(k)\| + \sigma\|\bar{\omega}(k)_a\|, \tag{16}$$

where $\sigma \in \mathbb{R}^+$ is a suitable designed parameter. Substituting (16) into (15), we have

$$\begin{aligned}W(k+1) - W(k) \leq& -\lambda_{\min}(Q)\|\hat{z}(k)\|^2 + \|2\Phi^T P\hat{B}K_L\|\sigma\|\hat{z}(k)\|^2\\ &+ \|2\Phi^T P\hat{B}K_L\|\sigma\|\hat{z}(k)\|\|\bar{\omega}(k)_a\|\\ &+ \|2\Phi^T P\|\|\hat{z}(k)\|\|\bar{\omega}(k)_a\|\\ &+ [K_L^T\hat{B}^T P\hat{B}K_L]\sigma^2[\|\hat{z}(k)\|^2 + \|\bar{\omega}(k)_a\|^2\\ &+ 2\|\hat{z}(k)\|\|\bar{\omega}(k)_a\|] + \|2P\hat{B}K_L\|\sigma\|\hat{z}(k)\|\|\bar{\omega}(k)_a\|\\ &+ \|2P\hat{B}K_L\|\sigma\|\bar{\omega}(k)_a\|^2 + P\|\bar{\omega}(k)_a\|^2.\end{aligned} \tag{17}$$

Let $\zeta_1 = \lambda_{\min}(Q)$, $\zeta_2 = \|2\Phi^T P\hat{B}K_L\|$, $\zeta_3 = \|2\Phi^T P\|$, $\zeta_4 = \lambda_{\max}(K_L^T\hat{B}^T P\hat{B}K_L)$, $\zeta_5 = \|2P\hat{B}K_L\|$, $\eta_2 = \lambda_{\max}(P)$, then

$$\begin{aligned}W(k+1) - W(k) \leq& -\zeta_1\|\hat{z}(k)\|^2 + \zeta_2\sigma\|\hat{z}(k)\|^2 + \zeta_2\sigma\|\hat{z}(k)\|\|\bar{\omega}(k)_a\|\\ &+ \zeta_3\|\hat{z}(k)\|\|\bar{\omega}(k)_a\| + \zeta_4\sigma^2\|\hat{z}(k)\|^2 + \zeta_4\sigma^2\|\bar{\omega}(k)_a\|^2\\ &+ \zeta_5\sigma\|\hat{z}(k)\|\|\bar{\omega}(k)_a\| + \zeta_5\sigma\|\bar{\omega}(k)_a\|^2 + \eta_2\|\bar{\omega}(k)_a\|^2\\ &+ 2\zeta_4\sigma^2\|\hat{z}(k)\|\|\bar{\omega}(k)_a\|\\ =& -(\zeta_1 - \zeta_2\sigma - \zeta_4\sigma^2)\|\hat{z}(k)\|^2 + (\zeta_2\sigma + \zeta_3 + \zeta_5\sigma\\ &+ 2\zeta_4\sigma^2)\|\hat{z}(k)\|\|\bar{\omega}(k)_a\| + (\zeta_4\sigma^2 + \zeta_5\sigma + \eta_2)\|\bar{\omega}(k)_a\|^2.\end{aligned} \tag{18}$$

Choosing σ that satisfies $\zeta_1 - \zeta_2\sigma - \zeta_4\sigma^2 > 0$ and letting $\zeta_6 = \zeta_1 - \zeta_2\sigma - \zeta_4\sigma^2$, $\zeta_7 = \zeta_2\sigma + \zeta_3 + \zeta_5\sigma + 2\zeta_4\sigma^2$, $\zeta_8 = \zeta_4\sigma^2 + \zeta_5\sigma + \eta_2$, $\zeta_9 = \frac{\zeta_7^2}{2\zeta_6} + \zeta_8$, then

$$W(k+1) - W(k) \leq -\zeta_6\|\hat{z}(k)\|^2 + \zeta_7\|\hat{z}(k)\|\|\bar{\omega}(k)_a\| + \zeta_8\|\bar{\omega}(k)_a\|^2. \tag{19}$$

Since for any positive real scalar δ, the following inequality holds:

$$\|\hat{z}(k)\|\|\bar{\omega}(k)_a\| \leq \frac{\|\hat{z}(k)\|^2}{2\delta} + \frac{\delta\|\bar{\omega}(k)_a\|^2}{2}, \qquad (20)$$

Thus, (19) becomes

$$W(k+1) - W(k) \leq -\zeta_6\|\hat{z}(k)\|^2 + \frac{\zeta_7}{2\delta}\|\hat{z}(k)\|^2 + \frac{\zeta_7\delta}{2}\|\bar{\omega}(k)_a\|^2 + \zeta_8\|\bar{\omega}(k)_a\|^2. \qquad (21)$$

Let $\delta = \frac{\zeta_7}{\zeta_6}$, then we obtain

$$W(k+1) - W(k) \leq -\zeta_6\|\hat{z}(k)\|^2 + \frac{\zeta_6}{2}\|\hat{z}(k)\|^2 + \frac{\zeta_7^2}{2\zeta_6}\|\bar{\omega}(k)_a\|^2 + \zeta_8\|\bar{\omega}(k)_a\|^2$$

$$= -\frac{\zeta_6}{2}\|\hat{z}(k)\|^2 + \zeta_9\|\bar{\omega}(k)_a\|^2. \qquad (22)$$

Define $\mu_1(\|\hat{z}(k)\|) = \lambda_{\min}(P)\|\hat{z}(k)\|^2$, $\mu_2(\|\hat{z}(k)\|) = \lambda_{\max}(P)\|\hat{z}(k)\|^2$, $\mu_3(\|\hat{z}(k)\|) = \frac{\zeta_6}{2}\|\hat{z}(k)\|^2$, $\mu_4(W(k)) = \mu_3 \circ \mu_2^{-1}(W(k)) = \frac{\zeta_6}{2\eta_2}W(k)$, $\mu_5(\|\bar{\omega}(k)_a\|) = \zeta_9\|\bar{\omega}(k)_a\|^2$; therefore we obtain

$$\mu_1(\|\hat{z}(k)\|) \leq W(k) \leq \mu_2(\|\hat{z}(k)\|), \qquad (23)$$

and

$$W(k+1) - W(k) \leq -\mu_3(\|\hat{z}(k)\|) + \mu_5(\|\bar{\omega}(k)_a\|)$$
$$\leq -\mu_4(W(k)) + \mu_5(\|\bar{\omega}(k)_a\|). \qquad (24)$$

Given that $\mu_1, \mu_2, \mu_3, \mu_5 \in \mathcal{K}_\infty$, it is evident that the function $W(k)$ is an ISS–Lyapunov function, implying the existence of a $\mathcal{KL}$-function $\beta_a : \mathbb{R}^+ \times \mathbb{R}^+ \to \mathbb{R}^+$ and a $\mathcal{K}$-function $\gamma_a : \mathbb{R}^+ \times \mathbb{R}^+$ such that

$$\|\hat{z}(k_0 + k)\| \leq \beta_a(\|\hat{z}(k_0)\|, k) + \gamma_a(\|\bar{\omega}_a\|_{-[k_0,k_0+k-1]}), \qquad (25)$$

where $k_0, k \geq 0$. Let $\hat{\mu}_4(\|\bar{\omega}_a\|)$ be any $\mathcal{K}_\infty$-lower bound of $\mu_4 \in \mathcal{K}_\infty$ such that $Id - \hat{\mu}_4 \in \mathcal{K}$. Hence, we can have $\hat{\mu}_4(\|\bar{\omega}_a\|) = \hat{h}_4\|\bar{\omega}_a\|$, where $\hat{h}_4 = \min(\frac{\zeta_6}{2\eta_2}, \hat{\theta}_a)$ with $\hat{\theta}_a \in (0,1)$. Let $\rho_1(\|\bar{\omega}_a\|) = h_\rho\|\bar{\omega}_a\|$ with $h_\rho \in (0,1)$, then according to [44], (25) holds with $\gamma_a = \mu_1^{-1} \circ \hat{\gamma}_a$ where $\hat{\gamma}_a(\|\bar{\omega}_a\|) = \frac{\zeta_9}{\hat{h}_4 h_\rho}\|\bar{\omega}_a\|^2$ and $\beta_a(s,t) = \mu_1^{-1}(\hat{\beta}_a(\mu_2(s)), t)$ for a $\mathcal{KL}$-function $\hat{\beta}_a : \mathbb{R}^+ \times \mathbb{R}^+ \to \mathbb{R}^+$; therefore, (25) can be written as

$$\|\hat{z}(k_0 + k)\| \leq \beta_a(\|\hat{z}(k_0)\|, k) + \sqrt{\frac{\zeta_9}{\hat{h}_4 h_\rho \lambda_{\min}(P)}}\|\bar{\omega}_a\|_{-[k_0,k_0+k-1]}$$

$$= \beta_a(\|\hat{z}(k_0)\|, k) + h_\Psi\|\bar{\omega}_a\|_{-[k_0,k_0+k-1]} \qquad (26)$$

with $h_\Psi = \sqrt{\frac{\zeta_9}{\hat{h}_4 h_\rho \lambda_{\min}(P)}}$.

Since $F_{j+1}(\alpha) = \text{diag}(c_{j+1}(\alpha_1), c_{j+1}(\alpha_2), \cdots, c_{j+1}(\alpha_n))$, its maximum norm can be obtained as

$$\|F_{j+1}(\alpha)\|_\infty = \max_i |c_{j+1}(\alpha_i)| \leq \max_i \frac{\alpha_i^{j+1}}{(j+1)!}. \qquad (27)$$

53

For simplicity, the maximum norm of matrix F will be expressed as $\|F\|$. Thus, the following inequality can be derived as

$$\|\bar{\omega}(k)_a\| \leq \|B_\omega\| q_\omega + \sum_{j=L+1}^{k} \|A_j\| \|z(k-j)_a\|$$

$$\leq \|B_\omega\| q_\omega + \sum_{j=L+1}^{k} \|A_j\| \|z\|_\infty$$

$$= \|B_\omega\| q_\omega + \sum_{j=L+1}^{k} \|F_{j+1}(\alpha)\| \|z\|_\infty$$

$$\leq \|B_\omega\| q_\omega + \sum_{j=L+1}^{k} \max_i \frac{\alpha_i^{j+1}}{(j+1)!} \|z\|_\infty$$

$$= \|B_\omega\| q_\omega + \max_i \phi_{\alpha_i}(L)_k \|z\|_\infty \tag{28}$$

where $\phi_{\alpha_i}(L)_k = \sum_{j=L+1}^{k} \frac{\alpha_i^{j+1}}{(j+1)!}$. Combining (26) with (28) results in

$$\|\hat{z}\|_\infty \leq \beta_a(\|\hat{z}(0)\|, 0) + h_\Psi \|B_\omega\| q_\omega + h_\Psi \max_i \phi_{\alpha_i}(L)_k \|z\|_\infty. \tag{29}$$

Due to the fact that $\|z\|_\infty \leq \|\hat{z}\|_\infty$, from (29), we obtain

$$\|\hat{z}\|_\infty \leq \beta_a(\|\hat{z}(0)\|, 0) + h_\Psi \|B_\omega\| q_\omega + h_\Psi \max_i \phi_{\alpha_i}(L)_k \|\hat{z}\|_\infty. \tag{30}$$

Consider $L \in \mathbb{N}_0$ that satisfies $0 < h_\Psi \max_i \phi_{\alpha_i}(L)_k < 1$ and define $d_z = [1 - h_\Psi \max_i \phi_{\alpha_i}(L)_k]^{-1} [\beta_a(\|\hat{z}(0)\|, 0) + h_\Psi \|B_\omega\| q_\omega]$; it then further implies $\|\hat{z}\|_\infty \leq d_z$. Hence, (28) becomes

$$\|\bar{\omega}(k)_a\| \leq \|B_\omega\| q_\omega + \max_i \phi_{\alpha_i}(L)_k d_z. \tag{31}$$

Furthermore, (26) turns into

$$\|\hat{z}(k)\| \leq \beta_a(\|\hat{z}(0)\|, k) + h_\Psi \left[\|B_\omega\| q_\omega + \max_i \phi_{\alpha_i}(L)_k d_z \right]$$

$$= \beta_a(\|\hat{z}(0)\|, k) + p_z \tag{32}$$

where $p_z = h_\Psi \left[\|B_\omega\| q_\omega + \max_i \phi_{\alpha_i}(L)_k d_z \right]$ and $\beta_a : \mathbb{R}^+ \times \mathbb{R}^+ \to \mathbb{R}^+$ is a $\mathcal{KL}$-function.

For any scalar $M \in \mathbb{N}$, the boundedness inequality of $\bar{\omega}_a$ can be written as

$$\|\bar{\omega}(k)_a\| \leq \|B_\omega\| q_\omega + \sum_{j=L+1}^{L+1+M} \|A_j\| \|z(k-j)_a\| + \sum_{j=L+2+M}^{k} \|A_j\| \|z(k-j)_a\|$$

$$\leq \|B_\omega\| q_\omega + \sum_{j=L+1}^{L+1+M} \|A_j\| \|z\|_{-[k-L-1-M,k-L-1]}$$

$$+ \sum_{j=L+2+M}^{k} \|A_j\| \|z\|_{-[0,k-L-2-M]}$$

$$\leq \|B_\omega\| q_\omega + \sum_{j=L+1}^{L+1+M} \|A_j\| \|z\|_{-[k-L-1-M,k-L]} + \max_i \phi_{\alpha_i}(L+1+M)_k d_z$$

$$\leq \|B_\omega\| q_\omega + \sum_{j=L+1}^{L+1+M} \max_i \frac{\alpha_i^{j+1}}{(j+1)!} \|z\|_{-[k-L-1-M,k-L]}$$

$$+ \max_i \phi_{\alpha_i}(L+1+M)_k d_z$$

$$\leq \|B_\omega\|q_\omega + \max_i \psi_{L\alpha_i}(M)\|z\|_{-[k-L-1-M,k-L]} + \max_i \phi_{\alpha_i}(L+1+M)_k d_z \quad (33)$$

where $\psi_{L\alpha_i}(M) = \sum_{j=L+1}^{L+1+M} \frac{\alpha_i^{j+1}}{(j+1)!}$. Consider for constant $p_l \geq 0$ and function $\beta_{al} : \mathbb{R}^+ \times \mathbb{R}^+ \to \mathbb{R}^+$, $l \in \mathbb{N}_0$ such that for any $r, s \in \mathbb{R}^+$, $\beta_{al}(r,s)$ is bounded and $\beta_{al}(r,s) \to 0$ as $s \to \infty$, the following inequality holds:

$$\|\hat{z}(k)\| \leq \beta_{al}(\|\hat{z}(0)\|, k) + p_l. \quad (34)$$

Step 1 ($l = 0$): Let $\beta_{a0}(r, s) = \beta_a(r, s)$ and $p_0 = p_z$, from (32) we then obtain

$$\|\hat{z}(k)\| \leq \beta_{a0}(\|\hat{z}(0)\|, k) + p_0. \quad (35)$$

Step 2 ($l > 0$): For a $v_l \in \mathbb{R}$ that satisfies $v_l \in (0, \min\{1, \frac{\kappa-\chi}{\chi} p_l\})$, where $\kappa \in (\chi, 1)$ and $\chi = h_\Psi \max_i \phi_{\alpha_i}(L)_k$, it then indicates $\chi(p_l + v_l) \leq \kappa p_l$. Choosing $v_{l+1} \in (0, \kappa v_l)$, there then exists a $k_l = k_l(v_{l+1})$ that for $k \geq k_l$, $\|z\|_{-[k-L,k]} \leq \|\hat{z}(k)\| \leq p_l + \frac{v_{l+1}}{2}$. This further implies that for any $M_l \in \mathbb{N}$, there exists a $k \geq \bar{k}_l = k_l + M_l + 2$ such that $\|z\|_{-[k-L-1-M_l,k-L]} \leq p_l + \frac{v_{l+1}}{2}$ holds. After combining with (33), we obtain

$$\|\bar{\omega}(k)_a\| \leq \|B_\omega\|q_\omega + \max_i \psi_{L\alpha_i}(M_l)(p_l + \frac{v_{l+1}}{2})$$
$$+ \max_i \phi_{\alpha_i}(L+1+M_l)_k d_z, \text{ for } k \geq \bar{k}_l. \quad (36)$$

By selecting M_l that satisfies $h_\Psi \max_i \phi_{\alpha_i}(L+1+M_l)_k d_z \leq \chi \frac{v_{l+1}}{2}$, from (26), we obtain

$$\|\hat{z}(\bar{k}_l+k)\| \leq \beta_a(\|\hat{z}(\bar{k}_l)\|, k) + h_\Psi\left[\max_i \psi_{L\alpha_i}(M_l)(p_l + \frac{v_{l+1}}{2})\right.$$
$$\left.+ \|B_\omega\|q_\omega + \max_i \phi_{\alpha_i}(L+1+M_l)_k d_z\right]. \quad (37)$$

Since for $L, M_l \in \mathbb{N}_0$, $\psi_{L\alpha_i}(M_l) \leq \phi_{\alpha_i}(L)_k$; hence,

$$\|\hat{z}(\bar{k}_l+k)\| \leq \beta_a(\|\hat{z}(\bar{k}_l)\|, k) + h_\Psi\|B_\omega\|q_\omega + h_\Psi \max_i \phi_{\alpha_i}(L)_k$$
$$(p_l + \frac{v_{l+1}}{2}) + \chi \frac{v_{l+1}}{2}$$
$$\leq \beta_a(\|\hat{z}(\bar{k}_l)\|, k) + h_\Psi\|B_\omega\|q_\omega + \chi(p_l + \frac{v_{l+1}}{2})$$
$$+ \chi \frac{v_{l+1}}{2}$$
$$\leq \beta_a(\|\hat{z}(\bar{k}_l)\|, k) + h_\Psi\|B_\omega\|q_\omega + \chi(p_l + v_l)$$
$$\leq \beta_a(\|\hat{z}(\bar{k}_l)\|, k) + h_\Psi\|B_\omega\|q_\omega + \kappa p_l. \quad (38)$$

Thus, combining with (34) gives

$$\|\hat{z}(k)\| \leq \beta_{a(l+1)}(\|\hat{z}(0)\|, k) + \kappa p_l + h_\Psi\|B_\omega\|q_\omega \quad (39)$$

where

$$\beta_{a(l+1)}(r,k) = \begin{cases} \beta_{al}(r,k) + (1-\kappa)p_l - h_\Psi\|B_\omega\|q_\omega, & k \in [0, \bar{k}_l-1] \\ \min\{\beta_{al}(r,k) + (1-\kappa)p_l - \\ \quad h_\Psi\|B_\omega\|q_\omega, \beta_a(\|\hat{z}(\bar{k}_l)\|, k-\bar{k}_l)\}, & k \in [\bar{k}_l, +\infty) \end{cases} \quad (40)$$

which recursively satisfies that $\beta_{a(l+1)}(r,k) \to 0$ as $k \to \infty$, and it can be noticed from (34) that the state will finally converge to p_l. Also, (39) can be written as $\|\hat{z}(k)\| \le \beta_{a(l+1)}(\|\hat{z}(0)\|, k) + p_{l+1}$, where

$$\begin{aligned} p_{l+1} &= \kappa p_l + h_\Psi \|B_\omega\| q_\omega \\ &= \kappa(\kappa p_{l-1} + h_\Psi \|B_\omega\| q_\omega) + h_\Psi \|B_\omega\| q_\omega \\ &= \kappa(\kappa(\kappa p_{l-2} + h_\Psi \|B_\omega\| q_\omega) + h_\Psi \|B_\omega\| q_\omega) + h_\Psi \|B_\omega\| q_\omega \\ &= \cdots \\ &= \kappa^{l+1} p_0 + h_\Psi \|B_\omega\| q_\omega \left(\sum_{j=0}^{l} \kappa^j \right). \end{aligned} \qquad (41)$$

As a result, (34) indicates

$$\|\hat{z}(k)\| \le \beta_{a\infty}(\|\hat{z}(0)\|, k) + p_\infty \qquad (42)$$

where $\beta_{a\infty}(\|\hat{z}(0)\|, k) \to 0$ as $k \to \infty$ and

$$p_\infty = \lim_{l \to \infty} p_l = h_\Psi \|B_\omega\| q_\omega \frac{\kappa}{1-\kappa}. \qquad (43)$$

In light of Assumption 2, $\|\hat{z}(0)\| = \|z(0)\|$ and $\|z(k)\| \le \|\hat{z}(k)\|$; thus,

$$\begin{aligned} \|z(k)\| &\le \beta_a(\|z(0)\|, k) + h_\Psi \|B_\omega\| q_\omega \frac{\kappa}{1-\kappa} \\ &= \beta_a(\|z(0)\|, k) + \gamma_a(q_\omega) \end{aligned} \qquad (44)$$

where $\gamma_a(r) = c_{\gamma a} r$ with $c_{\gamma a} = h_\Psi \|B_\omega\| \frac{\kappa}{1-\kappa}$. Therefore, under DoS attacks, the closed-loop fractional-order system (1) with controller (12) is globally ISS, and the control objective is achieved. □

Remark 3. *Although there has been considerable research into secure control for integer-order systems [32,35,37,38], comparatively little attention has been given to systems in fractional-order systems, and even less to those in the discrete-time domain. This research is the first to address the security control of discrete-time fractional-order systems under DoS attacks while taking into account the memory and heredity effects of fractional calculus.*

Remark 4. *References [39,40] respectively investigate the control problem for fractional-order multi-agent systems and complex networks which are vulnerable to DoS attacks in the continuous-time domain. The control issue of discrete-time fractional-order multi-agent systems under DoS attacks is studied in [41], yet the non-local characteristics of fractional-order calculus are ignored when designing the control scheme. Different from such mentioned works, the control for discrete-time fractional systems under the effect of DoS attacks that rigorously consider the unique hereditary and infinite memory properties of fractional calculus is addressed in this work for the first time.*

4. Numerical Example

Consider the fractional-order discrete-time system shown in (1) with

$$A = \begin{bmatrix} 1 & 1 \\ 1 & -1 \end{bmatrix}, B = \begin{bmatrix} 1 \\ 1 \end{bmatrix}, B_\omega = \begin{bmatrix} 0 & 0 \\ 0 & 1 \end{bmatrix}, C_2 = \begin{bmatrix} 1 & 1 \end{bmatrix},$$

$_0\Delta^\alpha_{k+1} z(k+1) = [_0\Delta^{0.1}_{k+1} z_1(k+1), _0\Delta^{0.4}_{k+1} z_n(k+1)]^T$ ($k \in \mathbb{N}_0$), $z_0 = [0.1, 0.5]^T$, and the external disturbance $\omega(k)$ is an uniformly distributed random signal with $q_\omega = 0.02$. The numerical example and its visualized results are both implemented in MATLAB. Details of technical implementation can refer to [16–18,45].

The results of the open-loop fractional-order system without control input, depicted in Figure 2, demonstrate its instability, as evidenced by the outputs z_1 and z_2. By choosing $L = 1$, $\sigma = 0.1$, and $K_L = [-1, 0.01, 0.01, 0.05]^T$, we can notice that even under the influence of DoS attacks, the closed-loop system is ISS under our proposed controller, as presented in Figures 3 and 4. Furthermore, it is presented in Figure 3 that under the proposed control input, both system outputs can be driven to zero instead of just being bounded, as illustrated in the proof of Theorem 1, which further indicates an interesting future work to explore the design of security control law for fractional-order systems to achieve asymptotic stability. Moreover, as displayed in Figures 5 and 6 where $K_L = [-1, 0.01]^T$ and $L = 0$, it is worth noting that with a proper selection of design parameters, the global stability of the closed-loop system in the presence of DoS attacks can be ensured under our proposed controller, even if only the current state is considered in designing the control strategy. Consequently, the effectiveness of the investigated control strategy is verified by the simulation results.

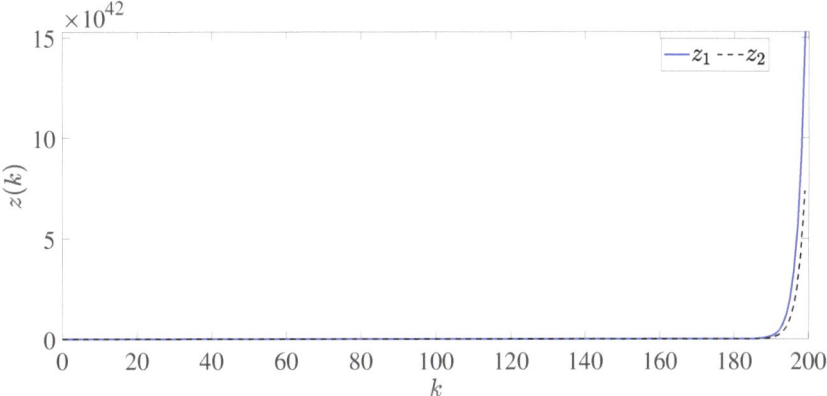

Figure 2. System output z_1 and z_2 without control effort.

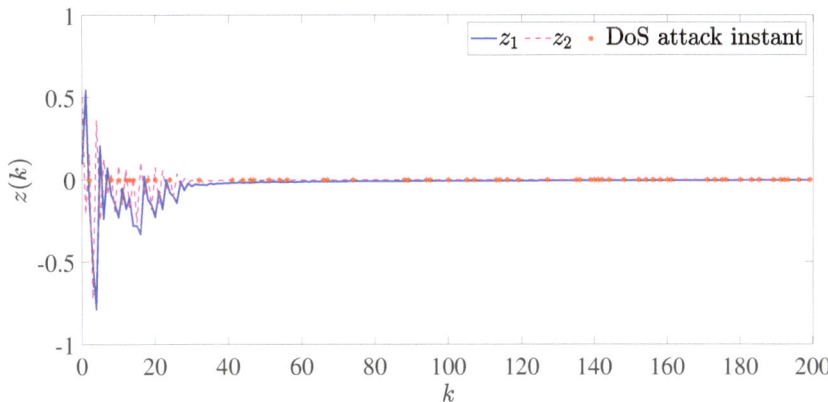

Figure 3. System output z_1 and z_2 with DoS attacks under the proposed control law where $L = 1$.

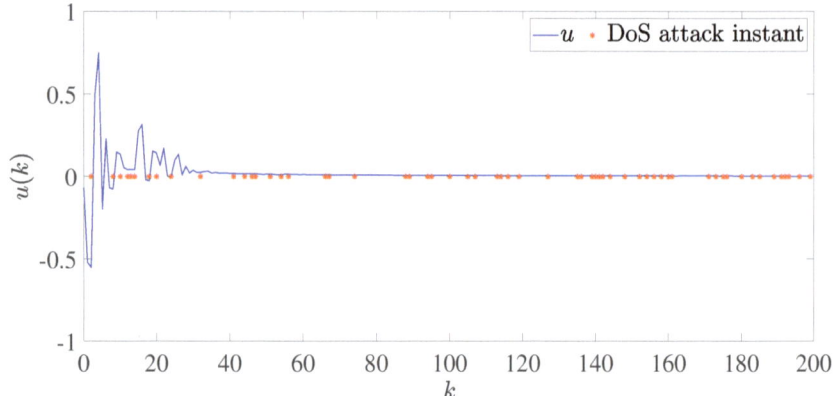

Figure 4. Control input u with $L = 1$.

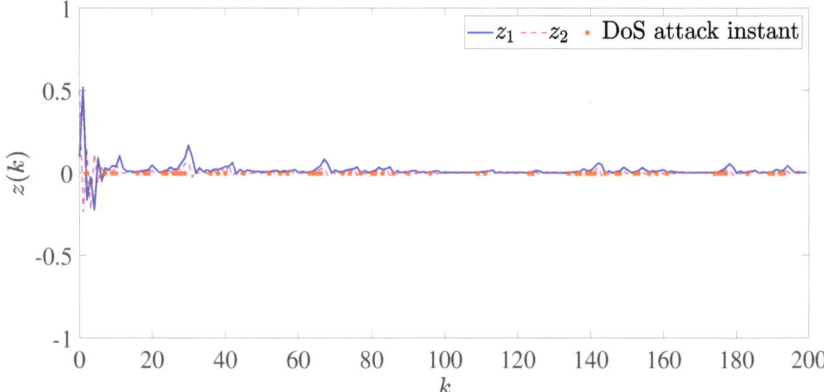

Figure 5. System output z_1 and z_2 with DoS attacks under the proposed control law where $L = 0$.

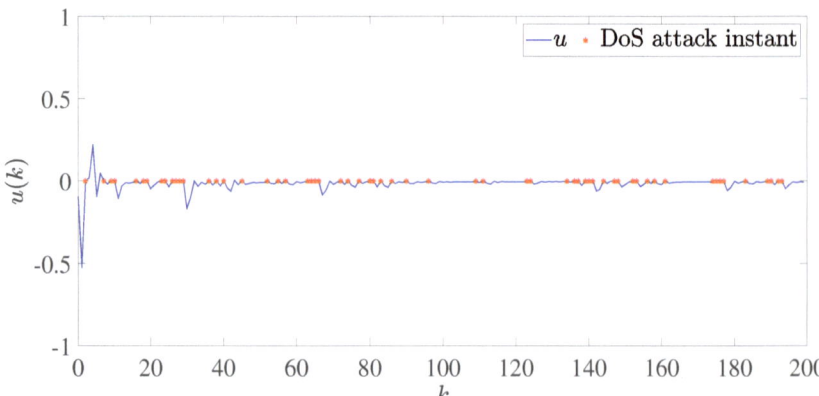

Figure 6. Control input u with $L = 0$.

5. Conclusions

The security control issue for discrete-time fractional-order linear systems under DoS attacks is addressed in this work. A finite-dimensional controller, which requires merely the information of a finite number of the previous state, and hence is practically useful, is proposed in this article. Our proposed control law is verified by numerical simulation, ensuring the global input-to-state stability of the associated closed-loop system. In practice, it is possible that the system matrices could not be known precisely, which consequently implies an interesting future topic for considering the study of adaptive finite-dimensional control for fractional systems under attack by introducing adaptive techniques in our work to estimate system uncertainties.

Author Contributions: Conceptualization, X.L.; Methodology, X.L.; Validation, X.L.; Formal analysis, X.L.; Investigation, X.L.; Writing—original draft, X.L.; Writing—review & editing, Y.Z., X.L. and C.D.; Visualization, Y.Z. and X.L.; Supervision, C.D.; Funding acquisition, Y.Z. and X.W. All authors have read and agreed to the published version of the manuscript.

Funding: This work is supported by the National Natural Science Foundation of China (62203164, 62203165), and the Scientific Research Fund of Hunan Provincial Education Department (Outstanding Young Project) (21B0499).

Data Availability Statement: The data presented in this study may be available on request from the corresponding author.

Conflicts of Interest: The authors declare no potential conflicts of interest with respect to the research, authorship, finance, and/or publication of this article.

References

1. Koeller, R. Applications of fractional calculus to the theory of viscoelasticity. *J. Appl. Mech.* **1984**, *51*, 299–307. [CrossRef]
2. Friedrich, C. Relaxation and retardation functions of the Maxwell model with fractional derivatives. *Rheol. Acta* **1991**, *30*, 151–158. [CrossRef]
3. Cao, H.; Deng, Z.; Li, X.; Yang, J.; Qin, Y. Dynamic modeling of electrical characteristics of solid oxide fuel cells using fractional derivatives. *Int. J. Hydrogen Energy* **2010**, *35*, 1749–1758. [CrossRef]
4. Hammouch, Z.; Mekkaoui, T. Circuit design and simulation for the fractional-order chaotic behavior in a new dynamical system. *Complex Intell. Syst.* **2018**, *4*, 251–260. [CrossRef]
5. Butzer, P.L.; Westphal, U.; Hilfer, R.; West, B.J.; Grigolini, P.; Zaslavsky, G.M.; Douglas, J.F.; Schiessel, H.; Friedrich, C.; Blumen, A.; et al. *Applications of Fractional Calculus in Physics*; World Scientific: Singapore, 2000; Volume 35.
6. Liu, L.; Xue, D.; Zhang, S. General type industrial temperature system control based on fuzzy fractional-order PID controller. *Complex Intell. Syst.* **2021**, *9*, 2585–2597. [CrossRef]
7. Guo, D.; Yang, G.; Feng, X.; Han, X.; Lu, L.; Ouyang, M. Physics-based fractional-order model with simplified solid phase diffusion of lithium-ion battery. *J. Energy Storage* **2020**, *30*, 101404. [CrossRef]
8. Wang, Y.; Li, M.; Chen, Z. Experimental study of fractional-order models for lithium-ion battery and ultra-capacitor: Modeling, system identification, and validation. *Appl. Energy* **2020**, *278*, 115736. [CrossRef]
9. Zou, C.; Zhang, L.; Hu, X.; Wang, Z.; Wik, T.; Pecht, M. A review of fractional-order techniques applied to lithium-ion batteries, lead-acid batteries, and supercapacitors. *J. Power Sources* **2018**, *390*, 286–296. [CrossRef]
10. Hakkar, N.; Dhayal, R.; Debbouche, A.; Torres, D.F. Approximate controllability of delayed fractional stochastic differential systems with mixed noise and impulsive effects. *Fractal Fract.* **2023**, *7*, 104. [CrossRef]
11. Johnson, M.; Vijayakumar, V. An analysis on the optimal control for fractional stochastic delay integrodifferential systems of order $1 < \gamma < 2$. *Fractal Fract.* **2023**, *7*, 284. [CrossRef]
12. Kavitha, K.; Vijayakumar, V. An analysis regarding to approximate controllability for Hilfer fractional neutral evolution hemivariational inequality. *Qual. Theory Dyn. Syst.* **2022**, *21*, 80. [CrossRef]
13. Guechi, S.; Dhayal, R.; Debbouche, A.; Malik, M. Analysis and optimal control of φ-Hilfer fractional semilinear equations involving nonlocal impulsive conditions. *Symmetry* **2021**, *13*, 2084. [CrossRef]
14. Podlubny, I. Fractional-order systems and $PI^\lambda D^\mu$-controllers. *IEEE Trans. Autom. Control* **1999**, *44*, 208–214. [CrossRef]
15. Chen, Y.; Petráš, I.; Xue, D. Fractional order control—A tutorial. In Proceedings of the 2009 American Control Conference, St. Louis, MO, USA, 10–12 June 2009; pp. 1397–1411.
16. Li, X.; Wen, C.; Liu, X.K. Sampled-data control based consensus of fractional-order multi-agent systems. *IEEE Control Syst. Lett.* **2021**, *5*, 133–138. [CrossRef]
17. Li, X.; Wen, C.; Liu, X.K. Finite-dimensional sampled-data control of fractional-order systems. *IEEE Control Syst. Lett.* **2022**, *6*, 181–186. [CrossRef]
18. Li, X.; Wen, C.; Li, X.; Deng, C. Stabilization for a general class of fractional-order systems: A sampled-data control method. *IEEE Trans. Circuits Syst. I Regul. Pap.* **2022**, *69*, 4643–4653. [CrossRef]
19. Li, Y.; Chen, Y.; Podlubny, I. Mittag–Leffler stability of fractional order nonlinear dynamic systems. *Automatica* **2009**, *45*, 1965–1969. [CrossRef]

20. Liu, H.; Pan, Y.; Li, S.; Chen, Y. Adaptive fuzzy backstepping control of fractional-order nonlinear systems. *IEEE Trans. Syst. Man Cybern. Syst.* **2017**, *47*, 2209–2217. [CrossRef]
21. Li, X.; Wen, C.; Zou, Y. Adaptive backstepping control for fractional-order nonlinear systems with external disturbance and uncertain parameters using smooth control. *IEEE Trans. Syst. Man Cybern. Syst.* **2021**, *51*, 7860–7869. [CrossRef]
22. Li, X.; He, J.; Wen, C.; Liu, X.K. Backstepping-based adaptive control of a class of uncertain incommensurate fractional-order nonlinear systems With external disturbance. *IEEE Trans. Ind. Electron.* **2022**, *69*, 4087–4095. [CrossRef]
23. Li, X.; Li, X.; Xing, L. Backstepping-based adaptive control for uncertain fractional-order nonlinear systems. In Proceedings of the 2021 IEEE 16th Conference on Industrial Electronics and Applications (ICIEA), Chengdu, China, 1–4 August 2021; pp. 12–17. [CrossRef]
24. Li, X.; Wen, C.; Li, X.; He, J. Adaptive fractional-order backstepping control for a general class of nonlinear uncertain integer-order systems. *IEEE Trans. Ind. Electron.* **2023**, *70*, 7246–7256. [CrossRef]
25. Kaczorek, T. Practical stability of positive fractional discrete-time linear systems. *Bull. Pol. Acad. Sci. Tech. Sci.* **2008**, *56*, 313–317.
26. Busłowicz, M.; Kaczorek, T. Simple conditions for practical stability of positive fractional discrete-time linear systems. *Int. J. Appl. Math. Comput. Sci.* **2009**, *19*, 263–269. [CrossRef]
27. Guermah, S.; Djennoune, S.; Bettayeb, M. A new approach for stability analysis of linear discrete-time fractional-order systems. In *New Trends in Nanotechnology and Fractional Calculus Applications*; Springer: Dordrecht, The Netherlands, 2010; pp. 151–162. [CrossRef]
28. Guermah, S.; Djennoune, S.; Bettayeb, M. Discrete-time fractional-order systems: Modeling and stability issues. In *Advances in Discrete Time Systems*; InTech: London, UK, 2012; pp. 183–212. [CrossRef]
29. Sopasakis, P.; Ntouskas, S.; Sarimveis, H. Robust model predictive control for discrete-time fractional-order systems. In Proceedings of the 2015 23rd Mediterranean Conference on Control and Automation (MED), Torremolinos, Spain, 16–19 June 2015; pp. 384–389. [CrossRef]
30. Sopasakis, P.; Sarimveis, H. Stabilising model predictive control for discrete-time fractional-order systems. *Automatica* **2017**, *75*, 24–31. [CrossRef]
31. Alessandretti, A.; Pequito, S.; Pappas, G.J.; Aguiar, A.P. Finite-dimensional control of linear discrete-time fractional-order systems. *Automatica* **2020**, *115*, 108512. [CrossRef]
32. Deng, C.; Wen, C.; Zou, Y.; Wang, W.; Li, X. A hierarchical security control framework of nonlinear CPSs against DoS attacks with application to power sharing of AC microgrids. *IEEE Trans. Cybern.* **2022**, *52*, 5255–5266. [CrossRef]
33. Cárdenas, A.A.; Amin, S.; Sastry, S. Research challenges for the security of control systems. In Proceedings of the 3rd Conference on Hot Topics in Security, San Jose, CA, USA, 29 July 2008; pp. 1–6.
34. De Persis, C.; Tesi, P. Input-to-state stabilizing control under denial-of-service. *IEEE Trans. Autom. Control* **2015**, *60*, 2930–2944. [CrossRef]
35. Zhao, L.; Yang, G.H. Adaptive fault-tolerant control for nonlinear multi-agent systems with DoS attacks. *Inf. Sci.* **2020**, *526*, 39–53. [CrossRef]
36. Zhang, D.; Liu, L.; Feng, G. Consensus of heterogeneous linear multiagent systems subject to aperiodic sampled-data and DoS attack. *IEEE Trans. Cybern.* **2019**, *49*, 1501–1511. [CrossRef]
37. Feng, Z.; Hu, G. Secure cooperative event-triggered control of linear multiagent systems Under DoS attacks. *IEEE Trans. Control Syst. Technol.* **2020**, *28*, 741–752. [CrossRef]
38. Chang, B.; Mu, X.; Yang, Z.; Fang, J. Event-based secure consensus of muti-agent systems under asynchronous DoS attacks. *Appl. Math. Comput.* **2021**, *401*, 126120. [CrossRef]
39. Narayanan, G.; Ali, M.S.; Alsulami, H.; Stamov, G.; Stamova, I.; Ahmad, B. Impulsive security control for fractional-order delayed multi-agent systems with uncertain parameters and switching topology under DoS attack. *Inf. Sci.* **2022**, *618*, 169–190. [CrossRef]
40. Bai, J.; Wu, H.; Cao, J. Secure synchronization and identification for fractional complex networks with multiple weight couplings under DoS attacks. *Comput. Appl. Math.* **2022**, *41*, 187. [CrossRef]
41. Narayanan, G.; Ali, M.S.; Ahamad, S. Cyber secure consensus of discrete-time fractional-order multi-agent systems with distributed delayed control against attacks. In Proceedings of the 2021 IEEE International Conference on Systems, Man, and Cybernetics (SMC), Melbourne, Australia, 17–20 October 2021; pp. 2191–2196. [CrossRef]
42. Ostalczyk, P. *Discrete Fractional Calculus: Applications in Control and Image Processing*; World Scientific: Hackensack, NJ, USA, 2016; Volume 4.
43. Chatterjee, S.; Romero, O.; Pequito, S. A separation principle for discrete-time fractional-order dynamical systems and its implications to closed-loop neurotechnology. *IEEE Control Syst. Lett.* **2019**, *3*, 691–696. [CrossRef]
44. Jiang, Z.P.; Wang, Y. Input-to-state stability for discrete-time nonlinear systems. *Automatica* **2001**, *37*, 857–869. [CrossRef]
45. Mendes, E.M.; Salgado, G.H.; Aguirre, L.A. Numerical solution of Caputo fractional differential equations with infinity memory effect at initial condition. *Commun. Nonlinear Sci. Numer. Simul.* **2019**, *69*, 237–247. [CrossRef]

Disclaimer/Publisher's Note: The statements, opinions and data contained in all publications are solely those of the individual author(s) and contributor(s) and not of MDPI and/or the editor(s). MDPI and/or the editor(s) disclaim responsibility for any injury to people or property resulting from any ideas, methods, instructions or products referred to in the content.

 *fractal and fractional*

Article

Alternate Admissibility LMI Criteria for Descriptor Fractional Order Systems with $0 < \alpha < 2$

Ying Di [1], Jin-Xi Zhang [2,*] and Xuefeng Zhang [1,*]

1. College of Sciences, Northeastern University, Shenyang 110819, China; 2100097@stu.neu.edu.cn
2. State Key Laboratory of Synthetical Automation for Process Industries, Northeastern University, Shenyang 110819, China
* Correspondence: zhangjx@mail.neu.edu.cn (J.-X.Z.); zhangxuefeng@mail.neu.edu.cn (X.Z.)

Abstract: The paper focuses on the admissibility problem of descriptor fractional-order systems (DFOSs). The alternate admissibility criteria are addressed for DFOSs with order in $(0,2)$ which involve a non-strict linear matrix inequality (LMI) method and a strict LMI method, respectively. The forms of non-strict and strict LMIs are brand new and distinguished with the existing literature, which fills the gaps of studies for admissibility. These necessary and sufficient conditions of admissibility are available to the order in $(0,2)$ without separating the order ranges into $(0,1)$ and $[1,2)$. Based on the special position of singular matrix, the non-strict LMI criterion has an advantage in handling the DFOSs with uncertain derivative matrices. For the strict LMI form, a method involving least real decision variables is derived which is more convenient to process the practical solution. Three numerical examples are given to illustrate the validity of the proposed results.

Keywords: descriptor fractional order systems; admissibility; unified criterion; linear matrix inequality

Citation: Di, Y.; Zhang, J.-X.; Zhang, X. Alternate Admissibility LMI Criteria for Descriptor Fractional Order Systems with $0 < \alpha < 2$. *Fractal Fract.* **2023**, *7*, 577. https://doi.org/10.3390/fractalfract7080577

Academic Editor: David Kubanek

Received: 24 June 2023
Revised: 18 July 2023
Accepted: 25 July 2023
Published: 27 July 2023

Copyright: © 2023 by the authors. Licensee MDPI, Basel, Switzerland. This article is an open access article distributed under the terms and conditions of the Creative Commons Attribution (CC BY) license (https://creativecommons.org/licenses/by/4.0/).

1. Introduction

Fractional calculus has a long period of development which has been broadly applied in different areas of engineering applications, such as systems theory [1], signal processing [2] and image fusion [3]. Recently, fractional-order systems (FOSs) have aroused extensive attention from scholars because more and more practical problems based on engineering requirements are well described by fractional calculus [4]. Many fundamental notions and crucial research achievements on integer order systems have been expanded to FOSs sucessfully, and hugely fruitful research has been published in stability analysis [5] and sliding mode control [6,7]. Furthermore, the special characteristics of fractional-order are broadly applied in electrical systems [8,9], power systems [10,11], economic systems [12] and fuzzy systems [13,14].

Stability analysis is a fundamental issue for all control systems, certainly including FOSs. Since the stability region of FOSs is quite different from integer order systems, exploration on stability becomes more challenging. Experts have developed many research works and a number of theories are obtained. In [15], based on the FOS stability region, the LMI stability conditions are first proposed for fractional order $0 < \alpha < 1$ and $1 < \alpha < 2$, respectively. However, the criterion for $0 < \alpha < 1$ contains complex numbers and is difficult to solve. In [16], the stability of FOSs with order in $(0,1)$ is studied and a method for the robust asymptotical stability with real matrices is proposed, but the result is inapplicable to the system eigenvalues on positive real part. In [17], the authors provide a unified LMI formulation to ensure the stability of FOSs for a given order in $(0,2)$ without separating into $(0,1)$ and $[1,2)$. Those criteria are necessary and sufficient conditions with least real decision variables of LMIs. In [18], the FOSs with arbitrary real order between 0 and 2 are considered and a method to quickly and robustly estimate the fractional integrals and derivatives of positions is presented. Robust stability analysis of an interval fractional-order plant with an interval time delay is investigated by a general form of fractional-order controllers in [19]. For the discrete-time systems, the finite-dimensional feedback control of FOSs with additive state disturbance is addressed in [20] and the stability regions of FOSs with interval uncertainties are analyzed in [21]. In [22], by using a boundary layer technique without any global and unknown information, the robust adaptive fault-tolerant consensus control for nonlinear fractional-order multi-agent systems is addressed.

Descriptor systems (also called singular systems, generalized state-space systems and implicit systems) are a special class of systems with a wider range of applications than normal systems, many of which have good performance [23,24]. With the emergence of FOSs, DFOSs have aroused great attention of scholars in different research directions. A great number of attainments on admissibility have been achieved because admissibility is one of the most important properties in DFOSs. For the fractional order in [1,2), the new admissibility conditions of DFOSs expressed in a set of strict LMIs are given in [25,26], and H_∞ control problems have been solved by designing a state feedback control based on bounded real lemma in [27]. For the fractional order in $(0,1)$, the authors in [28] provide necessary and sufficient conditions for admissibility of DFOSs and an observer-based controller is proposed to guarantee the system admissibility. However, the LMIs in the results involve complex matrices and complex numbers which cause difficulty in solving. In [29], the admissibility and robust stabilization of DFOSs with order in $(0,1)$ are investigated, and an approach with strict LMIs with real matrices is presented. In [30], a different method for admissibility is reported for order in $(0,1)$ and $[1,2)$, respectively, and robust stabilization problem of DFOSs with uncertain derivative matrices is solved. Although there are many papers on admissibility, most of the existing theorems divide order α into $(0,1)$ and $[1,2)$ to analysis admissibility, respectively, as shown above. A unified form of admissibility for a given fractional order interval $(0,2)$ is valuable and has been considered in few studies. In [31], a unified framework for admissibility and quadratic admissibility is provided in terms of LMIs, but it does not satisfy the condition of least real decision variables which can be improved.

Motivated by the above observations, we study the admissibility of DFOSs. The main contributions of this paper are summarized as follows:

(i) The alternate admissibility criteria with order in $(0,2)$ are presented with non-strict LMIs and strict LMIs, respectively. These necessary and sufficient conditions are fresh and have many good features of existing results, some of which are that these theorems do not involve any complex variables and are able to deal with the eigenvalues of system matrix with positive real part.

(ii) The methods are applicable to the order interval $(0,2)$ directly without separating the order ranges into $(0,1)$ and $[1,2)$ when discussing the admissibility of DFOSs, which overcomes the drawback brought by interval separation in [25–30].

(iii) A strict LMI approach with only one real decision variable is provided, which owns a simpler expression and is easier to simulate compared with the methods in [25–31].

(iv) When $E = I$ or $\alpha = 1$, the criteria in this paper are consistent with the results in [15,29] and [32], respectively. In additions, the method of non-strict LMIs is applicable to the DFOSs with uncertainties in singular matrix.

The paper is organized as follows. Section 2 presents some preliminaries which are applicable to the rest of the paper. In Section 3, for the fractional order α in $(0,2)$, two different methods of admissibility for DFOSs are proposed with non-strict and strict LMI formulations, respectively. Three numerical examples are given in Section 4 and a brief conclusion is provided in Section 5.

Notations : $\mathbb{R}^{n \times m}$ denotes the set of all $n \times m$ real matrices. $P < 0$ ($P \leq 0$, respectively,) means that P is negative definite (negative semi-definite, respectively). P^T represents the transpose of matrix P. $P > 0$ denotes that P is positive definite. $\det(A)$ is the determinant of A. $[x_{ij}]_{n \times n}$ represents a $n \times n$ matrix where x_{ij} is the element of the i-th row and the j-th column. $\text{sym}(P)$ and $\text{asym}(P)$ denote the expressions of $P + P^T$ and $P - P^T$, respectively. I_n is the identity matrix of order n. $\otimes$ stands for the Kronecker product of two matrices. $\text{spec}(E, A)$ is the spectrum of $\det(sE - A) = 0$. $\arg(z)$ denotes the argument of a complex number z. $\Gamma(\cdot)$ indicates Euler Gamma function. $\lfloor \alpha \rfloor$ ($\lceil \alpha \rceil$) is the floor function (ceiling function, respectively) which denotes the nearest integer less (greater) than or equal to α. The symbol $*$ represents the symmetric part of a matrix. The symbol $\star$ in a matrix denotes the part which is unrelated to the discussion. For convenience, let $\Theta = \begin{bmatrix} a & -b \\ b & a \end{bmatrix}$, $a = \sin(\frac{\alpha \pi}{2})$, $b = \cos(\frac{\alpha \pi}{2})$ in the sequel.

2. Problem Formulation and Preliminaries

Consider the following DFOS

$$ED^\alpha x(t) = Ax(t), \tag{1}$$

where $A \in \mathbb{R}^{n \times n}$ is a constant matrix; $E \in \mathbb{R}^{n \times n}$ is singular with $\text{rank}(E) = r < n$; $x(t) \in \mathbb{R}^n$ is state of the system; $D^\alpha x(t)$ is the Caputo fractional order derivative with the following definition

$$D^\alpha x(t) = \frac{1}{\Gamma(m-\alpha)} \int_0^t \frac{x^{(m)}(\tau)}{(t-\tau)^{\alpha+1-m}} d\tau,$$

where $m - 1 < \alpha \leq m$, m is an integer. If $E = I$, (1) is simplified to FOS

$$D^\alpha x(t) = Ax(t). \tag{2}$$

Lemma 1 ([29]). *Assume that System (1) is regular, and two invertible matrices G and W are found such that*

$$GEW = \begin{bmatrix} I_r & 0 \\ 0 & J_{n-r} \end{bmatrix}, GAW = \begin{bmatrix} \bar{A}_1 & 0 \\ 0 & I_{n-r} \end{bmatrix}, \tag{3}$$

where J_{n-r} is a nilpotent matrix; then, we have:
(a) *System (1) is impulse-free if $J_{n-r} = 0$.*
(b) *System (1) is stable if $|\arg(\text{spec}(\bar{A}_1))| > \alpha \frac{\pi}{2}$.*
(c) *System (1) is admissible if $J_{n-r} = 0$ and $|\arg(\text{spec}(\bar{A}_1))| > \alpha \frac{\pi}{2}$.*

Lemma 2 ([29]). *FOS (2) with $0 < \alpha < 1$ is stable if there exist matrices $X, Y \in \mathbb{R}^{n \times n}$ such that*

$$\begin{bmatrix} X & Y \\ -Y & X \end{bmatrix} > 0, \tag{4}$$

$$\text{sym}(A(aX - bY)) < 0. \tag{5}$$

Lemma 3 ([15]). *FOS (2) with $1 \leq \alpha < 2$ is stable if there exist positive matrix P such that*

$$\text{sym}(\Theta \otimes AP) < 0. \tag{6}$$

3. Main Results

In this section, for the DFOSs with order in $(0,2)$, new approaches of admissibility based on non-strict LMIs and strict LMIs are addressed, respectively.

3.1. Criteria of Admissibility Based on Non-Strict LMIs

Theorem 1. *DFOS (1) with $0 < \alpha < 1$ is admissible if A is nonsingular and there exist matrices $X, Y, Q \in \mathbb{R}^{n \times n}$, $Q > 0$ satisfying (4) and*

$$A(aX - bY)E^T + E(aX - bY)^T A^T + EQE^T \leq 0. \tag{7}$$

Proof. (Sufficiency). Since A is nonsingular, $\det(s^\alpha E - A) \neq 0$ for some $s \in \mathbb{C}$, so the system (1) is regular. Then, there exist two nonsingular matrices G and W such that (3) holds. Let

$$X = W \begin{bmatrix} X_1 & X_2 \\ X_2^T & X_3 \end{bmatrix} W^T, \quad X_1 = X_1^T > 0, \quad X_3 = X_3^T > 0, \tag{8}$$

$$Y = W \begin{bmatrix} Y_1 & Y_2 \\ -Y_2^T & Y_3 \end{bmatrix} W^T, \quad Y_1^T = -Y_1, \quad Y_3^T = -Y_3, \tag{9}$$

$$Q = W \begin{bmatrix} Q_1 & Q_2 \\ Q_2^T & Q_3 \end{bmatrix} W^T, \quad Q_1 = Q_1^T > 0, \quad Q_3 = Q_3^T > 0. \tag{10}$$

From the condition (4)

$$\begin{bmatrix} X & Y \\ -Y & X \end{bmatrix} = \begin{bmatrix} W & 0 \\ 0 & W \end{bmatrix} \begin{bmatrix} X_1 & X_2 & Y_1 & Y_2 \\ X_2^T & X_3 & -Y_2^T & Y_3 \\ -Y_1 & -Y_2 & X_1 & X_2 \\ Y_2^T & -Y_3 & X_2^T & X_3 \end{bmatrix} \begin{bmatrix} W^T & 0 \\ 0 & W^T \end{bmatrix} > 0, \tag{11}$$

it is easy to obtain

$$\begin{bmatrix} X_1 & Y_1 \\ -Y_1 & X_1 \end{bmatrix} > 0. \tag{12}$$

Substituting (3), (8), (9) and (10) into (7), we get

$$U = \begin{bmatrix} U_1 & U_2 \\ U_2^T & U_3 \end{bmatrix} \leq 0, \tag{13}$$

where

$$U_1 = \tilde{A}_1(aX_1 - bY_1) + (aX_1 - bY_1)^T \tilde{A}_1^T + Q_1,$$
$$U_2 = \tilde{A}_1(aX_2 - bY_2)J_{n-r}^T + (aX_2 + bY_2) + Q_2 J_{n-r}^T,$$
$$U_3 = (aX_3 - bY_3)J_{n-r}^T + J_{n-r}(aX_3 - bY_3)^T + J_{n-r}Q_3 J_{n-r}^T.$$

(13) implies $U_1 < 0$ or $U_1 \leq 0$. Considering $Q_1 > 0$, we have

$$\tilde{A}_1(aX_1 - bY_1) + (aX_1 - bY_1)^T \tilde{A}_1^T < 0. \tag{14}$$

Hence, X_1, Y_1 satisfy (12) and (14). By Lemma 2, we obtain that (1) is stable.

Without loss of generality, assume that the nilpotent matrix $J_{n-r} \neq 0$ which owns the Jordan form

$$J_{n-r} = \begin{bmatrix} 0 & & & \\ 1 & 0 & & \\ & \ddots & \ddots & \\ & & 1 & 0 \\ & & & 1 & 0 \end{bmatrix}. \tag{15}$$

Write X_3, Y_3, Q_3 as

$$X_3 = [x_{ij}]_{t \times t} > 0, \quad x_{ij} = x_{ji}, \tag{16}$$

$$Y_3 = [y_{ij}]_{t \times t}, \quad y_{ij} = -y_{ji} \ (i \neq j), \quad y_{ii} = 0, \tag{17}$$

$$Q_3 = [q_{ij}]_{t \times t} > 0, \quad q_{ij} = q_{ji}, \tag{18}$$

where $t = n - r$ and $i, j = 1, \cdots, n$. Then U_3, is rewritten as

$$\begin{bmatrix} 0 & ax_{11} & \star & \star \\ ax_{11} & 2(ax_{12} - by_{12}) + q_{11} & \star & \star \\ \star & \star & \star & \star \\ \star & \star & \star & \star \end{bmatrix}.$$

Since

$$\det\left(\begin{bmatrix} 0 & ax_{11} \\ ax_{11} & 2(ax_{12} - by_{12}) + q_{11} \end{bmatrix}\right) < 0,$$

U_3 contains two eigenvalues with different sign, so U is neither negative definite (negative semi-definite) nor positive definite (positive semi-definite) which conflicts with $U \leq 0$. It follows that $J_{n-r} = 0$. By Lemma 1, we get that (1) is impulse-free. This, together with the regularity and stability of (1), deduces that (1) is admissible.

(Necessity). According to Lemma 1 and the admissible condition of (1), there exist nonsingular matrices G, W such that (3) holds with $J_{n-r} = 0$, and $D^\alpha x_1(t) = \bar{A}_1 x_1(t)$ is stable. By Lemma 2, there exist matrices X_1, Y_1 satisfying (12) and (14) which deduces that $\bar{A}_1$ is invertible. Then, there exists a matrix $Q_1 > 0$ such that

$$\bar{A}_1(aX_1 - bY_1) + (aX_1 - bY_1)^T \bar{A}_1^T + Q_1 \leq 0. \tag{19}$$

From the invertible matrix $\bar{A}_1$ and (3), we get that A is also invertible.
Let

$$X = W \begin{bmatrix} X_1 & 0 \\ 0 & I_{n-r} \end{bmatrix} W^T, \quad Y = W \begin{bmatrix} Y_1 & 0 \\ 0 & 0 \end{bmatrix} W^T, \quad Q = W \begin{bmatrix} Q_1 & 0 \\ 0 & I \end{bmatrix} W^T. \tag{20}$$

From (12) and (20), we get

$$\begin{bmatrix} X & Y \\ -Y & X \end{bmatrix} = \begin{bmatrix} W & 0 \\ 0 & W \end{bmatrix} \begin{bmatrix} X_1 & 0 & Y_1 & 0 \\ 0 & I_{n-r} & 0 & 0 \\ -Y_1 & 0 & X_1 & 0 \\ 0 & 0 & 0 & I_{n-r} \end{bmatrix} \begin{bmatrix} W^T & 0 \\ 0 & W^T \end{bmatrix} > 0.$$

Substituting (3) and (20) into (7), we obtain

$$A(aX - bY)E^T + E(aX - bY)^T A^T + EQE^T$$
$$= G^{-1} \begin{bmatrix} A_1(aX_1 - bY_1) + (aX_1 - bY_1)^T \bar{A}_1^T + Q_1 & 0 \\ 0 & 0 \end{bmatrix} G^{-T} \leq 0 \cdot$$

□

Corollary 1. *DFOS (1) with $0 < \alpha < 1$ is admissible if A is nonsingular and there exist matrices $X, Y, \hat{Q} \in \mathbb{R}^{n \times n}$, $\hat{Q} > 0$ satisfying (4) and*

$$\begin{bmatrix} \text{sym}(A(aX - bY)E^T) & E \\ \star & -\hat{Q} \end{bmatrix} \leq 0. \tag{21}$$

Proof. Setting $\hat{Q} = Q^{-1}$, by Schur complement, it is easy to get that (21) is equivalent to (7). □

Remark 1. *The formulations in Theorem 1 are new and different from the existing literature; they enrich the research methods of admissibility for DFOSs. Moreover, this new approach can easily deal with the uncertainties in singular matrix based on the special position of E in (21).*

Corollary 2. DFOS (1) with $0 < \alpha < 1$ is admissible if A is nonsingular and there exist matrices P and $Q > 0$ such that

$$\begin{bmatrix} \text{sym}(P) & \text{asym}(P) \\ -\text{asym}(P) & \text{sym}(P) \end{bmatrix} > 0, \tag{22}$$

$$A\Phi E^T + E\Phi^T A^T + EQE^T \leq 0, \tag{23}$$

where $\Phi = a \cdot \text{sym}(P) - b \cdot \text{asym}(P)$.

Proof. According to (22), we get $\text{sym}(P) > 0$ and $(\text{asym}(P))^T = -\text{asym}(P)$. Let $\text{sym}(P) = X$, $\text{asym}(P) = Y$, where $X > 0$ and $Y^T = -Y$. It is easy to get

$$P = \frac{1}{2}(X+Y), \quad P^T = \frac{1}{2}(X-Y). \tag{24}$$

Therefore, (22) and (23) are equivalent to (4) and (7), respectively. By Theorem 1, one concludes that (1) is admissible. □

Remark 2. Corollary 2 provides a method to reduce the count of decision variables. Matrices X and Y are replaced by a single matrix P which simplifies the expressions in Theorem 1 and is easier to solve than the exiting approach.

Theorem 2. DFOS (1) with $1 \leq \alpha < 2$ is admissible if A is nonsingular and there exist two positive matrices $P, Q \in \mathbb{R}^{n \times n}$ such that

$$\Theta \otimes APE^T + \Theta^T \otimes EPA^T + I_2 \otimes EQE^T \leq 0. \tag{25}$$

Proof. Using the similar proof method of Theorem 1, we deduce that Theorem 2 holds. □

Corollary 3. DFOS (1) with $1 \leq \alpha < 2$ is admissible if A is nonsingular and there exist two positive matrices $P, \hat{Q} \in \mathbb{R}^{n \times n}$ such that

$$\begin{bmatrix} \text{sym}(\Theta \otimes APE^T) & I_2 \otimes E \\ * & -I_2 \otimes \hat{Q} \end{bmatrix} \leq 0. \tag{26}$$

Proof. The proof of Corollary 3 is similar to that in Corollary 1 and is omitted. □

Remark 3. For the order in $[1,2)$, a different criterion for admissibility is proposed in Theorem 2. Considering the special form of equation (26), this method is convenient to handle the DFOSs with uncertain singular matrix E.

Theorem 3. DFOS (1) with $0 < \alpha < 2$ is admissible if A is nonsingular and there exist matrices P and $Q > 0$ such that

$$\begin{bmatrix} \text{sym}(P) & \text{asym}(P) \\ \lfloor \alpha - 1 \rfloor \text{asym}(P) & \text{sym}(P) \end{bmatrix} > 0, \tag{27}$$

$$\text{sym}(\Theta_\alpha \otimes AP_\alpha E^T) + I_{\lceil \alpha \rceil} \otimes EQE^T \leq 0, \tag{28}$$

where $\Theta_\alpha = \Theta(\lceil \alpha \rceil)$, $\Theta(1) = \det(\Theta)$, $\Theta(2) = \Theta$, $P_\alpha = a^{-\lfloor \alpha - 1 \rfloor} \cdot \text{sym}(P) + b\lfloor \alpha - 1 \rfloor \text{asym}(P)$.

Proof. When $0 < \alpha < 1$, it is easy to get $\Theta_\alpha = 1$, $P_\alpha = a \cdot \text{sym}(P) - b \cdot \text{asym}(P)$. Then, we obtain that (27) and (28) yield to (4) and (7). Thus, Theorem 3 is equivalent to Theorem 1 in this case.

When $1 \leq \alpha < 2$, we have $\Theta_\alpha = \Theta$, $P_\alpha = \text{sym}(P)$. From equations (27) and (28), we obtain

$$\begin{bmatrix} P_\alpha & 0 \\ 0 & P_\alpha \end{bmatrix} > 0, \tag{29}$$

$$\text{sym}(\Theta \otimes AP_\alpha E^T) + I_2 \otimes EQE^T \leq 0. \tag{30}$$

It is easy to see that (29) and (30) are equivalent to $P_\alpha > 0$ and (25) in Theorem 2. □

Remark 4. *Theorem 3 is an unified form of Theorems 1 and 2, which are necessary and sufficient conditions without complex number and are able to handle eigenvalues of system matrix A with positive real part. In the case of E = I, Theorem 3 is consistent with Lemmas 2 and 3 for α in $(0,1)$ and $[1,2)$, respectively. When $\alpha = 1$, Theorem 3 is the same as admissibility conditions for integer systems in [32].*

Remark 5. *The inequality (28) cannot be solved directly because it contains an equality constraint. In order to tackle this issue, nonsingular matrices G, W and a column full rank matrix S which satisfies $ES = 0$ are introduced in the following theorems. Nonsingular matrices G and W satisfy (3) which is deduced by the nonsingular condition of A. Then, a strict LMI without equality constraint is further formulated.*

3.2. Criteria of Admissibility Based on Strict LMIs

Theorem 4. *DFOS (1) with $0 < \alpha < 1$ is admissible if A is nonsingular and there exist matrices X, Y satisfying (4) and*

$$A(aX - bY)E^T + E(aX - bY)^T A^T - (WG)^{-1}SS^T(WG)^{-T} < 0, \tag{31}$$

where W, G satisfy (3), and S is any matrix with full column rank which satisfies $ES = 0$.

Proof. The proof is similar to Theorem 1 and is simplified as follows:
(Sufficiency) Since A is nonsingular, there exist two invertible matrices G and W satisfying (3). Set the form of X, Y as (8) and (9), respectively. Under the condition (4), it is easy to obtain (12).

Let

$$S = W \begin{bmatrix} 0 \\ S_2 \end{bmatrix}, \tag{32}$$

which satisfies $ES = 0$. Therefore, $J_{n-r}S_2 = 0$. Substituting (3), (8), (9) and (32) into (31), we have

$$\tilde{U} = \begin{bmatrix} \tilde{U}_1 & \tilde{U}_2 \\ \tilde{U}_2^T & \tilde{U}_3 \end{bmatrix} < 0, \tag{33}$$

where

$$\tilde{U}_1 = \bar{A}_1(aX_1 - bY_1) + (aX_1 - bY_1)^T \bar{A}_1^T,$$
$$\tilde{U}_2 = \bar{A}_1(aX_2 - bY_2)J_{n-r}^T + (aX_2 + bY_2),$$
$$\tilde{U}_3 = (aX_3 - bY_3)J_{n-r}^T + J_{n-r}(aX_3 - bY_3)^T - S_2 S_2^T.$$

(33) implies $\tilde{U}_1 < 0$. According to $\tilde{U}_1 < 0$ and (12), by Lemma 2, one has that (1) is stable.
Without loss of generality, suppose that the nilpotent matrix $J_{n-r} \neq 0$ which owns the Jordan form (15).

Choose S_2 as

$$S_2 = \begin{bmatrix} 0 & 0 & \cdots & 0 \\ \vdots & \vdots & \ddots & \vdots \\ 0 & 0 & \cdots & 0 \\ s_{1t} & s_{2t} & \cdots & s_{tt} \end{bmatrix},$$

where $t = n - r$, $s_{it} \neq 0$ is an arbitrary real number for $i = 1, \cdots, n$, and S_2 satisfies $J_{n-r}S_2 = 0$.

Write X_3, Y_3 as (16), (17). Then, $\tilde{U}_3$ is rewritten as

$$\begin{bmatrix} 0 & ax_{11} & \star & \star \\ ax_{11} & 2(ax_{12} - by_{12}) & \star & \star \\ \star & \star & \star & \star \\ \star & \star & \star & \star \end{bmatrix}.$$

Since

$$\det\left(\begin{bmatrix} 0 & ax_{11} \\ ax_{11} & 2(ax_{12} - by_{12}) \end{bmatrix}\right) < 0,$$

$\tilde{U}_3$ contains two eigenvalues with different sign which is conflicted with $\tilde{U} < 0$. It follows that $J_{n-r} = 0$. Applying Lemma 1, one concludes that (1) is impulse-free. This together with the regularity and stability of (1) deduces that (1) is admissible.

(Necessity) According to Lemma 1 and the admissible condition of (1), there exist nonsingular matrices G, W such that (3) holds. By Lemma 2, there exist matrices X_1, Y_1 satisfying (12) and (14) which deduces that A is invertible. Setting the expressions of X, Y as (20), it is easy to see that (4) holds.

Choose S as

$$S = W \begin{bmatrix} 0 \\ I \end{bmatrix}, \tag{34}$$

which satisfies $ES = 0$. Substituting (3), (20) and (34) into (31), one has

$$A(aX - bY)E^T + E(aX - bY)^T A^T - (WG)^{-1}\hat{E}\hat{E}^T(WG)^{-T}$$
$$= G^{-1} \begin{bmatrix} A_1(aX_1 - bY_1) + (aX_1 - bY_1)^T A_1^T & 0 \\ 0 & -I \end{bmatrix} G^{-T} < 0.$$

□

Theorem 5. *DFOS (1) with $0 < \alpha < 1$ is admissible if A is nonsingular and there exists a matrix P satisfying (22) and*

$$A\Phi E^T + E\Phi^T A^T - (WG)^{-1}SS^T(WG)^{-T} < 0, \tag{35}$$

where $\Phi = a \cdot \text{sym}(P) - b \cdot \text{asym}(P)$.

Proof. The proof is similar to that in Corollary 2 and is therefore omitted. □

Theorem 6. *DFOS (1) with $1 \leq \alpha < 2$ is admissible if A is nonsingular and there exists a matrix $P > 0$ such that*

$$\Theta \otimes APE^T + \Theta^T \otimes EPA^T - I_2 \otimes (WG)^{-1}SS^T(WG)^{-T} < 0, \tag{36}$$

where W, G and S are given in Theorem 4.

Proof. Using the method of Theorem 4, we can easily obtain Theorem 6. □

Theorem 7. *DFOS (1) with $0 < \alpha < 2$ is admissible if A is nonsingular and there exist a matrix P satisfying (27) and*

$$\text{sym}(\Theta_\alpha \otimes AP_\alpha E^T) - I_{[\alpha]} \otimes (WG)^{-1}SS^T(WG)^{-T} < 0, \tag{37}$$

where Θ_α and P_α are given in Theorem 3.

Proof. The proof is similar to that in Theorem 3, so the details are omitted. □

Remark 6. *In Theorem 7, a strict LMI criterion of admissibility is proposed. This new approach is an unified form of Theorems 5 and 6, and it is easy to cope with the eigenvalues with positive real part. In addition, the LMIs in (27) and (37) only contain one real decision variable which is easy to solve. In the case of $E = I$, Theorem 7 is also consistent with Lemmas 2 and 3 for α in $(0,1)$ and $[1,2)$, respectively.*

4. Numerical Examples

Three numerical examples are provided to illustrate the effectiveness of theorems based on non-strict LMIs and strict LMIs.

Example 1. *Consider system (1) with $\alpha = 0.4$, and*

$$E = \begin{bmatrix} 1 & 0 & 0 \\ 0 & 1 & 0 \\ 0 & 0 & 0 \end{bmatrix}, \quad A = \begin{bmatrix} 1 & 2 & 0 \\ -2 & 1 & 0 \\ 0 & 0 & 1 \end{bmatrix}.$$

By solving non-strict LMIs in Theorem 3, we obtain the feasible solutions as follows:

$$P = \begin{bmatrix} 0.5621 & -0.4766 & 0 \\ 0.4766 & 0.5621 & 0 \\ 0 & 0 & 0.5000 \end{bmatrix}, \quad Q = \begin{bmatrix} 0.8814 & 0 & 0 \\ 0 & 0.8814 & 0 \\ 0 & 0 & 1.0000 \end{bmatrix}.$$

Remark 7. *The correctness of Theorem 3 is verified in Example 1 by solving Equations (27) and (28). Since (28) contains an equality constraint which cannot be solved by any simulation software directly, we need to convert the matrices A and E into the form of (3). A feasible approach to get the solution is solving the following strict LMI*

$$\bar{A}_1(aX_1 - bY_1) + (aX_1 - bY_1)^T \bar{A}_1^T + Q_1 < 0.$$

we can get the values of X_1, Y_1 and Q_1. Construct matrices X, Y and Q with the form of (20). Then, the feasible solutions of P and Q is obtained, where $P = \frac{1}{2}(X + Y)$.

Example 2. *Consider a DFOS in (1) with*

$$\alpha = 0.5, \; E = \begin{bmatrix} -3 & -1 & 2 & 5 \\ 1 & 1 & -1 & -3 \\ -3 & 1 & 2 & 3 \\ 1 & 1 & 1 & 1 \end{bmatrix}, \; A = \begin{bmatrix} 7 & 2 & 2 & 1 \\ -3 & -2 & -4 & -5 \\ 10 & 1 & -7 & -16 \\ 3 & 4 & -2 & -7 \end{bmatrix}.$$

Since A is nonsingular, the system (1) is regular. Due to $\deg(\det(sE - A)) = \mathrm{rank}(E) = 3$, the system (1) is impulse-free. The roots of $\det(sE - A) = 0$ are -2 and $1 \pm 3j$. By Lemma 1, it is easy to verify that the DFOS with parameters in Example 2 is admissible. By solving strict LMIs (27) and (37) in Theorem 7, we get the following feasible solution of real matrix P:

$$P = \begin{bmatrix} 2.3934 & -1.7708 & -0.7703 & 2.3777 \\ 1.8095 & 8.1164 & -2.3734 & 2.8106 \\ 0.2597 & -0.8788 & 4.7747 & -2.3535 \\ 2.1066 & -1.3637 & -2.5610 & 3.3455 \end{bmatrix}.$$

The state responses are displayed in Figure 1.

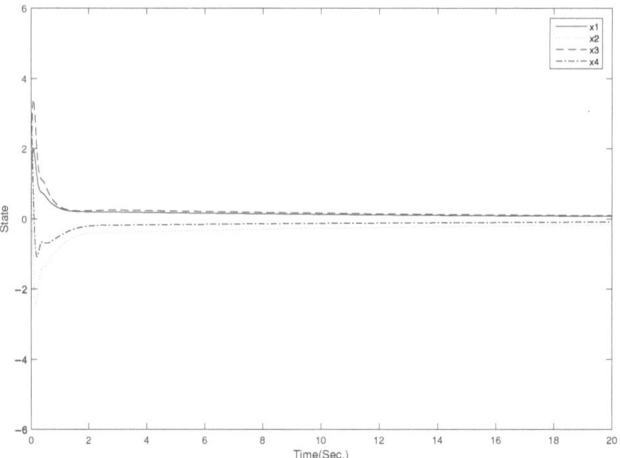

Figure 1. The state responses with $\alpha = 0.5$ in Example 2.

Example 3. *Consider a DFOS in (1) with $\alpha = 0.5$, $\alpha = 1$ and $\alpha = 1.5$, respectively, and*

$$E = \begin{bmatrix} 1 & 2 & 1 & 2 \\ 0 & 0 & -1 & -1 \\ -1 & 0 & -1 & 0 \\ 0 & 2 & 0 & 2 \end{bmatrix}, \quad A = \begin{bmatrix} -1 & -5 & -2 & -6 \\ 2 & 1 & 4 & 1 \\ 1 & -1 & 2 & 0 \\ 1 & -6 & 1 & -7 \end{bmatrix}.$$

By Lemma 1, it is easy to get that the DFOS in Example 3 is also admissible. By Theorem 7, we obtain the following feasible solution:

Case $\alpha = 0.5$,

$$P = \begin{bmatrix} 0.7020 & -0.0885 & -0.3003 & 0.0798 \\ 0.1775 & 0.4749 & 0.0800 & -0.4463 \\ -0.2594 & 0.0377 & 0.2139 & -0.0457 \\ -0.1554 & -0.4179 & -0.1077 & 0.4209 \end{bmatrix};$$

Case $\alpha = 1$,

$$P = \begin{bmatrix} 7.6362 & -3.4359 & -4.4911 & 3.2509 \\ -3.4359 & 3.4431 & 2.0794 & -3.1028 \\ -4.4911 & 2.0794 & 3.0249 & -2.0289 \\ 3.2509 & -3.1028 & -2.0289 & 2.9524 \end{bmatrix};$$

Case $\alpha = 1.5$,

$$P = \begin{bmatrix} 12.1598 & -6.1003 & -7.1349 & 5.7156 \\ -6.1003 & 5.0981 & 3.4141 & -4.4487 \\ -7.1349 & 3.4141 & 5.2904 & -3.3692 \\ 5.7156 & -4.4487 & -3.3692 & 4.2455 \end{bmatrix}.$$

From the state responses in Figure 2 which are simulated based on the data above, we can see that the system quickly reaches stability after 10 s.

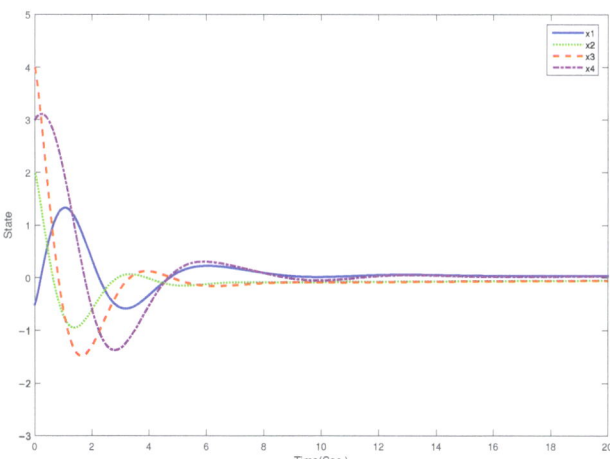

Figure 2. The state responses with $\alpha = 1.5$ in Example 3.

Remark 8. *For the arbitrary $\alpha \in (0,2)$, the effectiveness of Theorem 7 is verified by the simulation results in Example 3. Compared with the methods addressed in [15,28] with multiple complex variables, the LMIs in Theorems 3 and 7 are all composed of real matrices, which avoids the difficulty in solving brought by complex numbers. On the basis of the general approaches in [25,29,30], which divide order α into $(0,1)$ and $[1,2)$ to discuss admissibility, we propose a unified form without interval separation and enrich the theoretical research on admissibility.*

Remark 9. *The approaches reported in [33] are inapplicable to the case of matrix A with eigenvalues on positive real part, but our method has no the limitation of eigenvalues which has a wider range of applications. Compared with the necessary and sufficient criteria proposed in [25–31] with multiple decision variables, the Theorem 7 based on LMIs in this paper contains only one real decision variable in which is easy to obtain the feasible solution.*

5. Conclusions

This paper analyzes the problem concerning synthesis of DFOSs without any order interval separation. Novel and alternate admissibility approaches based on non-strict LMIs and strict LMIs are proposed, which fill the vacancy of previous achievements and have theoretical research value. For the non-strict LMI criterion, the position of singular matrix E is different from existing studies, which is convenient to tackle the uncertainties in derivative matrix. For the strict LMI criterion, the research object of using the least real decision variable to solve the problem of admissibility is achieved. All the methods are necessary and sufficient conditions without complex numbers and are applicable to the system eigenvalues with positive real part. When $E = I$ or $\alpha = 1$, the Theorems established in this paper are consistent with related FOSs results or descriptor integer system results in [15,29,32], which are regarded as the extensions of Lyapunov stability. Further works will focus on the controller design for the DFOSs with uncertain derivative matrices based on the methods established above.

Author Contributions: Conceptualization, methodology, validation, Y.D., X.Z. and J.-X.Z.; writing—original draft preparation, Y.D.; writing—review and editing, J.-X.Z. and X.Z. All authors have read and agreed to the published version of the manuscript.

Funding: This work was supported in part by the National Natural Science Foundation of China under Grant 62103093 and the Fundamental Research Funds for the Central Universities of China under Grant N2108003.

Data Availability Statement: Not applicable.

Conflicts of Interest: The authors declare no conflict of interest.

References

1. Ortigueira, M.D.; Ionescu, C.M.; Machado, J.T.; Trujillo, J.J. Fractional signal processing and applications. *Signal Process.* **2015**, *107*, 197. [CrossRef]
2. Zhao, Z.C,; Li, G. Synchrosqueezing-based short-time fractional fourier transform. *IEEE Trans. Image Process.* **2023**, *71*, 279–294. [CrossRef]
3. Yan, H.; Zhang, J. X.; Zhang, X.F. Injected infrared and visible image fusion via L_1 decomposition model and guided filtering. *IEEE Trans. Comput. Imag.* **2022**, *8*, 162–173. [CrossRef]
4. Liu, C.H.; Hu, M.H.; Jin, G.Q.; Xu, Y.D.; Zhai, J. State of power estimation of lithium-ion battery based on fractional-order equivalent circuit model. *J. Energy Storage* **2021**, *41*, 102954. [CrossRef]
5. Muresan, C.I.; Birs, I.; Ionescu, C.; Dulf, E.H.; De Keyser, R. A review of recent developments in autotuning methods for fractional-order controllers. *Fractal Fract* **2022**, *6*, 37. [CrossRef]
6. Wang, Z.; Fei, J.T. Fractional-order terminal sliding-mode control using self-evolving recurrent chebyshev fuzzy neural network for MEMS gyroscope. *IEEE Trans. Fuzzy Syst.* **2022**, *30*, 2747–2758. [CrossRef]
7. Fei, J.T.; Wang, Z.; Liang, X.; Feng, Z.L.; Xue, Y.C. Fractional sliding-mode control for microgyroscope based on multilayer recurrent fuzzy neural network. *IEEE Trans. Fuzzy Syst.* **2022**, *30*, 1712–1721. [CrossRef]
8. Radwan, A.G.; Emira, A.A.; Abdelaty, A.M.; Azar, A.T. Modeling and analysis of fractional order DC-DC converter. *ISA Trans.* **2018**, *82*, 184–199. [CrossRef]
9. Babes, B.; Mekhilef, S.; Boutaghane, A.; Rahmani, L. Fuzzy approximation-based fractional-order nonsingular terminal sliding mode controller for DC-DC buck converters. *IEEE Trans. Power Electron.* **2022**, *37*, 2749–2760. [CrossRef]
10. Yu, Z.M.; Sun, Y.; Dai, X. Stability and stabilization of the fractional-order power system with time delay. *IEEE Trans. Circuits Syst. II Express Briefs* **2021**, *68*, 3446–3450. [CrossRef]
11. Yang, F.; Shao, X.Y.; Muyeen, S.M.; Li, D.D.; Lin, S.F.; Fang, C. Disturbance observer based fractional-order integral sliding mode frequency control strategy for interconnected power system. *IEEE Trans. Power Syst.* **2021**, *35*, 5922–5932. [CrossRef]
12. Yousefpour, A.; Jahanshahi, H.; Munoz-Pacheco, J.; Bekiros, S.; Wei, Z.C. A fractional-order hyper-chaotic economic system with transient chaos. *Chaos Solitons Fractals* **2020**, *130*, 109400. [CrossRef]
13. Yang, W.G.; Zheng, W.X.; Yu, W.W. Observer-based event-triggered adaptive fuzzy control for fractional-order time-varying delayed MIMO systems against actuator faults. *IEEE Trans. Fuzzy Syst.* **2022**, *30*, 5445–5459. [CrossRef]
14. Fan, X.F.; Wang, Z.S. A fuzzy lyapunov function method to stability analysis of fractional-order T-S fuzzy systems. *IEEE Trans. Fuzzy Syst.* **2022**, *30*, 2769–2776. [CrossRef]
15. Farges, C.; Moze, M.; Sabatier, J. Pseudo-state feedback stabilisation of commensurate fractional order systems. *Automatica* **2010**, *46*, 1730–1734. [CrossRef]
16. Lu, J.G.; Chen, Y.Q. Robust stability and stabilization of fractional-order interval systems with the fractional order $\alpha : 0 < \alpha < 1$ case. *IEEE Trans. Autom. Control* **2010**, *55*, 152–158.
17. Zhang, X.F.; Lin, C.; Chen, Y.Q.; Boutat, D. A unified framework of stability theorems for LTI fractional order systems with $0 < \alpha < 2$. *IEEE Trans. Circuits Syst. II Express Briefs* **2020**, *67*, 3237–3241.
18. Tian, Y.; Wang, Z.B.; Liu, D.Y.; Boutat, D.; Liu, H.R. Non-asymptotic estimation for fractional integrals of noisy accelerations for fractional order vibration systems. *Automatica* **2022**, *135*, 109996. [CrossRef]
19. Ghorbani, M.; Tavakoli-Kakhki, M.; Tepljakov, A.; Petlenkov, E.; Farnam, A.; Crevecoeur, G. Robust stability analysis of interval fractional-order plants with interval time delay and general form of fractional-order controllers. *IEEE Control Syst. Lett.* **2021**, *6*, 1268–1273. [CrossRef]
20. Alessandretti, A.; Pequito, S.; Pappas, G.J.; Aguiar, A.P. Finite-dimensional control of linear discrete-time fractional-order systems. *Automatica* **2020**, *115*, 108512. [CrossRef]
21. Zhu, Z.; Lu, J.G. LMI-based robust stability analysis of discrete-time fractional-order systems with interval uncertainties. *IEEE Trans. Circuits Syst. I-Regul. Pap.* **2021**, *68*, 1671–1680. [CrossRef]
22. Gong, P.; Lan, W.Y.; Han, Q.L. Robust adaptive fault-tolerant consensus control for uncertain nonlinear fractional-order multi-agent systems with directed topologies. *Automatica* **2020**, *117*, 109011. [CrossRef]
23. Zhang, J.X.; Yang, G.H. Low-complexity tracking control of strict-feedback systems with unknown control directions. *IEEE Trans. Autom. Control* **2019**, *64*, 5175–5182. [CrossRef]
24. Zhang, J.X.; Yang, G.H. Fault-tolerant output-constrained control of unknown Euler-Lagrange systems with prescribed tracking accuracy. *Automatica* **2020**, *111*, 108606. [CrossRef]
25. Marir, S.; Chadli, M.; Bouagada, D. New admissibility conditions for singular linear continuous-time fractional-order systems. *J. Frankl. Inst.* **2017**, *354*, 752–766. [CrossRef]
26. Marir, S.; Chadli, M. Robust admissibility and stabilization of uncertain singular fractional-order linear time-invariant systems. *IEEE/CAA J. Autom. Sin.* **2019**, *6*, 685–692. [CrossRef]

27. Marir, S.; Chadli, M.; Basin, M.V. Bounded real lemma for singular linear continuous-time fractional-order systems. *Automatica* **2022**, *135*, 109962. [CrossRef]
28. Marir, S.; Chadli, M.; Bouagada, D. A novel approach of admissibility for singular linear continuous-time fractional-order systems. *Int. J. Control Autom. Syst.* **2017**, *15*, 959–964. [CrossRef]
29. Zhang, X.F.; Chen, Y.Q. Admissibility and robust stabilization of continuous linear singular fractional order systems with the fractional order α : The $0 < \alpha < 1$ case. *ISA Trans.* **2018**, *82*, 42–50.
30. Luo, S.Y.; Lu, J.G.; Qiu, X.Y. Robust normalization and stabilization of descriptor fractional-order systems with uncertainties in all matrices. *J. Frankl. Inst.* **2022**, *359*, 1113–1129. [CrossRef]
31. Wang, Y.Y., Zhang, X.F., Boutat, D.; Shi, P. Quadratic admissibility for a class of LTI uncertain singular fractional-order systems with $0 < \alpha < 2$. *Fractal Fract.* **2022**, *7*, 1.
32. Zhang, D.Q.; Zhang, Q.L. On the quadratic stability of descriptor systems with uncertainties in the derivative matrix. *Int. J. Syst. Sci.* **2009**, *40*, 695–702. [CrossRef]
33. Zhang, Q.H.; Lu, J.G. Necessary and sufficient conditions for extended strictly positive realness of singular fractional-order systems. *IEEE Trans. Circuits Syst. II Express Briefs* **2021**, *68*, 1997–2001. [CrossRef]

Disclaimer/Publisher's Note: The statements, opinions and data contained in all publications are solely those of the individual author(s) and contributor(s) and not of MDPI and/or the editor(s). MDPI and/or the editor(s) disclaim responsibility for any injury to people or property resulting from any ideas, methods, instructions or products referred to in the content.

Article

Prescribed Performance Tracking Control of Lower-Triangular Systems with Unknown Fractional Powers

Kai-Di Xu and Jin-Xi Zhang *

State Key Laboratory of Synthetical Automation for Process Industries, Northeastern University, Shenyang 110819, China; kaidixu@stumail.neu.edu.cn
* Correspondence: zhangjx@mail.neu.edu.cn

Abstract: This paper is concerned with the tracking control problem for the lower-triangular systems with unknown fractional powers and nonparametric uncertainties. A prescribed performance control approach is put forward as a means of resolving this problem. The proposed control law incorporates a set of barrier functions to guarantee error constraints. Unlike the previous works, our approach works for the cases where the fractional powers, the nonlinearities, and their bounding functions or bounds are totally unknown; no restrictive conditions on the powers, such as power order restriction, specific size limitation or homogeneous condition, are made. Moreover, neither the powers and system nonlinearities nor their bounding functions or bounds are needed. It achieves reference tracking with the preassigned tracking accuracy and convergence speed. In addition, our controller is simple, as it does not necessitate parameter identification, function approximation, derivative calculation, or adding a power integrator technique. At the end, a comparative simulation demonstrates the effectiveness and advantage of the proposed approach.

Keywords: fractional powers; lower-triangular systems; nonparametric uncertainties; prescribed performance; reference tracking

1. Introduction

Due to the theoretical challenge and practical needs, the issue of controlling uncertain nonlinear systems with odd powers has garnered significant attention. Examples of odd-power nonlinear systems in engineering include but are not limited to dynamical boiler–turbine units [1], jet engine compression systems [2], and under-actuated mechanical systems [3]. Compared with the strict feedback systems whose powers are one, odd-power nonlinear systems exhibit more general and complex behavior due to their exponential powers. It is worth claiming that such a system cannot conduct feedback linearization caused by the uncontrollability of its Jacobian matrix and is nonaffine with respect to the control input. Therefore, the control development of odd-power systems poses significant challenges and difficulties.

Various methods for the odd-power nonlinear systems have been developed, which are mainly based on adaptive control [4–14], neural or fuzzy control [15–20], funnel or prescribed performance control [14,17–21], and adding a power integrator technique [11,13,22–28]. The results [22–24] work well under the power order restriction (i.e., $p_1 \geq p_i \geq \ldots \geq p_n$, $i = 1, \cdots, n$, where $p_1, \ldots, p_n$ are positive odd powers), and they also extend to the odd-power stochastic nonlinear systems [5,8,29]. Later, this restriction was removed, but the powers need to be identical [30]. The above limitations were relaxed [3,4,16,17,20,25,31]; however, the sphere of application for the above methods is limited to integer powers. The control designs for the systems with fractional powers were performed in recent years [6,7,9,10,18,21,32,33]. Nonetheless, in all the aforementioned developments, the powers are required not less than one. In the literature [14,19], the powers can be odd numbers greater than zero and less than one. Notably, a common feature among the aforesaid

findings is that the powers should be known. Nevertheless, as summarized in Ref. [27], the aging of hardening spring and diverse operating conditions may result in time-varying and unknown powers in some particular cases, such as the boiler–turbine systems [1] and the under-actuated, weakly coupled mechanical systems [3]. It is noteworthy that the technique of adding a power integrator, an effective strategy for the odd-power systems, is not suitable for the unknown power systems due to its reliance on the system's homogeneous dominant part. To deal with this problem, numerous approaches were put forward in the literature [11,13,26–28], but the bounds of their powers need to be available for the control design. The prior knowledge of the bounds is eliminated, either by imposing order restriction [12] or by placing a specific size limitation on the powers [12,15]. Additionally, the system nonlinearities of the aforementioned results are either considered to be known [32] or constrained by known functions [3,5,8,22–24,30] or expressed as a form containing unknown parameters and known functions [11–13,28,29].

On the other hand, in the presence of unknown nonlinearities, the results [3,4,16,25,28,32] show only the tracking error's boundedness, but the specific behavior (e.g., the convergence speed and the accuracy) cannot be predetermined. To overcome this problem, researchers propose the prescribed performance (PPC) method [34,35], which enables quantitatively pre-specification of both transient and steady-state reference tracking behavior. This method has been applied to the first-order systems [36–38], feedback linearizable systems [39–41], strict-feedback systems [42,43], and odd-power systems [14,17–21]. However, there are some restrictive conditions on the powers and nonlinearities as mentioned above. Therefore, the control development for the odd-power nonlinear systems without the aforesaid requirements still remains open.

Inspired by the above discussion, this paper introduces a PPC strategy for the lower-triangular systems with unknown fractional powers and nonparametric uncertainties. The primary contributions and advantages are outlined:

1. Our approach works well when the fractional powers, the system nonlinearities, and their bounds or bounding functions are unknown, without the power order restriction [5,8,12,13,22–24,29], the specific size limitation [3–13,15–18,20–33], or the homogeneous condition [30].
2. It guarantees reference tracking with the prescribed convergence speed and accuracy in addition to the boundedness of the tracking error [3,4,16,25,28,32].
3. It exhibits simplicity, without function approximation [15–20,44,45], parameter identification [4–14], command filtering [44,45], or adding a power integrator technique [11,13,22–28].

This paper is structured as follows. Section 2 presents the system description and control objective. In Section 3, we state the composition of the proposed control scheme. Its feasibility is demonstrated in Section 4. The simulation results are detailed in Section 5. Finally, we draw the conclusion in Section 6.

Notations: The notations used in this paper are standard and are summarized as follows. $\Re^i$ denotes the i-dimensional Euclidean space, with $\Re^1 = \Re$; $sgn(\cdot)$ denotes the sign function.

2. Problem Description
2.1. System Description

Consider the lower-triangular systems with unknown fractional powers as follows:

$$\begin{cases} \dot{x}_i = f_i(\bar{x}_i) + x_{i+1}^{\frac{p_i}{q_i}}, \\ \dot{x}_n = f_n(\bar{x}_n) + u^{\frac{p_n}{q_n}}, \\ y = x_1, \end{cases} \qquad (1)$$

where $\bar{x}_i = [x_1, \cdots, x_i]^T \in \mathfrak{R}^i$, $i = 1, \cdots, n$; $\bar{x}_n$ is composed of the system state; $u \in \mathfrak{R}$ and $y \in \mathfrak{R}$ are the input and the output, respectively; p_i and q_i are positive odd integers, $i = 1, \cdots, n$; $f_i(\cdot) \in \mathfrak{R}$, $i = 1, \cdots, n$ denote the continuous nonlinear functions.

Remark 1. *Distinct from the available findings, only the basic structural properties of (1) are required for the subsequent control design. Specifically, the nonlinear function $f_i(\cdot)$ and the powers p_i and q_i are unknown, which helps to design the universal controller. In this case, the commonly used model-based technique of adding a power integrator cannot be applied to (1). Moreover, it is worth claiming that the fractional powers are allowed in this study rather than integers [3–5,8,16,17,20,22–25,29–31] and are not required to satisfy the power order restriction and specific size limitation [3–13,15–18,20–33].*

2.2. Control Objective

The control target for (1) is let $y(t)$ follow a reference $r(t)$, which meets the following assumption [14,16,23,32].

Assumption 1. *$r(t)$ and $\dot{r}(t)$ are bounded on $[0, \infty)$.*

To be specific, the desired tracking performance is prescribed by

$$|y(t) - r(t)| < \xi_1(t), \quad t \geq 0, \tag{2}$$

with

$$\xi_1(t) = (\xi_{10} - \xi_{1\infty})e^{-l_1 t} + \xi_{1\infty}, \tag{3}$$

where $l_1 > 0$ and $\xi_{1\infty} > 0$ are the convergence rate and the tracking accuracy, respectively. Both of them can be chosen by the designer according to the requirements. Moreover, $\xi_1(0)$ should satisfy

$$|y(0) - r(0)| < \xi_1(0). \tag{4}$$

We take into account the problem below.

Problem 1. *Develop a control for the odd-power systems with unknown fractional powers in (1) to ensure the fulfillment of the performance requirement stated in (2) and guarantee the boundedness of the closed-loop system signals.*

3. Control Design

We present a robust PPC approach to address Problem 1. The proposed controller design starts from

$$e_1(t) = x_1(t) - r(t). \tag{5}$$

Subsequently, a barrier function is utilized to confine $e_1(t)$:

$$\eta_1(t) = \tan\left(\frac{\pi}{2}\frac{e_1(t)}{\xi_1(t)}\right). \tag{6}$$

The resulting first intermediate control law is obtained by

$$\alpha_1(t) = -c_1\eta_1(t), \tag{7}$$

where $c_1 > 0$ denotes the constant control gain. Proceed with

$$e_i(t) = x_i(t) - \alpha_{i-1}(t), \tag{8}$$

$$\xi_i(t) = (\xi_{i0} - \xi_{i\infty})e^{-l_i t} + \xi_{i\infty}, \tag{9}$$

$$\eta_i(t) = \tan\left(\frac{\pi}{2} \frac{e_i(t)}{\xi_i(t)}\right), \tag{10}$$

$$\alpha_i(t) = -c_i \eta_i(t), \tag{11}$$

for $i = 2, \cdots, n$, in a recursive manner, where $c_i > 0$ represents the constant control gain; $l_i > 0$ and $\xi_{i\infty} > 0$ are freely designed by the designer; $\xi_i(0)$ is chosen such that

$$|e_i(0)| < \xi_i(0), \ i = 2 \cdots, n. \tag{12}$$

In the end, the final control is obtained as follows:

$$u(t) = \alpha_n(t). \tag{13}$$

The block diagram of the system with the controller is given in Figure 1.

Remark 2. *The presented design in (5)–(13) depends on neither the prior knowledge of the powers and the system nonlinearities nor their specific bounding functions or bounds. Even so, no attempt is made for parameter identification [4–14], function approximation [15–20,44,45], gain adaptation [46,47], or adding a power integrator technique [11,13,22–28]. Furthermore, the reference derivative and the intermediate control signal derivatives are not involved in the control law. Nevertheless, this is accomplished without dynamic surface control [44] or auxiliary filters [45]. Thus, the controller exhibits fewer demands and simplicity.*

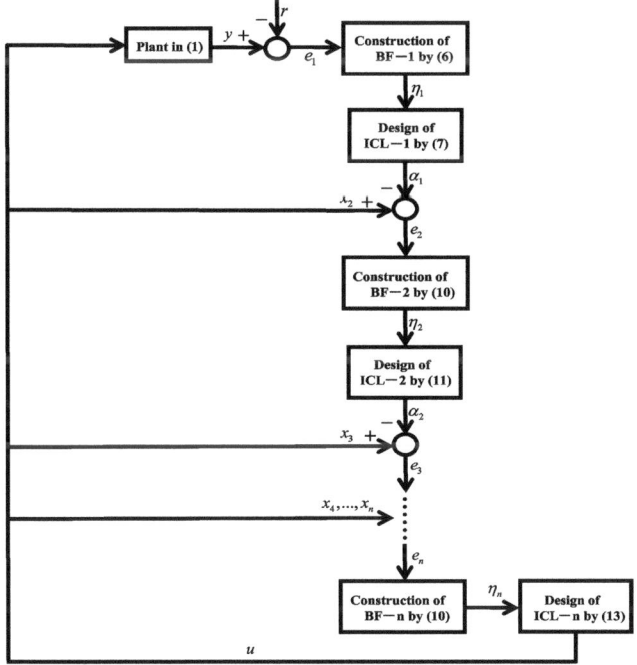

Figure 1. The block diagram of the system with the controller.

4. Theoretical Analysis

For ease of theoretical analysis, we first give a lemma.

Lemma 1. *For any $\epsilon > 0$, $\dot{\alpha}_i(t)$ is bounded on $[0, \epsilon)$, if*
1. *$e_i(t)$ evolves within $(-\xi_i(t), \bar{\xi}_i(t))$ but keeps away from the boundaries on $[0, \epsilon)$;*
2. *$\dot{e}_i(t)$ is bounded on $[0, \epsilon)$;*

with $i = 1, \cdots, n$.

Proof. Differentiating (7) and (11) by (6) and (10), respectively, yields

$$\dot{\alpha}_i(t) = -c_i \cdot \frac{\pi}{2} \cdot \frac{1}{\bar{\xi}_i(t)} \cdot \frac{1}{\gamma_i(t)} \cdot \psi_i(t), \quad i = 1, \cdots, n, \tag{14}$$

with

$$\gamma_i(t) = \cos^2\left(\frac{\pi}{2} \frac{e_i(t)}{\bar{\xi}_i(t)}\right), \tag{15}$$

$$\psi_i(t) = \dot{e}_i(t) - \frac{e_i(t)\dot{\bar{\xi}}_i(t)}{\bar{\xi}_i(t)}. \tag{16}$$

According to (3) and (9), we obtain

$$0 < \bar{\xi}_{i\infty} \le \bar{\xi}_i(t) \le \bar{\xi}_{i0}, \quad i = 1, \cdots, n, \tag{17}$$

and

$$-\rho_i(\bar{\xi}_{i0} - \bar{\xi}_{i\infty}) \le \dot{\bar{\xi}}_i(t) < 0, \quad i = 1, \cdots, n. \tag{18}$$

It follows that the reciprocal of (15) is bounded on $[0, \epsilon)$ provided that the first assumed condition is met. Note from (17) and (18) that $|\psi_i(t)| < \infty$, $t < \epsilon$, under the assumed conditions of Lemma 1. Thereby, $\dot{\alpha}_i(t)$ in (14) is bounded over $[0, \epsilon)$ under the same conditions. □

The result of theory is outlined next.

Theorem 1. *Under Assumption 1, as well as the initial conditions in (4) and (12), the control scheme developed in (5)–(11) and (13) effectively resolves Problem 1.*

Proof. The argument starts from positing the claim below.

$$|e_i(t)| < \bar{\xi}_i(t), \quad i = 1, \cdots, n, \quad t \ge 0, \tag{19}$$

This claim is demonstrated through the method of proof by contradiction. From (4) and (12), (19) is met at $t = 0$. Note that $\bar{x}_n(t)$ is continuous on $[0, \infty)$. The same holds for $r(t)$ under Assumption 1. Hence, $e_1(t)$ in (5) is continuous on $[0, \infty)$. This combined with the continuity of $\bar{\xi}_1(t)$ in (3) guarantees that $\eta_1(t)$ in (6) and $\alpha_1(t)$ in (7) are continuous if $|e_1(t)| < \bar{\xi}_1(t)$. Further, $e_2(t)$ in (8) does so under the same condition. Proceed with analyzing $e_3(t), \cdots, e_n(t)$, recursively. Then, we deduce that each $e_i(t)$ is continuous so long as $|e_\tau(t)| < \bar{\xi}_\tau(t)$, where τ varies from 1 to $i - 1$. This information indicates that the existence of $t^* > 0$ is a necessary condition for the breach of (19) so that

$$\lim_{t \to t^*} |e_\tau(t)| = \bar{\xi}_\tau(t^*), \quad \tau \in \{1, \cdots, n\}, \tag{20}$$

and

$$|e_i(t)| < \bar{\xi}_i(t), \quad i = 1, \cdots, n, \quad t < t^*. \tag{21}$$

Next, we posit (20) with (21) and proceed to examine each individual case defined in (20). To maintain concision, the subsequent discussion may omit some functions' dependence on time or state.

Case 1:

At the outset, we consider

$$\lim_{t \to t^*} |e_1(t)| = \zeta_1(t^*). \tag{22}$$

A necessary condition for (22) under (21) is

$$\lim_{t \to t^*} \frac{d|e_1(t)|}{dt} \geq \lim_{t \to t^*} \dot{\zeta}_1(t). \tag{23}$$

Based on (1) and (5), the differential equation for e_1 is obtained as follows:

$$\dot{e}_1 = f_1 + x_2^{\frac{p_1}{q_1}} - \dot{r}. \tag{24}$$

Rewrite (8) for $i = 2$ as follows:

$$x_2 = e_2 + \alpha_1. \tag{25}$$

Substituting (25) into (24) yields

$$\dot{e}_1 = f_1 - \dot{r} + (e_2 + \alpha_1)^{\frac{p_1}{q_1}}. \tag{26}$$

Therefore, it holds that

$$\lim_{t \to t^*} \frac{d|e_1(t)|}{dt} = \lim_{t \to t^*} \operatorname{sgn}(e_1(t))(f_1 - \dot{r}) + \lim_{t \to t^*} \operatorname{sgn}(e_1(t))(e_2 + \alpha_1)^{\frac{p_1}{q_1}}. \tag{27}$$

According to (5), (21) and Assumption 1, x_1 and e_2 are bounded on $[0, t^*)$. Further, due to the continuity of f_1 with respect to its arguments, it follows that $|f_1| < \infty$, $t < t^*$. Recalling that $\dot{r}$ is bounded on $[0, \infty)$, we know

$$\lim_{t \to t^*} |\operatorname{sgn}(e_1(t))(f_1 - \dot{r})| < \infty, \ t < t^*. \tag{28}$$

It follows from (6) and (22) that

$$\lim_{t \to t^*} \operatorname{sgn}(e_1(t))\eta_1 = +\infty. \tag{29}$$

By (7), there is

$$\lim_{t \to t^*} \operatorname{sgn}(e_1(t))\alpha_1 = -\infty. \tag{30}$$

Under (20), it holds that

$$\lim_{t \to t^*} \operatorname{sgn}(e_1(t))(e_2 + \alpha_1) = -\infty. \tag{31}$$

Noting that p_1 and q_1 are positive odd integers, we further obtain

$$\lim_{t \to t^*} (\operatorname{sgn}(e_1(t))(e_2 + \alpha_1))^{\frac{p_1}{q_1}} = -\infty. \tag{32}$$

Substituting (28) and (32) into (27) gives

$$\lim_{t \to t^*} \frac{d|e_1(t)|}{dt} = -\infty. \tag{33}$$

Note from (18) that

$$-\rho_1(\zeta_{10} - \zeta_{1\infty}) \leq \lim_{t \to t^*} \dot{\zeta}_1(t) < 0.$$

Apparently, (33) contradicts (23). Therefore, (22) is false. Instead, this implies the existence of a constant $o_1 > 0$ so that

$$|e_1(t)| \leq \xi_1(t) - o_1 < \xi_1(t), \quad t < t^*. \tag{34}$$

As a result, η_1 in (6) and α_1 in (7) are bounded for $t < t^*$. Further, by virtue of the boundedness of f_1, e_2 and $\dot{r}$ on $[0, t^*)$, the same holds for $\dot{e}_1$ in (26). This above facts imply by Lemma 1 that $\dot{\alpha}_1$ is bounded for $t < t^*$, which contributes to the analysis of e_2 next.

Case 2:

Proceed with supposing

$$\lim_{t \to t^*} |e_2(t)| = \xi_2(t^*), \tag{35}$$

which necessitates

$$\lim_{t \to t^*} \frac{d|e_2(t)|}{dt} \geq \lim_{t \to t^*} \dot{\xi}_2(t). \tag{36}$$

Differentiating (8) for $i = 2$ by (1) yields

$$\dot{e}_2 = f_2 + x_3^{\frac{p_2}{q_2}} - \dot{\alpha}_1. \tag{37}$$

One sees from (8) for $i = 3$ that

$$x_3 = e_3 + \alpha_2. \tag{38}$$

Substituting (38) into (37) leads to

$$\dot{e}_2 = f_2 - \dot{\alpha}_1 + (e_3 + \alpha_2)^{\frac{p_2}{q_2}}. \tag{39}$$

Then, there is

$$\lim_{t \to t^*} \frac{d|e_2(t)|}{dt} = \lim_{t \to t^*} \text{sgn}(e_2(t))(f_2 - \dot{\alpha}_1) + \lim_{t \to t^*} \text{sgn}(e_2(t))(e_3 + \alpha_2)^{\frac{p_2}{q_2}}. \tag{40}$$

Recall the boundedness of x_1 and α_1 on $[0, t^*)$. From (8) and (21) for $i = 2$, we have $|x_2| < \infty$, $t < t^*$. Due to the continuity of f_2 in its arguments, we know $|f_2| < \infty$, $t < t^*$. This, along with $|\dot{\alpha}_1| < \infty$ over $[0, t^*)$ established in Case 1, ensures

$$\lim_{t \to t^*} |\text{sgn}(e_2(t))(f_2 - \dot{\alpha}_1)| < \infty, \quad t < t^*. \tag{41}$$

Under (10), (11), and (35), it holds that

$$\lim_{t \to t^*} \text{sgn}(e_2(t))\alpha_2 = -\infty. \tag{42}$$

Proceed with (20), and we have

$$\lim_{t \to t^*} \text{sgn}(e_2(t))(e_3 + \alpha_2) = -\infty. \tag{43}$$

Noting that p_2 and q_2 are positive odd integers, it further holds that

$$\lim_{t \to t^*} (\text{sgn}(e_2(t))(e_3 + \alpha_2))^{\frac{p_2}{q_2}} = -\infty. \tag{44}$$

Inserting (41) with (44) into (40) yields

$$\lim_{t \to t^*} \frac{d|e_2(t)|}{dt} = -\infty, \tag{45}$$

which contradicts (36) due to (18). Hence, (35) is false. Then there exists a constant o_2 greater than zero so that

$$|e_1(t)| \leq \xi_2(t) - o_2 < \xi_2(t), \ t < t^*. \tag{46}$$

Thus, η_2 in (10) and α_2 in (11) are bounded during $t < t^*$. Recalling f_2, e_3 and $\dot{\alpha}_1$ are bounded over $[0, t^*)$ established above, $\dot{e}_2$ in (39) is bounded for $t < t^*$. This along with (46) ensures by Lemma 1 the boundedness of α_2 on $[0, t^*)$, which contributes to the analysis of e_3 next.

Case i (i = 3,...,n):
Adopt the same method as in Case 2 to analyze e_i, $i = 3, \ldots, n$, recursively. We can deduce that a constant o_i greater than zero exists, $i = 3, \cdots, n$, so that

$$|e_i(t)| \leq \xi_i(t) - o_i < \xi_i(t), \ i = 3, \cdots, n, \ t < t^*. \tag{47}$$

Now, we arrive at a contradiction between (34), (46), (47), and (20). Therefore, (20) is false, and instead

$$|e_i(t)| \leq \xi_i(t) - o_i < \xi_i(t), \ i = 1, \cdots, n, \ t \geq 0. \tag{48}$$

Obviously, (19) is correct. This means that the controller not only guarantees the error constraints but also excludes the boundary contact. Hence, the prescribed tracking performance as described in (2) is achieved.

It remains to demonstrate that the state variables, $x_1, \cdots, x_n$, the intermediate control law, $\alpha_1, \cdots, \alpha_{n-1}$, and the control input, u are all bounded. From (48), $\eta_i(t)$, $i = 1, \cdots, n$, in (6) and (10), $\alpha_i(t)$, $i = 1, \cdots, n-1$, in (7) and (11) and $u(t)$ in (13) are all bounded. Further, under (48) and Assumption 1, we know that x_i, $i = 1, \cdots, n$ are bounded on $[0, \infty)$. □

Remark 3. *Contrary to the classical Lyapunov stability theory, this study employs a constraint analysis based on dialectic by contradiction. It reveals the control system's robustness against the unknown fractional powers and the unknown uncertainties. This is attributed to the infinity property of the PPC method [34,35], as shown in (31). When it extends to the nonlinear system whose powers are unknown, the infinity property is preserved as shown in (32). This means that the controller has sufficient potential to suppress the effects of the above unknown terms. However, this does not mean that such an infinity phenonmenon would occur in the control implementation. The reason has been elaborated in the related works [48–50].*

Remark 4. *Due to the aging of hardening spring and diverse operating conditions, the powers are not fixed but varied within a range in some particular cases, such as the boiler–turbine systems [1] and the under-actuated, weakly coupled mechanical systems [3]. The proposed approach extends to the nonlinear systems with time-varying powers [26] as follows.*

$$\begin{cases} \dot{x}_i = f_i(\bar{x}_i) + [x_{i+1}]^{p_i(t)}, \\ \dot{x}_n = f_n(\bar{x}_n) + [u]^{p_n(t)}, \\ y = x_1, \end{cases} \tag{49}$$

where $p_i(t)$ is a time-varying continuous function, $i = 1, \cdots, n$; the power sign function $[\cdot]^\alpha$ is defined as $[\cdot]^\alpha = sgn(\cdot)|\cdot|^\alpha$ for a real number $\alpha > 0$. When extending the proposed approach to (49), the existence of $[\cdot]^\alpha$ has no influence on the infinity property in (33). Therefore, the robustness of the PPC method [34,35] against the time varying powers is exploited.

Remark 5. *In the presence of external disturbances, the predetermined transient and steady-state performance of the control system still holds, i.e., the stability of the system is still guaranteed. This is because the effect of external disturbances is finite, and it can be sufficiently counteracted by* feat of the infinity property of the PPC controller. Therefore, the control system is robust against external disturbances.

5. Simulation Study

To provide the illustration of the above theoretical findings, two simulation studies are carried out.

Case 1: Take account of the subsequent second-order lower-triangular systems with time varying powers

$$\begin{cases} \dot{x}_1 = -x_1 - x_1^3 + [x_2]^{1.2+\cos(t)}, \\ \dot{x}_2 = x_1 x_2^2 + u^{\frac{7}{5}}, \\ y = x_1. \end{cases} \quad (50)$$

In the simulation, let $x_1(0) = -1$, $x_2(0) = 1.5$. The control target for (50) is let $y(t)$ track $r(t) = 0.7 \sin(t)$ with

$$|y(t) - r(t)| < \xi_1(t) = (1.5 - 0.01)e^{-0.5t} + 0.01. \quad (51)$$

Following Theorem 1, a model-free controller is obtained with $c_1 = 8$, $c_2 = 10$ and

$$\xi_2(t) = (17 - 0.15)e^{-t} + 0.15. \quad (52)$$

Applying the above control scheme to (50), the simulation results are exhibited in Figures 2–6. Figure 2 displays that the output varies along with the reference. The tracking error, plotted in Figure 3, is inside the predefined performance funnel. Hence, the performance requirement in (51) is fulfilled. Likewise, Figure 4 shows that the prescribed specification of the intermediate error in (52) is also met. Lastly, Figures 5 and 6 depict the boundedness of the state variable, the intermediate control law and the input. Thus, our approach is effective.

To perform a comparative study, another controller employing backstepping design method is applied to (50). This is executed with the same control goal and under the same simulation condition. The controller is designed in the case where the nonlinear functions are known but the fractional powers are unknown. The simulation results are displayed in Figures 7 and 8. Figure 7 depicts a large basis between the output and the reference. It is demonstrated by Figure 8 that the tracking error violates the performance constraint in both the transient and steady-state phrases. Therefore, the control target in (51) fails to be achieved. Accordingly, the comparative findings show the advantages of our approach.

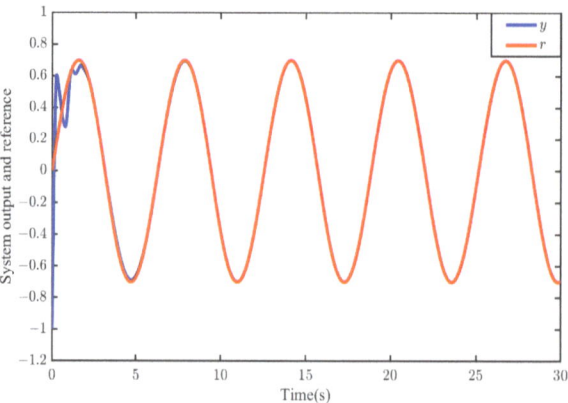

Figure 2. The system output and the reference.

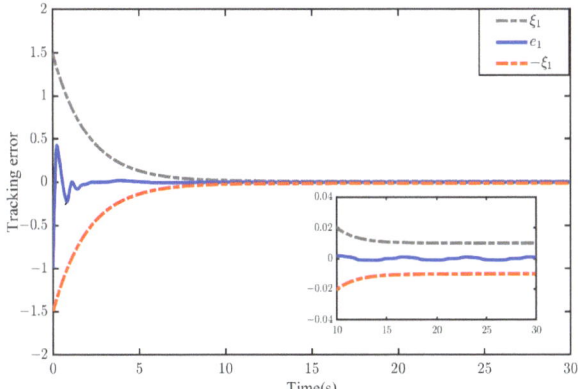

Figure 3. The tracking error and the prescribed boundaries.

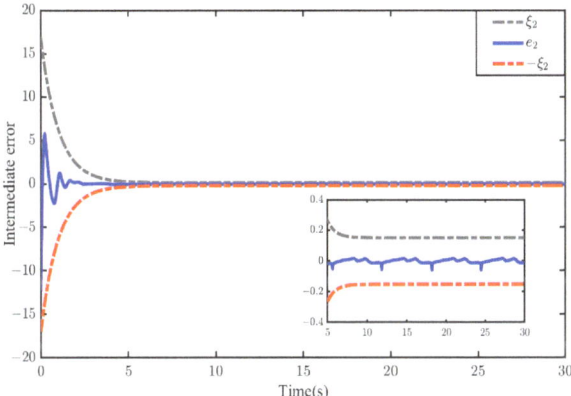

Figure 4. The intermediate error and the prescribed boundaries.

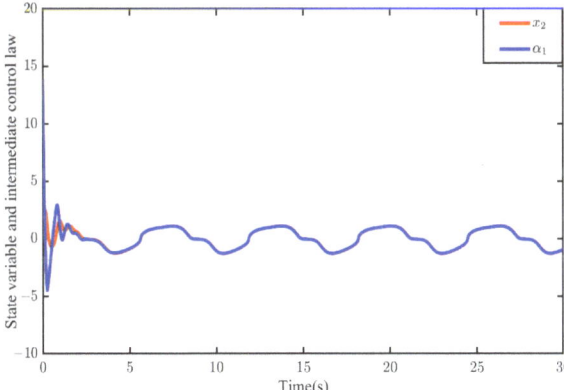

Figure 5. The state variable and the intermediate control signal.

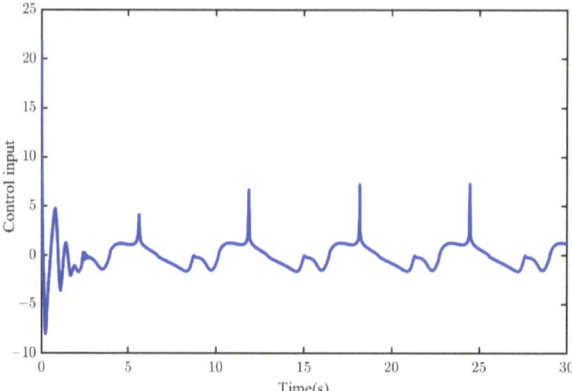

Figure 6. The control input.

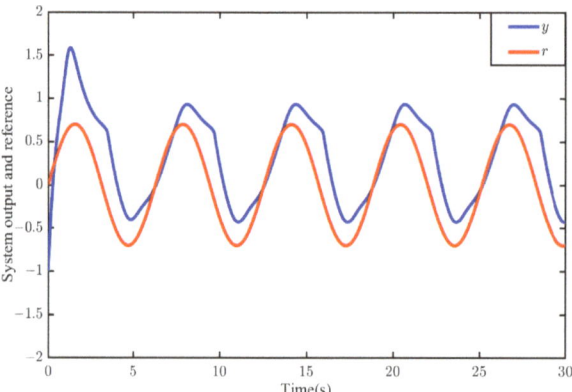

Figure 7. The system output and the reference by the comparative controller.

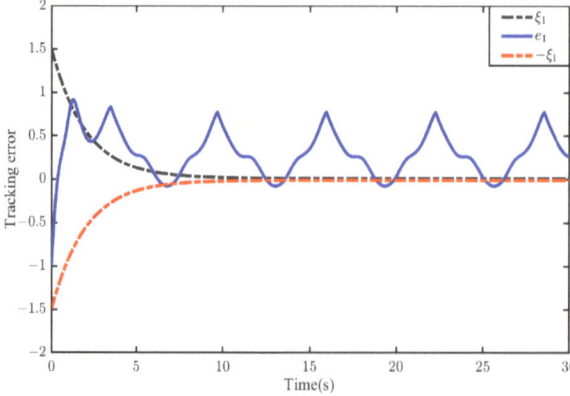

Figure 8. The tracking performance by the comparative controller.

Case 2: Consider the following three-order lower-triangular systems with positive powers:

$$\begin{cases} \dot{x}_1 = -x_1 - x_1^2 + x_2^{\frac{9}{7}}, \\ \dot{x}_2 = -x_2^2 + x_3, \\ \dot{x}_3 = x_3^3 + u^{\frac{7}{5}}, \\ y = x_1. \end{cases} \quad (53)$$

The control goal for (53) is steering its output to track $r(t) = 0.5\sin(0.2t)$ and satisfy

$$|y(t) - r(t)| < \xi_1(t) = (1.6 - 0.05)e^{-0.48t} + 0.05. \quad (54)$$

The performance functions are chosen as $\xi_2(t) = (9 - 0.45)e^{-0.5t} + 0.45$ and $\xi_3(t) = (13 - 0.2)e^{-0.8t} + 0.2$. According to the design procedure in (5)–(13), we can obtain a model-free controller. In the simulation, let $x_1(0) = 0.5$, $x_2(0) = 0.5$ and $x_3(0) = 0$. Applying the designed controller to (53), the simulation results are displayed in Figures 9–14. Figure 9 shows that the output nearly tracks the reference after $t = 10$ s. The tracking error, plotted in Figure 10, evolves within the prescribed performance envelope, and thus (54) is satisfied. Figures 11 and 12 exhibit that the intermediate tracking errors are also inside the performance funnel. Finally, Figures 13 and 14 show that the state variables, the intermediate control law, and the control input are all bounded. Accordingly, the above results verify the effectiveness of our approach.

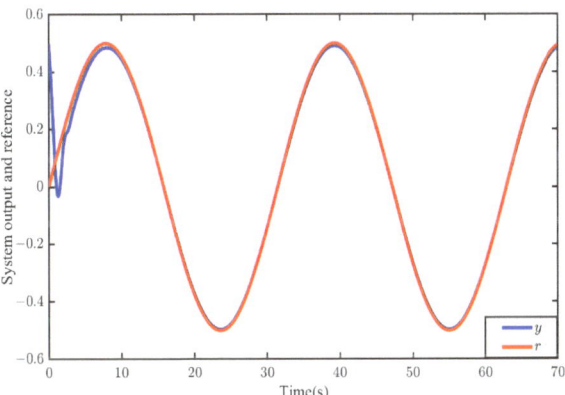

Figure 9. The system output and the reference.

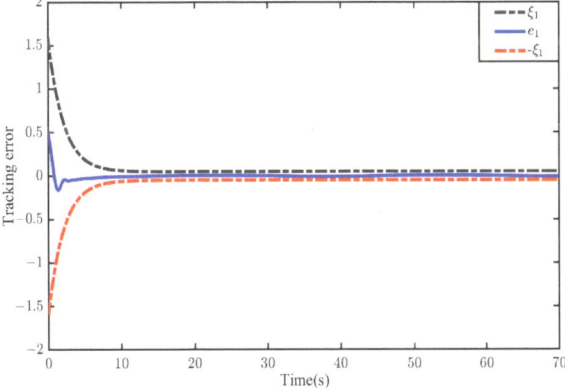

Figure 10. The tracking error and the prescribed boundaries.

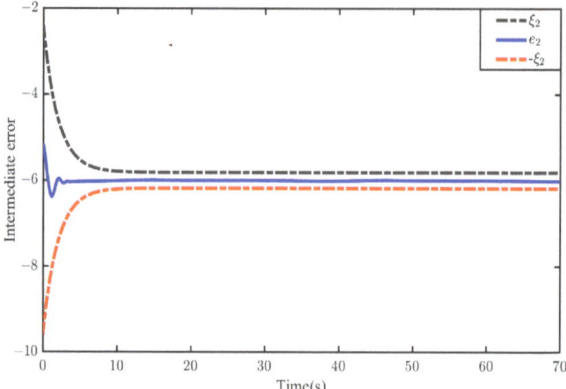

Figure 11. The intermediate error and the prescribed boundaries.

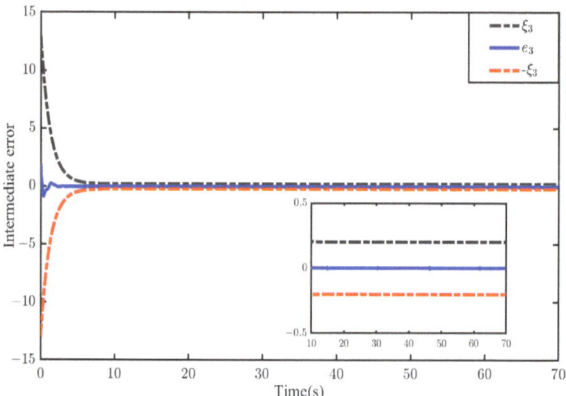

Figure 12. The intermediate error and the prescribed boundaries.

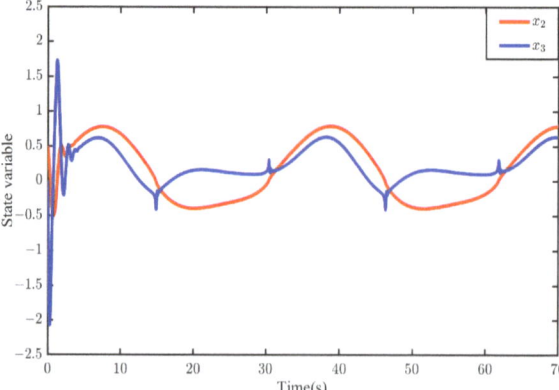

Figure 13. The state variable.

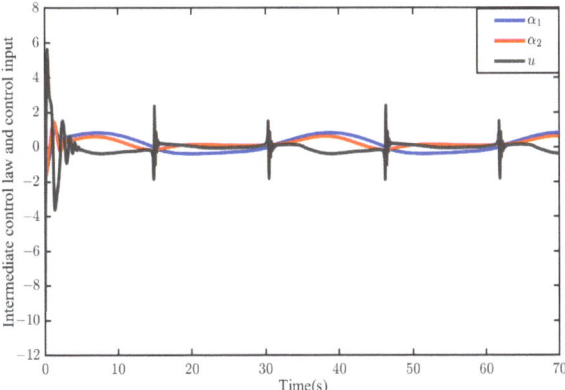

Figure 14. The intermediate control signals and the control input.

6. Conclusions

An approach for prescribed performance tracking control is put forward in this paper. It is capable of handling unknown fractional powers and unknown nonlinearities. It achieves the reference tracking with the arbitrarily preassigned accuracy and speed. It eliminates the power order restriction, the specific size limitation, and the homogeneous condition. Additionally, the powers, the system nonlinearities, and their bounds or bounding functions are totally unknown. The proposed control is simple in the sense that it does not involve derivative calculation, parameter identification, function approximation, or adding a power integrator technique. The simulation results validate the theoretical findings.

Author Contributions: Conceptualization, K.-D.X. and J.-X.Z.; Methodology, K.-D.X. and J.-X.Z.; Software, K.-D.X.; Validation, K.-D.X. ; Formal Analysis, K.-D.X.; Investigation, J.-X.Z. and K.-D.X.; Writing-original draft preparation, K.-D.X.; Writing—review and editing, J.-X.Z.; Visualization, K.-D.X.; Supervision, J.-X.Z.; Funding acquisition, J.-X.Z. All authors have read and agreed to the published version of the manuscript.

Funding: This research was funded by the National Natural Science Foundation of China under Grant 62103093 and the Fundamental Research Funds for the Central Universities of China under Grant N2108003.

Data Availability Statement: Not applicable.

Conflicts of Interest: The authors declare no conflict of interest.

References

1. Liu, J.Z.; Yan, S.; Zeng, D.L.; Hu, Y.; Lv, Y. A dynamic model used for controller design of a coal fired once-through boiler-turbine unit. *Energy* **2015**, *93*, 2069–2078. [CrossRef]
2. Krstic, M.; Kanellakopoulos, I.; Kokotovic, P.V. *Nonlinear and Adaptive Control Design*; Wiley: New York, NY, USA, 1995.
3. Xie, X.J.; Duan, N. Output Tracking of High-order stochastic nonlinear systems with application to benchmark mechanical system. *IEEE Trans. Autom. Control* **2010**, *55*, 1197–1202.
4. Lin, W.; Pongvuthithum, R. Adaptive output tracking of inherently nonlinear systems with nonlinear parameterization. *IEEE Trans. Autom. Control* **2003**, *48*, 1737–1749. [CrossRef]
5. Xie, X.J.; Tian, J. Adaptive state-feedback stabilization of high-order stochastic systems with nonlinear parameterization. *Automatica* **2009**, *45*, 126–133. [CrossRef]
6. Li, W.Q.; Jing, Y.W.; Zhang, S.Y. Adaptive state-feedback stabilization for a large class of high-order stochastic nonlinear systems. *Automatica* **2011**, *47*, 819–828. [CrossRef]
7. Li, W.Q.; Liu, X.H.; Zhang, S.Y. Further results on adaptive state-feedback stabilization for stochastic high-order nonlinear systems. *Automatica* **2012**, *48*, 1667–1675. [CrossRef]
8. Liu, L.; Yin, S.; Gao, H.J.; Alsaadi, F.; Hayat, T. Adaptive partial-state feedback control for stochastic high-order nonlinear systems with stochastic input-to-state stable inverse dynamics. *Automatica* **2015**, *51*, 285–291. [CrossRef]

9. Sun, Z.Y.; Xue, L.R.; Zhang, K.M. A new approach to finite-time adaptive stabilization of high-order uncertain nonlinear system. *Automatica* **2015**, *58*, 60–66. [CrossRef]
10. Sun, Z.Y.; Zhang, C.H.; Wang, Z. Adaptive disturbance attenuation for generalized high-order uncertain nonlinear systems. *Automatica* **2017**, *80*, 102–109. [CrossRef]
11. Man, Y.C.; Liu, Y.G. Global adaptive stabilization and practical tracking for nonlinear systems with unknown powers. *Automatica* **2019**, *100*, 171–181. [CrossRef]
12. Wang, M.; Liu, Y.; Man, Y. Switching adaptive controller for the nonlinear systems with uncertainties from unknown powers. *IEEE Trans. Syst. Man Cybern. Syst.* **2020**, *50*, 2375–2385. [CrossRef]
13. Guo, C.; Xie, R.M.; Xie, X.J. Adaptive control of full-state constrained high-order nonlinear systems with time-varying powers. *IEEE Trans. Syst. Man Cybern. Syst.* **2021**, *51*, 5189–5197. [CrossRef]
14. Lv, M.; Schutter, B.D.; Cao, J.; Baldi, S. Adaptive prescribed performance asymptotic tracking for high-order odd-rational-power nonlinear systems. *IEEE Trans. Autom. Control* **2023**, *68*, 1047–1053. [CrossRef]
15. Liu, Y.H.; Liu, Y.; Liu, Y.F.; Su, C.Y.; Zhou, Q.; Lu, R. Adaptive approximation-based tracking control for a class of unknown high-order nonlinear systems with unknown powers. *IEEE Trans. Cybern.* **2022**, *52*, 4559–4573. [CrossRef]
16. Ma, J.W.; Wang, H.Q.; Su, Y.K.; Liu, C.G.; Chen, M. Adaptive neural fault-tolerant control for nonlinear fractional-order systems with positive odd rational powers. *Fractal Fract.* **2022**, *6*, 622. [CrossRef]
17. Wang, N.; Wang, Y. Fuzzy adaptive quantized tracking control of switched high-order nonlinear systems: A new fixed-time prescribed performance method. *IEEE Trans. Circuits Syst. II Exp. Briefs* **2022**, *69*, 3279–3283. [CrossRef]
18. Sun, W.; Su, S.F.; Wu, Y.; Xia, J. Adaptive fuzzy event-triggered control for high-order nonlinear systems with prescribed performance. *IEEE Trans. Cybern.* **2022**, *52*, 2885–2895. [CrossRef]
19. Sui, S.; Chen, C.L.P.; Tong, S. Finite-time adaptive fuzzy prescribed performance control for high-order stochastic nonlinear systems. *IEEE Trans. Fuzzy Syst.* **2022**, *30*, 2227–2240. [CrossRef]
20. Fu, Z.; Wang, N.; Song, S.; Wang, T. Adaptive fuzzy finite-time tracking control of stochastic high-order nonlinear systems with a class of prescribed performance. *IEEE Trans. Fuzzy Syst.* **2022**, *30*, 88–96. [CrossRef]
21. Zhang, L.; Liu, X.; Hua, C. Prescribed-time control for stochastic high-order nonlinear systems with parameter uncertainty. *IEEE Trans. Circuits Syst. II Exp. Briefs* 2022, in press. [CrossRef]
22. Lin, W.; Qian, C.J. Adding one power integrator: A tool for global stabilization of high-order lower-triangular systems. *Syst Control Lett.* **2000**, *39*, 339–351. [CrossRef]
23. Lin, W.; Qian, C.J. Robust regulation of a chain of power integrators perturbed by a lower-triangular vector field. *Int. J. Robust Nonlin. Control* **2000**, *10*, 397–421. [CrossRef]
24. Qian, C.J.; Lin, W. Almost disturbance decoupling for a class of high-order nonlinear systems. *IEEE Trans. Autom. Control* **2000**, *45*, 1208–1214. [CrossRef]
25. Qian, C.J.; Lin, W. Practical output tracking of nonlinear systems with uncontrollable unstable linearization. *IEEE Trans. Autom. Control* **2002**, *47*, 21–36. [CrossRef]
26. Chen, C.C.; Qian, C.J.; Lin, X.Z.; Sun, Z.Y.; Liang, Y.W. Smooth output feedback stabilization for a class of nonlinear systems with time-varying powers. *Int. J. Robust Nonlin. Control* **2017**, *27*, 5113–5128. [CrossRef]
27. Su, Z.G.; Qian, C.J.; Shen, J. Interval homogeneity-based control for a class of nonlinear systems with unknown power drifts. *IEEE Trans. Autom. Control* **2017**, *62*, 1445–1450. [CrossRef]
28. Xie, X.J.; Guo, C.; Cui, R.H. Removing feasibility conditions on tracking control of full-state constrained nonlinear systems with time-varying powers. *IEEE Trans. Syst. Man, Cybern. Syst.* **2021**, *51*, 6535–6543. [CrossRef]
29. Xie, X.J.; Duan, N.; Yu, X. State-feedback control of high-order stochastic nonlinear systems with SiISS inverse dynamics. *IEEE Trans. Autom. Control* **2011**, *56*, 1921–1926.
30. Zhang, X.F.; Liu, Q.R.; Baron, L.; Boukas, E.K. Feedback stabilization for high order feedforward nonlinear time-delay systems. *Automatica* **2011**, *47*, 962–967. [CrossRef]
31. Min, H.F.; Xu, S.Y.; Gu, J.S.; Cui, G.Z. Adaptive finite-time control for high-order nonlinear systems with multiple uncertainties and its application. *IEEE Trans. Circuits Syst. I Reg. Pap.* **2020**, *67*, 1752–1761. [CrossRef]
32. Li, W.Q.; Wu, Z.J. Output tracking of stochastic high-order nonlinear systems with markovian switching. *IEEE Trans. Autom. Control* **2013**, *58*, 1585–1590. [CrossRef]
33. Zhao, C.Y.; Xie, X.J. Global stabilization of stochastic high-order feedforward nonlinear systems with time-varying delay. *Automatica* **2014**, *50*, 203–210. [CrossRef]
34. Bechlioulis, C.P.; Rovithakis, G.A. Robust adaptive control of feedback linearizable MIMO nonlinear systems with prescribed performance. *IEEE Trans. Autom. Control* **2008**, *53*, 2090–2099. [CrossRef]
35. Bechlioulis, C.P.; Rovithakis, G.A. Adaptive control with guaranteed transient and steady state tracking error bounds for strict feedback systems. *Automatica* **2009**, *45*, 532–538. [CrossRef]
36. Ilchmann, A.; Ryan, E.; Sangwin, C. Tracking with prescribed transient behaviour. *ESAIM Control Optim. Calc. Var.* **2002**, *7*, 471–493. [CrossRef]
37. Ilchmann, A.; Ryan, E.P.; Trenn, S. Tracking control: Performance funnels and prescribed transient behaviour. *Syst. Control Lett.* **2005**, *54*, 655–670. [CrossRef]

38. Hopfe, N.; Ilchmann, A.; Ryan, E.P. Funnel control with saturation: Nonlinear SISO systems. *IEEE Trans. Autom. Control* **2010**, *55*, 2177–2182. [CrossRef]
39. Berger, T.; Lê, H.H.; Reis, T. Funnel control for nonlinear systems with known strict relative degree. *Automatica* **2018**, *87*, 345–357. [CrossRef]
40. Berger, T.; Puche, M.; Schwenninger, F. Funnel control for a moving water tank. *Automatica* **2022**, *135*, 109999. [CrossRef]
41. Ilchmann, A.; Ryan, E.P.; Townsend, P. Tracking with prescribed transient behavior for nonlinear systems of known relative degree. *SIAM J. Control Optim.* **2007**, *46*, 210–230. [CrossRef]
42. Qiu, J.; Wang, T.; Sun, K.; Rudas, I.J.; Gao, H. Disturbance observer-based adaptive fuzzy control for strict-feedback nonlinear systems with finite-time prescribed performance. *IEEE Trans. Fuzzy Syst.* **2022**, *30*, 1175–1184. [CrossRef]
43. Zhao, K.; Wen, C.; Song, Y.; Lewis, F.L. Adaptive uniform performance control of strict-feedback nonlinear systems with time-varying control gain. *IEEE/CAA J. Autom. Sin.* **2023**, *10*, 451–461. [CrossRef]
44. Zhang, F.; Deng, X.F.; Wei, L.S. Adaptive dynamic surface control of strict-feedback fractional-order nonlinear systems with input quantization and external disturbances. *Fractal Fract.* **2022**, *6*, 698. [CrossRef]
45. Deng, X.F.; Wei, L.S. Adaptive neural network finite-time control of uncertain fractional-order systems with unknown dead-zone fault via command filter. *Fractal Fract.* **2022**, *6*, 494. [CrossRef]
46. Zhang, J.X.; Yang, G.H. Fault-tolerant output-constrained control of unknown Euler-Lagrange systems with prescribed tracking accuracy. *Automatica* **2020**, *111*, 108606. [CrossRef]
47. Zhang, J.X.; Yang, G.H. Robust adaptive fault-tolerant control for a class of unknown nonlinear systems. *IEEE Trans. Ind. Electron.* **2017**, *64*, 585–594. [CrossRef]
48. Zhang, J.X.; Yang, G.H. Low-complexity tracking control of strict-feedback systems with unknown control directions. *IEEE Trans. Autom. Control* **2019**, *64*, 5175–5182. [CrossRef]
49. Zhang, J.X.; Yang, G.H. Fuzzy adaptive output feedback control of uncertain nonlinear systems with prescribed performance. *IEEE Trans. Cybern.* **2018**, *48*, 1342–1354. [CrossRef] [PubMed]
50. Zhang, J.X.; Wang, Q.G.; Ding, W. Global output-feedback prescribed performance control of nonlinear systems with unknown virtual control coefficients. *IEEE Trans. Autom. Control* **2022**, *67*, 6904–6911. [CrossRef]

Disclaimer/Publisher's Note: The statements, opinions and data contained in all publications are solely those of the individual author(s) and contributor(s) and not of MDPI and/or the editor(s). MDPI and/or the editor(s) disclaim responsibility for any injury to people or property resulting from any ideas, methods, instructions or products referred to in the content.

fractal and fractional

Article

Backstepping Control with a Fractional-Order Command Filter and Disturbance Observer for Unmanned Surface Vehicles

Runan Ma, Jian Chen *, Chengxing Lv, Zhibo Yang and Xiangyu Hu

School of Information and Control Engineering, Qingdao University of Technology, Qingdao 266520, China; nancym1225@163.com (R.M.); lvchengxing@qut.edu.cn (C.L.); yangzhibo@qut.edu.cn (Z.Y.); huxiangyu@stu.qut.edu.cn (X.H.)
* Correspondence: chenjian@qut.edu.cn

Abstract: In the paper, a backstepping control strategy based on a fractional-order finite-time command filter and a fractional-order finite-time disturbance observer is proposed for the trajectory tracking control of an unmanned surface vehicle. A fractional-order finite-time command filter is presented to estimate the derivatives of the intermediate control, which cannot be directly calculated, thereby reducing the chattering generated by the integer-order command filter. The fractional-order finite-time disturbance observer is presented to approximate and compensate for the model uncertainty and unknown external disturbances in the system. Subsequently, the globally asymptotically stable nature of the closed-loop system is proved based on the Lyapunov method. The effectiveness of the method is proven by simulation experiments on unmanned surface vehicles.

Keywords: fractional-order; disturbance observer; unmanned surface vehicles; finite-time command filter

1. Introduction

Recently, with the increase of marine activities, such as resource exploration, maritime rescue, and environmental monitoring, unmanned surface vehicles (USVs) with low failure rates and high reliability have received more and more attention [1–3]. To promote a variety of applications of USVs, trajectory tracking is the core problem of USVs for marine operations. However, due to the complexity of the marine environment and the uncertainty in the modeling process, the control of USVs faces great challenges. Hence, it has important, realistic meaning to research the trajectory tracking control of USVs in complex environments.

At present, there are some control methods used in USVs, such as model predictive control (MPC) [4], sliding mode control (SMC) [5], backstepping control (BC) [6], and optimum control [7]. Among them, backstepping control is one of the most effective design tools for USV nonlinear systems. By continuously constructing Lyapunov functions, the intermediate control laws of each subsystem can be given, and the control inputs of the system can be obtained [8]. Nevertheless, the repeated derivation of the intermediate control law in the backstepping control will cause a complexity explosion. The first-order filter applied to dynamic surface control technology is the first effective solution to avoid the complexity explosion problem [9]. Although this method avoids the complexity explosion, it ignores the influence of compensation error, which also increases the difficulty of proving the stability of the controller. Nowadays, the command filter is the preferred choice to avoid the issue that the intermediate control law cannot be derived directly [10]. The backstepping control technology based on command filtering, which is proposed in [11], avoids the problem of direct derivation of intermediate control laws and eliminates the impact of command filtering errors by designing the auxiliary signal. In addition, most of the backstepping control is based on the infinite-time stability theory, which has the problem of slow convergence time. The finite-time command filter proposed in [12] adopts the error compensation mechanism to eliminate the filtering error, which not only ensures

Citation: Ma, R.; Chen, J.; Lv, C.; Yang, Z.; Hu, X. Backstepping Control with a Fractional-Order Command Filter and Disturbance Observer for Unmanned Surface Vehicles. *Fractal Fract.* **2024**, *8*, 23. https://doi.org/10.3390/fractalfract8010023

Academic Editors: Jin-Xi Zhang, Norbert Herencsar, Xuefeng Zhang, Da-Yan Liu and Driss Boutat

Received: 24 November 2023
Revised: 20 December 2023
Accepted: 21 December 2023
Published: 27 December 2023

Copyright: © 2023 by the authors. Licensee MDPI, Basel, Switzerland. This article is an open access article distributed under the terms and conditions of the Creative Commons Attribution (CC BY) license (https://creativecommons.org/licenses/by/4.0/).

the finite-time stability of the system, but also avoids the direct derivation problem of the intermediate control law of the system. However, adding auxiliary signals to the command filter will lead to more complexity in controller design and a slower convergence time for the filter. Properly increasing the gain can optimize these problems but also lead to higher actual control input or aggravate system chattering.

The modeling uncertainties and the external disturbances (winds, waves, and currents, etc.) caused by the complex environment of the USVs can be estimated and compensated by constructing a disturbance observer [13–15]. The adaptive sliding mode control system proposed by [15] uses the radial basis function neural network approximator to approach the modeling uncertainty and constructs the disturbance observer to estimate the influence of environmental disturbances while ensuring the stability of the unmanned underwater vehicle system. In [16], the fuzzy logic system (FLS) is used to approximate the uncertainty in the nonlinear USV model, and a disturbance observer with a learning factor is proposed to compensate for external disturbances, effectively improving the accuracy and speed of trajectory tracking. In [17], an adaptive control law based on a finite-time disturbance observer and neural network is proposed for USV containment with external environmental disturbances and obstacles. Consequently, the disturbance observer is used to accurately observe the unknown disturbances, and the cascade analysis and Lyapunov method are combined to guarantee the globally asymptotical stability of the unmanned submersible system. For all that, the above literature ignores the problem that the disturbance observer faces: excessive control input and the input chattering phenomenon.

Fractional calculus [18–20] is an extension of integer calculus. Then, fractional-order systems can also be regarded as an extension of integer-order systems. Fractional calculus has non-locality and a long memory, which makes it especially suitable for describing the development of system functions with historical dependence. Some scholars have added fractional calculus to traditional control method, such as fractional-order optimal control [21], fractional-order proportional-integral-derivative (FOPID) control [22,23], fractional-order sliding mode control (FOSMC) [24], fractional-order adaptive fuzzy control [25], and so on. The results show that the controller designed by fractional calculus has a better effect than the integer one on the steady-state and transient responses of the closed-loop system, as well as its robustness and immunity to uncertainty.

Based on the above statements, this paper combines fractional calculus with a disturbance observer and a command filter. A backstepping control scheme for unmanned submersibles based on a fractional-order disturbance observer and command filter is designed. The major contributions are listed as follows:

(1) The fractional-order finite-time command filter is proposed, which is proved to be finite-time stable. It can track the derivatives of the intermediate control well without adding additional compensation signals, and the direct derivation issue is avoided when designing a controller.
(2) A fractional-order finite-time disturbance observer is designed to compensate for unknown environmental disturbances and model uncertainty, which can improve the transient and steady-state performances of the USVs system.
(3) The controller in the paper can ensure the globally asymptotical stability of the closed-loop system. Thus, good control performance can be achieved. In addition, using the fractional-order command filter and disturbance observer can reduce chattering caused by the finite-time differentiator, which facilitates the application in practice.

2. Preliminaries and Problem Formulation

2.1. Fractional Calculus

It is necessary to have an understanding of basic fractional order concepts and properties, the model of the USVs system, and the control objectives before the main body of this paper.

Definition 1 ([26]). *The $\gamma-$order fractional integral of the given function $f(t) : (0, \infty) \to R$ is defined as*

$$_{t_0}I_t^\gamma f(t) = \frac{1}{\Gamma(\gamma)} \int_{t_0}^t \frac{f(\tau)}{(t-\tau)^{1-\gamma}} d\tau \tag{1}$$

where $\Gamma(\gamma) = \int_0^\infty t^{\gamma-1} e^{-t} dt$ is the Gamma function, and $\gamma > 0$.

Definition 2 ([27]). *The Caputo-type fractional differential of the function $f(t) : (0, \infty) \to R$ is defined as*

$$_{t_0}^C D_t^\gamma f(t) = \frac{1}{\Gamma(m-\gamma)} \int_{t_0}^t \frac{f^m(\tau)}{(t-\tau)^{-m+\gamma+1}} d\tau \tag{2}$$

where $m - 1 < \gamma < m$ and $m \in N$, and $\gamma > 0$.

Property 1 ([28]). *The Caputo-type fractional differentiation satisfies the linearity property:*

$$_{t_0}^C D_t^\gamma [\lambda_1 f(t) + \lambda_2 g(t)] = \lambda_1 (_{t_0}^C D_t^\gamma f(t)) + \lambda_2 {}_{t_0}^C D_t^\gamma g((t)) \tag{3}$$

where λ_1 and λ_2 are real numbers.

Property 2 ([28]). *For the Caputo-type fractional derivative, if the function $f(t) \in C[0, t]$ and $t > 0$, the following relation holds:*

$$_{t_0}^C D_t^\gamma ({}_{t_0}^C D_t^\beta f(t)) = {}_{t_0}^C D_t^{\gamma+\beta} f(t) \tag{4}$$

where $\gamma, \beta \in R^+$, and $\gamma + \beta \leq 1$.

According to basic fractional order concepts and properties, the lemmas are obtained as follows.

Lemma 1 ([29]). *The problem of solving the Caputo-type fractional-order equation ${}_{t_0}^C D_t^\gamma x(t) = f(t, x)$ can be converted to solving the homologous integer-order equation. The initial value issue of the fractional equation is presented as*

$$_{t_0}^C D_t^\gamma (x(t) - x_0) = f(t, x), \ \& \ x_0 = x(0) \tag{5}$$

where $0 < \gamma < 1$, and $f(t, x) \in C([0, T] \times R, R)$.

Lemma 2 ([29]). *Assume that $f(t, x) \in C(R_I, R)$, where $R_I = [(t, x) : 0 \leq t \leq c \ \& \ |x - x_0| \leq d]$ and $|f(t, x)| \leq M$ on R_I. There is at least a solution for fractional-order Equation (5) on $0 \leq t \leq \delta$, where $\delta = \min(c, [\frac{d}{M}\Gamma(\gamma+1)]^{1/\gamma})$ and $0 < \gamma < 1$. Then, a solution of the problem (5) is obtained by $x(t) = x^*(\frac{t^\gamma}{\Gamma(\gamma+1)})$, and $x^*(v)$ is the solution of the corresponding integer-order equation $\frac{d(x^*(v))}{dv} = g(v, x^*(v)) = f(t - (t^\gamma - v\Gamma(\gamma+1))^{1/\gamma}, x(t - (t^\gamma - v\Gamma(\gamma+1))^{1/\gamma}))$, with the original condition $x_0 = x^*(0)$.*

2.2. Problem Formulation

To describe the motion process of the USVs and simplify the design of the controller as much as possible, the three degrees of freedom model coordinate frames of the USV is shown in Figure 1.

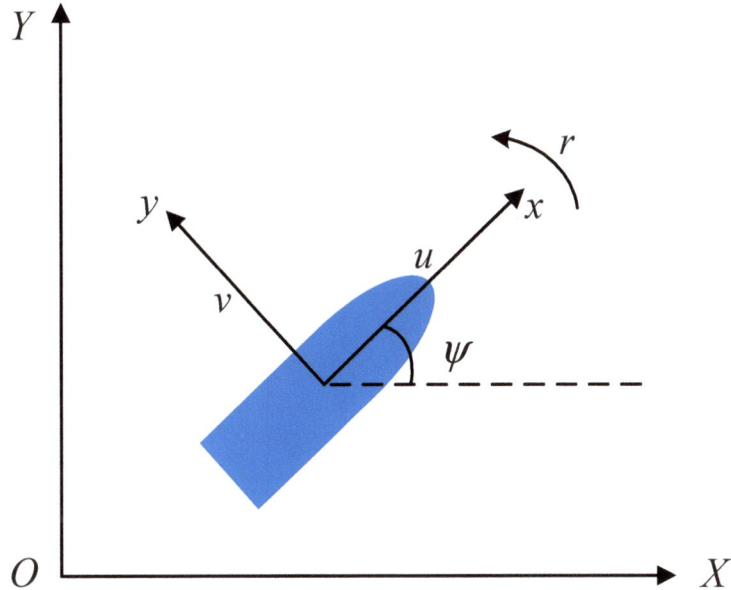

Figure 1. Ground-fixed (X, Y) and body-fixed (x, y) frames.

The kinematic equation of the USV is described as [30].

$$\begin{cases} \dot{x} = u\cos\psi - v\sin\psi \\ \dot{y} = u\sin\psi + v\cos\psi \\ \dot{\psi} = r \end{cases} \quad (6)$$

where $\eta = [x, y, \psi]^T$ consists of the position coordinates and the yaw angle in the ground coordinate system. $\nu = [u, v, r]^T$ is composed of the surge, sway, and yaw velocity of the USV in the vehicle body coordinate system.

The dynamic equation of the USV with unknown external disturbances and model uncertainties is described as [31].

$$\begin{cases} \dot{u} = \frac{\tau_u}{m_u} + \frac{m_v vr - X_u u - f_u(\nu)}{m_u} + \frac{\omega_u(t)}{m_u} \\ \dot{v} = \frac{-m_u ur - Y_v v - f_v(\nu)}{m_v} + \frac{\omega_v(t)}{m_v} \\ \dot{r} = \frac{\tau_r}{m_r} + \frac{(m_u - m_v)uv - N_r r - f_r(\nu)}{m_r} + \frac{\omega_r(t)}{m_r} \end{cases} \quad (7)$$

where m_u, m_v denote the additional mass and m_r represents the moment of inertia. τ_u, τ_r denote the surge force and the yaw moment of the actual control inputs, respectively. $\omega_u(t)$, $\omega_v(t)$ and $\omega_r(t)$ represent the environmental disturbances by the winds, waves, and currents. $f_u(\nu)$, $f_v(\nu)$, and $f_r(\nu)$ are uncertain hydrodynamic damping effects; this part will be explained in the simulation.

Remark 1: *The unmanned surface vehicles have only two control inputs, but have three control outputs, which is a typical underactuated system. At the same time, the USV model contains unknown uncertainty terms $f_i(\nu)(i = u, v, r)$ and unmeasurable external disturbances. These factors bring difficulties to the design of the actual controller.*

2.3. Control Objective

Let $\eta_d = [x_d, y_d, \psi_d]^T$ be the desired trajectory without a dynamic loop (7), which can be generated by

$$\begin{cases} \dot{x}_d = u_d \cos \psi_d \\ \dot{y}_d = u_d \sin \psi_d \\ \dot{\psi}_d = r_d \end{cases} \quad (8)$$

where $v_d = [u_d, 0, r_d]^T$ represents the reference speed velocity. The control target is to construct a controller such that the system output η is capable of tracking the reference trajectory η_d while ensuring all closed loop signals are global asymptotically stable. Assumptions are presented as follows.

Assumption 1. *The expected position coordinates x_d, y_d and the reference yaw angle ψ_d are bounded, differentiable and available.*

Assumption 2. *The marine disturbances $\omega_i(t)$, $i = u, v, r$ are bounded and differentiable. Moreover, $\dot{\omega}_i(t)$, $i = u, v, r$ is bounded, and there exists $\iota_i > 0$ satisfying $|\dot{\omega}_i(t)| \leq \iota_i$, $i = u, v, r$.*

3. Results Analysis

The controller will be designed for the USVs in this section. The errors of the system are provided as

$$\begin{cases} x_e = (x - x_d) \cos \psi + (y - y_d) \sin \psi \\ y_e = -(x - x_d) \sin \psi + (y - y_d) \cos \psi \\ \psi_e = \psi - \psi_d \end{cases} \quad (9)$$

The time differentiation of (9) is obtained as

$$\begin{cases} \dot{x}_e = u - u_d \cos \psi_e + y_e r \\ \dot{y}_e = v + u_d \sin \psi_e - x_e r \\ \dot{\psi}_e = r - r_d \end{cases} \quad (10)$$

where $\eta_e = [x_e, y_e, \psi_e]^T$ is the deviation between the actual trajectory and the expected trajectory.

3.1. Fractional-Order Finite-Time Command Filter

The integer-order command filter is defined as [32]

$$\begin{cases} \dot{z}_{i,1} = z_{i,2}, \\ z_{i,2} = -\zeta_{i1} |z_{i,1} - \alpha_i(t)|^{1/2} \text{sgn}(z_{i,1} - \alpha_i(t)) + \bar{z}_{i,2}, \\ \dot{\bar{z}}_{i,2} = -\zeta_{i2} \text{sgn}(\bar{z}_{i,2} - z_{i,2}). \end{cases} \quad (11)$$

where $z_{i,1}$, $z_{i,2}$, and $\bar{z}_{i,2}$ represent the state variables of the system. The measurable locally bound function $\alpha_i(t)$, $t \in [0, +\infty)$ is the intermediate control signal. There is a differential with Lipschitz's constant $\zeta > 0$. $\zeta_{i1}, \zeta_{i2} > \zeta$ are the adjustable positive real number. The sign function is defined as $\text{sgn}(\theta) = \begin{cases} -1 & \theta < 0 \\ 1 & \theta \geq 0 \end{cases}$.

Lemma 4 [33]: *It can be obtained that there is $\zeta_{i2} > \zeta > 0$, $0 < \frac{2(\zeta_{i2}+\zeta)}{\zeta_{i1}^2(\zeta_{i2}-\zeta)} < 1$ and a sufficiently large $\zeta_{i1} > 0$, such that $z_{i,2}, \dot{z}_{i,1}$ converge to $\dot{\alpha}_i$ and $z_{i,1}$ converges to α_i in the finite time.*

According to Lemma 4, it is known that the second-order command filter (11) is finite-time stable without additional compensation signals. However, using the integer-order command filter for nonlinear systems (9) and (10) will lead to the chattering phenomenon, which will affect the practical application effect.

The n-order integer-order nonlinear system corresponding to the fractional-order command filter is presented as [34]

$$\begin{aligned}
\dot{z}_{j,1} &= z_{j,2}, \\
z_{j,2} &= -\zeta_{j1}|z_{j,1} - \alpha_j|^{n/n+1} \operatorname{sgn}(z_{j,1} - \alpha_j) + \bar{z}_{j,2}, \\
\dot{\bar{z}}_{j,2} &= -\zeta_{j2}|\bar{z}_{j,2} - \dot{z}_{j,1}|^{n-1/n} \operatorname{sgn}(\bar{z}_{j,2} - \dot{z}_{j,1}) + \bar{z}_{j,3}, \\
\dot{\bar{z}}_{j,3} &= -\zeta_{j3}|\bar{z}_{j,3} - \dot{\bar{z}}_{j,2}|^{n-2/n-1} \operatorname{sgn}(\bar{z}_{j,3} - \dot{\bar{z}}_{j,2}) + \bar{z}_{j,4}, \\
&\vdots \\
\dot{\bar{z}}_{j,n+1} &= -\zeta_{j,n+1}\operatorname{sgn}(\bar{z}_{j,n+1} - \dot{\bar{z}}_{j,n}), \, j = 1,2,\ldots,n \, (n \in Z^+).
\end{aligned} \quad (12)$$

where $z_{j,1}, \bar{z}_{j,2}, \ldots \bar{z}_{j,n+1}, j = 1,2,\ldots,n$ represent the USV state variables, $\zeta_{j1}, \zeta_{j2}, \ldots \zeta_{j,n+1}, j = 1,2,\ldots,n$ denote the positive real number.

Lemma 5 [34]: *If the appropriate parameters are selected, the following equation is correct in the case of a finite-time transient process without input noises.*

$$\begin{aligned}
z_{j,1} &= \alpha_{j,0}(t), \\
\bar{z}_{j,k} &= \alpha_{j,0}^{(k)}(t), \, j = 1, 2, \ldots, n \, \& \, k = 2, 3, \ldots, n \, (n \in Z^+).
\end{aligned} \quad (13)$$

Therefore, the solutions of the system are finite-time stable.

Based on the integer-order system (12), the fractional-order finite-time command filter can be obtained as

$$\begin{aligned}
{}_{t_0}^{C}\mathbf{D}_t^{1/n} z_{j,1} &= z_{j,2}, \\
z_{j,2} &= -\zeta_{j1}|z_{j,1} - \alpha_j|^{n/n+1} \operatorname{sgn}(z_{j,1} - \alpha_j) + \bar{z}_{j,2}, \\
{}_{t_0}^{C}\mathbf{D}_t^{1/n} \bar{z}_{j,2} &= z_{j,3}, \\
z_{j,3} &= -\zeta_{j2}|\bar{z}_{j,2} - z_{j,2}|^{n-1/n} \operatorname{sgn}(\bar{z}_{j,2} - z_{j,2}) + \bar{z}_{j,3}, \\
{}_{t_0}^{C}\mathbf{D}_t^{1/n} \bar{z}_{j,3} &= z_{j,4}, \\
z_{j,4} &= -\zeta_{j3}|\bar{z}_{j,3} - z_{j,3}|^{n-2/n-1} \operatorname{sgn}(\bar{z}_{j,3} - z_{j,3}) + \bar{z}_{j,4}, \\
&\vdots \\
{}_{t_0}^{C}\mathbf{D}_t^{1/n} \bar{z}_{j,n+1} &= -\zeta_{j,n+1}\operatorname{sgn}(\bar{z}_{j,n+1} - z_{j,n}), \, j = 1,2,\ldots,n \, (n \in Z^+).
\end{aligned} \quad (14)$$

Theorem 1: *There is finite time t_s for any initial condition $z_{j,1}(0), \bar{z}_{j,2}(0), \cdots, \bar{z}_{j,n+1}(0)$; there are parameters $\zeta_{j1}, \zeta_{j2}, \ldots, \zeta_{j,n+1}$, such that $z_{j,1}, \bar{z}_{j,2}, \ldots, \bar{z}_{j,n+1}$ are able to converge to zero in the finite time t_s.*

Proof. Motivated by Lemma 2, the integer-order system corresponding to Equation (14) is expressed as

$$\begin{aligned}
\dot{z}_{j,1}^*(v) &= z_{j,2}^*(v), \\
\dot{z}_{j,2}^*(v) &= -\zeta_{j1}\left|z_{j,1}^*(v) - \alpha_j\right|^{n/n+1} \operatorname{sgn}(z_{j,1}^*(v) - \alpha_j) + \bar{z}_{j,2}^*(v), \\
\dot{\bar{z}}_{j,2}^*(v) &= -\zeta_{j2}\left|\bar{z}_{j,2}^*(v) - \dot{z}_{j,1}^*(v)\right|^{n-1/n} \operatorname{sgn}(\bar{z}_{j,2}^*(v) - \dot{z}_{j,1}^*(v)) + \bar{z}_{j,3}^*(v), \\
\dot{\bar{z}}_{j,3}^*(v) &= -\zeta_{j3}\left|\bar{z}_{j,3}^*(v) - \dot{\bar{z}}_{j,2}^*(v)\right|^{n-2/n-1} \operatorname{sgn}(\bar{z}_{j,3}^*(v) - \dot{\bar{z}}_{j,2}^*(v)) + \bar{z}_{j,4}^*(v), \\
&\vdots \\
\dot{\bar{z}}_{j,n+1}^*(v) &= -\zeta_{j,n+1}\operatorname{sgn}(\bar{z}_{j,n+1}^*(v) - \dot{\bar{z}}_{j,n}^*(v)), \ j = 1, 2, \ldots, n \ (n \in Z^+).
\end{aligned} \quad (15)$$

where v denotes the time scale, and $z_{j,1}^*(0) = z_{j,1}(0)$, $\bar{z}_{j,2}^*(0) = \bar{z}_{j,2}(0)$, $\ldots$, $\bar{z}_{j,n+1}^*(0) = \bar{z}_{j,n+1}(0)$ are the initial conditions. Motivated by Lemma 5, the stability of Equation (15) can be proved by the solutions of the integer-order Equation (12). □

Motivated by Lemma 2, the solutions of Equation (15) can be given as

$$\begin{aligned}
z_{j,1}(t) &= z_{j,1}^*(t)\left(\tfrac{t^\gamma}{\Gamma(\gamma+1)}\right), \\
\bar{z}_{j,k}(t) &= \bar{z}_{j,k}^*(t)\left(\tfrac{t^\gamma}{\Gamma(\gamma+1)}\right), \ j = 1, 2, \ldots, n \ \& \ k = 2, 3, \ldots, n \ (n \in Z^+).
\end{aligned} \quad (16)$$

For $\alpha = t - (t^\gamma - v\Gamma(\gamma+1))^{1/\gamma}$ of Lemma 2, $t_s = t_s - (t_s^\gamma - v_s\Gamma(\gamma+1))^{1/\gamma}$ with the time scale v_s being able to be maintained in a steady state. Thus, there is a corresponding relationship between the convergence time t_s of $z_{j,1}(t)$, $\bar{z}_{j,2}(t)$, $\ldots$, $\bar{z}_{j,n}(t)$, $j = 1, 2, \ldots, n$ and the integer-order command-filter convergence time v_s. □

Remark 2: *The fractional-order command filter (14) avoids the problem that the derivative of the intermediate control law cannot be calculated directly in the process of designing a controller. It can track the derivative of the intermediate control without adding an additional compensation signal because it is finite-time stable. In addition, the fractional-order command filter can suppress the chattering phenomenon well.*

3.2. Fractional-Order Finite-Time Disturbance Observer

According to Theorem 1, the n-order fractional-order disturbance observer can be given as follows:

$$\begin{aligned}
{}_{t_0}^{C}D_t^{1/n}\vartheta_{j,1} &= -\varsigma_{j1}\left|\vartheta_{j,1} - v_j(t)\right|^{n+1/n+2}\operatorname{sgn}(\vartheta_{j,1} - v_j(t)) + \vartheta_{j,2}, \\
{}_{t_0}^{C}D_t^{1/n}\vartheta_{j,2} &= -\varsigma_{j2}\left|\vartheta_{j,2} - {}_{t_0}^{C}D_t^{1/n}\vartheta_{j,1}\right|^{n/n+1}\operatorname{sgn}(\vartheta_{j,2} - {}_{t_0}^{C}D_t^{1/n}\vartheta_{j,1}) + \vartheta_{j,3}, \\
&\vdots \\
{}_{t_0}^{C}D_t^{1/n}\vartheta_{j,n} &= -\varsigma_{j,n}\left|\vartheta_{j,n} - {}_{t_0}^{C}D_t^{1/n}\vartheta_{j,n-1}\right|^{2/3}\operatorname{sgn}(\vartheta_{j,n} - {}_{t_0}^{C}D_t^{1/n}\vartheta_{j,n-1}) + \vartheta_{j,n+1} + g_j(v) + \tau_j, \\
&\vdots \\
{}_{t_0}^{C}D_t^{1/n}\vartheta_{j,n+2} &= -\varsigma_{j,n+2}\operatorname{sgn}(\vartheta_{j,n+2} - {}_{t_0}^{C}D_t^{1/n}\vartheta_{j,n+1}), \\
\hat{\omega}_j &= -\varsigma_{j,n}\left|\vartheta_{j,n} - {}_{t_0}^{C}D_t^{1/n}\vartheta_{j,n-1}\right|^{2/3}\operatorname{sgn}(\vartheta_{j,n} - {}_{t_0}^{C}D_t^{1/n}\vartheta_{j,n-1}) + \vartheta_{j,n+1}, \ j = 1, 2, \cdots, n \ (n \in Z^+).
\end{aligned} \quad (17)$$

where $\vartheta_{j,1}$, $\vartheta_{j,2}$, $\ldots$, $\vartheta_{j,n+2}$, $j = 1, 2, \ldots, n$ represent the variables of the disturbance observer, and ς_{j1}, ς_{j2}, $\ldots$, $\varsigma_{j,n+2}$, $j = 1, 2, \ldots, n$ represent the adjustable positive real number. τ_j and $g_j(v)$ represent the actual control input and known modeling error, respectively. $v_j(t)$ denotes the speed velocity of the dynamic model. $\hat{\omega}_j$ is the output of disturbance observer and represents the estimated value of the system disturbances and unknown model uncertainties.

Theorem 2: *There is a time t_r for any original conditions $\vartheta_{j,1}(0)$, $\vartheta_{j,2}(0)$, ..., $\vartheta_{j,n+2}(0)$; there are parameters ς_{j1}, ς_{j2}, ..., $\varsigma_{j,n+2}$, such that $\vartheta_{j,1}$, $\vartheta_{j,2}$, ..., $\vartheta_{j,n+2}$ are able to converge to zero in finite time t_r.*

Proof. According to the similar proof method of Theorem 1, it can be concluded that Theorem 2 holds. □

3.3. Controller Design

On the basis of the above section, the fractional-order backstepping controller block diagram is shown in Figure 2.

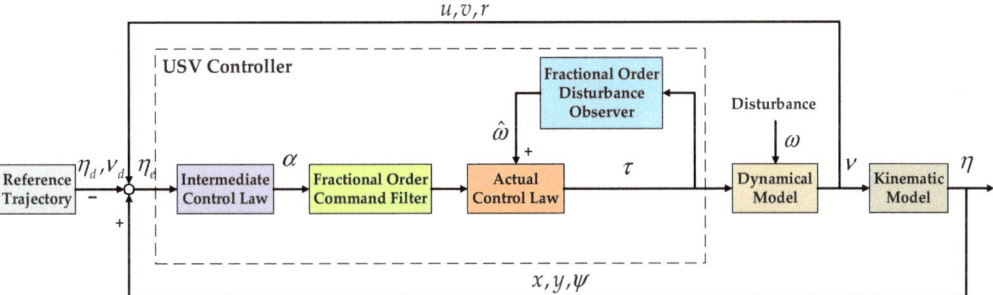

Figure 2. Overall control system block diagram.

The conversion of coordinates is defined as follows:

$$u_e = u - \alpha_u, \ \overline{\psi}_e = \psi_e - \alpha_\psi, \ r_e = r - \alpha_r. \tag{18}$$

The system intermediate control signals α_u, α_ψ, α_r are defined as

$$\begin{aligned}\alpha_u &= -c_x x_e + u_d \cos \psi_e - y_e r, \\ \alpha_\psi &= \tfrac{1}{u_d}(-c_y y_e - v + x_e r), \\ \alpha_r &= -c_\psi \overline{\psi}_e + \dot{r}_d + z_{\psi,n+1} - y_e u_d.\end{aligned} \tag{19}$$

where c_x, c_y, c_ψ are positive real numbers.

The actual control inputs τ_u, τ_r are designed as

$$\begin{aligned}\tau_u &= m_u\left(-c_u u_e - x_e + z_{u,n+1} - \tfrac{m_v v r - X_u u}{m_u} - \tfrac{\hat{\omega}_u}{m_u}\right), \\ \tau_r &= m_r\left(-c_r r_e - \overline{\psi}_e + z_{r,n+1} - \tfrac{(m_u - m_v)uv - X_r r}{m_r} - \tfrac{\hat{\omega}_r}{m_r}\right).\end{aligned} \tag{20}$$

where $c_u, c_r \in R^+$.

3.4. Stability Analysis

Consider the Lyapunov function as

$$V = V_x + V_y + V_\psi + V_u + V_r \tag{21}$$

and

$$\begin{aligned}V_x &= \tfrac{1}{2}x_e^2, \ V_y = \tfrac{1}{2}y_e^2, \ V_\psi = \tfrac{1}{2}\psi_e^2, \\ V_u &= \tfrac{1}{2}u_e^2, \ V_r = \tfrac{1}{2}r_e^2.\end{aligned} \tag{22}$$

The differential of (21) can be written as

$$\dot{V} = \dot{V}_x + \dot{V}_y + \dot{V}_\psi + \dot{V}_u + \dot{V}_r \qquad (23)$$

Combining (10) and (22), the differential of the Lyapunov function V_x is expressed as

$$\dot{V}_x = x_e \dot{x}_e = x_e(u - u_d \cos \psi_e + y_e r) \qquad (24)$$

According to Lemma 5, Theorem 1, (18), and (19), adding (14) to the Lyapunov function, where $z_{u,1} = \alpha_u$, (24) can then be simplified as

$$\dot{V}_x = x_e(u_e + \alpha_u - u_d \cos \psi_e + y_e r) = -c_x x_e^2 + x_e u_e \qquad (25)$$

Based on (11) and (22), the differential of the Lyapunov candidate V_y is given as

$$\dot{V}_y = y_e \dot{y}_e = y_e(v + u_d \sin \psi_e - x_e r) \qquad (26)$$

According to Lemma 5, Theorem 1, (14), (18), and (19), there is $z_{\psi,1} = \alpha_\psi$; then, (26) can be simplified as

$$\dot{V}_y = y_e(v + u_d(\overline{\psi}_e + \alpha_\psi) - x_e r) = -c_y y_e^2 + u_d y_e \overline{\psi}_e \qquad (27)$$

From Formulas (10) and (22), the differentiation of the Lyapunov candidate V_ψ is rewritten as

$$\dot{V}_\psi = \overline{\psi}_e \dot{\overline{\psi}}_e = \overline{\psi}_e(\dot{\psi}_e - \dot{\alpha}_\psi) = \overline{\psi}_e(r - r_d - \dot{\alpha}_\psi) \qquad (28)$$

Combining (14), (18), (19), Lemma 5, and Theorem 1, we can obtain $z_{r,1} = \alpha_r$ and ${}^C_{t_0}\mathbf{D}^{1/n}_t \overline{z}_{\psi,n} = z_{\psi,n+1} = \dot{\alpha}_\psi$. Thus, (28) can be simplified as

$$\dot{V}_\psi = \overline{\psi}_e((r_e + \alpha_r) - r_d - \dot{\alpha}_\psi) = -c_\psi \overline{\psi}_e^2 + \overline{\psi}_e r_e \qquad (29)$$

According to Lemma 5, Theorem 1, and Formula (14), there are ${}^C_{t_0}\mathbf{D}^{1/n}_t \overline{z}_{u,n} = z_{u,n+1} = \dot{\alpha}_u$ and ${}^C_{t_0}\mathbf{D}^{1/n}_t \overline{z}_{r,n} = z_{r,n+1} = \dot{\alpha}_r$. Based on Theorem 2, there is a finite time t_r such that $t > t_r$ has $\hat{\omega}_u(t) = \omega_u(t) - f_u(v)$ and $\hat{\omega}_r(t) = \omega_r(t) - f_r(v)$. Therefore, the time derivatives of the Lyapunov candidates V_u and V_r are expressed as

$$\begin{aligned}\dot{V}_u &= u_e \dot{u}_e = u_e(\dot{u} - \dot{\alpha}_u) \\ &= u_e(\tfrac{\tau_u}{m_u} + \tfrac{m_v vr - X_u u - f_u(v)}{m_u} + \tfrac{\omega_u(t)}{m_u} - \dot{\alpha}_u) \\ &= -c_u u_e^2 - u_e x_e\end{aligned} \qquad (30)$$

and

$$\begin{aligned}\dot{V}_r &= r_e \dot{r}_e = r_e(\dot{r} - \dot{\alpha}_r) \\ &= r_e(\tfrac{\tau_r}{m_r} + \tfrac{(m_u - m_v)uv - N_r r - f_r(v)}{m_r} + \tfrac{\omega_r(t)}{m_r} - \dot{\alpha}_r) \\ &= -c_r r_e^2 - \overline{\psi}_e r_e\end{aligned} \qquad (31)$$

Substituting (25), (27), and (29)–(31) into (23), we obtain

$$\dot{V} = -c_x x_e^2 - c_y y_e^2 - c_\psi \overline{\psi}_e^2 - c_u u_e^2 - c_r r_e^2 \qquad (32)$$

The Lyapunov function $V = V_x + V_y + V_\psi + V_u + V_r$ satisfies the relation

$$\begin{aligned}\dot{V} &= -c_x x_e^2 - c_y y_e^2 - c_\psi \overline{\psi}_e^2 - c_u u_e^2 - c_r r_e^2 \\ &< -CV\end{aligned} \qquad (33)$$

where $C = \min(2 * (c_x, c_y, c_\psi, c_u, c_r))$.

Theorem 3: For the USVs (6) and (7) with Assumptions 1 and 2, the reference signals are given as (8), the fractional-order finite-time command filter is denoted by (14), the fractional-order finite-time disturbance observer is provided as (17), the intermediate control signals are represented by (19), and the actual control inputs are designed as (20). By choosing appropriate positive parameters $c_x, c_y, c_\psi, c_u, c_r, \varsigma_{j1}, \varsigma_{j2}, \ldots, \varsigma_{j,n+2}$, and $\zeta_{j1}, \zeta_{j2}, \ldots, \zeta_{j,n+1}$, the solutions of the closed-loop nonlinear system are globally asymptotically stable in nature, and satisfy $\eta = \eta_d$ when $t \to \infty$.

Proof. According to formula (33), when $V = V_x + V_y + V_\psi + V_u + V_r > 0$, there is $\dot{V} < -CV$, then the closed-loop systems (6) and (7) are global asymptotically stable. Since the USV system satisfies the globally asymptotic stability, if the appropriate system parameters $c_x, c_y, c_\psi, c_u, c_r, \varsigma_{j1}, \varsigma_{j2}, \ldots, \varsigma_{j,n+2}$, and $\zeta_{j1}, \zeta_{j2}, \ldots, \zeta_{j,n+1}$ are selected, it is obvious that $\lim_{t \to \infty} |\eta - \eta_d| \to 0$. □

4. Simulation Results

To prove the effectiveness and superiority of the fractional-order backstepping controller, simulation experiments based on the USV model are proposed in this section. The same reference trajectory and system model are used for comparison experiments. The initial value of USV is defined as $\eta_0 = [0\text{ m}, 0\text{ m}, 0\text{ rad}]^T$, $v_0 = [1\text{ m/s}, 0\text{ m/s}, 0\text{ rad/s}]^T$. The hydrodynamic coefficients effects are assumed as $f_u(v) = X_{|u|u}|u|u$, $f_v(v) = Y_{|v|v}|v|v$, and $f_r(v) = N_{|r|r}|r|r$. The system parameters are denoted as $m_u = 25.8$ kg, $m_v = 33.8$ kg, $m_r = 2.76$ kg·m^2, $X_u = 12$ N, $X_v = 17$ N, $X_r = 0.5$ N·m, $X_{|u|u} = 2.5$, $Y_{|v|v} = 4.5$, and $N_{|r|r} = 0.1$.

Case 1: The unknown external disturbances are defined as $\dot{w}_u = -0.01w_u + 3$ rand, $\dot{w}_v = -0.01w_v + 2$ rand, $\dot{w}_r = -0.01w_r + 2.5$ rand, where rand is a random number with a mean value of 0, a variance of 0.5, and a sampling time of 1. The USV reference trajectory are given as $u_d = 1$ m/s, $v_d = 0$ m/s for $0 \leq t \leq 100$ s. $r_d = -0.2e^{-(15-t)}$rad/s for $0 \leq t \leq 15$ s, and $r_d = -0.2$ rad/s for $15 < t \leq 100$ s.

(1) For the fractional-order backstepping controller, the fractional-order command filter is (14), and the fractional-order disturbance observer is (18). When $n = 2$, the control parameters are selected as $c_x = 20$, $c_y = 10$, $c_\psi = 1$, $c_u = 1$, $c_r = 30$, $\zeta_{\psi 1} = \zeta_{u1} = \zeta_{r1} = 1$, $\zeta_{\psi 2} = \zeta_{u2} = \zeta_{r2} = 0.1$, $\zeta_{\psi 3} = 0.01$, $\zeta_{r3} = 0.01$, $\zeta_{u3} = 0.001$, $\varsigma_{u1} = \varsigma_{r1} = 5$, $\varsigma_{u2} = 0.1$, $\varsigma_{r2} = 1$, $\varsigma_{u3} = \varsigma_{r3} = 0.1$, $\varsigma_{u4} = \varsigma_{r4} = 0.001$.

(2) For the integer-order backstepping controller, the command filter is given as (11), and the integer-order disturbance observer is defined as

$$\dot{\vartheta}_{i,1} = -\varsigma_{i1}|\vartheta_{i,1} - v_i(t)|^{1/2}\text{sgn}(\vartheta_{i,1} - v_i(t)) + \vartheta_{i,2} + g_i(v) + \tau_i,$$
$$\dot{\vartheta}_{i,2} = -\varsigma_{i2}\text{sgn}(\vartheta_{i,2} - \dot{\vartheta}_{i,1}), \qquad (34)$$
$$\hat{w}_i = -\varsigma_{i1}|\vartheta_{i,1} - v_i(t)|^{1/2}\text{sgn}(\vartheta_{i,1} - v_i(t)) + \vartheta_{i,2}.$$

where $\vartheta_{i,2}$ and $\vartheta_{i,1}$ represent the state variables of the disturbance observer, ς_{i1}, ς_{i2} are the adjustable positive constants, $v_i(t)$ denotes the output of the dynamic equation, τ_i and $g_i(v)$ represent the actual control input and known modeling error, respectively. $\hat{w}_i$ is the output of the disturbance observer and represents the estimated value of the system disturbances and uncertainties.

Then, the control parameters are selected as $c_x = c_y = c_\psi = c_u = c_r = 4$, $\zeta_{\psi 1} = \zeta_{u1} = \zeta_{r1} = 10$, $\zeta_{\psi 2} = \zeta_{u2} = \zeta_{r2} = 0.001$, $\varsigma_{u1} = \varsigma_{r1} = 15$, $\varsigma_{u2} = \varsigma_{r2} = 0.01$.

In Case 1, the simulation results of the USV system with model uncertainty and external environmental disturbance are presented in Figures 3–12. Figures 3–5 present the trajectory tracking diagram and error diagram of the proposed fractional-order backstepping controller, and Figures 8–10 present the trajectory tracking of the integer-order controller. It can be seen from Figures 3 and 8 that the tracking error of the proposed controller is basically the same as that of the comparison controller; that is, the trajectory tracking effect of both is basically the same. Random numbers are used as disturbance sources in this paper. Figure 6 shows the disturbance observations of the fractional-order backstepping controller. It is clear that the original observation value of the observer of the fractional-order backstepping controller is small, and there is no chattering. Figure 11 presents the disturbance observations of the integer-order backstepping controller. It can be seen that the observed initial value of the integer-order controller is large, and chattering is always present during trajectory tracking. Figure 7 represents the actual control inputs of the fractional-order backstepping controller, and there is no chattering in the control inputs. Figure 12 denotes the actual control inputs of the integer-order controller, and it can be seen that the chattering phenomenon of the control inputs is severe. Combined with the local amplification view, it is clear that the control input chattering of the controller proposed in this paper is significantly improved compared with the integer-order controller under the condition that the trajectory tracking effect is basically the same.

Case 2: Comparative experiment of Case 1. Modify the reference trajectory of Case 1 without changing other conditions. The USV reference trajectory are given as $u_d = 1$ m/s, $v_d = 0.2$ m/s for $0 \leq t \leq 100$ s. $r_d = -0.1e^{-(30-t)}$ rad/s for $0 \leq t \leq 30$ s, $r_d = 0.15 + 0.1e^{-(50-t)}$ rad/s for $30 \leq t \leq 50$ s, $r_d = -\left(0.15 + 0.1e^{-(70-t)}\right)$ rad/s for $50 \leq t \leq 70$ s, and $r_d = -0.1e^{-(100-t)}$ rad/s for $70 < t \leq 100$ s.

(1) For fractional-order backstepping controller, when $n = 2$, the control parameters of USV system are selected as $c_x = 15$, $c_y = 20$, $c_\psi = 1$, $c_u = 1$, $c_r = 15$, $\zeta_{\psi 1} = \zeta_{u1} = \zeta_{r1} = 1$, $\zeta_{\psi 2} = \zeta_{u2} = \zeta_{r2} = 0.1$, $\zeta_{\psi 3} = 0.01$, $\zeta_{r3} = 0.01$, $\zeta_{u3} = 0.001$, $\varsigma_{u1} = \varsigma_{r1} = 5$, $\varsigma_{u2} = 0.1$, $\varsigma_{r2} = 1$, $\varsigma_{u3} = \varsigma_{r3} = 0.1$, $\varsigma_{u4} = \varsigma_{r4} = 0.001$.

(2) For integer-order backstepping controller, the control parameters of USV are selected as $c_x = c_y = c_\psi = c_u = c_r = 2$, $\zeta_{\psi 1} = \zeta_{u1} = \zeta_{r1} = 10$, $\zeta_{\psi 2} = \zeta_{u2} = \zeta_{r2} = 0.001$, $\varsigma_{u1} = \varsigma_{r1} = 15$, $\varsigma_{u2} = \varsigma_{r2} = 0.01$.

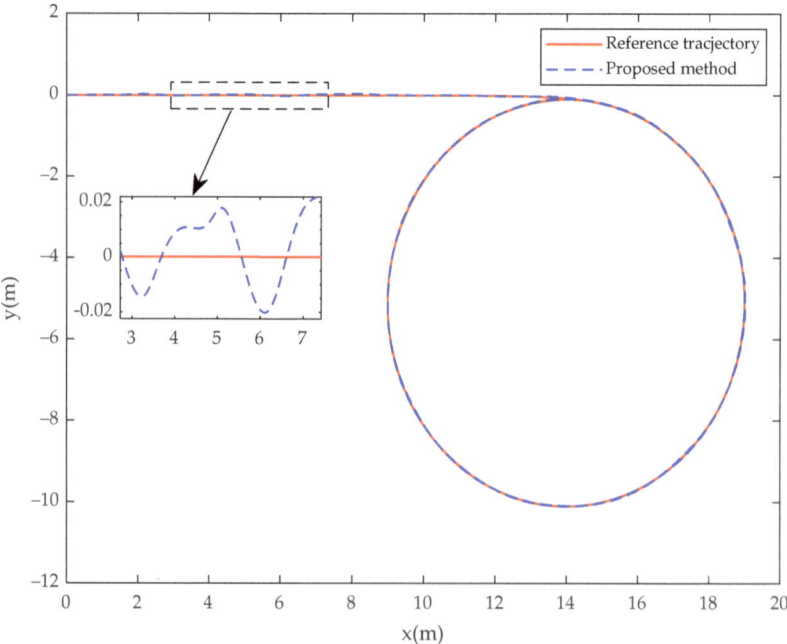

Figure 3. USV position (x, y) tracks the desired trajectory (x_d, y_d) for the fractional-order controller in Case 1.

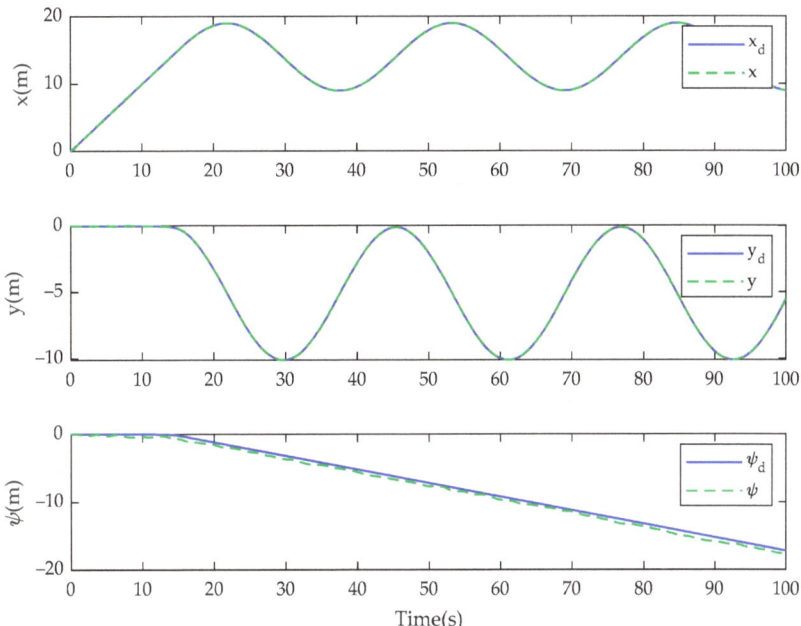

Figure 4. Tracking performance of x, y, ψ track the desired trajectory x_d, y_d, ψ_d for the fractional-order controller in Case 1.

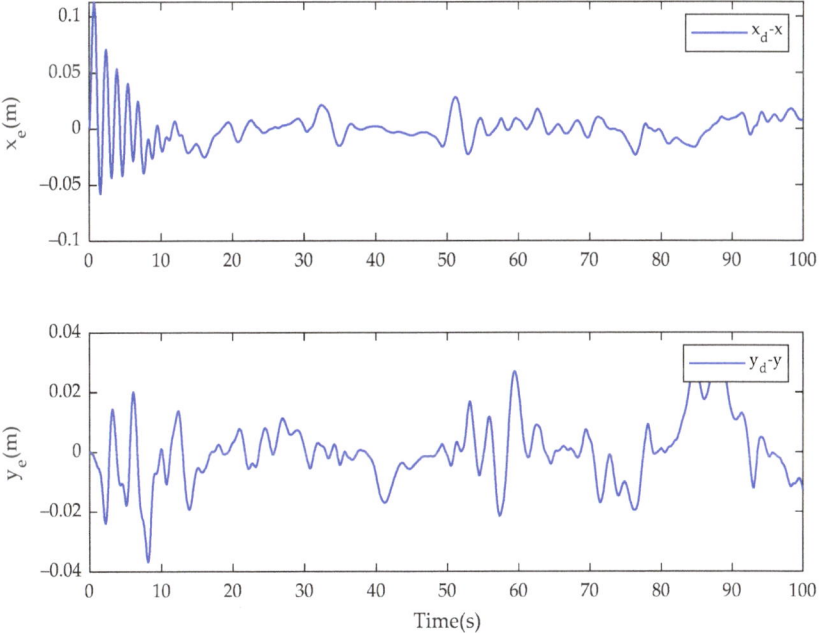

Figure 5. Tracking errors of x_e and y_e for the fractional-order controller in Case 1.

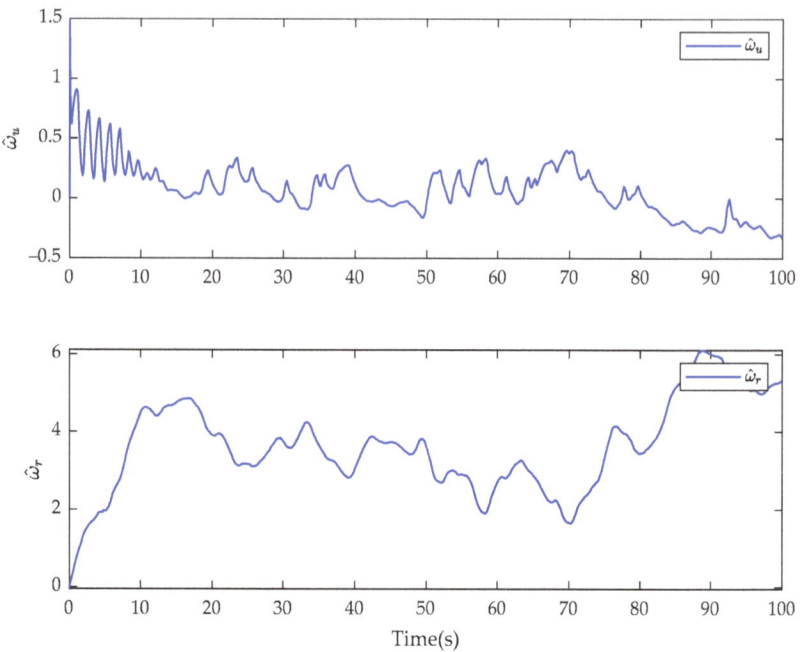

Figure 6. Estimate of fractional-order finite-time disturbance observer for $\hat{\omega}_u$ and $\hat{\omega}_r$ for fractional-order controller in Case 1.

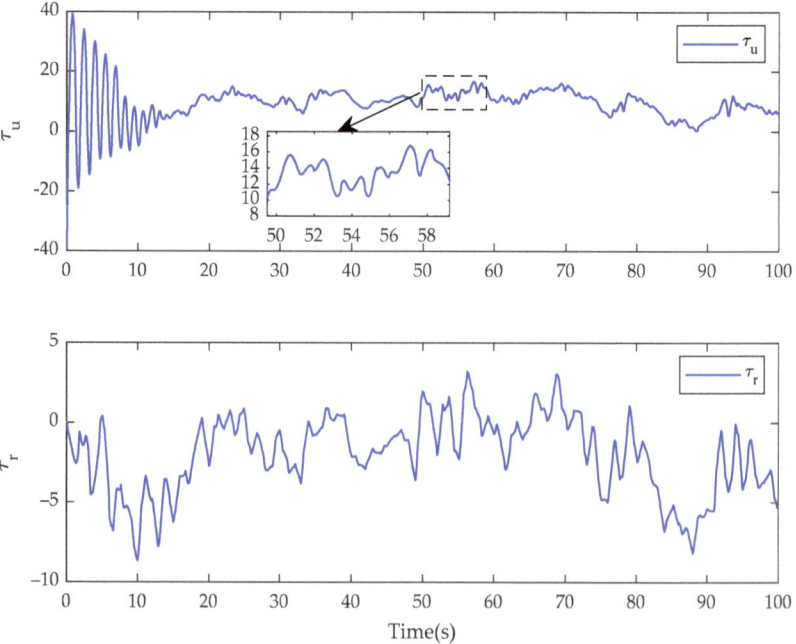

Figure 7. Control inputs of τ_u and τ_r for the fractional-order controller in Case 1.

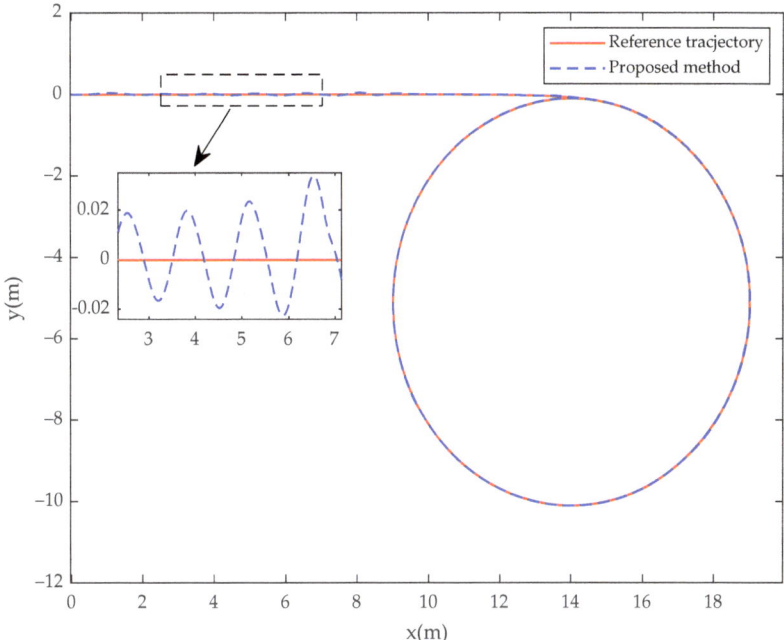

Figure 8. USV position (x, y) tracks the desired trajectory (x_d, y_d) for the integer-order controller in Case 1.

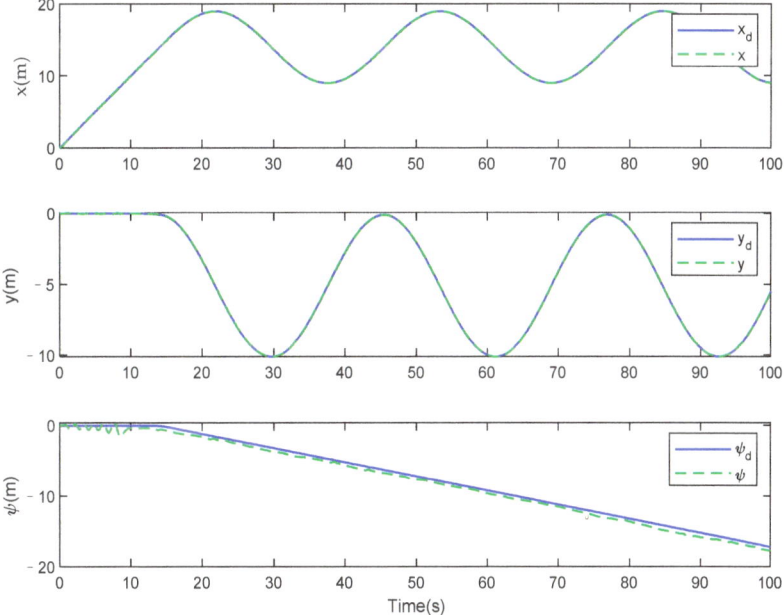

Figure 9. Tracking performance of x, y, ψ track the desired trajectory x_d, y_d, ψ_d for the integer-order controller in Case 1.

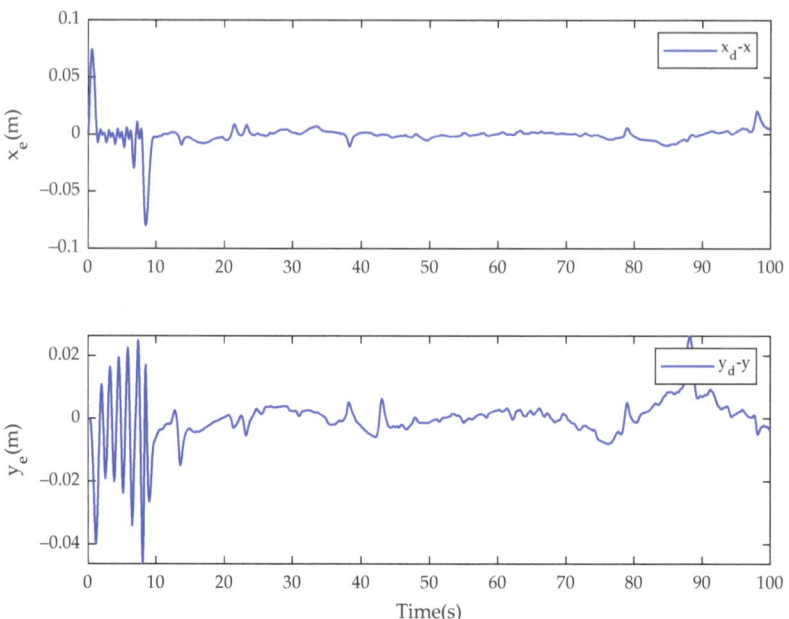

Figure 10. Tracking errors of x_e and y_e for the integer-order controller in Case 1.

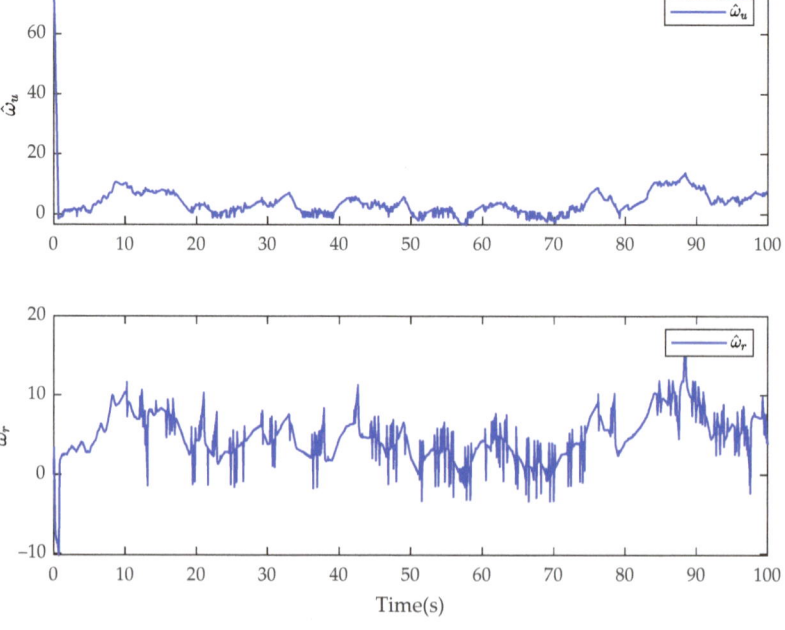

Figure 11. Estimate of fractional-order finite-time disturbance observer for $\hat{\omega}_u$ and $\hat{\omega}_r$ for the integer-order controller in Case 1.

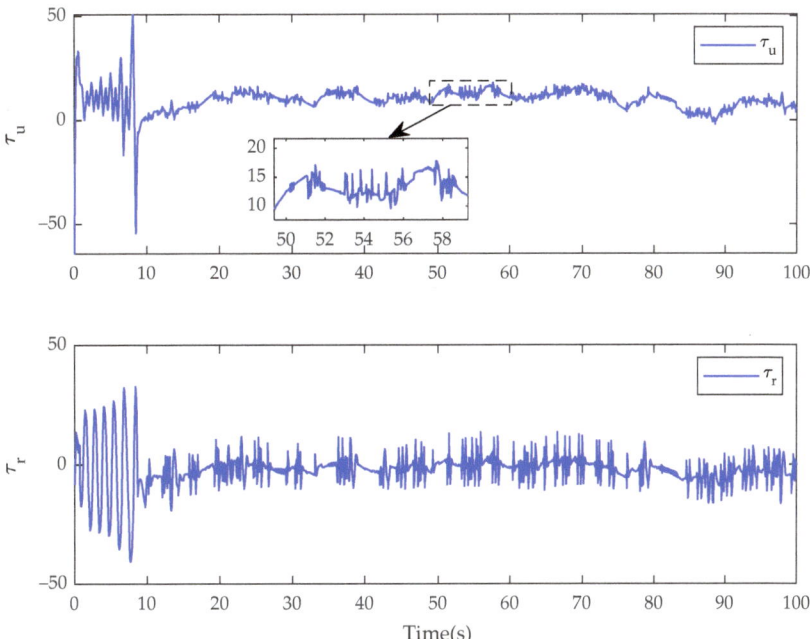

Figure 12. Control inputs of τ_u and τ_r for the integer-order controller in Case 1.

In Case 2, the simulation results of the USV system with model uncertainty and external environmental disturbance are presented in Figures 13–18. Figures 13 and 16 are the reference trajectory tracking plans of the fractional-order controller and the integer-order controller after changing the desired trajectory, respectively. Figures 14 and 17 are the disturbance observed values of the disturbance for the fractional-order controller and integer-order controller, respectively. Figures 15 and 18 are the actual control input values of the fractional-order controller and the integer-order controller after changing the desired trajectory, respectively. By comparing Figures 13 and 16, it can be seen that the proposed controller and the integer-order controller have the same trajectory tracking effect. It can be seen from the comparison between Figures 14 and 15 and Figures 17 and 18 that the disturbance observation value and control input chattering of the controller proposed in this paper are significantly improved compared with the integer-order controller. Comparing the experimental results with Case 1, it shows that the fractional-order controller is not sensitive to the motion reference trajectory of the USV.

Case 3: Comparative experiment with Case 1. Modify the disturbances in Case 1 without changing other conditions. The unknown external disturbances are defined as $\omega_u = 5 + 10\sin(0.5t + \pi/3)$, $\omega_v = 5\sin(0.5t + 2\pi/3)$, $\omega_r = 48\sin(0.5t)$.

(1) For fractional-order backstepping controller, when $n = 2$, the control parameters of USV system are given as $c_x = 21$, $c_y = 10$, $c_\psi = 1$, $c_u = 1$, $c_r = 30$, $\zeta_{\psi 1} = \zeta_{u1} = \zeta_{r1} = 1$, $\zeta_{\psi 2} = \zeta_{u2} = \zeta_{r2} = 0.1$, $\zeta_{\psi 3} = 0.01$, $\zeta_{r3} = 0.01$, $\zeta_{u3} = 0.001$, $\varsigma_{u1} = \varsigma_{r1} = 5$, $\varsigma_{u2} = 0.1$, $\varsigma_{r2} = 1$, $\varsigma_{u3} = \varsigma_{r3} = 0.1$, $\varsigma_{u4} = \varsigma_{r4} = 0.001$.

(2) For integer-order backstepping controller, the control parameters of system are given as $c_x = c_y = c_\psi = c_u = c_r = 3$, $\zeta_{\psi 1} = \zeta_{u1} = \zeta_{r1} = 10$, $\zeta_{\psi 2} = \zeta_{u2} = \zeta_{r2} = 0.001$, $\varsigma_{u1} = \varsigma_{r1} = 15$, $\varsigma_{u2} = \varsigma_{r2} = 0.01$.

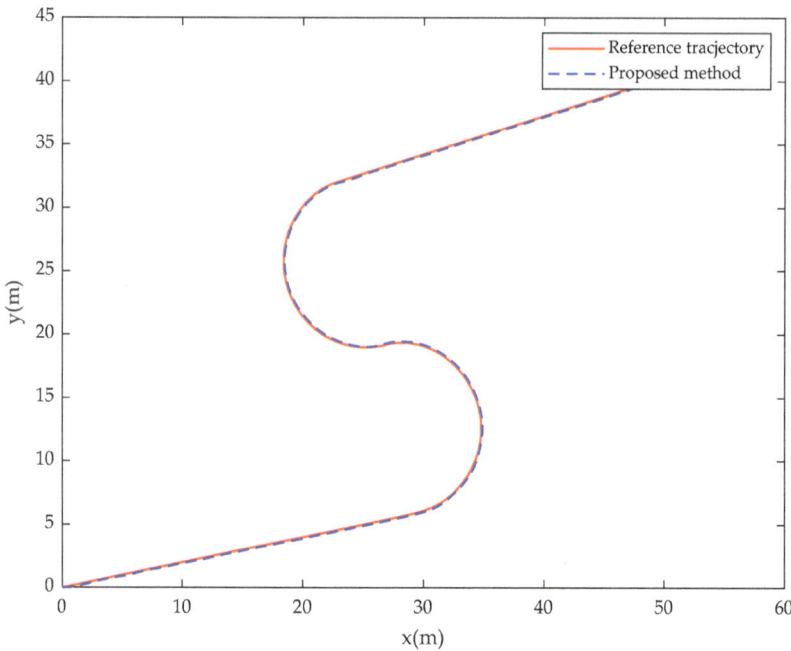

Figure 13. USV position (x, y) tracks the desired trajectory (x_d, y_d) for the fractional-order controller in Case 2.

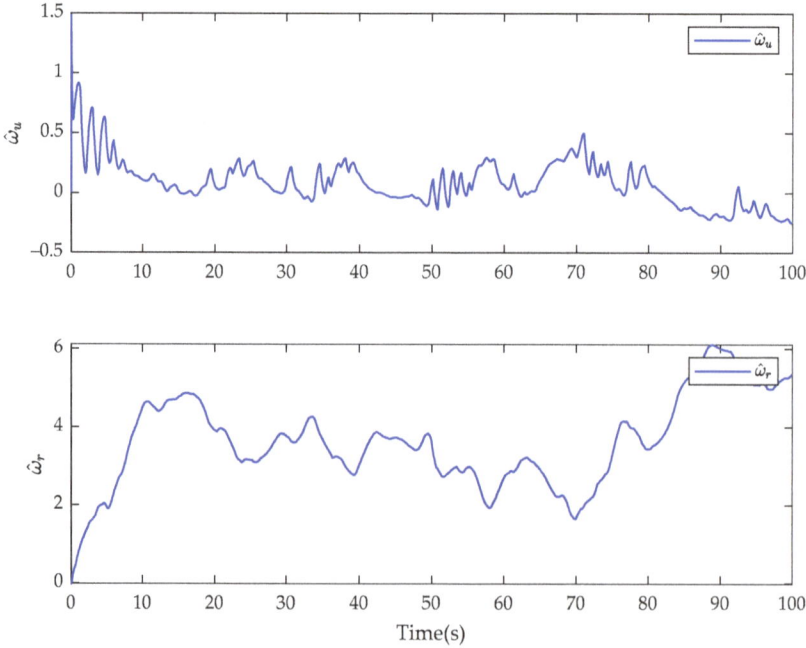

Figure 14. Estimate of fractional-order finite-time disturbance observer for $\hat{\omega}_u$ and $\hat{\omega}_r$ for the fractional-order controller in Case 2.

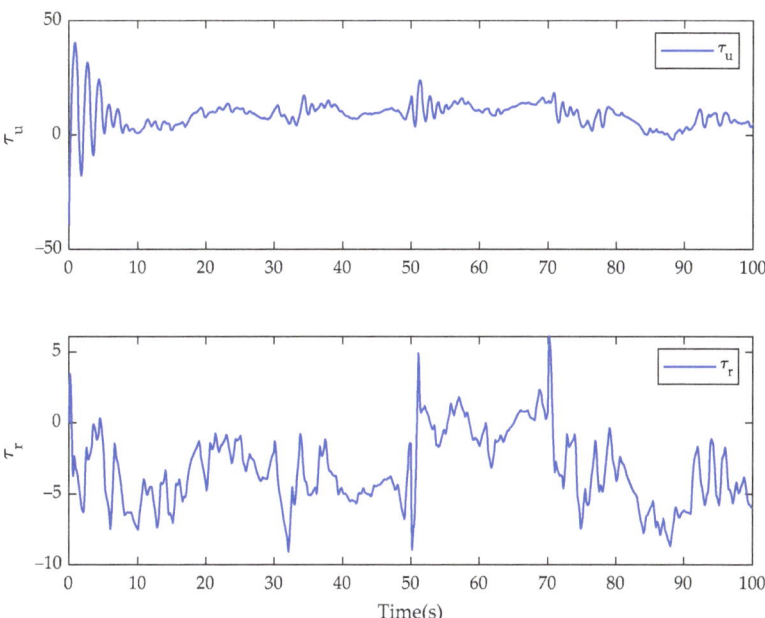

Figure 15. Control inputs of τ_u and τ_r for the fractional-order controller in Case 2.

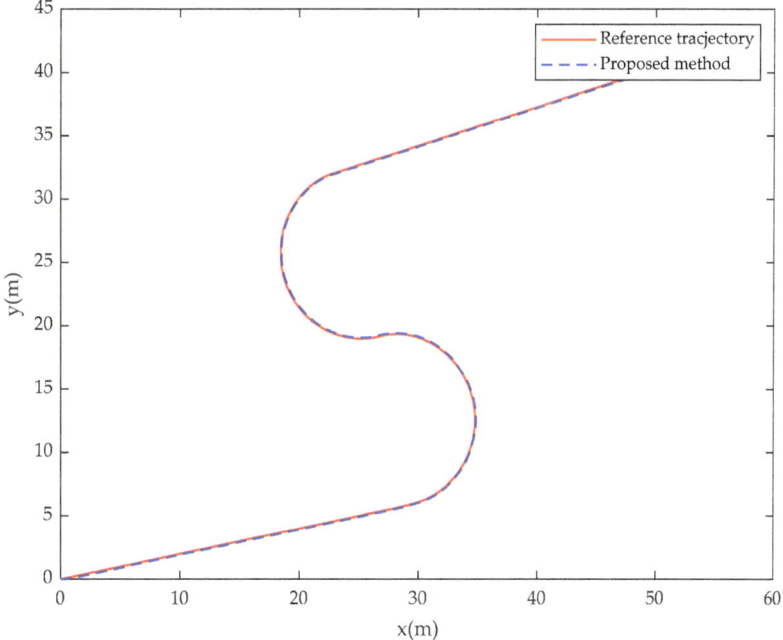

Figure 16. USV position (x, y) tracks the desired trajectory (x_d, y_d) for the integer-order controller in Case 2.

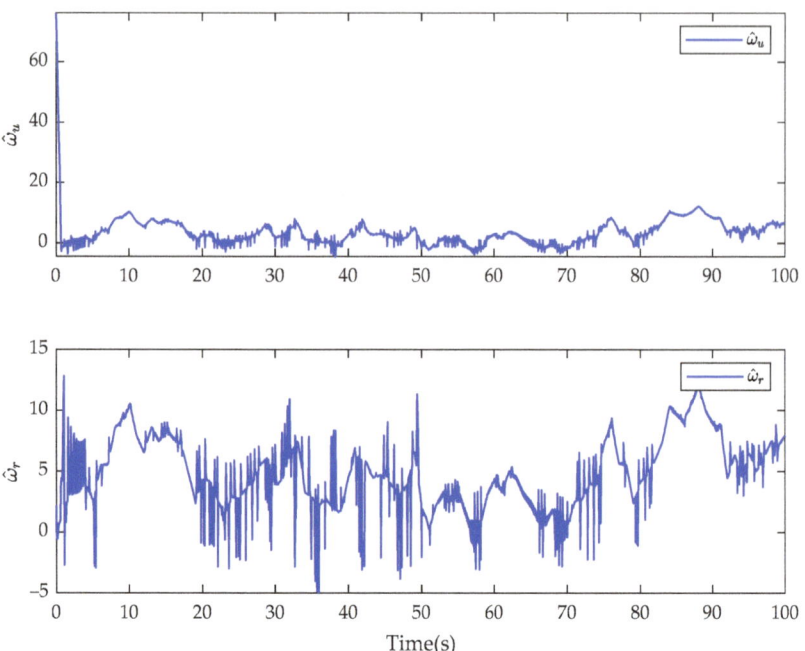

Figure 17. Estimate of fractional-order finite-time disturbance observer for $\hat{\omega}_u$ and $\hat{\omega}_r$ for the integer-order controller in Case 2.

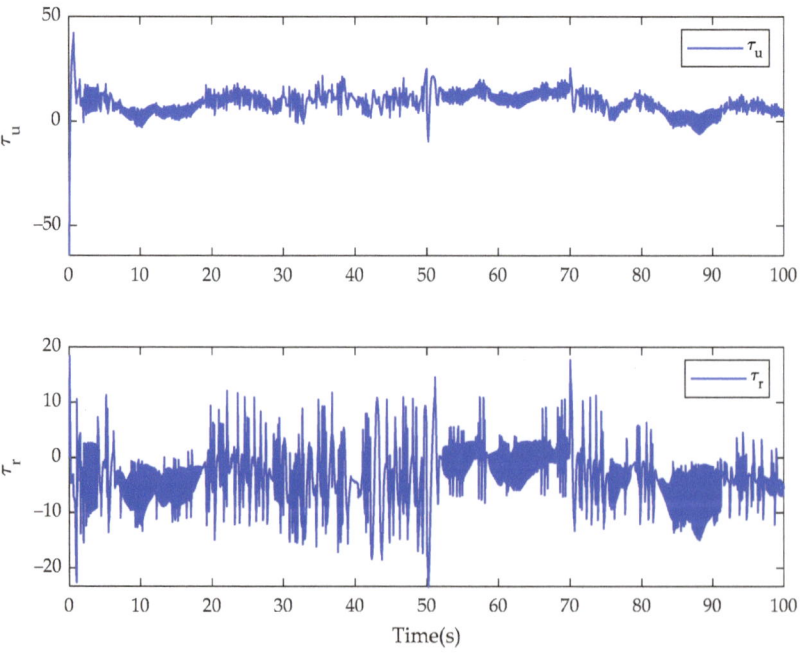

Figure 18. Control inputs of τ_u and τ_r for the integer-order controller in Case 2.

In Case 3, the simulation results of the USV system with model uncertainty and external environmental disturbance are presented in Figures 19–24. Figures 19 and 22 are the reference trajectory tracking plane diagrams of the fractional-order controller and the integer-order controller, respectively. The comparison between the two shows that the proposed controller and the integer-order controller have basically the same trajectory tracking effect. Figures 20 and 23 are the disturbance observations of the fractional-order controller and the integer-order controller after changing the disturbance, respectively. It can be seen that the fractional-order disturbance observer has a greater improvement in the chattering of the disturbance observation value than the integer-order disturbance observer. Figures 21 and 24 are the actual control input values of the fractional-order controller and the integer-order controller, respectively. It is obvious from the diagram that the controller proposed in this paper eliminates the input chattering of the integer-order controller. Therefore, when the trajectory tracking effect is basically the same, the fractional-order controller can improve the chattering phenomenon of the actual control input of the integer-order controller. Comparing the experimental results with Case 1, it can be seen that the fractional-order controller can improve the chattering of the control input when changing the system disturbance, indicating that the controller proposed in this paper is insensitive to the disturbance type.

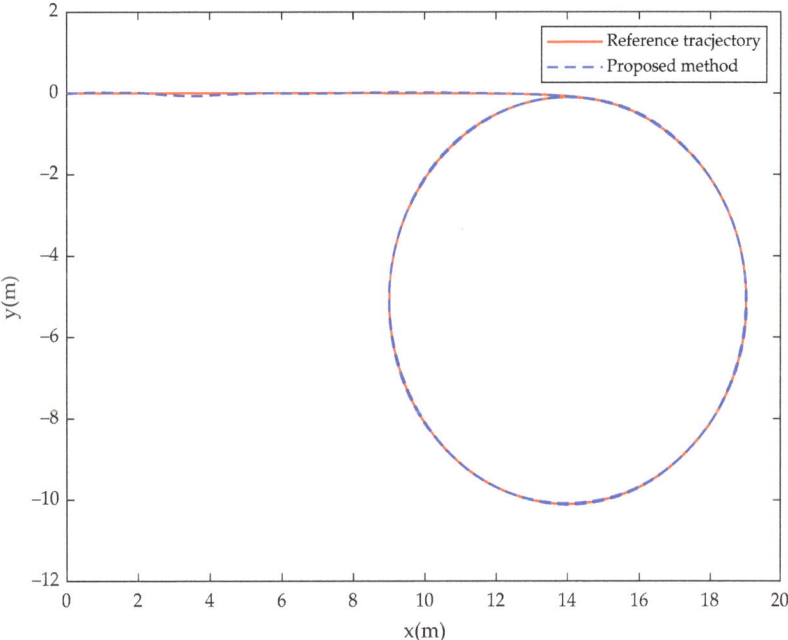

Figure 19. USV position (x, y) tracks the desired trajectory (x_d, y_d) for the fractional-order controller in Case 3.

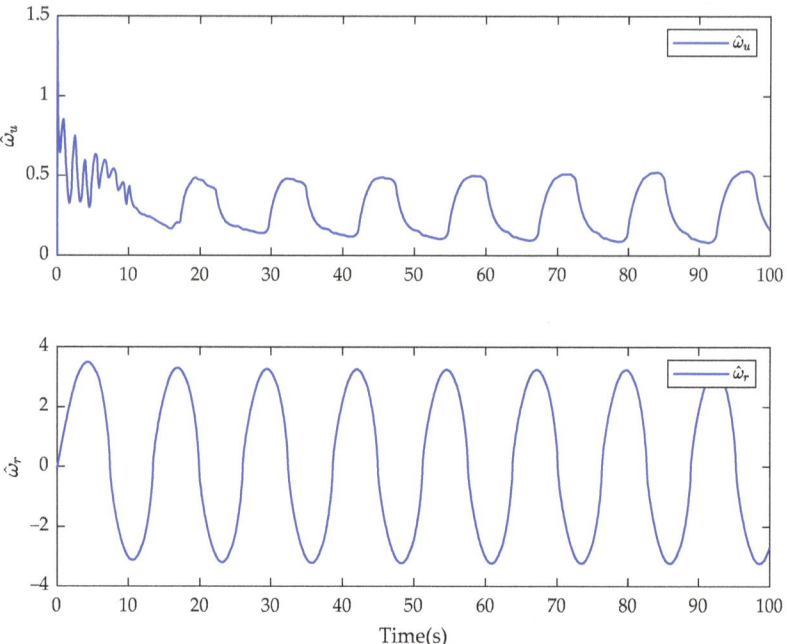

Figure 20. Estimate of fractional-order finite-time disturbance observer for $\hat{\omega}_u$ and $\hat{\omega}_r$ for the fractional-order controller in Case 3.

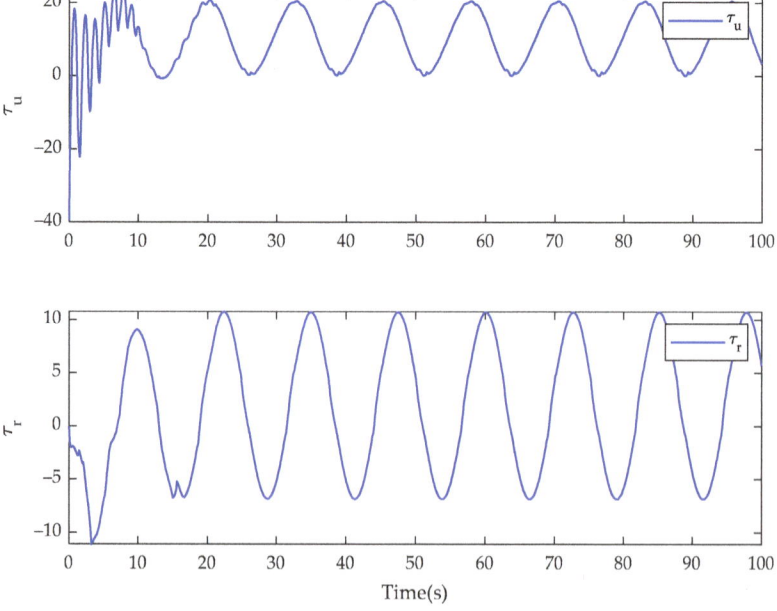

Figure 21. Control inputs of τ_u and τ_r for the fractional-order controller in Case 3.

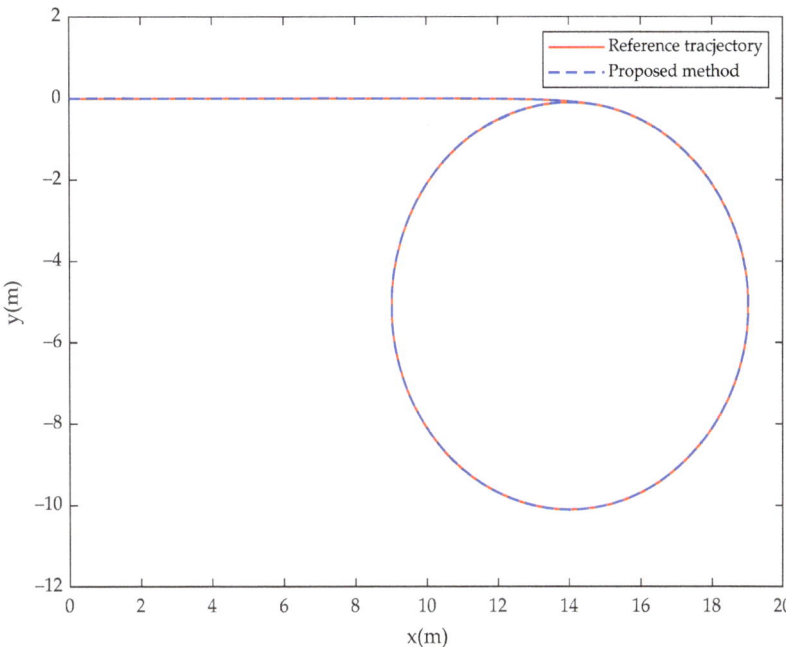

Figure 22. USV position (x, y) tracks the desired trajectory (x_d, y_d) for the integer-order controller in Case 3.

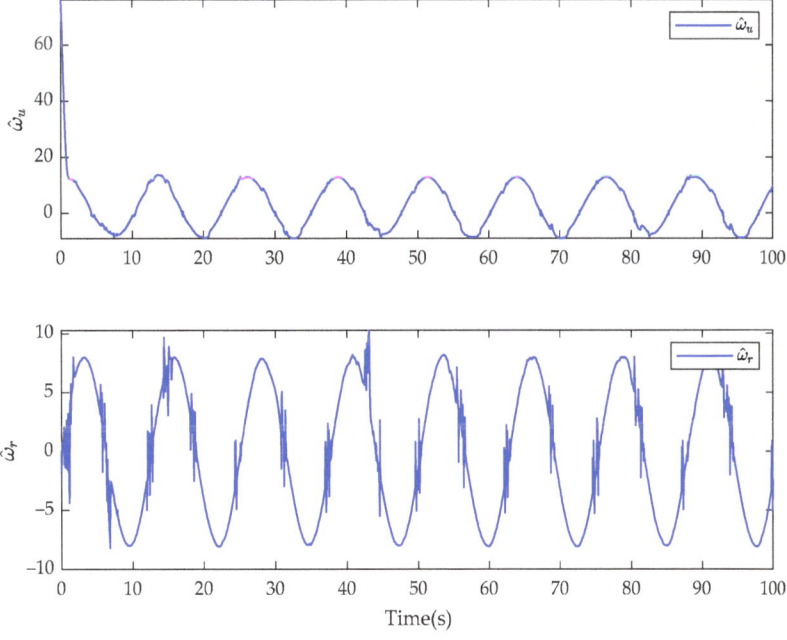

Figure 23. Estimate of fractional-order finite-time disturbance observer for $\hat{\omega}_u$ and $\hat{\omega}_r$ for the integer-order controller in Case 3.

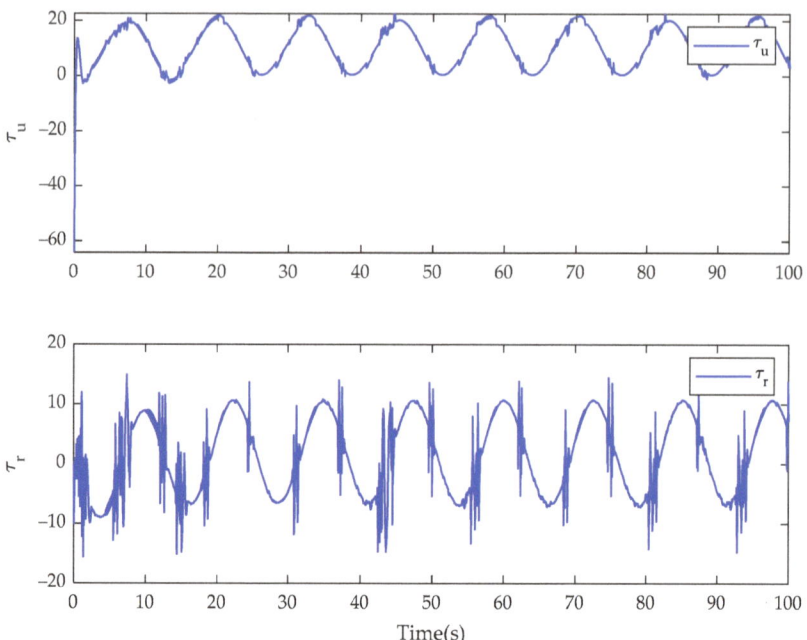

Figure 24. Control inputs of τ_u and τ_r for the integer-order controller in Case 3.

5. Conclusions

The backstepping control strategy, which combines a fractional-order command filter and a fractional-order finite-time disturbance observer, is presented for the trajectory tracking control of the USV with model uncertainty and unknown environmental disturbances in the paper. The fractional-order command filter is used to replace the original integer-order command filter, which reduces the chattering phenomenon of the integer-order command filter and avoids the problem that the controller cannot be directly derived. The fractional-order disturbance observer is adopted to compensate for the model uncertainty and environmental disturbances of the USV system. The simulation examples demonstrate that the fractional-order controller is capable of reducing the chattering phenomenon of the actual control inputs of the integer-order controller under the condition of consistent performance. At the same time, the controller proposed in this paper is not sensitive to the desired trajectory and disturbance type.

Author Contributions: Conceptualization, R.M., J.C. and C.L.; Methodology, R.M., J.C., C.L. and Z.Y.; Supervision, R.M., J.C., C.L. and Z.Y.; Validation, R.M. and J.C.; Writing—original draft, R.M. and X.H.; Writing—review, R.M., J.C., C.L. and Z.Y.; Writing—editing, R.M., J.C. and X.H. All authors have read and agreed to the published version of the manuscript.

Funding: This work was supported by the Qingdao Natural Science Foundation under Grant 23-2-1-154-zyyd-jch and 23-1-2-qljh-6-gx, the National Natural Science Foundation under Grant Nos. 62373209, 61803220, and 61573203 and the Shandong Natural Science Foundation under GrantZR2023MF017, ZR2023MF032, and 2022CXGC010608.

Data Availability Statement: The data presented in this study may be available on request from the corresponding author.

Conflicts of Interest: The authors declare no conflicts of interest.

References

1. Lv, C.X.; Yu, H.S.; Chen, J.; Zhao, N.; Chi, J.R. Trajectory tracking control for unmanned surface vessel with input saturation and disturbances via robust state error IDA-PBC approach. *J. Frankl. Inst.* **2022**, *359*, 1899–1924. [CrossRef]
2. Guo, X.H.; Narthsirinth, N.; Zhang, W.D.; Hu, Y.Z. Unmanned surface vehicles (USVs) scheduling method by a bi-level mission planning and path control. *Comput. Oper. Res.* **2024**, *162*, 106472. [CrossRef]
3. Li, J.P.; Fan, Y.S.; Liu, J.X. Adaptive NN formation tracking control for the multiple underactuated USVs with prescribed performance and input saturations. *Ocean Eng.* **2023**, *290*, 116274. [CrossRef]
4. Lim, C.S.; Lee, S.S.; Levi, E. Continuous-Control-Set Model Predictive Current Control of Asymmetrical Six- Phase Drives Considering System Nonidealities. *IEEE Trans. Ind. Electron.* **2023**, *70*, 7615–7626. [CrossRef]
5. Zhang, X.F.; Chen, S.N.; Zhang, J.X. Adaptive sliding mode consensus control based on neural network for singular fractional order multi-agent systems. *Appl. Math. Comput.* **2022**, *434*, 127442. [CrossRef]
6. Reis, J.; Xie, W.; Cabecinhas, D.; Silvestre, C. Nonlinear Backstepping Controller for an Underactuated ASV With Model Parametric Uncertainty: Design and Experimental Validation. *IEEE Trans. Intell. Veh.* **2023**, *8*, 2514–2526. [CrossRef]
7. Wang, Z.K.; Zhang, L.J.; Zhu, Z.Y. Game-based distributed optimal formation tracking control of underactuated AUVs based on reinforcement learning. *Ocean Eng.* **2023**, *287*, 115879. [CrossRef]
8. Liu, H.; Pan, Y.; Cao, J.; Wang, H.; Zhou, Y. Adaptive neural network backstepping control of fractional-order nonlinear systems with actuator faults. *IEEE Trans. Neural Netw. Learn. Syst.* **2020**, *31*, 5166–5177. [CrossRef]
9. Habibi, H.; Nohooji, H.R.; Howard, I. Backstepping Nussbaum gain dynamic surface control for a class of input and state constrained systems with actuator faults. *Inf. Sci.* **2019**, *482*, 27–46. [CrossRef]
10. Alsaadi, F.E.; Zhang, X.L.; Alassafi, M.O.; Alotaibi, R.M.; Ahmad, A.M.; Cao, J.D. Fuzzy Command Filter Backstepping Control for Incommensurate Fractional-Order Systems via Composite Learning. *Int. J. Fuzzy Syst.* **2022**, *24*, 3293–3307. [CrossRef]
11. Sheng, N.; Zhang, D.; Zhang, Q.C. Fuzzy Command Filtered Backstepping Control for Nonlinear System With Nonlinear Faults. *IEEE Access* **2021**, *9*, 60409–60418. [CrossRef]
12. Cui, G.Z.; Yu, J.P.; Shi, P. Observer-based finite-time adaptive fuzzy control with prescribed performance for nonstrict-feedback nonlinear systems. *IEEE Trans. Fuzzy Syst.* **2020**, *30*, 767–778. [CrossRef]
13. Lv, C.X.; Yu, H.S.; Chi, J.R.; Xu, T.; Zang, H.C.; Jiang, H.L.; Zhang, Z.W. A hybrid coordination controller for speed and heading control of underactuated unmanned surface vehicles system. *Ocean Eng.* **2019**, *176*, 222–230. [CrossRef]
14. Peng, Z.H.; Wang, D.; Wang, J. Data-Driven Adaptive Disturbance Observers for Model-Free Trajectory Tracking Control of Maritime Autonomous Surface Ships. *IEEE Trans. Neural Netw. Learn. Syst.* **2021**, *32*, 5584–5594. [CrossRef] [PubMed]
15. Chen, Z.; Zhang, Y.G.; Nie, Y.; Tang, J.Z.; Zhu, S.Q. Adaptive Sliding Mode Control Design for Nonlinear Unmanned Surface Vessel Using RBFNN and Disturbance-Observer. *IEEE Access* **2020**, *8*, 45457–45467. [CrossRef]
16. Chen, J.; Hu, X.Y.; Lv, C.X.; Zhang, Z.Y.; Ma, R.N. Adaptive event-triggered fuzzy tracking control for underactuated surface vehicles under external disturbances. *Ocean Eng.* **2023**, *283*, 115026. [CrossRef]
17. Deng, Y.; Peng, Y.; Qu, D.; Han, T.; Zhan, X.S. Neuro-adaptive containment control of unmanned surface vehicles with disturbance observer and collision-frees. *ISA Trans.* **2022**, *129*, 150–156. [CrossRef]
18. Zhang, X.F.; Chen, Y.Q. Admissibility and robust stabilization of continuous linear singular fractional order systems with the fractional order α: The $0 < α < 1$ case. *ISA Trans.* **2018**, *82*, 42–50.
19. Zhang, X.F.; Driss, D.; Liu, D.Y. Applications of fractional operator in image processing and stability of control systems. *Fractal Fract.* **2023**, *7*, 359. [CrossRef]
20. Zhang, X.F.; Lin, C.; Chen, Y.Q.; Boutat, D. A unified framework of stability theorems for LTI fractional order systems with $0 < alpha < 2$. *IEEE Trans. Circuits Syst. II* **2020**, *67*, 3237–3241.
21. Sabouri, J.; Effati, S.; Pakdaman, M. A neural network approach for solving a class of fractional optimal control problems. *Neural Process. Lett.* **2017**, *45*, 59–74. [CrossRef]
22. Acharya, D.S.; Mishra, S.K.; Swain, S.K.; Ghosh, S. Real-Time Implementation of Fractional-Order PID Controller for Magnetic Levitation Plant With Time Delay. *IEEE Trans. Instrum. Meas.* **2022**, *71*, 1–11. [CrossRef]
23. Zhang, D.D.; Li, F.; Ma, R.; Zhao, G.F.; Huangfu, Y.G. An Unknown Input Nonlinear Observer Based Fractional Order PID Control of Fuel Cell Air Supply System. *IEEE. Trans. Ind. Appl.* **2020**, *56*, 5523–5532.
24. Ren, H.-P.; Wang, X.; Fan, J.-T.; Kaynak, O. Fractional order sliding mode control of a pneumatic position servo control. *J. Frankl. Inst.* **2019**, *356*, 6160–6174. [CrossRef]
25. Liang, B.Y.; Zheng, S.Q.; Ahn, C.K.; Liu, F. Adaptive Fuzzy Control for Fractional-Order Interconnected Systems With Unknown Control Directions. *IEEE Trans. Fuzzy Syst.* **2022**, *30*, 75–87. [CrossRef]
26. Podlubny, I. *Fractional Differential Equations*, 1st ed.; Academic Press: San Diego, CA, USA, 1999; pp. 41–106.
27. Di, Y.; Zhang, J.X.; Zhang, X.F. Alternate admissibility LMI criteria for descriptor fractional order systems with $0 < α < 2$. *Fractal Fract.* **2023**, *7*, 577.
28. Li, C.P.; Deng, W.H. Remarks on fractional derivates. *Appl. Math. Comput.* **2007**, *187*, 777–784.
29. Demirci, E.; Ozalp, N. A method for solving differential equations of fractional order. *Comput. Appl. Math.* **2012**, *236*, 2754–2762. [CrossRef]
30. Li, S.L.; Zhu, Y.K.; Bai, J.G.; Guo, G. Dynamic obstacle avoidance of unmanned ship based on event-triggered adaptive nonlinear model predictive control. *Ocean Eng.* **2023**, *286*, 115626. [CrossRef]

31. Fossen, T.I. *Handbook of Marine Craft Hydrodynamics and Motion Control*, 2nd ed.; John Wiley& Sons: New York, NY, USA, 2011; pp. 133–142.
32. Levant, A. Robust exact differentiation via sliding mode technique. *Automatica* **1998**, *34*, 379–384. [CrossRef]
33. Shtessel, Y.; Edwards, C.; Fridman, L.; Levant, A. *Sliding Mode Control and Observation*, 1st ed.; Birkhauser Springer: New York, NY, USA, 2014; pp. 159–160.
34. Levant, A. Higher-order sliding modes, differentiation and output-feedback control. *Int. J. Control* **2003**, *76*, 924–941. [CrossRef]

Disclaimer/Publisher's Note: The statements, opinions and data contained in all publications are solely those of the individual author(s) and contributor(s) and not of MDPI and/or the editor(s). MDPI and/or the editor(s) disclaim responsibility for any injury to people or property resulting from any ideas, methods, instructions or products referred to in the content.

 *fractal and fractional*

Article

Adaptive Fractional-Order Multi-Scale Optimization TV-L1 Optical Flow Algorithm

Qi Yang [1,*], Yilu Wang [1], Lu Liu [2,3] and Xiaomeng Zhang [2,3]

1 The School of Mechanical Engineering, Shenyang Ligong University, Shenyang 110158, China; yiluwang6588699@163.com
2 The School of Marine Science and Technology, Northwestern Polytechnical University, Xi'an 710072, China; liulu12201220@nwpu.edu.cn (L.L.); zhangxiaomeng@mail.nwpu.edu.cn (X.Z.)
3 Research & Development Institute, Northwestern Polytechnical University, Shenzhen 518057, China
* Correspondence: yangqi@sylu.edu.cn; Tel.: +86-130-6657-7770

Abstract: We propose an adaptive fractional multi-scale optimization optical flow algorithm, which for the first time improves the over-smoothing of optical flow estimation under the total variation model from the perspective of global feature and local texture balance, and solves the problem that the convergence of fractional optical flow algorithms depends on the order parameter. Specifically, a fractional-order discrete L1-regularization Total Variational Optical Flow model is constructed. On this basis, the Ant Lion algorithm is innovatively used to realize the iterative calculation of the optical flow equation, and the fractional order is dynamically adjusted to obtain an adaptive optimization algorithm with strong search accuracy and high efficiency. In this paper, the flexibility of optical flow estimation in weak gradient texture scenes is increased, and the optical flow extraction rate of target features at multiple scales is greatly improved. We show excellent recognition performance and stability under the MPI_Sintel and Middlebury benchmarks.

Keywords: optical flow estimation; swarm intelligence optimization; fractional-order differential; adaptive

Citation: Yang, Q.; Wang, Y.; Liu, L.; Zhang, X. Adaptive Fractional-Order Multi-Scale Optimization TV-L1 Optical Flow Algorithm. *Fractal Fract.* **2024**, *8*, 179. https://doi.org/10.3390/fractalfract8040179

Academic Editors: Norbert Herencsar, Dayan Liu, Driss Boutat, Xuefeng Zhang and Jinxi Zhang

Received: 21 February 2024
Revised: 14 March 2024
Accepted: 18 March 2024
Published: 22 March 2024

Copyright: © 2024 by the authors. Licensee MDPI, Basel, Switzerland. This article is an open access article distributed under the terms and conditions of the Creative Commons Attribution (CC BY) license (https:// creativecommons.org/licenses/by/ 4.0/).

1. Introduction

The TV-L1 optical flow estimation algorithm is a method for estimating the optical flow field that combines the noise reduction advantage of L1 regularization and the global-scale smoothing performance of the total variation model [1]. The variation-based optical flow estimation unifies the calculation of optical flow quantities in a standard equation framework and reduces it to minimizing a global energy function, which consists of data terms and smoothness terms. Due to its standardized construction for computing models, it has quickly become the mainstream optical flow algorithm over the past two decades. Ant Lion optimization is a swarm intelligence optimization algorithm. In recent years, research on image processing optimization has focused on leveraging the advantages of Ant Lion swarm intelligence optimization in global optimization range, high convergence accuracy, and minimal parameter requirements [2,3]. Researchers have utilized Ant Lion optimization to improve search accuracy and robustness in various visual tasks. However, its application in optical flow estimation remains unexplored.

While studies [4,5] demonstrate that using the TV-L1 optical flow algorithm yields higher accuracy in weak texture regions compared to other methods, it can also lead to excessive smoothing and blurring of targets as well as contour edges. This cumulative error significantly impacts subsequent recognition results. Reference [6] employed multi-channel sampling interpolation to restore texture in motion-blurred images while reference [7] proposed a pixel-weight-based smoothing operation aimed at reducing edge blur caused by variational light path equations. Based on the work of Demetz O et al., reference [8] proposed the anisotropic smoothness constraint. However, this work presented a significant challenge for researchers. The graph-based method suggested for improving edge blurring can result in excessive segmentation of the foreground and background, leading to a loss in optical flow estimation. Consequently, penalty functions based on flow fields have been proposed to emphasize smooth edges and enhance them in order to mitigate excessive smoothing [9]. In addition, reference [10] employs super-resolution techniques to enhance contour edges and thereby increase the detection of displacement feature points at the edge. Generally speaking, projects aimed at improving Variational Optical Flow data seek to make their algorithms more robust against disturbances such as noise and illumination changes or enhance their ability to handle large motion displacements. The purpose behind enhancing the smoothing parameter is finding an optimal weight that is balanced between the data term and smoothing term. A reasonable choice of this parameter ensures stable results by appropriately considering each constituent term's contribution. Nevertheless, previous works completely overlook local-scale optical flow estimation while few researchers address the issue of multi-scale feature imbalance that hampers motion features' detection. Therefore, this work holds significance in terms of improvement within this field. The contributions made by this work are as follows:

- The TV-L1 optical flow objective function is discretized by the fractional-order differential operator, which makes the model pay extra attention to the local texture-scale optical flow features, increases the participation of effective optical flow, and improves the robustness of the model in multi-scale computation.
- The fractional order is regarded as one of the objects of the optimization problem, and the Ant Lion algorithm is used to realize the local sampling search, and the global smoothness advantage of the TV-L1 optical flow model is retained. The multi-scale objective function is optimized by multi-parameter optimization of the smoothness term weight and fractional order.
- The significant performance of our proposed model is verified on the MPI_Sintel and Middleburry datasets.

2. Materials and Methods

In this work, we propose an optical flow estimation algorithm based on the fractional order and the Ant Lion optimizer. As shown in Figure 1, the proposed optical flow model consists of the following main modules: a fractional-order TV-L1 optical flow estimation part to realize basic learning tasks, and an Ant Lion optimizer part responsible for adaptive parameters.

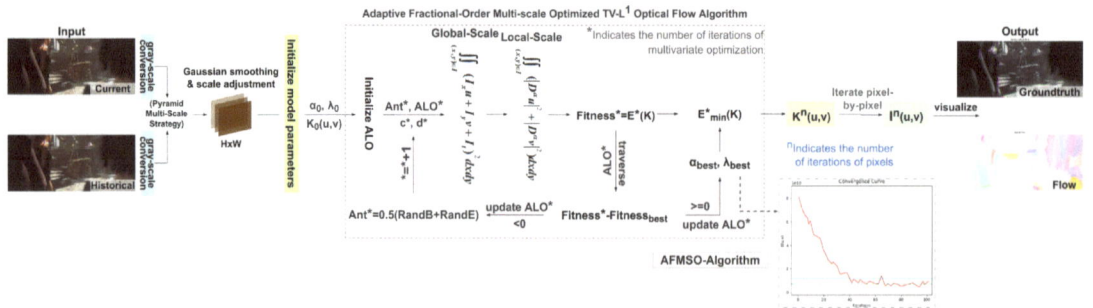

Figure 1. AFMSO-TVL1 optical flow algorithm's overall framework.

In Section 2.1, we first review the construction process of the TV-L1 optical flow model, and we carry out reasonable fractional discretization of it in Section 2.2. Next, we describe the iterative process of the Ant Lion optimization in detail in Section 2.3. Finally, we carry out the experimental analysis in Section 3, and give the discussion and conclusion in Sections 4 and 5.

2.1. Construction Process of TV-L1 Optical Flow Model

The conventional TV-L1 optical flow model is established and solved under the brightness constant constraint, which is as follows (1):

$$I(x,y,t) = I(x+u, y+v, t+1) \tag{1}$$

where $I(x,y,t)$ is the brightness function of the input image pixel, u and v are the components of the optical flow vector $\kappa(u,v)$ in the x and y directions, respectively, and t and $t+1$ represent the change in the number of frames. Based on the assumption of uniform velocity, the L1 regularization Total Variational Optical Flow equation can be obtained as Equation (2):

$$E(\kappa) = \iint ((I_x u + I_y v + I_t)^2 + \lambda(|\nabla u|^2 + |\nabla v|^2)) dx dy \tag{2}$$

where λ represents the weight of the smoothing term and is determined by the characteristics of the input data. Specifically, the smoothing term weight should be inversely proportional to the image quality. In Total Variational Optical Flow estimation tasks, the problem of solving the optical flow equation can be reformulated as an energy functional minimization problem, as represented by Equation (3). By solving the first derivative of the energy function using the Euler–Lagrange equation [11], Equations (3) and (4) can be obtained.

$$I_x^2 u + I_x I_y v = -\lambda^2 \nabla u - I_x I_t \tag{3}$$

$$I_y^2 v + I_x I_y u = -\lambda^2 \nabla v - I_y I_t \tag{4}$$

where $\nabla u = u - \overline{u}$, $\nabla v = v - \overline{v}$, $\overline{u}$, and $\overline{v}$ respectively represent the mean velocity in the x and y directions in the neighborhood; then, the components of the optical flow vector in the x and y directions can be obtained as Equations (5) and (6).

$$u = \overline{u} - \frac{I_x[I_x \overline{u} + I_y \overline{v} + I_t]}{\lambda^2 + I_x^2 + I_y^2} \tag{5}$$

$$v = \overline{v} - \frac{I_y[I_x \overline{u} + I_y \overline{v} + I_t]}{\lambda^2 + I_x^2 + I_y^2} \tag{6}$$

After simplifying the components of the optical flow field, the optical flow field can finally be obtained as Equation (7):

$$\kappa(\overline{u} - \frac{I_x[I_x \overline{u} + I_y \overline{v} + I_t]}{\lambda^2 + I_x^2 + I_y^2}, \overline{v} - \frac{I_y[I_x \overline{u} + I_y \overline{v} + I_t]}{\lambda^2 + I_x^2 + I_y^2}) \tag{7}$$

The iterative process of the optical flow field corresponds to the optimization process of the optical flow energy function. In this work, we employ the Ant Lion optimization algorithm to enhance the fractional-order Variational Optical Flow estimation model. This enhancement manifests in the iterative evolution of the optical flow field, representing the optimization of the energy functional associated with optical flow.

2.2. Subsection

The fractional order is derived on the basis of the integer order. Assuming that the function $f(x)$ is differentiable, the nth derivative of $f(x)$ with respect to x is as follows (8):

$$f^{(n)}(x) = \lim_{h \to 0} \frac{\sum_{i=0}^{n} (-1)^i \binom{n}{i} f(x - ih)}{h^n} \tag{8}$$

where $\binom{n}{i} = \frac{n(n-1)(n-2)\cdots(n-i+1)}{i!}$. According to the above derivation, the discretization expression of the objective function is shown in Equation (9).

$$_a^{GL}D_x^n f(x) = \lim_{h \to 0^+} h^{-n} \sum_{i=0}^{n} (-1)^i \binom{n}{i} f(x - ih) = \frac{1}{\Gamma(-n)} \int_a^x \frac{f(\tau)}{(x-n)^{n+1}} d\tau \qquad (9)$$

As outlined in the introduction, the utilization of fractional-order optimization has been prevalent in various fields such as control systems, image enhancement, and restoration tasks within the realm of image processing. This preference is attributed to the historical correlation advantages and overall smoothing capabilities offered by fractional-order methods. Notably, research has extensively explored the application of fractional-order optimization in image processing tasks [12]. For instance, in the context of image data processing, the discrete brightness function $I(c_x, c_y, t)$ derived from the image pixel (c_x, c_y) serves as a prominent example, with N denoting the total number of image pixels. From the definition of the G-L fractional-order differential derived in the previous subsection [13], it can be seen that its meaning is as follows: n pixels are sampled equidistantly in (a, t) at intervals of h, the object function $f(x)$ is a continuous function, and the domain of independent variable x is $(a, b), n \to \infty, h = (x - a)/n \to 0$. Thus, the α-order differential discretization of the brightness function $I(c_x, c_y, t)$ can be obtained as Equations (10)–(12) [14].

$$D_x^\alpha I(c_x, c_y, t) = \sum_{k=0}^{N} (-1)^k \binom{\alpha}{k} I(c_x - k, c_y, t) = I(c_x, c_y, t) + (-\alpha) I(c_x - 1, c_y, t) \\ + \frac{(-\alpha)(-\alpha+1)}{2} I(c_x - 2, c_y, t) + \cdots \frac{\Gamma(-\alpha+1)}{N!\Gamma(-\alpha+N+1)} I(c_x - N, c_y, t) \qquad (10)$$

$$D_y^\alpha I(c_x, c_y, t) = \sum_{k=0}^{N} (-1)^k \binom{\alpha}{k} I(c_x, c_y - k, t) = I(c_x, c_y, t) + (-\alpha) I(c_x, c_y - 1, t) \\ + \frac{(-\alpha)(-\alpha+1)}{2} I(c_x, c_y - 2, t) + \cdots \frac{\Gamma(-\alpha+1)}{N!\Gamma(-\alpha+N+1)} I(c_x, c_y - N, t) \qquad (11)$$

$$D_t^\alpha I(c_x, c_y, t) = \sum_{k=0}^{N} (-1)^k \binom{\alpha}{k} I(c_x, c_y, t - k) = I(c_x, c_y, t) + (-\alpha) I(c_x, c_y, t - 1) \\ + \frac{(-\alpha)(-\alpha+1)}{2} I(c_x, c_y, t - 2) + \cdots \frac{\Gamma(-\alpha+1)}{N!\Gamma(-\alpha+N+1)} I(c_x, c_y, t - N) \qquad (12)$$

In this section, drawing inspiration from the enhancements brought about by fractional-order methods in variational image denoising models [15], as illustrated in Equation (13), we incorporate fractional-order discretization to establish the L1 smoothness constraint based on fractional-order principles. This approach culminates in the derivation of the fractional TV-L1 optical flow. Equation (14) is finally obtained [16].

$$E_{FoSmooth}(\kappa) = \iint_\Omega (|D^\alpha u|^2 + |D^\alpha v|^2) dx dy \qquad (13)$$

$$E_{FoTVL1}(\kappa) = \iint_\Omega ((I_x u + I_y v + I_t)^2 + \lambda(|D^\alpha u|^2 + |D^\alpha v|^2)) dx dy \qquad (14)$$

The TV-L1 optical flow equation can be derived from the Euler–Lagrange equation as Equation (15):

$$J(u, v) = \int_\Omega ((I_x u + I_y v + I_t)^2 + \lambda(|D_x^\alpha u|^2 + |D_y^\alpha u|^2 + |D_x^\alpha v|^2 + |D_y^\alpha v|^2)) d\Omega \qquad (15)$$

where $|D^\alpha u| = \sqrt{|D_x^\alpha u|^2 + |D_y^\alpha u|^2}$, $|D^\alpha v| = \sqrt{|D_x^\alpha v|^2 + |D_y^\alpha v|^2}$, the optical flow components $u(x, y)$ and $v(x, y)$ have deviations $\eta(x, y)$ and $\xi(x, y)$, respectively, and the deviation parameter is ω; then, the current optical flow component is shown in Equations (16) and (17).

$$u^*(x,y) = u(x,y) + \omega\eta(x,y) \tag{16}$$

$$v^*(x,y) = v(x,y) + \omega\xi(x,y) \tag{17}$$

Therefore, the energy function can be reformulated as Equation (18):

$$J(\omega) = \int_\Omega ((I_x u^* + I_y v^* + I_t + \omega I_x \eta + \omega I_y \xi)^2 + \lambda(|D_x^\alpha u^* + \omega D_x^\alpha \eta|^2 \\ + \left|D_y^\alpha u^* + \omega D_y^\alpha \eta\right|^2 + |D_x^\alpha v^* + \omega D_x^\alpha \xi|^2 + \left|D_y^\alpha v^* + \omega D_y^\alpha \xi\right|^2))d\Omega \tag{18}$$

If $\omega = 0$, and at the same time the first derivative of the independent variable ω in the above equation is taken, then

$$J'(0) = \int_\Omega (\eta(KI_x + \lambda(D_x^{\alpha*}D_x^\alpha u^* + D_y^{\alpha*}D_y^\alpha u^*)) + \xi(KI_y + \lambda(D_x^{\alpha*}D_x^\alpha v^* + D_y^{\alpha*}D_y^\alpha v^*)))d\Omega \tag{19}$$

where $K = I_x u^* + I_y v^* + I_t$; thus, the simplified equation can be obtained as Equation (20):

$$(I_x u^* + I_y v^* + I_t)I_x + \lambda(D_x^{\alpha*}D_x^\alpha u + D_y^{\alpha*}D_y^\alpha u) = 0 \tag{20}$$

$$(I_x u + I_y v + I_t)I_y + \lambda(D_x^{\alpha*}D_x^\alpha v + D_y^{\alpha*}D_y^\alpha v) = 0 \tag{21}$$

After obtaining the simplified optical flow equation, the next step involves continuing the fractional-order differential solution based on the aforementioned approach. This further demonstrates that the functions acquired through the calculations mentioned above are discrete in nature. Assuming the number of pixels $p \times q$, then $c_x = 0, 1, \cdots, p-1$, $c_y = 0, 1, \cdots, q-1$, and $u(x,y) = I(c_x\Delta h, c_y\Delta h)$ in the processing of the optical flow vector; according to the Grünwald–Letnikov definition, the fractional-order differential discretization Equation (22) of optical flow κ can be derived as follows (22):

$$D_x^\alpha \kappa(c_x, c_y) = \sum_{k=0}^{\infty} w_k^{(\alpha)} \kappa(c_x - k, c_y) \tag{22}$$

where $w_0^{(\alpha)} = 1$; $w_k^{(\alpha)} = (1 - \frac{\alpha+1}{k})w_{k-1}^{(\alpha)}$ can be obtained from the discrete fractional-order differential properties as follows (23):

$$D_x^{\alpha*}D_x^\alpha u(c_x, c_y) = \sum_{k=-N}^{0} w_{|k|}^{(\alpha)} \nabla u(c_x - k, c_y) + \sum_{k=1}^{N} w_k^{(\alpha)} \nabla u(c_x - k, c_y) \tag{23}$$

$$D_y^{\alpha*}D_y^\alpha u(c_x, c_y) = \sum_{k=-N}^{0} w_{|k|}^{(\alpha)} \nabla u(c_x, c_y - k) + \sum_{k=1}^{N} w_k^{(\alpha)} \nabla u(c_x, c_y - k) \tag{24}$$

Thus, the following is true:

$$D_x^{\alpha*}D_x^\alpha u(c_x, c_y) + D_y^{\alpha*}D_y^\alpha u(c_x, c_y) \approx \sum_{(\overline{c_x}, \overline{c_y}) \in S(c_x, c_y)}^{0} w_{k_{\overline{c_x}\overline{c_y}}}^{(\alpha)} (u(\overline{c_x}, \overline{c_y}) - u(c_x, c_y)) \tag{25}$$

where $S(c_x, c_y)$ is the neighborhood of the current pixel point (c_x, c_y) participating in the computation, $k_{\overline{c_x}\overline{c_y}} = \max(|\overline{c_x} - c_x|, |\overline{c_y} - c_y|)$. Then, the v component can be obtained as follows:

$$D_x^{\alpha*}D_x^\alpha v(c_x, c_y) + D_y^{\alpha*}D_y^\alpha v(c_x, c_y) \approx \sum_{(\overline{c_x}, \overline{c_y}) \in S(c_x, c_y)}^{0} w_{k_{\overline{c_x}\overline{c_y}}}^{(\alpha)} (v(\overline{c_x}, \overline{c_y}) - v(c_x, c_y)) \tag{26}$$

Finally, the iterative calculation formula of the fractional TV-L1 optical flow equation can be obtained as Equations (27) and (28):

$$I_{xx}(c_x,c_y)u(c_x,c_y) + I_{xy}(c_x,c_y)v(c_x,c_y) + I_{xt}(c_x,c_y) + \lambda \sum_{(\overline{c_x},\overline{c_y})\in S(c_x,c_y)}^{0} w_{k_{\overline{c_x}\overline{c_y}}}^{(\alpha)}(u(\overline{c_x},\overline{c_y}) - u(c_x,c_y)) = 0 \quad (27)$$

$$I_{xy}(c_x,c_y)u(c_x,c_y) + I_{yy}(c_x,c_y)v(c_x,c_y) + I_{yt}(c_x,c_y) + \lambda \sum_{(\overline{c_x},\overline{c_y})\in S(c_x,c_y)}^{0} w_{k_{\overline{c_x}\overline{c_y}}}^{(\alpha)}(v(\overline{c_x},\overline{c_y}) - v(c_x,c_y)) = 0 \quad (28)$$

From the iterative formula, it is evident that when the order is an integer (1 in this case), the proposed fractional-order TV-L1 optical flow model simplifies into the original L1 regularization optical flow. Therefore, the iterative formula exhibits certain versatility in the choice of a termination criterion.

2.3. Iterative Calculation of Fractional TV-L1 Optical Flow Based on Ant Lion Optimization

The Ant Lion algorithm is applied to facilitate the numerical iteration for calculating fractional optical flow. While the Ant Lion algorithm is designed for discrete optimization problems, optical flow estimation involves continuous problem solving. However, since the fractional-order TV-L1 optical flow itself relies on pixel-level discretization, employing the Ant Lion algorithm for minimizing the function for the fractional-order TV-L1 optical flow model is theoretically viable.

In Ant Lion optimization [17], the following entities are defined: the Ant Lion, representing the candidate's better solution, and the Ant, which conducts a random walk around the candidate's better solution to explore the neighborhood for potential improvements. The Ant algorithm operates by updating the current optimal solution based on the fitness value of the solution. This can be seen as the Ant randomly occupying points within the neighborhood of the pixel. By obtaining fitness information from these points, the Ant Lion leverages the information returned by the Ants. The selection probability is determined using the roulette wheel method and weights. As the number of iterations increases, the Ants' territory narrows down, leading to more accurate searches in the Ant Lion neighborhood.

In this chapter, the Ant Lion algorithm is employed to replace the iterative method used in traditional optical flow algorithms for computing TV-L1 optical flow based on fractional-order theory discretization. Prior to this, it is essential to address two key points as the foundation of the entire problem [18]: defining the objective that must be accomplished during the numerical iteration process of fractional-order optical flow calculation and determining the desired outcome.

The numerical iterative process of the optical flow field is aimed at computing the motion of pixels between two images over a specific time interval. By modeling the intensity changes in each pixel in the input image sequence, the fractional TV-L1 algorithm can calculate the displacement vector of each pixel, representing its movement between the two images. During the iteration, the fractional TV-L1 algorithm computes the optical flow field by minimizing the overall error, which comprises three components: the luminance error, the fractional smoothness term that penalizes regions with large fractional gradients [19], and the L1-norm term, which effectively eliminates noise. Through iterative optimization of these three errors, the fractional TV-L1 algorithm accurately calculates the optical flow field. Ultimately, the TV-L1 algorithm with fractional iteration generates the optical flow vector for each individual pixel [20], signifying the displacement of that specific pixel between the two given images. These vectors can be utilized to calculate the motion of the entire image or to implement other computer vision applications such as object tracking, scene reconstruction, and virtual reality.

The parameters utilized in ALO optimization primarily involve the solution vector within the fractional TV-L1 algorithm, along with other parameters that affect the performance of the algorithm, such as the penalty parameter and the number of iterations. ALO adjusts the solution vector by updating the positions of the Ant colony and the Ant

Lion, and applies the updated solution vector to the numerical iterative computation in the fractional TV-L1 algorithm. The movement process of the Ant colony and the Ant Lion is affected by the fractional TV-L1 energy function value and the current solution vector, aiming to search for a solution vector with a lower energy function value. By simulating the behavior of an ant colony searching for food and ant lion predation, ALO optimizes the solution vector by combining the requirements of the fractional TV-L1 energy function. The movement of the Ant colony is affected by the pheromone concentration and the attraction of the solution vector, and the Ant colony will randomly choose the next position. The pheromone concentration in the Ant colony is updated according to the distance between the current optimal solution vector and the current position. The Ant Lion, on the other hand, chooses the predation position according to the energy function value of the current solution vector, and adjusts the solution vector by modeling the behavior of the Ant Lion in expectation of finding a better solution.

Overall, the objective of ALO is to optimize the solution vector within the fractional TV-L1 algorithm by leveraging the movement of the Ant colony and Ant Lion, aiming to enhance the convergence rate and achieve superior optimization outcomes. In summary, in this chapter, the pixel point and optical flow vector are used as the initial position and initial velocity of the Ant and the Ant Lion. Following the Ant Lion's flow involves these steps:

1. The initial values of pixels and optical flow vectors are initialized in the two populations, and the pheromone matrix of the Ants is established to record the pheromone concentration between each pixel. The search space of the Ants is defined as follows (29):

$$Q_z^t = \frac{(Q_z^t - a_z) \times (b_z - c_z^t)}{d_z^t - a_z} + c_z \quad (29)$$

where Q_z^t represents the position of the Ant individual in the z-th dimension in the solution space in the tth iteration, "z-th dimension" in this chapter refers to the coordinate axis space $z \in \{x, y\}$ of the image, a_z and b_z respectively represent the maximum value range of the random walk of the Ant individual in the z-th dimension, and $d_z^t = ALO_r^t + d^t$ and d_z^t respectively represent the minimum and maximum values of the random walk of the Ant individual in the z-th dimension in the t-th iteration.

2. The second step is to randomly initialize the positions of Ants and Ant Lions on the solution space, calculate the fitness value E_{FoTVL1} of each pixel, and take the pixel corresponding to the lowest value minE_{FoTVL1} as the L_B Ant Lion.

During the individual random walk process, the initial configuration of the trap and the selection of the Ant Lion significantly influence the outcome as follows:

$$c_z^t = ALO_r^t + c^t \quad (30)$$

$$d_z^t = ALO_r^t + d^t \quad (31)$$

where r represents the Ant Lion, ALO_r^t represents the position of the t-th Ant Lion in the r-th iteration, c^t represents the vector of all c's in the t-th iteration, and d^t represents the vector of all d's in the t-th iteration. The motion space of the Ant was centered around the position of the Ant Lion, gradually shrinking as the number of iterations increased, ultimately converging towards the optimal solution and yielding the final computation result. The minimization process is detailed in Equations (32) and (33):

$$c^t = \frac{c^t}{10^R \frac{t}{T}} \quad (32)$$

$$d^t = \frac{d^t}{10^R \frac{t}{T}} \tag{33}$$

where T is the parameter of iteration termination times set by initialization, and R is the relevant parameter, whose value is determined by t; when $t > 0.1T$, $R = 2$; when $t > 0.5T$, $R = 3$; when $t > 0.9T$, $R = 5$; and when $t > 0.95T$, $R = 6$.

3   For each Ant, a roulette wheel is used to select an Ant Lion as the target. Concurrently, the Ant will randomly move around the chosen Ant Lion as the best solution, and update its position and speed, calculate the position and speed of the next moment and the pheromone increment of the current position, and update the pheromone, that is, the path that the Ant has passed and the local optimal pixel solution.

4   When the fitness value of an Ant exceeds the optimal value from the previous iteration, the position is then updated to match the position of that particular Ant. In the selection and update of the Ant Lion, assuming that the random walk of L_B goes to $Rand_B^t$ and the random walk of L_E goes to $Rand_E^t$, the movement of the individual Ant around the Ant Lion trap domain is as follows (34):

$$Ant_z^t = \alpha Rand_B^t + \beta Rand_E^t \tag{34}$$

where α and β are weight parameters with sums equal to 1, and empirically default to 0.5 each. The update of the Ant Lion involves assigning the position information of the Ant with the best fitness value in the current iteration to the Ant Lion. Subsequently, for the new iteration, the position of the Ant is randomly generated within the solution space to prevent falling into local optima. This process helps to explore a wider search space and avoid getting trapped in suboptimal solutions.

5   The fifth step is to determine whether the convergence condition is satisfied, output the fractional order α, penalty parameter λ, and solution vector $\kappa = (u, v)$ corresponding to the current optimal solution, and stop the iteration, or otherwise return to step 3.

3. Experiments and Analysis

The algorithm in this chapter is based on the L1 regularization Total Variational Optical Flow model, which is improved by fractional discretization and numerical iteration. Therefore, the convergence performance of the new algorithm and the influence of the fractional-order parameter of the smoothing term on the optical flow tracker, that is, the index performance of the optical flow task, are two important criteria for investigating the algorithm. The following experiments are established on the conventional optical flow datasets known as the MPI_Sintel and MiddleBury sequences, and the optical flow performance indicators AEPE, AAE, PSNR, SSIM, and the visual coding map are selected. The proposed adaptive fractional multi-scale tracker was validated qualitatively and quantitatively in a Pytorch environment on a laptop with Intel(R) i7-12700F CPU, 16 GB RAM, and an NVIDIA GeForce RTX 3060Ti. This was used to evaluate the feasibility and reliability of the algorithm in this chapter.

3.1. Ablation Experiment

In order to verify the improved performance of the TV-L1 optical flow energy function by introducing fractional discretization, the empirical interval was used to sample the order at 0.1 intervals, and the two optical flow error indexes AEPE and AAE, PSNR, and SSIM were calculated. Table 1 shows the setting of the necessary default parameters of AFMSO-TVL1 in the following experiments. The results of the ablation experiments are shown in Tables 2 and 3. PSNR (Peak Signal-to-Noise Ratio) and SSIM (Structural Similarity Index) were selected to measure the stability and accuracy of pixel calculation in the process of optical flow calculation.

Table 1. The setting of fixed parameter values involved in the experimental analysis.

Parameter	Description	Default Value
τ	Time step	0.25
ε	Threshold	0.01
η	Zoom factor	0.5
N_{scales}	Number of scales	5
N_{warps}	Number of warps	5

Table 2. Under the MPI_Sintel random sequence, $\lambda = 79.4$, AEPE and AAE indexes are obtained by the FO-TVL1 optical flow algorithm traversing fractional order alpha in the interval $[0.5, 1]$.

	Parameter Selection	MPI_Sintel Sequence ($\lambda = 79.4$)							
		Ambush2	Ambush6	Shamen2	Bandage1	Market2	Temple3	Sleeping2	Cave4
AEPE	$\alpha = 0.4$	44.30	40.70	1.45	6.35	5.22	25.79	4.86	13.05
	$\alpha = 0.5$	44.26	39.78	1.40	6.30	4.86	16.99	7.15	13.10
	$\alpha = 0.6$	44.17	39.65	1.35	6.29	4.63	12.73	11.76	13.37
	$\alpha = 0.7$	44.29	39.64	1.40	6.27	4.21	11.89	4.75	13.04
	$\alpha = 0.8$	44.78	40.72	1.66	6.45	4.10	14.38	5.22	13.05
	$\alpha = 0.9$	45.90	44.48	2.11	6.66	4.75	19.17	6.12	13.09
	$\alpha = 1.0$	50.91	49.45	2.53	7.00	5.21	32.52	7.86	13.67
AAE	$\alpha = 0.4$	1.54	1.51	1.48	1.29	1.70	1.49	1.66	1.53
	$\alpha = 0.5$	1.61	1.42	1.69	1.42	1.79	1.70	1.68	1.51
	$\alpha = 0.6$	1.66	1.83	1.81	1.40	1.89	1.69	1.69	1.50
	$\alpha = 0.7$	1.57	1.8	1.50	1.33	2.29	1.44	1.77	1.62
	$\alpha = 0.8$	1.54	1.42	1.40	1.29	1.88	1.45	1.88	1.63
	$\alpha = 0.9$	1.61	1.74	1.43	1.41	1.66	1.44	1.84	1.63
	$\alpha = 1.0$	1.60	1.92	1.53	1.30	1.85	1.45	1.67	1.63

Table 3. Under the MiddleBury random sequence, $\lambda = 79.6$, AEPE and AAE indexes are obtained by the FO-TVL1 optical flow algorithm traversing fractional order alpha in the interval $[0.5, 3]$.

	Parameter Selection	MiddleBury Sequence ($\lambda = 79.6$)							
		Teddy	Urban	Woden	Mequn	Army	Scheflera	Grove	Yosemite
AEPE	$\alpha = 0.4$	0.68	0.69	0.15	0.21	0.13	0.26	0.50	0.10
	$\alpha = 0.5$	0.65	0.63	0.13	0.19	0.11	0.25	0.54	0.10
	$\alpha = 0.6$	0.65	0.56	0.15	0.18	0.12	0.25	0.57	0.13
	$\alpha = 0.7$	0.56	0.43	0.11	0.17	0.09	0.29	0.54	0.15
	$\alpha = 0.8$	0.63	0.66	0.15	0.20	0.09	0.27	0.51	0.09
	$\alpha = 0.9$	0.73	0.69	0.14	0.21	0.11	0.37	0.53	0.13
	$\alpha = 1.0$	0.79	0.90	0.20	0.24	0.14	0.42	0.58	0.18
AAE	$\alpha = 0.4$	2.46	2.20	3.00	3.03	3.35	4.72	2.61	2.71
	$\alpha = 0.5$	2.45	2.19	2.99	3.03	3.03	4.69	2.63	2.63
	$\alpha = 0.6$	2.43	2.17	3.01	2.97	2.99	4.65	2.63	2.60
	$\alpha = 0.7$	2.43	2.16	2.94	3.01	2.98	4.65	2.60	2.62
	$\alpha = 0.8$	2.45	2.17	3.01	3.00	3.04	4.62	2.58	2.64
	$\alpha = 0.9$	2.47	2.18	3.03	3.00	3.04	4.61	2.61	2.68
	$\alpha = 1.0$	2.66	2.30	3.33	3.44	3.07	5.11	3.05	3.01

In order to verify and analyze the contribution of the introduction of the fractional differential theory of the Grünwald–Letnikov method discretization to the TVL1 algorithm using the gradient descent method for numerical iteration, two ablation experiments were carried out, as shown in Tables 1–3.

(1) A fixed smoothing term parameter is set and the fractional order acting on the objective function is changed. The fractional order is in the interval $[0.5, 3]$ with a step of 0.1. Tables 2 and 3 intercept the results within the interval $[0.5, 1]$ for presentation.

When the smoothing parameter is 79.4, the evaluation results of the FO-TVL1 optical flow algorithm under the MPI_Sintel sequence significantly reflect that the fractional-order TV-L1 algorithm reduces the values of two error evaluation indexes compared with the integer-order TV-L1 algorithm. In terms of the AEPE index, the optical flow errors of eight test sequences in the optimal fractional order are reduced compared with the integer order: 6.7409, 9.8112, 1.1759, 0.7221, 1.1107, 20.6276, 3.1123, and 0.6305. In the AAE index, the optical flow angle error is decreased compared with the integer order: 0.061, 0.509, 0.1335, 0.0116, 0.1843, 0.0113, 0.0017, and 0.1259. For sequences with different attribute challenges, the fractional-order parameters to obtain the best results are different, which is due to the feature of fractional-order discretization based on image gradient calculation.

According to the principle of AEPE and AAE evaluation of optical flow algorithms [18], when the two error values reach the minimum value in balance, the optical flow algorithm can obtain ideal parameters. In the results shown in Table 2, taking the Shaman2 sequence as an example, even if AEPE and AAE achieve ideal results when alpha = 0.6 and alpha = 0.8, respectively, the optimization parameters cannot be simply determined on this basis. The two evaluation indexes must be considered at the same time; otherwise, it is difficult to avoid the algorithm falling into local optimality during the convergence process. Therefore, it is necessary to further use the ALO method for parameter optimization to obtain the ideal optical flow estimation results.

It can be seen from Table 3 that when the fractional-order value is from 0.7 to 1, the optical flow error increases with a high growth rate, and when the fractional-order value is from 0.4 to 0.7, the optical flow error shows a steady downward trend. The optical flow calculation under fractional-order differentiation is better than that under integer-order differentiation as a whole. And in the interval $\alpha = [0.3, 1]$, the best value is $\alpha = [0.5, 0.8]$; in this time flow error index, AEPE and AAE are overall low, indicating that the model in this interval performs well and has high accuracy under the influence of fractional-order differentials.

From the analysis of the challenging attributes of the test data, in the Army and Grove sequences with rich texture and clear edges, $\alpha = 0.8$ has the best comprehensive performance and the smallest error in time flow estimation. The Ambush2 sequence has rich contours, and the optimal order is $\alpha = 0.8$. The Market1 sequence has rich and complex scenes and targets with dramatic changes in motion state, and the optimal fractional order of data items is $\alpha = 0.9$. For the Mequn and Wall sequences with relatively simple motion and texture, the optimal orders are $\alpha = 0.6$ and $\alpha = 0.5$, respectively, and the comprehensive error result is the lowest. The Cave4 sequence is not rich in texture details, and the optimal order is $\alpha = 0.6$. The Wooden, Ambush2, and Market4 sequence have simple rules and sufficient illumination in the texture, and the optimal fractional order is $\alpha = 0.7$.

In summary, the following hypotheses can be obtained from the above experimental results: The optimal performance interval of the fractional order has a strong correlation with the data themselves, and the higher the complexity of the motion scene, texture, and lighting conditions, the higher the value of the optimal fractional order, and there is a concentrated law. After performing the above experiments on two optical flow datasets with completely different scene elements and target states, it can be obtained that the value of the optimal fractional order is closely related to the complexity of the scene and the target texture conditions of the input image.

(2) To validate the efficacy of the ALO module in optimizing parameters for TV-L1 energy function minimization during numerical iteration, this chapter involves conducting ablation experiments using the gradient descent method (GD, gradient descent), conjugate gradient method (CG, conjugate gradient), and ALO method as ablation components under different methods and compares the optical flow evaluation results. Additionally, convergence experiments are carried out with AFMSO-TVL1's smooth term parameters and fractional-order parameters.

From the analysis of the results in Table 3, when the smoothing parameter is fixed to 23.6, for the integer-order TVL1 algorithm, the AEPE of TVL1(ALO) using the ALO method for numerical iteration is reduced by 2.4614 and 0.4978, respectively, compared with TVL(GD) and TVL1(CG) using the gradient descent method and the conjugate gradient method. PSNR increased by 0.19% and 0.85%, while the SSIM index increased by 0.1017% and slightly decreased by 0.186%. Similarly, with the introduction of the ALO algorithm, the AEPE index of the FO-TVL1 algorithm is reduced by 3.0026 and 1.3616, the SSIM index is increased by about 0.9077% and 0.4059%, and the PSNR value is increased by about 0.0185 and 0.1446.

At the same time, it can be concluded from the statistical analysis results in Table 4 that the introduction of fractional differentiation or ALO alone can only lead to a maximum of two improvements in the evaluation results, which also confirms the necessity of the simultaneous contribution of fractional differentiation and ALO components based on the discretization of the Grünwald–Letnikov method.

Table 4. Based on integer-order TVL1 and fractional-order TVL1 algorithms, different iterative methods were used for ablation experiments.

Evaluation Index	Test Sequence—Cave2					
	TVL1 (GD) $\lambda = 23.6\ \alpha = 0.5$	TV-L1 (CG) $\lambda = 23.6\ \alpha = 0.5$	FO-TVL1 (GD − $\alpha = 0.5$)	FO-TVL1 (CG − $\alpha = 0.5$)	TVL1 (ALO)	FO-TVL1 (ALO)
AEPE	18.40	15.44	17.58	15.33	15.94	14.58
PSNR	12.94	12.93	12.97	12.85	12.94	12.99
SSIM	0.0295	0.0266	0.0249	0.0299	0.0276	0.0340

(3) The next step involves conducting an ablation experiment on the FO-TVL1 optical flow estimation algorithm to analyze the impact of the smoothing term parameter λ. Initially, various disturbance factors such as the number of iterations, population size, and initial parameters were determined (values provided in Table 1). The ablation component refers to the weight λ assigned to the smoothing term. The experimental optimization object is the objective function of optical flow estimation, and the fitness function is set as the error calculation function. The iteration process stops after reaching a predefined number ($N_{Iterations} = 100$). Throughout the experiment, convergence values for three evaluation indexes were recorded. In Table 5, fractional order alpha is set at a fixed value ($\alpha = 0.5$), and statistical analysis was performed on three evaluation results obtained from FO-TVL1 under different smoothing parameters.

Table 5. When the fixed fractional order alpha is 1.5, the optical flow error index, PSNR index, and SSIM index are obtained when the smoothing coefficient value is traversed with the step of 0.1 in the interval [0.5, 70].

Parameter Selection	Evaluation Index	MPI_Sintel Sequence			
		Ambush2	alley_1	Market_5	Cave2
$\lambda = 9.8$	AEPE	80.30	278.86	109.60	71.25
	PSNR	11.25	13.73	10.60	22.91
	SSIM	0.0130	0.0313	0.0062	0.1988
$\lambda = 11.3$	AEPE	80.01	247.92	101.71	65.80
	PSNR	11.24	13.75	10.62	22.87
	SSIM	0.0119	0.0280	0.0032	0.1900
$\lambda = 16.7$	AEPE	78.98	155.15	84.36	50.29
	PSNR	11.24	13.76	10.65	22.88
	SSIM	0.0127	0.0247	0.0113	0.2147
$\lambda = 19.5$	AEPE	78.81	138.70	80.79	44.79
	PSNR	11.24	13.78	10.65	22.89
	SSIM	0.0130	0.0229	0.0114	0.211

Table 5. *Cont.*

Parameter Selection	Evaluation Index	MPI_Sintel Sequence			
		Ambush2	alley_1	Market_5	Cave2
$\lambda = 33.6$	AEPE	77.44	96.22	69.40	26.09
	PSNR	11.24	13.72	10.59	22.69
	SSIM	0.0132	0.0370	0.0010	0.2074
$\lambda = 45.9$	AEPE	77.21	71.92	64.96	18.48
	PSNR	11.24	13.69	10.55	22.61
	SSIM	0.0132	0.0332	0.0017	0.2174
$\lambda = 64.2$	AEPE	76.53	49.79	61.50	14.33
	PSNR	11.24	13.72	10.49	22.53
	SSIM	0.0150	0.0278	0.0081	0.2165

In the experimental analysis results in Table 4, under the influence of different image scene attributes and image quality, the optical flow estimation results under different smoothing parameter values are different, but the data show that when the beta value is within the interval [35, 49], the three evaluation results perform well.

Figure 2 shows a convergence process curve drawn in the control variable experiment.

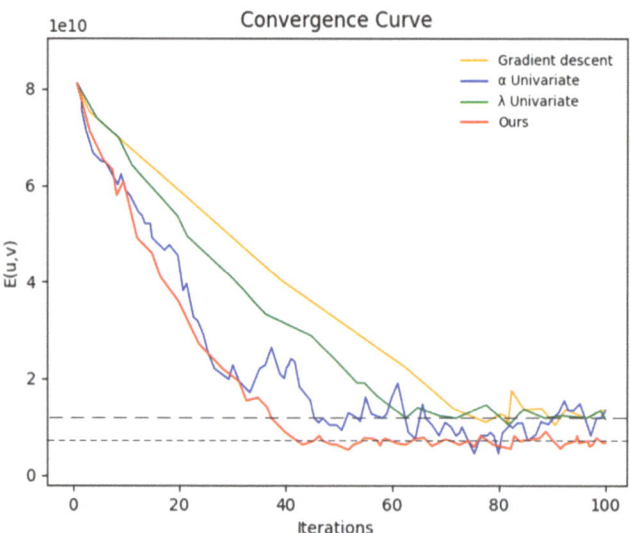

Figure 2. Comparison plots of convergence curves of numerical iterations using gradient descent method, univariate iteration (α or λ), and multivariate iteration (ours) based on the objective function of this paper when the number of iterations is set to 100 for random pixels.

3.2. Comparative Experiments

In order to verify the superiority of the algorithm in this chapter for the dataset performance, this chapter uses AFMSO-TVL1 to compare with TVL1-Flow, HS, FO-FFlow (the Fractional Order Farneback Flow Algorithm), FOTVL1-Flow, FOVOFM, and ADFOVOFM, and obtains the following optical flow performance of random sequences in the MPI_Sintel and Middlebury datasets under different algorithms.

As can be seen from the data in Table 5, the performance of the AFMSO-TVL1 algorithm proposed in this chapter for complex scenes is comprehensive and as fully able as possible to retain and estimate the moving optical flow from the texture information. In the scenes with complex texture structure and lighting conditions, the advantages of the algorithm in this chapter are stronger. The comparative experimental results are shown in Table 6.

Table 6. Optical flow error indexes obtained from parameter optimization experiments performed on MPI_Sintel sequences.

	Comparative Algorithms	MPI_Sintel Sequence			
		Ambush	Wall	Market	Cave
AEPE	TVL1-Flow	44.62	6.51	4.11	18.23
	HS	43.87	8.39	3.64	19.82
	FO-FFlow	38.69	6.45	3.64	18.05
	FOVOFM	44.15	6.55	4.23	17.71
	ADFOVOFM	42.35	6.27	3.58	16.18
	Ours	41.72	6.24	3.96	15.32

In Table 7, the AFMSO-TVL1 algorithm shows better results than the five contrasted algorithms in complex scenes, especially in scenes containing low light and high texture features (such as the Wall and Market sequences). Compared with the fractional-order moving optical flow estimation algorithm FOVOFM, the AEPE errors estimated by AFMSO-TVL1 in the four sequences are reduced by 2.4237, 0.3107, 0.2746, and 0.8499, respectively. In the Ambush sequence, the fractional-order parameter of AFMSO-TVL1 achieving the lowest convergence value is 2.1486, and the optimal value of the smoothing parameter is 67.9466.

Table 7. Optical flow error indexes derived from Middlebury sequence parameter optimization experiments.

	Comparative Algorithms	MiddleBury Sequence			
		Mequn	Yosemite	Grove	Teddy
AEPE	TVL1-Flow	0.24	0.16	0.62	0.41
	HS	0.18	0.19	0.49	0.32
	FO-FFlow	0.21	0.15	0.56	0.47
	FOVOFM	0.22	0.17	0.67	0.51
	ADFOVOFM	0.19	0.13	0.61	0.42
	Ours	0.17	0.11	0.57	0.39

When considering the average endpoint error indexes of the optical flow, PSNR, and SSIM indexes at the same time, the proposed work can provide 6.45% and 4.76% lower error rates than TVL1-Flow and FOVOFM in the Mequn and Yosemite sequences from MiddleBury. The accuracy of the Grove and Teddy sequences is slightly lower than that of FOVOFM and FO-FFlow at 55.67% and 48.89%.

As shown in Figure 3, (a), (b), and (c) respectively represent three random sequences, (1) represents the original input image, and (2), (3), (4), and (5) respectively represent the visual results of optical flow estimation by the four algorithms HS, TVL1-Flow, FOVOFM, and AFMSO-TVL1 for the four random data. It can be seen that in group (1), the estimation of optical flow mainly focuses on the contour with distinct features, and hardly involves the extraction of texture, and even the edge of the moving target cannot be accurately extracted. In (2), the visualization image obtained by the TVL1 group obviously increases the pixel participation in the estimation of complex texture regions, but the performance is not ideal, and excessive smoothing on the global scale causes serious texture blur. According to the statistical analysis conclusion in Section 3.1, this is caused by the difficulty in achieving optimal convergence of parameter values. In (4b), the general outline of human facial features can be displayed more clearly, but because the algorithm is difficult to adapt to adjust the fractional order according to the pixel gradient, the details of the hair and the details of the wall in the background cannot be estimated. It can be seen from (5c) and (5a) that the algorithm in this chapter fairly restores and preserves the complex textures of the front and back scenes, and the details of the necklace, head shadow texture, and background fence are richly estimated. The shell decoration in the background with very poor lighting conditions, the details of the figure's clothing, and the shape of the hand skeleton are all things that the previous works did not pay attention to or show. In this chapter, we make full use of pixel texture information and participate in optical flow calculation. The region selected by the red box in the image can highlight the improvements of our proposed AFMSO-TVL1 algorithm in texture detail and global feature extraction.

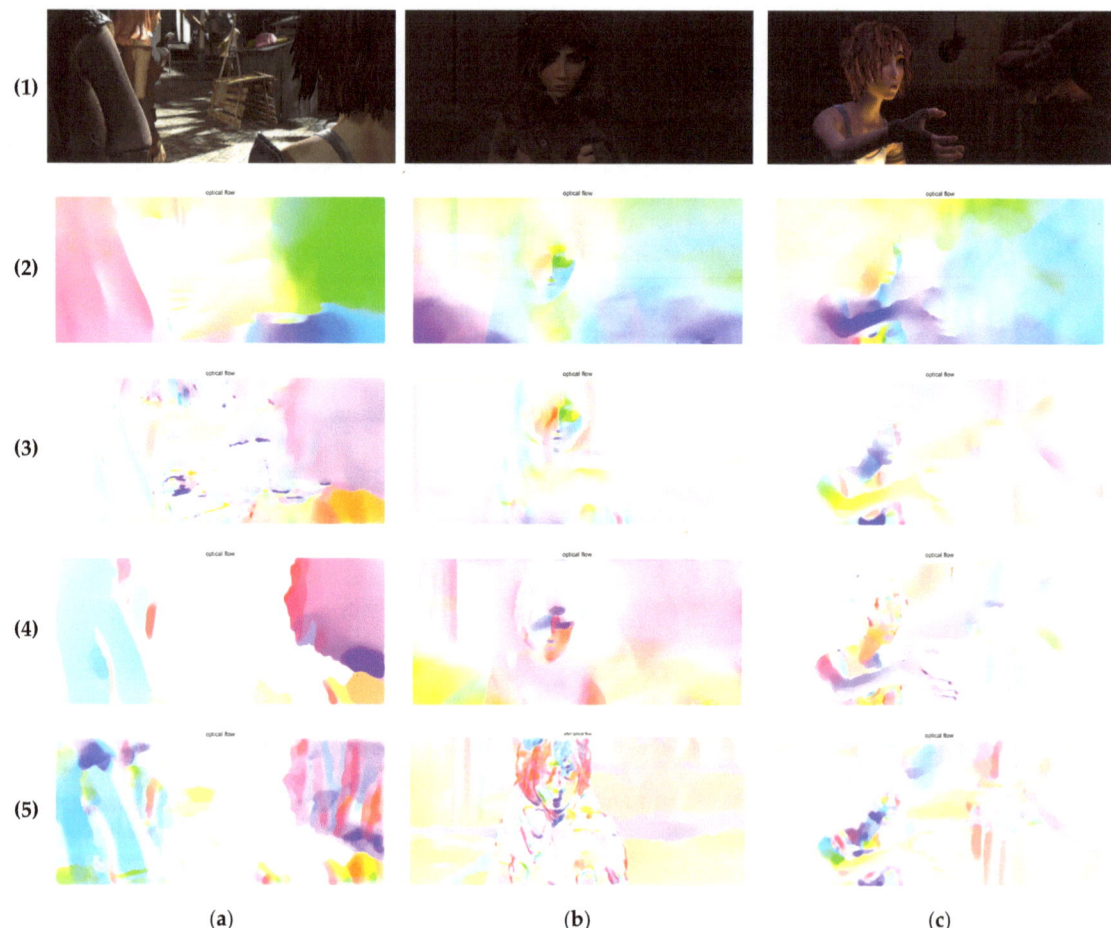

Figure 3. Visualization of optical flow estimation. (**a**) Sequence 1; (**b**) Sequence 2; (**c**) Sequence 3.

4. Discussion

Multiple sets of experimental data in Section 3 show that the robustness and accuracy of our proposed optical flow estimation model for dynamic feature capture and estimation of texture details in complex attribute scenes are clear. Ant Lion optimization plays an important role in the minimization of fractional-order optical flow equations, and it can realize the global optical flow estimation while preserving texture details in contrast to the estimation methods under the fractional-order differential. The proposed optimization method for the Variational Optical Flow model avoids to a large extent the local optimal problem, which is easy to fall into when using the bionic population optimization method to optimize the optical flow estimation model. This method does not affect the advantage of fractional-order differentials in texture feature mining in the optical flow estimation model, whereas our proposed AFMSO-TVL1 deftly improves the accuracy and robustness of the optical flow estimation model at multiple scales through a multi-parameter optimization strategy but inevitably sacrifices the real-time operation of the model. Compared with the previous work, the optical flow estimation time of the AFMSO-TVL1 model is longer, which is also something that future researchers can pay attention to and improve.

In the TVL1 optical flow algorithm, the fractional differential is used to replace the traditional integer differential, and the ALO algorithm is used for numerical iteration of optical flow estimation. It can be seen from the results of experiment 3 in Section 3.1 that such a design can better capture the local correlation and global distribution of pixels in the sequence. The optical flow estimation based on pixel features can generalize input data and avoid optical flow estimation errors caused by sequence scene complexity and unpredictability of target motion. This makes the proposed algorithm more widely applicable to scenarios. At the same time, the enhancement effect of the fractional order on texture and the characteristics of historical memory make the total variable spectral flow estimation result more robust after optimization by the ALO algorithm with global search ability. The test optical flow graphs of the three sequences in Figure 3 can be analyzed as follows: To a certain extent, the proposed algorithm effectively solves the over-smoothing problem of the total variable spectral flow estimation, and the local optimal problem that the fractional-order optical flow algorithm is easy to produce. However, since the fractional order is calculated based on the per-pixel gradient, the calculation amount is much higher than that of the integer order. Moreover, the computational update of pheromones and the search for solution space in the ALO iterative search are complicated. This is despite the fact that ALO has improved speed relative to other swarm intelligence algorithms. However, for some carriers requiring real-time performance, the proposed algorithm has the limitation of slow operation speed.

5. Conclusions

In the previous experiments and theoretical studies, we found that the optical flow estimation algorithm has a relatively large estimation loss for the target texture in some dynamic scenes. In fact, not all objects are suitable for tracking by extracting salient contours. When it is necessary to estimate the moving target from the texture characteristics, the existing optical flow estimation algorithms are difficult to adapt to real-world application. In order to solve the shortcomings of the previous optical flow algorithms in the generalized scenario, we present the work in this paper.

The fractional-order theory of the Grünwald–Letnikov method is introduced into the TV-L1 optical flow algorithm, and a new fractional-order TV-L1 optical flow objective function is reconstructed. The Ant Lion optimization method is used for the first time to optimize the new objective function with multiple parameters, so that two parameters affect the final optical flow estimation error: the fractional order for enhancing the local features and the smoothing term for smoothing the global features are balanced and optimized. It can be found that the introduction of fractional differentiation reduces the convergence value of the objective function of optical flow, and the visualized optical flow results are more fully displayed in the processing of texture region information than in previous work.

In this work, we design a novel AFMSO-TVL1 optical flow algorithm from the perspective of balancing global and texture features. The TV-L1 optical flow equation involves fractional-order discretization, and the Ant Lion algorithm is innovatively introduced to realize the optimization of adaptive multi-scale algorithm parameters. Our algorithm performs well in scenes with complex lighting and rich textures. This improvement adds flexibility to dynamic optical flow estimation in scene fitness, while greatly improving the optical flow extraction rate of multi-scale features. However, the AFMSO-TVL1 optical flow algorithm may lead to increased background interference in some dynamic tracking tasks, such as target localization in SLAM tasks. Since the information is fully utilized in the calculation process, the sampling area should be carefully segmented into special tasks to ensure operation accuracy and efficiency.

At the same time, the random walk of the Ant population around the elite Ant Lion ensures the convergence of the optimization process, and the roulette wheel strategy helps to improve the global search ability of the algorithm to a certain extent. However, the phasic contraction of the Ant Lion's predation radius with the increase in the number of iterations will lead to a gradual decrease in population diversity, and the convergence speed of the algorithm will be reduced under the leadership of a single elite. At the same time, compared with other optimization methods, the computational complexity of ALO optimization is relatively high. Therefore, future research can focus on how to improve the population renewal strategy and reduce the computational complexity of the algorithm.

Author Contributions: Conceptualization, Q.Y. and Y.W.; data curation, Y.W.; formal analysis, L.L.; funding acquisition, Q.Y.; investigation, X.Z.; methodology, Y.W.; project administration, X.Z.; resources, Q.Y.; software, Y.W.; supervision, Q.Y.; validation, Q.Y.; visualization, L.L.; writing—original draft, Y.W.; writing—review and editing, Q.Y. All authors have read and agreed to the published version of the manuscript.

Funding: This research was funded by the National Natural Science Foundation of China (Nos. 52371339 and 12172283), Shenzhen Science and Technology Program under Grant JCYJ20210324122010 027, Research Project of Key Laboratory of Underwater Acoustic Adversarial Technology (Grant No. JCKY2023207CH02), State Key Laboratory of Mechanics and Control of Mechanical Structures (Nanjing University of Aeronautics and astronautics) (Grant MCMS-E-0122G02), Research Project of State Key Laboratory of Mechanical System and Vibration (Grant No. MSV202310), China Postdoctoral Science Foundation under Grant 2020M673484, National Research and Development Project under Grant 2021YFC2803000, the National Natural Science Foundation of China (Grant No. 61971118), in part by the first batch of major science and technology projects in Liaoning Province unveiled and launched under Grant 2021020430-JH/104.

Data Availability Statement: Data are contained within the article.

Conflicts of Interest: The authors declare that they have no known competing financial interests or personal relationships that could have appeared to influence the work reported in this paper.

References

1. Bolme, D.; Beveridge, J.R.; Draper, B.A.; Lui, Y.M. Visual object tracking using adaptive correlation filters. In Proceedings of the 2010 IEEE Computer Society Conference on Computer Vision and Pattern Recognition, San Francisco, CA, USA, 13–18 June 2010; pp. 2544–2550. [CrossRef]
2. Zhang, J.-X.; Yang, T.; Chai, T. Neural Network Control of Underactuated Surface Vehicles With Prescribed Trajectory Tracking Performance. *IEEE Trans. Neural Netw. Learn. Syst.* **2023**, 1–14. [CrossRef] [PubMed]
3. Zhang, J.-X.; Xu, K.-D.; Wang, Q.-G. Prescribed performance tracking control of time-delay nonlinear systems with output constraints. *IEEE/CAA J. Autom. Sin.* **2023**, *67*, 6904–6911.
4. Wang, G.; Luo, C.; Sun, X.; Xiong, Z.; Zeng, W. Tracking by Instance Detection: A Meta-Learning Approach. In Proceedings of the 2020 IEEE/CVF Conference on Computer Vision and Pattern Recognition (CVPR), Seattle, WA, USA, 13–19 June 2020; pp. 6288–6297. [CrossRef]
5. Danelljan, M.; Bhat, G.; Khan, F.S.; Felsberg, M. ECO: Efficient Convolution Operators for Tracking. In Proceedings of the 2017 IEEE Conference on Computer Vision and Pattern Recognition (CVPR), Honolulu, HI, USA, 21–26 July 2017; pp. 6638–6646. [CrossRef]
6. Wei, H.; Qian, Z.; Bo, Q.; Yang, Y. Research on HS Optical Flow Algorithm Based on Motion Estimation Optimization. *J. Comput. Commun.* **2018**, *6*, 171–184. [CrossRef]
7. Brox, T.; Bruhn, A.; Papenberg, N.; Weickert, J. High Accuracy Optical Flow Estimation Based on a Theory for Warping. In Proceedings of the European Conference on Computer Vision, Prague, Czech Republic, 11–14 May 2004; pp. 25–36. [CrossRef]
8. Zhang, X.; Boutat, D.; Liu, D. Applications of Fractional Operator in Image Processing and Stability of Control Systems. *Fractal Fract.* **2023**, *7*, 359. [CrossRef]
9. Zhang, J.-X.; Chai, T. Proportional-integral funnel control of unknown lower-triangular nonlinear systems. *IEEE Trans. Autom. Control* **2023**, *69*, 1921–1927. [CrossRef]
10. Tu, Z.; Li, H.; Xie, W.; Liu, Y.; Zhang, S.; Li, B.; Yuan, J. Optical flow for video super-resolution: A survey. *Artif. Intell. Rev.* **2022**, *55*, 6505–6546. [CrossRef]

11. Zhang, J.-X.; Yang, G.-H. Fault-Tolerant Output-Constrained Control of Unknown Euler–Lagrange Systems with Prescribed Tracking Accuracy. *Automatica* **2020**, *111*, 108606. [CrossRef]
12. Zhang, X.; Lin, C.; Chen, Y.Q.; Boutat, D. A Unified Framework of Stability Theorems for LTI Fractional Order Systems with 0 < alpha < 2. *IEEE Trans. Circuits Syst. II Express Briefs* **2020**, *67*, 3237–3241. [CrossRef]
13. Zhang, X.; Chen, S.; Zhang, J.-X. Adaptive Sliding Mode Consensus Control Based on Neural Network for Singular Fractional Order Multi-Agent Systems. *Appl. Math. Comput.* **2022**, *434*, 127442. [CrossRef]
14. Yang, Q.; Chen, D.; Zhao, T.; Chen, Y. Fractional calculus in image processing: A review. *Fract. Calc. Appl. Anal.* **2016**, *19*, 1222–1249. [CrossRef]
15. Zhang, J.-X.; Wang, Q.-G.; Ding, W. Global Output-Feedback Prescribed Performance Control of Nonlinear Systems with Unknown Virtual Control Coefficients. *IEEE Trans. Autom. Control.* **2022**, *67*, 6904–6911. [CrossRef]
16. Zhang, G.-M.; Hu, Q.; Guo, L.-J. Medical image non-rigid registration based on adaptive fractional order. *Acta Autom. Sin.* **2020**, *46*, 1941–1951. [CrossRef]
17. Wang, Y. *Research and Application of Antlion Optimization Algorithm Based on Distance*; Hunan University: Changsha, China, 2017.
18. Kumar, P.; Kumar, S.; Raman, B. A fractional order variational model for the robust estimation of optical flow from image sequences. *Optik* **2016**, *127*, 8710–8727. [CrossRef]
19. Khan, M.; Kumar, P. A nonlinear modeling of fractional order based variational model in optical flow estimation. *Optik* **2022**, *261*, 169136. [CrossRef]
20. Kumar, P. A duality based approach for fractional order Tv-model in optical flow estimation. In Proceedings of the 2020 5th International Conference on Computing, Communication and Security (ICCCS), Patna, India, 14–16 October 2020; pp. 1–5.

Disclaimer/Publisher's Note: The statements, opinions and data contained in all publications are solely those of the individual author(s) and contributor(s) and not of MDPI and/or the editor(s). MDPI and/or the editor(s) disclaim responsibility for any injury to people or property resulting from any ideas, methods, instructions or products referred to in the content.

Article

Crop and Weed Segmentation and Fractal Dimension Estimation Using Small Training Data in Heterogeneous Data Environment

Rehan Akram , Jin Seong Hong , Seung Gu Kim, Haseeb Sultan, Muhammad Usman , Hafiz Ali Hamza Gondal, Muhammad Hamza Tariq, Nadeem Ullah and Kang Ryoung Park *

Division of Electronics and Electrical Engineering, Dongguk University, 30 Pildong-ro, 1-gil, Jung-gu, Seoul 04620, Republic of Korea; rehanakram@dgu.ac.kr (R.A.); turtle1990@dgu.ac.kr (J.S.H.); ismysg104@dgu.ac.kr (S.G.K.); haseebsltn@dgu.ac.kr (H.S.); musman@dgu.ac.kr (M.U.); alihamza@dgu.ac.kr (H.A.H.G.); mht92@dgu.ac.kr (M.H.T.); nadeempk@dgu.ac.kr (N.U.)
* Correspondence: parkgr@dongguk.edu; Tel.: +82-2-2260-3329

Citation: Akram, R.; Hong, J.S.; Kim, S.G.; Sultan, H.; Usman, M.; Gondal, H.A.H.; Tariq, M.H.; Ullah, N.; Park, K.R. Crop and Weed Segmentation and Fractal Dimension Estimation Using Small Training Data in Heterogeneous Data Environment. *Fractal Fract.* **2024**, *8*, 285. https://doi.org/10.3390/fractalfract8050285

Academic Editors: Dayan Liu, Driss Boutat, Xuefeng Zhang and Jinxi Zhang

Received: 20 March 2024
Revised: 8 May 2024
Accepted: 8 May 2024
Published: 10 May 2024

Copyright: © 2024 by the authors. Licensee MDPI, Basel, Switzerland. This article is an open access article distributed under the terms and conditions of the Creative Commons Attribution (CC BY) license (https://creativecommons.org/licenses/by/4.0/).

Abstract: The segmentation of crops and weeds from camera-captured images is a demanding research area for advancing agricultural and smart farming systems. Previously, the segmentation of crops and weeds was conducted within a homogeneous data environment where training and testing data were from the same database. However, in the real-world application of advancing agricultural and smart farming systems, it is often the case of a heterogeneous data environment where a system trained with one database should be used for testing with a different database without additional training. This study pioneers the use of heterogeneous data for crop and weed segmentation, addressing the issue of degraded accuracy. Through adjusting the mean and standard deviation, we minimize the variability in pixel value and contrast, enhancing segmentation robustness. Unlike previous methods relying on extensive training data, our approach achieves real-world applicability with just one training sample for deep learning-based semantic segmentation. Moreover, we seamlessly integrated a method for estimating fractal dimensions into our system, incorporating it as an end-to-end task to provide important information on the distributional characteristics of crops and weeds. We evaluated our framework using the BoniRob dataset and the CWFID. When trained with the BoniRob dataset and tested with the CWFID, we obtained a mean intersection of union (mIoU) of 62% and an F1-score of 75.2%. Furthermore, when trained with the CWFID and tested with the BoniRob dataset, we obtained an mIoU of 63.7% and an F1-score of 74.3%. We confirmed that these values are higher than those obtained by state-of-the-art methods.

Keywords: weed and crop semantic segmentation; deep learning; small training data; heterogeneous data; fractal dimension estimation

1. Introduction

Expanding crop efficiency is becoming increasingly important as food security concerns are increasing globally. However, it faces many challenges, such as a lack of manpower, uncertain environmental conditions, soil factors, and scarcity of water. To achieve high yields and address such problems, previous research used plant phenotyping methods and monitoring systems to strengthen crop productivity in precision agriculture [1,2]. Over time, traditional farming has shifted toward modern automated farming to increase yields and minimize labor costs, individual effort, and time.

Image processing has been widely adopted in various fields [3–11]. In addition, recently, deep learning methods have offered various solutions, and the use of computer vision has grown significantly in various applications including building monitoring, image enhancement, medical image processing, biomedical engineering, and underwater computer vision, where some research has adopted fractal-related perspectives, also in [9–16].

Although the studies adopt similar concepts of fractal dimension (FD) estimations [12,13,15], their applications are different in terms of building monitoring and medical image processing. Semantic segmentation also exhibits a fundamental role in the accurate recognition of crops and weeds [17,18]. Two mainstream methods exist for crop and weed detection. The first is box-based detection [19,20]; however, it has the drawback of overlooking specific regions in weeds and crops. The second type is semantic segmentation or pixel-based detection [21–23], which detects precise regions of weeds or crops at the pixel level. Therefore, correctly identifying the crop and weed segments is essential. Crop and weed segments typically have irregular shapes, and training with these irregularly shaped segments comes with an imbalance in the data. The irregular shapes of "sugar beets" (BoniRob) [24] and crop/weed field image datasets (CWFIDs) [25] are shown in Figure 1. A considerable amount of data is usually required during training, particularly in segmentation cases. To acquire more data, it may be necessary for experts to create a large number of annotations, which would require considerable time and effort. In some scenarios, if a considerable amount of training data are unavailable, the testing performance decreases. To avoid such a drop in performance owing to insufficient training data, a method using small amounts of training data was proposed by Nguyen et al. [26], which also achieved good performance. Homogenous data usually show satisfactory results; however, when applied to heterogeneous environments, where the testing and training datasets are completely different, the overall results decrease significantly. Abdalla et al. [27] showed that the efficacy of these algorithms is compromised in complex environments due to their heavy reliance on various factors, including lighting conditions and weed density, for feature extraction. Thus, it is essential to propose an effective and reliable framework that segments crops and weeds accurately, even in complex heterogeneous environments.

Figure 1. Sample images (**left**) and ground-truth masks (**right**) for crops (white pixels) and weeds (gray pixels) in BoniRob dataset (**upper**) and CWFID (**lower**).

To solve these issues, we propose an approach for weed and crop segmentation and fractal dimension estimation using a small amount of training data in a heterogeneous data environment. The contributions of this study include the following:

- This is the first study that considers the segmentation of crops and weeds within a heterogeneous environmental setup utilizing one training data sample. We rigorously investigate the factors that cause performance degradation in heterogeneous datasets, including variations in illumination and contrast. To address this problem, we propose a method that applies the Reinhard (RH) transformation, leveraging the mean and standard deviation (std) adjustments.

- We address the issue of high data availability for real-world applications. For this purpose, we improved the performance using a small amount of training data. The small amount of additional training data significantly improves the segmentation performance while requiring fewer computational resources and less training time.
- We introduce the FD estimation approach in our framework, which is seamlessly combined as an end-to-end task to provide important information on the distributional features of crops and weeds.
- It is noteworthy that our proposed framework [28] is publicly accessible for a fair comparison with other studies.

The structure of the remaining sections of this study is as follows: Multiple related studies are described in Section 2. In Section 3, we outline the proposed approach. Section 4 describes a comparison between the proposed framework and the state-of-the-art (SOTA) methods in terms of their performance. Section 5 presents a discussion, while Section 6 presents the conclusion and outlines future work.

2. Related Work

We classified previous studies on crop and weed segmentation into homogenous data-based methods and heterogeneous data-based methods as follows.

2.1. Homogenous Data-Based Methods

Homogeneous data-based methods mostly exhibit high accuracy because their training and testing data distributions originate from the same dataset. Many related studies using homogenous data have been conducted to date, and they have been highly effective in multiple domains, not only in agriculture. In general, the term "a large amount of training data" is used extensively in the literature. Typically, a considerable amount of training data is needed to efficiently train the model and achieve higher accuracy. Many prior studies have been conducted using a large amount of training data. Furthermore, learning-based methods are grouped into two main groups: the handcrafted feature-based and the deep learning-based methods.

2.1.1. Handcrafted Feature-Based Methods

Before the significant advancements in deep learning, features were often manually engineered, referred to as manual or handcrafted features, as they were developed progressively. In [29], a random forest classifier (RFC) is used to handle the overlap of together-grown different crops and weed plants. A Markov random field was also applied to smooth the sparse pixels. Another study by Lottes et al. [30] used the same RFC for vegetation detection using local and object-based features. Lottes et al. [31] used unmanned aerial vehicles (UAVs) and various robots to monitor weeds and crops. They implemented and evaluated plant-tailored feature extraction. Many systems rely on these techniques, primarily because they require fewer computations and have shorter execution times.

2.1.2. Deep Feature-Based Methods

Deep learning techniques utilizing deep features are advancing to automate precision agriculture [32], particularly by making intelligent decisions in the semantic segmentation of crops and weeds. Pixelwise classification networks play a crucial role in detecting objects and properly delimiting their boundaries so that automated robotic weeders can perform precision spraying and weeding operations. Commonly used base networks in semantic segmentation studies include DeepLab [33], fully convolutional networks [34], U-Net [35], and SegNet [36]. These networks, along with certain blocks proposed in various studies, employ an encoder–decoder architecture for crop and weed segmentation. The encoder architecture transforms input data into a compressed representation capturing their key features, while the decoder module upsamples and restores the spatial features of areas where the edges of objects are absent. The base U-Net encoder–decoder network has undergone modifications into multiple architectures, as seen in the work by

Zou et al. [37]. They achieved this by reducing feature extraction in the encoder and adding a skip connection at the output layer to recover object details, thereby enhancing model accuracy. They conducted two-stage training to accurately segment weeds and showcased greater applicability in the field. However, the robustness of these models has not been tested using heterogeneous datasets.

Milioto et al. [38] designed an end-to-end model identical to the previously used encoder–decoder format. This network is narrow and fast; however, the dataset used here covers a very small portion of crops and weeds. The model was developed by modifying Enet [39] and SegNet [36] through the replacement of convolutional (Conv) layers with residual blocks. Fathipoor et al. [40], based on an encoder–decoder in U-Net and U-Net++ [41] architectures, demonstrated promising overall results for weed segmentation in the early stages. In a prior study [18], a two-stage approach named MTS-CNN was proposed to segment crops and weeds utilizing U-Net with a visual geometry group (VGG)-16 [42]. The model separates object segmentation from crop and weed segmentation in two stages to enhance accuracy, also creating a loss function to address the class imbalance problem of the crop and weed dataset. However, errors made by the first model can impact overall model performance, and training takes a considerable amount of time. Another study [43] relied on images captured by different cameras mounted on an unmanned aerial vehicle (UAV) for crop and weed segmentation. The authors used a modified VGG-16 encoder and modified U-Net decoder architecture, concatenating images of different formats into channel directions to improve segmentation accuracy. Alongside recent developments in deep convolutional neural networks (CNNs), several new networks have been designed to enhance crop and weed segmentation. Dilated convolution [44] and atrous convolution [33] were integrated into the network alongside a universal function approximation block (UFAB) [45] to improve segmentation. However, these networks require inputs of near-infrared (NIR) light and red, green, and blue (RGB) channels that are unavailable in real time. Wang et al. [46] devised a dual attention network (DA-Net) bridging the gap between low- and high-level featured data using branch and spatial attention. The employed self-attention is computationally demanding due to the size of the spatial features. Siddiqui et al. [47] explored data augmentation (DA) using CNN methods to distinguish weeds from crops. In another study, Khan et al. [48] introduced a new cascaded encoder–decoder network (CED-Net) modifying the base network U-Net into four stages to distinguish between weeds and crops. The inclusion of stages in the network enhanced crop and weed segmentation accuracy. From the above discussion, we can conclude that these deep learning-based methods offer greater accuracy than handcrafted feature-based methods. However, all prior studies were conducted in a homogeneous data environment, where training and testing were performed using the same dataset.

2.2. Heterogeneous Data-Based Methods

Previous studies on crop and weed segmentation have not explored the use of heterogeneous data, where training and testing are conducted using different datasets. However, a model trained with the first dataset is often applied to the second dataset without intensive training using the second dataset. Additionally, sufficient training data cannot often be acquired for real-world applications. However, no previous studies have considered insufficient training data for crop or weed segmentation. Therefore, we propose a framework for weed and crop segmentation and FD estimation utilizing limited training data in a heterogeneous data environment. The strengths and weaknesses of the proposed framework for crop and weed segmentation relative to other techniques are listed in Table 1.

Table 1. Comparisons of proposed method with previous ones on crop and weed segmentation.

Data	Type	Method	Strength/Motivation	Weakness
Homogeneous data-based	Handcrafted feature-based	RFC [29]	Handling overlapping of crops and weeds	Overlapping of multiple plants with the same class cannot be split
		RFC + vegetation detection [30]	Detection of local and object-based features	Smoothing as post-processing on only local features
		Plant-tailored feature extraction [31]	UAV intra-row-space-based weed detection in challenging conditions	The number of weeds is much smaller in the datasets used
	Deep feature-based	MTS-CNN [18]	Separate object segmentation to avoid background-biased learning	Dependency of first stage network on second stage network
		Modified U-Net [37]	Effective two-stage training method with large applicability	Only weed-targeted segmentation
		SegNet + Enet [38]	Fast and more accurate pixelwise predictions	Images contain very small portions of crops and weeds
		U-Net and U-Net++ [40]	Detecting weeds in the early stages of growth	Uses a very small dataset and has no suitable real-time application
		Modified U-Net + modified VGG-16 [43]	Effective result for distribution estimation problem with graphics processing unit (GPU)-based embedded board	Not focusing on the exact location of weeds in the images
		UFAB [45]	Reducing redundancy by strengthening the model diversity	Unavailability of RGB and NIR input
		DA-Net [46]	Expanding receptive field without affecting the computational cost	Hard and time-consuming mechanism to parallelize the system using attention modules
		4-layered CNN + data augmentation [47]	Good for the early detection of weeds, improving production, and is easy to deploy because of the cheap cost	Minimizing accuracy if weeds are not detected at the early stages
		CED-Net [48]	Using a light model and achieving efficient results	Error at any level among the four levels affects the overall performance
Heterogeneous data-based		Proposed framework (proposed)	Use of small training images in a heterogeneous environment	Preprocessing steps are included

3. Proposed Method

3.1. Overview of Proposed Method

Figure 2 depicts an overview of the flow of our framework. During training, we train the conventional semantic segmentation model with Dataset A. Next, we preprocess the images of Dataset B using the RH transformation, which is based on the mean and std of Datasets A and B. This transformation adjusts the visual properties of the images, such as intensity, illumination, and contrast, to make them similar to the reference image in a heterogeneous environment. Then, we select one training data from the preprocessed Dataset B and perform DA on it to augment the training data. Afterward, we perform fine-tuning and train the model from scratch with Dataset A using the augmented data, and we perform the semantic segmentation of weeds and crops utilizing the testing data from Dataset B.

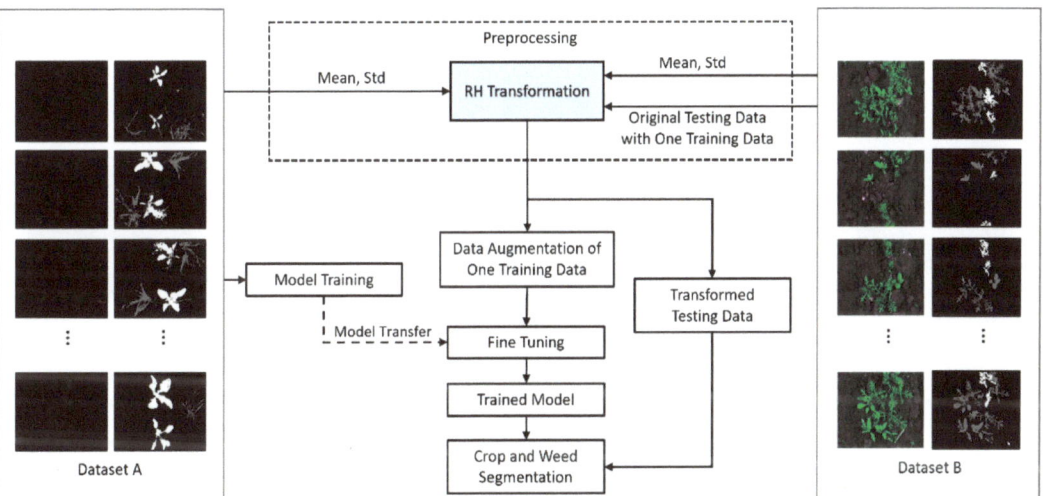

Figure 2. Overview of the proposed framework flow.

3.2. Preprocessing

3.2.1. RH Transformation

Many factors such as variations in intensity, illumination, and contrast cause performance degradation, particularly in heterogeneous environments. Transferring colors from one image (reference) to another (target) is a significant problem, particularly when the color information in the reference image does not match the newly generated image, causing quality and performance degradation. To address performance degradation using heterogeneous data, we adopted the RH transformation [49] with average mean and std adjustments to enhance the visual attributes of the images. Many prior transformation methods and color spaces enhance the visual characteristics of an image. In the l$\alpha\beta$ color space (LCS) [50], "l" indicates a brightness channel that captures the brightness independently of color attributes, the "α" channel encapsulates yellow and blue hues, and the "β" channel encloses the interplay between red and green shades. In the RH transformation, the LCS is used. The LCS minimizes the relative significance of each weight, with a matrix proposed for converting vectors from RGB to LCS. The RH transformation changes the mean and std values of the color channels based on the LCS that consistently represents the pixel colors in an image. As shown in Equation (1), it uses the f mapping function with δ parameters to transform the $dataB$ into preprocessed $dataB'$.

$$dataB' = f(dataB, \delta) \qquad (1)$$

For the transformation, the RGB images are manipulated in the LCS and then transformed into the long, medium, short (LMS) cone space, and the logarithmic of the LMS space is obtained to reduce skewness [49]. The mean and std for all the axes in the LCS are separately calculated to make images more synthetic. Moreover, the color space is normalized by subtracting the mean of the data points from the original data point value, as follows:

$$\hat{l} = l - l_m, \tag{2}$$

$$\hat{\alpha} = \alpha - \alpha_m, \tag{3}$$

$$\hat{\beta} = \beta - \beta_m \tag{4}$$

where l_m, α_m, β_m denote the average mean data point values of the l, α, and β data points, and $\hat{l}$, $\hat{\alpha}$, and $\hat{\beta}$ show the normalized space data points. Upon normalizing the space, data points are scaled by std σ_j^l, σ_j^α, σ_j^β for the reference images and σ_i^l, σ_i^α, σ_i^β for the target images. Finally, l°, α°, β° are the scaled points for the transformed images, as follows:

$$l^\circ = \frac{\sigma_i^l}{\sigma_j^l} \hat{l}, \tag{5}$$

$$\alpha^\circ = \frac{\sigma_i^\alpha}{\sigma_j^\alpha} \hat{\alpha}, \tag{6}$$

$$\beta^\circ = \frac{\sigma_i^\beta}{\sigma_j^\beta} \hat{\beta} \tag{7}$$

The pseudo-code of the RH transformation is provided in Algorithm 1.

Algorithm 1: RH transformation with pseudo-code

Input: {dataB} ^t_n; The total of t data samples, dataB: input dataset B images
dataA$_m$: training data from dataset A.
Output: (dataB′) the preprocessed sample
1: Compute the std of the dataset B (input images) by
   dataB _std = std (dataB (:, :))
2: Compute the mean of the dataB
   dataB _mean = mean (dataB (:, :))
3: Compute the average std of the training data from dataset A using
   dataA_std = avg (std (dataA$_m$ (:, :))
4: Compute the average mean of the training data from dataset A using
   dataA_mean = avg (mean (dataA$_m$ (:, :))
5: Apply the RH transformation
   for m = 1: x
     for n = 1: y
       dataB′ (m, n) = [(dataB (m, n) − dataB_mean) ×
       (dataA_std/dataB_std)] + dataA_mean
     end
   end
   return dataB′

Histograms of the RGB color channel distribution for the reference, target, and newly transformed images are shown in Figure 3a–c, respectively. The reference image is from Dataset A, the target image is from Dataset B, and the RH-transformed image is a new image generated by RH transformation. In Figure 3b, the histograms show only two channels; apparently, the red and blue channels overlap because they are replicas of each other [25]. The histogram shows the pixel values on the x-axis and the probability distribution of the pixels on the y-axis. As shown in Figure 3c, the histogram of the target image is more akin to that of the reference image in Figure 3a by RH transformation than to that of the target image in Figure 3b before RH transformation.

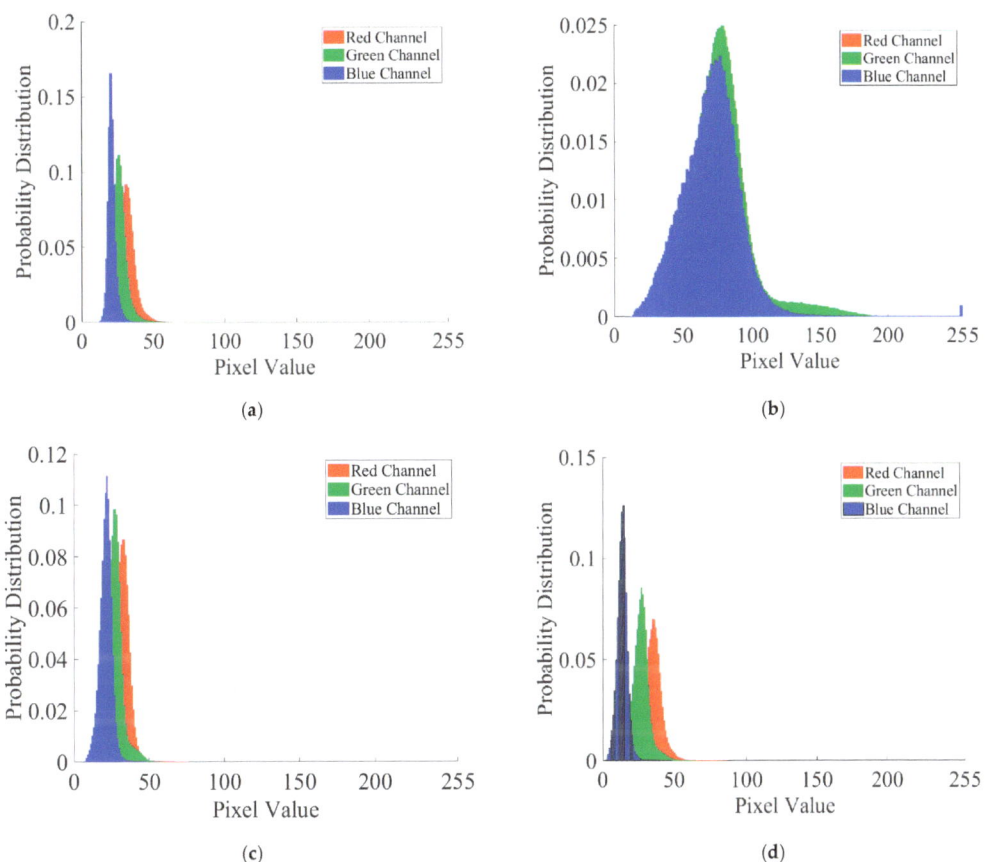

Figure 3. Sample histograms of (**a**) referenced image, (**b**) targeted image, (**c**) RH-transformed image, and (**d**) RH-transformed image with additional adjustment.

3.2.2. RH Transformation with Additional Adjustments

However, despite the RH transformation, there is still a difference in the relative probability distribution of each channel in Figure 3a,c. Therefore, we introduce an additional adjustment to obtain the relative probability distribution of each channel of the RH-transformed image that is more similar to that of the reference image as follows:

$$\min\nolimits_{\text{select}p_{iopt}} \left(R_t - (R_r - p_i)\right)^2, \tag{8}$$

$$\min\nolimits_{\text{select}q_{iopt}} \left(G_t - (G_r - q_i)\right)^2, \tag{9}$$

$$\min\nolimits_{\text{select}r_{iopt}} \left(B_t - (B_r - r_i)\right)^2 \tag{10}$$

where R_t, G_t, and B_t represent the pixels in the target image, and R_r, G_r, and B_r represent the pixels in the reference image. Moreover, p_{iopt}, q_{iopt}, and r_{iopt} are the optimal values generated by varying the p_i, q_i, and r_i values, respectively, to minimize the distance between the corresponding red, green, and blue channel distributions. To obtain this channel distribution, the following additional adjustments were made:

$$l_{adj} = l_m - p_{iopt}, \tag{11}$$

$$\alpha_{adj} = \alpha_m - q_{iopt}, \tag{12}$$

$$\beta_{adj} = \beta_m - r_{iopt} \tag{13}$$

where l_m, α_m, and β_m represent the average mean data point values, and p_{iopt}, q_{iopt}, and r_{iopt} represent the values that make the channel distribution look more similar among the reference and transformed images. These p_{iopt}, q_{iopt}, r_{iopt} values are subtracted from the average mean values to adjust the l_{adj}, α_{adj}, and β_{adj} data points. Furthermore, the transformation with additional adjustments is as follows:

$$l'' = l - l_{adj}, \tag{14}$$

$$\alpha'' = \alpha - \alpha_{adj}, \tag{15}$$

$$\beta'' = \beta - \beta_{adj} \tag{16}$$

where l_{adj}, α_{adj}, and β_{adj} are the different data point values for additional adjustments, which are experimentally chosen to make the channel distribution similar to the reference image. These values are subtracted from the l, α, β data points, and the result is l'', α'', and β'', which shows the normalized space data points. The newly generated histograms are visually presented in Figure 3d. As demonstrated in Figure 3d, the channel distributions resulting from the RH transformation with additional adjustments closely resemble those of the reference image in Figure 3a, in contrast to the RH without additional adjustment in Figure 3c.

Figure 4 illustrates the sample images of the referenced image, targeted image, RH-transformed image, and RH-transformed image with additional adjustments from the BoniRob dataset and CWFID.

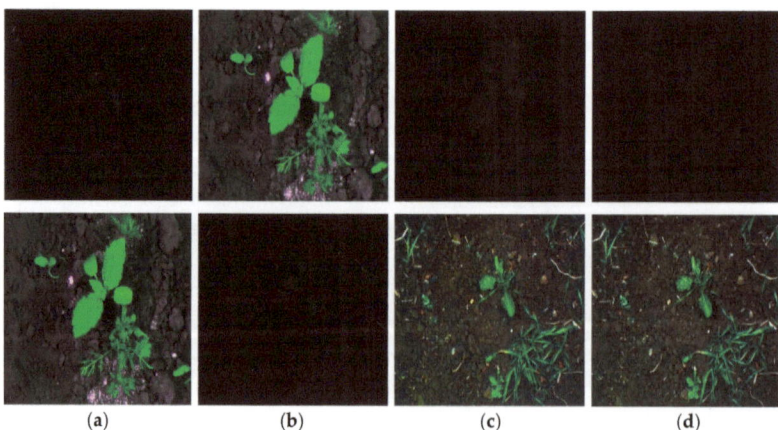

Figure 4. Sample images of the BoniRob dataset (**upper** images) and CWFID (**lower** images). (**a**) Referenced image, (**b**) targeted image, (**c**) RH-transformed image, and (**d**) RH-transformed image with additional adjustments.

3.3. Data Augmentation of One Training Data

Data augmentation (DA) involves employing various transformations on existing data to expand and diversify a training dataset artificially. In image datasets, DA can involve procedures such as in-plane rotation, flipping, zooming, and modifying the contrast and brightness levels of the images within the training dataset [51]. The purpose behind DA is to enhance the capacity of a model to generalize and perform effectively on novel and unseen data by exposing it to a broader spectrum of variations that may be encountered in real-world contexts. We randomly selected a single image from the training data and augmented it for training. By adding augmentation to this small training dataset, we improved the segmentation performance while reducing the training time. A simple 180-degree in-plane rotation was used for DA, as depicted in Figure 5.

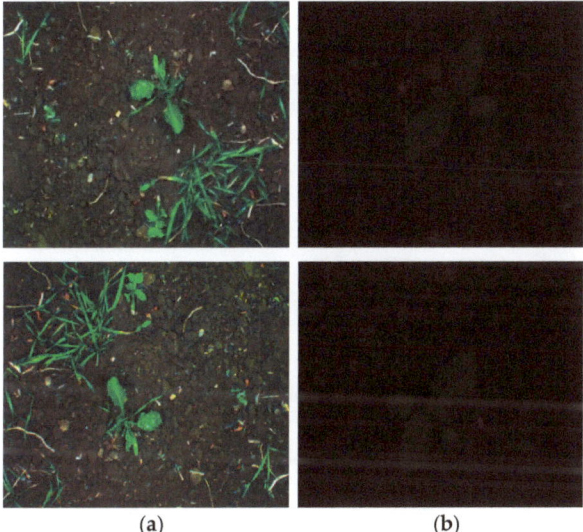

Figure 5. Sample training image (**upper**) and augmented image (**lower**) for training. (**a**) BoniRob dataset (**left** images) and (**b**) CWFID (**right** images).

3.4. Semantic Segmentation Networks

For the semantic segmentation of weeds and crops, the following conventional semantic segmentation models were adopted:

3.4.1. U-Net

U-Net [35] features a fully CNN with a U-shaped encoder–decoder framework. The input image of the encoder and the output image of the decoder have the same image size. The decoder is more or less symmetric than the encoder, and the encoder has a large feature channel for propagating contextual information to the high-resolution layer. The architecture includes two 3×3 Conv layers, each accompanied by a max-pooling (MP) layer of 2×2 kernel size, with stride 2, and a ReLU [52]. In the decoder, the tensor map was upsampled using a 2×2 up-convolution and concatenated with the encoder features. A final layer of 1×1 convolution was incorporated into the U-Net network. Figure 6 illustrates its architecture. Furthermore, the first stages of the encoder (including and before the first max-pooling layer as $Encoder_1$) and decoder (first up Conv layer with subsequent layers having the same spatial dimensions as $Decoder_1$) of the U-Net shown in Figure 6 are mathematically represented as follows:

$$Encoder_1 = P_1(C_1) \; where \; \begin{cases} C_1 = Conv(Conv(X, W_1)), \\ P_1 = Maxpool(C_1) \end{cases} \quad (17)$$

$$Decoder_1 = CR_1(C_{concat1}(C_{crop1}(U_1))), \qquad (18)$$

$$where \begin{cases} U_1 = Upconv(B, W_{up1}), \\ C_{crop1} = Crop(R, size(U_1)), \\ C_{concat1} = Concatenation(U_1, C_{crop1}), \\ CR_1 = Conv(Conv(C_{concat1}, W_{conv})) \end{cases}$$

In $Encoder_1$, X represents the input feature, and W_1 indicates the weight tensor for convolution operations. In every convolution operation for both the encoder and decoder, ReLU activation functions and batch normalization are applied. In $Decoder_1$, B represents the tensor of the previous layer, and W_{up1} in $Upconv(B, W_{up1})$ shows the weight tensor with an up-convolution operation. R in $Crop(R, size(U_1))$ indicates the input image size after convolutions from the encoder side with the same size as U_1, which is a result of the previous up-convolution. $C_{concat1}$ represents the concatenation of U_1 and C_{crop1} which are the final calculations for the previous layers. W_{Conv} represents weight tensors with convolution operations. Finally, after the convolution in the decoder, it is fed to CR_1, and the subsequent levels of decoder operations continue in a similar manner.

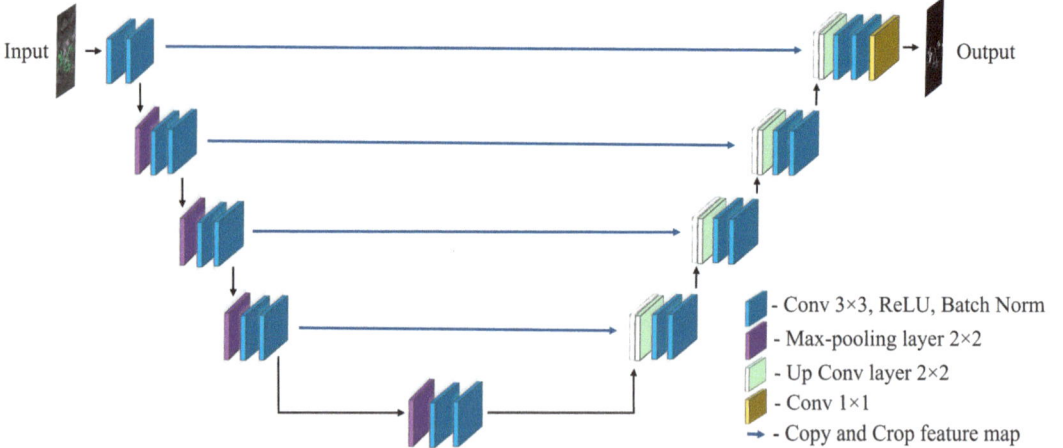

Figure 6. U-Net architecture.

3.4.2. Modified U-Net

Modified U-Net [37] is an updated variant of the U-Net, featuring an encoder–decoder framework. Like U-Net, the modified version includes two 3 × 3 Conv layers, each accompanied by an MP layer of 2 × 2 kernel size of stride 2, and an activation function named the exponential linear unit [53]. In the decoder, the tensor map is upsampled using a 2 × 2 up-convolution and concatenated with the encoder features. To overcome the overfitting issue, a dropout layer was placed between the Conv layers. A last layer with 1 × 1 Conv is used in the modified U-Net architecture. Moreover, the stochastic gradient descent optimization is replaced with the Adadelta algorithm. Figure 7 shows the structure of the modified U-Net. Furthermore, the first stages of the encoder (before and including the first pooling layer as $Encoder_1$) and decoder (first up Conv layer with the subsequent layer including convolutions as $Decoder_1$) of Figure 7 are mathematically expressed as follows:

$$Encoder_1 = P_1(C_1(D_1(B_1))) \; where \; \begin{cases} B_1 = Conv(X, W_{b1}), \\ D_1 = Dropout(B_1, dropout_{value}), \\ C_1 = Conv(D_1, W_{c1}), \\ P_1 = Maxpool(C_1) \end{cases} \quad (19)$$

$$Decoder_1 = CR_1(R_1(CB_1(U_1(CC_1)))), \quad (20)$$

$$where \; \begin{cases} CC_1 = Concatenate(B, D_n), \\ U_1 = Upconv(CC_1, W_{u1}), \\ CB_1 = Conv(U_1, W_{cb1}), \\ R_1 = Dropout(CB_1, dropout_{value}), \\ CR_1 = Conv(R_1, W_{cr1}) \end{cases}$$

In $Encoder_1$, X represents the input image, and W_{b1} represents the weight tensor for convolution operations. Following every Conv operation in both the encoder and decoder batch normalization, ELU is applied. In $ELU(Conv(D_1, W_{c1}))$, D_1 represents the dropout layer, which is further processed by convolution and ELU resulting in C_1. C_1 is downsampled using the MP layer. In $Decoder_1$, B represents the tensor map of the prior layer, and D_n represents the dropout feature map from the same level connection. W_{u1} in $Upconv(CC_1, W_{u1})$ represents the weight tensor with an upconvolution operation. Subsequently, a convolution is applied to the W_{cb1} weight tensor. R_1 has a dropout value on which convolution is applied with the W_{cr1} weight tensor. After the activation function, the final results are concluded in CR_1 with the completion of the first decoder-level operations.

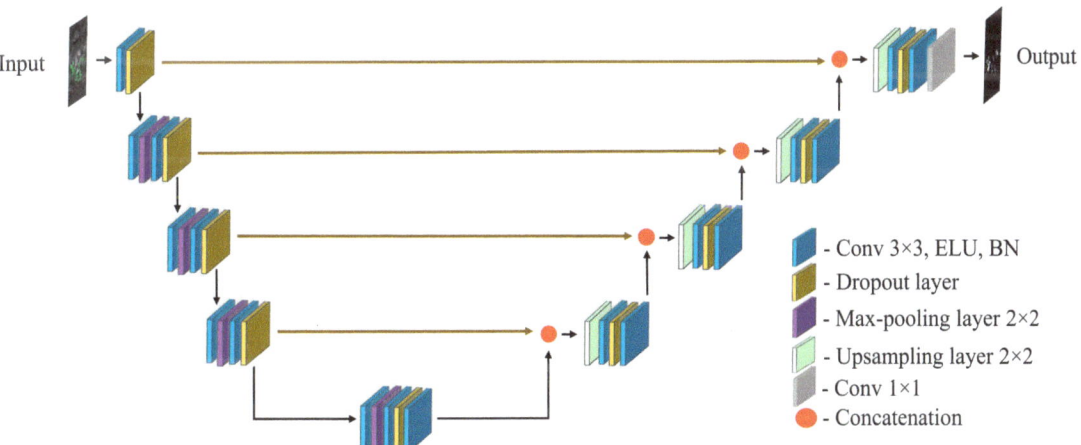

Figure 7. Modified U-Net architecture.

3.4.3. CED-Net

Although many other architectures for segmentation networks are deep, with a large number of parameters, CED-Net [48] is a simple cascading semantic segmentation model with a smaller number of parameters. The complete network comprises two training levels. Model 1 is trained at level 1 using the following steps. Model 1 is trained for predicting weeds, while Model 3 is trained for the prediction of crops. The results of Models 1 and 3 are upsampled and stitched to scale for each input image and then utilized as inputs for Models 2 and 4, respectively. The models are trained separately at each level. At Level 1, the images with their segmentation ground truths are reduced in size to spatial dimensions of 448 × 448. To train the Level 2 models, the 448 × 448 spatial dimension is upsampled to 896 × 896 using bilinear interpolation. The only difference from the U-Net structure is the highest feature map of 256 sizes in the bottleneck layer. All models and levels use the same encoder–decoder network architecture for CED-Net, as shown in Figure 8. Moreover, the first stages of CED-Net at each level in the model are akin to those of the U-Net encoder–decoder, other than the network depth and the number of convolutions. The encoder (including and before the first MP layer as $Encoder_1$) and decoder (first up Conv layer with more layers having convolutions as $Decoder_1$) of CED-Net, shown in Figure 8, are mathematically represented as follows:

$$Encoder_1 = P_1(D_1) \text{ where } \begin{cases} D_1 = Conv(Conv(Y, W_1)), \\ P_1 = Maxpool(C_1) \end{cases} \tag{21}$$

$$Decoder_1 = FR_1\big(C_{\text{concat1}}\big(C_{\text{crop1}}(U_1)\big)\big), \tag{22}$$

$$\text{where } \begin{cases} U_1 = Upconv(B, W_{up1}), \\ C_{crop1} = Crop(R, size(U_1)), \\ C_{concat1} = Concatenation(U_1, C_{crop1}), \\ FR_1 = Conv(Conv(Conv(C_{concat1}, W_{conv}))) \end{cases}$$

In $Encoder_1$, Y represents the input feature, and W_1 represents the weight tensor for the convolution operations. ReLU and batch normalization are employed in each Conv operation for both the encoder and decoder. In $Decoder_1$, B depicts the feature map of the prior layer, and W_{up1} in $Upconv(B, W_{up1})$ shows the weight tensor with an upconvolution operation. In $Crop(R, size(U_1))$, R represents the input image size after convolutions on the encoder side, converted to the same size as U_1, which is the result of a previous upconvolution. $C_{concat1}$ represents the concatenation of U_1 and C_{crop1} which are the final calculations for the previous layers. W_{Conv} represents weight tensors with convolution operations. Finally, after convolutions in the decoder, it is fed to FR_1, and the next stages of the decoder computations continue in a similar manner. At each level of CED-Net, a similar encoder–decoder architecture is used for network operations.

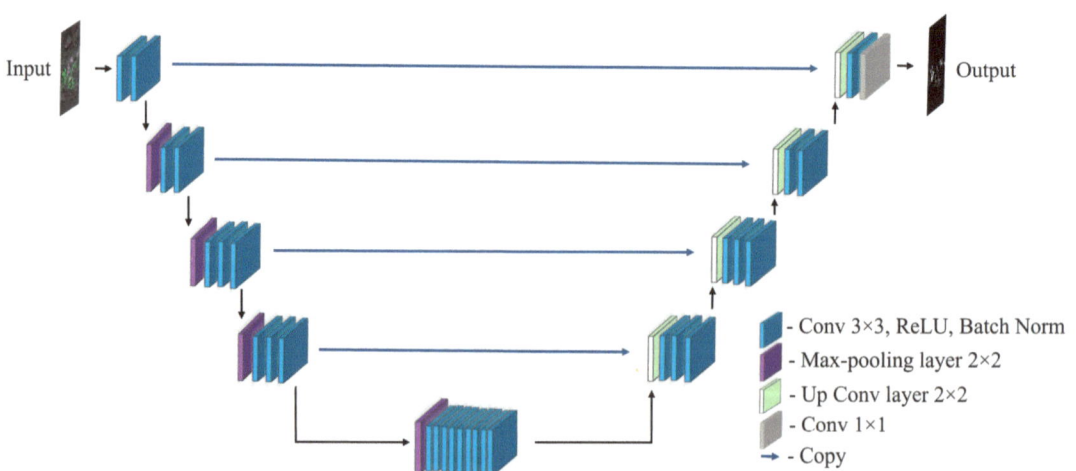

Figure 8. Encoder and decoder architecture of CED-Net.

4. Experimental Results

4.1. Experimental Dataset and Setup

We used two open datasets: the BoniRob dataset [24] as Dataset A and the CWFID [25] as Dataset B. The BoniRob dataset contains 496 images with pixel-level annotated masks, while the CWFID contains 60 images with the same pixel-level annotated masks. Both dataset images were captured by an autonomous robot in the field at a resolution of 1296 × 966 pixels. For small training datasets, we use only a single image, and augmentation produces an additional image. We utilized two images (one augmented and one small training data) for training. During training, we reduced the image size to 512 × 512 pixels. We experimented on a Windows-based desktop system with an Intel Core i5-2320 CPU @ 3.00 GHz processor [54], a GPU of NVIDIA GeForce GTX 1070 [55] with 8 gigabytes of memory, and 16 gigabytes of RAM. For development, we utilized the PyTorch [56] platform in Python version 3.8 [57].

4.2. Training Setup

For Experiment 1, Dataset A was first used for training with 70% of the data. Dataset B, transformed using the proposed method, was subsequently divided into two equal portions: one serving as testing data and the other as small training data. A single image of the small training data was then augmented and used for training, whereas the testing data remained unchanged. In Experiment 2, 70% of the data in Dataset B were used for training. Next, the data were preprocessed, and Dataset A was subsequently divided into two equal portions: one serving as testing data and the other as small training data. We augmented a single image of the small training data and further utilized it for training, while the test data remained unchanged. During training, the images underwent resizing to a resolution of 512 × 512 pixels, and the network was trained using a batch size of two for 150 epochs. We employed an Adam optimizer [58] with an initial learning rate (LR) of 1×10^{-5} and utilized a cosine annealing strategy [59] to steadily reduce the LR during training. The training loss was calculated using dice loss [60]. We trained the proposed framework using the U-Net, modified U-Net, and CED-Net architectures. Figure 9 depicts the loss and training graphs for the BoniRob dataset and the CWFID using U-Net. Furthermore, the convergence of the loss and accuracy curves of the validation and training data demonstrates that the network is adequately trained and avoids overfitting.

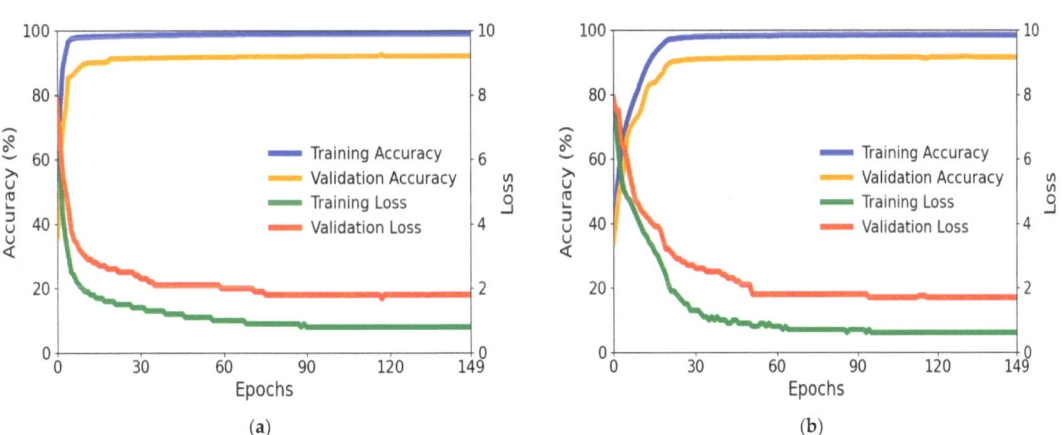

Figure 9. Accuracy and loss graphs of training and validation data from (**a**) BoniRob dataset and (**b**) CWFID.

4.3. Evaluation Metrics

The experiment aimed to assess the semantic segmentation performance across three classes (background, crop, and weed) using evaluation metrics including precision, the mean intersection of union (mIoU), recall, and weighted harmonic mean of precision and recall (F1-score), as outlined in Equations (23)–(27). These values were used to calculate the overall segmentation performance of the proposed framework. The number of classes was set to three. The evaluation metrics used to determine the accuracy of segmentation included true negative (TN), true positive (TP), false negative (FN), and false positive (FP) values. When the true and false labels match the prediction, the scenario is usually referred to as a TN or TP. FP and FN are terms used to describe scenarios in which an incorrect label is mistakenly anticipated as true and a valid label is mistakenly anticipated as a false label.

$$IoU = \frac{TP}{TP + FN + FP}, \tag{23}$$

$$mIoU = \frac{\sum_{j=1}^{Cls} IOU_j}{Cls}, \tag{24}$$

$$Recall = \frac{TP}{TP + FN}, \tag{25}$$

$$Precision = \frac{TP}{TP + FP}, \tag{26}$$

$$F1 - score = \frac{2 \times Precision \times Recall}{Precision + Recall} \tag{27}$$

4.4. Testing for the Proposed Framework

Below is the explanation of the experimental results of the proposed framework for semantic segmentation in Experiments 1 and 2.

4.4.1. Testing with CWFID after Training with BoniRob Dataset

Ablation Study

In the ablation studies, we conducted several experiments across various scenarios, encompassing six different cases outlined in Table 2.

Table 2. Representation of various cases.

Cases	RH Transformation	Using One Training Data	Data Augmentation
Case I			
Case II	✔		
Case III		✔	
Case IV	✔	✔	
Case V		✔	✔
Case VI	✔	✔	✔

We repeated these six cases in Experiments 1 and 2. Tables 3–5 present the results of Experiment 1 for semantic segmentation using segmentation networks including U-Net, modified U-Net, and CED-Net. Across all experiments, Case I showed the lowest performance, and Case VI (the proposed method) showed the highest performance. This confirms that the proposed schemes of using RH transformation, one training dataset, and DA can enhance segmentation accuracy in all the segmentation models. In addition, the semantic segmentation performance of Case VI and U-Net is the best.

Table 3. Comparisons of different cases using U-Net (Experiment 1) (Cr means crop, Wd means weed, Bg means background, Re means recall, and Pre means precision).

Model	Cases	mIoU	IoU (Cr)	IoU (Wd)	IoU (Bg)	Re	Pre	F1-Score
U-Net	Case I	0.384	0.001	0.195	0.384	0.643	0.403	0.495
	Case II	0.423	0.098	0.206	0.965	0.638	0.567	0.594
	Case III	0.493	0.322	0.175	0.982	0.621	0.605	0.611
	Case IV	0.589	0.472	0.309	0.985	0.732	0.721	0.724
	Case V	0.499	0.294	0.221	0.982	0.652	0.627	0.639
	Case VI (proposed)	0.620	0.524	0.349	0.986	0.762	0.749	0.752

An ablation study is presented in Table 6 to show the significance of the selection of the mean and std values for the RH transformation in the proposed framework. In this ablation study, we used the same training data as in the ablation study experiments with U-Net of Case VI (Table 3) and performed testing to validate the performance difference between the RH transformation and RH transformation with additional adjustment values that deviate from the selected values. We set the RH transformation with additional adjustment values to make the distribution of channels akin to that of the reference image in the histograms, as shown in Figure 3 and explained in Section 3.2.2. The performance results (F1-score) with additional adjustment values are 13.1% lower than those with the RH transformation without additional adjustments, as listed in Table 6. Although the RH transformation with additional adjustments makes the relative channel distributions similar between the target and reference images, as shown in Figure 3, it results in a greater decrease in the absolute numbers of red and green channels. Additionally, the mean of all channels decreases and moves toward zero, which reduces contrast and illumination, as shown in Figure 3. Moreover, the variance also increases, and all factors collectively cause the performance degradation of the RH transformation with additional adjustments.

Table 4. Comparisons of different cases using modified U-Net (Experiment 1) (Cr means crop, Wd means weed, Bg means background, Re means recall, and Pre means precision).

Model	Cases	mIoU	IoU (Cr)	IoU (Wd)	IoU (Bg)	Re	Pre	F1-Score
Modified U-Net	Case I	0.380	0.006	0.195	0.941	0.645	0.406	0.497
	Case II	0.427	0.104	0.209	0.968	0.657	0.563	0.601
	Case III	0.483	0.244	0.221	0.983	0.646	0.608	0.625
	Case IV	0.523	0.368	0.217	0.984	0.664	0.635	0.648
	Case V	0.471	0.195	0.234	0.983	0.656	0.615	0.634
	Case VI (proposed)	0.539	0.382	0.251	0.984	0.686	0.665	0.674

Table 5. Comparisons of different cases using CED-Net (Experiment 1) (Cr means crop, Wd means weed, Bg means background, Re means recall, and Pre means precision).

Model	Cases	mIoU	IoU (Cr)	IoU (Wd)	IoU (Bg)	Re	Pre	F1-Score
CED-Net	Case I	0.387	0.009	0.196	0.956	0.634	0.441	0.518
	Case II	0.396	0.018	0.209	0.962	0.616	0.465	0.528
	Case III	0.461	0.234	0.175	0.974	0.603	0.559	0.579
	Case IV	0.516	0.409	0.168	0.971	0.640	0.592	0.614
	Case V	0.466	0.235	0.188	0.974	0.617	0.564	0.589
	Case VI (proposed)	0.521	0.472	0.120	0.972	0.637	0.613	0.624

Table 6. Comparison of results between RH transformation and RH transformation with additional adjustments (Cr means crop, Wd means weed, Bg means background, Re means recall, and Pre means precision).

Experiment	mIoU	IoU (Cr)	IoU (Wd)	IoU (Bg)	Re	Pre	F1-Score
RH transformation	0.620	0.524	0.349	0.986	0.762	0.749	0.752
RH transformation with additional adjustments	0.468	0.199	0.229	0.975	0.631	0.615	0.621

Visual examples of the semantic segmentation results using U-Net, modified U-Net, and CED-Net are illustrated in Figure 10. In this illustration, red pixels represent the TP of crops, black pixels represent the TP of the background, and blue pixels signify the TP of the weed. Yellow pixels represent errors where crops were mistakenly identified as background or weeds, while orange pixels represent errors where weeds were mistakenly identified as background or crops. Gray pixels indicate errors where the background was mistakenly identified as weeds or crops. As depicted in the figure, the utilization of U-Net in the proposed framework demonstrates superior semantic segmentation accuracy.

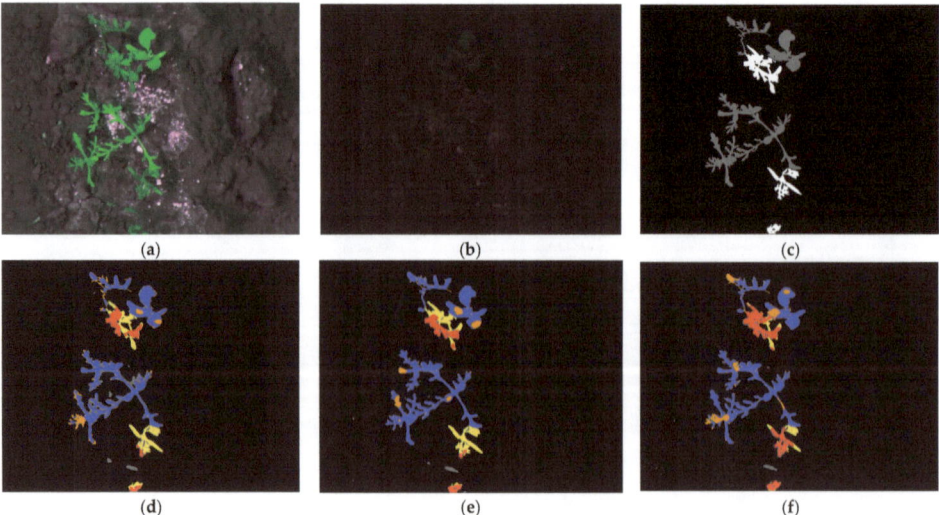

Figure 10. Visual comparisons of various semantic segmentation outputs with proposed framework (Experiment 1): (**a**) original image; (**b**) RH-transformed image; (**c**) ground-truth mask; semantic segmentation results with (**d**) CED-Net; (**e**) modified U-Net, and (**f**) U-Net.

Performance Comparisons of the Proposed Framework with SOTA Transformations

We analyzed the SOTA transformations with those of the proposed method employing U-Net, modified U-Net, and CED-Net, as outlined in Table 7. Our findings confirm that the proposed framework yields the highest outcomes across all segmentation networks. Additionally, Table 7 reveals that U-Net within the proposed framework attains the highest segmentation performance for both crops and weeds.

Visual examples of SOTA transformations and the proposed method using U-Net are shown in Figure 11. In this illustration, red pixels represent the TP of crops, black pixels represent the TP of the background, and blue pixels signify the TP of the weed. Yellow pixels represent errors where crops were mistakenly identified as background or weeds, while orange pixels represent errors where weeds were mistakenly identified as background or crops. Gray pixels indicate errors where the background was mistakenly identified as weeds or crops. As depicted in the figure, the proposed framework demonstrates the highest semantic segmentation accuracy.

Table 7. Performance comparisons of proposed method and SOTA transformations (Cr means crop, Wd means weed, Bg means background, Re means recall, and Pre means precision).

Segmentation Model	Transformation	mIoU	IoU (Cr)	IoU (Wd)	IoU (Bg)	Re	Pre	F1-Score
	Xiao et al. [61]	0.496	0.257	0.274	0.958	0.717	0.583	0.640
	Pitie et al. [62]	0.548	0.378	0.312	0.953	0.776	0.601	0.675
U-Net	Gatys et al. [63]	0.457	0.313	0.101	0.958	0.558	0.575	0.563
	Nguyen et al. [64]	0.487	0.486	0.010	0.964	0.563	0.580	0.569
	Proposed	0.620	0.524	0.349	0.986	0.762	0.749	0.752
	Xiao et al. [61]	0.387	0.066	0.161	0.934	0.651	0.494	0.558
	Pitie et al. [62]	0.462	0.200	0.221	0.966	0.716	0.569	0.630
Modified U-Net	Gatys et al. [63]	0.396	0.157	0.083	0.948	0.452	0.544	0.490
	Nguyen et al. [64]	0.427	0.136	0.185	0.959	0.518	0.580	0.545
	Proposed	0.539	0.382	0.251	0.984	0.686	0.665	0.674

Table 7. Cont.

Segmentation Model	Transformation	mIoU	IoU (Cr)	IoU (Wd)	IoU (Bg)	Re	Pre	F1-Score
	Xiao et al. [61]	0.390	0.036	0.204	0.928	0.618	0.447	0.518
	Pitie et al. [62]	0.394	0.109	0.180	0.894	0.673	0.472	0.553
CED-Net	Gatys et al. [63]	0.360	0.000	0.143	0.938	0.605	0.378	0.465
	Nguyen et al. [64]	0.310	0.000	0.065	0.865	0.479	0.349	0.402
	Proposed	0.521	0.472	0.120	0.972	0.637	0.613	0.624

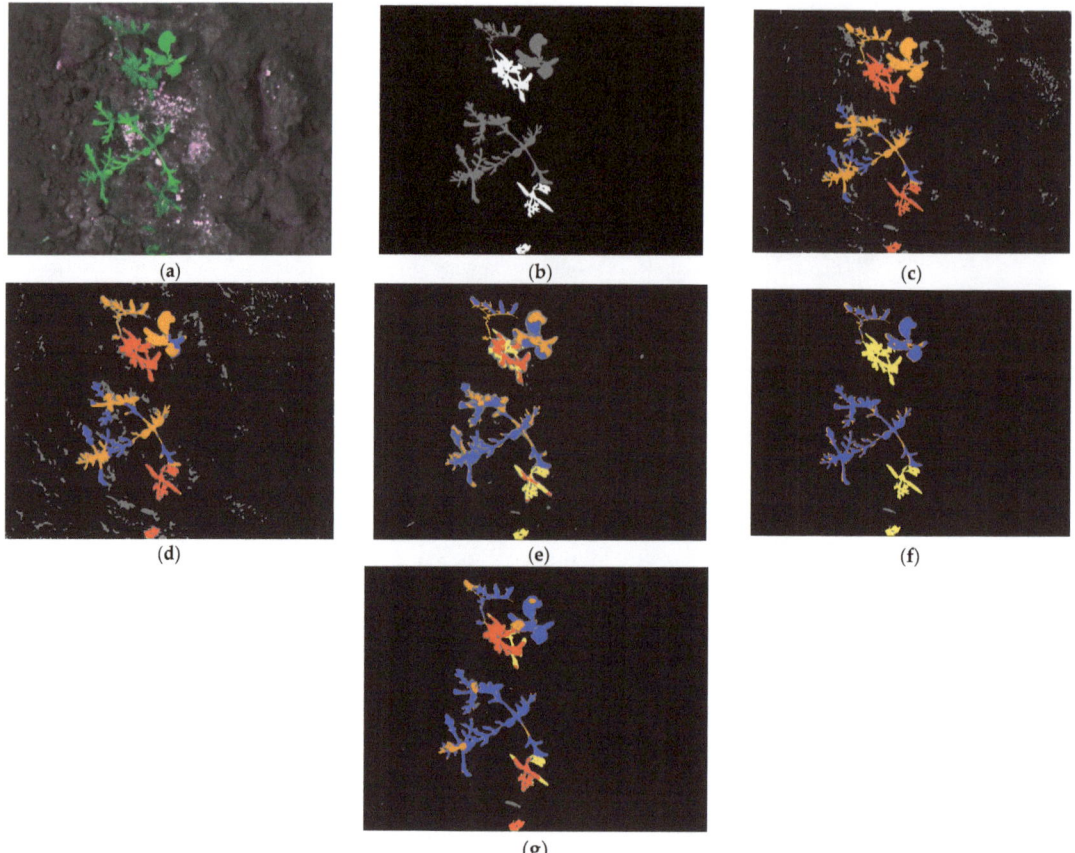

Figure 11. Visual comparisons of various SOTA transformations with the proposed framework using U-Net (Experiment 1): (**a**) original image; (**b**) ground-truth mask; semantic segmentation results with (**c**) Xiao et al.; (**d**) Pitie et al.; (**e**) Gatys et al.; (**f**) Nguyen et al.; and (**g**) proposed method.

4.4.2. Testing with BoniRob Dataset after Training with CWFID
Ablation Study

For the ablation studies, six cases were considered in Experiment 2, as described in the Ablation Study of Section 4.4.1. Tables 8–10 present the results of Experiment 2 for semantic segmentation using segmentation networks. From these tables, we can observe that the accuracy is lower for Cases I, III, and IV without RH transformation for the test data, but the performance improved when we used RH transformation in Cases II, IV, and VI. In Case VI, the proposed framework shows the highest accuracy among all segmentation networks and the best accuracy with U-Net.

Table 8. Comparison of different cases using U-Net (Experiment 2) (Cr means crop, Wd means weed, Bg means background, Re means recall, and Pre means precision).

Model	Cases	mIoU	IoU (Cr)	IoU (Wd)	IoU (Bg)	Re	Pre	F1-Score
U-Net	Case I	0.316	0.000	0.000	0.948	0.333	0.329	0.330
	Case II	0.570	0.230	0.508	0.971	0.704	0.679	0.688
	Case III	0.494	0.227	0.286	0.969	0.630	0.673	0.649
	Case IV	0.621	0.272	0.621	0.969	0.779	0.689	0.730
	Case V	0.507	0.232	0.322	0.968	0.645	0.679	0.659
	Case VI (proposed)	0.637	0.292	0.647	0.971	0.787	0.708	0.743

Table 9. Comparison of different cases using modified U-Net (Experiment 2) (Cr means crop, Wd means weed, Bg means background, Re means recall, and Pre means precision).

Model	Cases	mIoU	IoU (Cr)	IoU (Wd)	IoU (Bg)	Re	Pre	F1-Score
Modified U-Net	Case I	0.316	0.000	0.000	0.948	0.333	0.316	0.324
	Case II	0.529	0.235	0.383	0.970	0.682	0.665	0.668
	Case III	0.448	0.212	0.163	0.968	0.588	0.596	0.589
	Case IV	0.605	0.266	0.593	0.955	0.833	0.651	0.728
	Case V	0.477	0.232	0.232	0.966	0.633	0.611	0.619
	Case VI (proposed)	0.622	0.294	0.610	0.962	0.837	0.667	0.739

We can see the visual examples of semantic segmentation outputs using U-Net, modified U-Net, and CED-Net in Figure 12. In this illustration, red pixels represent the TP of crops, black pixels represent the TP of the background, and blue pixels signify the TP of the weed. Yellow pixels represent errors where crops were mistakenly identified as background or weeds, while orange pixels represent errors where weeds were mistakenly identified as background or crops. Gray pixels indicate errors where the background was mistakenly identified as weeds or crops. As depicted in the figure, the proposed framework with U-Net demonstrates the highest semantic segmentation accuracy.

Table 10. Comparison of different cases using CED-Net (Experiment 2) (Cr means crop, Wd means weed, Bg means background, Re means recall, and Pre means precision).

Model	Cases	mIoU	IoU (Cr)	IoU (Wd)	IoU (Bg)	Re	Pre	F1-Score
CED-Net	Case I	0.315	0.000	0.000	0.946	0.332	0.318	0.322
	Case II	0.487	0.176	0.336	0.951	0.699	0.564	0.621
	Case III	0.488	0.013	0.572	0.879	0.624	0.537	0.575
	Case IV	0.552	0.218	0.504	0.935	0.838	0.592	0.691
	Case V	0.485	0.0143	0.581	0.860	0.623	0.539	0.576
	Case VI (proposed)	0.570	0.244	0.519	0.946	0.836	0.611	0.703

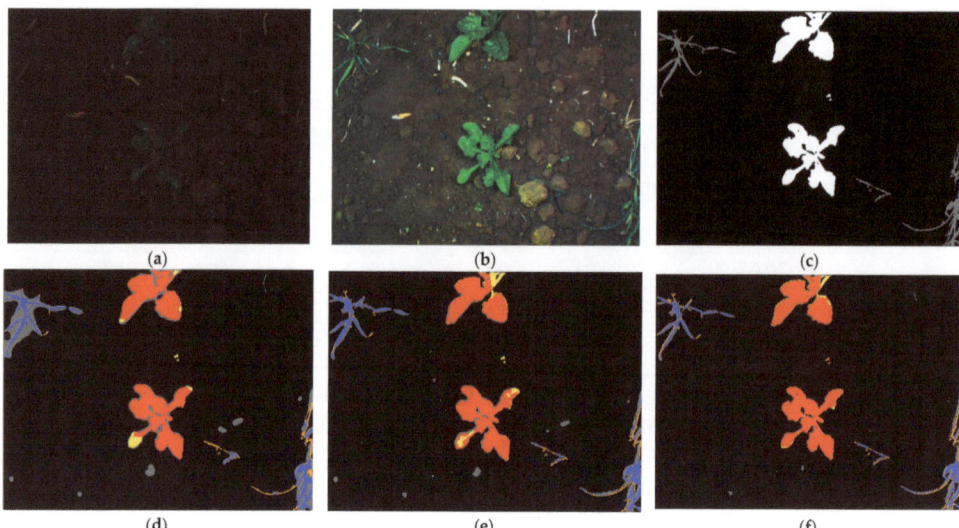

Figure 12. Visual comparisons of various semantic segmentation outputs with proposed framework (Experiment 1): (**a**) original image; (**b**) RH-transformed image; (**c**) ground-truth mask; semantic segmentation results with (**d**) CED-Net; (**e**) modified U-Net, and (**f**) U-Net.

Performance Comparisons of the Proposed Framework with SOTA Transformations

In this subsection, we compared the SOTA transformations with those of the proposed framework using U-Net, modified U-Net, and CED-Net, as listed in Table 11. We verify that the proposed framework shows superior performance over all segmentation networks. Moreover, Table 11 highlights that U-Net, when utilized within the proposed framework, obtained the highest semantic segmentation accuracy for crops and weeds.

Visual examples of SOTA transformations and the proposed method using U-Net are illustrated in Figure 13. In this illustration, red pixels represent the TP of crops, black pixels represent the TP of the background, and blue pixels signify the TP of the weed. Yellow pixels represent errors where crops were mistakenly identified as background or weeds, while orange pixels represent errors where weeds were mistakenly identified as background or crops. Gray pixels indicate errors where the background was mistakenly identified as weeds or crops. As illustrated in the figure, the proposed framework demonstrates the highest semantic segmentation accuracy.

Table 11. Comparisons of the performance of the proposed method and SOTA transformations (Cr means crop, Wd means weed, Bg means background, Re means recall, and Pre means precision).

Model	Transformation	mIoU	IoU (Cr)	IoU (Wd)	IoU (Bg)	Re	Pre	F1-Score
U-Net	Xiao et al. [61]	0.530	0.505	0.124	0.962	0.696	0.589	0.635
	Pitie et al. [62]	0.543	0.475	0.193	0.959	0.729	0.605	0.657
	Gatys et al. [63]	0.316	0.000	0.000	0.948	0.333	0.381	0.352
	Nguyen et al. [64]	0.332	0.049	0.000	0.946	0.352	0.417	0.379
	Proposed	0.637	0.647	0.292	0.971	0.787	0.708	0.743
Modified U-Net	Xiao et al. [61]	0.526	0.521	0.145	0.911	0.787	0.573	0.661
	Pitie et al. [62]	0.516	0.522	0.141	0.886	0.817	0.567	0.667
	Gatys et al. [63]	0.316	0.000	0.000	0.948	0.333	0.320	0.326
	Nguyen et al. [64]	0.187	0.014	0.031	0.516	0.387	0.368	0.375
	Proposed	0.622	0.610	0.294	0.962	0.837	0.667	0.739

Table 11. *Cont.*

Model	Transformation	mIoU	IoU (Cr)	IoU (Wd)	IoU (Bg)	Re	Pre	F1-Score
CED-Net	Xiao et al. [61]	0.423	0.339	0.067	0.862	0.709	0.475	0.566
	Pitie et al. [62]	0.466	0.442	0.107	0.850	0.807	0.524	0.632
	Gatys et al. [63]	0.318	0.005	0.018	0.932	0.338	0.340	0.339
	Nguyen et al. [64]	0.316	0.000	0.001	0.948	0.333	0.375	0.349
	Proposed	0.570	0.519	0.244	0.946	0.836	0.611	0.703

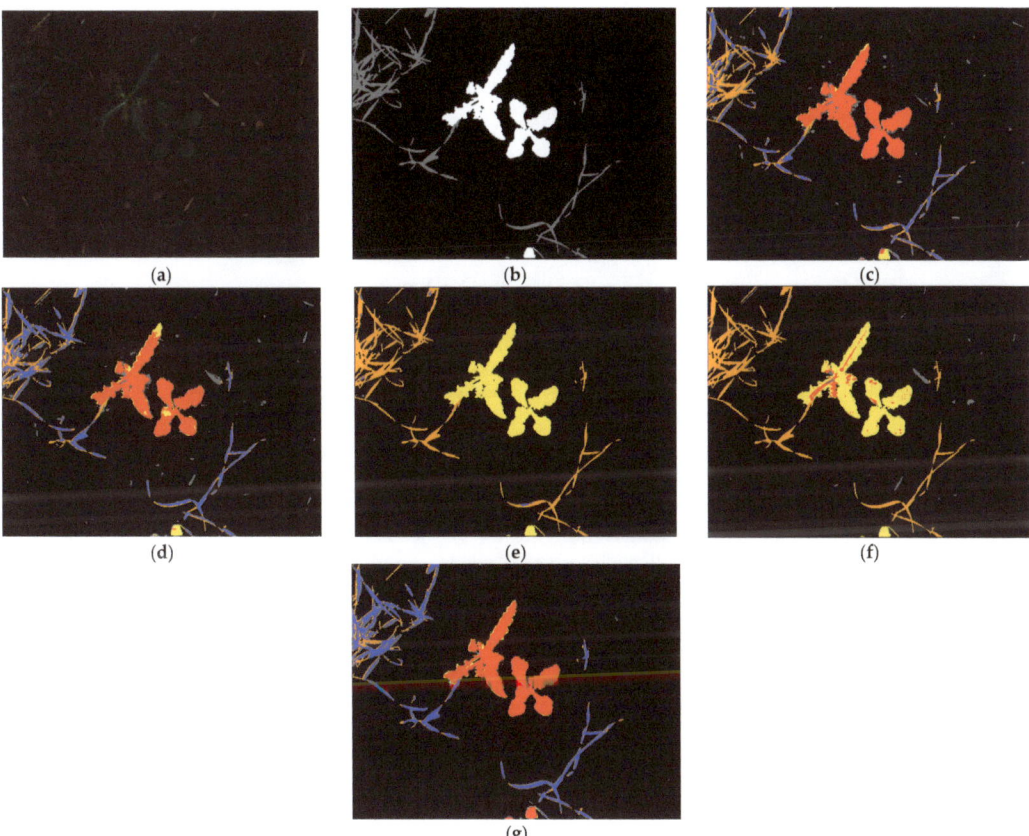

Figure 13. Visual comparisons of various SOTA transformations with proposed framework using U-Net (Experiment 1): (**a**) original image; (**b**) ground-truth mask; semantic segmentation results with (**c**) Xiao et al.; (**d**) Pitie et al.; (**e**) Gatys et al.; (**f**) Nguyen et al.; and (**g**) proposed method.

4.5. Fractal Dimension Estimation

The FD is used as a mathematical metric to characterize the complexity of geometric structures, particularly fractal shapes, which exhibit self-similarity across different scales. Fractal shapes possess similar patterns or structures across different scales, and the complexity of these shapes can be quantified using a numerical value of FD that generally ranges between one and two [65]. A higher FD value indicates greater complexity. A common method for computing the FD is the box-counting algorithm [66]. We refer to the box-counting algorithm [12] to compute the FD, which was implemented by the Py-

Torch [56] platform in Python version 3.8 [57]. Algorithm 2 provides the pseudo-code to measure the FD.

Algorithm 2: Pseudo-code for measuring FD

Input: image (path to the input image)
Output: Fractal dimension (FD) value
1:     Read the input image and further convert it into grayscale
2:     Set the maximum box-size with the power of 2 and ensure the dimensions
       s = 2^(log(max(size(image)))/log2)]
       Add the padding if required to match the dimensions
3:     Compute the number of boxes N(s) till minimum pixels
4:     Reduce box size by 2 and recalculate N(s) iteratively
       while s > 1
5:     Compute log(N(s)) and log(1/s) for each s
6:     Draw a fitted line to the points (log(N(s)) and log(1/s))
7:     FD value is the slope of the fitted line
       Return Fractal Dimension Value

The algorithm enables the calculation of the FD for both precise and approximate self-affine patterns and has wide applications across various natural and manmade systems [13,67]. The formula employed to estimate the FD utilizing the box-counting algorithm [12] is as follows:

$$FD = \lim_{s \to 0} \frac{\log(N(s))}{\log(1/s)} \tag{28}$$

where $N(s)$ represents the sum of boxes of size s, and FD signifies the fractal dimension defining the curve being analyzed. We employed a box-counting technique to calculate the approximate FD of various shapes. The method was evaluated using two datasets, BoniRob and CWFID. The experimental results are presented in Table 12, demonstrating the FD values and distribution of crops and weeds across different sections of the field. The 1st–3rd row FD values in Table 12 were computed from the 1st~3rd row images in Figure 14. In addition, the 4th~6th row FD values in Table 12 were computed from the 4th~6th row images in Figure 15. Higher FD values for crops and weeds represent the high complexities of crops and weeds, suggesting that farming experts or robots should pay more attention to discriminating between crops and weeds. This estimation technique can also automate farming systems by targeting and eliminating weeds through precise spraying in areas with high weed complexity, ultimately increasing the crop yield.

Table 12. FD values of images from CWFID and BoniRob dataset. The 1st~3rd row FD values are computed from the 1st~3rd row images of Figure 14. The 4th~6th row FD values are computed from the 4th~6th row images of Figure 15.

Dataset	Weed FD	Crop FD
	1.61	1.26
CWFID	0.76	1.43
	1.53	1.21
	1.27	0.91
BoniRob dataset	1.32	1.31
	0.97	1.54

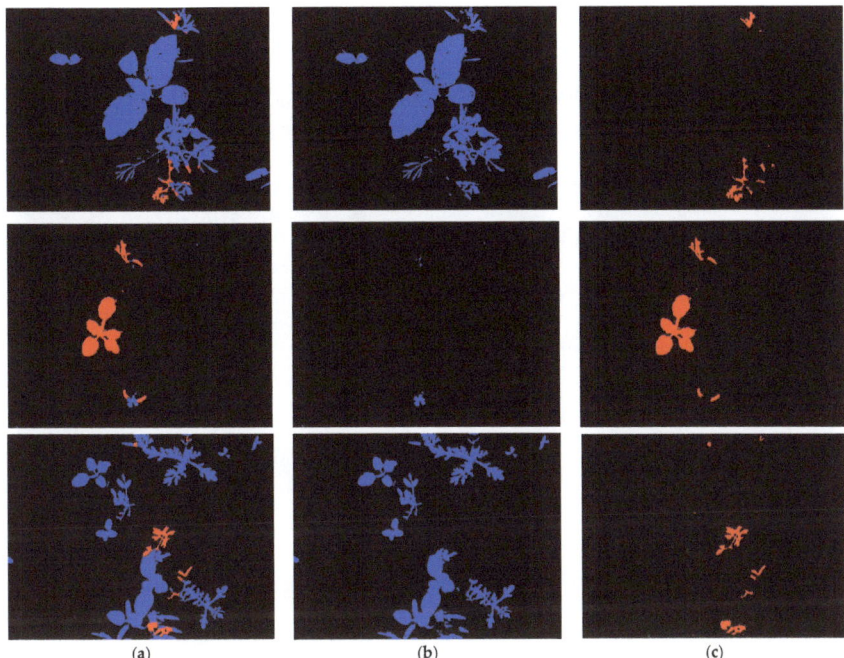

Figure 14. Visual representation of crops and weeds with samples from the CWFID for estimating FD values: (**a**) whole segmentation results; (**b**) weed segmentation result; and (**c**) crop segmentation result.

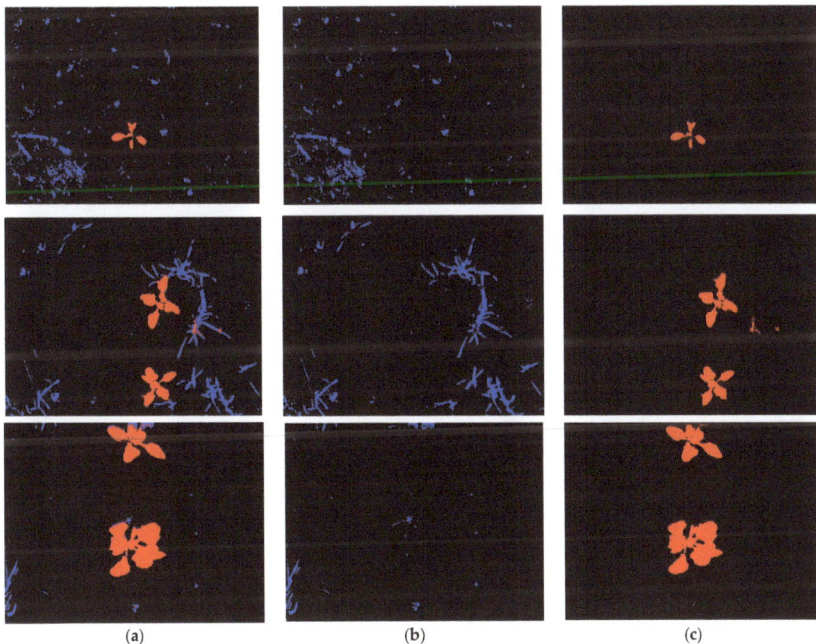

Figure 15. Visual representation of crops and weeds with samples from the BoniRob dataset for estimating FD values: (**a**) whole segmentation results; (**b**) weed segmentation result; and (**c**) crop segmentation result.

4.6. Comparisons of Processing Time

In this section, we compare the average processing times per image obtained using the proposed method with those obtained using the SOTA method. The unit ms denotes milliseconds. Table 13 illustrates that the method by Xiao et al. [61] exhibits the highest processing time, whereas the method by Nguyen et al. [64] demonstrates the lowest processing time. Interestingly, our proposed framework falls at the second lowest in processing time (as indicated in Table 13). Although the proposed framework has a higher processing time than Nguyen et al. [64], our goal is to achieve high accuracies of crop and weed segmentation. The proposed framework with U-Net yields better results than the SOTA methods, as evidenced in Tables 7 and 11 and Figures 11 and 13.

Table 13. Comparisons of average processing time by proposed and SOTA methods (unit: ms).

Methods	Processing Time
Xiao et al. [61]	1270
Pitie et al. [62]	2920
Gatys et al. [63]	2210
Nguyen et al. [64]	1030
Proposed	1080

5. Discussion

We performed statistical analysis using the Student's t-test [68] and calculated the Cohen's d-value [69]. For this purpose, we calculated the mean and std of the mIoU using our method with U-Net, as shown in Tables 7 and 11, respectively. Additionally, we calculated the mean and std of the mIoU using the second-best method (Pitie et al. [62]) with U-Net, as presented in Tables 7 and 11. The measured p-value is 0.041, showing a confidence level of 95% with a significant difference, as depicted in Figure 16, and Cohen's d-value is 0.936, representing a large effect size. This confirms that the proposed framework statistically surpasses the second-best method and achieves higher segmentation accuracy.

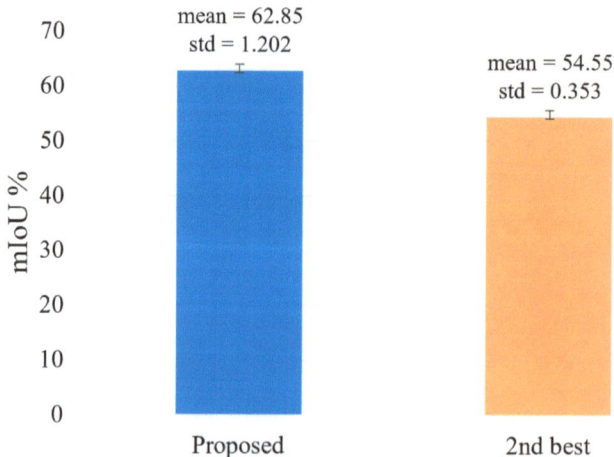

Figure 16. T-test results.

We also analyzed the semantic segmentation performance using the proposed method with U-Net based on gradient-weighted class activation mapping (Grad-CAM) [70], as depicted in Figure 17. Grad-CAM typically depicts important features as reddish and yellowish colors, whereas unimportant features are shown in bluish colors as explainable artificial intelligence. Figure 17 shows the Grad-CAM image, obtained after the fourth convolution layer of U-Net, illustrating the accurate extraction of crucial features for crop and weed segmentation, confirming that our method can generate correct images in heterogeneous datasets for the accurate segmentation of crops and weeds.

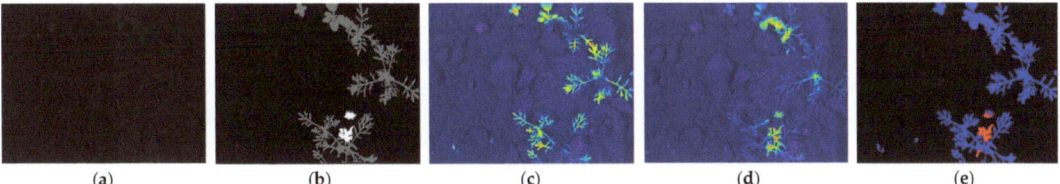

Figure 17. Sample images of the CWFID with Grad-CAM visualization after the 4th convolution layer. (**a**) Input image, (**b**) ground-truth mask (gray, white, and black pixels mean weeds, crops, and background, respectively), (**c**) Grad-CAM of class 1 (weed), (**d**) Grad-CAM of class 2 (crop), and (**e**) segmented results.

Figure 18 shows examples of incorrect segmentation using the proposed method with U-Net. In this illustration, red pixels represent the TP of crops, black pixels represent the TP of the background, and blue pixels signify the TP of the weed. Yellow pixels represent errors where crops were mistakenly identified as background or weeds, while orange pixels represent errors where weeds were mistakenly identified as background or crops. Gray pixels indicate errors where the background was mistakenly identified as weeds or crops. The reason for the incorrect segmentation is that crops and weeds have similar shapes and colors, making them hard to distinguish, especially in cases where objects possess thin regions.

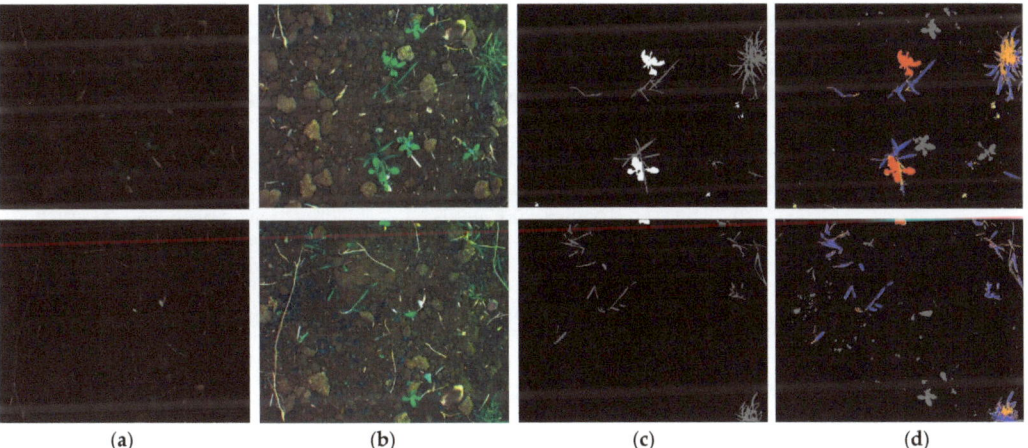

Figure 18. Samples of incorrect segmentation generated by proposed method with U-Net: (**a**) original image; (**b**) RH-transformed image; (**c**) ground-truth mask; and (**d**) semantic segmentation results.

As automation in agriculture is a subject of intensive research, it has led to many reformations in agriculture, such as saving time, reducing manpower, increasing yields through proper monitoring systems, and precise crop and weed detection. In agricultural precision for heterogeneous data, our proposed framework exhibits great performance, segregating crops and weeds accurately, which can increase yield and drive the transition to modern agriculture.

6. Conclusions

In this study, we introduce an approach for segmenting crops and weeds and estimating the FD using small amounts of training data in a heterogeneous data environment. This is the first study on the segmentation of crops and weeds within a heterogeneous environmental setup utilizing one training data sample. We rigorously investigated the factors that cause performance degradation in heterogeneous datasets, including variations in illumination and contrast. To solve this challenge, we proposed a framework that leverages mean and standard deviation adjustments using the RH transformation. Furthermore, we improved the performance using a small amount of training data. This additional small amount of training data significantly improves the segmentation performance with reduced computational power and training time. In addition, we introduced an FD estimation approach in our system, which was smoothly combined as an end-to-end task to furnish crucial insights into the distributional characteristics of crops and weeds. Through experiments using two open databases, we proved that our approach outperforms the SOTA method. Additionally, we confirmed that our approach showed statistically superior results than the second-best method in terms of the t-test and Cohen's d-value. Furthermore, using Grad-CAM images, we validated the capability of the proposed method to extract essential features necessary for the accurate segmentation of crops and weeds. Nonetheless, instances of inaccurate segmentation were observed in scenarios where crops and weeds exhibit comparable colors, shapes, and thin regions, as depicted in Figure 18.

To address this issue, we would research the generative adversarial network-based transformation method for the correct segmentation of small-sized and thin crops and weeds having similar colors and shapes in heterogeneous data environments. Moreover, we applied our method to other tasks, such as box-based detection or classification in heterogeneous data environments. In addition, we would check the possibility of applying our method to other application areas including crack detection for building monitoring, medical image detection, and underwater computer vision.

Author Contributions: Methodology, R.A.; conceptualization, J.S.H.; data curation, S.G.K.; formal analysis, H.S.; resources, M.U.; visualization, H.A.H.G.; software, M.H.T.; validation, N.U.; supervision, K.R.P.; writing—original draft, R.A.; writing—review and editing, K.R.P. All authors have read and agreed to the published version of the manuscript.

Funding: This research was supported in part by the National Research Foundation of Korea (NRF) funded by the Ministry of Science and ICT (MSIT) through the Basic Science Research Program (NRF-2022R1F1A1064291) and in part by MSIT, Korea, under the Information Technology Research Center (ITRC) support program (IITP-2024-2020-0-01789) supervised by the Institute for Information & Communications Technology Planning & Evaluation (IITP).

Data Availability Statement: The datasets are available in [24,25], and the proposed framework is available in [28].

Conflicts of Interest: The authors declare no conflicts of interest.

References

1. Jiang, Y.; Li, C. Convolutional Neural Networks for Image-Based High-Throughput Plant Phenotyping: A Review. *Plant Phenomics* **2020**, *2020*, 4152816. [CrossRef] [PubMed]
2. Fathipoor, H.; Arefi, H.; Shah-Hosseini, R.; Moghadam, H. Corn Forage Yield Prediction Using Unmanned Aerial Vehicle Images at Mid-Season Growth Stage. *J. Appl. Remote Sens* **2019**, *13*, 034503. [CrossRef]
3. Yang, Q.; Wang, Y.; Liu, L.; Zhang, X. Adaptive Fractional-Order Multi-Scale Optimization TV-L1 Optical Flow Algorithm. *Fractal Fract.* **2024**, *8*, 8040179. [CrossRef]
4. Huang, T.; Wang, X.; Xie, D.; Wang, C.; Liu, X. Depth Image Enhancement Algorithm Based on Fractional Differentiation. *Fractal Fract.* **2023**, *7*, 7050394. [CrossRef]
5. Bai, X.; Zhang, D.; Shi, S.; Yao, W.; Guo, Z.; Sun, J. A Fractional-Order Telegraph Diffusion Model for Restoring Texture Images with Multiplicative Noise. *Fractal Fract.* **2023**, *7*, 7010064. [CrossRef]
6. AlSheikh, M.H.; Al-Saidi, N.M.G.; Ibrahim, R.W. Dental X-ray Identification System Based on Association Rules Extracted by k-Symbol Fractional Haar Functions. *Fractal Fract.* **2022**, *6*, 6110669. [CrossRef]

7. Zhang, Y.; Yang, L.; Li, Y. A Novel Adaptive Fractional Differential Active Contour Image Segmentation Method. *Fractal Fract.* **2022**, *6*, 6100579. [CrossRef]
8. Zhang, Y.; Liu, T.; Yang, F.; Yang, Q. A Study of Adaptive Fractional-Order Total Variational Medical Image Denoising. *Fractal Fract.* **2022**, *6*, 6090508. [CrossRef]
9. Jiao, Q.; Liu, M.; Ning, B.; Zhao, F.; Dong, L.; Kong, L.; Hui, M.; Zhao, Y. Image Dehazing Based on Local and Non-Local Features. *Fractal Fract.* **2022**, *6*, 6050262. [CrossRef]
10. Zhang, X.; Dai, L. Image Enhancement Based on Rough Set and Fractional Order Differentiator. *Fractal Fract.* **2022**, *6*, 6040214. [CrossRef]
11. Zhang, X.; Liu, R.; Ren, J.; Gui, Q. Adaptive Fractional Image Enhancement Algorithm Based on Rough Set and Particle Swarm Optimization. *Fractal Fract.* **2022**, *6*, 6020100. [CrossRef]
12. Cheng, J.; Chen, Q.; Huang, X. An Algorithm for Crack Detection, Segmentation, and Fractal Dimension Estimation in Low-Light Environments by Fusing FFT and Convolutional Neural Network. *Fractal Fract.* **2023**, *7*, 7110820. [CrossRef]
13. An, Q.; Chen, X.; Wang, H.; Yang, H.; Yang, Y.; Huang, W.; Wang, L. Segmentation of Concrete Cracks by Using Fractal Dimension and UHK-Net. *Fractal Fract.* **2022**, *6*, 6020095. [CrossRef]
14. Sultan, H.; Owais, M.; Park, C.; Mahmood, T.; Haider, A.; Park, K.R. Artificial Intelligence-Based Recognition of Different Types of Shoulder Implants in X-Ray Scans Based on Dense Residual Ensemble-Network for Personalized Medicine. *J. Pers. Med.* **2021**, *11*, 11060482. [CrossRef] [PubMed]
15. Arsalan, M.; Haider, A.; Hong, J.S.; Kim, J.S.; Park, K.R. Deep Learning-Based Detection of Human Blastocyst Compartments with Fractal Dimension Estimation. *Fractal Fract.* **2024**, *8*, 8050267. [CrossRef]
16. González-Sabbagh, S.P.; Robles-Kelly, A. A Survey on Underwater Computer Vision. *ACM Comput. Surv.* **2023**, *55*, 1–39. [CrossRef]
17. Madokoro, H.; Takahashi, K.; Yamamoto, S.; Nix, S.; Chiyonobu, S.; Saruta, K.; Saito, T.K.; Nishimura, Y.; Sato, K. Semantic Segmentation of Agricultural Images Based on Style Transfer Using Conditional and Unconditional Generative Adversarial Networks. *Appl. Sci.* **2022**, *12*, 12157785. [CrossRef]
18. Kim, Y.; Park, K.R. MTS-CNN: MTS-CNN: Multi-Task Semantic Segmentation-Convolutional Neural Network for Detecting Crops and Weeds. *Comput. Electron. Agric.* **2022**, *199*, 107146. [CrossRef]
19. Wang, R.; Jiao, L.; Xie, C.; Chen, P.; Du, J.; Li, R. S-RPN: Sampling-Balanced Region Proposal Network for Small Crop Pest Detection. *Comput. Electron. Agric.* **2021**, *187*, 106290. [CrossRef]
20. Huang, S.; Wu, S.; Sun, C.; Ma, X.; Jiang, Y.; Qi, L. Deep Localization Model for Intra-Row Crop Detection in Paddy Field. *Comput. Electron. Agric.* **2020**, *169*, 105203. [CrossRef]
21. Kang, J.; Liu, L.; Zhang, F.; Shen, C.; Wang, N.; Shao, L. Semantic Segmentation Model of Cotton Roots In-Situ Image Based on Attention Mechanism. *Comput. Electron. Agric.* **2021**, *189*, 106370. [CrossRef]
22. Le Louëdec, J.; Cielniak, G. 3D Shape Sensing and Deep Learning-Based Segmentation of Strawberries. *Comput. Electron. Agric.* **2021**, *190*, 106374. [CrossRef]
23. Brilhador, A.; Gutoski, M.; Hattori, L.T.; de Souza Inácio, A.; Lazzaretti, A.E.; Lopes, H.S. Classification of Weeds and Crops at the Pixel-Level Using Convolutional Neural Networks and Data Augmentation. In Proceedings of the IEEE Latin American Conference on Computational Intelligence, Guayaquil, Ecuador, 11–15 November 2019; pp. 1–6. [CrossRef]
24. Chebrolu, N.; Lottes, P.; Schaefer, A.; Winterhalter, W.; Burgard, W.; Stachniss, C. Agricultural Robot Dataset for Plant Classification, Localization and Mapping on Sugar Beet Fields. *Int. J. Robot. Res.* **2017**, *36*, 1045–1052. [CrossRef]
25. Haug, S.; Ostermann, J. A Crop/Weed Field Image Dataset for the Evaluation of Computer Vision Based Precision Agriculture Tasks. In Proceedings of the Computer Vision—ECCV 2014 Workshops, Zurich, Switzerland, 6–7 and 12 September 2014; pp. 105–116. [CrossRef]
26. Nguyen, D.T.; Nam, S.H.; Batchuluun, G.; Owais, M.; Park, K.R. An Ensemble Classification Method for Brain Tumor Images Using Small Training Data. *Mathematics* **2022**, *10*, 10234566. [CrossRef]
27. Abdalla, A.; Cen, H.; Wan, L.; Rashid, R.; Weng, H.; Zhou, W.; He, Y. Fine-Tuning Convolutional Neural Network with Transfer Learning for Semantic Segmentation of Ground-Level Oilseed Rape Images in a Field with High Weed Pressure. *Comput. Electron. Agric.* **2019**, *167*, 105091. [CrossRef]
28. Crops and Weeds Segmentation Method in Heterogeneous Environment. Available online: https://github.com/iamrehanch/crops_and_weeds_semantic_segmentation (accessed on 9 March 2023).
29. Haug, S.; Michaels, A.; Biber, P.; Ostermann, J. Plant Classification System for Crop/Weed Discrimination without Segmentation. In Proceedings of the IEEE Winter Conference on Applications of Computer Vision, Steamboat Springs, CO, USA, 24–26 March 2014; pp. 1142–1149. [CrossRef]
30. Lottes, P.; Hörferlin, M.; Sander, S.; Stachniss, C. Effective Vision-Based Classification for Separating Sugar Beets and Weeds for Precision Farming: Effective Vision-Based Classification. *J. Field Robot.* **2017**, *34*, 1160–1178. [CrossRef]
31. Lottes, P.; Khanna, R.; Pfeifer, J.; Siegwart, R.; Stachniss, C. UAV-Based Crop and Weed Classification for Smart Farming. In Proceedings of the IEEE International Conference on Robotics and Automation, Singapore, Singapore, 29 May–3 June 2017; pp. 3024–3031. [CrossRef]
32. Yang, B.; Xu, Y. Applications of Deep-Learning Approaches in Horticultural Research: A Review. *Hortic. Res.* **2021**, *8*, 123. [CrossRef]

33. Chen, L.C.; Papandreou, G.; Schroff, F.; Adam, H. Rethinking Atrous Convolution for Semantic Image Segmentation. *arXiv* **2015**, arXiv:1706.05587v3.
34. Long, J.; Shelhamer, E.; Darrell, T. Fully Convolutional Networks for Semantic Segmentation. In Proceedings of the IEEE Conference on Computer Vision and Pattern Recognition, Boston, MA, USA, 7–12 June 2015; pp. 3431–3440. [CrossRef]
35. Ronneberger, O.; Fischer, P.; Brox, T. U-Net: Convolutional Networks for Biomedical Image Segmentation. In Proceedings of the Medical Image Computing and Computer-Assisted Intervention, Munich, Germany, 5–9 October 2015; pp. 234–241. [CrossRef]
36. Badrinarayanan, V.; Kendall, A.; Cipolla, R. SegNet: A Deep Convolutional Encoder-Decoder Architecture for Image Segmentation. *IEEE Trans. Pattern Anal. Mach. Intell.* **2017**, *39*, 2481–2495. [CrossRef]
37. Zou, K.; Chen, X.; Wang, Y.; Zhang, C.; Zhang, F. A Modified U-Net with a Specific Data Argumentation Method for Semantic Segmentation of Weed Images in the Field. *Comput. Electron. Agric.* **2021**, *187*, 106242. [CrossRef]
38. Milioto, A.; Lottes, P.; Stachniss, C. Real-Time Semantic Segmentation of Crop and Weed for Precision Agriculture Robots Leveraging Background Knowledge in CNNs. In Proceedings of the IEEE International Conference on Robotics and Automation, Brisbane, Australia, 21–25 May 2018; pp. 2235–2299. [CrossRef]
39. Paszke, A.; Chaurasia, A.; Kim, S.; Culurciello, E. ENet: A Deep Neural Network Architecture for Real-Time Semantic Segmentation. *arXiv* **2016**, arXiv:1606.02147v1.
40. Fathipoor, H.; Shah-Hosseini, R.; Arefi, H. Crop and Weed Segmentation on Ground_Based Images using Deep Convolutional Neural Network. In Proceedings of the ISPRS Annals of the Photogrammetry Remote Sensing and Spatial Information Sciences, Tehran, Iran, 13 January 2023; pp. 195–200. [CrossRef]
41. Zhou, Z.; Siddiquee, M.M.R.; Tajbakhsh, N.; Liang, J. UNet++: A Nested U-Net Architecture for Medical Image Segmentation. In Proceedings of the Deep Learning in Medical Image Analysis and Multimodal Learning for Clinical Decision Support, Granada, Spain, 20 September 2018; pp. 3–11. [CrossRef]
42. Simonyan, K.; Zisserman, A. Very Deep Convolutional Networks for Large-Scale Image Recognition. *arXiv* **2014**, arXiv:1409.1556v6.
43. Fawakherji, M.; Potena, C.; Bloisi, D.D.; Imperoli, M.; Pretto, A.; Nardi, D. UAV Image Based Crop and Weed Distribution Estimation on Embedded GPU Boards. In Proceedings of the Computer Analysis of Images and Patterns, Salerno, Italy, 6 September 2019; pp. 100–108. [CrossRef]
44. Chakraborty, R.; Zhen, X.; Vogt, N.; Bendlin, B.; Singh, V. Dilated Convolutional Neural Networks for Sequential Manifold-Valued Data. In Proceedings of the IEEE/CVF International Conference on Computer Vision, Seoul, South Korea, 27 October—2 November 2019; pp. 10620–10630. [CrossRef]
45. You, J.; Liu, W.; Lee, J. A DNN-Based Semantic Segmentation for Detecting Weed and Crop. *Comput. Electron. Agric.* **2020**, *178*, 10570. [CrossRef]
46. Wang, H.; Song, H.; Wu, H.; Zhang, Z.; Deng, S.; Feng, X.; Chen, Y. Multilayer Feature Fusion and Attention-Based Network for Crops and Weeds Segmentation. *J. Plant Dis. Prot.* **2022**, *129*, 1475–1489. [CrossRef]
47. Siddiqui, S.A.; Fatima, N.; Ahmad, A. Neural Network Based Smart Weed Detection System. In Proceedings of the International Conference on Communication, Control and Information Sciences, Idukki, India, 16–18 June 2021; pp. 1–5. [CrossRef]
48. Khan, A.; Ilyas, T.; Umraiz, M.; Mannan, Z.I.; Kim, H. CED-Net: Crops and Weeds Segmentation for Smart Farming Using a Small Cascaded Encoder-Decoder Architecture. *Electronics* **2020**, *9*, 9101602. [CrossRef]
49. Reinhard, E.; Adhikhmin, M.; Gooch, B.; Shirley, P. Color Transfer between Images. *IEEE Comput. Graph. Appl.* **2001**, *21*, 34–41. [CrossRef]
50. Ruderman, D.L.; Cronin, T.W.; Chiao, C.C. Statistics of Cone Responses to Natural Images: Implications for Visual Coding. *J. Opt. Soc. Am. A-Opt. Image Sci. Vis.* **1998**, *15*, 2036–2045. [CrossRef]
51. Mikołajczyk, A.; Grochowski, M. Data Augmentation for Improving Deep Learning in Image Classification Problem. In Proceedings of the International Interdisciplinary PhD Workshop, Świnoujście, Poland, 9–12 May 2018; pp. 117–122. [CrossRef]
52. Agarap, A.F. Deep Learning Using Rectified Linear Units (ReLU). *arXiv* **2019**, arXiv:1803.08375v2.
53. Clevert, D.A.; Unterthiner, T.; Hochreiter, S. Fast and Accurate Deep Network Learning by Exponential Linear Units (ELUs). *arXiv* **2015**, arXiv:1511.07289v5.
54. Intel Core i5-2320. Available online: https://www.intel.com/content/www/us/en/products/sku/53446/intel-core-i52320-processor-6m-cache-up_to-3-30-ghz/specifications.html (accessed on 5 October 2023).
55. NVIDIA GeForce GTX 1070. Available online: https://www.nvidia.com/en-gb/geforce/10-series/ (accessed on 5 October 2023).
56. PyTorch. Available online: https://pytorch.org/ (accessed on 5 October 2023).
57. Python 3.8. Available online: https://www.python.org/downloads/release/python-380/ (accessed on 5 October 2023).
58. Kingma, D.P.; Ba, J. Adam: A Method for Stochastic Optimization. *arXiv* **2014**, arXiv:1412.6980v9.
59. Loshchilov, I.; Hutter, F. SGDR: Stochastic Gradient Descent with Warm Restarts. *arXiv* **2016**, arXiv:1608.03983v5. Available online: https://arxiv.org/abs/1608.03983 (accessed on 5 October 2023).
60. Sudre, C.H.; Li, W.; Vercauteren, T.; Ourselin, S.; Cardoso, M.J. Generalised Dice Overlap as a Deep Learning Loss Function for Highly Unbalanced Segmentations. In Proceedings of the International Conference on Communication, Control and Information Sciences, Québec City, Canada, 9 September 2017; pp. 240–248. [CrossRef]
61. Xiao, X.; Ma, L. Color Transfer in Correlated Color Space. In Proceedings of the ACM International Conference on Virtual Reality Continuum and Its Applications, Hong Kong, China, 14 June 2006; pp. 305–309. [CrossRef]

62. Pitié, F.; Kokaram, A.C.; Dahyot, R. Automated Colour Grading Using Colour Distribution Transfer. *Comput. Vis. Image Underst.* **2007**, *107*, 123–137. [CrossRef]
63. Gatys, L.A.; Ecker, A.S.; Bethge, M. Image Style Transfer Using Convolutional Neural Networks. In Proceedings of the IEEE Conference on Computer Vision and Pattern Recognition, Las Vegas, NV, USA, 23–27 June 2016; pp. 2414–2423. [CrossRef]
64. Nguyen, R.M.H.; Kim, S.J.; Brown, M.S. Illuminant Aware Gamut-Based Color Transfer. *Comput. Graph. Forum* **2014**, *33*, 319–328. [CrossRef]
65. Rezaie, A.; Mauron, A.J.; Beyer, K. Sensitivity Analysis of Fractal Dimensions of Crack Maps on Concrete and Masonry Walls. *Autom.Constr.* **2020**, *117*, 103258. [CrossRef]
66. Wu, J.; Jin, X.; Mi, S.; Tang, J. An Effective Method to Compute the Box-counting Dimension Based on the Mathematical Definition and Intervals. *Results Eng.* **2020**, *6*, 100106. [CrossRef]
67. Xie, Y. The Application of Fractal Theory in Real-life. In Proceedings of the International Conference on Computing Innovation and Applied Physics, Qingdao, Shandong, China, 30 November 2023; pp. 132–136. [CrossRef]
68. Mishra, P.; Singh, U.; Pandey, C.M.; Mishra, P.; Pandey, G. Application of Student's t-test, Analysis of Variance, and Covariance. *Ann. Card. Anaesth.* **2019**, *22*, 407–411. [CrossRef]
69. Cohen, J. A Power Primer. *Psychol. Bull.* **1992**, *112*, 155–159. [CrossRef]
70. Selvaraju, R.R.; Cogswell, M.; Das, A.; Vedantam, R.; Parikh, D.; Batra, D. Grad-CAM: Grad-CAM: Visual Explanations from Deep Networks via Gradient-Based Localization. In Proceedings of the IEEE International Conference on Computer Vision, Venice, Italy, 22–29 October 2017; pp. 618–626. [CrossRef]

Disclaimer/Publisher's Note: The statements, opinions and data contained in all publications are solely those of the individual author(s) and contributor(s) and not of MDPI and/or the editor(s). MDPI and/or the editor(s) disclaim responsibility for any injury to people or property resulting from any ideas, methods, instructions or products referred to in the content.

 *fractal and fractional*

Article

Fractional-Order Modeling and Identification for an SCR Denitrification Process

Wei Ai [1], Xinlei Lin [1], Ying Luo [1,*] and Xiaowei Wang [2,*]

1. School of Automation Science and Engineering, South China University of Technology, Guangzhou 510640, China; aiwei@scut.edu.cn (W.A.); auxllin@mail.scut.edu.cn (X.L.)
2. School of Mechanical and Electrical Engineering, Guangzhou University, Guangzhou 511370, China
* Correspondence: yingluosase@scut.edu.cn (Y.L.); meewxw_ee@gzhu.edu.cn (X.W.)

Abstract: This paper presents an application of a fractional-order system on modeling an industrial process system with large inertia and time delay. The traditional integer-order model of the process system is extended to a fractional-order one in this work. To identify the parameters of the proposed fractional-order model, an output-error identification algorithm is presented. Based on the experimental step response data of the selective catalytic reduction (SCR) denitrification process in a power plant, this proposed fractional-order model shows a better fitting result compared with the typical integer-order models. An integer-order proportional–integral (PI) controller is designed for the process plant using a simple scheme according to the identified fractional-order and integer-order models, respectively. Validation tests are performed based on the obtained fractional-order and integer-order models, demonstrating the advantages of the proposed fractional-order model with the corresponding system identification approach for industrial processes with large inertia and time delay.

Keywords: fractional-order modeling and identification; selective catalytic reduction denitrification process; large inertia and time delay; proportional integral controller

Citation: Ai, W.; Lin, X.; Luo, Y.; Wang, X. Fractional-Order Modeling and Identification for an SCR Denitrification Process. *Fractal Fract.* **2024**, *8*, 524. https://doi.org/10.3390/fractalfract8090524

Academic Editors: Jinxi Zhang, Xuefeng Zhang, Driss Boutat and Dayan Liu

Received: 8 July 2024
Revised: 3 September 2024
Accepted: 5 September 2024
Published: 9 September 2024

Copyright: © 2024 by the authors. Licensee MDPI, Basel, Switzerland. This article is an open access article distributed under the terms and conditions of the Creative Commons Attribution (CC BY) license (https://creativecommons.org/licenses/by/4.0/).

1. Introduction

Fractional-order modeling has gained significant attention in recent years due to its ability to capture complex dynamics more accurately compared to its traditional integer-order counterparts [1]. Zheng et al. [2] proposed a fractional-order modeling approach for a permanent magnet synchronous motor (PMSM) speed servo system combining electromagnetic part modeling and mechanical part modeling; system identification, closed-loop control simulation, and experiments were conducted, showing the advantage of the proposed fractional-order model. Gan et al. [3] also presented a fractional-order electromagnetic modeling method for a PMSM speed servo system but from the perspective of voltage source inverter nonlinearity, and they proposed an improved inverter nonlinearity model and compensation method. Shi et al. [4] derived a fractional-order Euler–Lagrange equation and applied the proposed equation to describe the dynamics of a multiple-backbone continuum robot; the simulation illustrated that the fractional-order Lagrange dynamic model of the continuum robot had higher modeling accuracy. Sierociuk et al. [5] explored heat conduction under different initial and boundary conditions by analogizing it to electrical conduction, using an RC network as an electro-analog model of the diffusion process model of heat dissipation processes; in addition, a fractional-order model of the diffusion process and its modeling via a lumped RC network was used. A matrix method for solving fractional-order diffusion equations was introduced, and comparisons were made among analytical solutions, numerical solutions, and experimental measurements, demonstrating the effectiveness of the numerical approach. Wang et al. [6] established a fractional-order model of lithium-ion batteries based on a modified Randles model using the form of an equivalent circuit model. The parameters of the fractional-order model were identified based on time-domain test data by using a hybrid multiswarm particle swarm optimization algorithm. A comparison with the commonly used first-order RC equivalent circuit model demonstrates the superiority of the fractional-order model. Zeng et al. [7] established a high-precision fractional-order hysteresis-equivalent circuit model (FH-ECM) based on the second-order RC equivalent circuit model and Grunwald–Letnikov (G-L) definition, considering the open-circuit voltage hysteresis effect; identification was conducted using a particle swarm algorithm optimized by a genetic algorithm (GA-PSO), and the feasibility of the model and algorithm was verified under complex working conditions. Gude et al. [8] introduced a novel method for identifying dynamic systems aimed at deriving reduced-fractional-order models and applied them to processes exhibiting an S-shaped step response. The proposed method demonstrated its efficacy and simplicity through several illustrative examples. Haider et al. [9] proposed a novel method based on a hybrid of Bernoulli polynomials and block pulse functions (HBPBPFs) to identify fractional-order systems with time delays, and the approach was applied to a numerical and a real example of an industrial air heating process. Shalaby et al. [10] proposed a fractional-order model of an inverted pendulum system (IPS), extending the traditional integer-order IPS model to the fractional-order one. The parameters of the proposed fractional-order model were identified using the sine cosine algorithm (SCA), and comparison results showed superior fitting performance compared to the integer-order model. Controllers were designed using the same design approach for the identified fractional-order model, integer-order model, and theoretical nonlinear model (TNM), demonstrating the advantages of the proposed fractional-order modeling approach in control system design.

In the field of process control, considering the knowledge reserve of on-site operators, equipment computing power, and industrial control requirements for safety and stability, a low-order model such as a first-order plus time delay (FOPTD) model is normally used for identification and controller design [11]. However, due to the complex mechanisms, varying conditions, and multisource disturbances typically present in industrial processes, it is a struggle for lower-order models to accurately fit the responses of real systems. On the other hand, employing higher-order models increases the difficulty of controller design. From the above discussion, there is a significant advantage of fractional-order modeling in process control: a fractional-order model with much fewer parameters can achieve satisfactory fitting of system dynamics with significantly decreasing model complexity compared with a high-order model with many more parameters [8]. The selective catalytic reduction (SCR) denitrification process is a typical plant with complex dynamic characteristics, which has a strong need for modeling accuracy and control performance improvements. SCR technology has emerged as a cornerstone in the mitigation of nitrogen oxide (NO_x) emissions from industrial sources, crucial for environmental sustainability and regulatory compliance. Studying the modeling and control of the SCR denitrification process holds significant engineering importance. Pan et al. [12] proposed a simplified dynamical transfer function model of SCR denitrification reaction system adopting mechanism modeling. Li et al. [13] utilized historical data from the distributed control system (DCS) database of a 350 MW coal-fired power plant. The proposed method selects sufficiently excited data from the original historical operation data based on the condition number of the Fisher information matrix, and the asymptotic method is applied to identify the high-order auto-regressive with extra inputs (ARX) model of the SCR denitrification process. Wang et al. [14] proposed an identification method for the SCR flue gas denitration system of a 600 MW power plant under closed-loop operation conditions, based on a new fading memory recursive least squares (FMRLS) algorithm using the squared error loss function (SELF). The results demonstrate that this method offers advantages including a small deviation range, fast convergence speed, and high accuracy. Kang et al. [15] proposed a method that combines dynamic joint mutual information and Bi-LSTM, where the dynamic joint mutual information theory is used to estimate the reactor dynamic characteristics and system delay. Through the analysis of the formation mechanism of NOx and the reaction mechanism of the SCR reactor, Xie et al. [16] proposed a sequence-to-sequence dynamic prediction model, which can fit multivariable coupling, nonlinear, and large delay systems. An et al. [17] proposed a method based on hybrid data-driven approaches and model ensemble to dynamically estimate NO_x concentrations at the outlet of SCR systems. The approach includes outlier detection, time delay estimation, phase space reconstruction, and feature selection. Through model ensemble strategies integrating genetic algorithm-optimized neural networks, support vector machines, and gradient boosting models, a model accurately predicts NO_x emissions from SCR systems. Validation results demonstrate excellent dynamic tracking performance and prediction consistency in practical industrial applications.

Based on the above discussion, this paper explores an application of fractional-order systems in modeling the SCR denitrification process in a power plant which can be characterized by large inertia and time delays. It extends the traditional FOPTD model of such processes to a fractional-order model. To identify the parameters of the proposed model, an output-error identification algorithm is introduced. Using experimental step response data from the SCR denitrification process, the fractional-order model demonstrates superior fitting results compared to the integer-order model. An integer-order proportional–integral (PI) controller is designed for the process plant based on both the identified fractional-order model and the integer-order model. Validation tests confirm the advantages of the fractional-order model and the corresponding system identification approach for this industrial process.

The main contributions of this paper are summarized as follows:

(1) A fractional-order plus time delay modeling with a parameter identification approach for experimental step response data from an industrial power plant SCR denitrification process is proposed;
(2) Closed-loop control illustration using the PI controllers designed for the traditional integer-order models and the fractional-order one is conducted to show the advantages of the proposed fractional-order model with the corresponding system identification approach.

The rest of this paper is organized as follows: the main chemical reaction equation and dynamic mechanism model of the SCR denitrification process are discussed in Section 2; the fundamentals of fractional calculus, an integer-order approximation approach of fractional-order operators, and a time-domain identification method of fractional-order model are presented in Section 3; and parameter identification and control simulation based on experimental data of an SCR denitrification process in a power plant are conducted in Section 4. The conclusion is provided in the last section.

2. SCR Denitrification Process

The denitrification process of coal-fired units exhibits complex characteristics with large inertia and time delay, posing practical challenges in modeling and control. This section introduces the structure of the SCR denitrification system and its dynamic reaction mechanism.

2.1. Reaction Process of SCR Denitrification System

The schematic diagram of the SCR denitrification system for coal-fired units is shown in Figure 1 [18]. Flue gas generated by boiler combustion and ammonia gas diluted with air are introduced into the SCR reactor vessel simultaneously, and harmless nitrogen gas and water are produced, thereby strictly controlling the concentration of NO_x in the outlet flue gas. The main chemical reactions in this process are as follows [18]:

$$\begin{cases} 4NO + 4NH_3 + O_2 = 4N_2 + 6H_2O \\ 6NO + 4NH_3 = 5N_2 + 6H_2O \\ 6NO_2 + 8NH_3 = 7N_2 + 12H_2O \\ 2NO_2 + 4NH_3 + O_2 = 3N_2 + 6H_2O \end{cases} \quad (1)$$

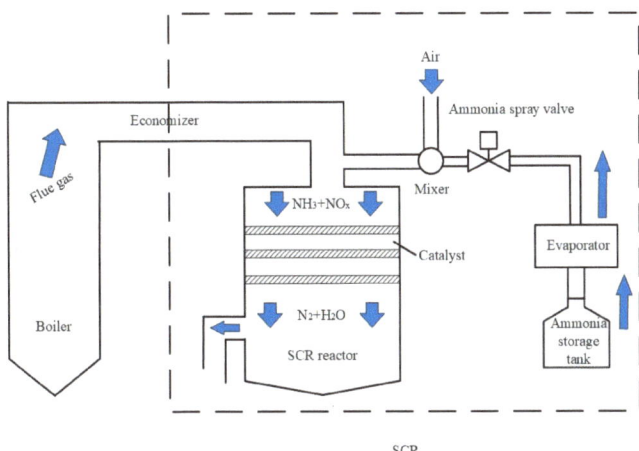

Figure 1. Schematic diagram of the selective catalytic reduction (SCR) denitrification system.

In the practical denitrification process, approximately 95% of the NO_x introduced into the reactor is NO; thus, the primary chemical reactions that occur are the first two reactions mentioned above.

The basic control diagram of the SCR denitrification process is shown in Figure 2. Adjusting the opening of the ammonia injection valve to control the amount of ammonia injected ensures sufficient reaction of NO_x in the flue gas. In the above-mentioned process, excessive ammonia injection leads to high outlet ammonia concentration, while insufficient injection results in NO_x concentration exceeding the standard [19].

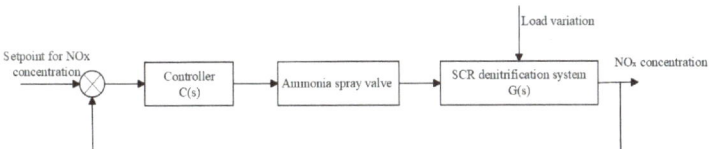

Figure 2. Basic control diagram of the SCR denitrification process.

2.2. Dynamic Mechanism of the SCR Denitrification Reaction

Investigating the reaction mechanism of the SCR denitrification process enhances comprehension of the intricate dynamic characteristics inherent to this process. Yao et al. [20] proposed a set of nonlinear differential equations to describe the dynamics of the SCR denitrification reaction:

$$\begin{aligned} \frac{dC_{NO}}{dt} &= \Theta(R_{ox} - R_{red}) + \frac{F}{V}\left(C_{NO}^{in} - C_{NO}\right) \\ \frac{d\theta_{NH_3}}{dt} &= R_{ads} - R_{des} - R_{red} - R_{ox} \\ \frac{dC_{NH_3}}{dt} &= \Theta(R_{des} - R_{ads}) + \frac{F}{V}\left(C_{NH_3}^{in} - C_{NH_3}\right) \end{aligned} \quad (2)$$

where C_{NO} and C_{NH_3} are the concentrations of NO and NH_3 in the SCR process; C_{NO}^{in} and $C_{NH_3}^{in}$ are the inlet concentration of NO and N; θ_{NH_3} is the coverage fraction of NH_3 on the catalyst surface; F and V are the flue gas flow and the volume of the reactor, respectively; Θ characterizes the adsorption capacity of the catalyst for NH_3 in the reactor; R_{ox}, R_{red}, R_{ads}, and R_{des} are the rates of oxidation, reduction, adsorption, and desorption, which can be calculated by

$$R_{ox} = k_{ox} \exp\left(-\frac{E_{ox}}{RT}\right)\theta_{NH_3}$$
$$R_{red} = k_{red} \exp\left(-\frac{E_{red}}{RT}\right)C_{NO}\theta_{NH_3}$$
$$R_{ads} = k_{ads} \exp\left(-\frac{E_{ads}}{RT}\right)C_{NH_3}(1-\theta_{NH_3})$$
$$R_{des} = k_{des} \exp\left(-\frac{E_{des}}{RT}\right)\theta_{NH_3}$$
(3)

where k_{ox}, k_{red}, k_{ads}, and k_{des} refer to oxidation rate coefficient, denitrification rate coefficient, adsorption rate coefficient, and desorption rate coefficient; E_{ox}, E_{red}, E_{ads}, and E_{des} stand for the activation energies in the corresponding reaction; and R and T refer to the universal gas constant and temperature, respectively. The units of the quantities are provided in Appendix B.

The adsorption and desorption of ammonia are intermediate processes in the entire denitrification reaction; hence, the coverage fraction of NH_3 (θ_{NH_3}) is regarded as an intermediate state variable in the dynamic model of the denitrification reaction. To simplify the model complexity, the concentration of the material inside the reactor is assumed to be equal to the outlet concentration. The inlet NH_3 molar concentration ($C_{NH_3}^{in}$) and inlet NO_x molar concentration (C_{NO}^{in}) are the inputs to the mechanism model, while the outlet NH_3 molar concentration (C_{NH_3}) and outlet NO_x molar concentration (C_{NO}) are the outputs of the mechanism model. k_{ox}, k_{red}, k_{ads}, k_{des}, E_{ox}, E_{red}, E_{ads}, E_{des}, and Θ remain constant during the reaction and can be obtained through identification. However, the concentration and flue gas flow fields within the reactor are nonuniform, and the flue gas temperature can only be measured at the reactor inlet, while the temperature inside the reactor is unmeasurable. Additionally, the aforementioned dynamics do not account for side reactions involving ammonia and other substances such as sulfur compounds in the flue gas, leading to poor generalization of the nonlinear model and difficulty in meeting control requirements. Consequently, black-box modeling methods are widely used in the denitrification process [13,14,18]. In practical applications, since the inlet NO_x concentration is relatively constant, the ammonia injection amount is often used as the input and the outlet NO_x concentration as the output for modeling.

3. Fractional Order Modeling and Identification

First, the fundamental concept of fractional calculus is introduced in this section, and then an implementation approximation method is presented, which approximates the fractional-order operators in the frequency domain. Furthermore, the approximation method of a fractional-order transfer function and time-domain identification method based on the fractional-order model are presented in the last two subsections.

3.1. Fundamental Concept of Fractional Calculus

The continuous fractional order integral–differential operator is defined as follows:

$$_{t_0}D_t^\alpha \triangleq \begin{cases} \frac{d^\alpha}{dt^\alpha} & \text{Re}(\alpha) > 0, \\ 1 & \text{Re}(\alpha) = 0, \\ \int_{t_0}^t (d\tau)^{-\alpha} & \text{Re}(\alpha) < 0, \end{cases}$$
(4)

where t_0 and t are the time limits of the integration and α is the fractional order, and $Re(\alpha)$ is the real part of α.

The Caputo definition of a fractional derivative is

$$_{t_0}D_t^\alpha f(t) = \frac{1}{\Gamma(n-\alpha)} \int_{t_0}^{t} (t-\tau)^{n-\alpha-1} f(\tau)\, d\tau \tag{5}$$

where n is an integer, satisfying $n-1 < \alpha < n$, and $\Gamma(x)$ is the Gamma function with the definition

$$\Gamma(x) = \int_0^\infty t^{x-1} e^{-t} dt. \tag{6}$$

The Laplace transform of the above-mentioned derivative is

$$\mathcal{L}\{_0D_t^\alpha f(t)\} = s^\alpha \mathcal{L}\{f(t)\} \tag{7}$$

where $n-1 < \alpha \leq n$.

3.2. Approximation of Fractional-Order Operator and System

The fractional-order system is infinite-dimensional, so approximation within a certain range is required in numerical simulation to approximate the behavior of a fractional-order system.

In this subsection, the fractional-order operator under discussion is s^γ, where $\gamma \in (-1, 1)$, and the fractional-order operator outside this range can be approximated by cascading with an integer-order operator [1].

Theoretically, the slope of the Bode magnitude characteristics of s^γ is 20γ dB/dec, while the slope of the asymptotic Bode plot for an integer-order transfer function is always a multiple of 20 dB/dec. Hence, it is not possible to achieve a completely consistent approximation of a fractional-order operator using an integer-order transfer function.

An Oustaloup filter [21] is a commonly used integer-order approximation method that approximates the Bode magnitude characteristics of fractional-order operators within a specific frequency range, using a set of integer-order poles and zeros to generate asymptotic Bode plots as shown in Figure 3 [22]. The slanted line in Figure 3 represents the ideal magnitude-frequency characteristic curve of the fractional-order operator, while the polyline is the approximation of the ideal magnitude-frequency curve within the specified frequency range.

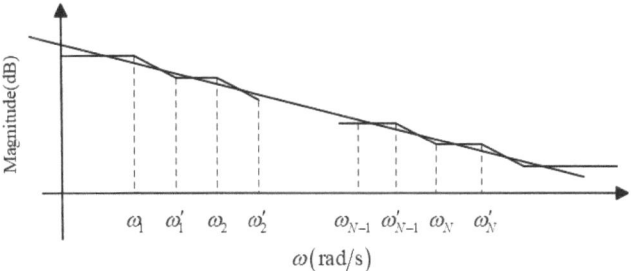

Figure 3. Illustration of the Bode plot of the Oustaloup filter.

The standard form of the Oustaloup filter is given as follows:

$$G_{flt}(s) = K_{flt} \prod_{i=1}^{N} \frac{s + \omega_i'}{s + \omega_i} \tag{8}$$

where K_{flt}, ω_i', and ω_i refer to the gain, zeros, and poles of the filter, respectively; N is the order of the filter.

Giving the frequency range (ω_L, ω_H) and the order N, the parameters of the Oustaloup filter can be calculated by

$$\begin{cases} \omega_m = \sqrt{\omega_H/\omega_L} \\ K_{flt} = \omega_H^\gamma \\ \omega_i' = \omega_L \omega_m^{(2i-1-\gamma)/N} \\ \omega_i = \omega_L \omega_m^{(2i-1+\gamma)/N}. \end{cases} \quad (9)$$

Fractional-order transfer functions can be used to describe the dynamics of the system. By replacing the fractional-order operator with the Oustaloup filter in a fractional-order transfer function, an integer-order approximation of the fractional-order model can be realized.

The frequency range affects the filter's ability to process signal frequencies, while the order determines the approximation capability and impacts model accuracy. When designing the Oustaloup filter, the rough estimation of the cutoff frequency of the plant is chosen as the midpoint of the frequency range for the filter. Since a larger frequency range and a higher order do not significantly increase the computation time of the filter parameters [22], a frequency range with the size of at least six decades and an order of 15 or higher are chosen to ensure that the output of the model closely approximates the actual plant.

3.3. Identification of the Fractional-Order Model with Time Delay

The proposed fractional-order plus time delay model to be identified is described as follows:

$$G(s) = \frac{K}{Ts^\alpha + 1} e^{-Ls} \quad (10)$$

where α is extended from a positive integer to any positive rational number; the FOPTD model is a specific instance of the above-mentioned model with $\alpha = 1$.

Known from the previous section, model (10) can be approximated by the following integer-order transfer function using an Oustaloup filter:

$$G_{approx}(s;x) = \frac{K \prod_{i=1}^{N}\left[s + \omega_L \left(\frac{\omega_H}{\omega_L}\right)^{(2i-1+\alpha)/N}\right]}{T\omega_H^\alpha \prod_{i=1}^{N}\left[s + \omega_L \left(\frac{\omega_H}{\omega_L}\right)^{(2i-1-\alpha)/N}\right] + \prod_{i=1}^{N}\left[s + \omega_L \left(\frac{\omega_H}{\omega_L}\right)^{(2i-1+\alpha)/N}\right]} e^{-Ls} \quad (11)$$

where $x = [K, T, L, \alpha]^T$ is the model parameter vector to be identified, while the frequency range (ω_L, ω_H) and the order N of the Oustaloup filter should be determined before the optimization procedure begins and stay consistent during the optimization process.

The classic graphical method is employed to obtain the initial model parameter vector $x_0 = [K_0, T_0, L_0, \alpha_0]^T$ and determine the frequency range and the order of the Oustaloup filter. The estimation of the cutoff frequency of the plant is denoted as $\omega_{est} = 1/T_0$, the frequency range of the filter is determined as $(\omega_{est}/1000, 1000\omega_{est})$, and the order is chosen to be 15.

The MATLAB function *lsim* is used to calculate the model (11) output $y_m(k;x)$ based on the input signal $u(k)$ and the model parameter vector x, where k represents the individual sample time point. The objective function of this optimization procedure is the root mean square error (RMSE) between the model output $y_m(k;x)$ and experimental output $y_e(k)$, i.e.,

$$f(x) = \sqrt{\frac{1}{n}\sum_{k=1}^{n}(y_e(k) - y_m(k;x))^2} \quad (12)$$

where n is the number of sample points.

The MATLAB function *fminunc* for finding the minimum value of an unconstrained multivariable function is applied in this work. Optimization is performed using the Broyden–Fletcher–Goldfarb–Shanno (BFGS) [23–26] quasi-Newton method within this function. The gradient of the objective function $g(x)$ and an approximation of the inverse of the Hessian matrix H are used in the iteration.

The gradient is calculated using the forward finite difference method:

$$g(x) = \nabla f(x) \approx \left[\frac{f\left(x + he^{(1)}\right) - f(x)}{h}, \frac{f\left(x + he^{(2)}\right) - f(x)}{h}, \ldots, \frac{f\left(x + he^{(m)}\right) - f(x)}{h} \right] \quad (13)$$

where h is the step size, with a recommended value of $\sqrt{eps}$ [27], and $eps = 2.2204 \times 10^{-16}$ is the relative floating-point precision in MATLAB; m is the dimension of x, and $e^{(l)}$ is an m-dimensional unit vector with the l-th element equal to 1, $l = 1, 2, \ldots, m$.

Before the iteration starts, the gradient at the initial point is calculated. If $\| g(x_0) \|_\infty < \epsilon$, where $\| \cdot \|_\infty$ denotes the infinity norm of a vector and $\epsilon = 1 \times 10^{-6}$ is the tolerance value, then the identification program terminates, and x_0 is returned as the optimal value x^*; otherwise, the matrix H is initialized to $H_0 = I_{m \times m}$, where $I_{m \times m}$ is the m-dimensional identity matrix. The iterative process is described as follows:

1. Line search: search along the given direction, determine the optimal step size, and update the solution.

    (a) Search direction p_j: quasi-Newton direction is determined as follows:

    $$p_j = -H_j g(x_j) \quad (14)$$

    where $j = 0, 1, \ldots, J - 1$, J is the maximum number of iterations (400 in this paper).

    (b) Step size λ_j: the Wolfe conditions are used to determine the search step size to ensure effective descent and improve convergence speed. The Wolfe conditions are defined as follows:

    $$\begin{cases} f\left(x_j + \lambda_j p_j\right) \leq f(x_j) + \rho \lambda_j g(x_j)^T p_j \\ g\left(x_j + \lambda_j p_j\right)^T p_j \geq \sigma g(x_j)^T p_j \end{cases} \quad (15)$$

    where $0 < \rho < \sigma < 1$. ρ ensures a significant descent in the objective function at the step size, while σ ensures that the gradient of the objective function changes sufficiently at the new point. In this paper, $\rho = 0.01$ and $\sigma = 0.9$. In each iteration, the initial step size is set to 1. If the current step size does not satisfy the Wolfe conditions, the step size is updated according to the following formula until the Wolfe conditions are met:

    $$\lambda_j = \rho \lambda_j. \quad (16)$$

    (c) Update solution x_{j+1}: according to the search direction and step size, the solution is updated as follows:

    $$x_{j+1} = x_j + \lambda_j p_j \quad (17)$$

2. Update the approximation of the inverse of the Hessian matrix: the BFGS method uses information from the previous iteration and related increments to update the approximation of the inverse of the Hessian matrix:

$$H_{j+1} = H_j + \frac{\Delta g(x_j) \Delta g(x_j)^T}{\Delta g(x_j)^T \Delta x_j} - \frac{H_j \Delta x_j \Delta x_j^T H_j^T}{\Delta x_j^T H_j \Delta x_j} \quad (18)$$

where $\Delta g(x_j) = g(x_{j+1}) - g(x_j)$ and $\Delta x_j = x_{j+1} - x_j$.

3. Termination: In each iteration, early termination is determined by checking if the gradient, solution increment, and objective function increment fall below predefined tolerance:

$$\begin{cases} \| g(x_{j+1}) \|_\infty < (1+ \| g(x_0) \|_\infty)\epsilon \\ \| \Delta x_j \|_\infty < \epsilon \\ |\frac{\Delta f(x_j)}{1+|f(x_j)|}| < \epsilon \end{cases} \quad (19)$$

where $\Delta f(x_j) = f(x_{j+1}) - f(x_j)$.

Algorithm 1 presents the pseudo-code for the identification procedure.

Algorithm 1 The pseudo-code of the identification procedure.

1:   Employ the classic graphical method to obtain $x_0 = [K_0, T_0, L_0, \alpha_0]^T$;
2:   Determine the cutoff frequency of the plant $\omega_{est} = 1/T_0$, the Oustaloup filter's frequency range $(\omega_{est}/1000, 1000\omega_{est})$ and its order (the recommended value is 15), and the approximated model (11);
3:   Form the objective function (12);
4:   $g(x_0) = $ Equation (13);
5:   **if** $\| g(x_0) \|_\infty < \epsilon$ **then**
6:     return $x^* = x_0$;
7:   **else**
8:     $f(x_0) = $ Equation (12);
9:     $H_0 = I_{m \times m}$;
10:    **for** $j = 0 : J - 1$ **do**
11:      $p_j = $ Equation (14);
12:      $\lambda_j = 1$;
13:      **while** Equation (15) is not satisfied **do**
14:        $\lambda_j = $ Equation (16);
15:      **end while**
16:      $x_{j+1} = $ Equation (17);
17:      $f(x_{j+1}) = $ Equation (12);
18:      $g(x_{j+1}) = $ Equation (13);
19:      $\Delta x_j = x_{j+1} - x_j$;
20:      $\Delta f(x_j) = f(x_{j+1}) - f(x_j)$;
21:      **if** Any condition in (19) is satisfied **then**
22:        return $x^* = x_{j+1}$;
23:      **end if**
24:      $\Delta g(x_j) = g(x_{j+1}) - g(x_j)$;
25:      $H_{j+1} = $ Equation (18);
26:    **end for**
27:    return $x^* = x_J$;
28:   **end if**

---

4. Fractional-Order Model Identification of the SCR Denitrification Process

In industrial processes, the FOPTD model's simplicity facilitates proper controller design. However, the SCR denitrification system's large inertia and delay characteristics lead to poor fitting when using FOPTD modeling, while the higher-order modeling method increases the complexity of controller design. Fractional-order modeling shows the advantages of both better fitting and easier controller design compared with traditional integer-order modeling.

4.1. Experimental Setup

In this paper, the research focuses on the SCR denitrification system employed in a 660 MW generator unit at the Honghaiwan Power Plant, Southern China Grid. Emerson's OVATION1.9 distributed control system (DCS) collects historical operation data, which provides advanced monitoring, control, and data analysis capabilities. It supports real-time data acquisition and optimization control strategies to enhance industrial process efficiency, safety, and reliability. The OVATION system is characterized by openness and scalability, seamlessly integrating with other equipment and systems to meet the demands of the complex industrial environment. The historical operational data used for identification are steady-state step open-loop test data conducted at 400 MW and 580 MW loads, with a sampling period of 3 s. Maintaining a steady-state condition of total airflow and coal quantity during data acquisition is essential to ensure the stable operation of the SCR denitrification process. Figure 4 shows the experimental conditions under 400 MW and 580 MW. The experimental data are extracted from the point that the input signal starts to change. The input and output signals should undergo incremental preprocessing before parameter identification.

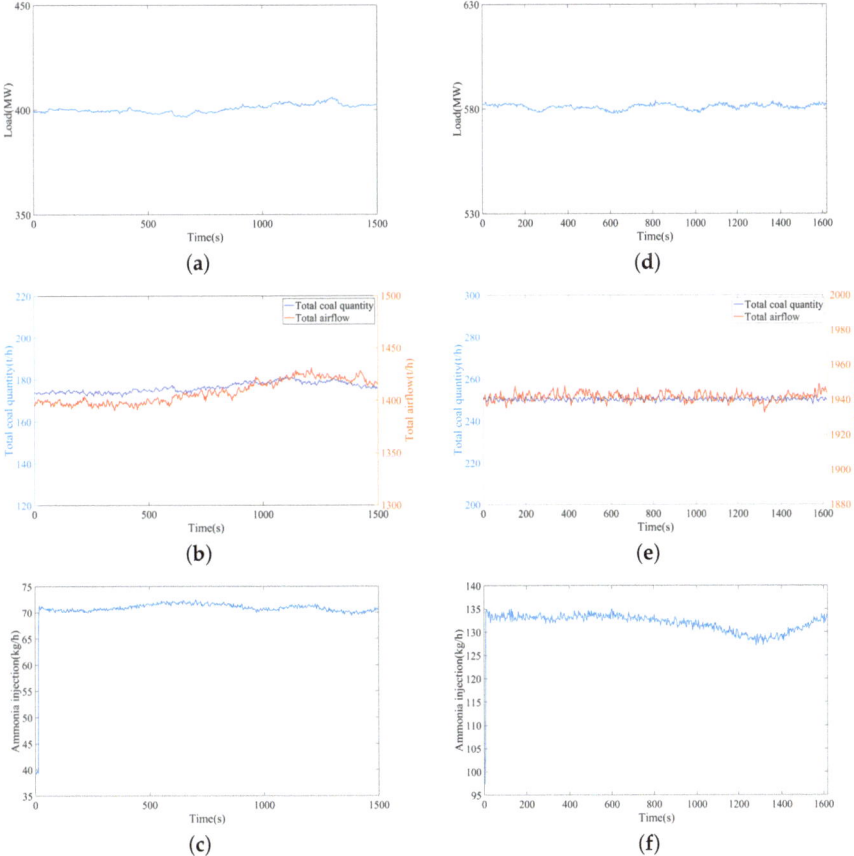

Figure 4. Experimental conditions under 400 MW and 580 MW. (**a**) 400 MW load curve. (**b**) Total airflow and coal quantity curves under 400 MW. (**c**) Input volume curve under 400 MW. (**d**) 580 MW load curve. (**e**) Total airflow and coal quantity curves under 580 MW. (**f**) Input volume curve under 580 MW.

4.2. System Identification

To confirm the effectiveness of the proposed fractional-order model, this subsection provides comparisons of the identification results between the proposed fractional-order model with the traditional FOPTD model and other integer-order models presented in [13,14].

Ref. [13] proposed an ARX model with parameters to be identified, which is

$$A\left(z^{-1}\right)y(k) = z^{-d}B\left(z^{-1}\right)u(k) \qquad (20)$$

where z^{-1} is a unit delay, k represents the time series, and d is the number of samples for the time delay. $u(k)$ and $y(k)$ stand for the input and output signals, respectively. $A\left(z^{-1}\right) = 1 + a_1 z^{-1} + a_2 z^{-2} + a_3 z^{-3} + a_4 z^{-4}$ and $B\left(z^{-1}\right) = b_0 + b_1 z^{-1} + b_2 z^{-2} + b_3 z^{-3}$, where a_1 to a_4, b_0 to b_3, and d are the parameters to be determined. The sampling period of the ARX model in our paper is 3 s as well.

Ref. [14] proposed a second-order transfer function model, which is

$$G_S(s) = \frac{K_p e^{-\tau s}}{As^2 + Bs + 1} \qquad (21)$$

where K_p, τ, A, and B are the parameters to be identified.

Figure 5 shows the identification results of the fractional-order model, the FOPTD model, and the two models mentioned above, respectively. Tables 1 and 2 present the identified models and the RMSE of each model, showing the advantage of the fractional-order model in better fitting.

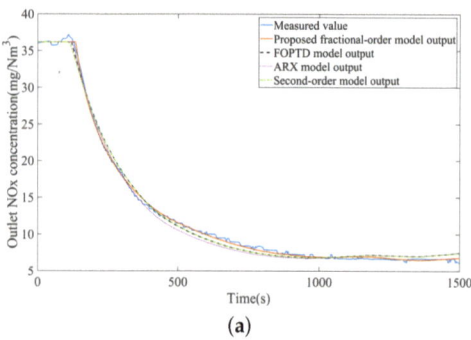
(a)

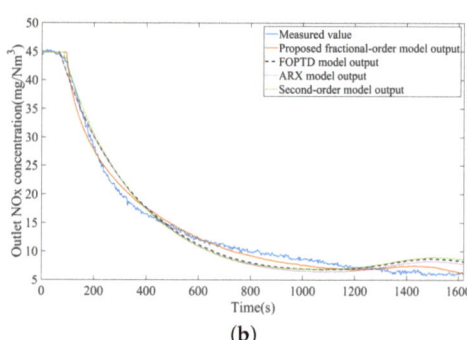
(b)

Figure 5. Comparison curves between model outputs and actual data under 400 MW and 580 MW. (a) 400 MW output curves. (b) 580 MW output curves.

Table 1. Identification result of dynamic characteristics of SCR denitrification system under 400 MW.

Model	Transfer Function of Ammonia Injection–Outlet NO$_x$ Concentration	RMSE (mg/Nm^3)
Fractional-order model	$\frac{-0.9864}{66.5126 s^{0.8157}+1} e^{-120s}$	0.2965
FOPTD model	$\frac{-0.9167}{185.6833 s+1} e^{-102s}$	0.6082
ARX model	$\frac{-0.0046 - 0.0098 z^{-1} + 0.0100 z^{-2} - 0.0167 z^{-3}}{1 - 0.7280 z^{-1} - 0.1798 z^{-2} - 0.0868 z^{-3} + 0.0175 z^{-4}} z^{-35}$	0.6887
Second-order model	$\frac{-0.9205}{1800.0249 s^2 + 197.8617 s + 1} e^{-90s}$	0.6162

Table 2. Identification result of dynamic characteristics of SCR denitrification system under 580 MW.

Model	Transfer Function of Ammonia Injection–Outlet NO$_x$ Concentration	RMSE (mg/Nm^3)
Fractional-order model	$\frac{-1.4372}{55.3038s^{0.6666}+1}e^{-90s}$	0.9390
FOPTD model	$\frac{-1.1243}{288.7331s+1}e^{-60s}$	1.6683
ARX model	$\frac{-0.0050-0.0117z^{-1}+0.0044z^{-2}-0.0109z^{-3}}{1-0.3947z^{-1}-0.2219z^{-2}-0.3155z^{-3}-0.0473z^{-4}}z^{-20}$	1.6944
Second-order model	$\frac{-1.1153}{4.1502\times10^{-6}s^2+266.7710s+1}e^{-75s}$	1.8092

The order of the fractional derivative has a significant impact on the solutions of fractional differential equations. Ref. [28] discusses the impact of the value of fractional order on the characteristics and dynamics of soliton solutions in the fractional nonlinear Schrödinger equation (fNLSE). Ref. [29] studies the boundary value problem for a fractional oscillator with random order and provides the random behavior of the solution to the fractional differential equation under different random processes for varying orders. Ref. [30] investigates an efficient iterative method for solving nonlinear fractional optimal control problems affected by external persistent disturbances and provides numerical simulation results for different fractional orders. The results indicate that the proposed method performs well for problems where the order is close to 1.

In this paper, to investigate the fitting performance of the fractional-order model under different given orders, model identification is performed for the experimental data based on each specified order.

Figure 6 shows the outputs of the fractional-order model for different given orders, while Tables 3 and 4 present the RMSE between the model output and the experimental data. The results indicate that as the given order approaches the previously identified order, the RMSE between the identified model output and the experimental data correspondingly decreases.

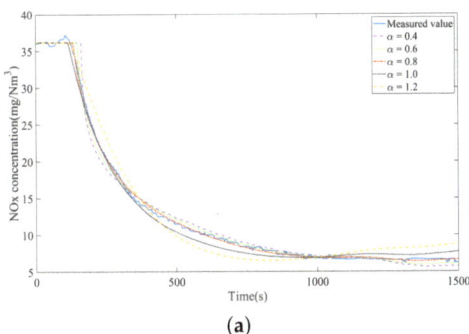
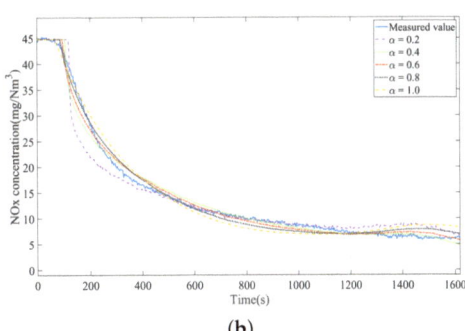

(a)   (b)

Figure 6. Fitting performance of the fractional-order model output under different given orders. (a) 400 MW load. (b) 580 MW load.

Table 3. RMSE between the fractional-order model output with given orders and the experimental data under 400 MW.

	$\alpha = 0.4$	$\alpha = 0.6$	$\alpha = 0.8$	$\alpha = 1.0$	$\alpha = 1.2$
RMSE (mg/Nm^3)	0.9328	0.5863	0.3179	0.6082	1.5523

Table 4. RMSE between the fractional-order model output with given orders and the experimental data under 580 MW.

	$\alpha = 0.2$	$\alpha = 0.4$	$\alpha = 0.6$	$\alpha = 0.8$	$\alpha = 1.0$
RMSE (mg/Nm³)	2.2985	1.2196	0.9825	1.1003	1.6683

4.3. Model Verification Based on Closed-Loop Control Step Response

To demonstrate the advantages of fractional-order modeling, this paper utilizes the MATLAB function *tfest* to fit a high-order model as a surrogate model for the actual plant. The MATLAB functions used in this paper can be found in Appendix A. The RMSE of the high-order model are 0.2306 mg/Nm³ and 0.3914 mg/Nm³ under 400 MW and 580 MW, respectively. Two groups of PI controllers are designed using the same scheme according to the identified fractional-order model and the other three models and applied to the high-order models. The fractional-order model is chosen to demonstrate the controller's design strategy. The transfer functions of the high-order models are as follows:

$$G_1(s) = \frac{-0.0071s^3 - 6.4832 \times 10^{-5}s^2 - 8.3457 \times 10^{-6}s - 2.2928 \times 10^{-8}}{s^4 + 0.0171s^3 + 0.0013s^2 + 1.4328 \times 10^{-5}s + 2.3691 \times 10^{-8}} e^{-117s} \quad (22)$$

and

$$G_2(s) = \frac{-0.0331s^3 - 0.0045s^2 - 3.7011 \times 10^{-4}s - 2.6082 \times 10^{-7}}{s^4 + 1.8427s^3 + 0.0652s^2 + 4.8645 \times 10^{-4}s + 1.1495 \times 10^{-7}} e^{-75s} \quad (23)$$

where $G_1(s)$ and $G_2(s)$ are the transfer functions of the high-order models under 400 MW and 580 MW, respectively.

The transfer function of the PI controller is

$$C(s) = K_p \left(1 + \frac{K_i}{s}\right) \quad (24)$$

where K_p and K_i are the proportional and integral gains, respectively.

The PI controller is designed with two frequency specifications: gain crossover frequency ω_c and phase margin ϕ_m, which satisfy

$$|C(\omega_c)G(\omega_c)| = 1, \quad (25)$$

$$Arg[C(\omega_c)G(\omega_c)] = -\pi + \phi_m. \quad (26)$$

The gain and phase of the PI controller and the identified fractional-order model are

$$|C(\omega)| = |K_p|\sqrt{1 + \frac{K_i^2}{\omega^2}}, \quad (27)$$

$$|G(\omega)| = \frac{|K|}{\sqrt{(1 + T\omega^\alpha \cos(\alpha\pi/2))^2 + (T\omega^\alpha \sin(\alpha\pi/2))^2}}, \quad (28)$$

$$Arg[C(\omega)] = -\tan^{-1}\left(\frac{K_i}{\omega}\right), \quad (29)$$

$$Arg[G(\omega)] = -\tan^{-1}\left(\frac{T\omega^\alpha \sin(\alpha\pi/2)}{1 + T\omega^\alpha \cos(\alpha\pi/2)}\right) - \omega L. \quad (30)$$

Based on the gain–frequency and phase–frequency relationships of the PI controller and the fractional-order model given in (27)–(30), considering the gain and phase conditions in (25) and (26) at the gain crossover frequency, the algebraic equations for the PI controller parameters are derived as follows:

$$|K_p|\sqrt{1+\frac{K_i^2}{\omega_c^2}}\frac{|K|}{\sqrt{(1+T\omega_c^\alpha \cos(\alpha\pi/2))^2+(T\omega_c^\alpha \sin(\alpha\pi/2))^2}}=1, \quad (31)$$

$$-\tan^{-1}\left(\frac{K_i}{\omega_c}\right)-\tan^{-1}\left(\frac{T\omega_c^\alpha \sin(\alpha\pi/2)}{1+T\omega_c^\alpha \cos(\alpha\pi/2)}\right)-\omega_c L = -\pi+\phi_m. \quad (32)$$

Solving the algebraic Equations (31) and (32), the PI controller parameters that ensure the control system meets the frequency domain specifications are obtained:

$$K_i = \omega_c \tan\left(\pi-\phi_m-\tan^{-1}\left(\frac{T\omega_c^\alpha \sin(\alpha\pi/2)}{1+T\omega_c^\alpha \cos(\alpha\pi/2)}\right)-\omega_c L\right),$$

$$|K_p| = \frac{\omega_c\sqrt{(1+T\omega_c^\alpha \cos(\alpha\pi/2))^2+(T\omega_c^\alpha \sin(\alpha\pi/2))^2}}{|K|\sqrt{\omega_c^2+K_i^2}}, \quad (33)$$

and the symbol of K_p should ensure that the closed-loop system is a negative feedback system, which means K_p should have the same sign as K.

$C_F(s)$, $C_I(s)$, $C_{ARX}(s)$, and $C_{SO}(s)$ are the transfer functions of the PI controller designed for the fractional-order model, FOPTD model, ARX model, and second-order model, respectively.

1. For 400 MW, $\omega_c = 0.004$ rad/s, and $\phi_m = 60°$:

$$C_F(s) = -0.6712\left(1+\frac{0.0074}{s}\right), \quad (34)$$

$$C_I(s) = -0.6752\left(1+\frac{0.0070}{s}\right), \quad (35)$$

$$C_{ARX}(s) = -0.6345\left(1+\frac{0.0073}{s}\right), \quad (36)$$

$$C_{SO}(s) = -0.6765\left(1+\frac{0.0070}{s}\right). \quad (37)$$

The open-loop Bode plots of the control system under 400 MW load with identified models are shown in Figure 7a.

Applying the designed PI controllers for the high-order system, a comparison between the identified model output and the high-order model output of each control system is shown in Figure 8. The RMSE between the identified model outputs and the high-order model output are shown in Table 5.

2. For 580 MW, $\omega_c = 0.005$ rad/s, and $\phi_m = 60°$:

$$C_F(s) = -0.8795\left(1+\frac{0.0075}{s}\right), \quad (38)$$

$$C_I(s) = -0.6063\left(1+\frac{0.0087}{s}\right), \quad (39)$$

$$C_{ARX}(s) = -1.0659\left(1+\frac{0.0053}{s}\right), \quad (40)$$

$$C_{SO}(s) = -1.0500\left(1 + \frac{0.0051}{s}\right). \tag{41}$$

The open-loop Bode plots of the control system under 580 MW load with identified models are shown in Figure 7b.

Applying the designed PI controllers for the high-order system, a comparison between the identified model output and the high-order model output of each control system is shown in Figure 9. The RMSE between the identified model outputs and the high-order model output are shown in Table 5.

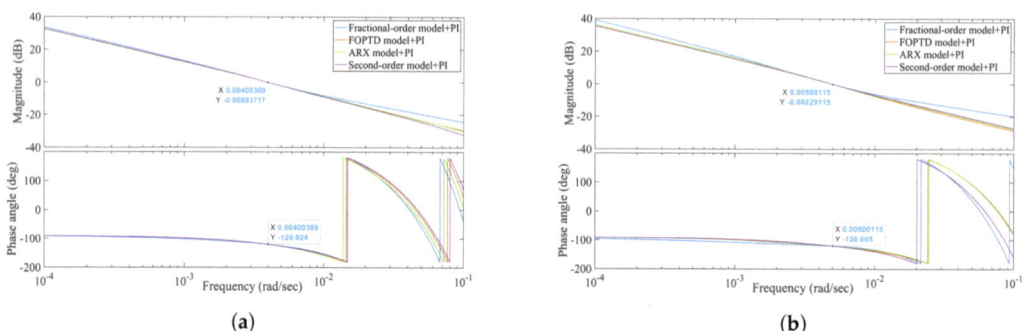

Figure 7. The open-loop plots of each control system under 400 MW and 580 MW. (**a**) 400 MW. (**b**) 580 MW.

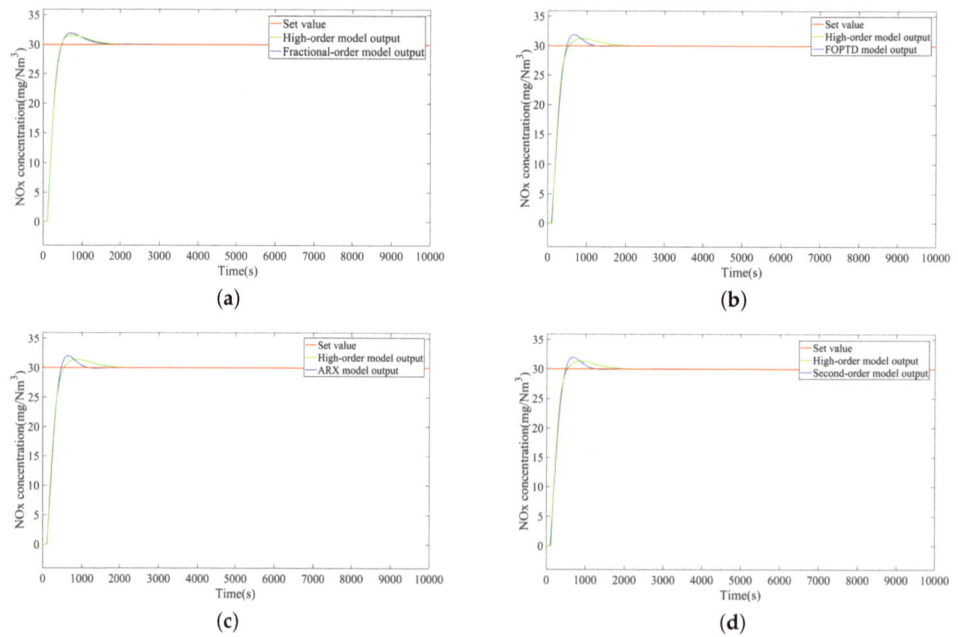

Figure 8. Step tracking responses under 400 MW. (**a**) Fractional-order model output and high-order model output. (**b**) FOPTD model output and high-order model output. (**c**) ARX model output and high-order model output. (**d**) Second-order model output and high-order model output.

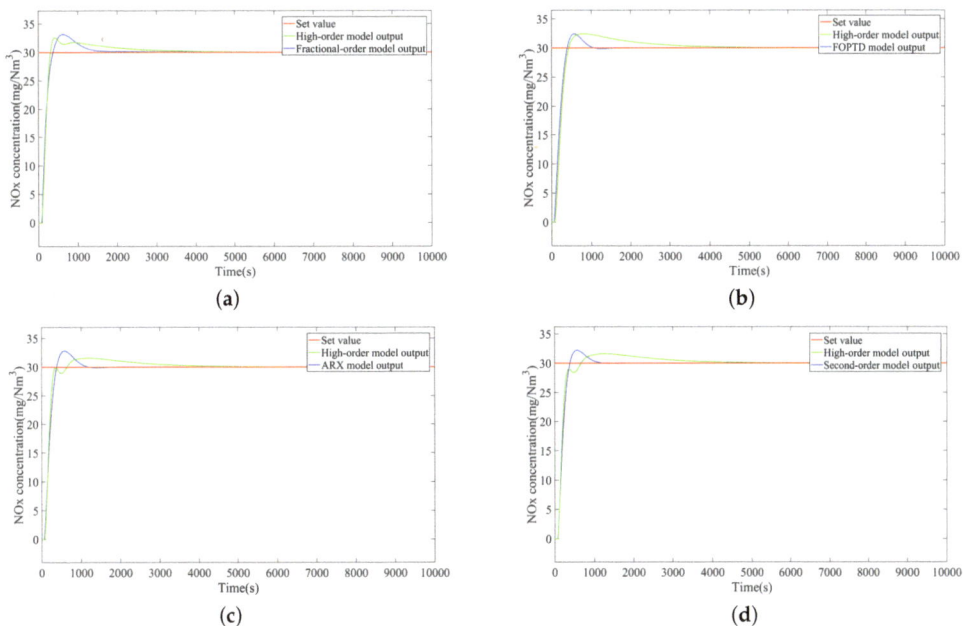

Figure 9. Step tracking responses under 580 MW. (**a**) Fractional-order model output and high-order model output. (**b**) FOPTD model output and high-order model output. (**c**) ARX model output and high-order model output. (**d**) Second-order model output and high-order model output.

Table 5. RMSE (mg/Nm^3) between identified model output and high-order model output of each system.

Load (MW)	Fractional-Order Model	FOPTD Model	ARX Model	Second-Order Model
400	0.0941	0.2860	0.3236	0.2850
580	0.5323	0.8309	0.8525	0.8250

5. Conclusions

To simultaneously achieve better fitting effects and facilitate controller design, this paper proposes a fractional-order system with a time-domain identification method for process control systems. The method extends the traditional integer-order first-order plus time delay model to the fractional-order one, improving the modeling accuracy while keeping the simple form. The proposed method is applied to the SCR denitrification process in a power plant and achieves a more accurate modeling effect over the traditional integer order method. Based on the identified integer-order and fractional-order models, controllers are designed using the same strategy and criteria, applied to control a high-order model that accurately characterizes system dynamics from the real experimental data. Closed-loop control results indicate that the response of the fractional order model-based controller is much closer to that of the high-order model compared with the integer-order model-based controller.

Future work will focus on the design of control strategies to mitigate the impact of large inertia and time delay. It is also necessary to consider identifying the system under more different loads and operating conditions and adjust control strategies based on identification results to improve control performance and reduce NO_x emissions.

Author Contributions: Conceptualization, Y.L.; Writing—original draft, X.L.; Writing—review & editing, W.A., Y.L. and X.W. All authors have read and agreed to the published version of the manuscript.

Funding: This research was funded by National Natural Science Foundation of China grant number 62173151.

Data Availability Statement: Data are contained within the article.

Conflicts of Interest: The authors declare no conflicts of interest.

Appendix A

This appendix provides a brief introduction to the MATLAB functions used in the paper. $fminunc$ is used to find the minimum value of an unconstrained multivariable function; $lsim$ calculates the simulated time response of a dynamic system to arbitrary inputs; $tfest$ estimates the transfer function model by input and output data. Basic syntax and description of the parameters of each function are presented in Table A1.

Table A1. Introduction to the MATLAB functions used in this paper.

Name	Basic Syntax	Parameter Descriptions
$fminunc$	x = fminunc(fun,x0)	x: Solution fun: Objective function x0: Initial solution
$lsim$	y = lsim(sys,u,t)	y: Simulated response data sys: Dynamic system u: Input signal t: Time samples
$tfest$	sys = tfest(tt,np,nz,iodelay)	sys: Identified transfer function tt: Timetable-based estimation data np: Number of poles nz: Number of zeros iodelay: Transport delay

Appendix B

This appendix provides the units for the quantities related to Section 2.2 and Table A2.

Table A2. Units of quantities in the dynamic equations for the denitrification reaction.

Quantity	Unit
F	m^3/s
V	m^3
R	$J/(mol \cdot K)$
T	K
C_{NO}	mol/m^3
C_{NH_3}	mol/m^3
C_{NO}^{in}	mol/m^3
$C_{NH_3}^{in}$	mol/m^3
θ_{NH_3}	dimensionless
Θ	mol/m^3
R_{ox}	s^{-1}
R_{red}	s^{-1}
R_{ads}	s^{-1}
R_{des}	s^{-1}
k_{ox}	$m^3/(mol \cdot s)$
k_{red}	$m^3/(mol \cdot s)$
k_{ads}	$m^3/(mol \cdot s)$

Table A2. Cont.

Quantity	Unit
k_{des}	$m^3/(mol \cdot s)$
E_{ox}	J/mol
E_{red}	J/mol
E_{ads}	J/mol
E_{des}	J/mol

References

1. Monje, C.A.; Chen, Y.; Vinagre, B.M.; Xue, D.; Feliu-Batlle, V. *Fractional-Order Systems and Controls: Fundamentals and Applications*; Springer Science & Business Media: Berlin/Heidelberg, Germany, 2010.
2. Zheng, W.; Luo, Y.; Chen, Y.; Pi, Y. Fractional-order modeling of permanent magnet synchronous motor speed servo system. *J. Vib. Control* **2016**, *22*, 2255–2280. [CrossRef]
3. Gan, H.; Cao, Z.; Chen, P.; Luo, Y.; Luo, X. Fractional-order electromagnetic modeling and identification for PMSM servo system. *ISA Trans.* **2024**, *147*, 527–539. [CrossRef] [PubMed]
4. Shi, H.; Liu, Y.; Chen, P.; Luo, Y.; Chen, Y. Fractional-Order Dynamics Modeling for Continuum Robots. In Proceedings of the 2023 International Conference on Fractional Differentiation and Its Applications (ICFDA), Ajman, United Arab Emirates, 14–16 March 2023; pp. 1–5.
5. Sierociuk, D.; Skovranek, T.; Macias, M.; Podlubny, I.; Petras, I.; Dzielinski, A.; Ziubinski, P. Diffusion process modeling by using fractional-order models. *Appl. Math. Comput.* **2015**, *257*, 2–11. [CrossRef]
6. Wang, B.; Li, S.E.; Peng, H.; Liu, Z. Fractional-order modeling and parameter identification for lithium-ion batteries. *J. Power Sources* **2015**, *293*, 151–161. [CrossRef]
7. Zeng, J.; Wang, S.; Cao, W.; Zhang, M.; Fernandez, C.; Guerrero, J.M. Improved fractional-order hysteresis-equivalent circuit modeling for the online adaptive high-precision state of charge prediction of urban-electric-bus lithium-ion batteries. *Int. J. Circuit Theory Appl.* **2024**, *52*, 420–438. [CrossRef]
8. Gude, J.J.; Bringas, P.G.; Herrera, M.; Rincón, L.; Di Teodoro, A.; Camacho, O. Fractional-order model identification based on the process reaction curve: A unified framework for chemical processes. *Results Eng.* **2024**, *21*, 101757. [CrossRef]
9. Haider, M.; Abid, M.; Khan, A.Q.; Mustafa, G. Identification of Fractional-Order Systems with Time Delays Using the Method of Hybrid of Bernoulli Polynomials and Block Pulse Functions. Available online: https://ssrn.com/abstract=4416424 (accessed on 3 September 2024).
10. Shalaby, R.; El-Hossainy, M.; Abo-Zalam, B. Fractional order modeling and control for under-actuated inverted pendulum. *Commun. Nonlinear Sci. Numer. Simul.* **2019**, *74*, 97–121. [CrossRef]
11. Ziegler, J.G.; Nichols, N.B. Optimum settings for automatic controllers. *Trans. Am. Soc. Mech. Eng.* **1942**, *64*, 759–765. [CrossRef]
12. Pan, Y.; Yan, F.; Yang, J.; Zeng, X.; Li, X.; Qi, X. Mechanism Modeling of SCR Flue Gas Denitration Reaction System. In Proceedings of the International Conference on Frontier Computing, Seoul, Republic of Korea, 13–17 July 2021; Springer: Berlin/Heidelberg, Germany, 2021; pp. 828–838.
13. Li, J.; Shi, R.; Xu, C.; Wang, S. Process identification of the SCR system of coal-fired power plant for de-NOx based on historical operation data. *Environ. Technol.* **2019**, *40*, 3287–3296. [CrossRef]
14. Wang, Y.; Zhao, J.; Zhu, X.; Jiao, Y. Model identification of SCR denitration system for 600 MW thermal power unit. In Proceedings of the 2017 Chinese Automation Congress (CAC), Jinan, China, 20–22 October 2017; pp. 1721–1726.
15. Kang, J.; Niu, Y.; Hu, B.; Li, H.; Zhou, Z. Dynamic modeling of SCR denitration systems in coal-fired power plants based on a bi-directional long short-term memory method. *Process. Saf. Environ. Prot.* **2021**, *148*, 867–878. [CrossRef]
16. Xie, P.; Gao, M.; Zhang, H.; Niu, Y.; Wang, X. Dynamic modeling for NOx emission sequence prediction of SCR system outlet based on sequence to sequence long short-term memory network. *Energy* **2020**, *190*, 116482. [CrossRef]
17. An, B.; Tang, M.; Qiu, J.; Li, Z.; Wang, W.; Zhang, Y.; Yan, Y. Dynamic NO x Prediction Model for SCR Denitrification Outlet of Coal-Fired Power Plants Based on Hybrid Data-Driven and Model Ensemble. *Ind. Eng. Chem. Res.* **2023**, *62*, 14286–14299. [CrossRef]
18. Wu, Z.; Sui, S.; Li, S.; Li, B.; Liu, Y.; Yang, L.; Li, D.; Chen, Y. Modified Active Disturbance Rejection Control Design Based on Gain Scheduling for Selective Catalytic Reduction Denitrification Processes. *IEEE Trans. Ind. Electron.* **2024**, 1–11. [CrossRef]
19. Tang, M.; An, B.; Yan, Y.; Zhang, Y.; Wang, W. Predictive control of SCR denitrification system in thermal power plants based on GA-BP and PSO. *Can. J. Chem. Eng.* **2023**, *101*, 5818–5831. [CrossRef]
20. Yao, C.; Long, D.; Lv, Y.; Liu, J. Study on mechanism modelling and control of SCR denitrification system in thermal power plant. *J. Eng. Therm. Energy Power* **2018**, *33*, 78–84.
21. Oustaloup, A.; Levron, F.; Mathieu, B.; Nanot, F.M. Frequency-band complex noninteger differentiator: Characterization and synthesis. *IEEE Trans. Circuits Syst. Fundam. Theory Appl.* **2000**, *47*, 25–39. [CrossRef]
22. Xue, D. *Fractional Calculus and Fractional-Order Control*; Science Press: Beijing, China, 2018.
23. Broyden, C.G. The convergence of a class of double-rank minimization algorithms 1. general considerations. *IMA J. Appl. Math.* **1970**, *6*, 76–90. [CrossRef]

24. Fletcher, R. A new approach to variable metric algorithms. *Comput. J.* **1970**, *13*, 317–322. [CrossRef]
25. Goldfarb, D. A Family of Variable-Metric Methods Derived by Variational Means. *Math. Comput.* **1970**, *24*, 23–26. [CrossRef]
26. Shanno, D.F. Conditioning of quasi-Newton methods for function minimization. *Math. Comput.* **1970**, *24*, 647–656. [CrossRef]
27. Conn, A.R.; Gould, N.I.; Toint, P.L. *Trust Region Methods*; SIAM: Philadelphia, PA, USA, 2000.
28. Bayındır, C.; Farazande, S.; Altintas, A.A.; Ozaydin, F. Petviashvili method for the fractional Schrödinger equation. *Fractal Fract.* **2022**, *7*, 9. [CrossRef]
29. Lopez-Cresencio, O.U.; Ariza-Hernandez, F.J.; Sanchez-Ortiz, J.; Arciga-Alejandre, M.P. A boundary value problem for a random-order fractional differential equation. *Results Appl. Math.* **2022**, *16*, 100328. [CrossRef]
30. Jajarmi, A.; Hajipour, M.; Mohammadzadeh, E.; Baleanu, D. A new approach for the nonlinear fractional optimal control problems with external persistent disturbances. *J. Frankl. Inst.* **2018**, *355*, 3938–3967. [CrossRef]

Disclaimer/Publisher's Note: The statements, opinions and data contained in all publications are solely those of the individual author(s) and contributor(s) and not of MDPI and/or the editor(s). MDPI and/or the editor(s) disclaim responsibility for any injury to people or property resulting from any ideas, methods, instructions or products referred to in the content.

 *fractal and fractional*

Article

Estimation of Fractal Dimension and Segmentation of Body Regions for Deep Learning-Based Gender Recognition

Dong Chan Lee, Min Su Jeong, Seong In Jeong, Seung Yong Jung and Kang Ryoung Park *

Division of Electronics and Electrical Engineering, Dongguk University, 30 Pildong-ro 1-gil, Jung-gu, Seoul 04620, Republic of Korea; dc8933@dongguk.edu (D.C.L.); wjdalstn9594@dgu.ac.kr (M.S.J.); jsi5668@dgu.ac.kr (S.I.J.); jsy19980305@dongguk.edu (S.Y.J.)
* Correspondence: parkgr@dongguk.edu; Tel.: +82-2-2260-3329

Abstract: There are few studies utilizing only IR cameras for long-distance gender recognition, and they have shown low recognition performance due to their lack of color and texture information in IR images with a complex background. Therefore, a rough body segmentation-based gender recognition network (RBSG-Net) is proposed, with enhanced gender recognition performance achieved by emphasizing the silhouette of a person through a body segmentation network. Anthropometric loss for the segmentation network and an adaptive body attention module are also proposed, which effectively integrate the segmentation and classification networks. To enhance the analytic capabilities of the proposed framework, fractal dimension estimation was introduced into the system to gain insights into the complexity and irregularity of the body region, thereby predicting the accuracy of body segmentation. For experiments, near-infrared images from the Sun Yat-sen University multiple modality re-identification version 1 (SYSU-MM01) dataset and thermal images from the Dongguk body-based gender version 2 (DBGender-DB2) database were used. The equal error rates of gender recognition by the proposed model were 4.320% and 8.303% for these two databases, respectively, surpassing state-of-the-art methods.

Keywords: gender recognition; infrared light images; fractal dimension; body segmentation; surveillance system

1. Introduction

With the advancement of technology, image processing has been widely adopted in various fields [1–6]. In addition, image-based intelligent surveillance systems have recently been utilized for various purposes such as crime prevention, security, criminal investigation, and suspect search. There is a growing demand for intelligent software in surveillance systems to automate the analysis of large volumes of images captured by closed circuit television (CCTV) cameras. This is particularly crucial for surveillance and security operations. When an image captured by a surveillance system is utilized to search for information on an individual that is stored in a database, gender recognition can enhance the efficiency of locating a person or a group of people of a specific gender. Gender recognition can also be employed to issue an alert regarding access to an area where only a specific gender is permitted [7]. Most previous studies on gender recognition have focused on high-resolution facial images. However, surveillance camera systems capture images from long distances, resulting in low resolution images, and it is often impractical to obtain high-quality facial images due to challenges such as human pose variation, changes in illumination, and occlusion. Consequently, there is a growing necessity for body-based gender recognition utilizing body images of individuals rather than facial images.

Previous studies on body-based gender recognition have primarily utilized images captured by visible light cameras in surveillance environments. With visible light images, high recognition performance can be achieved because of the abundance of information in the data, including color information and body shape details. However, it is essential to ensure the robust application of surveillance systems even during nighttime for tasks such as crime prevention, suspect tracking, and crime alarms. In low illumination environments such as nighttime, visible light camera images pose challenges for gender recognition due to the degradation of image quality caused by insufficient light. Conversely, infrared (IR) light images utilize light in the infrared wavelength band, invisible to the human eye, enabling the clear capture of a person's shape even in low illumination or nighttime conditions. In particular, leveraging thermal information based on a person's body temperature can ensure stable gender recognition performance despite environmental variations such as illumination changes, shadows, and foggy or dusty conditions. Therefore, a pressing need for research on gender recognition using IR images exists, but several challenges persist. Firstly, IR images are grayscale, lacking color information crucial for distinguishing gender characteristics like skin, hair, and clothing color. Secondly, the accurate extraction of body features may be hindered if the temperature of a body part closely matches the ambient temperature, potentially impacting gender recognition performance. Against this backdrop, this study proposes a method to enhance gender recognition performance by emphasizing human body regions in IR images through rough body segmentation. This approach aims to address the degradation of recognition performance caused by external environmental factors and the limited color information available in IR images.

The contributions of this study are as follows:

- To address the lack of color and texture information in IR images used in low illumination environments, a rough body segmentation-based gender recognition network (RBSG-Net) is proposed. In this network, rough body shape information is emphasized through a semantic segmentation network, thereby enhancing gender recognition performance.
- To mitigate the degradation of body segmentation performance in IR images when the contrast between the human region and the background is low, a novel anthropometric loss based on human anthropometric information is implemented into the semantic segmentation network.
- An adaptive body attention module (ABAM) is introduced, utilizing a binary rough segmentation map (BRSM) to identify the human body region in the image. The ABAM determines its attention based on anthropometric information to improve gender recognition performance by integrating segmentation and recognition tasks.
- To analyze the segmentation correctness capability within the proposed framework, the fractal dimension estimation technique is introduced to gain insights into the complexity and irregularity of the body regions. Additionally, the RBSG-Net code is available on the GitHub website [8].

This paper is organized as follows: Section 2 analyzes previous studies on body-based gender recognition. Section 3 describes the method proposed in this work. Section 4 presents and analyzes the experimental results. Section 5 provides the conclusion of this study.

2. Related Work

Previous studies on body-based gender recognition can be categorized into methods based on visible light images, methods combining visible light and IR images, and methods solely using IR images, depending on the type of images employed.

2.1. Using Visible Light Images

There are numerous open datasets available for visible light images [9–11], leading to a proliferation of related studies. Ng et al. [12] applied a shallow convolutional neural network (CNN) model comprising two convolutional layers, two subsampling layers, and one fully connected layer to a body-based gender recognition task. Antipov et al. [13] demonstrated that gender recognition performed better with learned features extracted through deep learning model training than with handcrafted features on heterogeneous datasets. Cai et al. [14] proposed an effective method called histogram of oriented gradients

(HOG)-assisted deep feature learning (HDFL). It enhances gender recognition performance by integrating handcrafted features, such as the weighted HOG feature, with deep-learned features obtained through model training. However, these studies did not consider noise elements (background or occlusion) present in the images as they relied solely on global features from full-body images. Subsequently, studies utilizing local features have emerged to address performance degradation caused by background noise [15–18]. Raza et al. [15] proposed a method for gender recognition by parsing pedestrians in an image using a deep decomposition network (DDN) [16], followed by inputting both the full-body and upper-body images into the CNN model. In a subsequent study, Raza et al. [18] enhanced gender recognition performance by employing a stacked sphere autoencoder (SSAE) instead of a CNN for human full-body images obtained using a DDN. These studies aimed to enhance gender recognition by extracting only the human silhouette in an image. However, since human parsing is applied universally to all images, there is a limitation whereby gender recognition performance may be influenced by the results of the parsing model. Liu et al. [11] improved performance by proposing HydraPlus-Net (HP-Net), utilizing an attentive feature network (AF-Net) that applies attention in multiple directions to a multi-scale feature map extracted from a CNN. Tang et al. [19] introduced an attribute localization module (ALM) based on a weakly supervised attention method to enhance recognition performance. This module identifies the most discriminative region for a classification label in an input image. Jia et al. [20] split existing datasets containing identical identities in training and test sets into a zero-shot setting akin to real-world environments. They compared a robust baseline method for training the model with conventional state-of-the-art (SOTA) methods. Roxo and Proença [21] proposed YinYang-Net (YY-Net) to improve performance. It detects the head using key points extracted by AlphaPose [22] to utilize the head part, crucial for gender recognition, and merges each feature extracted from the head and body images into a learnable matrix. Fan et al. [23] introduced a transformer-based multi-task pedestrian attribute recognition network (PARFormer), which is a vision transformer-based method based on the Swin Transformer [24] as its backbone. As described above, many studies on body-based gender recognition tasks have utilized visible light images instead of IR images due to the availability of more data for model training and readily usable color information. However, the drawback is a significant deterioration in recognition performance in environments with insufficient external light (nighttime, dark indoors, dark weather, etc.).

2.2. Using Visible Light and IR Images

As previously discussed, recognizing gender using visible light images in low illumination environments, such as nighttime, presents challenges. Consequently, in areas where nighttime usage is prevalent, such as intelligent surveillance systems, relying solely on visible light images may limit recognition performance. To circumvent this limitation, research has explored the use of IR images, which are well suited for night vision. Nguyen and Park [25] extracted HOG features from visible light and IR images, reduced feature dimensionality using principal component analysis (PCA), and performed gender recognition by fusing the respective scores obtained from a support vector machine (SVM) classifier. In a subsequent study, Nguyen and Park [26] enhanced gender recognition performance by concentrating features more on the foreground area of the image. This was achieved through a method that amplified HOG features extracted from both the visible light and thermal images by weighting the mean and standard deviation of pixels within each patch of the IR image. However, the application of near-infrared (NIR) images is limited due to unclear foreground–background distinctions and differing features compared to long-wave infrared (LWIR) images. Baek et al. [27] augmented the resolution of visible light images using a two-step method involving denoising and super-resolution (SR) models. They then combined scores extracted from IR and visible light images using ResNet-101 [28] to enhance gender recognition performance based on body images. These approaches offer the advantage of improving performance by supplementing degradation elements (such as low illumination, shadows, and clothing types) in visible light images with IR images. However, the simultaneous use of both types of data entails disadvantages, including increased computational complexity in feature extraction and fusion processes, as well as heightened system costs due to the necessity of employing both visible light and IR cameras simultaneously. Consequently, gender recognition studies utilizing only IR images have been pursued to address this challenge.

2.3. Using IR Images

In comparison to gender recognition based on visible light images, gender recognition utilizing IR images has not received extensive attention in prior studies on body-based gender recognition. This is primarily due to the relatively limited availability of data and lower image quality associated with IR images. Nevertheless, there has been a growing demand for research focused on gender recognition using solely IR images, driven by the necessity for robust performance in low-illumination environments and the importance of privacy protection. Previous studies on IR image-based gender recognition can be categorized as either without body segmentation or with body segmentation.

2.3.1. Without Body Segmentation

Previous research [29] curated a dataset comprising images extracted in frame units from video data captured by thermal cameras. Subsequently, they employed a CNN model consisting of 15 layers to extract features for individual images. They then trained the model with gait features, which can be extracted from image sequences using a bidirectional gated recurrent units (BGRUs) layer, for gender recognition. However, their method did not address performance degradation resulting from background presence in the image. Moreover, being an image sequence-based approach, it entails greater computational intensity compared to single image-based methods.

2.3.2. With Body Segmentation

During gender recognition, it becomes imperative to eliminate background elements unrelated to gender, as these elements can significantly impact recognition performance. This issue is particularly pronounced in thermal images, where the contrast between the body and background is minimal when the ambient temperature closely matches that of the body, resulting in diminished recognition accuracy. While open datasets exist for visible light images with annotated human body parts [18,30], there is currently no database providing similar annotations for IR images. Consequently, gender recognition research applying semantic segmentation to IR images is lacking. To address this gap, RBSG-Net is proposed in this study for rough segmentation-based gender recognition of human body regions.

3. Proposed Methodology

3.1. Overall Procedure of the Proposed Method

The overall procedure of the proposed RBSG-Net is schematically depicted in Figure 1. Upon input of an IR image, a prediction map in pixel units for the human body region is generated by the pre-trained semantic segmentation network. This prediction map facilitates the extraction of the human body region corresponding to the rough human body region. Subsequently, the ABAM computes the ratio of human anthropometric pixels representing the head, upper body, and lower body parts within the extracted human body region, ensuring each ratio falls within a predefined specific range. If the ratio meets this criterion, the body attention module (BAM) is activated for processing the input image; otherwise, the original input image is directly forwarded to the gender classification network. Ultimately, gender is determined using the gender classification network.

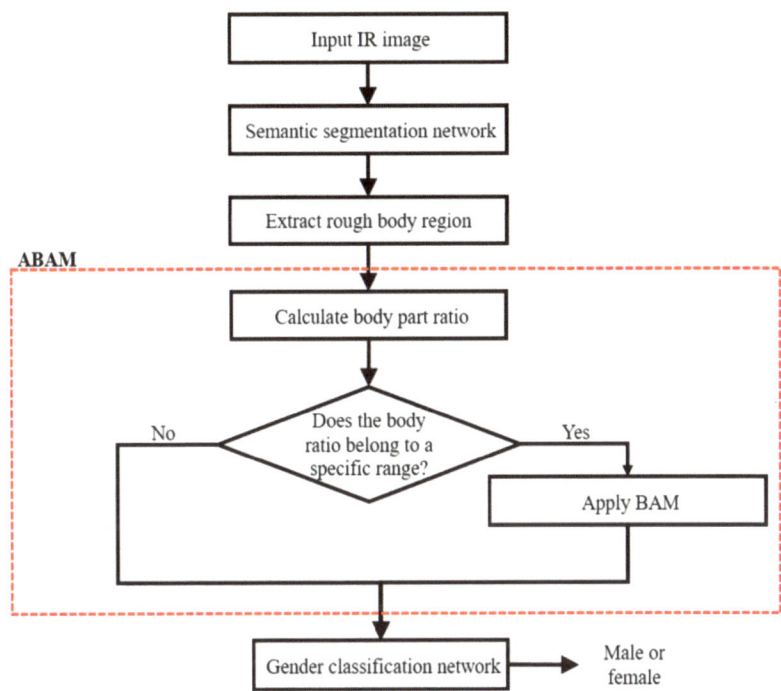

Figure 1. The overall procedure of the proposed method.

3.2. RBSG-Net

Since IR images lack color information, their extractable features are comparatively limited to those of visible light images. Additionally, noise generated from external environmental factors contributes to the degradation of gender recognition performance. To address these constraints, this study introduces a noise-robust RBSG-Net, which compensates for the absence of color information by enhancing structural features, such as body shape, in the IR image through a semantic segmentation network. Figure 2 shows the structural framework of the RBSG-Net. The RBSG-Net is designed to delineate the human body region based on the prediction map extracted from a pre-trained semantic segmentation network. It subsequently employs adaptive attention via the ABAM before sequentially transmitting the outcome to the gender classification network. Therefore, the performance of the semantic segmentation network significantly impacts the classification network. However, anticipating high segmentation performance is challenging due to the absence of annotations for the body region in IR images. To address this challenge, the ABAM is proposed, which assesses the segmentation result quality based on anthropometric information and selectively applies it to the image instead of employing all segmentation outcomes. Adaptive attention through the ABAM alleviates the decline in gender recognition performance resulting from reduced semantic segmentation network efficacy, while also facilitating the extraction of features emphasizing body shape information by the classification network.

3.2.1. Semantic Segmentation Network

When training the semantic segmentation network to segment the body region, training the data with annotation information for the body region is necessary. However, given the absence of an open dataset containing IR image-based body annotation information, this study addresses the issue by leveraging human anthropometric information as compensation for insufficient training data. Such information, rooted in the ratio of each body part, facilitates rough yet effective segmentation, thereby enhancing gender recognition accuracy. Figure 3 shows the training process of the semantic segmentation network based on human anatomical information for rough body segmentation. The prediction map, extracted from the input image via the semantic segmentation network, is partitioned into the head, upper body, and lower body according to specific ratios for each body part. Subsequently, the divided prediction map generated through this process is utilized to compute segmentation loss and anthropometric loss. This approach aims to complement the limited annotated training data available for human body segmentation by encouraging the segmentation network to consider and recognize the structural characteristics of the body. Detailed explanations of how the model integrates this anthropometric information into the training process are provided in Section 3.2.1.

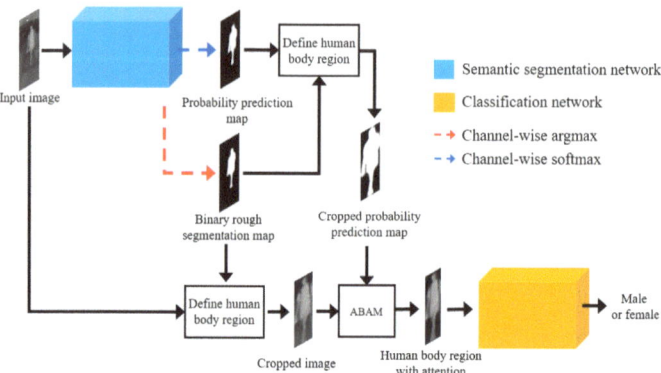

Figure 2. The architecture of the proposed RBSG-Net, including the adaptive body attention module (ABAM).

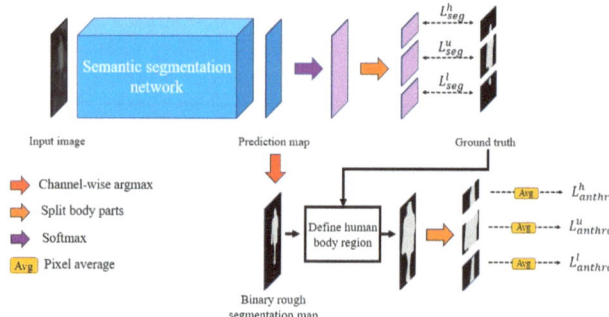

Figure 3. Training of the semantic segmentation network on rough body segmentation based on human anthropometric information.

Model Overview

In this study, a conventional U-Net [31] was employed for binary semantic segmentation, aiming to segment the human full body from the background in an IR image. The primary rationale behind selecting U-Net as the segmentation model lies in its robust performance, even with a limited quantity of annotated training data. This was verified through experiments, details of which are provided in Sections 4.4.1 and 4.5.1.

Figure 3 elaborates on the comprehensive process of training the semantic segmentation model. Initially, the input image undergoes processing by the encoder and decoder components of U-Net to generate a prediction map corresponding to the human body. Subsequently, the prediction map is transformed into probabilities using the SoftMax function and split based on a predefined ratio. In this study, the original image height is utilized to split the top 15% as the head, the middle 45% as the upper body, and the bottom 40% as the lower body, without overlap. The optimal ratio value was determined by comparing gender recognition performance using the training data. To utilize the ratio of human body parts within an image as anthropometric information, the BRSM for the human body is derived from the prediction map, as represented by Equation (1):

$$BRSM_{i,j} = \underset{k}{\mathrm{argmax}}\ P_{i,j,k} \tag{1}$$

where $P \in \mathbb{R}^{H \times W \times C}$ is the prediction map, i and j represent the indices of image height and width, respectively, k denotes the channel of the prediction map, representing the index for background and foreground, and BRSM is a binary map representing the human body at the corresponding pixel (i, j).

Based on the detected BRSM, the human body region is defined, and the ratio of each body part including the head, upper body, and lower body is utilized within the body region as anthropometric information by dividing each proportionally. In detail, for the detected BRSM(x, y), the minimum and maximum coordinates $(x_{min}, y_{min}, x_{max},$ and $y_{max})$ with BRSM$(x, y) = 1$ denote the four vertices of the body region. Utilizing the obtained human body region excludes the influence of background, facilitating the extraction of features crucial for gender recognition. Subsequently, the human body region is divided into body parts, the head, upper body, and lower body, as depicted in Figure 3, to compute the anthropometric loss, detailed in the following subsection. The effectiveness of the human body region extractor is demonstrated through the ablation study in Section 4.4.1, and examples of extracted human body regions are provided in Figure 4.

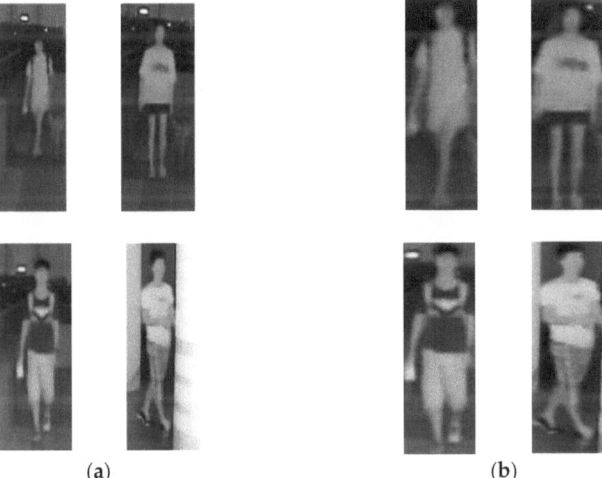

Figure 4. Examples of extracted human body regions: (**a**) original and (**b**) human body regions.

Loss Functions for Training the Semantic Segmentation Network

The loss function employed in this study to optimize the semantic segmentation network is defined as follows:

$$L_{total} = (1 - \lambda_{anthro})L_{seg} + \lambda_{anthro}L_{anthro} \tag{2}$$

where L_{seg} and L_{anthro} are the segmentation and anthropometric losses, respectively, and λ_{anthro} is a parameter balancing the anthropometric loss within the overall loss. In this study, it was set to 0.05, representing the optimal parameter for achieving the highest gender recognition accuracy with the training data. L_{seg} is calculated as the sum of the cross-entropy loss (CE) [32] for each body part after dividing the prediction map (P) and ground truth (G) into [P_h; P_u; P_l], [G_h; G_u; G_l], respectively, as follows:

$$L_{seg} = \sum_{k \in \{h,u,l\}} \frac{1}{H_k W} \sum_{i=0}^{H_k-1} \sum_{j=0}^{W-1} CE(P_k(i,j), G_k(i,j)) \quad (3)$$

In this case, each body part is delineated according to the specific ratio suggested in Section Model Overview: 15% for the head, 45% for the upper body, and 40% for the lower body, without overlap. Additionally, a novel anthropometric loss is proposed, utilizing anthropometric information to address the challenge of insufficient segmentation annotated training data. The anthropometric loss is computed as the sum of the mean squared errors between predefined values (y_h, y_u, and y_l) based on the method for calculating the proportion of pixels for each body part (head, upper body, and lower body) in the image. Equation (4) shows the calculation of the anthropometric loss:

$$L_{anthro} = \sum_{k \in \{h,u,l\}} \left\{ \frac{1}{H_k W} \sum_{i=0}^{H_k-1} \sum_{j=0}^{W-1} BRSM_k(i,j) - y_k \right\}^2 \quad (4)$$

Here, $BRSM_h$, $BRSM_u$, and $BRSM_l$ represent the BRSM split in ratios corresponding to the head, upper body, and lower body parts, with the human body region defined. In this study, the lower bound (l) and upper bound (u) of the pixel ratio for each body part (head, upper body, and lower body) within the BRSM were set. Specifically, (l_h, u_h) = (0.3, 0.6), (l_u, u_u) = (0.6, 0.9), and (l_l, u_l) = (0.4, 0.6) were assigned, considering various poses. The values of y_h, y_u, and y_l were set to the average of each lower and upper bounds, specifically 0.45, 0.75, and 0.5, respectively. These selections were made as they resulted in the highest gender recognition accuracy with the training data. Consequently, the anthropometric loss guides the model to predict the distribution of body parts more accurately in an image based on the pixel proportion of each body part. This aspect is particularly crucial, given the insufficiency of annotated training data. Through this approach, the model acquires knowledge about the typical range of ratios occupied by various body parts, enhancing the generalization capability of the segmentation network, even with limited data. This contributes to consistent segmentation performance for human images of diverse sizes and poses.

3.2.2. ABAM

The ABAM proposed in this study serves the purpose of accentuating the human body shape in the input image processed by the human body region extractor. After applying the SoftMax function in the channel direction to the prediction map (P) derived from the semantic segmentation network, the BAM for the human body region is generated as demonstrated in the following Equation (5):

$$BAM(i,j) = \begin{cases} 1 & \text{if } P(i,j) \geq T \\ (1-T) + P(i,j) & \text{otherwise} \end{cases} \quad (5)$$

Each pixel value in the prediction map (P) represents the probability for the human region and ranges between 0 and 1. If the value of P is greater than or equal to the threshold (T), it is set to 1; otherwise, the pixel value of the region predicted as the human body is preserved by adding (1 − T) to the existing value. In other cases, the existing pixel value is reduced to enhance the contrast between the human body and the background. In this scenario, the optimal T was set to 0.2, a value determined to yield the highest gender recognition accuracy with the training data. For the BAM generated in this manner, the shape is aligned with the input image by extracting the same human body region as the input image from the human body region extractor. However, since the semantic segmentation network was trained with limited annotation data, achieving high segmentation performance is challenging. To address this, an ABAM is proposed that assesses the quality of a segmentation mask based on anthropometric information and decides whether to selectively apply the BAM to the input image according to the results. To assess the quality, the region obtained by the human body region extractor is extracted from the BRSM generated by the semantic segmentation network. Then, the human full body is divided into three parts (head, upper body, and lower body), and the pixel ratio for each part is calculated as shown in the following equation:

$$r_h = \frac{n_h}{H_h \times W}, \quad r_u = \frac{n_u}{H_u \times W}, \quad r_l = \frac{n_l}{H_l \times W} \quad (6)$$

where n_h, n_u, and n_l represent the number of pixels with BRSM = 1 for the divided head, upper body, and lower body parts, respectively, H_h, H_u, and H_l denote the height of each part, and W represents the width of BRSM.

As shown in Equation (7), the value α is defined, which indicates whether the pixel ratio (r) for each part is between the set lower bound (l) and the upper bound (u) presented in Section Loss Functions for Training the Semantic Segmentation Network:

$$\alpha_k = \begin{cases} 1, & if\ l_k \leq r_k \leq u_k \\ 0, & otherwise \end{cases}, k \in \{h,\ u,\ l\} \quad (7)$$

This value is multiplied for all parts to calculate α_{final}, the value for the final decision of attention:

$$\alpha_{final} = \alpha_h \times \alpha_u \times \alpha_l \quad (8)$$

Suppose the input image is I, then the ABAM-applied image (E) is defined as follows:

$$E(i,j) = \begin{cases} I(i,j) \circledast BAM(i,j) & if\ \alpha_{final} = 1 \\ I(i,j) & otherwise \end{cases} \quad (9)$$

where $\circledast$ denotes element-wise multiplication.

3.2.3. Gender Recognition Network

In this study, the semantic segmentation network detects the human body region in the input image, and based on this detection, the emphasized human body region, achieved using the human body region extractor and the ABAM, serves as the input to the gender classification network. The classification network chosen for gender recognition in human full-body images is the dual attention vision transformer (DaViT) [33], depicted in Figure 5.

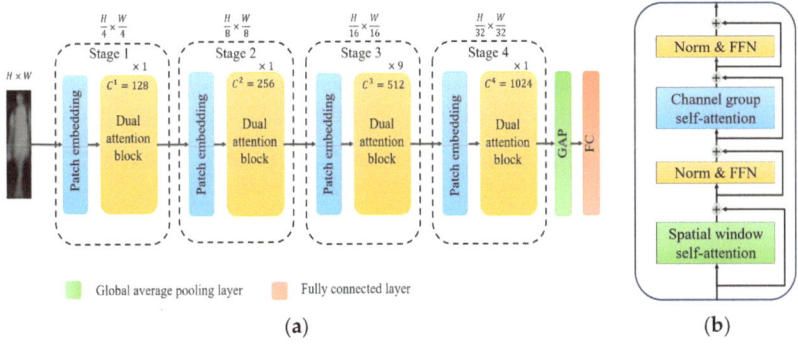

Figure 5. Architecture of DaViT: (**a**) overall model, and (**b**) dual attention block.

Figure 5a shows the architecture of DaViT. Like hierarchical vision transformers [24,34], it consists of four stages. Furthermore, each stage consists of a patch embedding layer and a dual attention block [33]. The patch embedding layer splits the image into multiple patches via overlapped convolution and converts them into embedding vectors. Afterward, the spatial window self-attention [24,33] and channel group self-attention [33] operations are sequentially performed in the dual attention block. Spatial window self-attention focuses on local features by computing attention scores between spatial tokens within non-overlapping windows. However, this approach loses the ability to capture global features. To address this issue, channel group self-attention is introduced, which focuses on learning relationships between tokens by dividing the channels into several groups and performing self-attention within each group. Consequently, the resulting feature map attains a size of $\mathbb{R}^{1024 \times \frac{H}{32} \times \frac{W}{32}}$. This feature map is subsequently converted into a feature vector through the global average pooling layer. Finally, the fully connected layer facilitates the classification of each individual as male or female.

Given that this study delves into gender recognition grounded in the human body's appearance in an IR image, it becomes imperative to incorporate global context information, encompassing data pertaining to the entire body. Transformer series models, exemplified by DaViT, excel in capturing global features more effectively than CNN-based models by leveraging correlations among multiple patches extracted from the input image [35]. The DaViT-Base stands out due to its superior recognition performance compared to alternative models. Comparative experiments involving the classification network are outlined in Sections 4.4.1 and 4.5.1.

4. Experimental Results

4.1. Experimental Database and Environment

Previous gender recognition studies have predominantly utilized datasets comprising visible light images, rendering them unsuitable for experiments focused on IR image-based gender recognition. Consequently, this study exclusively employed IR images sourced from the Sun Yat-sen University multiple modality re-identification version 1 database (SYSU-MM01) [36], an open-access database offering both visible light and IR images, alongside the Dongguk body-based gender version 2 (DBGender-DB2) [25] dataset. SYSU-MM01 encompasses 15,495 NIR images featuring 490 individuals, comprising 275 males and 215 females. These images were captured utilizing NIR cameras across various settings, including dark indoor environments and cluttered outdoor environments. To assess the effectiveness of the proposed method across different IR image wavelengths, experiments were conducted using DBGender-DB2 as a supplementary experimental dataset. This dataset consists of thermal images captured by a thermal imaging camera [37] utilizing the long-wave infrared (LWIR) range of 7.5 to 13.5 µm. It includes 4120 images obtained from outdoor settings, featuring a total of 412 individuals, comprising 254 males and 158 females. Notably, both the SYSU NIR dataset and the DBGender-DB2 thermal dataset exhibit variations in image sizes due to the extraction of IR images at different distances in human units. To the best of our knowledge, there is no IR image open dataset that provides gender information as ground truth considering various environmental conditions, except for the two experimental databases, SYSU-MM01 and DBGender-DB2. To maintain consistency in model training and validation while preserving the human body's appearance, the input image size was standardized to 384 × 128 pixels in this study. Figure 6 shows sample images from the datasets utilized in this investigation.

K-fold cross-validation was conducted to validate the experiments. For the SYSU-MM01 NIR dataset, 2-fold cross-validation was utilized due to its sufficiently large size. Conversely, for the relatively small DBGender-DB2 thermal dataset, 5-fold cross-validation was employed. Ensuring the inclusion of individuals with different identities (open-world setting) in both the train and test sets was crucial to enhance the reliability of the experiments and simulate real-world conditions. To create a validation set for model evaluation, images corresponding to 10% of the total individuals were separated from the training set. During training, data augmentation involved applying horizontal flips exclusively to the training set. Table 1 summarizes the dataset composition for the experiments.

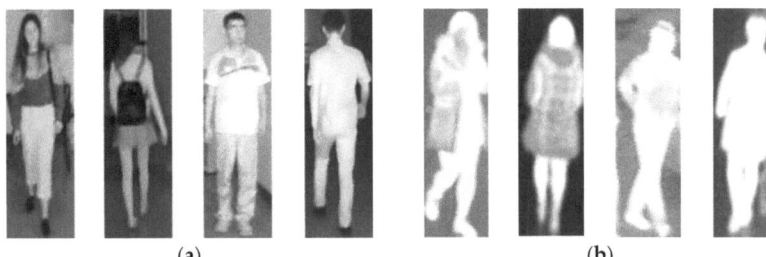

(a)   (b)

Figure 6. Example full body images from both experimental datasets, illustrating the front (**left image**) and back (**right image**) appearance of a female and a male. Example images from the (**a**) SYSU-MM01 NIR and (**b**) DBGender-DB2 thermal datasets.

Table 1. A summary of the experimental IR datasets: 'M' denotes the number of males; 'F' denotes the number of females.

Dataset	Fold	Training Set		Validation Set		Test Set	
		People (M/F)	Images (M/F)	People (M/F)	Images (M/F)	People (M/F)	Images (M/F)
SYSU-MM01 NIR	1	221 (125/96)	7011 (4018/2993)	24 (13/11)	760 (380/380)	245 (137/108)	7724 (4338/3386)
	2	221 (122/99)	6968 (3862/3106)	24 (15/9)	756 (476/280)	245 (138/107)	7771 (4398/3373)
DBGender-DB2 thermal	1	297 (186/111)	2970 (1860/1110)	33 (16/17)	330 (160/170)	82 (52/30)	820 (520/300)
	2	297 (180/117)	2970 (1800/1170)	32 (21/11)	320 (210/110)	83 (53/30)	830 (530/300)
	3	297 (183/114)	2970 (1830/1140)	32 (21/11)	320 (210/110)	83 (50/33)	830 (500/330)
	4	297 (183/114)	2970 (1830/1140)	33 (23/10)	330 (230/100)	82 (48/34)	820 (480/340)
	5	297 (184/113)	2970 (1840/1130)	33 (19/14)	330 (190/140)	82 (51/31)	820 (510/310)

The experiments were conducted using PyTorch version 1.13.0 [38], Intel® Core i7-12700F, with 32 GB of memory, and an NVIDIA GeForce RTX 4070 graphics processing unit (GPU) [39]. For segmentation annotation, manual labeling was performed using the Roboflow (version 1.0) software [40].

4.2. Training

The training process of the RBSG-Net proposed in this study comprises two parts: the training of the semantic segmentation network and the training of the classification network. Initially, the semantic segmentation network was trained using an Adam optimizer [41] with a learning rate of 10^{-4}. During training, random brightness contrast and cutout [42] were applied online for additional augmentation to address the limited amount of data. The mini-batch size was set to eight, and training was conducted for a total of 300 epochs.

Upon completion of the training for the semantic segmentation network, its parameters were frozen to prevent further updates. Subsequently, the classification network was fine-tuned by initializing its weights with pre-trained ImageNet-1K weights and using the Adam optimizer. The cosine learning rate decay method [43] was applied to decay the initial learning rate from 10^{-4} to a minimum of 10^{-6}. The weight decay was set to 10^{-4}, and only horizontal flipping was applied for data augmentation. The mini-batch size remained at eight, with training conducted for 30 epochs on SYSU-MM01 NIR and 60 epochs on DBGender-DB2 thermal. The cross-entropy loss function was employed for training the classification network. Figure 7 shows the graphs of training loss and validation loss for both the semantic segmentation network and the classification network. In all instances, the train loss converged with increasing epochs, indicating sufficient training on the training data for both networks. Furthermore, the validation loss also converged as the epoch count increased, suggesting that neither network was overfitted to the training data.

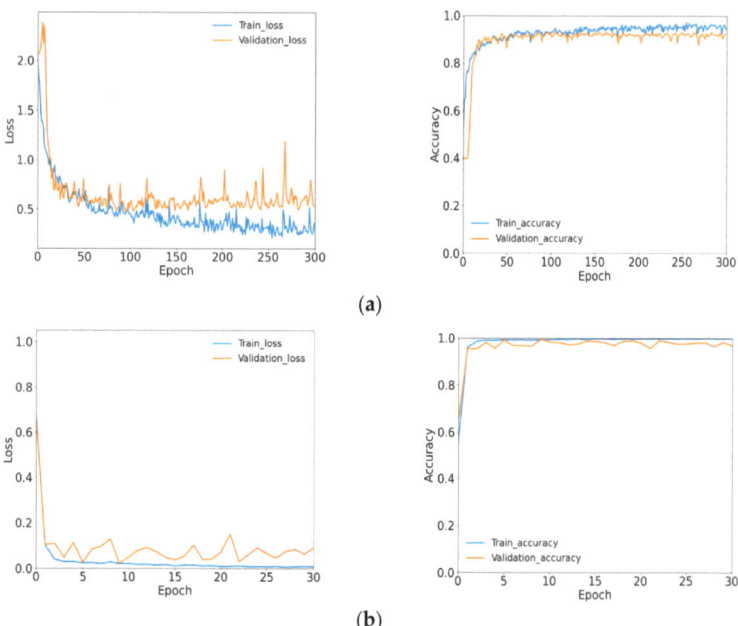

Figure 7. Learning curves (loss and accuracy) of the proposed model: (**a**) the semantic segmentation network and (**b**) the classification network.

4.3. Evaluation Metric and Fractal Dimension Estimation

The equal error rate (EER) was employed as the primary metric to assess the performance of the gender recognition model proposed in this study, utilizing the SYSU-MM01 NIR dataset. The EER, commonly utilized in biometrics and applicable to soft biometrics such as gender recognition [25], is derived from *Type I* and *Type II* errors. True positive (*TP*) represents cases where the model recognizes a female as a female, true negative (*TN*) represents cases where a male is recognized as a male, false negative (*FN*) represents cases where a female is incorrectly recognized as a male, and false positive (*FP*) represents cases where a male is incorrectly recognized as a female. Then, the *Type I* and *Type II* errors are calculated as follows:

$$Type\ I\ error = \frac{FP}{FP + TN} \tag{10}$$

$$Type\ II\ error = \frac{FN}{FN + TP} \tag{11}$$

Thus, the *Type I* error is the percentage of males misclassified as females, whereas the *Type II* error is the proportion of females misclassified as males. Typically, these values exhibit a trade-off relationship as the gender recognition threshold adjusts. The EER denotes the error rate where *Type I* and *Type II* errors intersect. In this research, the EER served as the principal performance metric for the gender recognition model.

Fractals are intricate forms that exhibit self-similarity and deviate from conventional geometric principles [44]. The fractal dimension (FD) measures the complexity of a shape, showing whether it is concentrated or spread out. In this research, binary masks predicted for human body regions are generated using a semantic segmentation network trained with proposed anthropometric loss, where the FD ranges from one to two, representing varying levels of complexity. Within this interval, the FD spans numerous representations for binary images, with higher values signifying greater shape intricacy. The FD for the human body is determined through the box counting method [45]. Here, N denotes the number of boxes that uniformly divide each body part, and ϵ stands for the scaling factor of the boxes. The FD is computed using the following Equation (12):

$$FD = \lim_{\epsilon \to 0} \left(-\frac{\log(N(\epsilon))}{\log(\epsilon)} \right) \quad (12)$$

where $FD \in [1, 2]$, and for all $\epsilon > 0$, there exists an $N(\epsilon)$. The pseudocode for estimating the FD of the generated human body parts of the U-Net using the box-counting method is provided in Algorithm 1.

Algorithm 1: The Pseudocode for FD Estimation

Input: *Img*: input is the produced output by U-Net
Output: FD
1: Determine the largest dimension of box size and adjust it to the nearest power of 2
Max_dim = max(size(*Img*))
$\epsilon = 2\char`\^[\log_2(Max\_dim)]$
2: If the size is smaller than ϵ, pad the image to match the dimension of ϵ
if size(*Img*) < size(ϵ)
pad_width = ((0, ϵ - *Img*.shape [0]), (0, ϵ - *Img*.shape[1]))
padded_Img = pad(*Img*, *pad_width*, mode='constant', constant_values=0)
else
padded_Img = *Img*
3: Initialize an array storing the number of boxes for each dimension size
n = zeros(1, ϵ +1)
4: Compute the number of boxes, '$N(\epsilon)$' containing at least one pixel of body region
$n[\epsilon + 1]$ = sum(I[:])
5:   While $\epsilon > 1$:
a. Diminish the size of ϵ: $\epsilon = \epsilon /2$
b. Update the number of '$N(\epsilon)$'
6:   Compute $\log(N(\epsilon))$ and $\log(\epsilon)$ for each 'ϵ'
7:   Fit line to [($\log(\epsilon)$, $\log(N(\epsilon))$] using the least squares method
8:   Fractal dimension is determined by the slope of the fitted line
Return FD

4.4. Testing the Proposed Method with the SYSU-MM01 NIR Dataset

4.4.1. Ablation Studies

Ablation studies were conducted to understand the impact of the semantic segmentation network trained with the anthropometric loss (L_{anthro}) and segmentation loss (L_{seg}) described in Section Loss Functions for Training the Semantic Segmentation Network on the final gender recognition performance of the RBSG-Net. First, the results of the ablation study according to the loss term used to train the semantic segmentation network are presented in Table 2. When the semantic segmentation network trained with both L_{seg} and L_{anthro} was applied to the RBSG-Net, the best EER performance was observed. In addition, Table 3 shows the recognition performance according to the value of λ_{anthro}, the weight of the L_{anthro} term. In this experiment, it was found that the best performance was obtained when the value of λ_{anthro} was 0.05. In subsequent experiments, this optimal value was used, based on the results of Tables 2 and 3.

Table 2. Effect of loss term of training semantic segmentation network (unit: %).

L_{seg}	L_{anthro}	EER
		5.395
✔		4.997
	✔	5.194
✔	✔	4.320

Table 3. Effect of adjusting λ_{anthro} weights on gender recognition performance (unit: %).

λ_{anthro}	EER
0.01	4.840
0.1	4.606
0.05	4.320

Next, the results of the ablation study for the human body region extractor and the ABAM, introduced in Section Model Overview and Section 3.2.2, respectively, are presented. Case 1 in Table 4 is the result of using only the classification network without the semantic segmentation network. In case 2, the EER of the ABAM alone is 5.180%, which is 0.23% lower than case 1. Case 3 shows an EER of 4.863% when using only the human body region extractor, which is a 0.547% reduction compared to case 1. Finally, case 4 uses both the human body region extractor and the ABAM, with an EER of 4.320%, suggesting the best improvement in gender recognition performance.

Table 4. An ablation study on the impact of the human body region extractor and the ABAM on gender recognition performance (unit: %).

Case	Human Body Region Extractor	ABAM	EER
1			5.410
2		✔	5.180
3	✔		4.863
4	✔	✔	4.320

In the following ablation study, the effectiveness of the ABAM was demonstrated by comparing cases of adaptive versus non-adaptive (i.e., uniform across all images) application of the BAM, as presented in Table 5. Specifically, only the adaptivity of BAM application was compared under the conditions of case 4 in Table 4. In Table 5, case 1 represents the results obtained solely with the application of the human body region extractor, while case 2 shows the outcomes of applying BAM in a non-adaptive manner. Comparing case 1 and case 2, the non-adaptive application of the attention map hinders feature extraction due to an image with an unsophisticated attention map, resulting in an increase in the EER compared to an image without the BAM. On the other hand, in case 3, the adaptively applied BAM compensates for this degradation and improves the recognition performance. The results of anthropometric loss and the ABAM can be found in Tables 2 and 4 in Section 4.4.1. Table 2 presents the results of the ablation study for the anthropometric loss in training the semantic segmentation network and shows the changes in gender recognition performance accordingly. Table 4 presents the results of the ablation study for the ABAM and shows the changes in gender recognition performance. The results in Tables 2 and 4 indicate that the ABAM gives the main result, and the anthropometric loss gives the secondary result.

Table 5. Comparative analysis of gender recognition performance between adaptive and non-adaptive body attention modules (unit: %).

Case	Adaptive BAM	Non-Adaptive BAM	EER
1			4.863
2		✔	5.581
3	✔		4.320

The results of comparative experiments are presented in Tables 6 and 7 to verify the robustness of the proposed RBSG-Net against various semantic segmentation networks and classification networks. First, to demonstrate the robustness of the proposed RBSG-Net to various semantic segmentation networks, comparative experiments were conducted using the CNN-based models of U-Net [31], DeepLabV3Plus [46], HRNet [47], DDRNet [48], and the transformer-based models of SegFormer [49]. The DaViT-Base model, presented in Section 3.2.3, was used as the classification network. As shown in Table 6, in all cases using various semantic segmentation networks, the EER is lower than 5.410%, compared to when only the classification network was used. This indicates that the RBSG-Net ensures robust improvement in gender recognition performance, regardless of the segmentation network type. In particular, the lowest EER of 4.320% was achieved using the U-Net. In the following experiments, the U-Net was adopted as the semantic segmentation network with the best performance and conducted comparative experiments on various classification networks.

Table 6. Comparisons of different segmentation networks for RBSG-Net on the SYSU-MM01 NIR (unit: %).

Method	EER
DeepLabV3Plus [46]	5.347
HRNet [47]	4.878
DDRNet [48]	5.339
SegFormer [49]	5.239
U-Net [31]	4.320
w/o segmentation	5.410

Table 7. Comparisons of different classification networks for RBSG-Net on the SYSU-MM01 NIR dataset (unit: %).

Model		EER	
		w/o	w/
CNN	InceptionV3 [50]	5.284	5.149
	ResNet-101 [28]	5.411	4.913
	ConvNeXt-Base [51]	5.135	4.777
Transformer	Swin-Base [24]	6.257	5.693
	DeiT-Large [52]	7.303	6.920
	DaViT-Base [33]	5.410	4.320

Secondly, comparative experiments were conducted to demonstrate the robustness of the proposed RBSG-Net to various classification networks. For a fair comparison, all classification networks were pre-trained with ImageNet-1K. The performance of the RBSG-Net was evaluated on various types of CNN-based models, including InceptionV3 [50], ResNet-101 [28], and ConvNeXt-Base [51], as well as transformer-based models such as

Swin-Base [24], DeiT-Large [52], and DaViT-Base [33]. In Table 7, 'w/o' is the result of using only classification network in the RBSG-Net, and 'w/' is the result of training using both the human body region extractor and the ABAM in the RBSG-Net.

As shown in Table 7, the experimental results show that when both the human body region extractor and the ABAM based on semantic segmentation network were applied, there was a performance improvement in all classification networks of the CNN and the transformer. Among them, DaViT-Base [33] showed the best performance with an EER of 4.320% and was utilized as a classification network in other experiments.

4.4.2. Comparisons of Gender Recognition Accuracy with SOTA Methods

Since this study focused on body-based gender recognition using IR images, it is necessary to compare the performance with distant gender recognition methods that use human full body images instead of faces. However, since there is not much research on gender recognition using only IR images, the proposed method is compared with existing methods using only visible light images, HP-Net [11], ALM [19], Strong Baseline [20], YY-Net [21], and PARFormer [23], and methods using only IR images, 1-ch ResNet-101 [27] and 15-layer CNN [29]. The experiments were performed with 2-fold cross-validation, and the average EER of each method is shown. According to Table 8, the RBSG-Net achieved an EER of 1.747% lower than the second-best model, Strong Baseline [20].

Table 8. Comparisons of gender recognition accuracies with SOTA methods using the SYSU-MM01 NIR dataset (unit: %).

Method	EER
HP-Net [11]	11.404
1-ch ResNet-101 [27]	11.312
ALM [19]	8.757
Strong Baseline [20]	6.067
15-layer CNN [29]	7.221
YY-Net [21]	6.422
PARFormer-B [23]	6.777
PARFormer-L [23]	6.319
RBSG-Net (proposed)	4.320

Figure 8 shows the receiver operating characteristic (ROC) curve and the EER line to compare the gender recognition performance of the proposed method and other SOTA models. The intersection points of the ROC curve and the EER line of each model are the points where the *Type I error* and *Type II error* are equalized, which represents the EER. As shown in Figure 8, the RBSG-Net proposed in this study has better gender recognition performance than the SOTA methods.

4.4.3. Comparisons of Gender Recognition Accuracy with SOTA Methods: 5-Fold Cross-Validation

The SYSU-MM01 NIR dataset has more images than the DBGender-DB2 thermal dataset, so a 2-fold cross-validation was performed. However, the body-based gender recognition dataset is characterized by low diversity of the training set because it is divided into a training set and a test set based on human identity. Therefore, to further improve the reliability of the generalization performance of the model, 5-fold cross-validation was performed.

Table 9 shows the average EER obtained by 5-fold cross-validation of the SOTA method in Section 4.4.2. From Table 9, the average EER of the RBSG-Net is 2.429%, which is the lowest compared to SOTA methods. The results in Tables 8 and 9 demonstrate that the RBSG-Net has a high generalization performance compared to SOTA methods in different experimental settings. Figure 9 shows the ROC curve and the EER line to visually represent the results.

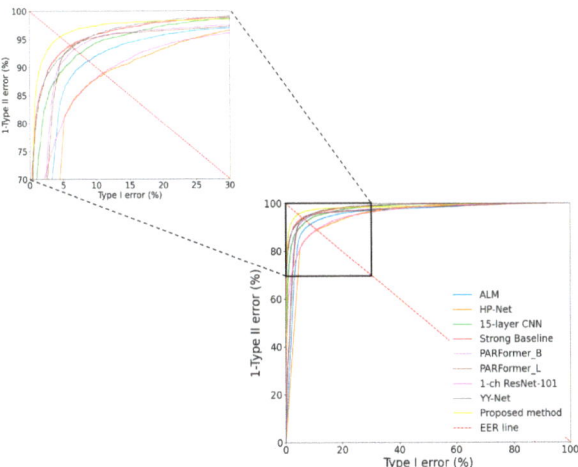

Figure 8. ROC curves for comparing gender recognition accuracies across SOTA and proposed methods using the SYSU-MM01 NIR dataset.

Table 9. The 5-fold cross-validation comparisons of gender recognition accuracies with SOTA methods using the SYSU-MM01 NIR dataset (unit: %).

Method	EER
HP-Net [11]	7.650
1-ch ResNet-101 [27]	7.053
ALM [19]	4.530
Strong Baseline [20]	2.970
15-layer CNN [29]	4.394
YY-Net [21]	2.925
PARFormer-B [23]	3.489
PARFormer-L [23]	2.929
RBSG-Net (proposed)	2.429

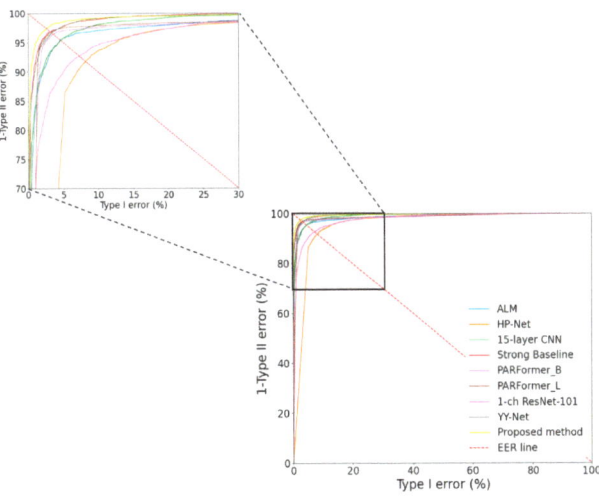

Figure 9. ROC curves for comparing 5-fold cross-validation performance across SOTA and proposed methods using the SYSU-MM01 NIR dataset.

4.5. Testing of Proposed Method with DBGender-DB2 Dataset

NIR images utilize infrared light at wavelengths close to visible light, so they have a higher resolution than LWIR images, which are thermal images. Due to these characteristics, NIR images tend to outperform LWIR images in gender recognition tasks. However, NIR images require an additional illuminator to acquire, and are more difficult to acquire in low light conditions than LWIR images and are more sensitive to changes in the surrounding environment. In contrast, LWIR images are acquired using the heat of the object, so no additional illuminator is required, and images can be acquired even under low illumination conditions, so they have a wider range of applications than NIR images.

In this subsection, to compare the performance of the proposed method for gender recognition in images using infrared light of various wavelengths, the DBGender-DB2 thermal dataset, consisting of LWIR images, is used as the second experimental data.

4.5.1. Ablation Study: Comparative Analysis of RBSG-Net with Various Networks

Ablation studies were conducted to demonstrate the effectiveness of the RBSG-Net on various semantic segmentation and classification networks using the DBGender-DB2 thermal dataset. The experimental setup was the same as the models mentioned in Section 4.3. In Table 10, 'w/o segmentation' refers to the gender recognition performance using only the classification network, DaViT-Base, without the semantic segmentation network. As shown in Table 10, the RBSG-Net can use various semantic segmentation networks to improve performance compared to using only a classification network. In particular, the lowest EER of 8.303% was achieved using the U-Net, so the U-Net was adopted as the semantic segmentation network for further experiments.

Table 10. A comparison of different semantic segmentation networks on the DBGender-DB2 thermal dataset (unit: %).

Method	EER
DeepLabV3Plus [46]	9.224
HRNet [47]	9.361
DDRNet [48]	9.055
SegFormer [49]	9.307
U-Net [31]	8.303
w/o segmentation	9.491

Table 11 shows the results of the gender recognition performance comparison experiment when various classification networks are used in the RBSG-Net. In Table 11, 'w/' refers to the EER performance of the RBSG-Net using segmentation information to perform gender recognition. The experimental results show that performance was improved for all classification networks. Compared to the different models, the DaViT-Base model showed the best performance. These results demonstrate that the RBSG-Net can flexibly utilize various networks in gender recognition tasks for LWIR images.

Table 11. A comparison of different classification networks on the DBGender-DB2 thermal dataset (unit: %).

Method		EER	
		w/o	w/
CNN	InceptionV3 [50]	10.271	9.776
	ResNet-101 [28]	13.476	12.167
	ConvNeXt-Base [51]	9.687	9.356
Transformer	Swin-Base [24]	14.151	13.870
	DeiT-Large [52]	10.561	9.523
	DaViT-Base [33]	9.491	8.303

4.5.2. Comparisons of Gender Recognition Accuracy with SOTA Methods

To compare the performance of body-based gender recognition in this study, a comparative experiment was conducted with the SOTA method. As shown in Table 12, the average EER of the second-best model, PARFormer-L, was 11.668%, and the average EER of the proposed model, the RBSG-Net, was 8.303%, which is a reduction of about 3.365%.

Table 12. Comparisons of gender recognition accuracies with SOTA methods using the DBGendr-DB2 thermal dataset (unit: %).

Method	EER
HP-Net [11]	20.811
1-ch ResNet-101 [27]	21.315
ALM [19]	13.348
Strong Baseline [20]	12.536
15-layer CNN [29]	12.872
YY-Net [21]	12.784
PARFormer-B [23]	12.743
PARFormer-L [23]	11.668
RBSG-Net (proposed)	8.303

The following Figure 10 shows the ROC curves of the SOTA and proposed methods for gender recognition of the DBGender-DB2 thermal dataset. The intersection of the EER line and the ROC curve represents the EER value, and it is visually shown that the proposed method, the RBSG-Net, has the lowest EER value among the other comparison models.

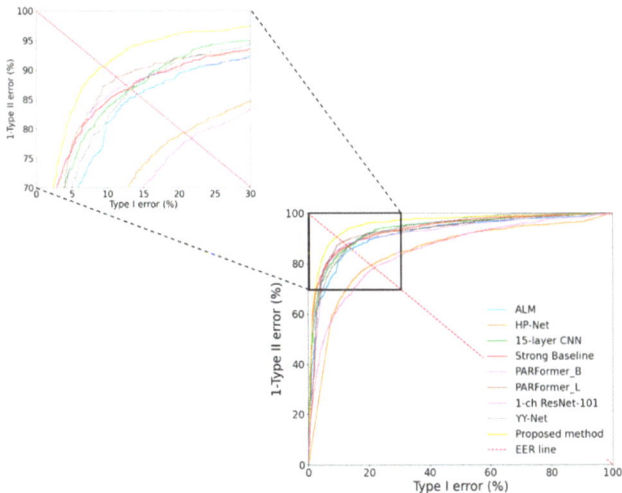

Figure 10. ROC curves for comparing gender recognition accuracy across the SOTA and proposed methods using the DBGender-DB2 thermal dataset.

4.6. Comparison of Gender Recognition Accuracy across Heterogeneous Datasets with SOTA Methods

LWIR and NIR images are acquired using different wavelengths of infrared light, each of which has unique image characteristics. In this subsection, experiments are conducted on a heterogeneous dataset using images of different wavelengths. The results of the experiments are shown in Table 13. Using the SYSU-MM01 NIR dataset as the training set and the DBGender-DB2 thermal dataset as the test set, the EER of the proposed method was measured to be 22.777%. On the other hand, when training with the DBGender-DB2 thermal dataset and testing with the SYSU-MM01 NIR dataset, the EER was found to be

26.728%. Compared with other methods, these results show that the RBSG-Net has a high gender recognition ability despite the domain differences between IR images, indicating that the model has a good generalization performance that can be practically applied in various environmental conditions and IR wavelengths. This has important implications for the use of IR images in different wavelengths in security, surveillance, and workforce management systems.

Table 13. EERs of different methods with heterogeneous datasets: 'S' denotes the SYSU-MM01 NIR dataset, and 'D' denotes the DBGender-DB2 thermal dataset (unit: %).

Models	Training Dataset → Test Dataset	
	S → D	D → S
HP-Net [11]	54.325	48.706
1-ch ResNet-101 [27]	40.014	46.809
ALM [19]	51.260	42.970
Strong Baseline [20]	41.098	33.904
15-layer CNN [29]	43.071	40.735
YY-Net [21]	37.983	32.989
PARFormer-B [23]	33.777	30.199
PARFormer-L [23]	30.838	28.337
RBSG-Net (proposed)	22.777	26.728

4.7. Testing of Proposed Method with Visible Light Images

As demonstrated in Sections 4.3–4.5, the proposed RBSG-Net outperformed existing methods in gender recognition using infrared light images. However, to show that the proposed method also works well for visible light images acquired in a surveillance environment, additional experiments were conducted using the visible light datasets used in previous studies of Table 8.

4.7.1. Visible Light Datasets and Evaluation Metrics

The pedestrian attribute (PETA) [9] dataset, which has been widely used in previous body-based gender recognition studies, was utilized in this study. The PETA dataset consists of 19,000 pedestrian images from visible light surveillance cameras. To compare the proposed method with existing methods, experiments were conducted using two protocols. The first protocol follows the method of [21] and divides the dataset into training, validation, and test sets (protocol 1). The second protocol follows the method of [53], excluding the MIT dataset, a subset of the PETA dataset, as the training set and using the MIT dataset as the test set (protocol 2). The details of each training, validation, and test dataset configuration are shown in Table 14, and samples of the PETA dataset and MIT dataset are shown in Figure 11.

Table 14. A summary of the visible light image dataset: protocol 1 is same setting as described in [21], and protocol 2 is same setting as described in [53] 'M' denotes the number of males and 'F' denotes the number of females.

Protocol	Training Set (M/F)	Validation Set (M/F)	Test Set (M/F)
1	9500 (5240/4260)	1900 (1034/866)	7600 (4147/3453)
2	13,555 (6778/6777)	3389 (1694/1695)	888 (600/288)

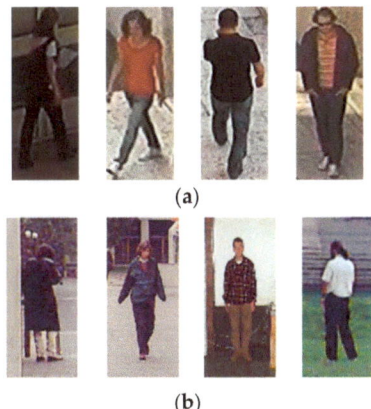

Figure 11. Example images of visible light datasets: (**a**) the PETA dataset, (**b**) the MIT dataset, with a mixed view of a female and male from left to right.

For a fair comparison with existing methods, overall accuracy and mean accuracy were used as indicators of gender recognition performance. These two metrics are defined by the following Equations (13) and (14).

$$Overall\ accuracy = \frac{TP+TN}{TP+TN+FP+FN} \qquad (13)$$

$$Mean\ accuracy = \frac{1}{2} \times \left(\frac{TP}{TP+FN} + \frac{TN}{TN+FP} \right) \qquad (14)$$

4.7.2. Comparisons of Gender Recognition Accuracy with SOTA Methods

In the proposed method, the RBSG-Net, which was the U-Net, was used for the semantic segmentation network, and DeiT-Large [52] was used for the classification network. The U-Net was trained using the Pedestrian Parsing Surveillance Scene (PPSS) dataset [16], and the classification network was pretrained on the ImageNet-1K dataset as described in Section 4.2. Table 15 compares the gender recognition performance measured in the protocol 1 setting. In the protocol 1 setting, the mean accuracy of RBSG-Net is 95.10%, which is about 0.19% higher than the second-best method, DeiT-Large [52]. Also, in the protocol 2 setting, as shown in Table 16, the overall accuracy and mean accuracy of the RBSG-Net are 92.7% and 91.2%, respectively, which are 1% and 0.6% higher than the second-best method, ViT-PGC [53]. This shows that the proposed RBSG-Net works well for visible light images and shows higher recognition performance than the SOTA methods.

Table 15. Performance comparisons with SOTA methods using protocol 1 setting (unit: %).

Method	Mean Accuracy
ALM [19]	92.28
DeepMar [54]	92.33
APR [55]	92.84
VAC [56]	92.85
Strong Baseline [20]	93.13
YY-Net [21]	93.39
DaViT-Base [33]	93.74
DeiT-Large [52]	94.91
RBSG-Net (proposed)	95.10

Table 16. Performance comparisons with SOTA methods using protocol 2 setting (unit: %).

Method	Overall Accuracy	Mean Accuracy
Upper body (CNN) [15]	82.8	81.4
Full body (CNN) [15]	82.0	80.7
HDFL [14]	74.3	-
SSAE [18]	82.4	81.6
U+M+L (CNN-3) [17]	81.3	-
J-LDFR [57]	82.0	77.3
CSVFL [58]	85.2	-
DaViT-Base [33]	86.2	84.6
DeiT-Large [52]	90.9	90.5
ViT-PGC [53]	91.7	90.7
RBSG-Net (Proposed)	92.7	91.3

5. Discussion

5.1. Comparisons of Algorithm Computational Complexity

In this subsection, the computational complexity between the proposed method is compared with other SOTA methods. The input image size was 384 × 128 pixels. The average processing time per image was measured in both the desktop computer environment, as presented in Section 4.1, and the embedded environment. For the embedded environment, the NVIDIA Jetson TX2 [59] board, shown in Figure 12, was used, which can be used in surveillance systems. The NVIDIA Jetson TX2 consists of an NVIDIA Pascal™ architecture GPU (256 CUDA cores) with 1.33 trillion floating point operations per second (TFLOPS) and 8 GB of memory.

Figure 12. Jetson TX2 board.

Table 17 compares the computational complexity of the RBSG-Net and SOTA methods in terms of the number of parameters in the model, Giga floating point operations (GFLOPs), and memory usage. Among the SOTA methods, the ALM [19], Strong Baseline [20], and the 15-layer CNN [29] are the lightweight real-time models used in surveillance environments. The RBSG-Net is a sequential structure that extracts prediction maps for human body regions through a semantic segmentation network, followed by feature extraction in a classification network, so it requires more parameters and computation than other models. This means that it is not the best in terms of computational complexity. However, in a desktop environment, the image processing speed is about 58.9 (1000/16.98) frames per second (fps), which can be processed in real time, so it can be used for video surveillance like other models except the HP-Net [11].

Table 17. Comparisons of processing time and computational complexity in the proposed method and SOTA methods (ms, M, and MB represent millisecond, mega, and mega-bytes, respectively).

Models	Processing Time per an Image (ms)		Number of Parameters (M)	GFLOPs	Memory Usage (MB)
	Desktop	Jetson TX2			
HP-Net [11]	89.746	922.345	20.799	10.306	80.173
1-ch ResNet-101 [27]	6.026	73.425	42.498	7.627	162.827
ALM [19]	7.051	60.053	11.021	2.113	42.793
Strong Baseline [20]	3.501	41.934	23.510	4.047	89.919
15-layer CNN [29]	1.762	14.155	6.996	1.335	26.728
YY-Net [21]	6.503	84.656	47.018	8.095	200.975
PARFormer-B [23]	6.961	156.662	86.680	15.169	336.421
PARFormer-L [23]	9.229	296.868	194.900	34.082	747.369
RBSG-Net (proposed)	16.980	345.798	117.917	58.168	454.951

In addition, as shown in Tables 8, 9, 12, 13, 15 and 16, and Figures 8–10, the RBSG-Net performs the best in terms of gender recognition accuracy compared to other models. RBSG-Net outperforms the other models on the heterogeneous dataset shown in Table 13, showing high performance in terms of gender recognition accuracy and infrared spectrum generalization. Although there may be some challenging issues in terms of processing time, the proposed model is better than others in terms of gender recognition accuracy, which is the main purpose of this research.

5.2. Analysis with Grad-CAM

It is a challenging task to analyze the reasons for the inference results of deep learning-based gender recognition models. In this subsection, gradient-weighted class activation mapping (GradCAM) [60] was used to analyze the reasons for the inference results of the RBSG-Net. GradCAM provides the interpretability of the trained model by mapping the feature regions in the input image that have the most influence on the inference results. Figure 13a,b show the GradCAMs obtained at each stage of the DaViT-Base [33] model for the front and back view of a female and male image from the SYSU-MM01 NIR and DBGender-DB2 thermal datasets. The GradCAM shown in Figure 13 is an indicator of the degree of activation of the feature values for model prediction, with regions colored in red indicating strong activation and regions colored in blue indicating weak activation.

As can be seen in Figure 13, the deep stage, or deep layer, captures semantic features, while the shallow stage focuses on primitive features. Since the proposed RBSG-Net in this study focuses on the human body regions extracted from the semantic segmentation network, it focuses on the primitive features such as texture and edges within the human body regions for all the images in the shallow layer. This shows that feature extraction was performed by focusing on the features present within the human body region, which is the foreground region for gender recognition. The features extracted in stage 4 are the semantic features used for gender recognition, which are also features captured within the human body region. These features are the key features that allow the model to distinguish between females and males.

For females, the focus is on the facial area in the front image and the hairstyle in the back image. Also, unlike males, females are often dressed in short shorts or skirts, so you can see that the focus is also on the exposed legs, which is a female feature. On the other hand, the male focuses on the face and shoulders in the front view and the head and shoulders in the back view. In this way, there is a visual difference in the areas the model focuses on when recognizing gender.

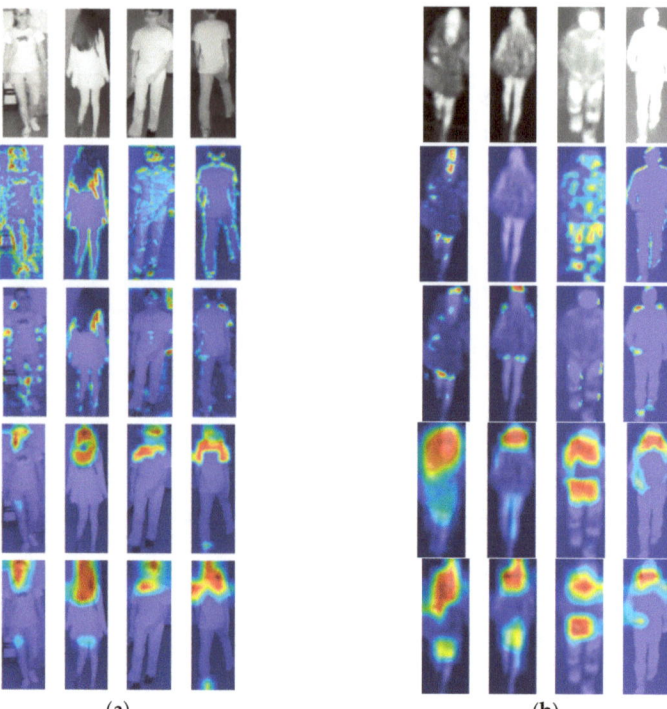

Figure 13. GradCAMs of the proposed method at four different network stages: the first row represents the input image and the second to fifth rows represent the GradCAM images extracted from stages 1 to 4 of DaViT-Base, respectively. Each row consists of females on the left and males on the right. (**a**) shows visualizations for female and male inferences on the SYSU-MM01 NIR dataset; (**b**) and for the DBGender-DB2 thermal dataset.

5.3. Statistical Analysis

In this subsection, the statistical significance between the proposed method and the second-best model is analyzed. Figure 14 shows the *t*-test result [61] between the second-best model, YY-Net [21], and the proposed method in Table 9, which compares the gender recognition performance on the SYSU-MM01 NIR dataset. The *t*-test resulted in a *p*-value of 0.45×10^{-1}, which means that there is a statistically significant difference at the 95% confidence interval. In addition, the Cohen's d-value [62] is used to verify the effect size of the proposed method. If the Cohen's d-value is close to 0.2, it indicates a small effect size; if it is close to 0.5, it indicates a medium effect size; and if it is close to 0.8, it indicates a large effect size. The Cohen's d-value of the proposed RBSG-Net in this study is 1.641, which indicates a large effect size. This confirms that the proposed method is statistically and significantly more accurate than the second-best model, YY-Net.

Figure 15 shows the *t*-test result between the second-best model, PARFormer-L [23], and the proposed method in Table 12, which compares the gender recognition performance on the DBGender-DB2 dataset. The *t*-test result shows that the *p*-value is 0.18×10^{-1}, which means that there is a statistically significant difference at the 95% confidence interval. Also, the Cohen's d-value is 0.961, indicating a large effect size. These analyses show that the proposed method has high accuracy on both DBGender-DB2 thermal and SYSU-MM01 NIR datasets with statistical significance compared to the second-best model.

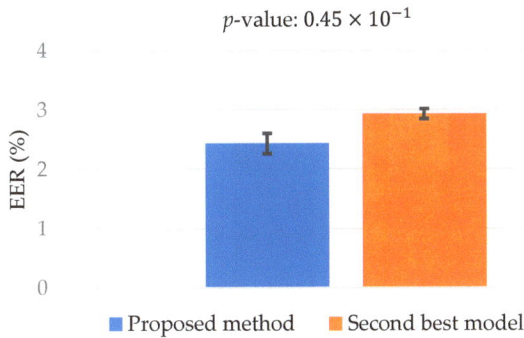

Figure 14. The *t*-test result of gender recognition accuracy achieved by the proposed method and the second-best model with the SYSU-MM01 NIR dataset.

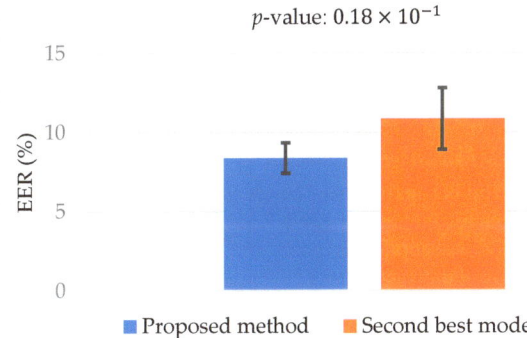

Figure 15. The *t*-test result of gender recognition accuracy achieved by our proposed method and the second-best model with the DBGender-DB2 dataset.

5.4. Analysis about Correct and Incorrect Cases

In this subsection, the correct and incorrect recognition cases where the RBSG-Net performed gender recognition are analyzed. To understand the areas that caused the RBSG-Net to recognize gender correctly or incorrectly, only the GradCAM obtained from stage 4 of the classification network DaViT-Base was visualized. Figure 16a,b shows an example image and the GradCAM of a case with correct classification of a female and a male, respectively. Even when some body parts are occluded by objects, as shown on the right side of Figure 16a and on the left side of Figure 16b, the features required for gender recognition within the human body region are well located. It can also be seen that accurate gender recognition is performed even with images taken in a dark environment.

Figure 17 shows an incorrect case of the RBSG-Net. In Figure 17a, a female with a short hairstyle is misclassified as male by focusing on the hairstyle as shown in the GradCAM image because it is difficult to distinguish the gender of the female based on the back view alone, while in the image on the left in Figure 17b, a male is misclassified as female based on the hairstyle. The image on the right in Figure 17b is misclassified as female because of the exposed leg area, which is an important female feature. This shows that when the RBSG-Net recognizes gender in cases where it is difficult to see the face from the back, hairstyle or body parts can affect the recognition performance.

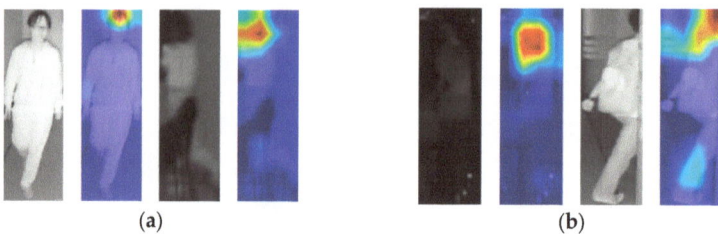

(a) (b)

Figure 16. Correct cases of the RBSG-Net: (**a**) correctly recognizing a female (TP) (**b**) correctly recognizing a male (TN).

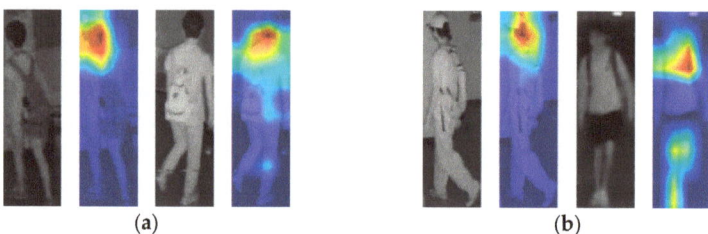

(a) (b)

Figure 17. Incorrect cases of the RBSG-Net: (**a**) incorrectly recognizing a female as a male (FN) (**b**) incorrectly recognizing a male as a female (FP).

5.5. FD Estimation for Human Body Segmentation

The FD analysis was conducted on the segmented human regions within the input images for the task of gender recognition. To calculate the FD score, the box-counting method was applied as outlined in Algorithm 1 of Section 4.3, and subsequently computed the correlation coefficient (C) between the box size (ϵ) and the corresponding number of boxes $N(\epsilon)$, as well as the coefficient of determination (R^2) for the regression line.

Figure 18a presents images where attention was determined by the proposed ABAM method, whereas Figure 18b shows those where it was not determined for different body parts of the head, upper body, and lower body. Figures 19–21 depict the human body masks generated by the U-Net and the corresponding FD values for each body part, as presented in Figure 18. The first row in Figures 19–21 shows the human body masks generated by the U-Net, where the pixels corresponding to the human body are represented in white. The second row displays the log–log plots for each mask, including the FD score, the correlation coefficient (C), and the coefficient of determination (R^2) calculated by Algorithm 1. The FD value serves as an indicator of the complexity of shapes or patterns within the mask. A higher FD value indicates more complex structures within the image. As shown in Figure 19c,d, the FD score for Figure 19a (1.6226) is higher than that for Figure 19b (1.2156), indicating that the mask where attention was determined by the ABAM exhibits greater complexity. The FD score represents the slope of the regression line in the log–log plots presented in Figures 19, 20 and 21c,d. The reliability of the FD value increases with the strength of the correlation between the number of boxes $N(\epsilon)$ and the box size (ϵ) during the regression process. In this context, the correlation coefficients for the two samples in Figure 19 are 0.9971 and 0.9961, respectively, indicating a strong positive correlation. Additionally, the R^2 values of 0.994 and 0.992 for both samples suggest that the regression line provides an excellent fit to the data. The same phenomena can be observed in Figures 20 and 21.

A higher FD value indicates more complex structures and patterns within the image, thereby reflecting the complexity of the segmentation mask. Table 18 presents the FD, R^2, and C values for each of the masks shown in Figures 19–21. Across all body parts, the samples of Figures 19, 20 and 21a with ABAM-determined attention demonstrate higher FD values compared to the samples of Figures 19, 20 and 21b without ABAM attention.

This observation suggests that the masks selected by the ABAM for gender recognition are indeed reliable, as the ABAM selectively passes only those results that satisfy the reliability criteria based on the percentage of pixel presence in the segmentation mask.

Figure 18. Examples of images with attention determined by the ABAM: (**a**) is an image where attention has been determined by the ABAM, and (**b**) is an image where attention was not determined.

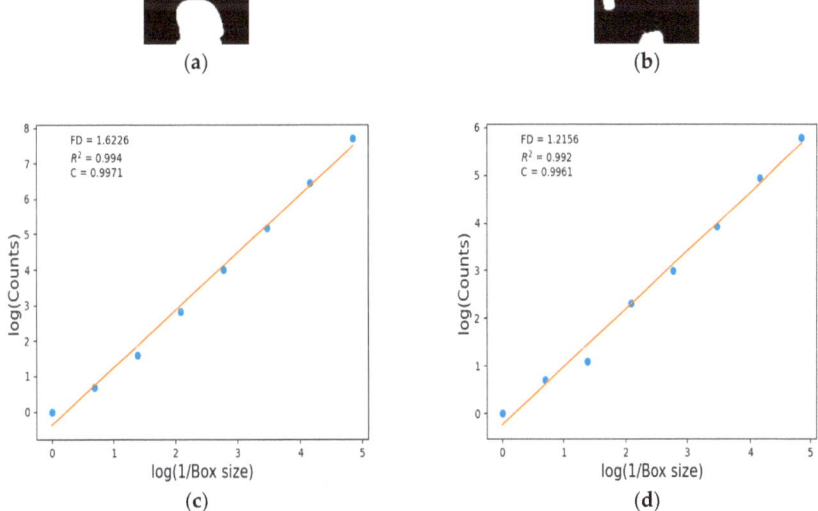

Figure 19. FD analysis for head segmentation: The first row presents the head mask generated by U-Net. The second row shows the FD value computed using Equation (12), accompanied by R^2 and C values for the head mask. (**c**,**d**) are the graphs computed from the images of (**a**,**b**), respectively.

Table 18. FD, R^2, and C values of the head, upper body, lower body from Figures 19–21.

Results	Head		Upper Body		Lower Body	
	Figure 19a	Figure 19b	Figure 20a	Figure 20b	Figure 21a	Figure 21b
FD	1.6226	1.2156	1.8039	1.6802	1.6237	1.5123
R^2	0.994	0.992	0.996	0.997	0.997	0.991
C	0.9971	0.9961	0.9981	0.9983	0.9984	0.9956

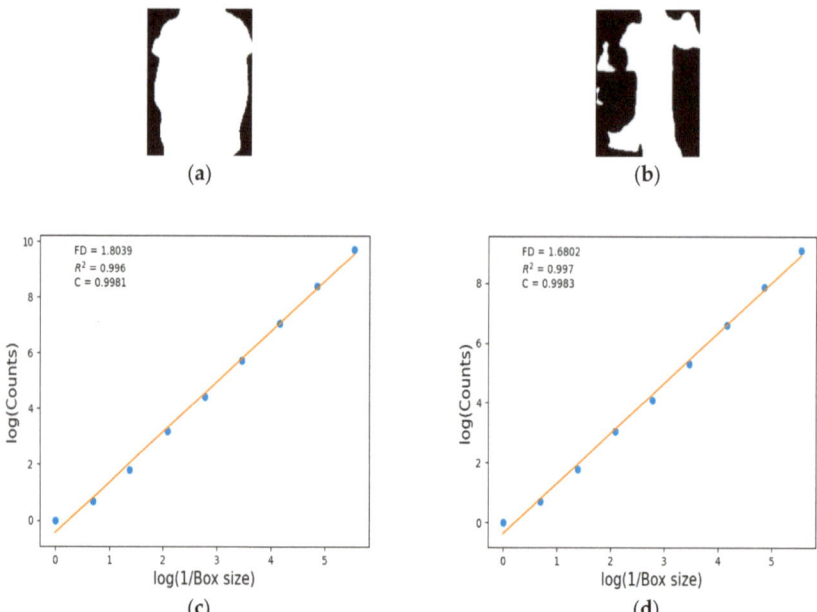

Figure 20. FD analysis for upper body segmentation: The first row presents the upper body mask generated by U-Net. The second row shows the FD value computed using Equation (12), accompanied by R^2 and C values for the upper body mask. (**c**,**d**) are the graphs computed from the images of (**a**,**b**), respectively.

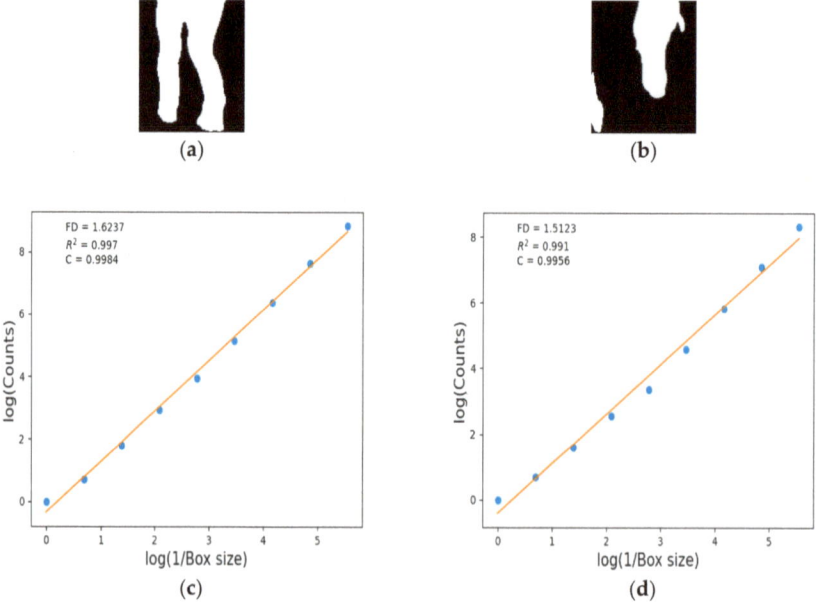

Figure 21. FD analysis for lower body segmentation: The first row presents the lower body mask generated by U-Net. The second row shows the FD value computed using Equation (12), accompanied by R^2 and C values for the lower body mask. (**c**,**d**) are the graphs computed from the images of (**a**,**b**), respectively.

In a broader context, the FD serves as a critical measure of irregularity, with higher FD values typically indicating more complex and irregular shapes [63]. This makes FD analysis particularly valuable in predicting human body silhouettes in infrared images, thereby improving not only gender recognition but also pedestrian attribute recognition and identity recognition in surveillance environments by addressing gaps in information. Moreover, the FD enables researchers to assess and compare the complexity of shapes both within and across datasets, thereby playing a crucial role in the understanding and analysis of human identity and behavior.

6. Conclusions

In this study, a new gender recognition method using only infrared images was proposed for use in night and low-light environments. To solve the problems of infrared images such as a lack of color information, background clutter, and a lack of training data annotated with body segmentation, a new loss function considering human body proportions was introduced to enable the semantic segmentation network to perform approximate segmentation. The RBSG-Net was proposed to improve gender recognition performance by defining human body regions using human body region prediction maps and removing unnecessary background elements.

The performance of the proposed method was evaluated using two IR image open databases and two visible light open databases. Four experimental databases, SYSU-MM01, DBGender-DB2, PETA, and MIT, cover a variety of environments (e.g., urban surveillance and different climates). The experimental results show that the RBSG-Net achieves the highest gender recognition performance compared to other SOTA methods in the four datasets, and the proposed method extracts features important for gender classification within the human body region by using GradCAM to interpret the model. Furthermore, the t-test and Cohen's d-value between the proposed model and the second-best model confirm that the proposed method has a statistically, significantly higher accuracy than the second-best model. It is meaningful that the RBSG-Net using human body segmentation maps can pay more specific and detailed attention than other attention-based methods, which can increase the reliability of classification results. To analyze the segmentation correctness capability within the proposed framework, the fractal dimension estimation technique was introduced to gain insights into the complexity and irregularity of the body regions. However, the experimental results showed that in cases where it is difficult to see the face from the back, hairstyle or body parts can affect the recognition performance, as shown in Figure 17.

In future work, the method considering face observation for gender recognition should be studied. In addition, performance enhancement of the segmentation model should be researched by applying an unsupervised segmentation methodology that includes anthropometric information to compensate for the small amount of human body segmentation annotation. Furthermore, a light model method that combines segmentation and classification in an end-to-end form should be explored to solve the computation and processing time problems of the RBSG-Net, while also applying knowledge distillation techniques to further improve its computational efficiency.

Author Contributions: Methodology, Writing—original draft, D.C.L.; Conceptualization, M.S.J.; Data curation, S.I.J.; Investigation, S.Y.J.; Supervision, Writing—review and editing, K.R.P. All authors have read and agreed to the published version of the manuscript.

Funding: This research was supported by the Ministry of Science and ICT (MSIT), Korea, under the Information Technology Research Center (ITRC) support program (IITP-2024-2020-0-01789) supervised by the Institute for Information and Communications Technology Planning and Evaluation (IITP).

Data Availability Statement: The proposed RBSG-Net models are publicly available via the Github site (https://github.com/DongChan2/RBSG-Net.git, accessed on 14 February 2024).

Conflicts of Interest: The authors declare no conflicts of interest.

References

1. Jiao, Q.; Liu, M.; Ning, B.; Zhao, F.; Dong, L.; Kong, L.; Hui, M.; Zhao, Y. Image Dehazing Based on Local and Non-Local Features. *Fractal Fract.* **2022**, *6*, 262. [CrossRef]
2. Zhang, Y.; Yang, L.; Li, Y. A Novel Adaptive Fractional Differential Active Contour Image Segmentation Method. *Fractal Fract.* **2022**, *6*, 579. [CrossRef]
3. Zhang, Y.; Liu, T.; Yang, F.; Yang, Q. A Study of Adaptive Fractional-Order Total Variational Medical Image Denoising. *Fractal Fract.* **2022**, *6*, 508. [CrossRef]
4. Zhang, X.; Dai, L. Image Enhancement Based on Rough Set and Fractional Order Differentiator. *Fractal Fract.* **2022**, *6*, 214. [CrossRef]
5. Zhang, X.; Liu, R.; Ren, J.; Gui, Q. Adaptive Fractional Image Enhancement Algorithm Based on Rough Set and Particle Swarm Optimization. *Fractal Fract.* **2022**, *6*, 100. [CrossRef]
6. Bai, X.; Zhang, D.; Shi, S.; Yao, W.; Guo, Z.; Sun, J. A Fractional-Order Telegraph Diffusion Model for Restoring Texture Images with Multiplicative Noise. *Fractal Fract.* **2023**, *7*, 64. [CrossRef]
7. Ng, C.B.; Tay, Y.H.; Goi, B.M. Vision-based human gender recognition: A survey. *arXiv* **2012**, arXiv:1204.1611. [CrossRef]
8. RBSG-Net. Available online: https://github.com/DongChan2/RBSG-Net.git (accessed on 14 February 2024).
9. Deng, Y.; Luo, P.; Loy, C.C.; Tang, X. Pedestrian attribute recognition at far distance. In Proceedings of the 22nd ACM International Conference on Multimedia, Orlando, FL, USA, 3–7 November 2014; pp. 789–792. [CrossRef]
10. Li, D.; Zhang, Z.; Chen, X.; Ling, H.; Huang, K. A richly annotated dataset for pedestrian attribute recognition. *arXiv* **2016**, arXiv:1603.07054. [CrossRef]
11. Liu, X.; Zhao, H.; Tian, M.; Sheng, L.; Shao, J.; Yi, S.; Yan, J.; Wang, X. HydraPlus-Net: Attentive deep features for pedestrian analysis. In Proceedings of the IEEE International Conference on Computer Vision (ICCV), Venice, Italy, 22–29 October 2017; pp. 350–359. [CrossRef]
12. Ng, C.-B.; Tay, Y.-H.; Goi, B.-M. A convolutional neural network for pedestrian gender recognition. In *Advances in Neural Networks—ISNN 2013, Lecture Notes in Computer Science*; Springer: Berlin/Heidelberg, Germany, 2013; Volume 7951, pp. 558–564. [CrossRef]
13. Antipov, G.; Berrani, S.-A.; Ruchaud, N.; Dugelay, J.-L. Learned vs. handcrafted features for pedestrian gender recognition. In Proceedings of the 23rd ACM International Conference on Multimedia, Brisbane, QLD, Australia, 26–30 October 2015; pp. 1263–1266. [CrossRef]
14. Cai, L.; Zhu, J.; Zeng, H.; Chen, J.; Cai, C.; Ma, K.-K. HOG-assisted deep feature learning for pedestrian gender recognition. *J. Frankl. Inst.* **2018**, *355*, 1991–2008. [CrossRef]
15. Raza, M.; Zonghai, C.; Rehman, S.U.; Zhenhua, G.; Jikai, W.; Peng, B. Part-wise pedestrian gender recognition via deep convolutional neural networks. In Proceedings of the 2nd IET International Conference on Biomedical Image and Signal Processing (ICBISP), Wuhan, China, 13–14 May 2017; pp. 1–6. [CrossRef]
16. Luo, P.; Wang, X.; Tang, X. Pedestrian parsing via deep decompositional network. In Proceedings of the IEEE International Conference on Computer Vision (ICCV), Sydney, NSW, Australia, 3–6 December 2013; pp. 2648–2655. [CrossRef]
17. Ng, C.B.; Tay, Y.-H.; Goi, B.-M. Pedestrian gender classification using combined global and local parts-based convolutional neural networks. *Pattern Anal. Appl.* **2018**, *22*, 1469–1480. [CrossRef]
18. Raza, M.; Sharif, M.; Yasmin, M.; Khan, M.A.; Saba, T.; Fernandes, S.L. Appearance based pedestrians' gender recognition by employing stacked auto encoders in deep learning. *Future Gener. Comput. Syst.* **2018**, *88*, 28–39. [CrossRef]
19. Tang, C.; Sheng, L.; Zhang, Z.; Hu, X. Improving pedestrian attribute recognition with weakly-supervised multi-scale attribute-specific localization. In Proceedings of the IEEE/CVF International Conference on Computer Vision (ICCV), Seoul, Republic of Korea, 27 October–2 November 2019; pp. 4997–5006. [CrossRef]
20. Jia, J.; Huang, H.; Yang, W.; Chen, X.; Huang, K. Rethinking of pedestrian attribute recognition: Realistic datasets with efficient method. *arXiv* **2020**, arXiv:2005.11909. [CrossRef]
21. Roxo, T.; Proença, H. YinYang-Net: Complementing face and body information for wild gender recognition. *IEEE Access* **2022**, *10*, 28122–28132. [CrossRef]
22. Fang, H.-S.; Li, J.; Tang, H.; Xu, C.; Zhu, H.; Xiu, Y.; Li, Y.-L.; Lu, C. AlphaPose: Whole-body regional multi-person pose estimation and tracking in real-time. *IEEE Trans. Pattern Anal. Mach. Intell.* **2022**, *45*, 7157–7173. [CrossRef] [PubMed]
23. Fan, X.; Zhang, Y.; Lu, Y.; Wang, H. PARFormer: Transformer-based multi-task network for pedestrian attribute recognition. *IEEE Trans. Circuits Syst. Video Technol.* **2023**, *34*, 411–423. [CrossRef]
24. Liu, Z.; Lin, Y.; Cao, Y.; Hu, H.; Wei, Y.; Zhang, Z.; Lin, S.; Guo, B. Swin Transformer: Hierarchical vision Transformer using shifted windows. In Proceedings of the IEEE/CVF International Conference on Computer Vision (ICCV), Montreal, QC, Canada, 10–17 October 2021; pp. 9992–10002. [CrossRef]
25. Nguyen, D.T.; Park, K.R. Body-based gender recognition using images from visible and thermal cameras. *Sensors* **2016**, *16*, 156. [CrossRef]
26. Nguyen, D.T.; Park, K.R. Enhanced gender recognition system using an improved Histogram of Oriented Gradient (HOG) feature from quality assessment of visible light and thermal images of the human body. *Sensors* **2016**, *16*, 1134. [CrossRef] [PubMed]
27. Baek, N.R.; Cho, S.W.; Koo, J.H.; Truong, N.Q.; Park, K.R. Multimodal camera-based gender recognition using human-body image with two-step reconstruction network. *IEEE Access* **2019**, *7*, 104025–104044. [CrossRef]

28. He, K.; Zhang, X.; Ren, S.; Sun, J. Deep residual learning for image recognition. In Proceedings of the IEEE Conference on Computer Vision and Pattern Recognition, Las Vegas, NV, USA, 27–30 June 2016; pp. 770–778. [CrossRef]
29. Baghezza, R.; Bouchard, K.; Gouin-Vallerand, C. Recognizing the age, gender, and mobility of pedestrians in smart cities using a CNN-BGRU on thermal images. In Proceedings of the ACM Conference on Information Technology for Social Good, Limassol, Cyprus, 7–9 September 2022; pp. 48–54. [CrossRef]
30. Wang, L.; Shi, J.; Song, G.; Shen, I. Object detection combining recognition and segmentation. In Proceedings of the 8th Asian Conference on Computer Vision (ACCV), Tokyo, Japan, 18–22 November 2007; pp. 189–199. [CrossRef]
31. Ronneberger, O.; Fischer, P.; Brox, T. U-Net: Convolutional networks for biomedical image segmentation. In Proceedings of the Medical Image Computing and Computer Assisted Intervention (MICCAI), Munich, Germany, 5–9 October 2015; pp. 234–241. [CrossRef]
32. Gordon-Rodriguez, E.; Loaiza-Ganem, G.; Pleiss, G.; Cunningham, J.P. Uses and abuses of the cross-entropy loss: Case studies in modern deep learning. *arXiv* **2020**, arXiv:2011.05231. [CrossRef]
33. Ding, M.; Xiao, B.; Codella, N.; Luo, P.; Wang, J.; Yuan, L. DaViT: Dual attention vision Transformers. In Proceedings of the European Conference on Computer Vision (ECCV), Tel Aviv, Israel, 23–27 October 2022; pp. 74–92. [CrossRef]
34. Yang, J.; Li, C.; Zhang, P.; Dai, X.; Xiao, B.; Yuan, L.; Gao, J. Focal self-attention for local-global interactions in vision Transformers. *arXiv* **2021**, arXiv:2107.00641. [CrossRef]
35. Dosovitskiy, A.; Beyer, L.; Kolesnikov, A.; Weissenborn, D.; Zhai, X.; Unterthiner, T.; Dehghani, M.; Minderer, M.; Heigold, G.; Gelly, S.; et al. An image is worth 16×16 words: Transformers for image recognition at scale. *arXiv* **2021**, arXiv:2010.11929. [CrossRef]
36. Wu, A.; Zheng, W.-S.; Yu, H.-X.; Gong, S.; Lai, J. RGB-infrared cross-modality person re-identification. In Proceedings of the IEEE International Conference on Computer Vision (ICCV), Venice, Italy, 22–29 October 2017; pp. 5390–5399.
37. FLIR Tau2. Available online: https://www.flir.com/products/tau-2/?vertical=lwir&segment=oem (accessed on 10 January 2024).
38. Paszke, A.; Gross, S.; Massa, F.; Lerer, A.; Bradbury, J.; Chanan, G.; Killeen, T.; Lin, Z.; Gimelshein, N.; Antiga, L. Pytorch: An imperative style, high-performance deep learning library. *arXiv* **2019**, arXiv:1912.01703. [CrossRef]
39. GeForce RTX 4070 Family. Available online: https://www.nvidia.com/en-us/geforce/graphics-cards/40-series/rtx-4070-family (accessed on 15 January 2024).
40. Dwyer, B.; Nelson, J.; Solawetz, J. Roboflow (Version 1.0) [Software]. 2022. Available online: https://roboflow.com (accessed on 14 February 2024).
41. Zhang, Y.; Chen, C.; Shi, N.; Sun, R.; Luo, Z.-Q. Adam can converge without any modification on update rules. In Proceedings of the 36th Conference on Neural Information Processing Systems, New Orleans, LA, USA, 28 November–9 December 2022; Volume 35, pp. 28386–28399. [CrossRef]
42. DeVries, T.; Taylor, G.W. Improved regularization of convolutional neural networks with cutout. *arXiv* **2017**, arXiv:1708.04552. [CrossRef]
43. Lewkowycz, A. How to decay your learning rate. *arXiv* **2021**, arXiv:2103.12682. [CrossRef]
44. Brouty, X.; Garcin, M. Fractal properties; information theory, and market efficiency. *Chaos Solitons Fractals* **2024**, *180*, 114543. [CrossRef]
45. Yin, J. Dynamical fractal: Theory and case study. *Chaos Solitons Fractals* **2023**, *176*, 114190. [CrossRef]
46. Chen, L.-C.; Zhu, Y.; Papandreou, G.; Schroff, F.; Adam, H. Encoder-decoder with atrous separable convolution for semantic image segmentation. In Proceedings of the European Conference on Computer Vision (ECCV), Munich, Germany, 8–14 September 2018; pp. 801–818. [CrossRef]
47. Sun, K.; Xiao, B.; Liu, D.; Wang, J. Deep high-resolution representation learning for human pose estimation. In Proceedings of the IEEE/CVF Conference on Computer Vision and Pattern Recognition (CVPR), Long Beach, CA, USA, 15–20 June 2019; pp. 5686–5696. [CrossRef]
48. Hong, Y.; Pan, H.; Sun, W.; Jia, Y. Deep dual-resolution networks for real-time and accurate semantic segmentation of road scenes. *arXiv* **2021**, arXiv:2101.06085. [CrossRef]
49. Xie, E.; Wang, W.; Yu, Z.; Anandkumar, A.; Alvarez, J.M.; Luo, P. SegFormer: Simple and efficient design for semantic segmentation with Transformers. In Proceedings of the advances in Neural Information Processing Systems (NeurIPS), Virtual, 6–14 December 2021; pp. 12077–12090. [CrossRef]
50. Szegedy, C.; Vanhoucke, V.; Ioffe, S.; Shlens, J.; Wojna, Z. Rethinking the inception architecture for computer vision. In Proceedings of the IEEE Conference on Computer Vision and Pattern Recognition (CVPR), Las Vegas, NV, USA, 27–30 June 2016; pp. 2818–2826.
51. Liu, Z.; Mao, H.; Wu, C.-Y.; Feichtenhofer, C.; Darrell, T.; Xie, S. A convnet for the 2020s. In Proceedings of the IEEE/CVF Conference on Computer Vision and Pattern Recognition (CVPR), New Orleans, LA, USA, 21–24 June 2022; pp. 11966–11976. [CrossRef]
52. Touvron, H.; Cord, M.; Jégou, H. DeiT III: Revenge of the ViT. In Proceedings of the European Conference on Computer Vision (ECCV), Tel Aviv, Israel, 23–27 October 2022; pp. 516–533. [CrossRef]
53. Abbas, F.; Yasmin, M.; Fayyaz, M.; Asim, U. ViT-PGC: Vision Transformer for pedestrian gender classification on small-size dataset. *Pattern Anal. Appl.* **2023**, *26*, 1805–1819. [CrossRef]
54. Li, D.; Chen, X.; Huang, K. Multi-attribute learning for pedestrian attribute recognition in surveillance scenarios. In Proceedings of the Asian Conference on Pattern Recognition (ACPR), Kuala Lumpur, Malaysia, 3–6 November 2015; pp. 111–115. [CrossRef]

55. Lin, Y.; Zheng, L.; Zheng, Z.; Wu, Y.; Hu, Z.; Yan, C.; Yang, Y. Improving person re-identification by attribute and identity learning. *Pattern Recognit.* **2019**, *95*, 151–161. [CrossRef]
56. Guo, H.; Zheng, K.; Fan, X.; Yu, H.; Wang, S. Visual Attention Consistency Under Image Transforms for Multi-Label Image Classification. In Proceedings of the 2019 IEEE/CVF Conference on Computer Vision and Pattern Recognition (CVPR), Long Beach, CA, USA, 15–20 June 2019; pp. 729–739. [CrossRef]
57. Fayyaz, M.; Yasmin, M.; Sharif, M.; Raza, M. J-LDFR: Joint low-level and deep neural network feature representations for pedestrian gender classification. *Neural Comput. Appl.* **2021**, *33*, 361–391. [CrossRef]
58. Cai, L.; Zeng, H.; Zhu, J.; Cao, J.; Wang, Y.; Ma, K.-K. Cascading scene and viewpoint feature learning for pedestrian gender recognition. *IEEE Internet Things J.* **2021**, *8*, 3014–3026. [CrossRef]
59. Jetson TX2 Module. Available online: https://developer.nvidia.com/embedded/jetson-tx2 (accessed on 1 February 2024).
60. Selvaraju, R.R.; Cogswell, M.; Das, A.; Vedantam, R.; Parikh, D.; Batra, D. Grad-CAM: Visual explanations from deep networks via gradient-based localization. *Int. J. Comput. Vis.* **2020**, *128*, 336–359. [CrossRef]
61. Student's t-test. Available online: https://en.wikipedia.org/wiki/Student's_t-test (accessed on 21 February 2024).
62. Cohen, J. A power primer. *Psychol. Bull.* **1992**, *112*, 1155–1159. [CrossRef] [PubMed]
63. Mandelbrot, B. How long is the coast of Britain? Statistical self-similarity and fractional dimension. *Science* **1967**, *156*, 636–638. [CrossRef]

Disclaimer/Publisher's Note: The statements, opinions and data contained in all publications are solely those of the individual author(s) and contributor(s) and not of MDPI and/or the editor(s). MDPI and/or the editor(s) disclaim responsibility for any injury to people or property resulting from any ideas, methods, instructions or products referred to in the content.

Article

Fractal Dimension-Based Multi-Focus Image Fusion via Coupled Neural P Systems in NSCT Domain

Liangliang Li [1], Xiaobin Zhao [1,2,*], Huayi Hou [3], Xueyu Zhang [1], Ming Lv [4], Zhenhong Jia [4] and Hongbing Ma [5]

- [1] School of Information and Electronics, Beijing Institute of Technology, Beijing 100081, China
- [2] Tianjin Key Laboratory of Autonomous Intelligence Technology and Systems, Tiangong University, Tianjin 300387, China
- [3] Hubei Key Laboratory of Optical Information and Pattern Recognition, Wuhan Institute of Technology, Wuhan 430205, China
- [4] School of Computer Science and Technology, Xinjiang University, Urumqi 830046, China
- [5] Department of Electronic Engineering, Tsinghua University, Beijing 100084, China
- * Correspondence: xiaobinzhao@bit.edu.cn

Abstract: In this paper, we introduce an innovative approach to multi-focus image fusion by leveraging the concepts of fractal dimension and coupled neural P (CNP) systems in nonsubsampled contourlet transform (NSCT) domain. This method is designed to overcome the challenges posed by the limitations of camera lenses and depth-of-field effects, which often prevent all parts of a scene from being simultaneously in focus. Our proposed fusion technique employs CNP systems with a local topology-based fusion model to merge the low-frequency components effectively. Meanwhile, for the high-frequency components, we utilize the spatial frequency and fractal dimension-based focus measure (FDFM) to achieve superior fusion performance. The effectiveness of the method is validated through extensive experiments conducted on three benchmark datasets: Lytro, MFI-WHU, and MFFW. The results demonstrate the superiority of our proposed multi-focus image fusion method, showcasing its potential to significantly enhance image clarity across the entire scene. Our algorithm has achieved advantageous values on metrics $Q_{AB/F}$, Q_{CB}, Q_{CV}, Q_E, Q_{FMI}, Q_G, Q_{MI}, and Q_{NCIE}.

Keywords: multi-focus image; image fusion; fractal dimension; CNP; NSCT

Citation: Li, L.; Zhao, X.; Hou, H.; Zhang, X.; Lv, M.; Jia, Z.; Ma, H. Fractal Dimension-Based Multi-Focus Image Fusion via Coupled Neural P Systems in NSCT Domain. *Fractal Fract.* **2024**, *8*, 554. https://doi.org/10.3390/fractalfract8100554

Academic Editors: Carlo Cattani, Dayan Liu, Driss Boutat, Xuefeng Zhang and Jinxi Zhang

Received: 10 August 2024
Revised: 5 September 2024
Accepted: 7 September 2024
Published: 25 September 2024

Copyright: © 2024 by the authors. Licensee MDPI, Basel, Switzerland. This article is an open access article distributed under the terms and conditions of the Creative Commons Attribution (CC BY) license (https://creativecommons.org/licenses/by/4.0/).

1. Introduction

Multi-focus image fusion (MFIF) is a sophisticated process used in image processing that involves combining multiple images taken with different focus settings into a single image where all objects are in focus [1]. This technique is particularly useful in scenarios where the depth of field is limited and parts of the scene are out of focus in each image. By integrating these images, multi-focus image fusion produces a composite that is entirely sharp and clear [2].

The process of multi-focus image fusion involves several key techniques and steps: (1) Image registration: aligning the multiple images accurately is crucial, as even slight misalignments can lead to poor fusion results; (2) Focus measurement: this involves assessing the focus level of different parts of each image, often using clarity or sharpness metrics; (3) Fusion algorithm: the core of the process, where algorithms decide how to combine the sharp portions of each input image into the final composite. Techniques vary from simple averaging to complex wavelet-based methods; (4) Post-processing: enhancing the fused image to improve visual quality or to prepare it for analysis, including tasks like contrast adjustment or noise reduction [3,4].

MFIF is not without its challenges. These include handling misalignments, reducing artifacts that can arise during fusion, and dealing with variations in exposure and color balance among the source images. Advances in computational photography, machine learning, and deep learning have led to more sophisticated fusion algorithms that can more effectively address these challenges, resulting in higher-quality fused images. Various algorithms and techniques, including multi-resolution analysis, image decomposition, and feature-based methods, have been developed to effectively fuse multi-focus images. One of the key challenges in image fusion is to ensure that important information from both input images is preserved and enhanced in the fused image, without introducing artifacts or losing critical details [5–7].

In traditional image fusion algorithms, the multi-scale transforms such as nonsubsampled contourlet transform (NSCT) [8] and nonsubsampled shearlet transform (NSST) [9] are commonly employed. These are mathematical tools that are used for image analysis and processing. They offer an enhanced representation of local features and multi-scale analysis capabilities, making them particularly suitable for tasks like image fusion. Li et al. [10] introduced the medical image fusion approach using NSST. Lv et al. [11] proposed MFIF via parameter-adaptive pulse-coupled neural network and fractal dimension in NSST domain. Li et al. [12] introduced the image fusion algorithm based on spatial frequency and improved sum-modified-Laplacian in NSST domain. Coupled neural P (CNP) systems were proposed by Peng et al. [13] in 2019, and Li et al. [14] proposed the medical image fusion method based on coupled neural P systems (CNP) in NSST domain; the experiments show that the CNP systems achieve excellent results in image fusion. Although the algorithm achieves good image fusion results, it is only suitable for images of size $m \times m$. For images of size $m \times n$, due to the necessity of preprocessing the image with NSST to obtain an $m \times m$ or $n \times n$ image, followed by decomposition, applying different fusion rules to obtain the fused image, and finally resizing the image back to $m \times n$, information loss and distortion occur to varying degrees during this process. Therefore, NSST is more suitable for the image fusion processing of $m \times m$-sized images. NSCT can directly process images with size $m \times n$, which can reduce image distortion and information loss. Li et al. [15] proposed the MFIF method via NSCT and achieved an excellent fusion effect.

To improve the clarity and information complementarity of the fused images, we propose a novel MFIF method based on fractal dimension and coupled neural P systems (CNP) in NSCT domain. The main contributions of our paper are as follows:

(1) The coupled neural P systems (CNP) are used to process low-frequency components in order to obtain better background information;
(2) A fractal dimension-based focus measure (FDFM) combined with spatial frequency (SF) is used to process high-frequency components, thereby obtaining more detailed image information;
(3) Through extensive qualitative and quantitative experiments conducted on three datasets, our method consistently outperforms state-of-the-art (SOTA) techniques, demonstrating superior performance.

The remainder of the article is structured into six sections. Section 2 provides an overview of related works. In Section 3, the nonsubsampled contourlet transform is introduced. Section 4 presents the introduction of CNP systems. The proposed method is detailed in Section 5. Section 6 covers experimental results and discussions, while Section 7 delves into further discussions.

2. Related Works

In this section, we provide a concise overview of the existing literature on MFIF, categorizing it into three main approaches: spatial domain-based methods, transform domain-based methods, and deep learning-based methods [16].

2.1. Spatial Domain-Based Image Fusion

Spatial domain-based fusion methods involve the direct manipulation of pixel values using specific algorithms designed for image fusion. Among them, image fusion algorithms based on edge-preserving filtering are the most commonly used. These filters typically include guided image filtering [17], rolling guidance filtering [18], Gaussian curvature filter [19], etc. Fiza et al. [20] proposed a technique for MFIF specifically tailored for satellite images. It addresses issues such as visual distortion and spatial inconsistencies at sharp edges by introducing the edge discriminative diffusion filter (EDDF). EDDF combines anisotropic diffusion (AD) with guided filter (GF) to discriminate between local and global features, preserving edges while maintaining spatial consistency. The technique involves transforming source images into detail and base layers to extract low-pass and high-pass information, processing saliency maps through EDDF to generate weight maps, and, finally, combining fused detail and base layers to produce the desired fused image. Quantitative and qualitative tests demonstrate that the proposed technique outperforms some SOTA alternatives.

Yan et al. [21] introduced a novel MFIF approach, utilizing dictionary learning alongside a rolling guidance filter to accommodate both registered and mis-registered input images. Initially, a dictionary is learned from classical multi-focus images blurred by the rolling guidance filter. Then, a model is proposed for identifying focus regions by applying the learned dictionary to input images, generating focus feature maps. These maps are compared to derive an initial decision map, which is optimized and applied to the input images to produce fused images. Experimental results demonstrate the competitiveness of the proposed algorithm with the current state of the art, particularly excelling when handling both well-registered and mis-registered input images.

Adeel et al. [22] introduced a two-stage spatial domain framework for MFIF, which finds applications in computer vision. Initially, the salient features of focused regions are detected using Gaussian curvature filter (GCF) and range filtering. Subsequently, morphological filters refine the initial focus detection map. Experimental results demonstrate the method's speed and robustness, outperforming recent multi-focus fusion schemes.

Tang et al. [23] introduced the image fusion technique that utilizes a simple weighted least squares filter. In their approach, source images are first decomposed into base and detail layers using this filter. The detail layers are then fused through a sub-window variance filter. For the base layer, they developed a fusion strategy that integrates visual saliency mapping with adaptive weight assignment techniques. Although the algorithm enhances the details, the fusion image as a whole suffers from some distortion.

2.2. Transform Domain-Based Image Fusion

Image fusion approaches via transform domains involve processing the transformed coefficients of source images using various transforms such as contourlet transform [24,25], shearlet transform [26,27], gradient domain [28], sparse representation [29,30], etc. Subsequently, these coefficients are inversely transformed back into the spatial domain. This approach typically comprises three primary stages: image transform, coefficient fusion, and inverse transform.

Jie et al. [31] proposed a method for enhancing full-field optical angiography (FFOA) images to achieve full focus, thereby improving its clinical utility. Existing FFOA techniques suffer from a limited depth of focus, resulting in partially unclear images. The method utilizes NSCT and contrast spatial frequency to fuse FFOA images effectively. Firstly, source images are decomposed into low-pass and bandpass images. Then, a sparse representation-based rule fuses low-pass images, while a contrast spatial frequency rule fuses bandpass images, considering pixel correlation and gradient relationships. Finally, a fully focused image is reconstructed. Experimental results demonstrate the superiority of the proposed method over SOTA approaches in both qualitative and quantitative evaluations, offering promising prospects for clinical applications in disease prevention and diagnosis.

Lu et al. [32] presented a novel focus measure called the sum of Gaussian-based fractional order differentiation (SGFD) to improve the accuracy of detecting low-frequency regions in MFIF. SGFD outperforms traditional focus measures by retaining more low-frequency information. The fusion process involves initial fusion using the NSST and SGFD, followed by refinement of the initial decision map through quadtree decomposition. Residual regions are identified and removed to generate the final fused image. Comparative experiments with SOTA approaches demonstrate that the SGFD-based approach excels in both subjective visual quality and objective metrics, offering promising advancements in MFIF.

Paul et al. [28] introduced a method for fusing color images that addresses both multi-exposure and multi-focus scenarios. It achieves this by blending the gradients of the luminance components of input images, prioritizing the maximum gradient magnitude at each pixel location. The fused luminance is then obtained through a Haar wavelet-based image reconstruction approach.

Tang et al. [33] proposed a sparse representation-based fusion approach for image fusion. Traditional methods often suffer from including redundant information during dictionary learning, leading to artifacts and increased computational time. To address this, the proposed method introduces a novel dictionary construction method based on joint patch grouping and informative sampling. Nonlocal similarity is utilized for joint patch grouping across all source images, simplifying the calculation by selecting only one class of informative image patches. Sparse coefficients are obtained using the orthogonal matching pursuit (OMP) algorithm, and a max-L1 fusion rule is employed for image reconstruction. Experimental results demonstrate the superiority of the proposed approach in effectively fusing multi-focus images.

Chen et al. [34] introduced an image fusion approach via a complex sparse representation (CSR) model. This model employs hypercomplex signal properties to derive directional information from real-valued signals by extending them into the complex domain. Following this, the directional aspects of the input signal are separated into sparse coefficients using corresponding directional dictionaries.

2.3. Deep Learning-Based Image Fusion

Deep learning has been widely applied in the field of image processing, including tasks such as image classification [35], image segmentation [36], object detection [37], image enhancement [38], image fusion [39], etc. The commonly used deep learning models have CNNs [40], GANs [41], autoencoders [42], etc. There has been extensive research into leveraging deep learning techniques for image fusion [43]. This has led to the emergence of numerous methods that utilize deep learning for MFIF. Zhang et al. [44] introduced the IFCNN fusion framework, a convolutional neural network (CNN)-based approach that offers a comprehensive fusion solution. Notably, it can undergo end-to-end training without necessitating preprocessing steps. Hu et al. [45] proposed a ZMFF method based on a deep prior network. Zhang et al. [46] introduced a fast unified image fusion network called PMGI. This network addresses various image fusion tasks like medical image fusion and MFIF. The key idea is to maintain the proportional relationship between texture and intensity information from source images. Xu et al. [47] introduced an innovative unified and unsupervised end-to-end image fusion network (U2Fusion).

Traditional algorithms have the following two advantages compared to deep learning: (1) Traditional algorithms typically operate based on mathematical models and specific rules, making their results easier to interpret and control; (2) Researchers can clearly understand how each step influences the final fusion outcome and can adjust parameters and methods according to their needs.

3. Nonsubsampled Contourlet Transform

The nonsubsampled contourlet transform (NSCT) is an advanced mathematical tool used for signal and image analysis, extending the principles of the contourlet transform but with significant improvements in handling images [48–50]. Developed to overcome some of the limitations of previous multi-scale and multi-directional transforms, the NSCT offers a flexible, multi-resolution, multi-direction, and shift-invariant framework for image decomposition. The NSCT decomposes images into components at multiple scales and orientations. It performs this through two main stages: a nonsubsampled pyramid (NSP) structure for capturing point discontinuities and a series of nonsubsampled directional filter banks (NSDFB) for linking point discontinuities into linear structures. This approach is adept at capturing edges and textures in an image, which are essential features in many image processing tasks. Figure 1a displays an overview of the proposed NSCT. The structure consists of a bank of filters that splits the 2-D frequency plane in the sub-bands illustrated in Figure 1b.

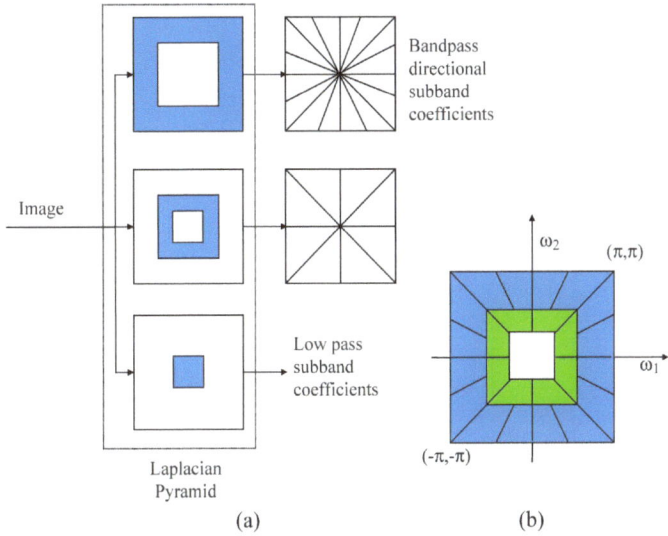

Figure 1. Nonsubsampled contourlet transform. (**a**) Nonsubsampled filter bank structure that implements the NSCT; (**b**) Idealized frequency partitioning obtained with the proposed structure.

The NSCT requires selecting appropriate scale and directional parameters, which can significantly impact the final processing results and necessitate experience and experimentation to optimize. Due to its involvement with multi-scale and multidirectional data representations, NSCT requires high memory demands, especially when processing large-scale data.

4. Coupled Neural P Systems

For the fusion of multi-focus images, coupled neural P (CNP) systems are designed as an array of neurons with local topology, i.e., CNP systems with local topology [13,14].

A CNP system with local topology, of degree $m \times n$, is delineated as follows:

$$\Pi = (O, \sigma_{11}, \sigma_{12}, \cdots, \sigma_{1n}, \cdots, \sigma_{m1}, \sigma_{m2}, \cdots, \sigma_{mn}, \text{syn}) \tag{1}$$

where

(1) $O = \{a\}$ is an alphabet (the objective a is known as the spike);
(2) $\sigma_{11}, \sigma_{12}, \cdots, \sigma_{mn}$ are an array of $m \times n$ coupled neurons of the form

$$\sigma_{ij} = (x_{ij}, y_{ij}, z_{ij}, R_{ij}), \ 1 \le i \le h, \ 1 \le j \le w$$

where

(a) $x_{ij} \in R$ is the value of spikes in feeding input unit in neuron σ_{ij};
(b) $y_{ij} \in R$ is the value of spikes in linking input unit in neuron σ_{ij};
(c) $z_{ij} \in R$ is the value of spikes in dynamic threshold unit in neuron σ_{ij};
(d) R_{ij} denotes the finite set of spiking rules, of the form $E/(a^x, a^y, a^z) \rightarrow a^p$, where E is the firing condition, $p \ge 0$, $\tau \ge 0$, and $p \le u(1+v)$.

(3) syn = $\{(ij,kl)|1 \leq i \leq h, 1 \leq j \leq w, |k-i| \leq r, |l-j| \leq r, i \neq k, j \neq l\}$, where r is the neighborhood radius.

Suppose that I is an input image with size $h \times w$ and I_{BC} is the matrix containing the base components (BC) obtained from the image decomposition method. Figure 2 shows the relationship between CNP system Π and base components matrix I_{BC}.

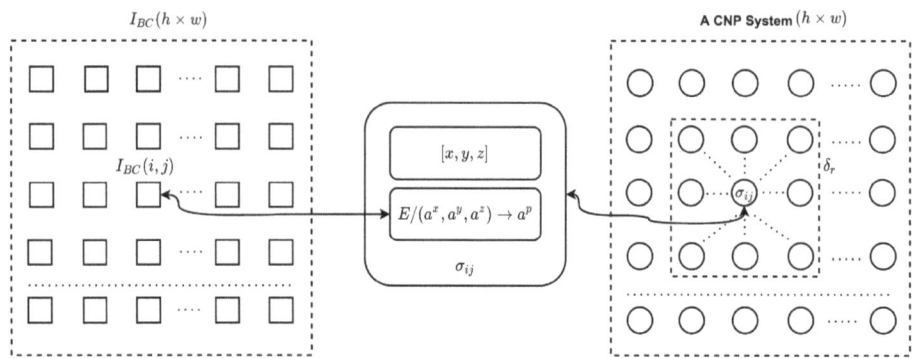

Figure 2. A CNP system Π and the corresponding base component matrix I_{BC}.

In CNP system Π, each coupled neuron only communicates with its neighboring neurons, i.e., local topology. An r-neighborhood of neurons σ_{ij} is defined as follows, as shown in Figure 2:

$$\delta_r(\sigma_{ij}) = \{\sigma_{kl} | |k-i| \leq r, |l-j| \leq r\} \quad (2)$$

The spiking rule of neuron σ_{ij} is defined as follows [14]:

$$E/(a^x, a^y, a^z) \to a^p \quad (3)$$

where E is a firing condition denoted as follows [14]:

$$E \equiv (n_i(t) \geq z_i(t)) \wedge (x_i(t) \geq x) \wedge (y_i(t) \geq y) \wedge (z_i(t) \geq z) \quad (4)$$

where $n_{ij}(t) = x_{ij}(t)(1 + y_{ij}(t))$, which represents a nonlinear modulation mechanism. According to the spiking mechanism, the state equation for neuron σ_{ij} can be given by

$$x_{ij}(t+1) = \begin{cases} x_{ij}(t) - x + C_{ij} + \sum_{\sigma_{kl} \in \delta_r} \omega_{kl} p_{kl}(t), & \text{if } \sigma_{ij} \text{ fires} \\ x_{ij}(t) + C_{ij} + \sum_{\sigma_{kl} \in \delta_r} \omega_{kl} p_{kl}(t), & \text{otherwise} \end{cases} \quad (5)$$

$$y_{ij}(t+1) = \begin{cases} y_{ij}(t) - y + \sum_{\sigma_{kl} \in \delta_r} \omega_{kl} p_{kl}(t), & \text{if } \sigma_{ij} \text{ fires} \\ y_{ij}(t) + \sum_{\sigma_{kl} \in \delta_r} \omega_{kl} p_{kl}(t), & \text{otherwise} \end{cases} \quad (6)$$

$$z_{ij}(t+1) = \begin{cases} z_{ij}(t) - z + p, & \text{if } \sigma_{ij} \text{ fires} \\ z_{ij}(t), & \text{otherwise} \end{cases} \quad (7)$$

where $p_{kl}(t)$ is the value of the spikes received by neuron σ_{ij} from neighboring neuron σ_{kl} and $\omega_{kl}(t)$ is the corresponding local weight, and C_{ij} is an external stimulus. p is the value of spikes generated by neuron σ_{ij} when it fires. Peng et al. [51] introduced the MFIF method based on CNP systems in NSCT domain, and the algorithm has achieved good fusion results.

5. The Proposed Method

We present a novel approach for MFIF utilizing fractal dimension and coupled neural P systems in NSCT domain. The main steps can be concluded as follows: NSCT decomposition, low-frequency coefficient fusion, high-frequency coefficient fusion, and inverse NSCT transform. Figure 3 illustrates the architecture of the proposed method.

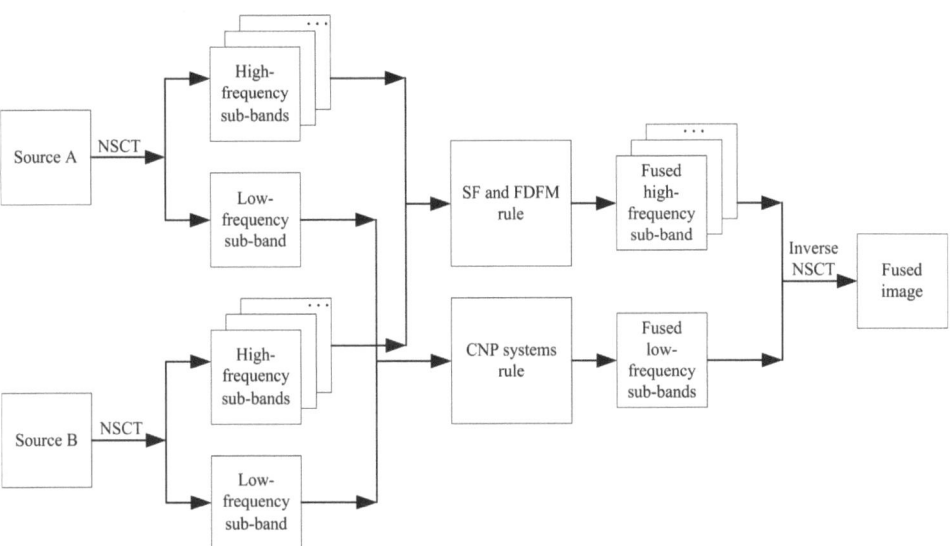

Figure 3. The structure of the proposed method.

5.1. NSCT Decomposition

Assume that A and B are the input images, the NSCT is used to decompose the two images, and the low- and high-frequency components are generated, named as $\left\{L_A, H_A^{l,k}\right\}$ and $\left\{L_B, H_B^{l,k}\right\}$, respectively.

5.2. Low-Frequency Coefficient Fusion

The low-frequency components have the most brightness and energy information; the fusion strategy for low-frequency components has a significant impact on the final fusion quality. In this section, the CNP systems-based low-frequency fusion rule is designed. Suppose that $\prod_A$ and $\prod_B$ are two CNP systems with local topology; the low-frequency coefficients of two multi-focus images are regarded as the external inputs of $\prod_A$ and $\prod_B$. Starting from the initial state, the two CNP systems work constantly until iteration number t_{max} is reached. Then, they halt. Denoted by T_A and T_B, the excitation number matrixes are associated with $\prod_A$ and $\prod_B$, i.e., $T_A = \left(t_{ij}^A\right)_{h \times w}$ and $T_B = \left(t_{ij}^B\right)_{h \times w}$, where t_{ij}^A (or t_{ij}^B) is the number of times that σ_{ij} fires in $\prod_A$ (or $\prod_B$). The fusion rules for low-frequency NSCT coefficients are formulated based on the information provided by the two excitation number matrices as follows [14]:

$$L_F(i,j) = \begin{cases} L_A(i,j) & \text{if } t_{ij}^A \geq t_{ij}^B \\ L_B(i,j) & \text{if } t_{ij}^A < t_{ij}^B \end{cases} \quad (8)$$

where $L_A(i,j)$ and $L_B(i,j)$ are the low-frequency coefficients of two source images at position (i,j), respectively, and $L_F(i,j)$ is the fused low-frequency coefficients.

5.3. High-Frequency Coefficient Fusion

The high-frequency coefficients contain richer texture and detailed information, as well as some of the image's noise. Fractal and fractional have extensive applications in image processing [52–63]. In this section, the spatial frequency (SF) [64] and fractal dimension-based focus measure (FDFM) [52] are defined as follows:

$$SF^{H_A^{l,k}}(i,j) = \sum_{i \in M, j \in N} \left(H_A^{l,k}(i,j) - H_A^{l,k}(i-1,j)\right)^2 + \left(H_A^{l,k}(i,j) - H_A^{l,k}(i,j-1)\right)^2 \quad (9)$$

$$SF^{H_B^{l,k}}(i,j) = \sum_{i \in M, j \in N} \left(H_B^{l,k}(i,j) - H_B^{l,k}(i-1,j)\right)^2 + \left(H_B^{l,k}(i,j) - H_B^{l,k}(i,j-1)\right)^2 \quad (10)$$

$$FDFM^{H_A^{l,k}}(i,j) = g_{max}^{H_A^{l,k}}(i,j) - g_{min}^{H_A^{l,k}}(i,j) \quad (11)$$

$$FDFM^{H_B^{l,k}}(i,j) = g_{max}^{H_B^{l,k}}(i,j) - g_{min}^{H_B^{l,k}}(i,j) \quad (12)$$

where $g_{max}^{X(i,j)}$ and $g_{min}^{X}(i,j)$ are the maximum and minimum intensities, respectively, over a 3×3 window centered at the $(i,j)^{th}$ pixel of $X \in \{H_A^{l,k}, H_B^{l,k}\}$. FDFM can measure such small activity levels, which also affect the fusion results.

The fused high-frequency coefficients are generated by

$$H_F^{l,k}(i,j) = \begin{cases} H_A^{l,k}(i,j) & \text{if } SF^{H_A^{l,k}}(i,j) \times FDFM^{H_A^{l,k}}(i,j) \\ & \geq SF^{H_B^{l,k}}(i,j) \times FDFM^{H_B^{l,k}}(i,j) \\ H_B^{l,k}(i,j) & \text{else} \end{cases} \quad (13)$$

where $H_F^{l,k}(i,j)$ shows the fused high-frequency coefficients.

5.4. Inverse NSCT Transform

The final fused image F can be generated by using inverse NSCT transform performed on the fused low- and high-frequency coefficients $\{L_F, H_F^{l,k}\}$.

The main steps of the proposed method can be summarized as in Algorithm 1.

Algorithm 1 Proposed MFIF method

Input: the source images: A and B
Parameters: The number of NSCT decomposition levels: L, the number of directions at each decomposition level: $K(l), l \in [1, L]$
Main step:
Step 1: NSCT decomposition
For each source image $X \in \{A, B\}$
    Perform NSCT decomposition on X to generate $\{L_X, H_X^{l,k}\}, l \in [1, L], k \in [1, K(l)]$;
End
Step 2: Low-frequency components fusion
For each source image $X \in \{A, B\}$
    Calculate the CNP for L_X using Equations (1)–(7);
End
Merge L_A and L_B using Equation (8) to generate L_F;
Step 3: High-frequency components fusion
For each level $l = 1 : L$
    For each direction $k = 1 : K(l)$

Algorithm 1 Cont.

      For each source image $X \in \{A, B\}$
      Calculate the SF for $H_X^{l,k}(i,j)$ using Equations (9) and (10);
      Calculate the FDFM for $H_X^{l,k}(i,j)$ using Equations (11) and (12);
      End
        Merge $H_A^{l,k}$ and $H_B^{l,k}$ using Equation (13);
    End
End
Step 4: Inverse NSCT
Perform inverse NSCT on $\{L_F, H_F^{l,k}\}$ to generate F;
Output: the fused image F.

6. Experimental Results and Discussion

6.1. Experimental Setup

In this section, the classical Lytro [65], MFI-WHU [66], and MFFW [67] datasets are used in the experiments, as shown in Figure 4. Eight image fusion methods, named GD [28], PMGI [46], MFFGAN [66], LEGFF [68], U2Fusion [47], CBFM [69], FUFusion [70], and EgeFusion [23], are used to compare. The metrics $Q_{AB/F}$ [64,71], Q_{CB} [72], Q_{CV} [72], Q_E [72], Q_{FMI} [73], Q_G [72], Q_{MI} [64], and Q_{NCIE} [72] are used to evaluate the fusion results. The source code of these compared methods is available or shared by the authors, and the relevant parameter settings are set according to the original papers. In our method, the NSCT decomposition levels is 4, and the corresponding directions are 2, 4, 8, and 8. The parameters in CNP systems are set to i_{max}, $z_0 = 0.3$, $r = 7$, and $p = 1$. $W_{7 \times 7} = \{\omega_{ij}\}_{7 \times 7}$ is determined as follows: (i) $\omega_{44} = 0$; (ii) $\omega_{ij} = 1/\text{sqrt}\left((i-4)^2 + (j-4)^2\right)$ for $i \neq 4, j \neq 4$, $1 \leq i \leq 7, 1 \leq j \leq 7$.

Figure 4. Examples of the Lytro, MFI-WHU, and MFFW datasets.

6.2. Fusion Results and Discussion

(1) Results on the Lytro Dataset

We conduct qualitative and quantitative evaluations to evaluate the performance of different image fusion methods. Figure 5 displays the fused images of Data 1 from the Lytro dataset. The fused image generated by GD exhibits over-brightness in certain areas, leading to the loss of some fine details and the presence of artifacts. The PMGI algorithm results in severe distortion, with the visual effect of the image appearing dim and blurry, and a significant loss of information. The brightness of the image generated by MFFGAN is insufficient, especially in areas such as the hair. The LEGFF algorithm achieved a relatively good fusion result, but there is slight darkness observed in the brightness of the hair section. The U2Fusion algorithm generated an image with some dim areas, particularly noticeable in regions like the hat and hair, as well as the watch section, where usable information is not observable. The CBFM generates a fused image that darkens the area around the arm. The FUFusion produces a blurry fused image, making it difficult to obtain some image information. The EgeFusion results in a significant distortion and loss of image information in the fused image. Compared to other algorithms, our method demonstrates a superior fusion result, featuring higher clarity and moderate brightness. Information pertaining to arm, watch, clothing, hat, golf club, and grass in the image is distinctly observable.

Figure 5. *Cont.*

(g) (h) (i)

Figure 5. Visual comparison for Data 1 in the Lytro dataset. (**a**) GD; (**b**) PMGI; (**c**) MFFGAN; (**d**) LEGFF; (**e**) U2Fusion; (**f**) CBFM; (**g**) FUFusion; (**h**) EgeFusion; (**i**) Proposed.

Table 1 presents the numerical values of various indicators corresponding to different algorithms depicted in Figure 5. These indicators serve as quantitative metrics for evaluating the performance of each algorithm in the context of the depicted data. By examining these values, we gain insights into the effectiveness of each algorithm in achieving the desired objectives. From Table 1, it is evident that our algorithm has achieved optimal values for the eight indicators, with respective values of $Q_{AB/F}$ (0.7524), Q_{CB} (0.7745), Q_{CV} (6.5508), Q_E (0.8862), Q_{FMI} (0.9380), Q_G (0.7382), Q_{MI} (6.5466), and Q_{NCIE} (0.8245).

Table 1. Quantitative comparative analysis of different methods for Data 1 in the Lytro dataset.

	Year	$Q_{AB/F}$	Q_{CB}	Q_{CV}	Q_E	Q_{FMI}	Q_G	Q_{MI}	Q_{NCIE}
GD	2016	0.7220	0.6684	63.5814	0.8144	0.9222	0.6985	3.1161	0.8096
PMGI	2020	0.5466	0.6070	70.2785	0.6316	0.9169	0.5156	5.1347	0.8169
MFFGAN	2021	0.6860	0.7026	23.3439	0.8451	0.9296	0.6599	5.5783	0.8190
LEGFF	2022	0.6923	0.6857	38.6156	0.8205	0.9306	0.6658	4.8919	0.8158
U2Fusion	2022	0.6575	0.6164	56.5810	0.7952	0.9206	0.6338	5.2894	0.8176
CBFM	2023	0.7201	0.7403	13.3863	0.8720	0.9334	0.6974	5.4462	0.8184
FUFusion	2024	0.7202	0.6652	47.2751	0.8146	0.9259	0.6967	5.6856	0.8197
EgeFusion	2024	0.3120	0.3356	468.3896	0.4318	0.8892	0.3080	2.6294	0.8084
Proposed		0.7524	0.7745	6.5508	0.8862	0.9380	0.7382	6.5466	0.8245

Figure 6 displays the fused images of Data 2 from the Lytro dataset. The image clarity obtained by the GD and PMGI algorithms is not high. The MFFGAN, LEGFF, and U2Fusion methods produce unevenly fused images, in which some regions are clear while others are dark, such as the neck area being too dim, obscuring detailed information. The fusion image generated by CBFM is dark and exhibits low brightness and clarity, resulting in a significant loss of information. The fused image produced by the FUFusion method is overall blurry, with a severe loss of detailed information. The EgeFusion algorithm produces an image with significant distortion, although some sharpening is applied to enhance detailed information; this sharpening also results in varying degrees of block effects in the image. Compared to other algorithms, our algorithm achieved the best fusion result, including image brightness, contrast, etc., allowing for a genuine observation of people and objects in the image.

Table 2 presents the numerical values of various indicators corresponding to different algorithms depicted in Figure 6. By analyzing the data in Table 2, we can conclude that our algorithm has achieved the optimal values in all eight indicators, with values as follows:

$Q_{AB/F}$ (0.7445), Q_{CB} (0.6870), Q_{CV} (5.3153), Q_E (0.8672), Q_{FMI} (0.8732), Q_G (0.7369), Q_{MI} (7.6750), and Q_{NCIE} (0.8339).

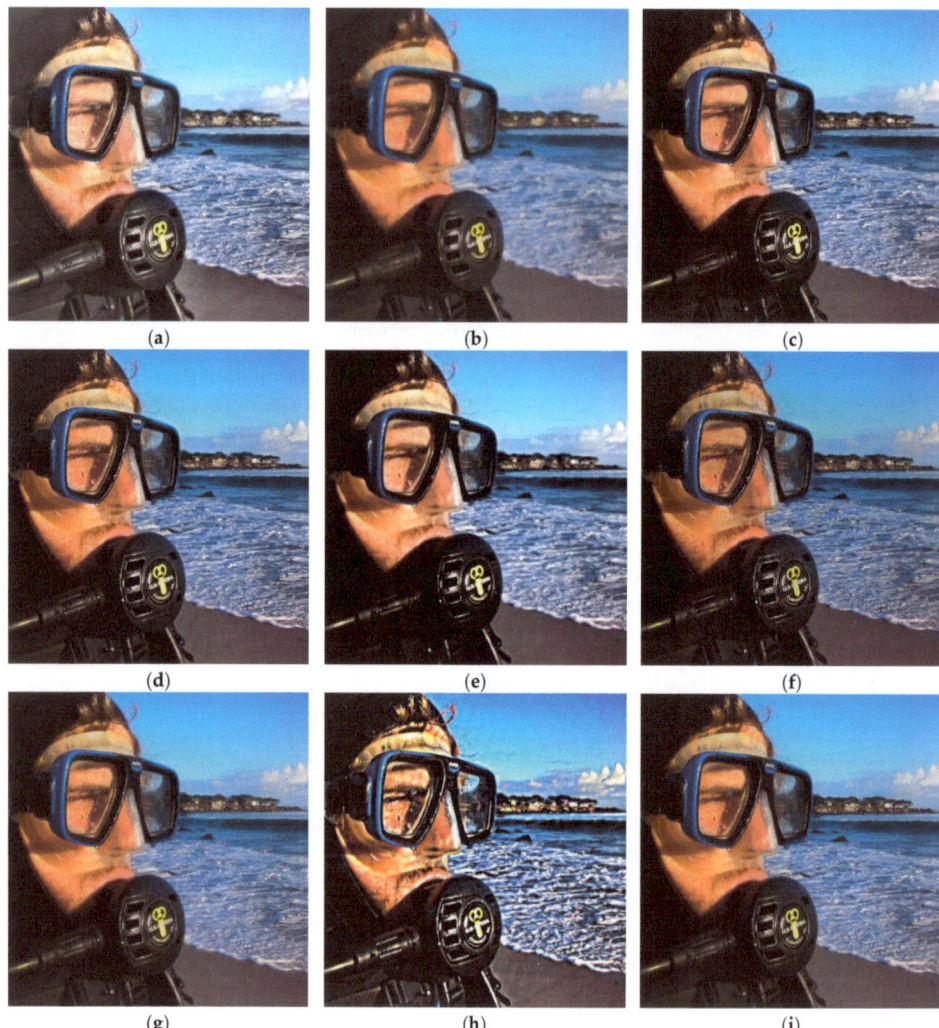

Figure 6. Visual comparison for Data 2 in the Lytro dataset. (**a**) GD; (**b**) PMGI; (**c**) MFFGAN; (**d**) LEGFF; (**e**) U2Fusion; (**f**) CBFM; (**g**) FUFusion; (**h**) EgeFusion; (**i**) Proposed.

Figure 7 depicts a line chart of the metrics for different data in the Lytro dataset (20 sets of data were used in this experiment), allowing for an observation of fluctuations in the indicator data. Additionally, we have computed the average indicators, as shown in both Figure 7 and Table 3. Considering that a lower value of Q_{CV} indicates better performance, we take its negative value (i.e., $-Q_{CV}$) to illustrate the sub-figure of Q_{CV}. The horizontal axis represents the number of image groups in the dataset, and the vertical axis represents the metric value. From the Figure 7 and Table 3, we can observe that our method has achieved the optimal average values for all the indicators, with values as follows: $Q_{AB/F}$ (0.7390), Q_{CB} (0.7388), Q_{CV} (31.4085), Q_E (0.8772), Q_{FMI} (0.8989), Q_G (0.7362), Q_{MI} (6.9683), and Q_{NCIE} (0.8296).

Table 2. Quantitative comparative analysis of different methods for Data 2 in the Lytro dataset.

	Year	$Q_{AB/F}$	Q_{CB}	Q_{CV}	Q_E	Q_{FMI}	Q_G	Q_{MI}	Q_{NCIE}
GD	2016	0.6823	0.6135	85.4217	0.7559	0.8645	0.6660	4.2116	0.8156
PMGI	2020	0.4798	0.5977	53.3298	0.5816	0.8573	0.4592	6.3071	0.8251
MFFGAN	2021	0.6609	0.6291	28.2393	0.7931	0.8651	0.6440	6.4491	0.8260
LEGFF	2022	0.6770	0.6466	22.7596	0.7920	0.8680	0.6603	5.8173	0.8225
U2Fusion	2022	0.5951	0.4969	168.9820	0.6838	0.8619	0.5786	6.1325	0.8242
CBFM	2023	0.7116	0.6634	31.8620	0.8348	0.8690	0.7019	5.9728	0.8234
FUFusion	2024	0.7226	0.6400	16.7184	0.8511	0.8671	0.7088	7.0218	0.8294
EgeFusion	2024	0.2492	0.3688	490.2211	0.3210	0.8429	0.2419	3.2940	0.8127
Proposed		0.7445	0.6870	5.3153	0.8672	0.8732	0.7369	7.6750	0.8339

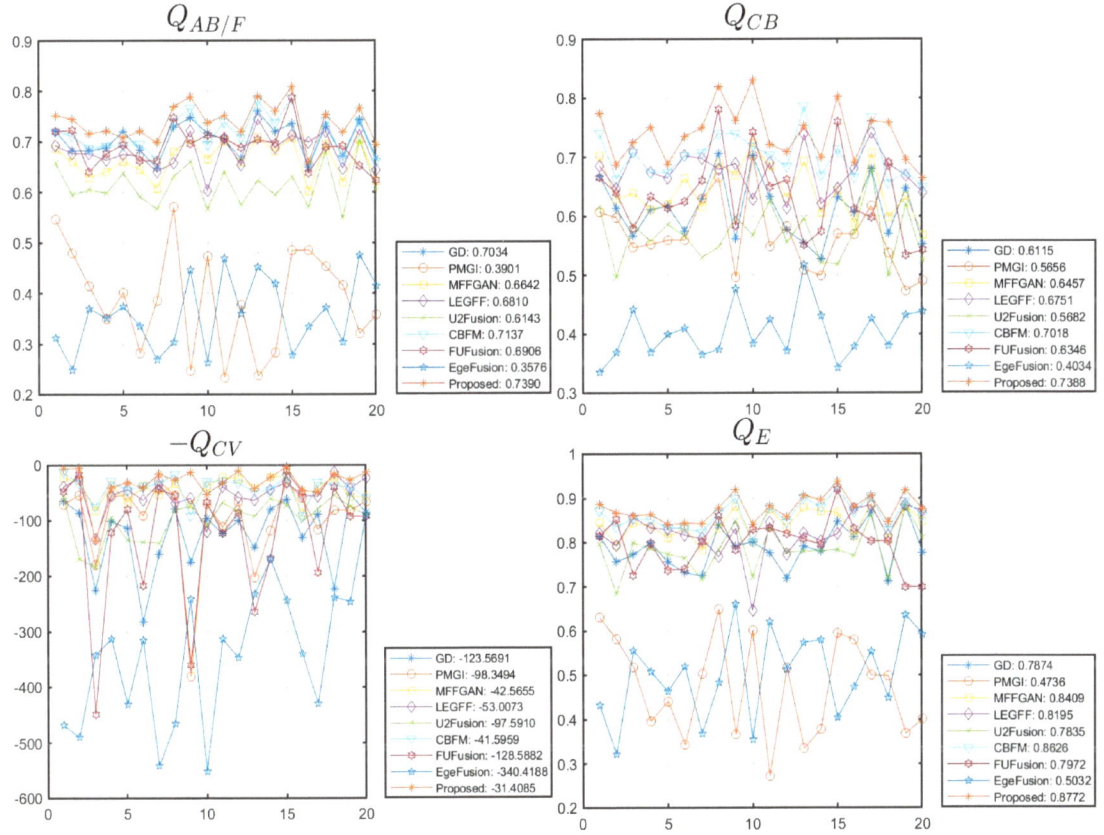

Figure 7. Cont.

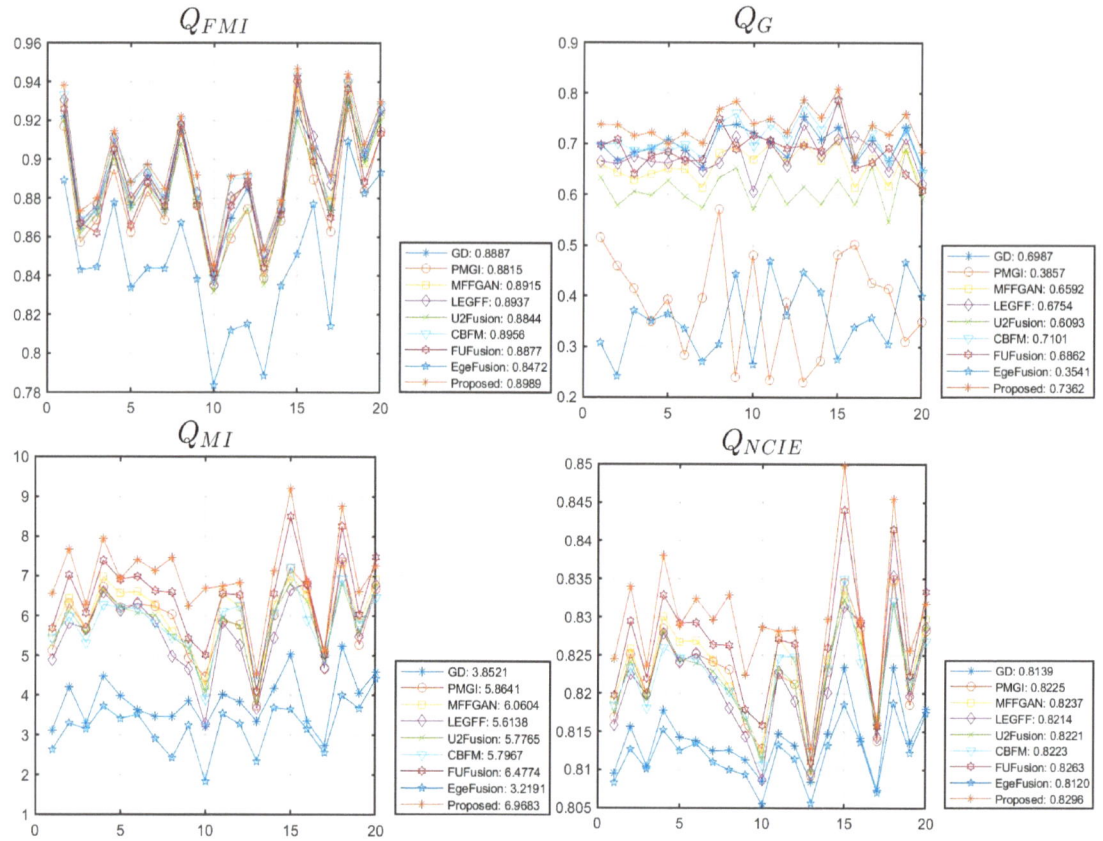

Figure 7. The line chart illustrates the metrics of various data in the Lytro dataset.

Table 3. Quantitative average comparative analysis of different methods on the Lytro dataset.

	Year	$Q_{AB/F}$	Q_{CB}	Q_{CV}	Q_E	Q_{FMI}	Q_G	Q_{MI}	Q_{NCIE}
GD	2016	0.7034	0.6115	123.5691	0.7874	0.8887	0.6987	3.8521	0.8139
PMGI	2020	0.3901	0.5656	98.3494	0.4736	0.8815	0.3857	5.8641	0.8225
MFFGAN	2021	0.6642	0.6457	42.5655	0.8409	0.8915	0.6592	6.0604	0.8237
LEGFF	2022	0.6810	0.6751	53.0073	0.8195	0.8937	0.6754	5.6138	0.8214
U2Fusion	2022	0.6143	0.5682	97.5910	0.7835	0.8844	0.6093	5.7765	0.8221
CBFM	2023	0.7137	0.7018	41.5959	0.8626	0.8956	0.7101	5.7967	0.8223
FUFusion	2024	0.6906	0.6346	128.5882	0.7972	0.8877	0.6862	6.4774	0.8263
EgeFusion	2024	0.3576	0.4034	340.4188	0.5032	0.8472	0.3541	3.2191	0.8120
Proposed		0.7390	0.7388	31.4085	0.8772	0.8989	0.7362	6.9683	0.8296

(2) Results on the MFI-WHU Dataset

Figure 8 depicts the fused images of Data 1 from the MFI-WHU dataset. The images produced by GD exhibit some slight pseudo-shadow artifacts. The PMGI algorithm generates blurry fused images; for instance, the details of the roof and mural cannot be accurately captured. The MFFGAN and U2Fusion algorithms achieve higher brightness fusion results in certain regions, such as the glass display area. However, there are also areas with lower brightness. For instance, MFFGAN exhibits shadows around the base of the display cabinet, while U2Fusion produces significant shadowing along the edges of the roof and the bench, hindering the retrieval of complete information. The fused image produced by LEGFF has a higher clarity. The fused images produced by the CBFM and FUFusion algorithms have some areas with shadows, such as on the side of a bench. Although the EgeFusion algorithm enhances the texture information in the image, it also introduces some degree of distortion. Upon comprehensive comparison, our algorithm outperforms others in the fusion experiment, enhancing the overall fusion effect by reducing pseudo-shadows and dark areas, while simultaneously improving the brightness and clarity of the fused image.

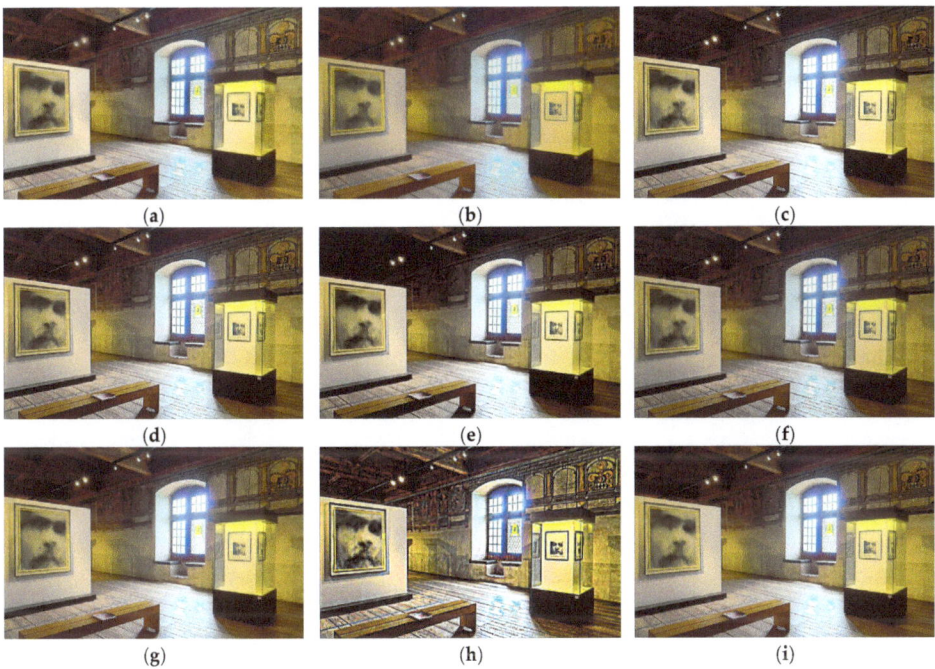

Figure 8. Visual comparison for Data 1 in the MFI-WHU dataset. (**a**) GD; (**b**) PMGI; (**c**) MFFGAN; (**d**) LEGFF; (**e**) U2Fusion; (**f**) CBFM; (**g**) FUFusion; (**h**) EgeFusion; (**i**) Proposed.

Table 4 presents the numerical values of various indicators corresponding to different algorithms depicted in Figure 8. From Table 4, it is evident that our algorithm has achieved optimal values for the eight indicators, with respective values of $Q_{AB/F}$ (0.7281), Q_{CB} (0.8256), Q_{CV} (6.4076), Q_E (0.8534), Q_{FMI} (0.9000), Q_G (0.7288), Q_{MI} (9.0964), and Q_{NCIE} (0.8476).

Figure 9 depicts the fused images of Data 2 from the MFI-WHU dataset. The GD method produced a fused image with low clarity. The PMGI method generated a low-quality fused image with varying degrees of shadowing in objects such as the vehicle, windowsill, sky, and trees. The images produced by the MFFGAN and LEGFF algorithms cause the windowsill area to become darker. The U2Fusion method generated fused image with uneven brightness distribution, such as a darker area in the windowsill region and a brighter area in the vehicle region. The fused images produced by the CBFM and FUFusion algorithms have relatively low brightness. The EgeFusion algorithm causes distortion in the fused image. Through comprehensive comparison, our algorithm produces the optimal fusion result, with balanced brightness and high clarity, which are beneficial for information retrieval.

Table 4. Quantitative comparative analysis of different methods for Data 1 in the MFI-WHU dataset.

	Year	$Q_{AB/F}$	Q_{CB}	Q_{CV}	Q_E	Q_{FMI}	Q_G	Q_{MI}	Q_{NCIE}
GD	2016	0.6739	0.6571	82.3636	0.7953	0.8906	0.6829	4.1802	0.8180
PMGI	2020	0.3769	0.6528	25.6514	0.4425	0.8883	0.3772	7.0843	0.8320
MFFGAN	2021	0.6371	0.6336	37.0591	0.7936	0.8950	0.6337	6.9928	0.8315
LEGFF	2022	0.6253	0.6348	37.4732	0.7451	0.8959	0.6345	6.2296	0.8271
U2Fusion	2022	0.5571	0.4815	140.7225	0.7173	0.8867	0.5574	6.2829	0.8273
CBFM	2023	0.6846	0.7014	28.2899	0.8218	0.8963	0.6835	6.5658	0.8290
FUFusion	2024	0.7024	0.7546	24.4700	0.8452	0.8970	0.7039	8.0555	0.8390
EgeFusion	2024	0.2691	0.3308	453.2295	0.3956	0.8557	0.2720	3.1227	0.8148
Proposed		0.7281	0.8256	6.4076	0.8534	0.9000	0.7288	9.0964	0.8476

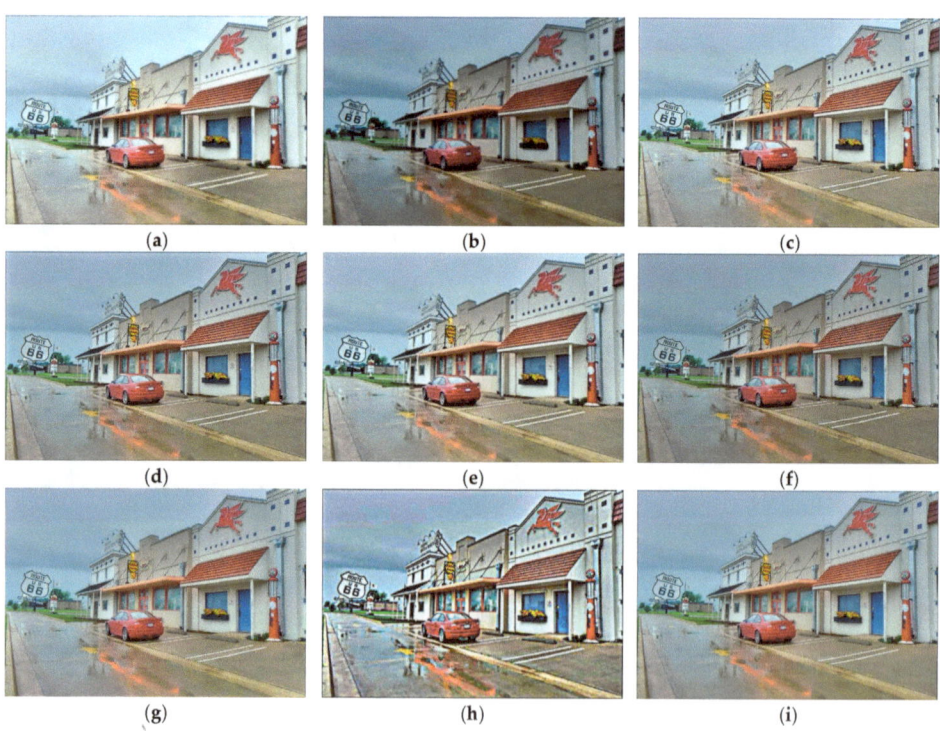

Figure 9. Visual comparison for Data 2 in the MFI-WHU dataset. (**a**) GD; (**b**) PMGI; (**c**) MFFGAN; (**d**) LEGFF; (**e**) U2Fusion; (**f**) CBFM; (**g**) FUFusion; (**h**) EgeFusion; (**i**) Proposed.

Table 5 presents the numerical values of various indicators corresponding to different algorithms depicted in Figure 9. From Table 5, it is evident that our algorithm has achieved optimal values for seven indicators, with respective values of $Q_{AB/F}$ (0.7408), Q_{CB} (0.8250), Q_E (0.8550), Q_{FMI} (0.8795), Q_G (0.7409), Q_{MI} (7.8104), and Q_{NCIE} (0.8348). The FUFusion algorithm achieved the optimal value on the Q_{CV} metric, with a value of 30.6077. Our algorithm ranked second in the Q_{CV} metric, with a value of 38.0683.

Figure 10 depicts a line chart of the metrics of different data in the MFI-WHU dataset (30 sets of data were used in this experiment), allowing for the observation of fluctuations in the indicator data. Additionally, we have computed the average indicators, as shown in both Figure 10 and Table 6. We can observe that our algorithm has achieved optimal values for seven indicators, with respective values of $Q_{AB/F}$ (0.7296), Q_{CB} (0.8072), Q_E (0.8453), Q_{FMI} (0.8772), Q_G (0.7254), Q_{MI} (7.8107), and Q_{NCIE} (0.8371). The FUFusion algorithm achieved the optimal value on the Q_{CV} metric, with a value of 23.7140. Our algorithm ranked second in the Q_{CV} metric, with a value of 36.4954.

Table 5. Quantitative comparative analysis of different methods for Data 2 in the MFI-WHU dataset.

	Year	$Q_{AB/F}$	Q_{CB}	Q_{CV}	Q_E	Q_{FMI}	Q_G	Q_{MI}	Q_{NCIE}
GD	2016	0.6876	0.5795	137.2797	0.7862	0.8655	0.6842	3.9284	0.8140
PMGI	2020	0.5906	0.4640	97.4159	0.6549	0.8559	0.5880	5.1975	0.8190
MFFGAN	2021	0.6536	0.5945	64.3859	0.7661	0.8695	0.6497	5.3730	0.8198
LEGFF	2022	0.6546	0.5709	58.2280	0.7660	0.8744	0.6462	4.8070	0.8173
U2Fusion	2022	0.6053	0.5280	86.2756	0.7221	0.8578	0.6035	5.1287	0.8187
CBFM	2023	0.7031	0.6458	59.4391	0.8212	0.8757	0.7015	5.3351	0.8196
FUFusion	2024	0.7070	0.7063	30.6077	0.8411	0.8784	0.7061	5.9021	0.8224
EgeFusion	2024	0.3031	0.2703	653.9751	0.3296	0.8315	0.2953	2.8712	0.8110
Proposed		0.7408	0.8250	38.0683	0.8550	0.8795	0.7409	7.8104	0.8348

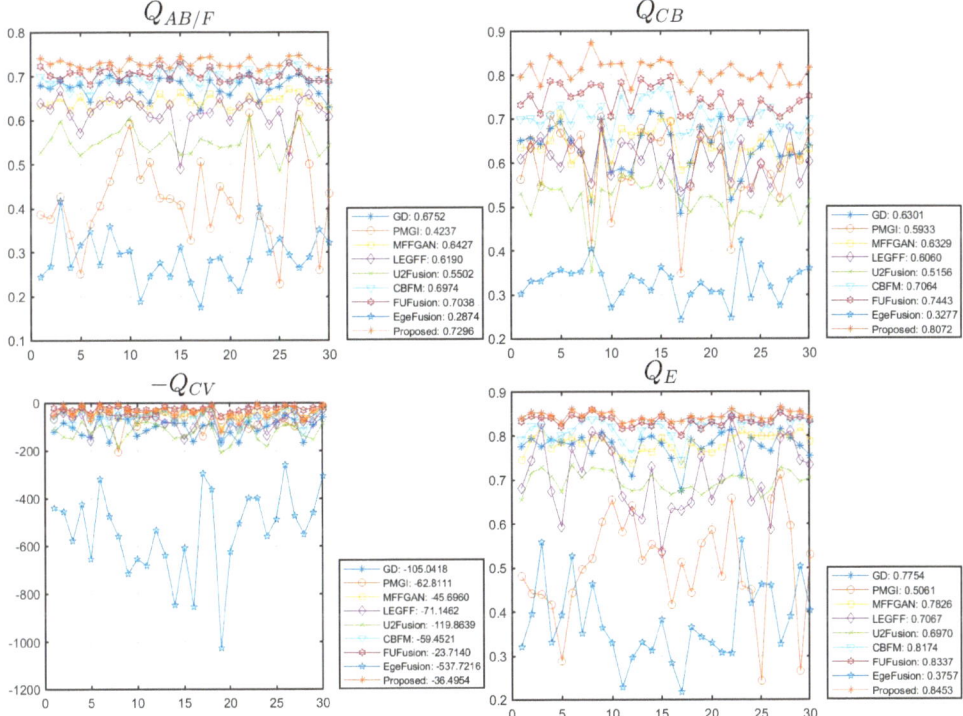

Figure 10. *Cont.*

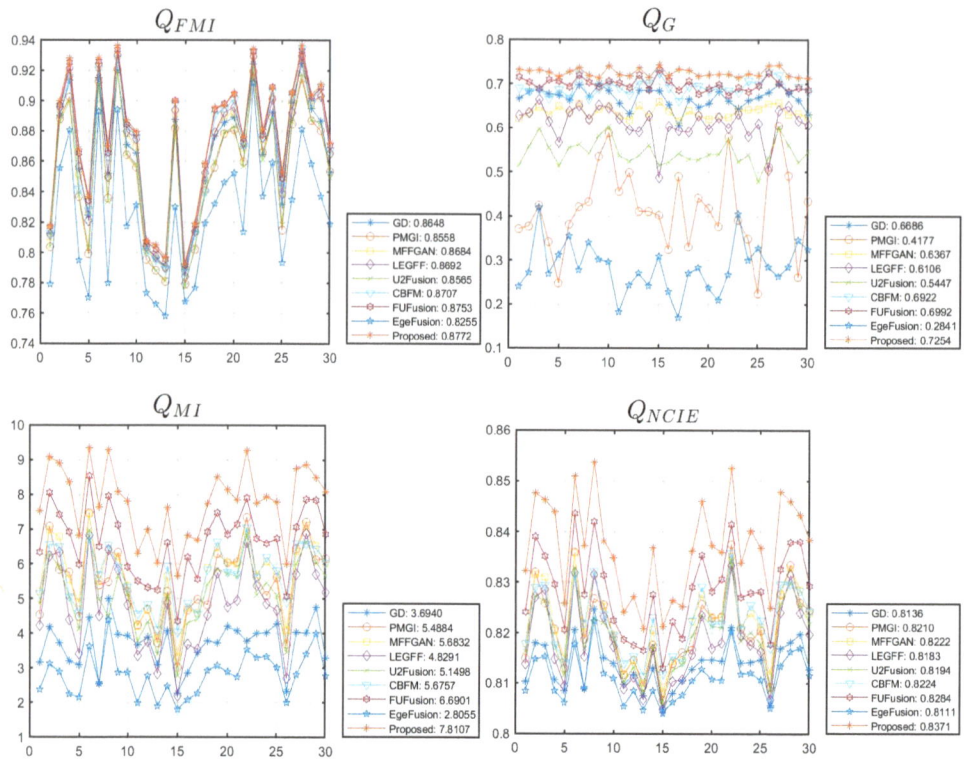

Figure 10. The line chart illustrates the metrics of various data in the MFI-WHU dataset.

Table 6. Quantitative average comparative analysis of different methods on the MFI-WHU dataset.

	Year	$Q_{AB/F}$	Q_{CB}	Q_{CV}	Q_E	Q_{FMI}	Q_G	Q_{MI}	Q_{NCIE}
GD	2016	0.6752	0.6301	105.0418	0.7754	0.8648	0.6686	3.6940	0.8136
PMGI	2020	0.4237	0.5933	62.8111	0.5061	0.8558	0.4177	5.4884	0.8210
MFFGAN	2021	0.6427	0.6329	45.6960	0.7826	0.8684	0.6367	5.6832	0.8222
LEGFF	2022	0.6190	0.6060	71.1462	0.7067	0.8692	0.6106	4.8291	0.8183
U2Fusion	2022	0.5502	0.5156	119.8639	0.6970	0.8565	0.5447	5.1498	0.8194
CBFM	2023	0.6974	0.7064	59.4521	0.8174	0.8707	0.6922	5.6757	0.8224
FUFusion	2024	0.7038	0.7443	23.7140	0.8337	0.8753	0.6992	6.6901	0.8284
EgeFusion	2024	0.2874	0.3277	537.7216	0.3757	0.8255	0.2841	2.8055	0.8111
Proposed		0.7296	0.8072	36.4954	0.8453	0.8772	0.7254	7.8107	0.8371

(3) Results on the MFFW Dataset

Figure 11 depicts the fused images of Data 1 from the MFFW dataset. The fused images produced by the GD, PMGI, and FUFusion algorithms are blurry and have lower clarity. The fused images produced by the MFFGAN and LEGFF methods cause the center of the rose to appear darker, with shadowing present. The U2Fusion causes the piano keys and the rose in the fused image to appear darker. The fused images produced by the CBFM and FUFusion algorithms exhibit varying degrees of artifacts. Although the EgeFusion algorithm enhances the texture information in the fused image, it also introduces a certain degree of distortion. By comparison with other algorithms, our method achieves a superior fusion result, attaining effective information complementarity.

Table 7 presents the numerical values of various indicators corresponding to different algorithms depicted in Figure 11. From Table 7, it is evident that our algorithm has achieved optimal values for six indicators, with respective values of Q_{CB} (0.6155), Q_{CV} (33.3908), Q_E (0.8290), Q_{FMI} (0.8987), Q_{MI} (6.6801), and Q_{NCIE} (0.8290). The GD algorithm achieved optimal values for the $Q_{AB/F}$ and Q_G metrics, with values of 0.7297 and 0.6829, respectively.

Figure 12 depicts a line chart of the metrics of different data in the MFFW dataset (13 sets of data were used in this experiment), allowing for the observation of fluctuations in the indicator data. Additionally, we have computed the average indicators, as shown in both Figure 12 and Table 8. We can observe that our algorithm has achieved optimal values for five indicators, with respective values of $Q_{AB/F}$ (0.6377), Q_{CV} (116.0756) Q_E (0.8048), Q_{FMI} (0.8799), and Q_G (0.6224). The CBFM algorithm achieved the optimal value for the Q_{CB} metric, with a value of 0.6408. Our algorithm ranked second in the Q_{CB} metric, with a value of 0.6362. The FUFusion algorithm achieved the optimal value on the Q_{MI} and Q_{NCIE} metrics, with values of 5.3456 and 0.8196, respectively. Our method ranked second in these two metrics, with values of 5.0505 and 0.8180, respectively.

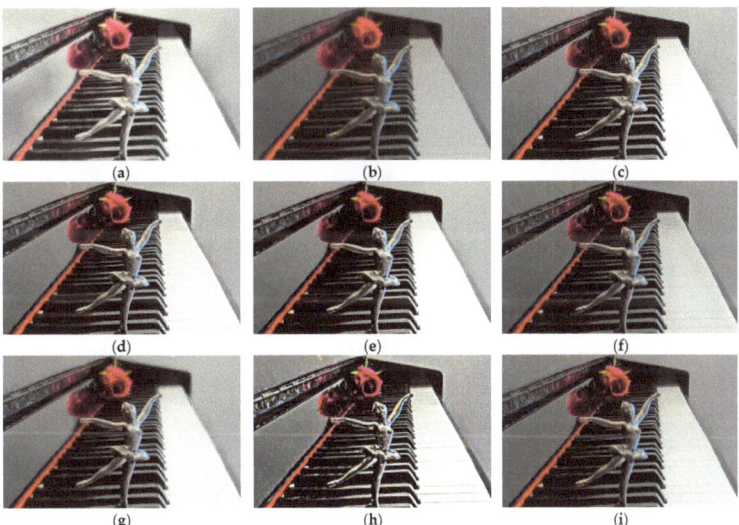

Figure 11. Visual comparison for Data 1 in the MFFW dataset. (**a**) GD; (**b**) PMGI; (**c**) MFFGAN; (**d**) LEGFF; (**e**) U2Fusion; (**f**) CBFM; (**g**) FUFusion; (**h**) EgeFusion; (**i**) Proposed.

Table 7. Quantitative comparative analysis of different methods for Data 1 in the MFFW dataset.

	Year	$Q_{AB/F}$	Q_{CB}	Q_{CV}	Q_E	Q_{FMI}	Q_G	Q_{MI}	Q_{NCIE}
GD	2016	0.7297	0.4875	110.5392	0.6970	0.8882	0.6829	4.7958	0.8195
PMGI	2020	0.4084	0.4709	61.0451	0.3863	0.8842	0.3766	6.5896	0.8282
MFFGAN	2021	0.6626	0.5677	57.0983	0.7777	0.8923	0.6165	6.3993	0.8272
LEGFF	2022	0.7001	0.5947	60.1930	0.7886	0.8968	0.6457	6.1499	0.8258
U2Fusion	2022	0.5914	0.5325	101.9227	0.6879	0.8790	0.5539	6.2297	0.8262
CBFM	2023	0.7037	0.6146	51.8537	0.8237	0.8933	0.6588	6.0571	0.8254
FUFusion	2024	0.6992	0.5522	76.2735	0.7652	0.8897	0.6479	6.6305	0.8285
EgeFusion	2024	0.3877	0.4132	365.6116	0.4142	0.8406	0.3611	4.2145	0.8173
Proposed		0.7013	0.6155	33.3908	0.8290	0.8987	0.6571	6.6801	0.8290

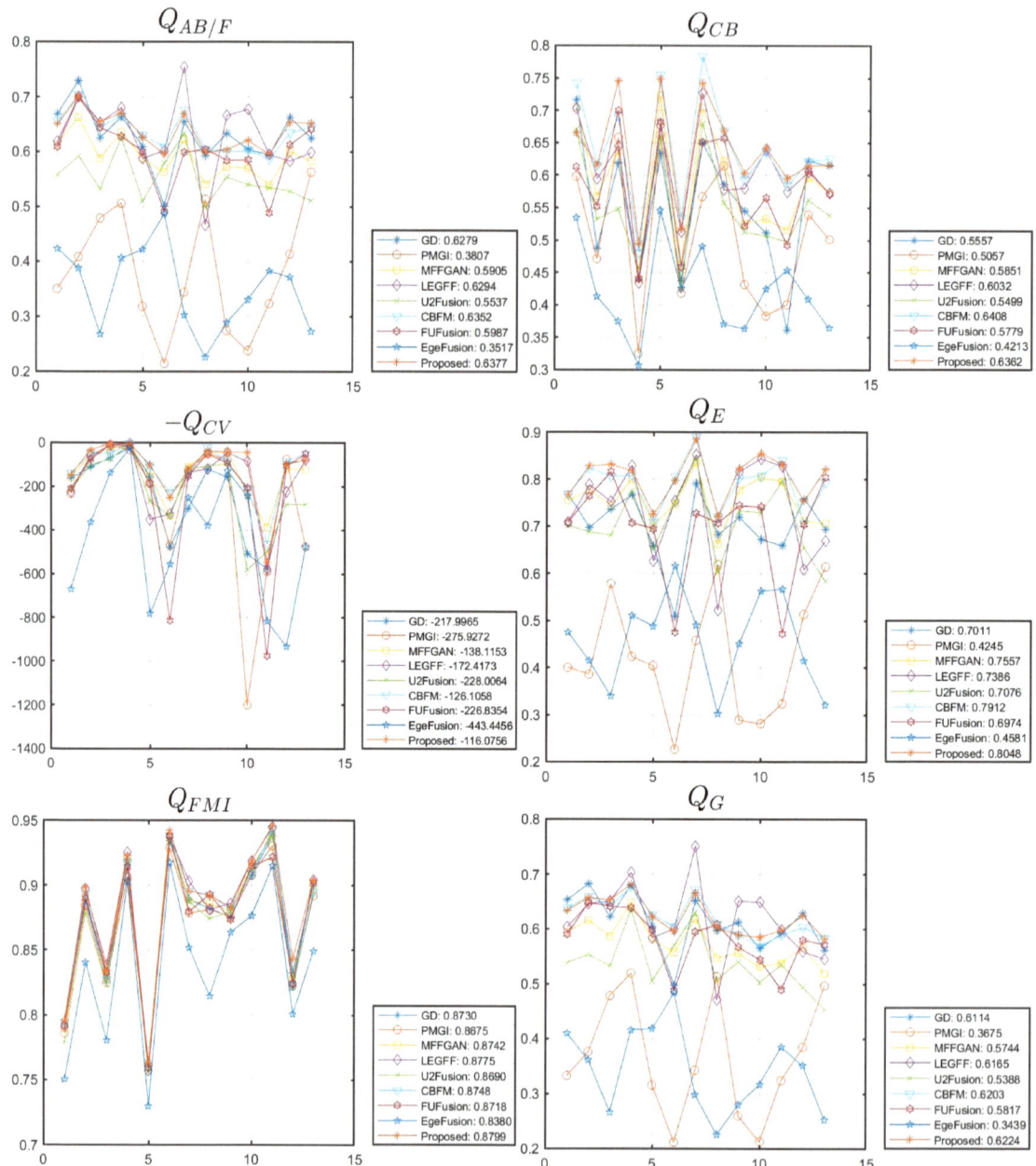

Figure 12. *Cont.*

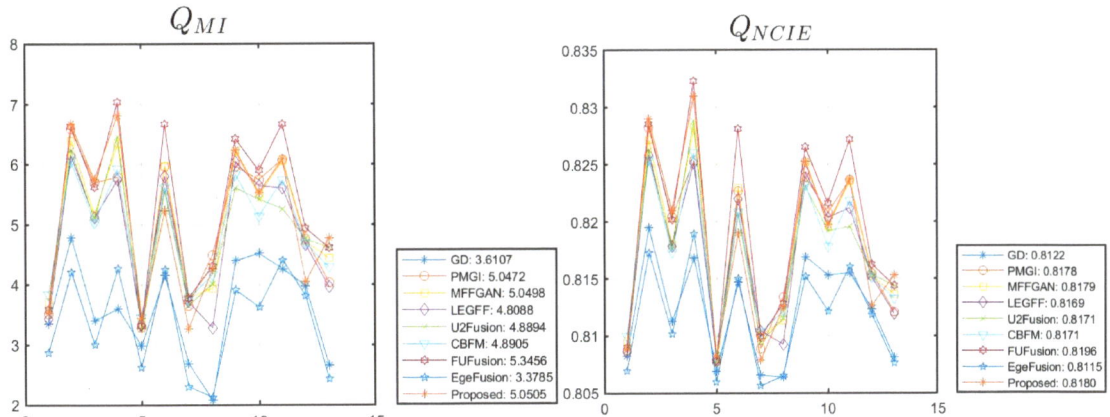

Figure 12. The line chart illustrates the metrics of various data in the MFFW dataset.

Table 8. Quantitative average comparative analysis of different methods on the MFFW dataset.

	Year	$Q_{AB/F}$	Q_{CB}	Q_{CV}	Q_E	Q_{FMI}	Q_G	Q_{MI}	Q_{NCIE}
GD	2016	0.6279	0.5557	217.9965	0.7011	0.8730	0.6114	3.6107	0.8122
PMGI	2020	0.3807	0.5057	275.9272	0.4245	0.8675	0.3675	5.0472	0.8178
MFFGAN	2021	0.5905	0.5851	138.1153	0.7557	0.8742	0.5744	5.0498	0.8179
LEGFF	2022	0.6294	0.6032	172.4173	0.7386	0.8775	0.6165	4.8088	0.8169
U2Fusion	2022	0.5537	0.5499	228.0064	0.7076	0.8690	0.5388	4.8894	0.8171
CBFM	2023	0.6352	0.6408	126.1058	0.7912	0.8748	0.6203	4.8905	0.8171
FUFusion	2024	0.5987	0.5779	226.8354	0.6974	0.8718	0.5817	5.3456	0.8196
EgeFusion	2024	0.3517	0.4213	443.4456	0.4581	0.8380	0.3439	3.3785	0.8115
Proposed		0.6377	0.6362	116.0756	0.8048	0.8799	0.6224	5.0505	0.8180

6.3. Application Extension

In this section, we extend the proposed algorithm to the application of multi-modal medical image fusion. We utilized two medical datasets from the Whole Brain Atlas [74]. When processing color medical images (such as magnetic resonance (MR) and positron emission tomography (PET)), the PET images need to be converted between the RGB and YUV color spaces. The Y channel of the PET image is fused with the MR image, and then the fused Y channel is converted back to the RGB space along with the U and V channels of the PET image to obtain the final color fusion image. The corresponding schematic diagram is shown in Figure 13. From the experimental results shown in Figure 14, it is evident that our algorithm performs exceptionally well for medical image fusion, achieving significantly enhanced information complementarity in the fused images.

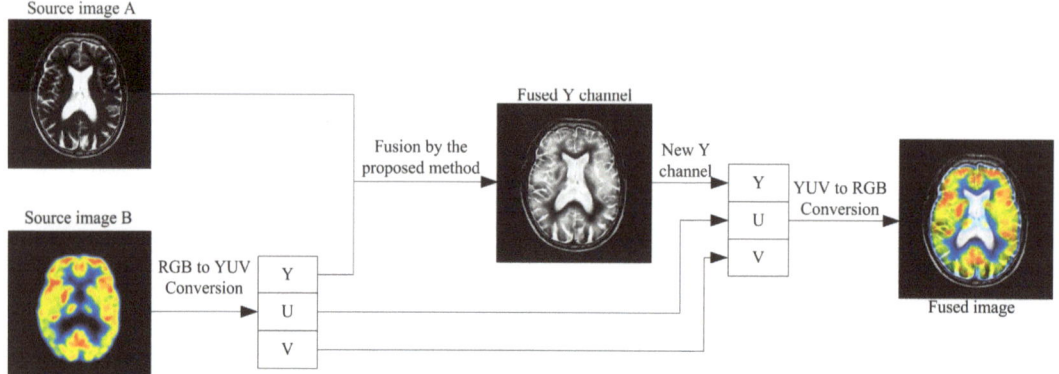

Figure 13. Structure of the proposed method for multi-modal medical images in the YUV color space.

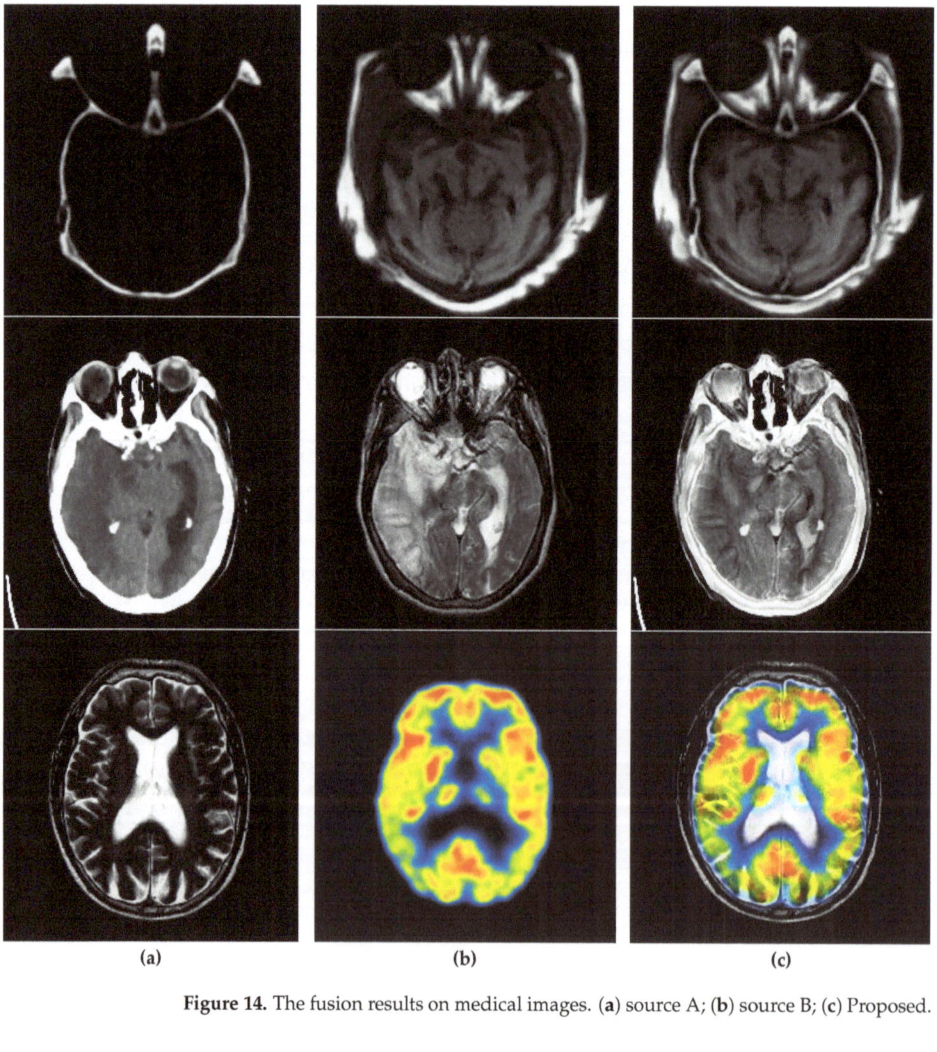

Figure 14. The fusion results on medical images. (**a**) source A; (**b**) source B; (**c**) Proposed.

7. Conclusions

This paper presents a novel approach to multi-focus image fusion that integrates fractal dimension and CNP systems in NSCT domain. Our fusion technique utilizes CNP systems with a local topology-based fusion model to effectively merge low-frequency components. Additionally, for high-frequency components, we employ a focus measure based on spatial frequency and FDFM to achieve superior fusion performance. Extensive experiments conducted on three classic datasets (Lytro, MFI-WHU, and MFFW), validate the effectiveness of the proposed method. In security surveillance, fusing images with different focal points can enhance the detail and clarity of the monitoring footage, improving target recognition capabilities. Furthermore, we have extended and applied this method to the field of medical image fusion, achieving the complementary integration of multi-modal medical image information. The number of decomposition levels in NSCT affects the effectiveness of image fusion. However, too many levels increase algorithm complexity. Therefore, choosing an optimal number of decomposition levels is our research focus. In future work, we will attempt to improve this algorithm and expand its application to the fusion of SAR (synthetic aperture radar) and optical images [48]. Additionally, the application of image fusion in multimodal finger knuckle print identification and image change detection are also worthwhile directions to explore [75–79].

Author Contributions: The experimental measurements and data collection were carried out by L.L., X.Z. (Xiaobin Zhao), H.H., X.Z. (Xueyu Zhang), M.L., Z.J. and H.M. The manuscript was written by L.L. with the assistance of X.Z. (Xiaobin Zhao), H.H., X.Z. (Xueyu Zhang), M.L., Z.J. and H.M. Writing—original draft, L.L. and H.M.; Writing—review & editing, X.Z. (Xiaobin Zhao), H.H., X.Z. (Xueyu Zhang), M.L. and H.M. All authors have read and agreed to the published version of the manuscript.

Funding: This work was supported by the National Natural Science Foundation of China under Grant No. 62261053; the Tianshan Talent Training Project-Xinjiang Science and Technology Innovation Team Program (2023TSYCTD0012); the Cross-Media Intelligent Technology Project of Beijing National Research Center for Information Science and Technology (BNRist) under Grant No. BNR2019TD01022; the Hubei Key Laboratory of Optical Information and Pattern Recognition, Wuhan Institute of Technology under Grant No. 202305; and the Open Project of Tianjin Key Laboratory of Autonomous Intelligence Technology and Systems (No. AITS-20240001).

Data Availability Statement: The original contributions presented in the study are included in the article, further inquiries can be directed to the corresponding author.

Acknowledgments: The authors would like to thank the Tianjin Key Laboratory of Autonomous Intelligence Technology and Systems (Tiangong University) for the financial support (No. AITS-20240001).

Conflicts of Interest: The authors declare no conflicts of interest.

References

1. Wang, C.; Yan, K. Focus-aware and deep restoration network with transformer for multi-focus image fusion. *Digit. Signal Process.* **2024**, *149*, 104473. [CrossRef]
2. Zhang, J.; Liao, Q.; Ma, H. Exploit the best of both end-to-end and map-based methods for multi-focus image fusion. *IEEE Trans. Multimed.* **2024**, *26*, 6411–6423. [CrossRef]
3. Qiao, L.; Wu, S.; Xiao, B. Boosting robust multi-focus image fusion with frequency mask and hyperdimensional computing. *IEEE Trans. Circuits Syst. Video Technol.* **2024**, *34*, 3538–3550. [CrossRef]
4. Li, B.; Zhang, L.; Liu, J.; Peng, H. Multi-focus image fusion with parameter adaptive dual channel dynamic threshold neural P systems. *Neural Netw.* **2024**, *179*, 106603. [CrossRef] [PubMed]
5. Liu, Y.; Liu, S.; Wang, Z. A general framework for image fusion based on multi-scale transform and sparse representation. *Inf. Fusion* **2015**, *24*, 147–164. [CrossRef]
6. Lv, M.; Li, L.; Jin, Q.; Jia, Z.; Chen, L.; Ma, H. Multi-focus image fusion via distance-weighted regional energy and structure tensor in NSCT domain. *Sensors* **2023**, *23*, 6135. [CrossRef] [PubMed]
7. Liu, Y.; Qi, Z.; Cheng, J.; Chen, X. Rethinking the effectiveness of objective evaluation metrics in multi-focus image fusion: A statistic-based approach. *IEEE Trans. Pattern Anal. Mach. Intell.* **2024**, *46*, 5806–5819. [CrossRef] [PubMed]
8. Wang, G.; Li, J. Fusion of full-field optical angiography images via gradient feature detection. *Front. Phys.* **2024**, *12*, 1397732. [CrossRef]

9. Wu, M.; Yang, L.; Chai, R. Research on multi-scale fusion method for ancient bronze ware X-ray images in NSST domain. *Appl. Sci.* **2024**, *14*, 4166. [CrossRef]
10. Li, L.; Wang, L.; Wang, Z.; Jia, Z. A novel medical image fusion approach based on nonsubsampled shearlet transform. *J. Med. Imaging Health Inform.* **2019**, *9*, 1815–1826.
11. Lv, M.; Jia, Z.; Li, L.; Ma, H. Multi-focus image fusion via PAPCNN and fractal dimension in NSST domain. *Mathematics* **2023**, *11*, 3803. [CrossRef]
12. Li, L.; Si, Y.; Wang, L.; Jia, Z.; Ma, H. A novel approach for multi-focus image fusion based on SF-PAPCNN and ISML in NSST domain. *Multimed. Tools Appl.* **2020**, *79*, 24303–24328. [CrossRef]
13. Peng, H.; Wang, J. Coupled neural P systems. *IEEE Trans. Neural Netw. Learn. Syst.* **2019**, *30*, 1672–1682. [CrossRef]
14. Li, B.; Peng, H. Medical image fusion method based on coupled neural P systems in nonsubsampled shearlet transform domain. *Int. J. Neural Syst.* **2021**, *31*, 2050050. [CrossRef] [PubMed]
15. Li, L.; Ma, H.; Jia, Z.; Si, Y. A novel multiscale transform decomposition based multi-focus image fusion framework. *Multimed. Tools Appl.* **2021**, *80*, 12389–12409. [CrossRef]
16. Qi, Y.; Yang, Z. A multi-channel neural network model for multi-focus image fusion. *Expert Syst. Appl.* **2024**, *247*, 123244. [CrossRef]
17. Li, S.; Kang, X.; Hu, J. Image fusion with guided filtering. *IEEE Trans. Image Process.* **2013**, *22*, 2864–2875.
18. Li, L.; Lv, M.; Jia, Z.; Jin, Q.; Liu, M.; Chen, L.; Ma, H. An effective infrared and visible image fusion approach via rolling guidance filtering and gradient saliency map. *Remote Sens.* **2023**, *15*, 2486. [CrossRef]
19. Huo, X.; Deng, Y.; Shao, K. Infrared and visible image fusion with significant target enhancement. *Entropy* **2022**, *24*, 1633. [CrossRef]
20. Fiza, S.; Safinaz, S. Multi-focus image fusion using edge discriminative diffusion filter for satellite images. *Multimed. Tools Appl.* **2024**, *83*, 66087–66106. [CrossRef]
21. Yan, X.; Qin, H.; Li, J. Multi-focus image fusion based on dictionary learning with rolling guidance filter. *J. Opt. Soc. Am. A-Opt. Image Sci. Vis.* **2017**, *34*, 432–440. [CrossRef]
22. Adeel, H.; Riaz, M. Multi-focus image fusion using curvature minimization and morphological filtering. *Multimed. Tools Appl.* **2024**, *83*, 78625–78639. [CrossRef]
23. Tang, H.; Liu, G.; Qian, Y. EgeFusion: Towards edge gradient enhancement in infrared and visible image fusion with multi-scale transform. *IEEE Trans. Comput. Imaging* **2024**, *10*, 385–398. [CrossRef]
24. Do, M.N.; Vetterli, M. The contourlet transform: An efficient directional multiresolution image representation. *IEEE Trans. Image Process.* **2005**, *14*, 2091–2106. [CrossRef] [PubMed]
25. Li, L.; Ma, H. Pulse coupled neural network-based multimodal medical image fusion via guided filtering and WSEML in NSCT domain. *Entropy* **2021**, *23*, 591. [CrossRef]
26. Guo, K.; Labate, D. Optimally sparse multidimensional representation using shearlets. *SIAM J. Math. Anal.* **2007**, *39*, 298–318. [CrossRef]
27. Li, L.; Ma, H. Saliency-guided nonsubsampled shearlet transform for multisource remote sensing image fusion. *Sensors* **2021**, *21*, 1756. [CrossRef]
28. Paul, S.; Sevcenco, I.; Agathoklis, P. Multi-exposure and multi-focus image fusion in gradient domain. *J. Circuits Syst. Comput.* **2016**, *25*, 1650123. [CrossRef]
29. Li, L.; Lv, M.; Jia, Z.; Ma, H. Sparse representation-based multi-focus image fusion method via local energy in shearlet domain. *Sensors* **2023**, *23*, 2888. [CrossRef]
30. Luo, Y.; Luo, Z. Infrared and visible image fusion: Methods, datasets, applications, and prospects. *Appl. Sci.* **2023**, *13*, 10891. [CrossRef]
31. Jie, Y.; Li, X.; Wang, M.; Tan, H. Multi-focus image fusion for full-field optical angiography. *Entropy* **2023**, *25*, 951. [CrossRef] [PubMed]
32. Lu, J.; Tan, K. Multi-focus image fusion using residual removal and fractional order differentiation focus measure. *Signal Image Video Process.* **2024**, *18*, 3395–3410. [CrossRef]
33. Tang, D.; Xiong, Q. A novel sparse representation based fusion approach for multi-focus images. *Expert Syst. Appl.* **2022**, *197*, 116737. [CrossRef]
34. Chen, Y.; Liu, Y.; Ward, R.K.; Chen, X. Multi-focus image fusion with complex sparse representation. *IEEE Sens. J.* **2024**. Early Access.
35. Shen, D.; Hu, H.; He, F.; Zhang, F.; Zhao, J.; Shen, X. Hierarchical prototype-aligned graph neural network for cross-scene hyperspectral image classification. *Remote Sens.* **2024**, *16*, 2464. [CrossRef]
36. Akram, R.; Hong, J.S.; Kim, S.G. Crop and weed segmentation and fractal dimension estimation using small training data in heterogeneous data environment. *Fractal Fract.* **2024**, *8*, 285. [CrossRef]
37. Zhou, M.; Li, B.; Wang, J. Optimization of hyperparameters in object detection models based on fractal loss function. *Fractal Fract.* **2022**, *6*, 706. [CrossRef]
38. Zhao, P.; Zheng, H.; Tang, S. DAMNet: A dual adjacent indexing and multi-deraining network for real-time image deraining. *Fractal Fract.* **2023**, *7*, 24. [CrossRef]

39. Fang, J.; Ning, X. A multi-focus image fusion network combining dilated convolution with learnable spacings and residual dense network. *Comput. Electr. Eng.* **2024**, *117*, 109299. [CrossRef]
40. Wang, S.; Chen, Z.; Qi, F. Fractal geometry and convolutional neural networks for the characterization of thermal shock resistances of ultra-high temperature ceramics. *Fractal Fract.* **2022**, *6*, 605. [CrossRef]
41. Sun, H.; Wu, S.; Ma, L. Adversarial attacks on GAN-based image fusion. *Inf. Fusion* **2024**, *108*, 102389. [CrossRef]
42. Yu, Y.; Qin, C. An end-to-end underwater-image-enhancement framework based on fractional integral retinex and unsupervised autoencoder. *Fractal Fract.* **2023**, *7*, 70. [CrossRef]
43. Zhang, X. Deep learning-based multi-focus image fusion: A survey and a comparative study. *IEEE Trans. Pattern Anal. Mach. Intell.* **2022**, *44*, 4819–4838. [CrossRef]
44. Zhang, Y.; Liu, Y.; Sun, P. IFCNN: A general image fusion framework based on convolutional neural network. *Inf. Fusion* **2020**, *54*, 99–118. [CrossRef]
45. Hu, X.; Jiang, J.; Liu, X.; Ma, J. ZMFF: Zero-shot multi-focus image fusion. *Inf. Fusion* **2023**, *92*, 127–138. [CrossRef]
46. Zhang, H.; Xu, H.; Xiao, Y. Rethinking the image fusion: A fast unified image fusion network based on proportional maintenance of gradient and intensity. In Proceedings of the AAAI Conference on Artificial Intelligence, New York, NY, USA, 7–12 February 2020; Volume 34, pp. 12797–12804.
47. Xu, H.; Ma, J.; Jiang, J. U2Fusion: A unified unsupervised image fusion network. *IEEE Trans. Pattern Anal. Mach. Intell.* **2022**, *44*, 502–518. [CrossRef]
48. Li, J.; Zhang, J.; Yang, C.; Liu, H.; Zhao, Y.; Ye, Y. Comparative analysis of pixel-level fusion algorithms and a new high-resolution dataset for SAR and optical image fusion. *Remote Sens.* **2023**, *15*, 5514. [CrossRef]
49. Li, L.; Si, Y.; Jia, Z. Remote sensing image enhancement based on non-local means filter in NSCT domain. *Algorithms* **2017**, *10*, 116. [CrossRef]
50. Li, L.; Si, Y.; Jia, Z. A novel brain image enhancement method based on nonsubsampled contourlet transform. *Int. J. Imaging Syst. Technol.* **2018**, *28*, 124–131. [CrossRef]
51. Peng, H.; Li, B. Multi-focus image fusion approach based on CNP systems in NSCT domain. *Comput. Vis. Image Underst.* **2021**, *210*, 103228. [CrossRef]
52. Panigrahy, C.; Seal, A.; Mahato, N.K. Fractal dimension based parameter adaptive dual channel PCNN for multi-focus image fusion. *Opt. Lasers Eng.* **2020**, *133*, 106141. [CrossRef]
53. Zhang, X.; Boutat, D.; Liu, D. Applications of fractional operator in image processing and stability of control systems. *Fractal Fract.* **2023**, *7*, 359. [CrossRef]
54. Zhang, X.; Dai, L. Image enhancement based on rough set and fractional order differentiator. *Fractal Fract.* **2022**, *6*, 214. [CrossRef]
55. Zhang, X.; Chen, S.; Zhang, J. Adaptive sliding mode consensus control based on neural network for singular fractional order multi-agent systems. *Appl. Math. Comput.* **2022**, *434*, 127442. [CrossRef]
56. Zhang, X.; Lin, C. A unified framework of stability theorems for LTI fractional order systems with $0 < \alpha < 2$. *IEEE Trans. Circuit Syst. II-Express* **2020**, *67*, 3237–3241.
57. Di, Y.; Zhang, J.; Zhang, X. Robust stabilization of descriptor fractional-order interval systems with uncertain derivative matrices. *Appl. Math. Comput.* **2023**, *453*, 128076. [CrossRef]
58. Zhang, X.; Chen, Y. Admissibility and robust stabilization of continuous linear singular fractional order systems with the fractional order α: The $0 < \alpha < 1$ case. *ISA Trans.* **2018**, *82*, 42–50.
59. Zhang, J.; Yang, G. Low-complexity tracking control of strict-feedback systems with unknown control directions. *IEEE Trans. Autom. Control* **2019**, *64*, 5175–5182. [CrossRef]
60. Zhang, J.; Wang, Q.; Ding, W. Global output-feedback prescribed performance control of nonlinear systems with unknown virtual control coefficients. *IEEE Trans. Autom. Control* **2022**, *67*, 6904–6911. [CrossRef]
61. Zhang, J.; Ding, J.; Chai, T. Fault-tolerant prescribed performance control of wheeled mobile robots: A mixed-gain adaption approach. *IEEE Trans. Autom. Control* **2024**, *69*, 5500–5507. [CrossRef]
62. Zhang, J.; Xu, K.; Wang, Q. Prescribed performance tracking control of time-delay nonlinear systems with output constraints. *IEEE/CAA J. Autom. Sin.* **2024**, *11*, 1557–1565. [CrossRef]
63. Di, Y.; Zhang, J.-X.; Zhang, X. Alternate admissibility LMI criteria for descriptor fractional order systems with $0 < \alpha < 2$. *Fractal Fract.* **2023**, *7*, 577. [CrossRef]
64. Qu, X.; Yan, J.; Xiao, H. Image fusion algorithm based on spatial frequency-motivated pulse coupled neural networks in nonsubsampled contourlet transform domain. *Acta Autom. Sin.* **2008**, *34*, 1508–1514. [CrossRef]
65. Nejati, M.; Samavi, S.; Shirani, S. Multi-focus image fusion using dictionary-based sparse representation. *Inf. Fusion* **2015**, *25*, 72–84. [CrossRef]
66. Zhang, H.; Le, Z. MFF-GAN: An unsupervised generative adversarial network with adaptive and gradient joint constraints for multi-focus image fusion. *Inf. Fusion* **2021**, *66*, 40–53. [CrossRef]
67. Xu, S.; Wei, X.; Zhang, C. MFFW: A newdataset for multi-focus image fusion. *arXiv* **2020**, arXiv:2002.04780.
68. Zhang, Y.; Xiang, W. Local extreme map guided multi-modal brain image fusion. *Front. Neurosci.* **2022**, *16*, 1055451. [CrossRef] [PubMed]
69. Li, X.; Li, X.; Liu, W. CBFM: Contrast balance infrared and visible image fusion based on contrast-preserving guided filter. *Remote Sens.* **2023**, *15*, 2969. [CrossRef]

70. Jie, Y.; Chen, Y.; Li, X.; Yi, P.; Tan, H.; Cheng, X. FUFusion: Fuzzy sets theory for infrared and visible image fusion. *Lect. Notes Comput. Sci.* **2024**, *14426*, 466–478.
71. Yang, H.; Zhang, J.; Zhang, X. Injected infrared and visible image fusion via L_1 decomposition model and guided filtering. *IEEE Trans. Comput. Imaging* **2022**, *8*, 162–173.
72. Liu, Z.; Blasch, E.; Xue, Z. Objective assessment of multiresolution image fusion algorithms for context enhancement in night vision: A comparative study. *IEEE Trans. Pattern Anal. Mach. Intell.* **2012**, *34*, 94–109. [CrossRef]
73. Haghighat, M.; Razian, M. Fast-FMI: Non-reference image fusion metric. In Proceedings of the IEEE 8th International Conference on Application of Information and Communication Technologies, Astana, Kazakhstan, 15–17 October 2014; pp. 424–426.
74. Available online: http://www.med.harvard.edu/AANLIB/home.html (accessed on 1 March 2024).
75. Aiadi, O.; Khaldi, B.; Korichi, A. Fusion of deep and local gradient-based features for multimodal finger knuckle print identification. *Clust. Comput.* **2024**, *27*, 7541–7557. [CrossRef]
76. Li, L.; Ma, H.; Jia, Z. Multiscale geometric analysis fusion-based unsupervised change detection in remote sensing images via FLICM model. *Entropy* **2022**, *24*, 291. [CrossRef] [PubMed]
77. Li, L.; Ma, H.; Zhang, X.; Zhao, X.; Lv, M.; Jia, Z. Synthetic aperture radar image change detection based on principal component analysis and two-level clustering. *Remote Sens.* **2024**, *16*, 1861. [CrossRef]
78. Li, L.; Ma, H.; Jia, Z. Change detection from SAR images based on convolutional neural networks guided by saliency enhancement. *Remote Sens.* **2021**, *13*, 3697. [CrossRef]
79. Li, L.; Ma, H.; Jia, Z. Gamma correction-based automatic unsupervised change detection in SAR images via FLICM model. *J. Indian Soc. Remote Sens.* **2023**, *51*, 1077–1088. [CrossRef]

Disclaimer/Publisher's Note: The statements, opinions and data contained in all publications are solely those of the individual author(s) and contributor(s) and not of MDPI and/or the editor(s). MDPI and/or the editor(s) disclaim responsibility for any injury to people or property resulting from any ideas, methods, instructions or products referred to in the content.

Article

Artificial Intelligence-Based Segmentation and Classification of Plant Images with Missing Parts and Fractal Dimension Estimation

Ganbayar Batchuluun, Seung Gu Kim, Jung Soo Kim, Tahir Mahmood and Kang Ryoung Park *

Division of Electronics and Electrical Engineering, Dongguk University, 30 Pildong-ro 1-gil, Jung-gu, Seoul 04620, Republic of Korea; ganabata87@gmail.com (G.B.); ismysg104@dgu.ac.kr (S.G.K.); k_jungsoo@dgu.ac.kr (J.S.K.); tahirmahmood@dongguk.edu (T.M.)
* Correspondence: parkgr@dongguk.edu; Tel.: +82-2-2260-3329

Abstract: Existing research on image-based plant classification has demonstrated high performance using artificial intelligence algorithms. However, limited camera viewing angles can cause parts of the plant to be invisible in the acquired images, leading to an inaccurate classification. However, this issue has not been addressed by previous research. Hence, our study aims to introduce a method to improve classification performance by taking these limitations into account; specifically, we incorporated both segmentation and classification networks structured as shallow networks to expedite the processing times. The proposed shallow plant segmentation network (Shal-PSN) performs adversarial learning based on a discriminator network; and a shallow plant classification network (Shal-PCN) with applied residual connections was also implemented. Moreover, the fractal dimension estimation is used in this study for analyzing the segmentation results. Additionally, this study evaluated the performance of the proposed Shal-PSN that achieved the dice scores (DSs) of 87.43% and 85.71% with PlantVillage and open leaf image (OLID-I) open datasets, respectively, in instances where 40–60% of plant parts were missing. Moreover, the results demonstrate that the proposed method increased the classification accuracy from 41.16% to 90.51% in the same instances. Overall, our approach achieved superior performance compared to the existing state-of-the-art classification methods.

Keywords: plant images; missing plant parts; limited camera viewing angle; deep learning; plant image classification and segmentation; fractal dimension

Citation: Batchuluun, G.; Kim, S.G.; Kim, J.S.; Mahmood, T.; Park, K.R. Artificial Intelligence-Based Segmentation and Classification of Plant Images with Missing Parts and Fractal Dimension Estimation. *Fractal Fract.* **2024**, *8*, 633. https://doi.org/10.3390/fractalfract8110633

Academic Editors: Jinxi Zhang, Xuefeng Zhang, Driss Boutat and Dayan Liu

Received: 11 September 2024
Revised: 23 October 2024
Accepted: 25 October 2024
Published: 27 October 2024

Copyright: © 2024 by the authors. Licensee MDPI, Basel, Switzerland. This article is an open access article distributed under the terms and conditions of the Creative Commons Attribution (CC BY) license (https://creativecommons.org/licenses/by/4.0/).

1. Introduction

A variety of systems based on cameras and artificial intelligence algorithms are being developed for rapid plant recognition. These systems are widely utilized in diverse fields, such as crop disease detection and classification [1–3], plant health diagnosis [4], fruit classification [5–8], and plant classification [9–12]. Existing methods for recognizing plants using camera-acquired images have been based on a variety of algorithms, including detection [3] and deblurring [13], as well as methods using hand-crafted algorithms and manually processed image datasets [14]. However, limited camera viewing angles pose a challenge to plant recognition, particularly when parts of plants are obscured in images (Figure 1). Despite the significance of this issue, it remains unaddressed in existing research, leading to notable deterioration in the accuracy of plant image classification when these scenarios actually arise.

To tackle this issue, our study proposes a method to enhance the accuracy and efficiency of plant recognition through the integration of image segmentation, processing, and classification. In the segmentation network, we utilized residual blocks and trained the network on the concept of a generative adversarial network (GAN) [15]. The images obtained from the segmentation network were processed through image processing algorithms such as masking, coordinate detection, cropping, and resizing before being input into the classification network, which also utilized residual blocks. Experiments were conducted using the PlantVillage open dataset, dividing the dataset into original image data and those with parts of plants removed. The part-removed plant image data were varied, creating sets with 20–40%, 40–60%, and 60% or more of plants removed. In segmentation, both the original and the part-removed image datasets were used for training and testing. In classification, experiments were conducted using only the original image dataset, separately with the part-removed image datasets, and with all the datasets combined; various outcomes obtained in all these cases were compared.

Figure 1. Example plant images from a PlantVillage open dataset [16] (**a**–**d**) and an open leaf image dataset (OLID-I) [17] (**e**–**h**): (**a**,**e**) original images; (**b**–**d**,**f**–**h**) images with missing parts of the same plant parts shown in (**a**,**e**), respectively.

The key contributions of this study are as follows:
- Previous research on plant image classification did not consider images with parts of the plant removed, resulting in poor recognition owing to insufficient plant information within the image. This study is the first to propose a method that aims to solve this recognition issue.
- To resolve the aforementioned issues, our study introduced a novel approach for plant segmentation and classification. The proposed method consists of segmentation and classification networks, designed as shallow networks to decrease the processing time. The suggested shallow plant segmentation network (Shal-PSN) performs adversarial learning based on a discriminator network. Furthermore, a shallow plant classification network (Shal-PCN), applying residual connections has also been introduced.
- For enhancing the diagnosis of the proposed Shal-PSN, the fractal dimension (FD) estimation is utilized for analyzing segmentation results in this study. In addition, the models and source code employed in our proposed plant classification method are made available for other researchers via the GitHub site [18].

A detailed discussion of existing plant image-based research is presented in Section 2. The specific methodologies proposed in this research are described in Section 3. All experimental results and analyses utilizing the proposed methods are presented in Section 4. Finally, a discussion of the results and our conclusions are presented in Sections 5 and 6, respectively.

2. Related Work

This section provides an overview of existing research on plant recognition based on plant imagery. Various studies to date, utilizing plant images for detection, diagnosis, deblurring, identification, and classification, have employed image data to create three subsections: thermal image-, visible light image-, and combined visible and thermal image-based methods. Moreover, studies about the fractal dimension are presented in a subsection.

2.1. Thermal Image-Based Studies

Previous research on thermal images of plants includes studies, such as the one by Lydia et al. [19], who conducted experiments with a self-collected dataset. This study proposed a data collection method to identify diseased plants, notably without employing computer devices or algorithms. Similarly, Zhu et al. [4] used a self-collected dataset for their experiments and proposed a method for diagnosing diseased plants, utilizing the maximum temperature difference (MTD) during the diagnostic process. However, the aforementioned methods relied solely on visual inspection and analysis by humans for identification and diagnosis, a process that can be time-consuming. To address this issue, research has been conducted on plant disease classification using computational devices and algorithms. For instance, Batchuluun et al. [1] introduced the plant deep explainable artificial intelligence (PlantDXAI) model and conducted various experiments with the paddy crop dataset [20] and their self-dataset. In this study, a self-designed convolutional neural network (CNN)-16 was utilized for plant classification, and the performance of CNN-16 was enhanced by incorporating a class activation map [21] and a discriminator network for additional training in plant disease classification. The above methods only utilized thermal information from images, neglecting color information. Therefore, alternative approaches have been developed that leverage visible light images to use the color information of plants for analogous objectives.

2.2. Visible Light Image-Based Studies

Research utilizing visible light images of plants includes significant contributions, such as those from Abawatew et al. [9], Ashwinkumar et al. [10], and Chakraborty et al. [11], who introduced classification techniques employing attention-augmented residual (AAR) networks, optimal mobile network-based convolutional neural networks (OMNCNNs), and DenseNet-121 networks, respectively, and conducted classification experiments with the PlantDoc database [22]. Chompookham et al. [23] also utilized this dataset to conduct experiments with five types of networks, namely NASNetMobile, MobileNetV1, MobileNetV2, Xception, and DenseNet-121. Wang et al. [12] expanded their experiments to include the PlantDoc and PlantVillage open datasets and proposed a trilinear convolutional neural network model (T-CNN), specifically designed for these plant image datasets. An attention-based fruit classification method by Shahi et al. [5] suggested a lightweight deep learning model based on MobileNetV2, using the MobileNetV2 pre-trained model with ImageNet as a backbone. This research utilized a dataset collection composed of three fruit-related datasets [24–26].

Kader et al. [6] conducted a series of experiments on fruit recognition, using the Fruits-360 image dataset. Additionally, their research explored and compared results using a variety of feature extraction methods, including hu moments, haralick texture, and color histograms, alongside a range of machine learning techniques, such as decision trees, k-nearest neighbors, linear discriminant analysis, logistic regression, naïve Bayes, random forests, and support vector machines (SVMs). Biswas et al. [7] proposed a multiclass CNN model, experimenting with the FIDS30 and Fruits-360 datasets. Hossain et al. [8] introduced two deep learning models (CNN and VGG-16), including lightweight and pre-trained models, and used both a supermarket-produce dataset and a self-collected dataset for experimentation. Siddiqi [27] proposed FruitNet and compared it against 14 deep learning methods using the Fruit-360 dataset for accuracy assessment. Hamid et al. [28] employed a bag of features (BoF), conventional CNN, and AlexNet for classification experiments, and compared these methods using the Fruit-360 dataset. Katarzyna et al. [29] utilized a CNN with the Fruit-360 dataset, and additionally employed YOLO-V3 to create regions of interest (ROIs) from original apple images for classification. However, the aforementioned methods face challenges in environments without external lighting, such as nighttime or low-light conditions; furthermore, detecting plant diseases invisible to the human eye using only color information can be difficult. Consequently, methods combining thermal and visible light images have been developed to leverage the advantages of thermal imaging and address these challenges.

2.3. Thermal and Visible Light Image-Based Studies

Research combining thermal and visible light images has developed as follows. Anasta et al. [2] conducted experiments using a self-collected dataset and utilized thermal images alongside an if–then rule to detect diseased regions in visible light images. However, these detected regions were analyzed solely by human observation, a time-consuming process. To address this issue, research has been conducted on plant disease classification using computer devices and algorithms. Batchuluun et al. [30] performed research with nonaligned thermal and visible light images, constructing and proposing the plant classification residual (PlantCR) network. This network inputs visible light and thermal images simultaneously, combining features extracted from both to perform multiclass classification. Raza et al. [3] proposed a method based on thermal and visible light images for binary classification, using three types of camera sensors to capture thermal and stereo visible light images. By combining these three image types, the accuracy of classifying healthy and diseased plant images was improved. Features extracted using manual methods were then used for binary classification through an analysis of variance (ANOVA) [31–33] and an SVM. Batchuluun et al. [34] utilized the plant super-resolution (PlantSR) network to upscale images for input into the plant multiclass classification (PlantMC) network, enhancing classification performance with the simultaneous use of visible light and thermal images. This study also employed a self-collected dataset. Sections 2.1–2.3 describe various experiments conducted with diverse camera devices, algorithms, AI-based methods, and datasets. However, all these studies used conventional plant images without missing parts, and none addressed the issue of images with missing plant parts owing to camera angle limitations for classification. To solve these issues, this research introduced new methods, namely Shal-PSN and Shal-PCN. Table 1 compares the proposed methods to existing plant image-based approaches, categorizing them by image type, dataset, method, and task.

Table 1. Summarized comparison of the proposed and existing plant image-based studies.

Category	Image Type	Task	Dataset	Method	Advantage	Disadvantage
Normal plant images	Thermal images	Identification	Self-collected	Manual approach [19]	- Extraction of features based on thermal information, which is robust to night and low-illumination environments - Adequate amount of information is provided to recognize plants	- Lower detection accuracy owing to usage of low quality images of thermal - Poor performance when recognizing plants with inadequate information
		Diagnosis		MTD [4]		
		Classification	Paddy crop, self-collected	PlantDXAI [1]		
	Thermal and visible light images	Detection	Self-collected	If-then rule [2]	- Extraction of features based on both visual and thermal information - Robust to night and low-illumination environments - High accuracy using high-quality visible light images - Adequate amount of information is provided to recognize plants	- Higher system cost - Different viewing angles of cameras - Higher processing time requirement - Poor performance when recognizing plants with inadequate information
		Classification		PlantCR [30]; SVM [3]; PlantMC [32]		
	Visible light images	Classification	Supermarket produce, self-collected	VGG16-based [8]	- High accuracy using high-quality visible light images - Adequate amount of information is given to recognize plants	- Ineffective at night and in low-illumination environments - Poor performance when recognizing plants with inadequate information
			FIDS30	CNN-based [7]		
			Fruits-360	SVM [6]; FruitNet [27]; CNN and Alexnet [28]; CNN and YOLO-V3 [29]		
			Dataset collection	MobileNetV2 [5]		
			PlantVillage, PlantDoc	T-CNN [12]		
			PlantDoc	AAR [9]; OMNCNN [10]; DenseNet-121 [11]; DenseNet-121 [23]		
Plant images with missing parts			PlantVillage, OLID-I	Sha1-PSN + Sha1-PCN (proposed method)	- High accuracy using plant images with inadequate information	- Cannot be used at night and in low-illumination environments - Poor performance if the given information is lower than 20%

2.4. The Fractal Dimension-Based Studies

The fractal dimension has been widely used in a variety of fields, including medical image analysis [35], biology [36], brain tumor identification [37], and urbanization studies [38]. In this study, FD estimation was introduced into the proposed segmentation framework. This analysis provides valuable insights into the structural complexity and irregularity of plant segmentation. The understanding of plant segmentation ultimately contributed to the advancement of plant segmentation research, and it aided in diagnosis and prognosis, which were improved by characterizing the complex morphology of plant segmentation. Fractals are complex shapes with self-similarity that defy traditional rules of geometry [39]. Fractal dimension (FD) quantifies complexity, indicating whether the structure is concentrated or dispersed. The box-counting technique [40] was used to calculate the FD of plant segmentation.

3. Proposed Methodology

3.1. Overview of the Proposed Method

In this section, we detail the methods proposed in this study. The flowchart in Figure 2 illustrates the process of the proposed method. When images with missing parts of plants (as shown in Figure 2) are input, the proposed Shal-PSN segments the plant area, and based on this segmentation information, an ROI for the plant area is defined (Section 3.2). Subsequently, this image is input into the proposed Shal-PCN, ultimately yielding the plant classification results (Section 3.3).

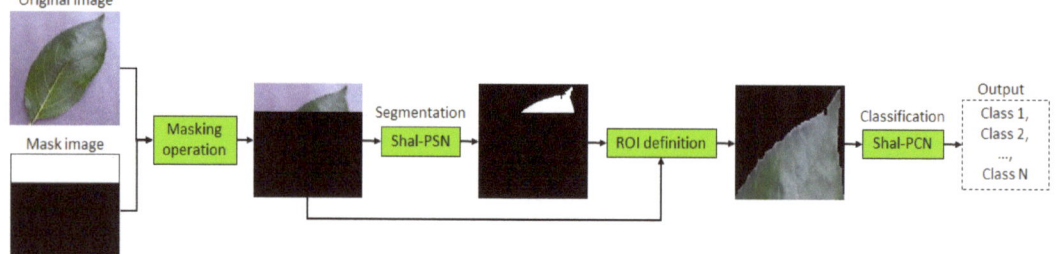

Figure 2. Flowchart of the proposed method. The input image is from the PlantVillage open dataset [16].

3.2. Detailed Description of Shal-PSN

This section elaborates on the structure of the proposed Shal-PSN. Table 2 presents the architecture of Shal-PSN, wherein the size of input and output images is $256 \times 256 \times 3$. As shown in Table 2, the architecture of Shal-PSN utilized an input layer (input), convolution layer (conv2d), additional operation layer (add), parametric rectified linear unit (p_relu), upsampling layer (up_sampling2d), and activation layer (tanh). The padding size for conv2d_0–conv2d_5 layers was zero (see Table 2) and one for the remaining layers. Moreover, the stride size for conv2d_2, conv2d_5, and conv2d_13 layers was two and one for the remaining layers. The filter size for conv2d_1 and conv2d_4 was four, and three for the remaining layers. Additionally, the filter numbers for conv2d_0–conv2d_2, conv2d_3–conv2d_12, and conv2d_13 were 64, 128, and 512, respectively. Here, "#" denotes "number of" throughout. Figure 3 visually represents the Shal-PSN. As illustrated in Table 2, the residual blocks, (.), were constructed in a manner that connects conv2d_5 to conv2d_7, add_0 to conv2d_9, and add_1 to conv2d_11. The formulation of the residual block is given by Equation (1).

$$(f_i, \omega) = C_{\omega_e}\left(C_{\omega_g}(f_i)\right) + f_i, \quad (1)$$

(.), f_i, and ω represent the residual block, input tensor, and weight, respectively; $C_{\omega_e}(.)$ and $C_{\omega_g}(.)$ denote the convolution layers that possess the weights ω_e and ω_g, respectively. The process of extracting the output image (I_{out}) in the final layer of Shal-PSN is mathematically represented by Equation (2) as follows:

$$O = t(\mathcal{C}_{\omega_q}(f_i)), \qquad (2)$$

$O \in R^{H \times W \times C}$, $t(.)$, $\mathcal{C}_{\omega_g}(.)$, and f_i signify the output image, the tanh activation function, a convolution layer, and the input tensor, respectively. Additionally, as outlined in Table 2, Shal-PSN serves as the generator network utilized within a GAN, and its discriminator network structure is identical to the Shal-PCN architecture shown in Table 3, with the number of classes being two (real or fake). The minmax loss function was employed for the GAN, as illustrated in Equation (5).

$$\min_{G} = E_n[\log(1 - D(G(n)))], \qquad (3)$$

$$\min_{D} = E_i[\log(D(i))], \qquad (4)$$

$$\min_{G} \max_{D} F(G, D) = E_n\left[\log\left(1 - D(G(n))\right)\right] + E_i[\log(D(i))], \qquad (5)$$

E_n is the expected value over all real data instances. Equation (3) illustrates the generator loss, where n, $G(n)$, and $D(G(n))$ represent the input image, output image by the generator (fake or segmented image), and discriminator output, respectively. Equation (4) denotes the loss when using a real (ground truth) image as input, with i and $D(i)$ representing the real image and output of the discriminator, respectively. Equation (5) reflects the adversarial (discriminator) loss, where the generator is trained to minimize $E_n[\log(1 - D(G(n)))]$ and the discriminator is trained to maximize Equation (5).

Table 2. Structure of Shal-PSN (#, conv2d, p_relu, add, up_sampling2d, tanh, and Params represent "number of", convolution layer, parametric rectified linear unit, addition layer, upsampling layer, tanh activation layer, and parameters, respectively).

Layer	Output Shape	# Params	Connected to
input	256, 256, 3	0	
conv2d_0	256, 256, 64	1792	input
conv2d_1	256, 256, 64	36,928	conv2d_0
conv2d_2	128, 128, 64	36,928	conv2d_1
conv2d_3	128, 128, 128	73,856	conv2d_2
conv2d_4	128, 128, 128	147,584	conv2d_3
conv2d_5	128, 128, 128	147,584	conv2d_4
conv2d_6	128, 128, 128	147,584	conv2d_5
p_relu_0	128, 128, 128	128	conv2d_6
conv2d_7	128, 128, 128	147,584	p_relu_0
add_0	128, 128, 128	0	conv2d_5 and conv2d_7
conv2d_8	128, 128, 128	147,584	add_0
p_relu_1	128, 128, 128	128	conv2d_8
conv2d_9	128, 128, 128	147,584	p_relu_1
add_1	128, 128, 128	0	add_0 and conv2d_9
conv2d_10	128, 128, 128	147,584	add_1
p_relu_2	128, 128, 128	128	conv2d_10
conv2d_11	128, 128, 128	147,584	p_relu_2
add_2	128, 128, 128	0	add_1 and conv2d_11
conv2d_12	128, 128, 128	147,584	add_2
up_sampling2d	256, 256, 128	0	conv2d_12
conv2d_13	256, 256, 1	1153	up_sampling2d
tanh	256, 256, 1	0	conv2d_13
# Trainable Params: 1,479,297			

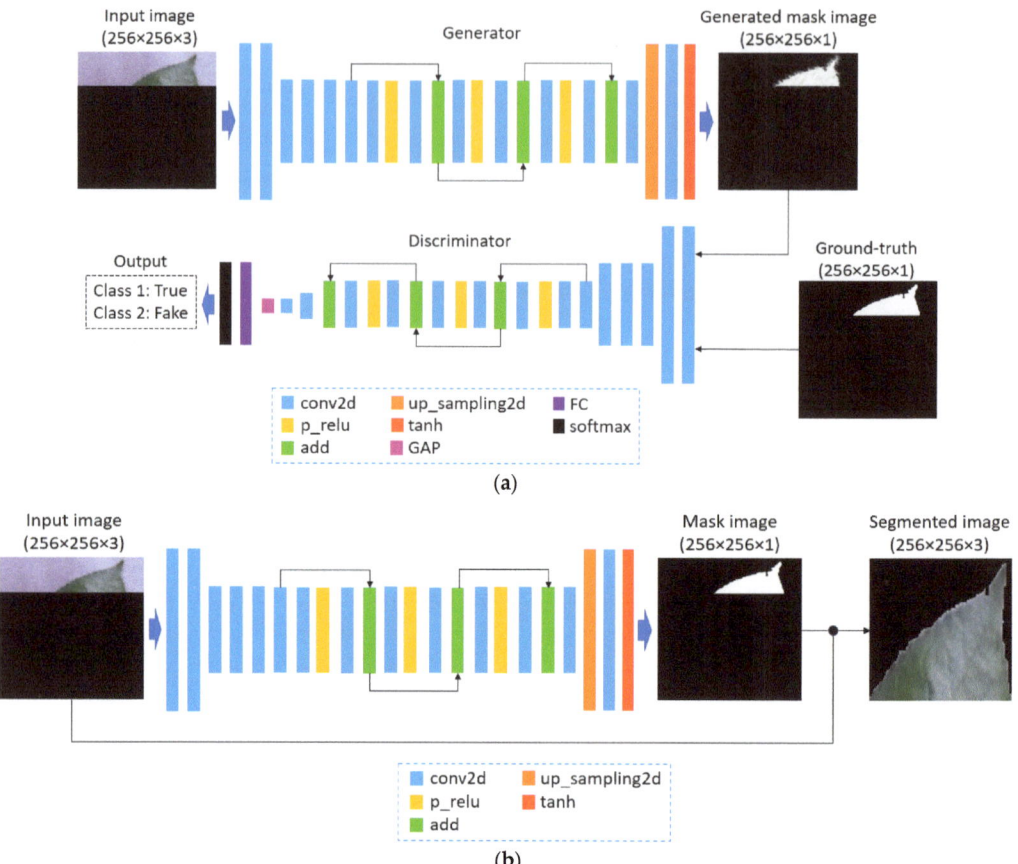

Figure 3. Architecture of proposed Shal-PSN (conv2d, up_sampling2d, FC, p_relu, tanh, softmax, add, and GAP represent convolution layer, upsampling layer, fully connected layer, parametric rectified linear unit, tanh activation layer, softmax function, addition layer, and global average pooling layer, respectively). (**a**) Generator and discriminator networks in training phase; (**b**) generator network in testing phase. The input image is from the PlantVillage open dataset [16].

In the proposed method, training was conducted with a structure that included both a generator and discriminator, as shown in Figure 3a, and during the testing, the trained generator was utilized, as depicted in Figure 3b. In the segmentation process, illustrated in Figure 3, images with missing parts of plants were input into Shal-PSN to generate a mask image. The next step, shown in Figure 2, involved defining the ROI using the generated mask image to specify the ROI of the plant in the input image, thereby obtaining the final segmented image. This segmented image was then used as the input for Shal-PCN. The explanation of the classification method is presented in Section 3.3. This process is described as follows:

$$ö(x) = \mathcal{C}\left(\check{S}(x^{w \times h \times d})\right) \tag{6}$$

$$ɣ(x) = \mathfrak{m}\left(\check{S}(x^{w \times h \times d})\right) \tag{7}$$

$$p = \zeta\left(R\left(H(ö(x), ɣ(x))\right)\right) \tag{8}$$

In Equation (6), $x^{w \times h \times d}$, $w \times h \times d$, $\check{S}(.)$, and $\acute{C}(.)$ represent the input image, dimension of the input image, segmentation network, and coordinate detection, respectively, while in Equation (7), $\mathfrak{m}(.)$ denotes the masking operation. Furthermore, in Equation (8), $H(.)$, $R(.)$, $\zeta(.)$, and p stand for image cropping, resizing, classification network, and output probability, respectively. Additionally, in Equation (8), $H(\ddot{o}(x), Y(x))$ refers to cropping the masked image, $Y(x)$, based on the plant coordinates $\ddot{o}(x)$.

Table 3. Structure of Shal-PCN (#, conv2d, p_relu, add, GAP, FC, softmax, and Params represent "number of", convolution layer, parametric rectified linear unit, addition layer, global average pooling layer, fully connected layer, softmax function, and parameters, respectively).

Layer	Output Shape	# Params	Connected to
input	256, 256, 3	0	
conv2d_0	254, 254, 64	1792	input
conv2d_1	251, 251, 64	65,600	conv2d_0
conv2d_2	125, 125, 64	36,928	conv2d_1
conv2d_3	123, 123, 128	73,856	conv2d_2
conv2d_4	120, 120, 128	262,272	conv2d_3
conv2d_5	59, 59, 128	147,584	conv2d_4
conv2d_6	59, 59, 128	147,584	conv2d_5
p_relu_0	59, 59, 128	128	conv2d_6
conv2d_7	59, 59, 128	147,584	p_relu_0
add_0	59, 59, 128	0	conv2d_5 and conv2d_7
conv2d_8	59, 59, 128	147,584	add_0
p_relu_0	59, 59, 128	128	conv2d_8
conv2d_9	59, 59, 128	147,584	p_relu_0
add_1	59, 59, 128	0	add_0 and conv2d_9
conv2d_10	59, 59, 128	147,584	add_1
p_relu_1	59, 59, 128	128	conv2d_10
conv2d_11	59, 59, 128	147,584	p_relu_1
add_2	59, 59, 128	0	add_1 and conv2d_11
conv2d_12	57, 57, 128	147,584	add_2
conv2d_13	28, 28, 512	590,336	conv2d_12
GAP	512	0	conv2d_13
FC	28	14,364	GAP
softmax	28	0	FC
# Trainable Params: 2,226,204			

3.3. Detailed Description of Shal-PCN

This section delves into the Shal-PCN structure of the proposed method. Table 3 displays the architecture of the proposed Shal-PCN, which accepts an input image size of $256 \times 256 \times 3$ and outputs 28 classes.

As shown in Table 3, the Shal-PCN structure included an input layer (input), convolution layer (conv2d), additional operation layer (add), parametric rectified linear unit (p_relu), global average pooling (GAP), fully connected layer (FC), and softmax function (softmax). The padding size was zero for conv2d_0–conv2d_5 layers and one for the remaining layers. The stride size was two for conv2d_2, conv2d_5, and conv2d_13 layers and one for the rest. The filter size was four for conv2d_1 and conv2d_4 and three for other layers. Additionally, the filter numbers for conv2d_0–conv2d_2, conv2d_3–conv2d_12, and conv2d_13 were 64, 128, and 512, respectively. Figure 4 visually represents the Shal-PCN.

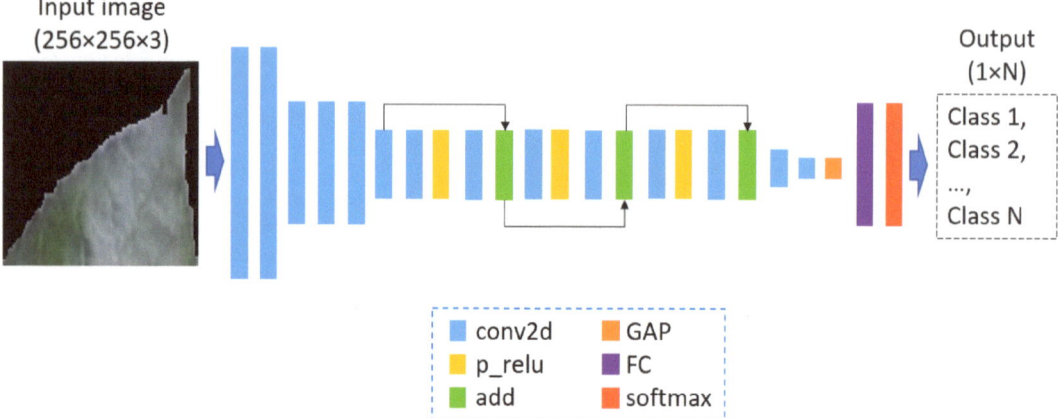

Figure 4. The architecture of the Shal-PCN (conv2d, GAP, p_relu, FC, add, and softmax represent convolution layer, global average pooling layer, parametric rectified linear unit, fully connected layer, addition layer, and softmax function, respectively). The input image is from the PlantVillage open dataset [16].

3.4. Description of the OLID-I Open Dataset

This section describes the OLID-I open dataset in detail with tables and figures. The OLID-I dataset contains 57 classes, of which 49 are plant disease and 8 are non-disease (healthy) classes. As this study does not focus on plant disease recognition, only the images of 8 healthy classes were used. The size and file extension of images in the dataset are $3024 \times 3024 \times 3$ and "jpg", respectively. The images were captured at three different sites in Bangladesh in natural field settings. Information on these 8 classes is described below, with example images shown in Figure 5.

Figure 5. Example images from the OLID-I open dataset. From the left to right: eggplant, cucumber, ridge gourd, and snake gourd [17].

Table 4 lists the number of images per class and names of the plants used in the experiments; a total of 19,650 images were used. In Table 4, "# Images" denotes the number of original images, while "# Images 20–40%", "# Images 40–60%", and "# Images 60% or more" represent the numbers of image datasets with plant parts removed to the extent of the ranges specified. Moreover, example images with missing plant parts used in the experiments in this study are shown in Figure 6.

Table 4. Description of the OLID-I open dataset (# means "number of").

# Class	Class Name	# Images	# Images 20–40%	# Images 40–60%	# Images 60% or More
1	Ash gourd	83	664	664	664
2	Bitter gourd	181	1448	1448	1448
3	Bottle gourd	31	248	248	248
4	Cucumber	34	272	272	272
5	Eggplant	92	736	736	736
6	Ridge gourd	70	560	560	560
7	Snake gourd	59	472	472	472
8	Tomato	236	1888	1888	1888
Total of each set		786	6288	6288	6288
Total					19,650

Figure 6. Example images with missing parts based on the OLID-I open dataset [17]. From top to bottom: plant parts reduced by 20–40%, 40–60%, and 60% or more.

3.5. Description of the PlantVillage Open Dataset

In this section, the PlantVillage open dataset is described in detail with tables and figures. The open dataset, named PlantVillage, contains 38 classes, of which 26 are plant disease and 12 are non-disease (healthy) classes. As this study does not focus on plant disease recognition, only the 12 healthy classes were used. Information on these 12 classes is described below, with example images shown in Figure 7.

Figure 7. Example images from PlantVillage open dataset [16]. From left to right: apple, blueberry, cherry, and corn leaves.

Table 5 lists the number of images per class and names of the plants used in the experiments with the PlantVillage open dataset; a total of 128,700 images were used. "# Images" indicates the number of original images, while "# Images 20–40%", "# Images 40–60%", and "# Images 60% or more" denote the numbers of image datasets with plants removed to the extent of the ranges specified. Figure 8 demonstrates how information is variably removed depending on the plant's position within the image, with examples of 50% removal shown in Figure 8a–c, illustrating approximately 50%, 40%, and 60%, respectively, of the plant removed. Table 6 presents other details related to the images in the PlantVillage open dataset.

Table 5. Description of PlantVillage open dataset (# means "number of").

# Class	Class Name	# Images	# Images 20–40%	# Images 40–60%	# Images 60% or More
1	Apple	476	3808	3808	3808
2	Blueberry	448	3584	3584	3584
3	Cherry	464	3712	3712	3712
4	Orange	448	3584	3584	3584
5	Grape	448	3584	3584	3584
6	Peach	448	3584	3584	3584
7	Pepper bell	444	3552	3552	3552
8	Potato	160	1280	1280	1280
9	Raspberry	452	3616	3616	3616
10	Soybean	448	3584	3584	3584
11	Strawberry	456	3648	3648	3648
12	Tomato	456	3648	3648	3648
Total of each set		5148	41,184	41,184	41,184
Total			128,700		

Figure 8. (**a**–**c**) Example images with missing parts based on PlantVillage open dataset [16].

Table 6. Other details of PlantVillage open dataset.

Item	Visible Light Image	Units
Image size	256 × 256 × 3	pixel
Image depth	24	bit
Class number	38	-
Image extension	jpg	-

4. Experimental Results

4.1. Training

In this subsection, we describe the training setup, hyperparameters, hardware, and software used in this study. Table 7 details the computer specifications and software implemented, and Table 8 outlines the training setup and hyperparameters for the proposed method. The hyperparameters were optimized by training the models with various hyperparameters in our experiments.

Table 7. Hardware and software utilized in the proposed method.

	Hardware	Software	
		Library	Version
Memory	32 GB RAM (Samsung electronics, Republic of Korea)	Python [41]	3.5.4
GPU	Nvidia GeForce TITAN X (12 GB)	TensorFlow [42]	1.9.0
Processor	Intel(R) Core™ i7-6700 CPU@3.40 GHz (8 CPUs)	OpenCV [43]	4.3.0
		Keras API [44]	2.1.6-tf

Table 8. Training setup and hyperparameters utilized in the proposed method.

Parameter	Shal-PSN	Shal-PCN
Loss	Categorical cross-entropy	Binary cross-entropy
Optimizer	Adam	Adam
# Epochs	100	200
Learning rate	0.001	0.001
Batch size	16	16

Specifically, the expression for the binary cross-entropy loss (BCE) [45] is given by Equation (9).

$$\text{BCE}(i) = -\frac{1}{N} \sum_{i=1}^{N} (x(i) \log(p(i)) + (1 - x(i)) \log(1 - p(i))) \qquad (9)$$

N signifies the total number of samples; and $x(i)$ and $p(i)$ represent the true and predicted classes of the ith sample, respectively. Here, x is either 1 or 0. The expression for the categorical cross-entropy loss (CCE) [46] is given by Equation (10).

$$\text{CCE}(i) = -\log\left(\frac{\exp(s(i))}{\sum_{j}^{N} \exp(s(j))}\right) \qquad (10)$$

Here, the exponential function exp(.) is applied to each element of the input vector s and output value ($\exp(s(i))$), which is then normalized by the sum of all exponentials ($\sum_{j}^{N} \exp(s(j))$). Furthermore, an adaptive moment estimation (Adam) optimizer [47] was employed for the training. All experiments were conducted using a two-fold cross-validation method, where half of the total data were used as the training subset and the other half as the testing subset for the first-fold validation. Then, the training and testing subsets were swapped for the second-fold validation, with the average accuracy serving as the final accuracy. In total, 10% of the training data were used as the validation subset for each fold. In addition, the segmentation and classification models were trained separately on the datasets. By training models separately, a model is more focused on its own task (segmentation or classification) and achieves higher performance rather than focusing on two tasks. It also takes a longer time to train parameters when segmentation and classification tasks are connected and trained end to end.

Figure 9 illustrates the training loss curves of Shal-PCN. Specifically, Figure 9a,b display the training loss curves for classification methods using the OLID-I and PlantVillage open datasets, respectively, per epoch, alongside the validation loss curves. As epochs progressed, the training loss curves converged, indicating that the proposed network was adequately trained on the training data. Similarly, the validation loss curves (Figure 9c,d) converged with progressing epochs, demonstrating that the proposed network did not overfit the training data. Furthermore, loss curves shown in Figure 9b,d were obtained using a segmented image dataset as shown in Figures 3b and 10b. As shown in Figure 9, the training and validation loss curves when using both the original image data and image data with missing parts of plants decreased more compared to the training and validation loss curves when using only the original image data. This is because, as shown in Tables 4 and 5, the number of images in the training dataset containing both the original image data and the image data with missing plant parts at each training epoch is much larger compared to that in the training dataset containing only the original image data.

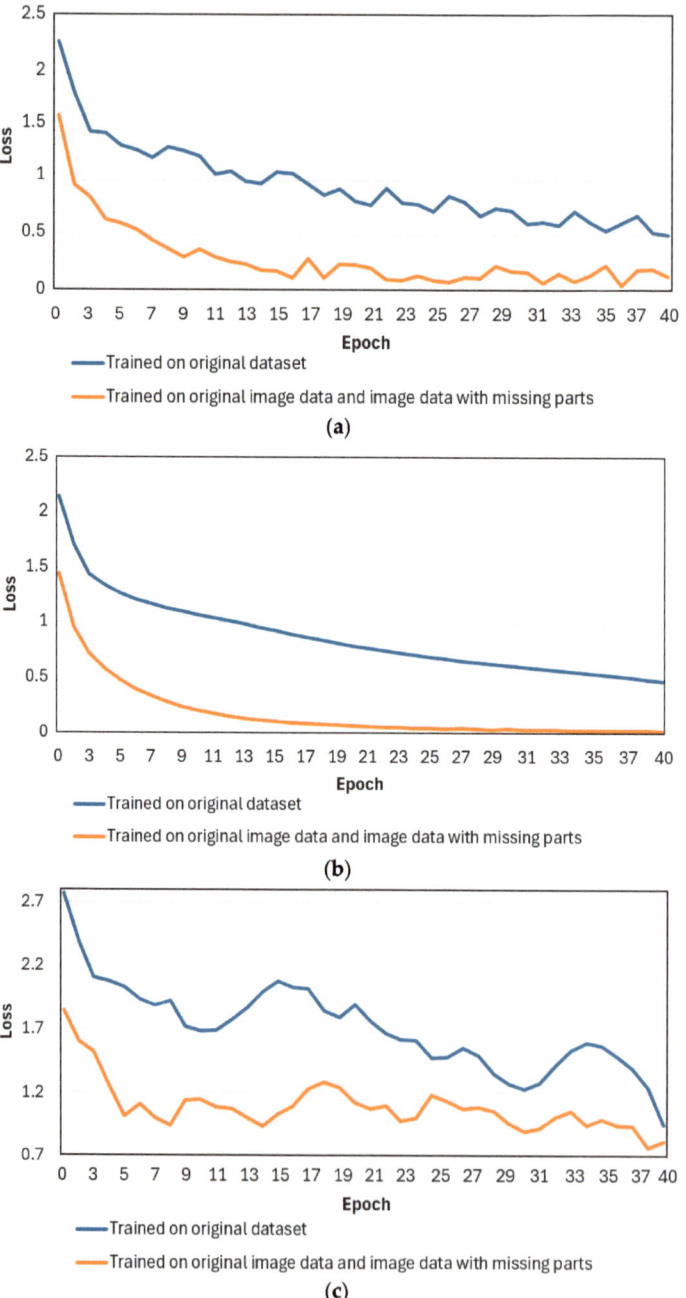

Figure 9. *Cont.*

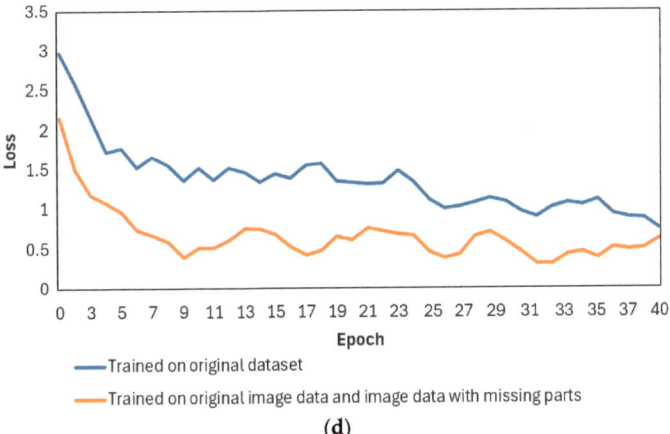

(d)

Figure 9. Training and validation loss curves of the proposed Shal-PCN. Training loss curves obtained from the OLID-I open dataset (**a**) and the PlantVillage open dataset (**b**). Validation loss curves obtained from the OLID-I open dataset (**c**) and the PlantVillage open dataset (**d**).

Figure 10. Example images [16] used in the experiments: (**a**) images with missing parts of 60% or more; (**b**) images with remaining parts obtained through segmentation.

4.2. Testing

4.2.1. Evaluation Metrics

To measure the experimental results of the plant image segmentation, three metrics (Equations (11)–(13)) were used. These metrics involve calculating the dice score (DS) [48] of Equation (11), the intersection over union (IoU) [48] of Equation (12), and the fractal dimension [39] of Equation (13). DS and IoU metrics are widely used in image segmentation tasks to calculate overlapping regions of two binary images.

$$DS = \frac{2 \times TP}{2 \times TP + FP + FN} \tag{11}$$

$$IoU = \frac{TP}{TP + FP + FN} \tag{12}$$

TP, FP, and FN stand for true positive, false positive, and false negative pixels, respectively.
FD calculates the complexity of shapes that reveals as shown in Algorithm 1 [49] if the structure of segmented images is dispersed or concentrated by scaling images.

$$FD(j) = \lim_{j \to 0} \frac{log(N(j))}{log(1/j)} \quad (13)$$

FD, j, and N are the fractal dimension, the size of the boxes, and the number of boxes, respectively.

Algorithm 1: Pseudo code of FD estimation [49]

	Steps	Descriptions
1	Input: I Output: FD	Segmented binary image by Shal-PSN Fractal dimension
2	p = 2^[log(max(size(I)))/log2]	Set the maximum box size and make its dimensions powers of 2
3	if size(I) < size(p): pad(I) = p end	Padding I for making its dimension equal to j
4	b = zeros(1, p + 1)	Pre-allocating the number of boxes
5	b(p + 1) = sum(I(:)) While p > 1:	Calculate the number of boxes "N(j)"
6	p = p/2 N(p)	Reduce box size Recalculate
7	Calculate log(N(p)) and log(1/p) for each "p"	
8	Fit line to [(log(1/p), log(N(p))] using least squares	
9	FD is used to make the slope of lines	

To measure the experimental results of the plant image classification, three equations from powers [50] were used (Equations (14)–(16)). These equations involve calculating the true positive rate (TPR), using TP and FN; positive predictive value (PPV) using TP and FP; and F1 score (F1) using TPR and PPV. TP, FN, and FP in Equations (14)–(16) are true positive, false negative, and false positive, respectively. The symbol "#" represents the "number of".

$$TPR = \# TP/(\# TP + \# FN) \quad (14)$$

$$PPV = \# TP/(\# TP + \# FP) \quad (15)$$

$$F1 = 2 \cdot PPV \cdot TPR/(PPV + TPR) \quad (16)$$

4.2.2. Ablation Study

This study involves comparing various experimental results obtained by partially removing parts of plants from the images. Table 9 compares the experimental results with the model trained using the original images (Figures 5 and 7). As shown in the table, the test accuracy with the original images was the highest, while the accuracies with images with missing plant parts (Figures 6 and 8) were lower. In all cases of missing parts, applying Shal-PSN before Shal-PCN showed higher accuracy than that with Shal-PCN alone.

Segmentation results obtained by the proposed Shal-PSN are DS = 87.43% and IoU = 81.27%, and DS = 85.71% and IoU = 80.38%, respectively, on PlantVillage and OLID-I open datasets, in instances where 40–60% of plant parts were missing. Segmentation results obtained by using images with different sizes of missing parts.

Table 10 compares the experimental results obtained using the proposed models (Shal-PCN and Shal-PSN + Shal-PCN) trained using both the original (Figures 5 and 7) and images with missing plant parts (Figures 6 and 8). In contrast to the results presented in Table 9, the results for the original images tested with Shal-PCN alone were lower than those with Shal-PSN + Shal-PCN. According to the results of Table 9, the proposed methods trained on the original image dataset provide lower performance on testing image datasets with fewer plant parts (missing parts: 20–60% and more). Moreover, all the accuracies in all cases for Shal-PSN + Shal-PCN in Table 10 are significantly higher than those in Table 9. Consequently, it was observed that classification accuracy increased when training the model using plant images with missing parts. Furthermore, a significant enhancement in the classification accuracy was noticed when using the proposed Shal-PSN + Shal-PCN.

Table 9. Classification results by proposed methods trained on original image dataset (unit: %).

Input Images	Methods	PlantVillage			OLID-I		
		TPR	PPV	F1	TPR	PPV	F1
Original	Shal-PCN	77.42	78.68	77.08	76.49	78.32	76.62
	Shal-PSN + Shal-PCN	70.39	72.20	68.02	69.51	71.58	67.44
Missing parts: 20–40%	Shal-PCN	48.45	70.97	46.61	48.17	70.85	45.81
	Shal-PSN + Shal-PCN	66.53	71.87	66.20	66.23	71.69	65.96
Missing parts: 40–60%	Shal-PCN	25.16	10.67	14.34	24.96	10.54	14.16
	Shal-PSN + Shal-PCN	42.75	53.30	41.16	42.39	52.77	40.40
Missing parts: 60% or more	Shal-PCN	8.60	3.98	1.89	7.73	3.49	1.84
	Shal-PSN + Shal-PCN	24.45	37.88	23.93	23.64	37.28	23.32

Table 10. Classification results by proposed method trained on original images plus images with missing parts (unit: %).

Input Images	Methods	PlantVillage			OLID-I		
		TPR	PPV	F1	TPR	PPV	F1
Original	Shal-PCN	8.33	0.73	1.34	8.33	0.73	1.34
	Shal-PSN + Shal-PCN	94.81	91.15	92.53	95.01	91.59	92.89
Missing parts: 20–40%	Shal-PCN	8.33	0.73	1.34	8.33	0.73	1.34
	Shal-PSN + Shal-PCN	95.20	94.91	94.95	95.42	95.34	95.10
Missing parts: 40–60%	Shal-PCN	8.33	0.73	1.34	8.33	0.73	1.34
	Shal-PSN + Shal-PCN	90.93	90.39	90.51	91.55	90.80	91.47
Missing parts: 60% or more	Shal-PCN	8.33	0.73	1.34	8.33	0.73	1.34
	Shal-PSN + Shal-PCN	46.15	52.80	46.76	47.03	53.03	47.37

Identical F1 scores (as shown in Table 10) were obtained with Shal-PCN because Shal-PCN classifies all input images into the same class when Shal-PCN is trained on both original images and images with missing parts, which means that the other methods were not trained properly, so they misclassified all the input images into one class. Therefore, all accuracies are the same in the table except those of the proposed method. Conversely, when Shal-PCN is only trained on the original images, Shal-PCN yields different F1 scores, as shown in Table 9. This shows that the Shal-PCN model did not converge properly when training the model using a dataset with a mixture of original images and images with missing parts (Figure 10a). However, the Shal-PCN model converged properly (as shown in Figure 9) when training the model using a dataset with a mixture of original images and images with missing parts (Figure 10b) that were obtained through a segmentation process by Shal-PSN. The success of classification with Shal-PSN + Shal-PCN is attributed to the training on images segmented by Shal-PSN, as depicted in Figure 10b.

4.3. Comparisons with State-of-the-Art (SOTA) Methods

Next, we conducted experiments to compare the proposed method with existing SOTA plant image-based segmentation methods. We compared the methods based on

DEEPLABV3+ [51], YOLOv8-Seg [52], Mask-RCNN [53], Modified U-Net [54], and CNN-based semantic segmentation (CNN-SS) [55]. Table 11 shows the results from models trained on all images including original and images with missing parts. The results are mean values of results obtained from the two open datasets. As shown in Table 11, among all the results tested with the two datasets, the proposed Shal-PSN was the best.

Table 11. Segmentation results by proposed and SOTA plant-based methods trained on all images including original and images with missing parts (unit: %).

Input Images	Model/Method	DS	IoU	mAP
Original	DEEPLABV3+ [51]	84.01	73.48	73.50
	YOLOv8-Seg [52]	88.10	80.74	81.26
	Mask-RCNN [53]	85.55	77.51	78.09
	Modified U-Net [54]	88.49	80.87	81.43
	CNN-SS [55]	86.90	79.73	81.19
	Shal-PSN (proposed)	92.30	84.81	84.65
Missing parts: 20–40%	DEEPLABV3+ [51]	81.03	71.54	72.91
	YOLOv8-Seg [52]	85.49	78.86	80.88
	Mask-RCNN [53]	82.85	74.84	75.62
	Modified U-Net [54]	86.17	79.87	80.40
	CNN-SS [55]	83.57	72.23	70.60
	Shal-PSN (proposed)	87.37	82.31	82.61
Missing parts: 40–60%	DEEPLABV3+ [51]	80.16	70.68	71.63
	YOLOv8-Seg [52]	83.31	76.64	76.86
	Mask-RCNN [53]	80.75	73.02	74.92
	Modified U-Net [54]	85.79	77.07	77.02
	CNN-SS [55]	82.25	75.86	75.90
	Shal-PSN (proposed)	86.57	80.82	80.93
Missing parts: 60% or more	DEEPLABV3+ [51]	72.04	64.47	64.52
	YOLOv8-Seg [52]	75.51	68.36	68.55
	Mask-RCNN [53]	73.67	65.49	65.30
	Modified U-Net [54]	77.60	73.98	73.27
	CNN-SS [55]	74.61	67.07	68.25
	Shal-PSN (proposed)	79.38	78.18	78.78

Moreover, we conducted experiments to compare the proposed method with existing SOTA plant image-based classification methods. We compared the methods based on artificial neural networks (ANNs) [56], EfficientNet B5 [57], SVMs [58], and the convolutional neural network—grape leaf species (CNN-GLS) model [59]. Table 12 presents the results from models trained only on original images, while Table 13 presents the results from models trained on both original and images with missing parts of plants. As shown in Table 12, among all the results tested with the original images, CNN-GLS was the best. However, among those tested with images with missing plant parts, the proposed Shal-PSN + Shal-PCN was the best.

Table 12. Classification results by proposed and SOTA plant-based methods trained on original image dataset (unit: %).

Input Images	Model/Method	PlantVillage			OLID-I		
		TPR	PPV	F1	TPR	PPV	F1
Original	ANN-based [56]	74.43	77.42	74.91	74.21	77.08	74.73
	EfficientNet B5 [57]	74.46	77.43	76.36	74.09	76.79	76.03
	SVM-based [58]	76.71	77.00	75.34	76.44	76.32	75.20
	CNN-GLS [59]	79.76	80.26	77.73	78.78	79.72	77.40
	Shal-PCN (proposed)	77.42	78.68	77.08	76.49	78.32	76.62
	Shal-PSN + Shal-PCN (proposed)	70.39	72.20	68.02	69.51	71.58	67.44

Table 12. *Cont.*

Input Images	Model/Method	PlantVillage			OLID-I		
		TPR	PPV	F1	TPR	PPV	F1
Missing parts: 20–40%	ANN-based [56]	46.53	70.34	45.10	46.49	69.57	44.55
	EfficientNet B5 [57]	48.03	70.56	45.67	47.71	70.22	44.78
	SVM-based [58]	48.06	69.92	45.91	47.25	69.89	45.37
	CNN-GLS [59]	47.78	69.28	46.34	47.65	68.61	45.51
	Shal-PCN (proposed)	48.45	70.97	46.61	48.17	70.85	45.81
	Shal-PSN + Shal-PCN (proposed)	66.53	71.87	66.20	66.23	71.69	65.96
Missing parts: 40–60%	ANN-based [56]	23.71	10.56	13.58	22.98	9.92	12.93
	EfficientNet B5 [57]	24.72	8.85	13.24	24.18	8.00	12.77
	SVM-based [58]	23.67	10.53	12.41	22.88	9.62	11.96
	CNN-GLS [59]	24.54	10.42	14.28	23.55	10.32	14.13
	Shal-PCN (proposed)	25.16	10.67	14.34	24.96	10.54	14.16
	Shal-PSN + Shal-PCN (proposed)	42.75	53.30	41.16	42.39	52.77	40.40
Missing parts: 60% or more	ANN-based [56]	7.75	2.98	1.49	7.64	2.80	1.43
	EfficientNet B5 [57]	7.25	3.60	0.24	6.54	3.13	0.23
	SVM-based [58]	7.94	3.14	0.43	7.91	2.64	0.32
	CNN-GLS [59]	8.26	2.75	0.88	7.77	2.18	0.71
	Shal-PCN (proposed)	8.60	3.98	1.89	7.73	3.49	1.84
	Shal-PSN + Shal-PCN (proposed)	24.45	37.88	23.93	23.64	37.28	23.32

Table 13. Classification results by proposed and SOTA plant-based methods trained on original images plus images with missing parts (unit: %).

Input Images	Model/Method	PlantVillage			OLID-I		
		TPR	PPV	F1	TPR	PPV	F1
Original	ANN-based [56]	8.33	0.73	1.34	8.33	0.73	1.34
	EfficientNet B5 [57]	8.33	0.73	1.34	8.33	0.73	1.34
	SVM-based [58]	8.33	0.73	1.34	8.33	0.73	1.34
	CNN-GLS [59]	8.33	0.73	1.34	8.33	0.73	1.34
	Shal-PCN (proposed)	8.33	0.73	1.34	8.33	0.73	1.34
	Shal-PSN + Shal-PCN (proposed)	94.81	91.15	92.53	95.01	91.59	92.89
Missing parts: 20–40%	ANN-based [56]	8.33	0.73	1.34	8.33	0.73	1.34
	EfficientNet B5 [57]	8.33	0.73	1.34	8.33	0.73	1.34
	SVM-based [58]	8.33	0.73	1.34	8.33	0.73	1.34
	CNN-GLS [59]	8.33	0.73	1.34	8.33	0.73	1.34
	Shal-PCN (proposed)	8.33	0.73	1.34	8.33	0.73	1.34
	Shal-PSN + Shal-PCN (proposed)	95.20	94.91	94.95	95.42	95.34	95.10
Missing parts: 40–60%	ANN-based [56]	8.33	0.73	1.34	8.33	0.73	1.34
	EfficientNet B5 [57]	8.33	0.73	1.34	8.33	0.73	1.34
	SVM-based [58]	8.33	0.73	1.34	8.33	0.73	1.34
	CNN-GLS [59]	8.33	0.73	1.34	8.33	0.73	1.34
	Shal-PCN (proposed)	8.33	0.73	1.34	8.33	0.73	1.34
	Shal-PSN + Shal-PCN (proposed)	90.93	90.39	90.51	91.55	90.80	91.47
Missing parts: 60% or more	ANN-based [56]	8.33	0.73	1.34	8.33	0.73	1.34
	EfficientNet B5 [57]	8.33	0.73	1.34	8.33	0.73	1.34
	SVM-based [58]	8.33	0.73	1.34	8.33	0.73	1.34
	CNN-GLS [59]	8.33	0.73	1.34	8.33	0.73	1.34
	Shal-PCN (proposed)	8.33	0.73	1.34	8.33	0.73	1.34
	Shal-PSN + Shal-PCN (proposed)	46.15	52.80	46.76	47.03	53.03	47.37

Additionally, as seen in Table 13, the accuracy of Shal-PSN + Shal-PCN was the highest. The SOTA methods produced the same results (identical F1 scores) as Table 10, and the reasons are explained in Section 4.2.2 with Figure 10.

Additionally, we compared our proposed method with SOTA deep learning methods, using techniques such as CoAtNet [60], MaxViT [61], model soups [62], and DaViT [63]. Table 14 displays the results with the aforementioned models trained only on original images, while Table 15 shows results from the same models trained on original images plus images with missing parts of plants. As can be observed from Table 14, with regard to tests with original images, MaxViT yielded the highest outcome, while among those tested with images with missing plant parts, the proposed method, i.e., Shal-PSN + Shal-PCN, returned the best results.

Table 14. Classification results by proposed and SOTA deep learning methods trained on original image dataset (unit: %).

Input Images	Model/Method	PlantVillage			OLID-I		
		TPR	PPV	F1	TPR	PPV	F1
Original	CoAtNet [60]	81.03	79.10	79.22	80.93	78.13	78.92
	MaxViT [61]	80.78	80.83	80.38	80.60	80.73	79.84
	Model soups [62]	77.93	79.45	78.39	76.96	79.09	77.99
	DaViT [63]	79.51	81.70	78.02	79.06	81.06	77.66
	Shal-PCN (proposed)	77.42	78.68	77.08	76.49	78.32	76.62
	Shal-PSN + Shal-PCN (proposed)	70.39	72.20	68.02	69.51	71.58	67.44
Missing parts: 20–40%	CoAtNet [60]	50.28	71.88	47.25	49.50	71.51	46.74
	MaxViT [61]	49.58	71.06	48.29	48.87	70.92	47.62
	Model soups [62]	49.08	72.04	47.83	48.90	71.75	46.86
	DaViT [63]	49.87	72.20	46.91	49.73	71.56	46.81
	Shal-PCN (proposed)	48.45	70.97	46.61	48.17	70.85	45.81
	Shal-PSN + Shal-PCN (proposed)	66.53	71.87	66.20	66.23	71.69	65.96
Missing parts: 40–60%	CoAtNet [60]	26.94	11.11	15.90	26.08	10.40	15.47
	MaxViT [61]	26.16	12.05	14.39	25.34	11.13	13.76
	Model soups [62]	25.40	11.18	14.77	24.86	10.40	14.43
	DaViT [63]	26.77	12.58	16.02	26.74	12.19	15.14
	Shal-PCN (proposed)	25.16	10.67	14.34	24.96	10.54	14.16
	Shal-PSN + Shal-PCN (proposed)	42.75	53.30	41.16	42.39	52.77	40.40
Missing parts: 60% or more	CoAtNet [60]	9.85	4.81	3.11	9.38	4.55	2.12
	MaxViT [61]	9.25	4.41	2.03	8.90	3.75	1.95
	Model soups [62]	9.22	5.16	2.57	8.52	5.16	2.09
	DaViT [63]	9.77	5.74	3.32	8.78	4.89	3.23
	Shal-PCN (proposed)	8.60	3.98	1.89	7.73	3.49	1.84
	Shal-PSN + Shal-PCN (proposed)	24.45	37.88	23.93	23.64	37.28	23.32

Additionally, as presented in Table 15, the accuracy achieved with Shal-PSN + Shal-PCN was the highest. The SOTA methods produced the same results as presented in Table 10, for reasons explained in Section 4.2.2 with Figure 10.

Additionally, images with missing parts caused by environmental issues and the preprocessing of input images are used in the experiments. As shown in Figure 11a, plants may lose their parts due to insects and plant diseases. Moreover, as shown in Figure 11b, parts of a plant may not be visible because of the process of cropping images. In deep learning methods, original images are mostly cropped into images with smaller sizes for the preparation of inputs to models. For example, the original size of plant images of this dataset is $3024 \times 4032 \times 3$, and the images included multiple plants and leaves; the images are cropped automatically into smaller images with sizes of $256 \times 256 \times 3$ by using shifting and cropping operations. This operation generates images of plants with missing parts as shown in Figure 11b.

In these images, the missing parts have various sizes and patterns. In the experiments, the images were not divided into subsets like "20–40%", "40–60%", and "60% or more" as in Table 15. As shown in Table 16, the proposed method showed the highest performance compared to other existing methods.

Table 15. Classification results by proposed and SOTA deep learning methods on original images plus images with missing parts (unit: %).

Input Images	Model/method	PlantVillage			OLID-I		
		TPR	PPV	F1	TPR	PPV	F1
Original	CoAtNet [60]	8.33	0.73	1.34	8.33	0.73	1.34
	MaxViT [61]	8.33	0.73	1.34	8.33	0.73	1.34
	Model soups [62]	8.33	0.73	1.34	8.33	0.73	1.34
	DaViT [63]	8.33	0.73	1.34	8.33	0.73	1.34
	Shal-PCN (proposed)	8.33	0.73	1.34	8.33	0.73	1.34
	Shal-PSN + Shal-PCN (proposed)	94.81	91.15	92.53	95.01	91.59	92.89
Missing parts: 20–40%	CoAtNet [60]	8.33	0.73	1.34	8.33	0.73	1.34
	MaxViT [61]	8.33	0.73	1.34	8.33	0.73	1.34
	Model soups [62]	8.33	0.73	1.34	8.33	0.73	1.34
	DaViT [63]	8.33	0.73	1.34	8.33	0.73	1.34
	Shal-PCN (proposed)	8.33	0.73	1.34	8.33	0.73	1.34
	Shal-PSN + Shal-PCN (proposed)	95.20	94.91	94.95	95.42	95.34	95.10
Missing parts: 40–60%	CoAtNet [60]	8.33	0.73	1.34	8.33	0.73	1.34
	MaxViT [61]	8.33	0.73	1.34	8.33	0.73	1.34
	Model soups [62]	8.33	0.73	1.34	8.33	0.73	1.34
	DaViT [63]	8.33	0.73	1.34	8.33	0.73	1.34
	Shal-PCN (proposed)	8.33	0.73	1.34	8.33	0.73	1.34
	Shal-PSN + Shal-PCN (proposed)	90.93	90.39	90.51	91.55	90.80	91.47
Missing parts: 60% or more	CoAtNet [60]	8.33	0.73	1.34	8.33	0.73	1.34
	MaxViT [61]	8.33	0.73	1.34	8.33	0.73	1.34
	Model soups [62]	8.33	0.73	1.34	8.33	0.73	1.34
	DaViT [63]	8.33	0.73	1.34	8.33	0.73	1.34
	Shal-PCN (proposed)	8.33	0.73	1.34	8.33	0.73	1.34
	Shal-PSN + Shal-PCN (proposed)	46.15	52.80	46.76	47.03	53.03	47.37

Figure 11. *Cont.*

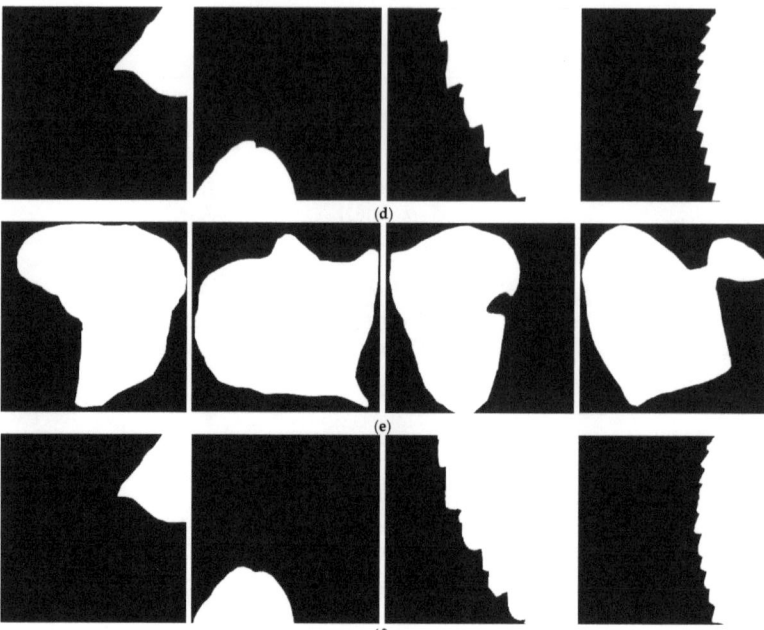

Figure 11. Example images [64] used in the experiments: images with various missing parts due to (**a**) insects and diseases; (**b**) the process of cropping images for input to classification models; (**c**,**d**) corresponding ground truth images; and (**e**,**f**) segmentation results by the proposed method.

Table 16. Classification results by proposed and SOTA deep learning methods on images with missing parts due to environmental effects (unit: %).

Input Images	Model/Method	PlantVillage		
		TPR	PPV	F1
Missing parts in various ways	CoAtNet [60]	58.68	74.94	66.81
	MaxViT [61]	52.08	78.16	65.12
	Model soups [62]	58.08	79.24	68.66
	DaViT [63]	56.48	77.26	66.87
	Shal-PCN (proposed)	49.81	78.58	64.20
	Shal-PSN + Shal-PCN (proposed)	86.32	83.27	84.79

4.4. Comparison of Algorithm Complexity

In this subsection, we compare the algorithm complexity between the proposed method and SOTA methods.

Table 17 details the processing time per image, giga floating-point operations per second (GFLOPs), number of parameters, and model size for our method and various SOTA models. Although our method does not show the lowest algorithm complexity, the accuracies of our method are higher than those of all the SOTA methods as shown in Tables 11–14, which is the main goal of our research.

Table 17. Comparison of processing times, GFLOPs, # parameters, and model sizes of proposed and SOTA methods (# means "number of").

Model	Processing Time (Unit: ms)	GFLOPs	# Parameters (Unit: Mega)	Model Size (Unit: MB)
ANN-based [56]	122.7	108.4	5.4	24.7
EfficientNet B5 [57]	135.8	115	30	56.4
CNN-GLS [59]	118.2	92.9	3.1	30.4
CoAtNet [60]	172.4	361	275	101.3
MaxViT [61]	153.6	63.4	120	89.6
Model soups [62]	363.1	1224	2440	494
DaViT [63]	281.4	1038	1437	337
Shal-PCN (proposed)	62.8	51.7	2.2	25.5
Shal-PSN + Shal-PCN (proposed)	121.4	106.2	3.6	31.2

5. Discussion

5.1. Error Cases and Statistical Analysis

Figure 12 presents the error cases from experiments involving images with missing parts of plants. In Figure 12a,b, even though only parts of plants are visible in the input images, correct classification was achieved. However, as shown in Figure 12c,d, when the remaining plant information in partially removed images constituted less than 10% of the plant's body, the given information was insufficient for plant recognition; this led to incorrect identification.

Figure 12. Examples of correctly and erroneously classified images with missing parts of plants based on PlantVillage open dataset [16]. From left to right: original images, images with missing parts of plants, and segmented images by the proposed method. (**a**,**b**) Correctly classified images; (**c**,**d**) incorrectly classified images.

In addition, gradient-weighted class activation mapping (Grad-CAM) [65] images were analyzed to verify that the proposed model extracts important features (reddish and yellowish colors in Figure 13) for correct classification and to interpret the model's decisions. In Figure 13, "images with missing parts of 0%" indicates the second images in Figure 13a,b; here, 0% means the background of the images was removed by the segmentation process, and the plant parts were not removed. As shown in Figure 13, we confirm that important features can be extracted by our method irrespective of the size of missing parts.

As shown in Table 14, the proposed method showed much higher accuracies than the other methods when input images have missing parts of 20–60% or more. This is because the other classification methods used input images with large black backgrounds (Figure 10a) without using the additional segmentation method, while our proposed method uses the additional segmentation method proposed in this study to solve the problem of classifying images with missing parts, and used input images with small black backgrounds (Figure 10b). Without using an additional segmentation method, the background of the image input to the classification model will be large and the region containing plant information will be small. Therefore, we proposed and used an additional segmentation method compared to the traditional method to remove the large empty background.

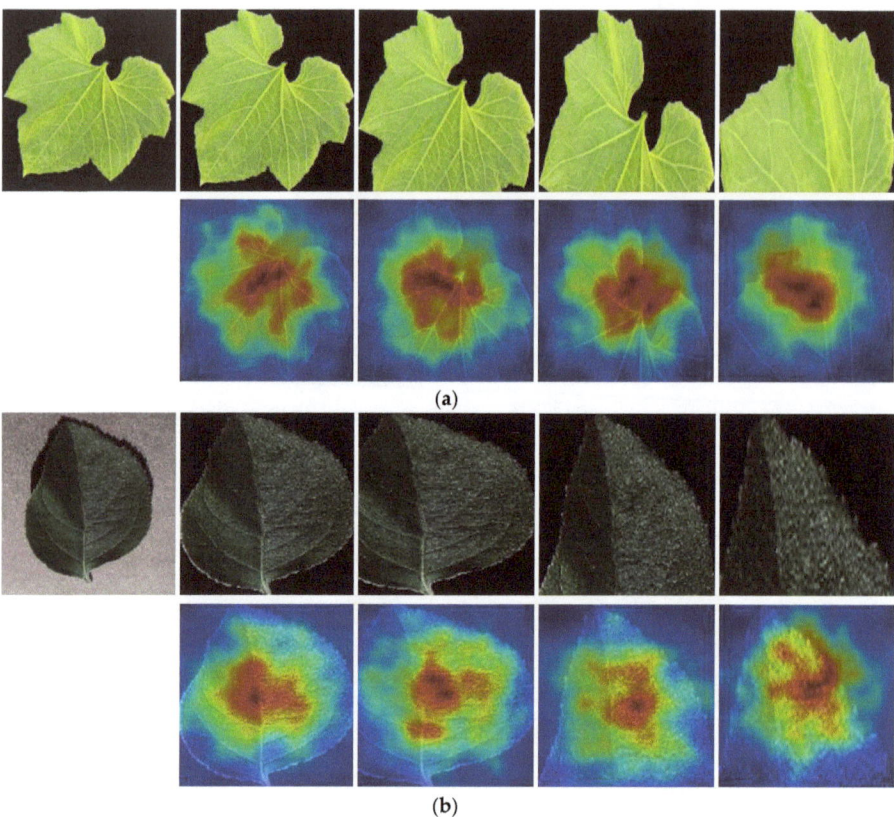

Figure 13. Example images of Grad-CAM [65] (the 2nd rows of **a**, **b**). From the left to right of the 1st two images of (**a**,**b**): original images and images with missing parts of 0%, 20–40%, 40–60%, and 60% or more. (**a**) OLID-I dataset [17]; (**b**) PlantVillage dataset [16].

Additionally, up to 75% of the information in the images was automatically removed. As shown in Figure 6, we removed 25%, 50%, and 75% of the images in various ways. However, depending on the location and size of plants in images, more than 80% were removed, and the image with the smallest plant information had a missing part of 95.66%.

In addition, for statistical validation, a t-test [66] and Cohen's d-value [67] were measured based on the F1 scores obtained by the proposed method and the second-best method of Tables 11 and 13. Cohen's d-value around 0.2 represents a small effective size, 0.5 means a medium effective size, and 0.8 means a large effective size. The p-value and Cohen's d-value between the second-best (SOTA plant-based) method and the proposed method were measured using the PlantVillage and OLID-I open datasets as shown in Figure 14. The p-values and Cohen's d-values of the result obtained by using the PlantVillage dataset were 0.052 and 0.029, and 6.69 and 7.94, respectively. The p-values and Cohen's d-values of the result obtained by using the OLID-I dataset were 0.013 and 0.012, and 18.4

and 8.95, respectively. These values confirm that our method statistically outperforms the SOTA method.

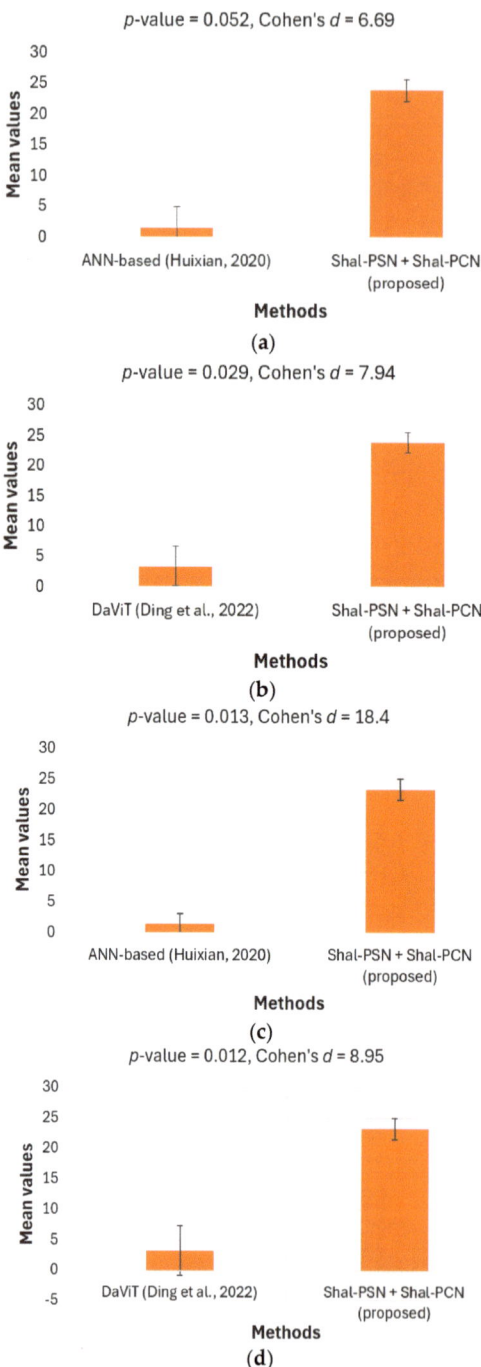

Figure 14. Comparison of *t*-test results between the proposed method and the second-best methods (DaViT [63] and ANN-based [56]) based on F1 scores. Results acquired using PlantVillage (**a**,**b**) and OLID–I (**c**,**d**) open datasets.

5.2. Fractal Dimension Estimation for Plant Image Segmentation

The box-counting method is applied for the estimation of FD for analyzing plant images from the PlantVillage open dataset, as shown in Figures 15 and 16. In Figure 15, input, ground truth, and output images are shown. In Figure 16, FD analysis performed by using segmented images shown in Figure 15 is illustrated. In Table 18, methods are compared using correlation coefficient (C), coefficient of determination (R^2), and FD values. Images in Figure 15a,b–h are input color images and binary images, respectively, where the white regions represent objects, whereas the black regions represent backgrounds. As shown in Figure 15, the segmented binary image by the proposed method (c) is the most similar to the ground truth image (b).

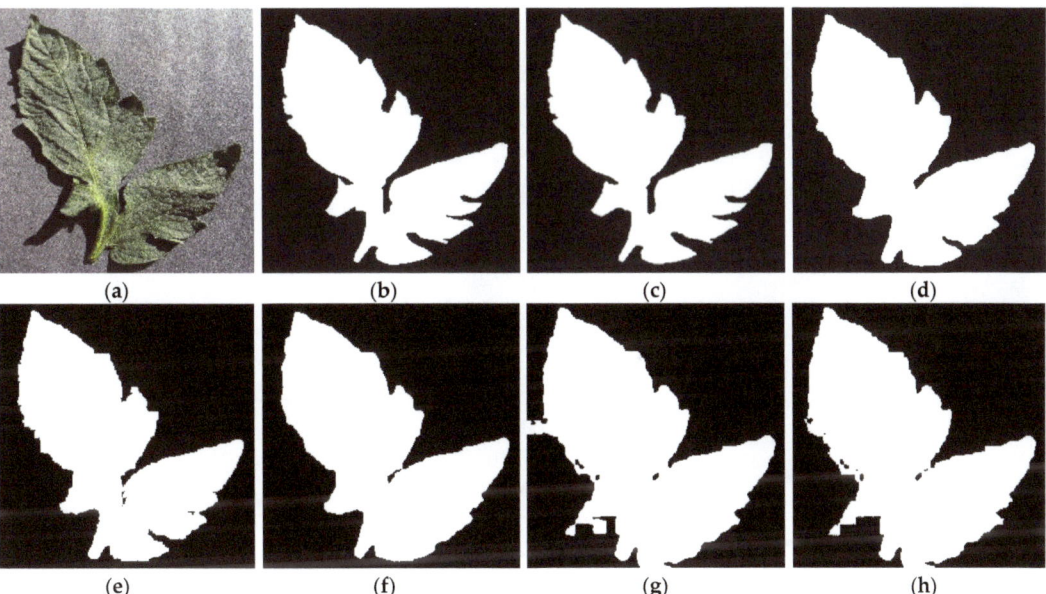

Figure 15. Example images used for analyzing FD for the segmentation. Input (**a**) [16] and ground truth (**b**) [16] images and segmentation results of the proposed Shal-PSN (**c**), Modified U-Net [54] (**d**), YOLOv8-Seg [52] (**e**), CNN-SS [55] (**f**), Mask-RCNN [53] (**g**), and DEEPLABV3+ [51] (**h**) models.

Table 18. FD, R^2, and C values, and the number of smallest boxes (s#), the number of boxes (Box#), and the size of boxes (S#) used in the analysis of segmentation results.

Methods	FD	C	R^2	Box#	S#	s#
Ground truth	2.2523	0.9888	0.8768	150,458	51	46,336
DEEPLABV3+ [51]	2.2414	0.9896	0.9025	139,075	51	46,592
YOLOv8–Seg [52]	2.2659	0.9916	0.9344	159,184	52	58,624
Mask–RCNN [53]	2.2429	0.9901	0.9043	140,833	52	46,592
Modified U–Net [54]	2.2513	0.9906	0.8973	149,874	52	44,544
CNN–SS [55]	2.2109	0.9893	0.9154	138,419	51	46,592
Shal–PSN (proposed)	2.2523	0.9888	0.8742	150,620	51	46,336

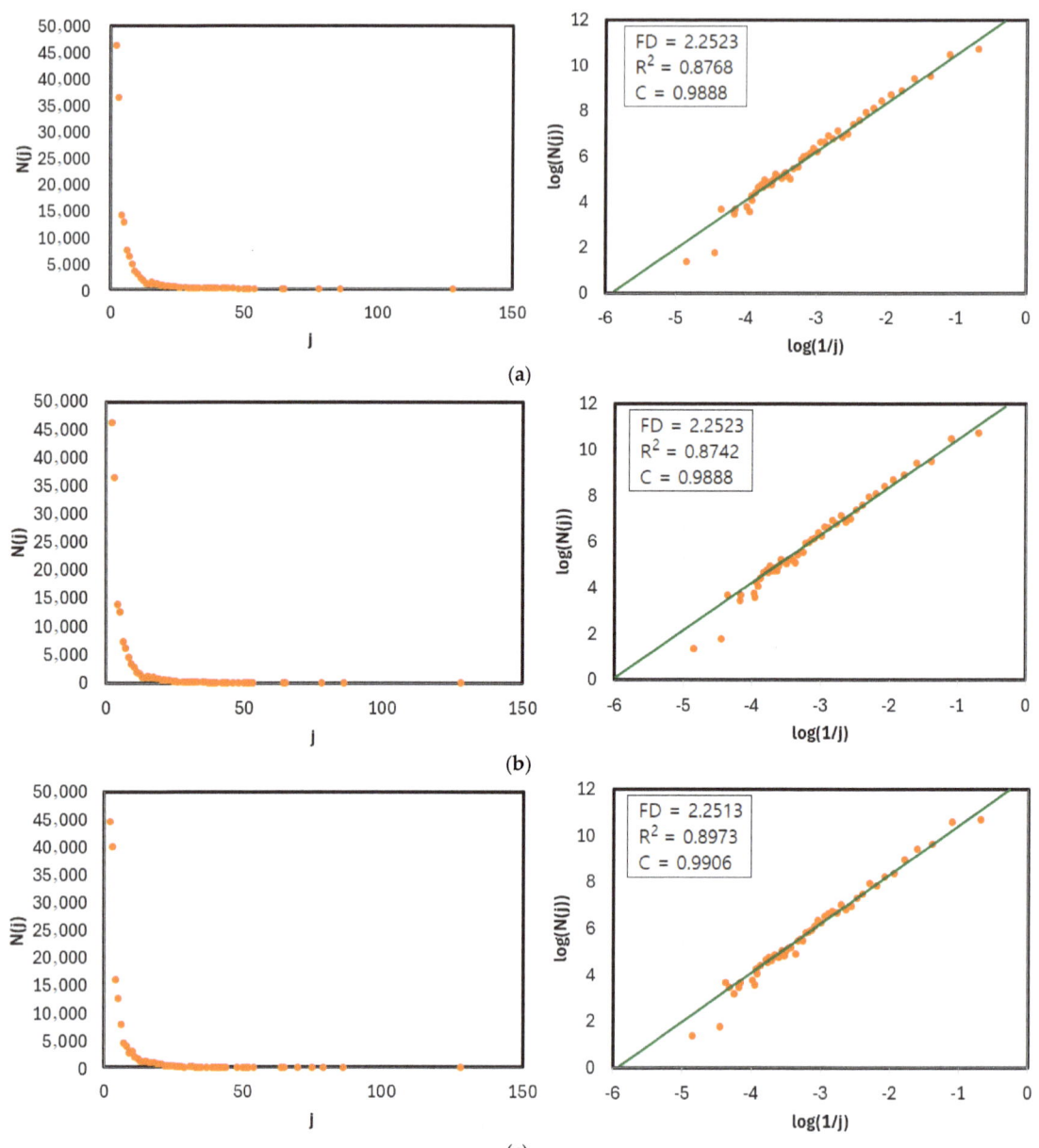

Figure 16. *Cont.*

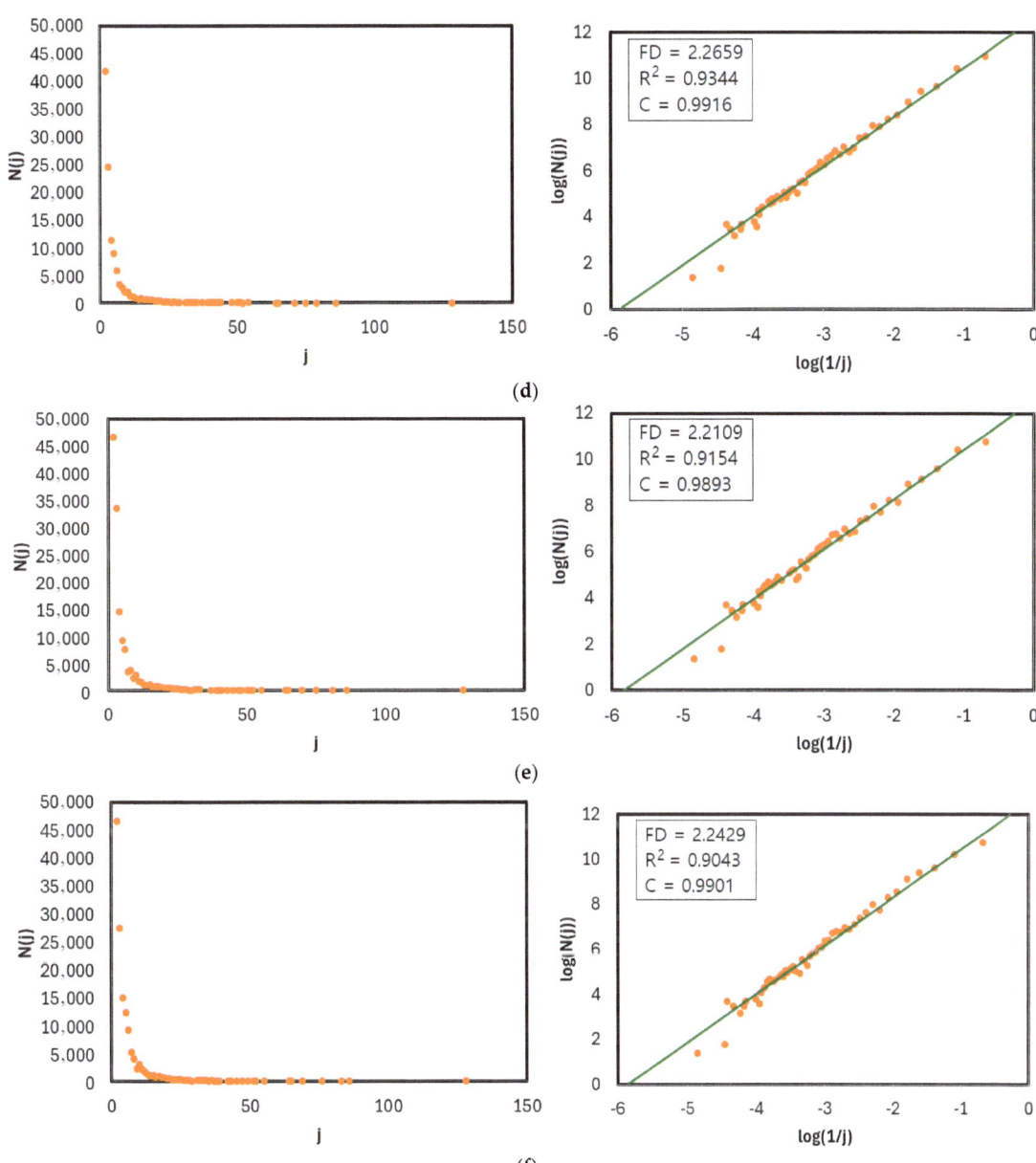

Figure 16. *Cont.*

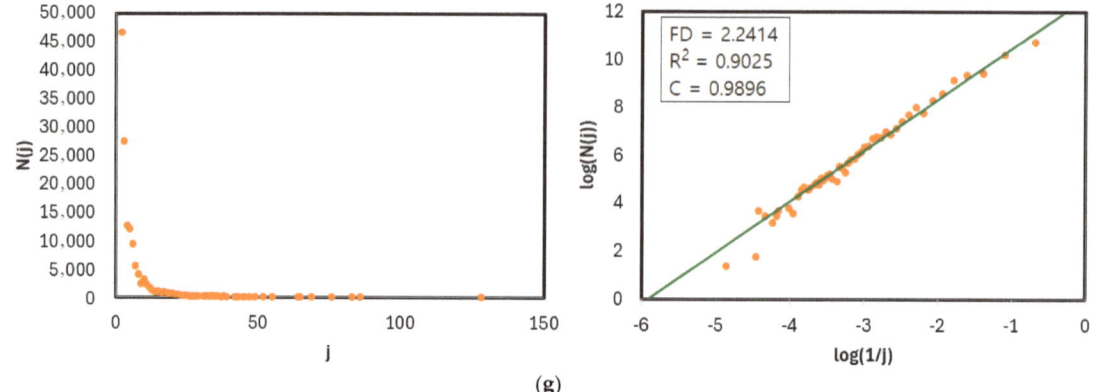

(g)

Figure 16. Analysis of FD for the segmentation. The number of boxes (N(j)) and size of boxes (j) are shown on the left side. FD, R^2, and C are shown on the right side. These results were obtained by using a ground truth image (**a**), and binary images (Figure 15) segmented by the proposed Shal–PSN (**b**), Modified U–Net [54] (**c**), YOLOv8–Seg [52] (**d**), CNN–SS [55] (**e**), Mask–RCNN [53] (**f**), and DEEPLABV3+ [51] (**g**) models.

These binary images are essential for the subsequent FD analysis. Data to calculate FD are obtained by covering binary images with boxes of different sizes and counting the number of boxes that intersect with plants. FD values in Figure 16 indicate the irregularity and complexity of the shape of segmented images. As shown in Figure 16, lower FD values indicate shapes with less complexity, and higher values indicate shapes with more complexity.

In Table 18, "Box#" represents the total number of boxes including boxes with different sizes that are illustrated on the left side of Figure 16. Moreover, "S#" represents how many different sizes of boxes are used for calculating FD values. Here, we can see that the images were not analyzed by using the same size of boxes because of their complex shapes. The smallest and biggest box sizes were 2×2 and 128×128, respectively. Furthermore, the total number of boxes also represents the complexity of shapes; the higher number means more boxes are required to analyze an image.

As shown in Table 18, the segmented images by the proposed Shal-PSN (Figure 15c) and YOLOv8-Seg models [52] (Figure 15e) show higher FD values because the image of Shal-PSN has deeper convexity defects than the other images whereas the image of YOLOv8-Seg [52] has many undesirable small convexity defects as shown in Figure 15. Thus, YOLOv8-Seg [52] showed the highest FD value and the proposed Shal-PSN showed the second highest FD value in Table 18. Moreover, the segmented image by CNN-SS [55] (Figure 15f) shows the lowest FD value because it has fewer convexity defects than other images. Furthermore, the image that showed the highest FD value (YOLOv8-Seg [52]) used more boxes than other images for the analysis whereas the image that showed the lowest FD value (CNN-SS [55]) used fewer boxes than other images, which indicates that the image by YOLOv8-Seg [52] is more complex and the image by CNN-SS [55] is less complex than other images.

In addition, FD, C, and R^2 values, and Box#, S#, and s# obtained from the image by Shal-PSN, are most similar to those of the ground truth image compared to other images as shown in Table 18. This proves that the binary image segmented by the proposed Shal-PSN is more similar to the ground truth image than the other images. In other words, the proposed Shal-PSN showed better segmentation performance compared to other methods.

Additionally, as shown in Table 18, "s#" denotes the number of smallest boxes (with a size of 2×2) used to analyze images, where an image segmented by YOLOv8-Seg [52] used 58,624 smallest boxes which is the highest number in Table 18, and which means that the image has more small undesirable convexity defects than other images. Moreover, an image segmented by the proposed method used 46,336 smallest boxes, which is the fifth highest number in Table 18, which means that the image has fewer small convexity defects than the other four images.

6. Conclusions

This study proposed a novel method combining a shallow plant segmentation network (Shal-PSN) and shallow plant classification network (Shal-PCN) to address the issue of improper plant image classification when parts of plants are not visible owing to limited camera angles. Various experiments using OLID-I and PlantVillage open datasets demonstrated that our proposed method achieved high classification accuracy, outperforming some of the SOTA methods. The proposed method was the third or fourth ranked in algorithm complexity compared with SOTA methods, and the statistical difference between our method and the second-best methods was confirmed through t-test and Cohen's d-value measurements. However, when the input images contained minimal plant information, the proposed method also struggled to effectively perform segmentation and classification. Moreover, the experimental results in Tables 9–14 showed that models trained on a dataset with a mixture of original images and images with missing parts had very poor classification performance compared to models trained on original images. This is due to the models being poorly trained on images with missing plant parts that have more empty space than plant parts, as shown in Figure 10a. However, as shown in Figure 10b, after removing the empty space from the images and training the model with those images, the classification performance of the model improved significantly. Therefore, we applied the segmentation method (Shal-PSN) for this task, and the proposed method (Shal-PSN + Shal-PCN) achieved promising results, as shown in Tables 9–14.

As shown in Tables 11–18, the proposed method improved classification performance on plant images with missing parts. The models trained on only normal (original) images showed higher accuracies than the models trained on images with missing parts. However, the proposed classification model with an additional segmentation model achieved higher accuracy than the existing plant image classification models. Here, we can see that segmentation models are effective for the classification model.

In this study, we also analyzed the segmentation results using fractal dimension estimation and compared the results using result images, graphs, and tables as shown in Section 5.2. As shown in the segmentation results, the result values of FD obtained from the generated images by the proposed method and the ground truth images showed similar FD values.

In future works, we plan to explore methods to improve segmentation and classification accuracy for images with minimal plant information. Additionally, we aim to explore strategies for improving plant segmentation and classification accuracy in scenarios not only affected by limited camera angles but also by other noise conditions, such as camera optical and motion blurring and low illumination.

Author Contributions: G.B.: methodology, writing—original draft. S.G.K.: conceptualization. J.S.K.: data curation. T.M.: investigation. K.R.P.: supervision, writing—review and editing. All authors have read and agreed to the published version of the manuscript.

Funding: This research was supported in part by the National Research Foundation of Korea (NRF), funded by the Ministry of Science and ICT (MSIT) through the Basic Science Research Program (NRF-2022R1F1A1064291), and in part by the MSIT, Korea, under the Information Technology Research Center (ITRC) support program (IITP-2024-2020-0-01789), supervised by the Institute for Information & Communications Technology Planning & Evaluation (IITP).

Data Availability Statement: The open datasets are available in [16,17]. In addition, our models and source code are available in [18].

Conflicts of Interest: The authors declare that they have no conflicting financial interests or personal relationships that could have appeared to affect the work presented in this paper.

References

1. Batchuluun, G.; Nam, S.H.; Park, K.R. Deep learning-based plant classification and crop disease classification by thermal camera. *J. King Saud Univ.-Comput. Inf. Sci.* **2022**, *34*, 1319–1578. [CrossRef]
2. Anasta, N.; Setyawan, F.X.A.; Fitriawan, H. Disease detection in banana trees using an image processing-based thermal camera. In *IOP Conference Series: Earth and Environmental Science*; IOP Publishing: Bristol, UK, 2021; Volume 739, p. 012088.
3. Raza, S.E.; Prince, G.; Clarkson, J.P.; Rajpoot, N.M. Automatic detection of diseased tomato plants using thermal and stereo visible light images. *PLoS ONE* **2015**, *10*, e0123262. [CrossRef] [PubMed]
4. Zhu, W.; Chen, H.; Ciechanowska, I.; Spaner, D. Application of infrared thermal imaging for the rapid diagnosis of crop disease. *IFAC-Pap.* **2018**, *51*, 424–430. [CrossRef]
5. Shahi, T.B.; Sitaula, C.; Neupane, A.; Guo, W. Fruit classification using attention-based MobileNetV2 for industrial applications. *PLoS ONE* **2022**, *17*, e0264586. [CrossRef]
6. Kader, A.; Sharif, S.; Bhowmick, P.; Mim, F.H.; Srizon, A.Y. Effective workflow for high-performance recognition of fruits using machine learning approaches. *Int. Res. J. Eng. Tech.* **2020**, *7*, 1516–1521.
7. Biswas, B.; Ghosh, S.K.; Ghosh, A. A robust multi-label fruit classification based on deep convolution neural network. In *Computational Intelligence in Pattern Recognition. Advances in Intelligent Systems and Computing*; Das, A., Nayak, J., Naik, B., Pati, S., Pelusi, D., Eds.; Springer: Singapore, 2020; Volume 999. [CrossRef]
8. Hossain, M.S.; Al-Hammadi, M.; Muhammad, G. Automatic fruit classification using deep learning for industrial applications. *IEEE Trans. Ind. Inform.* **2019**, *15*, 1027–1034. [CrossRef]
9. Abawatew, G.Y.; Belay, S.; Gedamu, K.; Assefa, M.; Ayalew, M.; Oluwasanmi, A.; Qin, Z. Attention augmented residual network for tomato disease detection and classification. *Turk. J. Electr. Eng. Comput. Sci.* **2021**, *29*, 2869–2885.
10. Ashwinkumar, S.; Rajagopal, S.; Manimaran, V.; Jegajothi, B. Automated plant leaf disease detection and classification using optimal MobileNet based convolutional neural networks. *Mater. Today* **2022**, *51*, 480–487. [CrossRef]
11. Chakraborty, A.; Kumer, D.; Deeba, K. Plant leaf disease recognition using Fastai image classification. In Proceedings of the 5th International Conference on Computing Methodologies and Communication, Erode, India, 8–10 April 2021; pp. 1624–1630. [CrossRef]
12. Wang, D.; Wang, J.; Li, W.; Guan, P. T-CNN: Trilinear convolutional neural networks model for visual detection of plant diseases. *Comput. Electron. Agric.* **2021**, *190*, 106468. [CrossRef]
13. Yun, C.; Kim, Y.W.; Lee, S.J.; Im, S.J.; Park, K.R. WRA-Net: Wide receptive field attention network for motion deblurring in crop and weed image. *Plant Phenomics* **2023**, *5*, 0031. [CrossRef]
14. Wang, J.; Wu, B.; Kohnen, M.V.; Lin, D.; Yang, C.; Wang, X.; Qiang, A.; Liu, W.; Kang, J.; Li, H.; et al. Classification of rice yield using UAV-based hyperspectral imagery and lodging feature. *Plant Phenomics* **2021**, *2021*, 9765952. [CrossRef] [PubMed]
15. Goodfellow, I.J.; Pouget-Abadie, J.; Mirza, M.; Xu, B.; Warde-Farley, D.; Ozair, S.; Courville, A.; Bengio, Y. Generative adversarial networks. *arXiv* **2014**, arXiv:1406.2661. [CrossRef]
16. PlantVillage Dataset. Available online: https://www.kaggle.com/datasets/emmarex/plantdisease (accessed on 8 February 2024).
17. OLID-I Dataset. Available online: https://www.kaggle.com/datasets/raiaone/olid-i?resource=download (accessed on 8 February 2024).
18. Plants with Missing Parts. Available online: https://github.com/ganav/Plants-with-Missing-Parts/tree/main (accessed on 8 February 2024).
19. Lydia, M.S.; Aulia, I.; Jaya, I.; Hanafiah, D.S.; Lubis, R.H. Preliminary study for identifying rice plant disease based on thermal images. In Proceedings of the 4th International Conference on Computing and Applied Informatics, Medan, Indonesia, 26 November 2019.
20. Paddy Crop Dataset. Available online: https://www.kaggle.com/sujaradha/thermal-images-diseased-healthy-leaves-paddy (accessed on 8 February 2024).
21. Zhou, B.; Khosla, A.; Lapedriza, A.; Oliva, A.; Torralba, A. Learning deep features for discriminative localization. In Proceedings of the IEEE Conference on Computer Vision and Pattern Recognition, Las Vegas, NV, USA, 27–30 June 2016; pp. 2921–2929.
22. Singh, D.; Jain, N.; Jain, P.; Kayal, P.; Kumawat, S.; Batra, N. PlantDoc: A dataset for visual plant disease detection. In Proceedings of the 7th ACM IKDD CoDS and 25th COMAD, Hyderabad, India, 5–7 January 2020; pp. 249–253. [CrossRef]
23. Chompookham, T.; Surinta, O. Ensemble methods with deep convolutional neural networks for plant leaf recognition. *ICIC Express Lett.* **2021**, *15*, 553–565.
24. Meshram, V.; Thanomliang, K.; Ruangkan, S.; Chumchu, P.; Patil, K. FruitsGB: Top Indian Fruits with Quality. IEEE Dataport. 2020. Available online: https://ieee-dataport.org/open-access/fruitsgb-top-indian-fruits-quality (accessed on 8 February 2024).
25. Rocha, A.; Hauagge, D.C.; Wainer, J.; Goldenstein, S. Automatic fruit and vegetable classification from images. *Comput. Electron. Agric.* **2010**, *70*, 96–104. [CrossRef]
26. Waltner, G.; Schwarz, M.; Ladstätter, S.; Weber, A.; Luley, P.; Lindschinger, M.; Schmid, I.; Scheitz, W.; Bischof, H. Personalized dietary self-management using mobile vision-based assistance. In Proceedings of the International Conference on Image Analysis and Processing, Catania, Italy, 11–15 September 2017; pp. 385–393.
27. Siddiqi, R. Comparative performance of various deep learning based models in fruit image classification. In Proceedings of the 11th International Conference on Advances in Information Technology, Bangkok, Thailand, 1–3 July 2020; pp. 1–9. [CrossRef]

28. Hamid, N.N.A.A.; Razali, R.A.; Ibrahim, Z. Comparing bags of features, conventional convolutional neural network and AlexNet for fruit recognition. *Indones. J. Elect. Eng. Comput. Sci.* **2019**, *14*, 333–339. [CrossRef]
29. Katarzyna, R.; Paweł, M.A. Vision-based method utilizing deep convolutional neural networks for fruit variety classification in uncertainty conditions of retail sales. *Appl. Sci.* **2019**, *9*, 3971. [CrossRef]
30. Batchuluun, G.; Nam, S.H.; Park, K.R. Deep learning-based plant classification using nonaligned thermal and visible light images. *Mathematics* **2022**, *10*, 4053. [CrossRef]
31. Analysis of Variance. Available online: https://en.wikipedia.org/wiki/Analysis_of_variance (accessed on 8 February 2024).
32. Anscombe, F.J. The Validity of Comparative Experiments. *J. R. Stat. Soc.* **1948**, *111*, 181–211. [CrossRef]
33. Gelman, A. Analysis of variance? Why it is more important than ever. *Ann. Stat.* **2005**, *33*, 1–53. [CrossRef]
34. Batchuluun, G.; Nam, S.H.; Park, C.; Park, K.R. Super-resolution reconstruction based plant image classification using thermal and visible-light images. *Mathematics* **2023**, *11*, 76. [CrossRef]
35. Sabir, Z.; Bhat, S.A.; Wahab, H.A.; Camargo, M.E.; Abildinova, G.; Zulpykhar, Z. A bio inspired learning scheme for the fractional order kidney function model with neural networks. *Chaos Solitons Fractals* **2024**, *180*, 114562. [CrossRef]
36. Havlin, S.; Buldyrev, S.V.; Goldberger, A.L.; Mantegna, R.N.; Ossadnik, S.M.; Peng, C.-K.; Simons, M.; Stanley, H. Fractals in biology and medicine. *Chaos Solitons Fractals* **1995**, *6*, 171–201. [CrossRef]
37. Zook, J.M.; Iftekharuddin, K.M. Statistical analysis of fractal-based brain tumor detection algorithms. *Magn. Reason. Imaging* **2005**, *23*, 671–678. [CrossRef] [PubMed]
38. Chen, Y.; Wang, Y.; Li, X. Fractal dimensions derived from spatial allometric scaling of urban form. *Chaos Solitons Fractals* **2019**, *126*, 122–134. [CrossRef]
39. Brouty, X.; Garcin, M. Fractal properties, information theory, and market efficiency. *Chaos Solitons Fractals* **2024**, *180*, 114543. [CrossRef]
40. Yin, J. Dynamical fractal: Theory and case study. *Chaos Solitons Fractals* **2023**, *176*, 114190. [CrossRef]
41. Python. Available online: https://www.python.org/ (accessed on 8 February 2024).
42. TensorFlow. Available online: https://www.tensorflow.org/ (accessed on 8 February 2024).
43. OpenCV. Available online: http://opencv.org/ (accessed on 8 February 2024).
44. Chollet, F.; California, U.S. Keras. Available online: https://keras.io/ (accessed on 8 February 2024).
45. Wali, R. Xtreme Margin: A tunable loss function for binary classification problems. *arXiv* **2022**, arXiv:2211.00176.
46. Zhang, Z.; Sabuncu, M.R. Generalized cross entropy loss for training deep neural networks with noisy labels. *arXiv* **2018**, arXiv:1805.07836.
47. Kingma, D.P.; Ba, J.B. ADAM: A method for stochastic optimization. In Proceedings of the 3rd International Conference on Learning Representations, San Diego, CA, USA, 7–9 May 2015; pp. 1–15.
48. Bertels, J.; Eelbode, T.; Berman, M.; Vandermeulen, D.; Maes, F.; Bisschops, R.; Blaschko, M.B. Optimizing the dice score and jaccard index for medical image segmentation: Theory & practice. In Proceedings of the 22nd International Conference on Medical Image Computing and Computer-Assisted Intervention, Shenzen, China, 13–17 October 2019; pp. 92–100. [CrossRef]
49. Sultan, H.; Ullah, N.; Hong, J.S.; Kim, S.G.; Lee, D.C.; Jung, S.Y.; Park, K.R. Estimation of Fractal Dimension and Segmentation of Brain Tumor with Parallel Features Aggregation Network. *Fractal Fract.* **2024**, *8*, 357. [CrossRef]
50. Powers, D.M.W. Evaluation: From precision, recall and f-measure to roc, informedness, markedness and correlation. *Mach. Learn. Technol.* **2011**, *2*, 37–63.
51. Yang, T.; Zhou, S.; Xu, A.; Ye, J.; Yin, J. An Approach for Plant Leaf Image Segmentation Based on YOLOV8 and the Improved DEEPLABV3+. *Plants* **2023**, *12*, 3438. [CrossRef] [PubMed]
52. Wang, P.; Deng, H.; Guo, J.; Ji, S.; Meng, D.; Bao, J.; Zuo, P. Leaf Segmentation Using Modified YOLOv8-Seg Models. *Life* **2024**, *14*, 780. [CrossRef] [PubMed]
53. Ward, D.; Moghadam, P.; Hudson, N. Deep Leaf Segmentation Using Synth. Data. *arXiv* **2018**, arXiv:1807.10931.
54. Shoaib, M.; Hussain, T.; Shah, B.; Ullah, I.; Shah, S.M.; Ali, F.; Park, S.H. Deep learning-based segmentation and classification of leaf images for detection of tomato plant disease. *Front. Plant Sci.* **2022**, *13*, 1031748. [CrossRef]
55. Milioto, A.; Lottes, P.; Stachniss, C. Real-time Semantic Segmentation of Crop and Weed for Precision Agriculture Robots Leveraging Background Knowledge in CNNs. In Proceedings of the 2018 IEEE International Conference on Robotics and Automation (ICRA), Brisbane, Australia, 21–25 May 2018; pp. 2229–2235.
56. Huixian, J. The analysis of plants image recognition based on deep learning and artificial neural network. *IEEE Access* **2020**, *8*, 68828–68841. [CrossRef]
57. Arun, Y.; Viknesh, G.S. Leaf classification for plant recognition using EfficientNet architecture. In Proceedings of the IEEE Fourth International Conference on Advances in Electronics, Computers and Communications, Bengaluru, India, 10–11 January 2022; pp. 1–5. [CrossRef]
58. Keerthika, P.; Devi, R.M.; Prasad, S.J.S.; Venkatesan, R.; Gunasekaran, H.; Sudha, K. Plant classification based on grey wolf optimizer based support vector machine (GOS) algorithm. In Proceedings of the 7th International Conference on Computing Methodologies and Communication, Erode, India, 23–25 February 2023; pp. 902–906. [CrossRef]
59. Sun, Y.; Tian, B.; Ni, C.; Wang, X.; Fei, C.; Chen, Q. Image classification of small sample grape leaves based on deep learning. In Proceedings of the IEEE 7th Information Technology and Mechatronics Engineering Conference, Chongqing, China, 15–17 September 2023; pp. 1874–1878. [CrossRef]

60. Dai, Z.; Liu, H.; Le, V.Q.; Tan, M. CoAtNet: Marrying convolution and attention for all data sizes. In Proceedings of the Annual Conference on Neural Information Processing Systems, Vancouver, BC, Canada, 8–14 December 2019; pp. 1–13.
61. Tu, Z.; Talebi, H.; Zhang, H.; Yang, F.; Milanfar, P.; Bovik, A.; Li, Y. MaxViT: Multi-axis vision transformer. *arXiv* **2022**, arXiv:2204.01697.
62. Wortsman, M.; Ilharco, G.; Yitzhak Gadre, S.; Roelofs, R.; Gontijo-Lopes, R.; Morcos, A.S.; Namkoong, H.; Farhadi, A.; Carmon, Y.; Kornblith, S.; et al. Model soups: Averaging weights of multiple fine-tuned models improves accuracy without increasing inference time. *arXiv* **2022**, arXiv:2203.05482.
63. Ding, M.; Xiao, B.; Codella, N.; Luo, P.; Wang, J.; Yuan, L. DaViT: Dual attention vision transformers. *arXiv* **2022**, arXiv:2204.03645.
64. Var_dataset. Available online: https://github.com/ganav/data/blob/main/dataset (accessed on 8 February 2024).
65. Selvaraju, R.R.; Cogswell, M.; Das, A.; Vedantam, R.; Parikh, D.; Batra, D. Grad-CAM: Visual explanations from deep networks via gradient-based localization. *arXiv* **2016**, arXiv:1610.02391.
66. Student's *t*-Test. Available online: https://en.wikipedia.org/wiki/Student's_t-test (accessed on 14 April 2024).
67. Cohen, J. A power primer. *Psychol. Bull.* **1992**, *112*, 155. [CrossRef]

Disclaimer/Publisher's Note: The statements, opinions and data contained in all publications are solely those of the individual author(s) and contributor(s) and not of MDPI and/or the editor(s). MDPI and/or the editor(s) disclaim responsibility for any injury to people or property resulting from any ideas, methods, instructions or products referred to in the content.

Article

Estimation of Fractal Dimension and Detection of Fake Finger-Vein Images for Finger-Vein Recognition

Seung Gu Kim, Jin Seong Hong, Jung Soo Kim and Kang Ryoung Park *

Division of Electronics and Electrical Engineering, Dongguk University, 30 Pildong-ro 1-gil, Jung-gu, Seoul 04620, Republic of Korea; ismysg104@dgu.ac.kr (S.G.K.); turtle1990@dgu.ac.kr (J.S.H.); k_jungsoo@dgu.ac.kr (J.S.K.)
* Correspondence: parkgr@dongguk.edu; Tel.: +82-2-2260-3329

Abstract: With recent advancements in deep learning, spoofing techniques have developed and generative adversarial networks (GANs) have become an emerging threat to finger-vein recognition systems. Therefore, previous research has been performed to generate finger-vein images for training spoof detectors. However, these are limited and researchers still cannot generate elaborate fake finger-vein images. Therefore, we develop a new densely updated contrastive learning-based self-attention generative adversarial network (DCS-GAN) to create elaborate fake finger-vein images, enabling the training of corresponding spoof detectors. Additionally, we propose an enhanced convolutional network for a next-dimension (ConvNeXt)-Small model with a large kernel attention module as a new spoof detector capable of distinguishing the generated fake finger-vein images. To improve the spoof detection performance of the proposed method, we introduce fractal dimension estimation to analyze the complexity and irregularity of class activation maps from real and fake finger-vein images, enabling the generation of more realistic and sophisticated fake finger-vein images. Experimental results obtained using two open databases showed that the fake images by the DCS-GAN exhibited Frechet inception distances (FID) of 7.601 and 23.351, with Wasserstein distances (WD) of 18.158 and 10.123, respectively, confirming the possibility of spoof attacks when using existing state-of-the-art (SOTA) frameworks of spoof detection. Furthermore, experiments conducted with the proposed spoof detector yielded average classification error rates of 0.4% and 0.12% on the two aforementioned open databases, respectively, outperforming existing SOTA methods for spoof detection.

Keywords: spoof attack; spoof detection; finger-vein recognition; fractal dimension estimation; generative adversarial network; convolutional neural network

1. Introduction

The evolution of identity verification in security technologies can be characterized as follows: (1) methods using keys, security cards, IDs, etc. These carry the risk of loss as the item must always be carried. (2) Methods using passwords, personal identification numbers (PINs), pattern locks, etc. These require memorization and may be exposed through external factors. (3) Methods using biometric data like fingerprints, faces, irises, and finger-veins. These are advantageous for security as they are unique to each individual, require neither possession nor memorization, and are less susceptible to external exposure. With advantages such as high accuracy and convenience, biometrics has been extensively studied for application to a variety of tasks and is now used in many security fields. However, biometric recognition systems which use pattern recognition techniques to compare enrolled-user biometric images with real-time input remain vulnerable to spoof attacks that exploit stolen images or data through data breaches or hacking [1]. Therefore, there is a need for specialized research on the anti-spoofing of biometric systems.

With the advancement of deep learning technologies, spoofing techniques have also evolved. Generative adversarial networks (GANs) are being studied for their capability to train generators and discriminators in an adversarial relationship, enabling the creation of image samples that are similar to original images with respect to characteristic distribution. Although images generated by GANs typically contain a unique GAN fingerprint, so that detection is straightforward via classifiers like convolutional neural networks (CNNs), researchers have confirmed that spoof attacks are possible with post-processed generated images through the use of various low-pass filters (Gaussian filter, median filter, average filter, etc.) following the discovery of high-frequency components in existing research [2]. These findings cause biometric recognition systems to fail in detecting adversarial spoof attacks. A spoof attack on post-processed generated images can cause conventional spoof detection mechanisms to fail, leading to inaccurate results. This enables unauthorized users to repeatedly gain access to sensitive information, potentially causing significant social, organizational, and financial losses.

Accordingly, previous research has adopted cycle-consistent adversarial networks (CycleGANs) to generate finger-vein images for the training of spoof detectors [3]. However, these approaches show limitations in generating elaborate fake finger-vein image samples. To overcome this challenge, a novel method is developed for generating fake finger-vein images, as well as a corresponding spoof detector for finger-veins. By integrating the fake finger-vein images generated by our method into conventional spoof detectors for additional training, or by directly applying our proposed spoof detection method, the security level of a finger-vein recognition system can be significantly enhanced, improving its robustness against spoof attacks.

Compared with previous works, our study has the following contributions:

- To resolve the issue of the generation of less elaborate fake finger-vein images by the existing methods, our study introduces a novel method for generating elaborate fake finger-vein images that can attack conventional finger-vein-recognition systems. We propose the densely updated contrastive learning-based self-attention generative adversarial network (DCS-GAN);
- The DCS-GAN is trained using the adaptive moment estimation (Adam) optimizer with sharpness-aware minimization (SAM) to improve the model's generalization. This allows for the creation of high-quality fake images. Furthermore, by updating the loss through a comparison of generated images and real images using a DenseNet-161 that is pre-trained on finger-vein data, the model can create fake images with a distribution similar to the original ones. Additionally, the inclusion of a self-attention layer in the generator emphasizes the finger-vein patterns, enhancing the quality of the generated images;
- The performance of spoof detection is improved by an enhanced convolutional network for a next-dimension (ConvNeXt) with a large kernel attention (LKA). This not only takes into account the adaptability in the spatial dimension, inherent to traditional self-attention, but also considers adaptability in the channel dimension, thereby computing long-range correlations and improving spoof detection;
- To improve the spoof detection performance of the proposed method, we introduce fractal dimension estimation to analyze the complexity and irregularity of class activation maps from real and fake finger-vein images, enabling the generation of more realistic and sophisticated fake finger-vein images. In addition, we freely share our DCS-GAN, enhanced ConvNeXt, algorithm codes, and generated fake finger-vein images through [4], so that researchers can utilize them for further study and ensure fair evaluations.

The rest of this manuscript is organized as follows. Section 2 analyzes the existing research, while Section 3 provides a thorough explanation of the proposed method. Section 4 presents the experimental results, which are then discussed in Section 5. Finally, Section 6 concludes the study.

2. Related Work

The research on finger-vein spoof attacks and detection can be categorized into two areas: spoof attacks and spoof detection. Therefore, the existing research related to spoof attacks, relying on fabricated objects and generated images, is analyzed herein. We also categorize and examine the existing research related to spoof detection based on machine learning and deep learning.

2.1. Spoof Attack

2.1.1. Using Fake Fabricated Artifacts

Previous research on finger-vein spoof attacks has mainly used handcrafted fake images to attempt spoof attacks. Nguyen et al. [5] printed 56 real finger-vein images on three types of paper—overhead project (OHP) films, A4 paper, and matte paper—using a LaserJet printer at various resolutions: 300 (low-resolution), 1200 (middle-resolution), and 2400 (high-resolution) dots per inch (dpi). They considered the texture of the paper and details based on resolution to generate the total of 7560 fake finger-vein images. They then attached these to fingers and attempted spoof attacks. Tome et al. [6] printed 220 real images on paper using a LaserJet printer and enhanced the vein outlines using a board marker to carry out spoof attacks. Singh et al. [7] printed 468 real images on glossy paper using an inkjet printer and improved the quality of the vein patterns using an existing algorithm [8] to generate 468 fake images. Raghavendra and Busch [9] used 100 real images and printed them on LaserJet and inkjet printers and replayed them smartphone displays, creating a total of 300 fake images. Additionally, Krishnan et al. [10] used a prosthesis with an inkjet-printed finger-vein image attached and a thin rubber cap. Schuiki et al. [11] used a finger-vein image printed on a LaserJet printer and attached it to wax. However, such fabricated artifacts for print and display attacks have limitations. Although they may look similar to the original (real) images, they suffer from issues like paper texture, resolution, and noise due to the acquisition environment. Furthermore, they lack effectiveness against recently improved CNN-based spoof detectors.

2.1.2. Using Fake Generated Images

The evolving GANs, developed by many researchers, generate data via training through competition between their generator and discriminator networks. This has brought about the following positive effects. (1) They can be used as a data augmentation method in small datasets where data acquisition is difficult [12,13]. (2) They can generate labeled data in segmentation fields where labeling is challenging or expensive to carry out [14,15]. (3) They can address image degradation issues caused by low or high illumination, blur, noise, etc. [16,17]. However, the ability of GANs to produce images with high similarity to the original images has led to risks of spoof attacks in the biometric recognition field, including deep fakes. Although there has been considerable research on spoof detection against generated (fake) images in the domains of face, iris, and fingerprint recognition, there has been very little research on spoof detection for finger-vein recognition. Previous research using CycleGAN [18] to create fake finger-vein images similar to real images for spoof attacks had the drawback of not generating highly elaborate fake finger-vein images [3].

2.2. Spoof Detection

2.2.1. Machine Learning-Based Methods

Finger-vein images display low-quality characteristics, As described in Chapter 1, they contain extensive noise, including scattering blurring, as they use the pattern of veins under the skin of a finger illuminated by near-infrared (NIR) light. Therefore, conventional image processing methods have been applied in previous finger-vein spoof detection research. Raghavendra and Busch [9] applied a steerable pyramid to extract information about the various sizes and directions in finger-vein images and used a support vector machine (SVM) for spoof detection and binary classification (real or fake). Tirunagari et al. [19]

employed dynamic mode decomposition (DMD), a technique for analyzing the dynamic characteristics of data, and specifically used a windowed dynamic mode decomposition (W-DMD) approach, moving a sliding window across the entire time range of the data. Features of the images were then extracted and classified using SVM. Kocher et al. [20] employed extension binary patterns (LBP) to extract image features and performed real and fake classification through a linear SVM. Similarly, Nguyen et al. [5] translated the input images into the frequency domain through Fourier transformation (FT) to extract information about the frequency bands in the image, or decomposed the low- and high-frequency components using Haar and Daubechies wavelet transformation to extract information, and then performed spoof detection through SVM. Additionally, Bok et al. [21] extracted heart rate and blood flow signal characteristics from finger-vein videos using discrete FT and used them to train an SVM for spoof detection. However, a drawback of the aforementioned studies is the degradation of spoof detection performance due to various spoof data creation methods.

2.2.2. Deep Learning-Based Methods

Recent advancements in deep learning technology have led to research on spoof detection using CNNs. Nguyen et al. [1] used modified models of visual geometry group (VGG)-Net [22] and AlexNet [23] to extract feature maps from images. Subsequently, they performed dimensionality reduction on these feature maps with the help of principal component analysis (PCA), and conducted fake classification via SVM. Shaheed et al. [24] employed only the entry flow of Xception [25] for feature extraction and performed spoof detection through a linear SVM. Kim et al. [3] used two types of ensemble networks, denseNet-161 and denseNet-169 [26], to obtain spoof detection scores. They then conducted score-fusion via SVM to classify them as real or fake. Additionally, Singh et al. [7] utilized SfS-Net [27] to acquire two types of images: normal-map and diffuse-map. They then extracted features using texture descriptors like LBP, local phase quantization (LPQ), and binarized statistical image features (BSIF), and used a linear SVM to obtain three different spoof detection scores. They classified real and fake data through SUM-rule fusion. However, the limitation of the aforementioned methods is that they do not achieve high accuracy in the spoof detection of more elaborately generated fake finger-vein images. To mitigate this problem, a spoof detection approach using an enhanced network of ConvNeXt-Small is proposed in this study. Table 1 shows the comparisons of existing and proposed methods for spoof attack and spoof detection in finger-vein recognition.

Table 1. Comparison of existing and proposed methods for spoof attack and spoof detection in finger-vein recognition.

Category		Methods	Advantages	Disadvantages
Spoof attack	Using fake fabricated artifacts	Printed on OHP film, matte paper, and A4 paper using a LaserJet printer at resolutions of 300, 1200, 2400 dpi and then applied to the finger [5]		- The quality of the fake image is not high due to not emphasizing the vein pattern - Labor-intensive and costly to produce fabricated artifacts
		Printed using an inkjet printer and applied to a prosthesis and a thin rubber cap [10]	Considers even the curvature of the finger during the spoof attack	
		Printed using a LaserJet printer and applied to wax [11]		
		Printed using laser and inkjet printers and replayed on smartphone display [9]	Provides more realistic motion information through display replaying	
		Printed using a LaserJet printer and enhanced the vein outline with a black whiteboard marker [6]	Improved vein pattern quality by applying post-processing after printing	- Very low image quality compared to generated images - Spoof attack performance against CNN-based detector is not high
		Printed on glossy paper using an inkjet printer and enhanced the vein pattern using Ramachandra et al. [8]'s algorithm [7]		
	Using fake generated images	Generated fake finger-vein images using CycleGAN [3]	The first study to use generated finger-vein images for both spoof attack and detection	Unable to generate elaborate fake finger-vein images
		Generates fake finger-vein images using DCS-GAN (Proposed method)	Generates fake data that is similar to the characteristic distribution of original finger-vein images	Unlike the structure of the existing research model CycleGAN, requires two discriminators and a multilayered perceptron (MLP)
Spoof detection	Machine learning-based	Steerable pyramid + SVM [9]	Requires less time for training compared to deep learning-based methods	Performance degradation in spoof detection depending on various spoof data generation methods
		W-DMD + SVM [19]		
		FT, Haar and Daubechies wavelet + SVM [5]		
		Discrete FT + SVM [21]		
	Deep learning-based	Modified network of AlexNet or VGG-Net + PCA + SVM [1]	Enables diverse spoof detection through learning CNN filters for efficient feature extraction	Lower accuracy in spoof detection against elaborately created fake finger-vein images
		Xception (entry flow) + linear SVM [24]		
		Ensemble network of DenseNet-161 and DenseNet-169 + SVM [3]		
		StS-Net + linear SVM [7]		
		Enhanced network of ConvNeXt-Small (Proposed method)	- Processes in one stage, eliminating the need for a separate classifier - High accuracy in spoof detection against elaborately created fake finger-vein images	The time required for CNN training is significant

3. Proposed Method

3.1. Flow Diagram of the Proposed Method

In this subsection, an overview of the proposed model, which is depicted in Figure 1, is described. Initially, for the spoof attack procedure, we extract the region of interest (ROI) from the input finger-vein image using the preprocessing method explained in Section 3.2. The extracted ROI image is then used as an input to the DCS-GAN to generate a fake finger-vein image. Subsequently, through low-pass filtering-based image blurring, such as median filter, Gaussian filter, and average filter blurring, we remove the GAN fingerprints present in the fake sample produced by the DCS-GAN, thus creating a more elaborate fake image. In the spoof detection procedure, the finger-vein image that has undergone post-processing is used as an input to the ConvNeXt with LKA, which ultimately classifies it as either a real or fake finger-vein image.

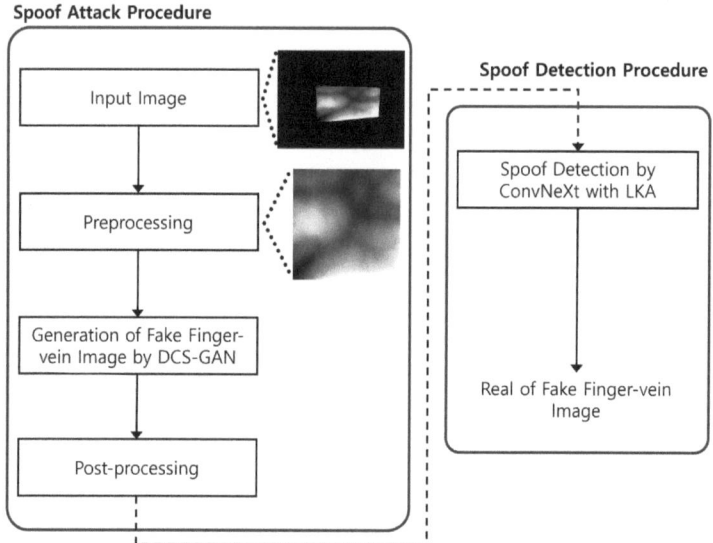

Figure 1. Overall flowchart of proposed method.

In our research, the synthesis of fake images and our model's recognition (i.e., learning) do not occur in one cycle of calculations. The synthesis of fake images (spoof attack procedure shown in Figure 1) occurs in advance. Afterwards, with the synthesized fake images, our recognition model is trained and recognizes which images are fake after the training of recognition model is finished (Spoof Detection Procedure of Figure 1). That is, the synthesis of fake images and our model's recognition (i.e., learning) are performed separately. Therefore, the recognition system which was not trained with the synthesized fake images does not know which images are fake.

3.2. The Preprocessing of the Finger-Vein Images

The preprocessing step is to remove the background and detect the finger ROI in the original finger-vein image, which serves as an input to the finger-vein recognition system. In the finger-vein recognition system, NIR lighting is used, resulting in a structure that blocks external lighting. Consequently, the areas outside the finger contain a black background. To remove this background, it is necessary to detect the finger boundaries at the top, bottom, left, and right. For detecting the left and right boundaries, this study employed the average pixel brightness. Specifically, we calculated the average pixel value along the y-axis for each x-axis position and detected the right and left boundaries based on the x-axis positions where this average value exceeded a certain threshold. Because the penetration amount of the NIR light varies depending on the skin and thickness of the user's finger, the threshold was adaptively determined on the basis of the average brightness from the input image. For the top and bottom finger boundaries, we detected the lines through filter operations using a 4 × 20 mask [28]. To address errors that may have occurred in the detection of the upper or lower boundaries, we compared the distance between the average value of all detected y-axis boundary coordinates and each detected y-axis boundary coordinate, eliminating outlier points that showed significant differences from the average, and then refined the boundary lines with the remaining points. Based on the refined boundaries, we apply bilinear interpolation to the obtained finger region to acquire the finger ROI of 224×224 pixels, which is used as the input to the pre-trained DCS-GAN.

3.3. Spoof Attack Procedure

3.3.1. Generation of Fake Finger-Vein Image Using DCS-GAN

In this study, the structure of the DCS-GAN used to produce fake finger-vein image samples is displayed in Figure 2. Detailed content about the DCS-GAN generator and discriminator is provided in Tables 2 and 3, respectively. In the DCS-GAN, the correlation between patches in the features attained by the encoder of the input real image and patches in the feature map extracted from the encoder of the generated fake image is calculated through a patch sample MLP composed of two dense layers, updating the loss. Additionally, the generator's encoder and an additional encoder share weights, enabling the maximization of mutual information by applying contrastive learning [29].

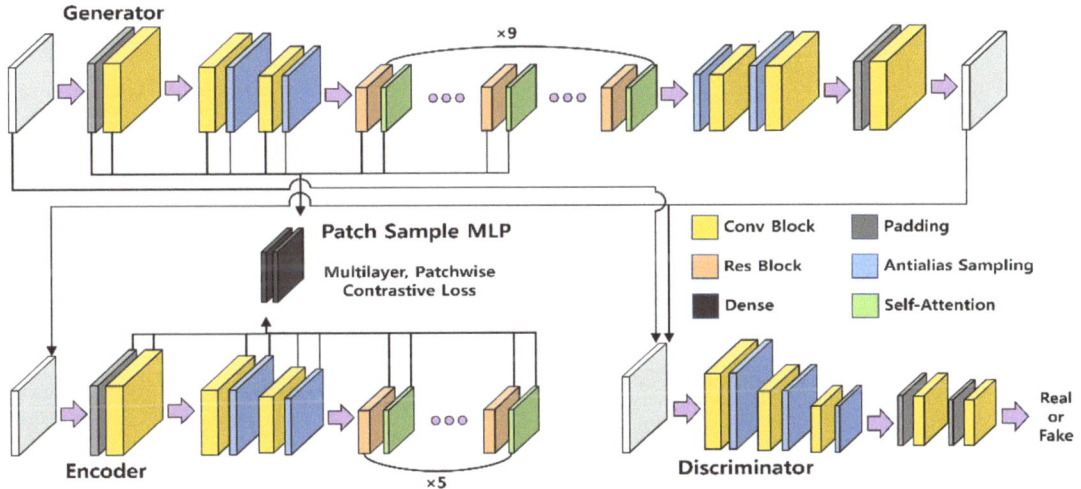

Figure 2. Architecture of DCS-GAN.

Table 2. Descriptions of the generator in the DCS-GAN (NA means "not available").

Layer Type		Kernel Size	Number of Filters	Stride	Input Size	Output Size
Input		NA	NA	NA	224 × 224 × 3	224 × 224 × 3
3 × 3 Padding (Reflect)		NA	NA	NA	224 × 224 × 3	230 × 230 × 3
1st Conv Block *	Conv	7	64	1	230 × 230 × 3	224 × 224 × 64
	Instance Norm (ReLU)	NA	NA	NA	224 × 224 × 64	224 × 224 × 64
2nd Conv Block * (ReLU)		3	128	1	224 × 224 × 64	224 × 224 × 128
Antialiasing Sampling (Down)		4	NA	NA	224 × 224 × 128	112 × 112 × 128

Table 2. *Cont.*

Layer Type		Kernel Size	Number of Filters	Stride	Input Size	Output Size
3rd Conv Block * (ReLU)		3	256	1	$112 \times 112 \times 128$	$112 \times 112 \times 256$
Antialiasing Sampling (Down)		4	NA	NA	$112 \times 112 \times 256$	$56 \times 56 \times 256$
1st Res Block	1×1 Padding (Reflect)	NA	NA	NA	$56 \times 56 \times 256$	$58 \times 58 \times 256$
	4th Conv Block * (ReLU)	3	256	1	$58 \times 58 \times 256$	$56 \times 56 \times 256$
	1×1 Padding (Reflect)	NA	NA	NA	$56 \times 56 \times 256$	$58 \times 58 \times 256$
	5th Conv Block * (Linear)	3	256	1	$58 \times 58 \times 256$	$56 \times 56 \times 256$
1st Self-attention		NA	NA	NA	$56 \times 56 \times 256$	$56 \times 56 \times 256$
2nd–8th Res Blocks with Self-attentions		NA	NA	NA	$56 \times 56 \times 256$	$56 \times 56 \times 256$
9th Res Block		3	256	1	$56 \times 56 \times 256$	$56 \times 56 \times 256$
9th Self-attention		NA	NA	NA	$56 \times 56 \times 256$	$56 \times 56 \times 256$
Antialiasing Sampling (Up)		4	NA	NA	$56 \times 56 \times 256$	$112 \times 112 \times 256$
22nd Conv Block * (ReLU)		3	128	1	$112 \times 112 \times 256$	$112 \times 112 \times 128$
Antialiasing Sampling (Up)		4	NA	NA	$112 \times 112 \times 128$	$224 \times 224 \times 128$
23rd Conv Block * (ReLU)		3	64	1	$224 \times 224 \times 128$	$224 \times 224 \times 64$
3×3 Padding (Reflect)		NA	NA	NA	$224 \times 224 \times 64$	$230 \times 230 \times 64$
24th Conv Block (Tanh)		7	3	1	$230 \times 230 \times 64$	$224 \times 224 \times 3$
Output		NA	NA	NA	$224 \times 224 \times 3$	$224 \times 224 \times 3$

* indicates that instance normalization is included after the corresponding layer.

Table 3. Descriptions of the discriminator in the DCS-GAN (NA means "not available").

Layer	Kernel Size	Number of Filters	Stride	Input Size	Output Size
Input	NA	NA	NA	$224 \times 224 \times 3$	$224 \times 224 \times 3$
25th Conv Block (Leaky ReLU)	4	64	1	$224 \times 224 \times 3$	$224 \times 224 \times 64$
Antialiasing Sampling (Down)	4	NA	n/1	$224 \times 224 \times 64$	$112 \times 112 \times 64$
26th Conv Block * (Leaky ReLU)	4	128	1	$112 \times 112 \times 64$	$112 \times 112 \times 128$
Antialiasing Sampling (Down)	4	NA	NA	$112 \times 112 \times 128$	$56 \times 56 \times 128$
27th Conv Block * (Leaky ReLU)	4	256	1	$56 \times 56 \times 128$	$56 \times 56 \times 256$
Antialiasing Sampling (Down)	4	NA	NA	$56 \times 56 \times 256$	$28 \times 28 \times 256$
1×1 Padding (Constant)	NA	NA	NA	$28 \times 28 \times 256$	$30 \times 30 \times 256$
28th Conv Block * (Leaky ReLU)	4	512	1	$30 \times 30 \times 256$	$27 \times 27 \times 512$
1×1 Padding (Constant)	NA	NA	NA	$27 \times 27 \times 512$	$29 \times 29 \times 512$
29th Conv Block (Linear)	4	1	1	$29 \times 29 \times 512$	$26 \times 26 \times 1$
Output	NA	NA	NA	$26 \times 26 \times 1$	$26 \times 26 \times 1$

* indicates that instance normalization is included after the corresponding layer.

When acquiring finger-vein images, a NIR camera is used to capture the finger-vein, which is illuminated by NIR light, and the acquired images will show fingerprint marks. In this study, we improved the image reality by adding self-attention [30] after each residual block, as indicated in Table 2, to both preserve the fingerprint texture and emphasize the patterns of veins in the fake image.

$$Attention(Q, K, V) = softmax\left(\frac{QK^T}{\sqrt{d_k}}\right)V \quad (1)$$

Equation (1) relates to self-attention, where the query, key, and value are represented by Q, K, and V, respectively. A query is an information vector generated at a specific location in the input data, and a key represents an information vector generated at another location in the input data. A value represents the actual information generated at each location in the input data. First, the similarity (relevance) is computed through the dot product between the query and key (QK^T), and scaling by $\sqrt{d_k}$ is applied for smoother model training. Second, a softmax activation function is applied to obtain the probability distribution, which is finally applied to the input data (V) as a self-attention map to emphasize relevant information.

For training the DCS-GAN, we used SAM [31] along with Adam [32] as the optimizer. Adam, which is widely used in existing research, generally offers excellent performance in training data compared with other optimizers, but it poses the risk of overfitting, leading to weaker performance on validation and testing data [33]. SAM helps to reach global minima by smoothing sharp minima during training. As a result, the model can avoid the risk of overfitting (i.e., not being overly tailored to training data) and show improved generalization performance on new data. Therefore, using SAM and Adam together, we were able to improve the generalization performance, which is crucial in generative models, and generate high-quality images. Equations (2)–(6) describe the operations of SAM.

$$L_D(\omega) \leq L_S(\omega + \epsilon) + h(\|\omega\|_2^2/\sigma^2) \quad (2)$$

$$L_D(\omega) \leq \max_{\|\epsilon\|_2 \leq \sigma} [L_S(\omega + \epsilon) - L_S(\omega)] + L_S(\omega) + h(\|\omega\|_2^2/\sigma^2) \quad (3)$$

$$L_S^{SAM}(\omega) + \mu \|\omega\|_2^2 \text{ where } L_S^{SAM}(\omega) \triangleq L_S(\omega + \epsilon) \quad (4)$$

$$\nabla_\omega L_S^{SAM}(\omega) \approx \nabla_\omega L_S(\omega + \hat{\epsilon}(\omega)) = \frac{d(\omega + \hat{\epsilon}(\omega))}{d\omega} \nabla_\omega L_S(\omega)|_{\omega + \hat{\epsilon}(\omega)}$$
$$= \nabla_\omega L_S(\omega)|_{\omega + \hat{\epsilon}(\omega)} + \frac{d\hat{\epsilon}(\omega)}{d(\omega)} \nabla_\omega L_S(\omega)|_{\omega + \hat{\epsilon}(\omega)} \quad (5)$$

$$\nabla_\omega L_S^{SAM}(\omega) \approx \nabla_\omega L_S(\omega)|_{\omega + \hat{\epsilon}(\omega)} \quad (6)$$

In Equations (2) and (3), ω is the vector of the classifier parameters, and h is a strictly increasing function. One of the differences between Equations (2) and (3) is that $L_S(\omega)$ is added in Equation (3). In this model, the term $\max_{\|\epsilon\|_2 \leq \sigma}[L_S(\omega + \epsilon) - L_S(\omega)]$ represents the sharpness, indicating the level of variation in the loss value when ω is altered by ϵ, while the term $L_S(\omega)$ signifies the loss value of the training data, as in other existing methods. Additionally, the term $h(\|\omega\|_2^2/\sigma^2)$ represents the term of regularization related to the size of ω. Here, the term of regularization employs an L2 regularizer. As a result, both the sharpness and training loss are minimized, enabling the model to find a relatively flat region. On the basis of this, the problem of selecting optimal parameter values for solving the SAM drawback is formulated in Equation (4). Consequently, while the SAM loss would be calculated as shown in Equation (5), the term $\frac{d\hat{\epsilon}(\omega)}{d(\omega)} \nabla_\omega L_S(\omega)|_{\omega + \hat{\epsilon}(\omega)}$ involves calculating the Hessian matrix, which is computationally expensive and thus not used to avoid slowing down the training. Therefore, Equation (6) becomes the final SAM loss.

To address the issue of the vanishing gradient in the generator caused by the sigmoid cross-entropy loss function that is traditionally employed to train the discriminator in GANs, Mao et al. [34] updated the generator by using the least square loss. This computes the distances between the distributions of the original samples not as divergence but as a least square error, thus penalizing the image samples that are not close to the decision boundary and enabling the generation of samples closer to real images. For that reason, we selected the least squares GAN (LSGAN) loss for smooth training of the GAN.

$$L_{Discriminator}(G_{en}, D_{is}, X, Y) = \frac{1}{2}\mathbb{E}_{y \sim Y}\left[(D_{is}(y) - b)^2\right] + \frac{1}{2}\mathbb{E}_{x \sim X}\left[(D_{is}(G_{en}(x)) - a)^2\right] \quad (7)$$

$$L_{Generator}(G_{en}, D_{is}, X) = \frac{1}{2}\mathbb{E}_{x \sim X}\left[(D_{is}(G_{en}(x)) - c)^2\right] \quad (8)$$

Equation (7) describes the LSGAN formulation used for training the DCS-GAN discriminator in this study, where a and b, respectively, denote the labels for fake and real images, and D_{is} and G_{en} represent the discriminator model and the generator model. To minimize the value of this equation, the term $\frac{1}{2}\mathbb{E}_{y \sim Y}\left[(D_{is}(y) - b)^2\right]$ must become $D_{is}(y) = b$, and in $\frac{1}{2}\mathbb{E}_{x \sim X}\left[(D_{is}(G_{en}(x)) - a)^2\right]$, $D_{is}(G_{en}(x)) = a$ must be achieved. More specifically, Equation (7) ensures that the discriminator model correctly classifies real images as y, the real image label, and fake images generated by the generator as x, the fake image label. Conversely, Equation (8) is for training the generator, and to minimize its value, $\frac{1}{2}\mathbb{E}_{x \sim X}\left[(D_{is}(G_{en}(x)) - c)^2\right]$ in the term must become $D_{is}(G_{en}(x)) = c$. Essentially, the data generated as $c \neq a$ finger-vein images should not be classified by the discriminator as having fake image labels.

In this study, besides the typical generator and discriminator constituting a GAN, we also employed a separate encoder section of the generator and an additional patch sample MLP to maximize the amount of mutual information. Based on this, we calculated a multilayer, patchwise contrastive loss aimed at correlating the same patches in the feature maps of real and fake images while not correlating the different patches, as shown in Equation (9).

$$L_{Patch}\left(G_{en}, M_{lp}, X\right) = \mathbb{E}_{x \sim X}\sum_{l=1}^{L}\sum_{s=1}^{S_l} \updownarrow\left(\hat{z}_l^s, z_l^s, z_l^{S/s}\right) \quad (9)$$

In Equation (9), M_{lp} is the MLP, L denotes the number of layers as $l \in \{1,2,3,\ldots,L\}$, and S denotes the number of spatial locations as $s \in \{1,2,3,\ldots,S\}$. Therefore, the term $\mathbb{E}_{x \sim X}\sum_{l=1}^{L}\sum_{s=1}^{S_l} \updownarrow\left(\hat{z}_l^s, z_l^s, z_l^{S/s}\right)$ results from inputting the output feature maps from the layers of the encoder into the MLP by using their spatial locations. The obtained feature map is then encoded into the image that is output from the generator.

In the case of GANs for general image-to-image translation, the main objective lies in mapping the input images to the output images while preserving their shapes but altering their internal structures. However, our objective is to generate fake images through GANs that the conventional finger-vein spoof detector cannot distinguish from input real images. Therefore, we have additionally applied perceptual loss [35] that allows for the comparison of feature maps between input real images and output fake images. The conventional perceptual loss employs a VGG-16 model pre-trained on ImageNet. As this study aims to spoof attack detection for finger-vein images, DenseNet-161 [3], pre-trained on real and fake finger-vein images, is used as a feature extractor.

$$L_{perceptual}(G_{en}, X, Y) = \frac{1}{H_{i,j}W_{i,j}C_{i,j}}\sum_{h=1}^{H_{i,j}}\sum_{w=1}^{W_{i,j}}\sum_{c=1}^{C_{i,j}}(\varnothing_{i,j}(G_{en}(x))_{h,w,c} - \varnothing_{i,j}(y)_{h,w,c})^2 \quad (10)$$

In Equation (10), $\varnothing_{i,j}$ refers to the feature map obtained after the jth convolution and before the ith maxpooling in the pre-trained DenseNet-161 model. $H_{i,j}$, $W_{i,j}$, and $C_{i,j}$ represent the dimensions of the feature map, respectively. Therefore, the term $(\varnothing_{i,j}(G_{en}(x))_{h,w,c} - \varnothing_{i,j}(y)_{h,w,c})^2$ signifies the Euclidean distance between the generated fake image sample and the real sample. Finally, Equation (11) combines Equations (8) and (10) to represent the loss used for training the generator in this study.

$$L_{Generator}(G_{en}, D_{is}, X) + L_{Patch}\left(G_{en}, M_{lp}, X\right) + L_{perceptual}(G_{en}, X, Y) \qquad (11)$$

In this study, to generate fake images that are as similar as possible to real images, we used real images as the input images during the DCS-GAN training process. For the target image, we excluded the input image itself and used one of the remaining real images within the input image's intra-class. The target image was randomly chosen to facilitate smooth learning through the use of diverse inputs. Figure 3 represents the samples of inputs for the DCS-GAN.

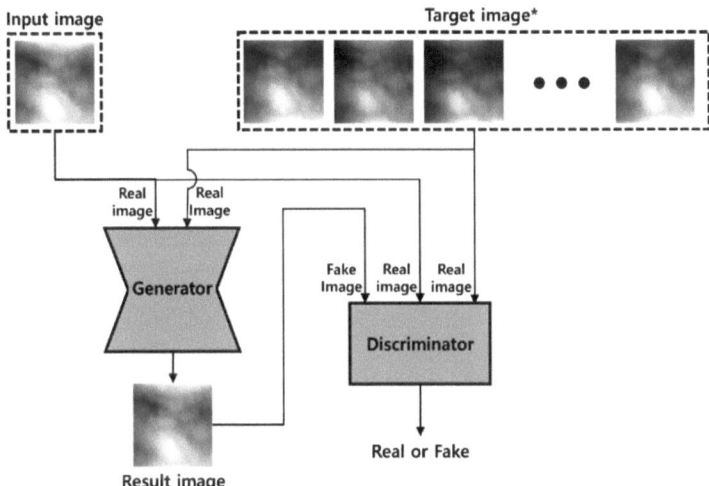

Figure 3. Samples for the selection of input and target image for training the generator and discriminator of DCS-GAN. * denotes one image randomly chosen in the intra-class of the input image, excluding the input image.

3.3.2. The Post-Processing Stage for the Generation of Fake Finger-Vein Images

In the spoof attack procedure in Figure 1, post-processing involves removing the traces of fake image generation. Previously, synthetic images generated by GANs contained a 'GAN fingerprint,' so spoof detection was relatively straightforward. However, researchers have found that such high-frequency components can be removed by low-pass filters like the median filter, Gaussian filter, and average filter [2]. Due to this, the risk of spoofing through GANs has increased. Therefore, in this study, we applied the Gaussian filter, median filter, and average filter individually and compared their effects on the spoof detection performance.

3.4. Spoof Detection Procedure
Spoof Detection of Fake-Vein Image by Enhanced ConvNeXt

In this study, we chose ConvNeXt-Small [36] as the base model for detecting fake finger-vein images. ConvNeXt achieves SOTA performance through various improvements such as the use of a stage compute ratio, stem layer (patchify), and inverted bottleneck. For these reasons, and considering computational efficiency, we used ConvNeXt-Small as the base model for spoof detection in this study. ConvNeXt-Small consists of a structure with ConvNeXt Block (1) × 3, ConvNeXt Block (2) × 3, ConvNeXt Block (3) × 27, and ConvNeXt Block (4) × 3. Here, ConvNeXt Blocks (1)–(4) are different blocks, and the × number indicates the number of repetitions. Unlike conventional CNN models, ConvNeXt Blocks utilize a 7 × 7-size kernel to expand the receptive field, thereby enhancing the model's performance. To further improve the performance of the existing ConvNeXt model, this study proposes an enhanced ConvNeXt-Small model that additionally employs LKA [37] after the last ConvNeXt Block to enable self-adaptation and long-range correlations. This allows emphasized feature maps to be transmitted to the classifier for the spoof detection problem, which involves real or fake classification (binary classification). The structure of the enhanced ConvNeXt-Small is detailed in Figure 4 and Table 4.

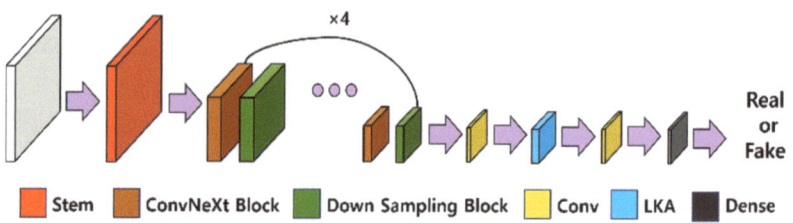

Figure 4. Architecture of enhanced ConvNeXt-Small.

Table 4. Descriptions of enhanced ConvNeXt-Small (NA means "not available").

Layer		Number of Blocks	Kernel Size	Number of Filters	Stride	Input Size	Output Size
Input		NA	NA	NA	NA	224 × 224 × 3	224 × 224 × 3
Stem	Conv *	NA	4 × 4	96	4	224 × 224 × 3	56 × 56 × 96
1st ConvNeXt Block	Depthwise Conv *	3	7 × 7	96	1	56 × 56 × 96	56 × 56 × 96
	Dense (GELU)		1 × 1	384	1	56 × 56 × 96	56 × 56 × 384
	Dense		1 × 1	96	1	56 × 56 × 384	56 × 56 × 96
1st Down Sampling Block	Layer Norm	1	NA	NA	NA	56 × 56 × 96	56 × 56 × 96
	Conv		2 × 2	192	2	56 × 56 × 96	28 × 28 × 192
2nd ConvNeXt Block		3	7 × 7	192	1	28 × 28 × 192	28 × 28 × 192
			1 × 1	768	1	28 × 28 × 192	28 × 28 × 768
			1 × 1	192	1	28 × 28 × 768	28 × 28 × 192
2nd Down Sampling Block		1	NA	NA	NA	28 × 28 × 192	28 × 28 × 192
			2 × 2	384	2	28 × 28 × 192	14 × 14 × 384
3rd ConvNeXt Block		27	7 × 7	384	1	14 × 14 × 384	14 × 14 × 384
			1 × 1	1536	1	14 × 14 × 384	14 × 14 × 1536
			1 × 1	384	1	14 × 14 × 1536	14 × 14 × 384
3rd Down Sampling Block		1	NA	NA	NA	14 × 14 × 384	14 × 14 × 384
			2 × 2	768	2	14 × 14 × 384	7 × 7 × 768
4th ConvNeXt Block		3	7 × 7	768	1	7 × 7 × 768	7 × 7 × 768
			1 × 1	3072	1	7 × 7 × 768	7 × 7 × 3072
			1 × 1	768	1	7 × 7 × 3072	7 × 7 × 768
Conv (GELU)		NA	1 × 1	768	1	7 × 7 × 768	7 × 7 × 768
LKA	Conv	NA	5 × 5	768	1	7 × 7 × 768	7 × 7 × 768
	Dilation Conv	NA	7 × 7	768	1	7 × 7 × 768	7 × 7 × 768
	Conv	NA	1 × 1	768	1	7 × 7 × 768	7 × 7 × 768
	multiply	NA	NA	NA	NA	7 × 7 × 768	7 × 7 × 768
Conv		NA	1 × 1	768	1	7 × 7 × 768	7 × 7 × 768
Add		NA	NA	NA	NA	7 × 7 × 768	7 × 7 × 768
Global Average Pooling		NA	NA	NA	NA	7 × 7 × 768	768
Dense (Softmax)		NA	NA	2	NA	768	2

* indicates that layer normalization is included after the corresponding layer.

3.5. Fractal Dimension Estimation

Fractals are complex structures that display self-similarity and diverge from traditional geometric rules [38]. The fractal dimension (FD) quantifies the complexity of a shape, indicating whether it is more concentrated or dispersed. In this study, a binary image representing the activated region of finger-vein images (real or fake) is used for FD estimation. The FD in this context ranges between almost one and two, reflecting different degrees of complexity. This range encompasses various representations of binary class activation maps (BCAMs), with higher FD values corresponding to greater shape intricacy. The FD for the activated region is calculated using the box-counting method [39,40], where C represents the number of boxes that evenly cover each activated region, and δ is the scaling factor of the boxes. The FD is determined using Equation (12).

$$FD = \lim_{\delta \to 0} \frac{\log(C(\delta))}{\log(1/\delta)} \quad (12)$$

where $1 \leq FD \leq 2$, and for all $\delta > 0$, there exists a $C(\delta)$. The pseudocode for estimating the FD of the activated part of the finger-vein image using the box-counting method is provided in Algorithm 1.

Algorithm 1 Pseudocode for Fractal Dimension (FD) Estimation

Input: *BCAM:* Binary class activation map extracted from DSC-GAN's encoder
Output: FD: Fractal dimension
1: Find the largest dimension of the box size and adjust it to the nearest power of 2
Max_dimension = max(size(*BCAM*))
$\delta = 2^{\lceil \log_2(Max\_dimension) \rceil}$
2: If the size is smaller than δ, pad the image to match δ's dimension
    if size(*BCAM*) < size(δ)
        Pad_width = ((0, δ − *BCAM*.shape [0]), (0, δ − *BCAM*.shape [1]))
        Pad_ BCAM= pad(*BCAM*, *Pad_width*, mode = 'constant', constant_values = 0)
    else
        Pad_ BCAM = *BCAM*
3: Initialize an array to store the number of boxes corresponding to each dimension size
n = zeros(1, δ + 1)
4: Compute the number of boxes, $C(\delta)$ containing at least one pixel of the positive region
$n[\delta + 1]$ = sum(*BCAM*[:])
5: While $\delta > 1$:
    a. Divide the size of δ by 2
    b. Reassign the number of boxes $C(\delta)$
6: Compute the $\log(C(\delta))$ and $\log(\delta)$ for each δ
7: Fit a line to the points [($\log(\delta)$, $\log(C(\delta))$] using the least squares method
8: The fractal dimension (FD) is found by the slope of the fitted line
Return FD

---

4. Experimental Results

4.1. Experimental Database and Setups

For the performance evaluation of the DCS-GAN for generating fake finger-vein images in the spoof attack procedure and the enhanced ConvNeXt-Small for detecting forgeries in the spoof detection procedure, we used real finger-vein images from two open databases: the ISPR database [1] and the Idiap database [41]. The ISPR database consists of a total of 3300 real images captured from all fingers of both hands of 33 individuals, each captured 10 times (10 trials × 33 individuals × 2 hands × 5 fingers). The Idiap database comprises a total of 440 real images captured from the index fingers from both hands of 110 individuals, each captured twice (2 trials × 110 individuals × 2 hands × 1 finger). In Table 5, a description of the ISPR and Idiap databases is presented, and Figure 5 shows examples from both databases.

Table 5. Detailed description of the ISPR and Idiap databases.

Database	Number of Trials	Number of Individuals	Number of Hands	Number of Fingers	Total Number of Images
ISPR	10	33	2	5	3300
Idiap	2	110	2	1	440

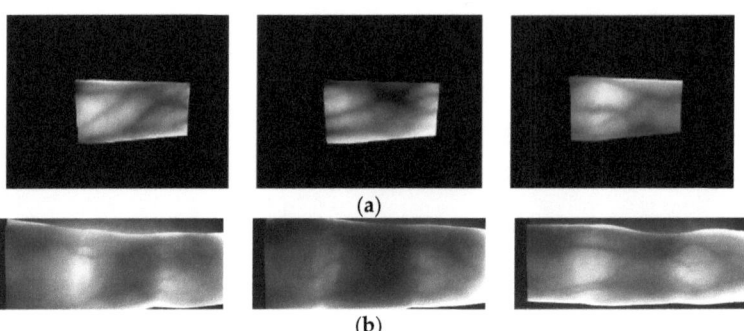

Figure 5. Sample images of real finger-veins in the databases. (**a**) Examples from the ISPR database and (**b**) examples from the Idiap database.

The experimental work of this study was performed using a desktop computer equipped with an Intel® Core (TM) i7-9700F central processing unit (CPU) operating at 3.0 GHz, supplemented by 32 GB of RAM and an NVIDIA GeForce RTX 3060 graphics processing unit (GPU). This graphics card includes 3584 compute unified device architecture (CUDA) cores and has a total of 12 GB of dedicated graphics memory [42].

4.2. Training of the Proposed Networks

All experiments in this study were carried out using two-fold cross-validation. Specifically, in the first fold validation, half of the total data were used for training of the network, while the remaining half were used to test the network. In the second fold validation, this was reversed. The final testing accuracy was calculated by averaging the testing accuracies from the two folds. From the training data, 10% of the data were used as a validation set to avoid model overfitting. For effective training, the ISPR database images were resized to 256 × 256 and then subjected to random crop augmentation to a size of 224 × 224. Particularly, in the Idiap database, due to the high risk of overfitting with the use of only 440 real images, each real image was subjected to 10-pixel shifts in all four directions (up, down, left, and right), resulting in a total of 1760 training images (440 images × 4 directions). Figure 6 shows examples of the shift augmentation applied to the Idiap database.

4.2.1. Training of DCS-GAN for Spoof Attack

For the spoof attack procedure, the DCS-GAN was trained for the generation of fake images that are similar to the real images. The initial learning rate was set at 0.0002, and it decayed at a rate of 0.9 every 10,000 steps, completing a total of 400 epochs. Table 6 provides details about the training parameters. Figure 7a refers to the training loss graphs for both the generator and the discriminator. This graph indicate sufficiently converged training results from the training split. Figure 7b displays the validation loss graphs for the generator and the discriminator, confirming that the DCS-GAN did not overfit on the training data.

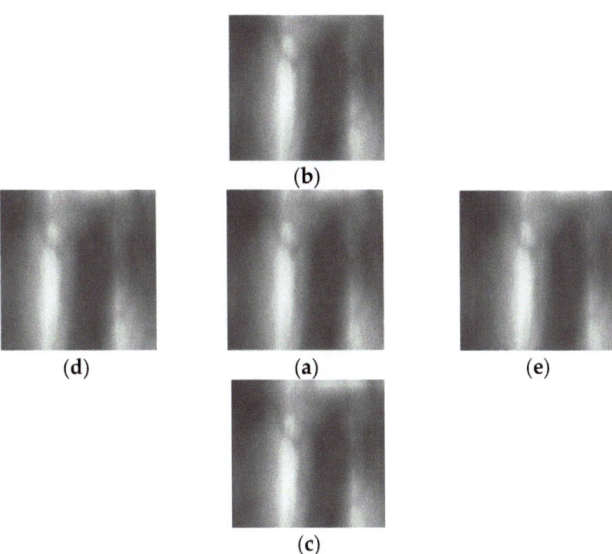

Figure 6. Examples of data augmentation on the Idiap database. (**a**) Original image, (**b**) image shifted upward, (**c**) image shifted downward, (**d**) image shifted to the left, (**e**) image shifted to the right.

Table 6. Hyperparameters used to train DCS-GAN.

Parameter Types	Value
Learning decay step	10,000
Learning decay rate	0.9
Learning rate	2×10^{-4}
Optimizer	Adam + SAM
Beta 1	0.5
Beta 2	0.999
Batch size	1
Epochs	400
Adversarial loss	LSGAN
Additional loss	Patch, Perceptual

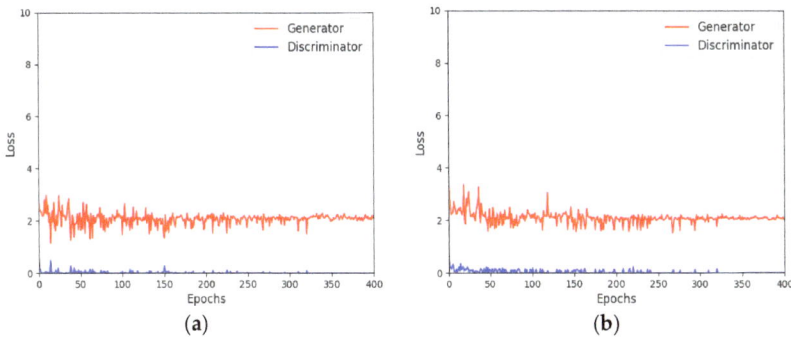

Figure 7. Graphs for the training and validation loss of DCS-GAN. (**a**) Training loss graph of the generator and the discriminator. (**b**) Validation loss graph of the generator and the discriminator.

4.2.2. Training of Enhanced ConvNeXt-Small for Spoof Detection

In the procedures for detecting spoof attacks with fake finger-vein images obtained by the DCS-GAN, Adam was used as the optimizer and cross-entropy loss was employed as the loss function. Table 7 details the training parameters.

Table 7. Hyperparameters used to train enhanced ConvNeXt-Small.

Parameter Types	Value
Learning decay step	None
Learning decay rate	None
Learning rate	1×10^{-6}
Beta 1	0.9
Beta 2	0.999
Epsilon	1×10^{-7}
Batch size	4
Epochs	30
Loss	Cross entropy

To train the enhanced ConvNeXt-Small for spoof detection, we mixed the original (real) images with the generated (fake) images from the DCS-GAN and trained it with two-fold cross validation. Figure 8a presents the resulting training accuracy and loss graphs for the enhanced ConvNeXt-Small. This demonstrates that, with the increase in epochs, both the accuracy and loss converge, indicating sufficient training on the data. Figure 8b presents the validation accuracy and loss graphs of the enhanced ConvNeXt-Small, confirming that the model has not overfitted on the training data.

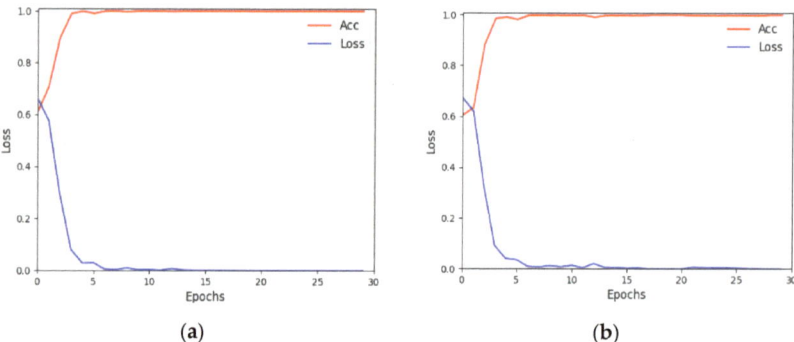

Figure 8. Training and validation accuracy (Acc) and loss (Loss) graphs of the enhanced ConvNeXt-Small. (**a**) Training accuracy and loss graphs. (**b**) Validation accuracy and loss graphs.

4.3. Testing of Proposed Model
4.3.1. Evaluation Metrics

In this study, the quality of the generated images by the GAN was evaluated using the Frechet inception distance (FID) [43] as per Equation (13), which was commonly used in previous research [3,29]. Additionally, the Wasserstein distance [44] was also used to evaluate the quality of uneven illumination-corrected vein images as in Equation (14) [17]. The quality was assessed by comparing real (original) images with fake (generated) images.

$$FID = \left| \mu_{real} - \mu_{fake} \right|^2 + Tr\left(\sum\nolimits_{real} + \sum\nolimits_{fake} - 2 \sum\nolimits_{real} \sum\nolimits_{fake} \right) \qquad (13)$$

$$WD_p(\mathbb{P}, \mathbb{Q}) = \left(\inf_{\gamma \in \Pi(P,Q)} \int_{\mathbb{R}^d \times \mathbb{R}^d} \left| I_{real} - I_{fake} \right|^p d\gamma \right)^{1/p} \qquad (14)$$

In Equation (13), μ_{real} and μ_{fake} represent the average pixel values of the real and fake image samples, respectively; Tr represents the diagonal sum function obtained from Inception-v3, pre-trained on ImageNet; and Σ_{real} and Σ_{fake} represent the covariance matrices. In Equation (14), $\Pi(P, Q)$ signifies the joint probability distribution, $\mathbb{R}^d \times \mathbb{R}^d$ represents the marginal probability distribution, and $d\gamma$ denote the measure according to the joint distribution γ.

To test the performance of the model's spoof detection, we used the attack presentation classification error rate (APCER), as per Equation (15), according to the ISO/IEC-30107 standard [45]. We also used the bona fide presentation classification error rate (BPCER) in Equation (16) to indicate the error rate of incorrectly classifying real images as fake. Additionally, the average classification error rate (ACER) was calculated using Equation (17), representing the average error rate between the APCER and BPCER.

$$APCER = 1 - (\frac{1}{I_{fake}}) \sum_{i=1}^{I_{fake}} Detector_i \quad (15)$$

$$BPCER = \frac{1}{I_{real}} \sum_{i=1}^{I_{real}} Detector_i \quad (16)$$

$$ACER = \frac{1}{2}(APCER + BPCER) \quad (17)$$

I_{real} refers to the number of real (original) images, and I_{fake} refers to that of fake (generated) images. Additionally, $Detector_i$ refers to the predicted labels obtained from the spoof detector. Therefore, in Equation (15), i takes a value of 1 if a fake image is correctly classified, and in the case of incorrect classification, a value of 0 is assigned. In Equation (16), i takes a value of 0 if a real image is correctly classified, and in the case of incorrect classification, a value of 1 is assigned.

4.3.2. Performance Test of the Spoof Attack

4.3.2.1. Ablation Studies

As the foremost step of our ablation study to measure the performance of the spoof attack, we compared the performance by incrementally removing the key modules of the DCS-GAN through the ISPR database. As indicated in Table 8, we confirmed that the WD metric by the CUT model (without SAM and self-attention) with a Dense perceptual was the best, but that the FID metric by the DCS-GAN model was the best. However, the goal of this research is to improve the performance of attacks against spoofing detectors. The FID metric reflects the performance of spoofing attacks against spoof detector CNNs, and it uses features obtained from pre-trained Inception V3 models [46]. The WD metric is usually used to evaluate the simple quality of uneven illumination-corrected images based on differences in pixel distribution [17]. Therefore, the FID metric can provide a more accurate measure of performance than the WD. To check the quality of the fake finger-vein images, we evaluated their effectiveness in spoof attacks using existing finger-vein spoof detectors. Specifically, we used DenseNet-161 and DenseNet-169, as in previous research [3], to evaluate the images' performance using the ACER metric on the generated images as listed in Table 8. As is evident from Table 9, the DCS-GAN model with all proposed modules generated fake images that yielded the highest spoof detection error rates: an average ACER of 1.05% for DenseNet-161 and 1.03% for DenseNet-169. This confirms that our fully equipped DCS-GAN model produces fake images that are the most similar to real images. For the next ablation study, we compared our results with the performance of data augmentation techniques applied to the Idiap database, for which there was a shortage of real images during DCS-GAN training. As demonstrated in Table 10, applying data augmentation via random cropping from 256 × 256 to 224 × 224 and shifting in four directions (up, down, left, right) resulted in the highest performance.

Table 8. Performance variation depending on the modules composing DCS-GAN ("Perceptual" refers to the cases where pre-trained VGG-16 was used for calculating perceptual loss as per Equation (10), and "Dense perceptual" indicates the cases where DenseNet-161 [3] was used in the same manner).

Perceptual Loss	Dense Perceptual	SAM	Self-Attention	FID			WD		
				1-Fold Validation	2-Fold Validation	Average	1-Fold Validation	2-Fold Validation	Average
				19.261	25.869	22.565	30.380	7.010	18.695
✓				16.365	18.927	17.646	19.576	7.180	13.378
	✓			13.149	14.689	13.919	4.286	6.428	5.357
	✓	✓		12.283	5.457	8.870	25.039	20.554	22.797
	✓	✓	✓	8.531	5.671	7.101	19.782	17.050	18.416

Table 9. Comparison of spoof attack performance by generated images on DenseNet-161 and DenseNet-169 ("Perceptual" refers to the cases where pre-trained VGG-16 was used for calculating perceptual loss as per Equation (10), and "Dense perceptual" indicates the cases where DenseNet-161 [3] was used in the same manner) (metric: ACER, unit: %).

Classification Model	Generation Model				1-Fold Validation	2-Fold Validation	Average
	Perceptual Loss	Dense Perceptual	SAM	Self-Attention			
					0.27	0.27	0.27
	✓				0.36	0.33	0.35
DenseNet-161		✓			0.46	0.49	0.48
		✓	✓		0.73	0.79	0.76
		✓	✓	✓	0.94	1.15	1.05
					0.36	0.42	0.39
	✓				0.64	0.70	0.67
DenseNet-169		✓			0.67	0.73	0.70
		✓	✓		0.73	0.82	0.77
		✓	✓	✓	1.06	1.00	1.03

Table 10. Comparison of fake image generation performance depending on data augmentation (# means "number of" and × means "none").

Augmentation		FID			WD		
Random Crop	# Directions for Shift	1-Fold Validation	2-Fold Validation	Average	1-Fold Validation	2-Fold Validation	Average
256 → 224	×	29.579	26.997	28.288	40.141	61.686	50.914
300 → 224		27.765	26.571	27.168	35.086	37.973	36.530
256 → 224	2	30.377	26.366	28.372	20.282	40.532	30.407
300 → 224		30.062	23.533	26.798	30.382	46.741	38.562
256 → 224	4	24.810	21.891	23.351	8.614	11.632	10.123
300 → 224		27.548	24.965	26.257	28.814	50.336	39.575
256 → 224	8	25.685	28.129	26.907	16.505	18.805	17.655
300 → 224		27.702	24.758	26.230	24.214	25.905	25.060

For the next ablation study, we compared our results to those of spoof detection performance based on the post-processing described in Section 3.3.2. All spoof detection training in this work was performed under the assumption that the actual conditions of spoof attacks were unknown, specifically how the fake images were generated. We trained our model using fake images without post-processing, while fake images with post-processing were only used for testing. The experimental results, as shown in Table 11, reveal that fake images generated from the ISPR database and post-processed with a median 5 × 5 filter led to the highest spoof detection errors: 5.74% for DenseNet-161 and 7.31% for DenseNet-169. Specifically, post-processing with the median 5 × 5 filter produced fake images that were the most similar to real images, hindering the spoof detection. For all subsequent experiments using the ISPR database, we used images post-processed with the median 5 × 5 filter. Additionally, as shown in Table 12, the fake images generated from the Idiap database and post-processed with the Gaussian 3 × 3 filter also exhibited the highest spoof detection errors: 2.5% for both DenseNet-161 and DenseNet-169. Hence, using the Gaussian 3 × 3 filter for post-processing produced the fake images that were the most similar to real images, effectively challenging the spoof detection. For all subsequent experiments using the Idiap database, we used images post-processed with the Gaussian 3 × 3 filter.

Table 11. Comparison of spoof attack performance by type of post-processing on DenseNet-161 and DenseNet-169 using the ISPR database (metric: ACER, unit: %).

Classification Model	Post Processing	Kernel Size	1-Fold Validation	2-Fold Validation	Average
DenseNet-161	Average filter	3 × 3	0.30	0.49	0.40
		5 × 5	0.06	0.09	0.08
	Gaussian filter	3 × 3	0.85	1.33	1.09
		5 × 5	0.18	0.30	0.24
	Median filter	3 × 3	3.49	3.67	3.58
		5 × 5	6.25	5.22	5.74
DenseNet-169	Average filter	3 × 3	0.70	0.64	0.67
		5 × 5	0.24	0.42	0.33
	Gaussian filter	3 × 3	0.64	0.94	0.79
		5 × 5	0.36	0.40	0.38
	Median filter	3 × 3	2.31	3.09	2.70
		5 × 5	8.04	6.58	7.31

4.3.2.2. Comparing Image Quality by the Proposed and SOTA Approaches

We compared the similarities between both fake images generated by our DCS-GAN and real (original) images and those generated by the SOTA methods. As shown in Table 13, the DCS-GAN outperformed all other methods when it was evaluated using the FID metric. In contrast, when using the WD metric, Pix2Pix or Pix2PixHD showed the highest results. As explained in Section 4.3.2.1, the FID metric provides a more accurate measure of performance than the WD metric. In some evaluation metrics, the difference between the DCS-GAN and SOTA methods is small. However, the final goal of this study is to generate more realistic fake images, which makes detecting spoof attacks more difficult than it is when using the SOTA methods, and this was verified in Section 4.3.3.2. Figure 9 shows examples of the fake finger-vein images generated for spoof attacks using the DCS-GAN and the SOTA methods. As can be seen, the DCS-GAN effectively creates fake images which are more similar to the real images than those generated by the SOTA methods. The spoof detection results of the SOTA spoof attack methods and the proposed DCS-GAN method are compared in Section 4.3.3.2.

Table 12. Comparison of spoof attack performance by type of post-processing on DenseNet-161 and DenseNet-169 using the Idiap database (metric: ACER, unit: %).

Classification Model	Post Processing	Kernel Size	1-Fold Validation	2-Fold Validation	Average
DenseNet-161	Average filter	3 × 3	1.82	2.27	2.05
		5 × 5	0.91	0.68	0.80
	Gaussian filter	3 × 3	2.27	2.73	2.50
		5 × 5	1.82	2.73	2.28
	Median filter	3 × 3	1.14	1.14	1.14
		5 × 5	0.00	0.45	0.23
DenseNet-169	Average filter	3 × 3	1.36	1.82	1.59
		5 × 5	0.91	2.28	1.60
	Gaussian filter	3 × 3	2.27	2.73	2.50
		5 × 5	1.36	1.36	1.36
	Median filter	3 × 3	2.05	0.91	1.48
		5 × 5	1.59	0.23	0.91

Table 13. Comparing the image quality testing of generated fake finger-vein images by DCS-GAN with testing of those generated by the SOTA methods.

Database	Model	FID	WD
ISPR	Pix2Pix [47]	32.193	7.887
	Pix2PixHD [48]	13.875	10.305
	CycleGAN [18]	23.576	13.792
	CUT [29]	22.565	18.695
	DCS-GAN (Proposed)	7.601	18.158
Idiap	Pix2Pix [47]	55.062	5.750
	Pix2PixHD [48]	24.200	2.625
	CycleGAN [18]	33.176	2.868
	CUT [29]	24.196	3.109
	DCS-GAN (Proposed)	23.351	10.123

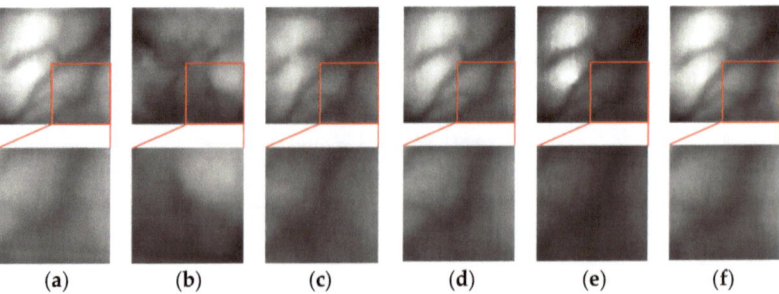

Figure 9. Sample images of fake finger-vein images generated by DCS-GAN and other SOTA methods. Examples of (**a**) original image and images generated by (**b**) Pix2Pix, (**c**) Pix2PixHD, (**d**) CycleGAN, (**e**) CUT, and (**f**) DCS-GAN.

4.3.2.3. FD Estimation for Evaluating Generated Image Quality by the Proposed Method

To evaluate the fake finger-vein images generated by the proposed method, we performed FD estimation, which can serve as a metric to analyze the complexity of and assess the similarity between real and fake images. In this approach, we utilized Eigen-CAM [49] to extract the class activation map (CAM). It can generate the CAM without requiring class labels. Unlike traditional CAM techniques, which are typically used to visualize activation maps corresponding to specific class labels, Eigen-CAM identifies key activation regions in feature maps independently of any class. First, we obtained a CAM that represents important regions from the final layer of the generator's encoder in the DCS-GAN model, and the extracted activation map was then binarized to produce a binary class activation map (BCAM), which was subsequently used for FD estimation. In our research, we did not turn the grayscale finger-vein images into black and white ones. Instead, we turned the red-green-blue color images of the class activation maps for the real and fake finger-vein images into black and white ones for fractal dimension estimation, as shown in Figure 10. In detail, we used the fixed threshold of 180 for the binarization of the red images, where the pixel whose value is higher than or the same as 180 is presented as a white pixel in both cases of real and fake finger-vein images, whereas a pixel with a value less than 180 is presented as a black pixel, as shown in Figure 10. That is because the pixels with a high red value indicate important features in the class activation map [49].

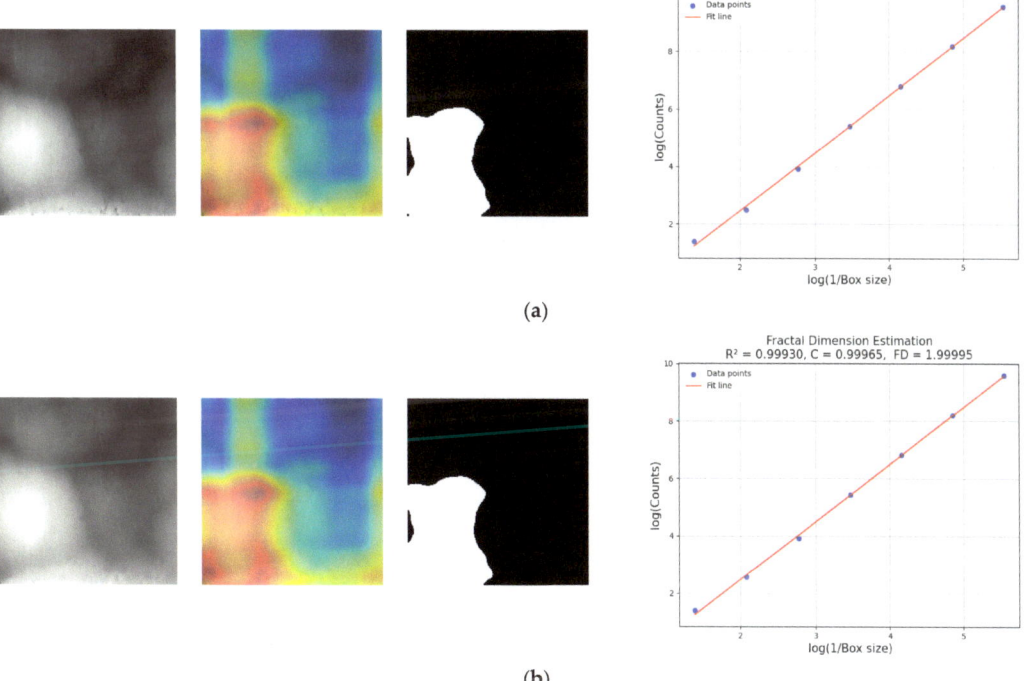

(a)

(b)

Figure 10. *Cont.*

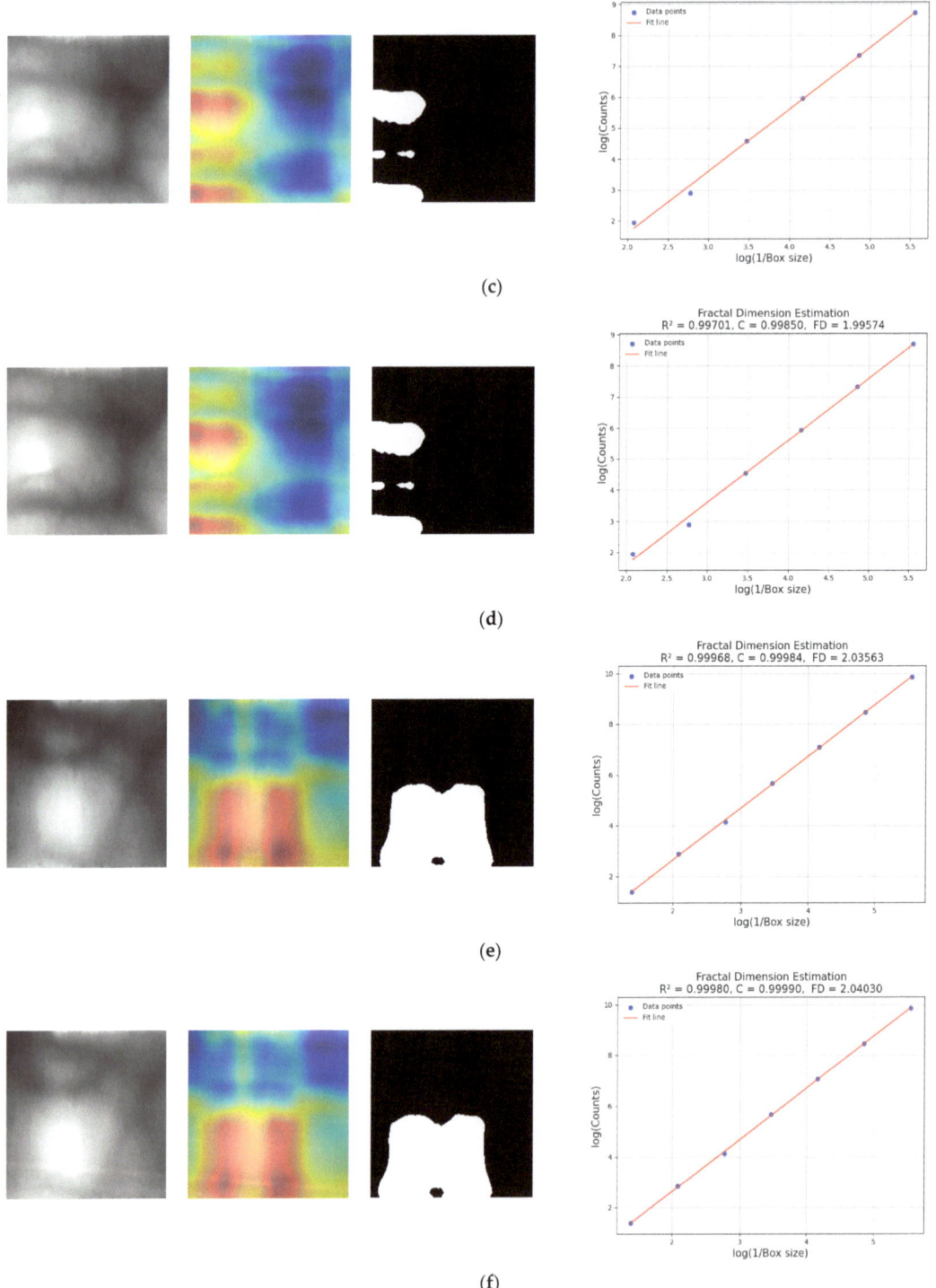

Figure 10. Cont.

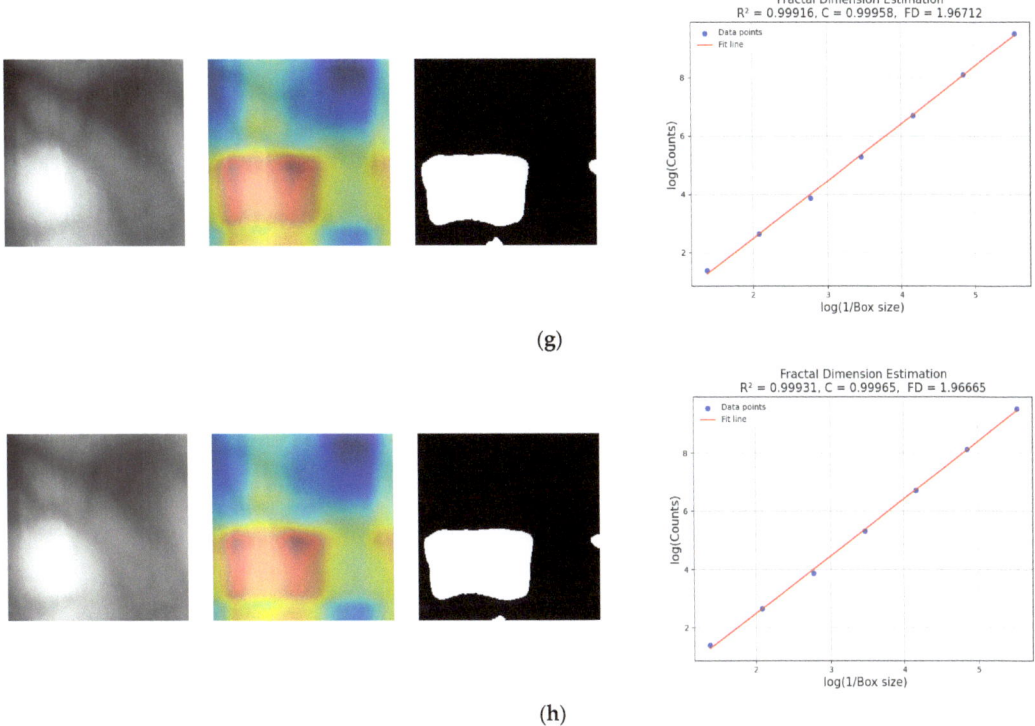

Figure 10. FD estimation analysis for comparison between real and fake vein images: the first to the fourth images, from the left, in (**a–h**) mean finger vein image, CAM, BCAM, and FD graph, respectively. (**a,c,e,g**) show the real finger-vein images whereas (**b,d,f,h**) present the corresponding fake finger-vein images.

The FD values represent the complexity of the BCAM of the finger-vein images. As shown in both Figure 10 and Table 14, the FD values of the real and fake finger-vein images are similar. This indicates that the fake image generated by the DCS-GAN has almost the same level of complexity as the real image, suggesting that the fake image is generated nearly identically to the real one. Therefore, it can be concluded that the fake images produced by the method proposed in this paper are highly similar to the real images while preserving the genuine characteristics of the real images. Furthermore, this suggests that this method can play a crucial role in enhancing the security level of finger-vein recognition systems.

Table 14. FD, R^2, and C values from Figure 10.

Results	Case 1		Case 2		Case 3		Case 4	
	Real Figure 10a	Fake Figure 10b	Real Figure 10c	Fake Figure 10d	Real Figure 10e	Fake Figure 10f	Real Figure 10g	Fake Figure 10h
R^2	0.99903	0.99930	0.99689	0.99701	0.99968	0.99980	0.99916	0.99931
C	0.99952	0.99965	0.99844	0.99850	0.99984	0.99990	0.99958	0.99965
FD	2.00286	1.99995	2.00492	1.99574	2.03563	2.04030	1.96712	1.96665

4.3.3. Performance Test of Spoof Detection

4.3.3.1. Ablation Study

To test the performance of the spoof detection, an ablation study was performed comparing the results of the enhanced ConvNeXt to those of the conventional ConvNeXt when attempting a spoof attack using fake finger-vein images generated by our method. Table 15 shows the performances of the conventional ConvNeXt and enhanced ConvNeXt on the ISPR and Idiap databases.

Table 15. Comparison of performance between enhanced ConvNeXt and conventional ConvNeXt (unit: %).

Model	Database	1-Fold			2-Fold			Average		
		APCER	BPCER	ACER	APCER	BPCER	ACER	APCER	BPCER	ACER
ConvNeXt-Tiny	ISPR	0.24	2.37	1.31	0.12	1.15	0.64	0.18	1.76	0.98
	Idiap	0.00	0.91	0.45	0.00	0.45	0.23	0.00	0.68	0.34
Enhanced ConvNeXt-Tiny	ISPR	0.67	0.97	0.82	0.00	0.61	0.30	0.34	0.79	0.56
	Idiap	0.00	0.45	0.23	0.00	0.45	0.23	0.00	0.45	0.23
ConvNeXt-Small	ISPR	0.79	1.40	1.09	0.42	0.61	0.52	0.61	1.01	0.81
	Idiap	0.91	0.00	0.45	0.00	0.45	0.23	0.46	0.23	0.34
Enhanced ConvNeXt-Small (Proposed)	ISPR	0.43	0.91	0.67	0.06	0.18	0.12	0.25	0.55	0.40
	Idiap	0.00	0.45	0.23	0.00	0.00	0.00	0.00	0.23	0.12

On the ISPR database, the enhanced ConvNeXt-Small (proposed method) reduced the average ACER to 0.4% during one- and two-fold validation, a 0.41% decrease compared with the conventional ConvNeXt-Small. Moreover, the enhanced ConvNeXt-Tiny showed a reduction to 0.56%, a 0.42% decrease compared with the conventional ConvNeXt-Tiny, albeit with a slightly higher error rate than the enhanced ConvNeXt-Small. A relatively higher error rate of 0.16% was observed. In the Idiap database, the enhanced ConvNeXt-Tiny also outperformed the conventional ConvNeXt-Tiny, and the enhanced ConvNeXt-Small (proposed method) showed the best result, with an ACER of 0.12%.

4.3.3.2. Comparisons of Spoof Detection Accuracies by Proposed and SOTA Methods

In this subsection, the spoof detection accuracy of the proposed spoof detector is compared with that of the SOTA spoof detectors. First, for a fair performance evaluation, we compared the performance based on various score-fusion methods used in existing research [3] and a detector trained on generated images from the DCS-GAN, as shown in Table 16. Table 16 presents the performance of existing spoof detectors on these fake finger-vein images obtained by the DCS-GAN. In the experiments on the ISPR database, an ACER of 0.82% was observed, and for the Idiap database, it was 0.34%. In comparison, using the fake-image generation method in the existing study [3], the ACER increased to 0.32% on the ISPR database and 0.23% on the Idiap database, marking increases of 0.5% and 0.11%, respectively. This confirms that spoof attacks using fake images produced by the DCS-GAN more effectively prevent spoof detection compared with the method used in the existing research [3].

Table 16. Performance comparison based on various score-fusion methods used in existing research.

Database	Method		1-Fold			2-Fold			Average		
			APCER	BPCER	ACER	APCER	BPCER	ACER	APCER	BPCER	ACER
ISPR	SVM	Linear	0.06	2.31	1.18	0.00	1.03	0.52	0.03	1.67	0.85
		RBF	0.06	2.31	1.18	0.00	1.03	0.52	0.03	1.67	0.85
		Poly	0.06	2.19	1.12	0.00	1.03	0.52	0.03	1.61	0.82
		Sigmoid	0.00	4.86	2.43	0.00	2.00	1.00	0.00	3.43	1.72
Idiap	SVM	Linear	0.00	0.91	0.45	0.00	0.45	0.23	0.00	0.68	0.34
		RBF	0.00	0.91	0.45	0.00	0.45	0.23	0.00	0.68	0.34
		Poly	0.00	0.91	0.45	0.00	0.45	0.23	0.00	0.68	0.34
		Sigmoid	0.00	3.18	1.59	0.00	0.91	0.45	0.00	2.05	1.02

Next, we compared the performance of the proposed spoof detector with that of the SOTA detectors, as shown in Tables 17 and 18. As confirmed in Tables 17 and 18, the proposed spoof detector exhibits the best performance. Moreover, we verified the equal error rate (EER), as shown in Figure 11, using the receiver operating characteristic (ROC) curves of the true positive rate (TPR) (Equation (18)) according to the false positive rate (FPR) (Equation (19)), similar to previous research [50].

$$TPR = 1 - \left(\frac{1}{I_{real}}\right)\sum_{i=1}^{I_{real}} Detector_i \quad (18)$$

$$FPR = 1 - \left(\frac{1}{I_{fake}}\right)\sum_{i=1}^{I_{fake}} Detector_i \quad (19)$$

Table 17. Comparisons of spoof detection testing errors by the proposed and the SOTA methods on ISPR database (unit: %).

Method	1-Fold			2-Fold			Average		
	APCER	BPCER	ACER	APCER	BPCER	ACER	APCER	BPCER	ACER
Ensemble Networks + SVM [3]	0.06	2.19	1.12	0.00	1.03	0.52	0.03	1.61	0.82
Modified Xception + LSVM [24]	0.61	2.61	1.61	0.30	1.03	0.67	0.46	1.82	1.14
Steerable pyramid + SVM [9]	7.83	2.79	5.31	6.43	1.76	4.10	7.13	2.28	4.71
Modified VGG16 + PCA + SVM [1]	2.79	0.00	1.40	3.46	0.12	1.79	3.13	0.06	1.60
MaxViT-Small [51]	2.31	1.28	1.79	2.31	2.00	2.15	2.31	1.64	1.97
Enhanced ConvNeXt-Small (Proposed)	0.43	0.91	0.67	0.06	0.18	0.12	0.25	0.55	0.40

In Equations (18) and (19), I_{real} denotes the number of real (original) images, and I_{fake} refers the number of fake (generated) images. Additionally, $Detector_i$ refers to the predicted labels obtained from the spoof detector. Therefore, in Equation (18), i will take the value of 1 if the input real image is incorrectly classified as a fake image, and the value of 0 if it is correctly classified as a real image. Additionally, in Equation (19), i will take the value of 0 if the input fake image is incorrectly classified as a real image, and the value of 1 if it is correctly classified as a fake image. As indicated in Figure 11, we confirmed that the proposed spoof detector exhibits the best performance.

Table 18. Comparisons of spoof detection testing errors by the proposed and the SOTA methods on Idiap database (unit: %).

Method	1-Fold			2-Fold			Average		
	APCER	BPCER	ACER	APCER	BPCER	ACER	APCER	BPCER	ACER
Ensemble Networks + SVM [3]	0.00	0.91	0.45	0.00	0.45	0.23	0.00	0.68	0.34
Modified Xception + LSVM [24]	0.00	1.36	0.68	0.00	3.64	1.82	0.00	2.50	1.25
Steerable pyramid + SVM [9]	0.00	1.82	0.91	0.00	2.27	1.14	0.00	2.05	1.03
Modified VGG16 + PCA + SVM [1]	0.45	2.27	1.36	0.91	0.45	0.68	0.68	1.36	1.02
MaxViT-Small [51]	0.91	0.45	0.68	1.36	0.45	0.91	1.14	0.45	0.80
Enhanced ConvNeXt-Small (Proposed)	0.00	0.45	0.23	0.00	0.00	0.00	0.00	0.23	0.12

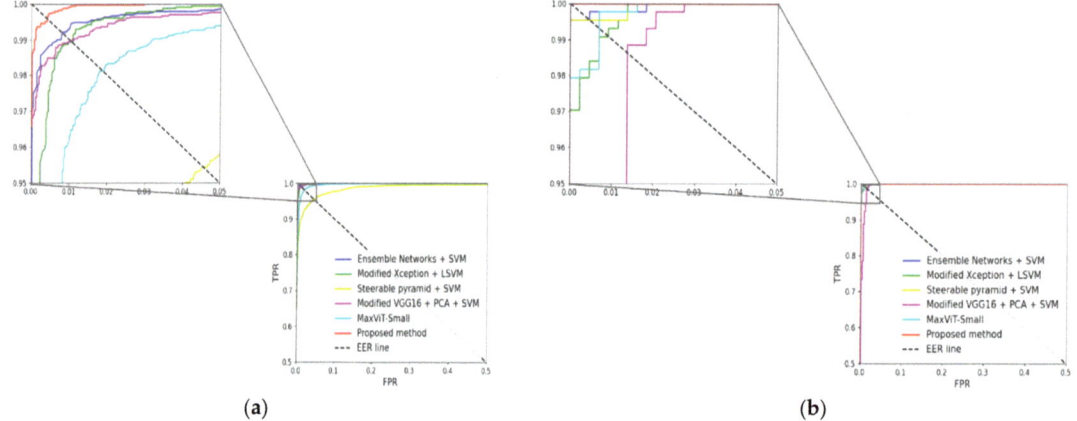

Figure 11. ROC curves of TPR according to FPR by the proposed and the SOTA methods on (**a**) ISPR database and (**b**) Idiap database.

Subsequently, we performed comparisons of the spoof detection testing errors with the use of the images generated by the DCS-GAN and the SOTA methods using the proposed enhanced ConvNeXt-Small detector, which showed the best detection performance, in Tables 17 and 18 and Figure 11. As listed in Table 19, the proposed DCS-GAN had the highest ACER, confirming that the DCS-GAN is the most effective at generating fake images that are the hardest to detect, thus being the closest to real images.

Table 19. Comparisons of spoof detection testing errors with the generated images by the DCS-GAN and the SOTA methods using the proposed enhanced ConvNeXt-Small detector (unit: %).

Database	Model	1-Fold			2-Fold			Average		
		APCER	BPCER	ACER	APCER	BPCER	ACER	APCER	BPCER	ACER
ISPR	Pix2Pix [47]	0.00	0.55	0.27	0.24	0.18	0.21	0.12	0.37	0.24
	Pix2PixHD [48]	0.30	0.49	0.39	0.14	0.28	0.21	0.22	0.39	0.30
	CycleGAN [18]	0.79	0.12	0.46	0.00	0.55	0.27	0.40	0.34	0.37
	CUT [29]	0.00	0.67	0.33	0.28	0.57	0.42	0.14	0.62	0.38
	DCS-GAN (Proposed)	0.43	0.91	0.67	0.06	0.18	0.12	0.25	0.55	0.40

Table 19. Cont.

Database	Model	1-Fold			2-Fold			Average		
		APCER	BPCER	ACER	APCER	BPCER	ACER	APCER	BPCER	ACER
Idiap	Pix2Pix [47]	0.00	0.00	0.00	0.00	0.00	0.00	0.00	0.00	0.00
	Pix2PixHD [48]	0.00	0.00	0.00	0.00	0.00	0.00	0.00	0.00	0.00
	CycleGAN [18]	0.00	0.00	0.00	0.00	0.00	0.00	0.00	0.00	0.00
	CUT [29]	0.00	0.00	0.00	0.00	0.00	0.00	0.00	0.00	0.00
	DCS-GAN (Proposed)	0.00	0.45	0.23	0.00	0.00	0.00	0.00	0.23	0.12

4.3.3.3. Comparisons of Algorithm Complexity

In this subsection, we evaluate the number of trainable parameters (param.), the number of floating point operations per second (FLOPs), and the GPU memory usage of the proposed method. Additionally, we computed the average processing time on a Jetson TX2 board to assess its feasibility in resource-constrained environments. As given in Figure 12, the Jetson TX2 board is equipped with an NVIDIA Pascal™-family GPU consisting of 256 compute unified device architecture (CUDA) cores [52].

Figure 12. Jetson TX2 board.

As indicated in Table 20, the processing time of our method on the Jetson TX2 system is 97.22 ms (10.29 (1000/97.22) frames per second (fps)), with GPU memory usage of 219.16 megabytes (MB), the number of parameters being 51.29 mega (M), and the number of FLOPs being 17.17 Giga (G). While not the best in all metrics shown in Table 20, the proposed method still shows the best accuracies in spoof detection compared with the existing SOTA methods, as demonstrated in Tables 17 and 18 and Figure 11. We also confirmed that the proposed spoof detector operates effectively even on the resource-limited Jetson TX2 embedded board. Although the Modified VGG16 + PCA + SAM [1] and Modified Xception + LSVM [24] were faster in terms of processing time compared to the proposed method, they had certain drawbacks. The Modified VGG16 + PCA + SAM required 2.46 times more GPU memory, while the Modified Xception + LSVM showed higher ACER values, with 0.74% on the ISPR database and 1.13% on the Idiap database, when compared to the proposed method.

Table 20. Comparison of the proposed method and the SOTA methods in terms of average processing time per image, GPU memory usage, number of parameters, and FLOPs on the Jetson TX2 board.

Method	Processing Time (Unit: ms (fps))	GPU Memory Usage (Unit: MB)	Number of Param. (Unit: M)	FLOPs (Unit: G)
Ensemble Networks + SVM [3]	113.30 (8.83)	190.66	39.34	22.27
Modified Xception + LSVM [24]	27.87 (35.88)	96.58	1.40	3.03
Modified VGG16 + PCA + SVM [1]	61.70 (16.20)	538.85	14.71	30.95
MaxViT-Small [51]	218.06 (4.59)	314.98	68.23	22.32
Enhanced ConvNeXt-Small (Proposed)	97.22 (10.29)	219.16	51.29	17.17

5. Discussions

In the spoof attack procedure, the DCS-GAN exhibited performance improvements of 6.274 and 0.845 in FID on the ISPR and Idiap databases, respectively, compared to the second-best model. Additionally, as illustrated in Figure 9, the images generated by the DCS-GAN appear to be more similar to the original images than those generated by the SOTA methods. In the spoof detection procedure, the enhanced ConvNeXt-Small model showed an improvement in ACER of 0.42% on the ISPR database and of 0.22% on the Idiap database compared to the second-best model. Unlike the existing spoof detection methods for finger-vein recognition systems, our proposed method operates without requiring additional classifiers (i.e., SVM) and demonstrates a reasonable processing time, as illustrated in Table 20, making it suitable for resource-constrained embedded environments. However, Figures 13 and 14, respectively, display examples of correct and incorrect spoof detection for real images from the ISPR and Idiap databases, as well as fake images generated by the DCS-GAN. As shown in Figure 13, the proposed spoof detector can accurately distinguish between real and fake images that are nearly indistinguishable to the naked eye. As in Figure 14, camera noise and fingerprint residues present in the real images are mostly eliminated in the fake images. These factors are believed to contribute to the incorrect spoof detection results.

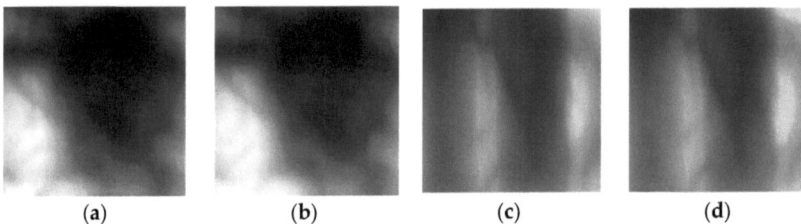

(a) (b) (c) (d)

Figure 13. Examples of correct spoof detection by the proposed method. (**a**) and (**c**) are examples of real images from the ISPR and Idiap databases, respectively, and (**b**) and (**d**) are corresponding examples of fake images.

Additionally, to identify the criteria used by the enhanced ConvNeXt-Small to discriminate real and fake images, we examined the extracted features through gradient-weighted class activation mapping (Grad-CAM) images [53]. Figure 15a shows the Grad-CAM images for real images, while Figure 15b displays the Grad-CAM images for fake images generated from those in Figure 15a. Starting from the leftmost images in Figure 15a,b, the images represent the Grad-CAM visualizations acquired from the first ConvNeXt Block, second ConvNeXt Block, third ConvNeXt Block, fourth ConvNeXt Block, and LKA attention shown in Table 4. In Figure 15, the activation map in red indicates significant features, while blue indicates insignificant features. Comparing Figure 15a,b, we observe that different activation maps are displayed for real and fake images that appear identical to the naked eye. This confirms that the proposed enhanced ConvNeXt-Small effectively extracts crucial features for spoof detection.

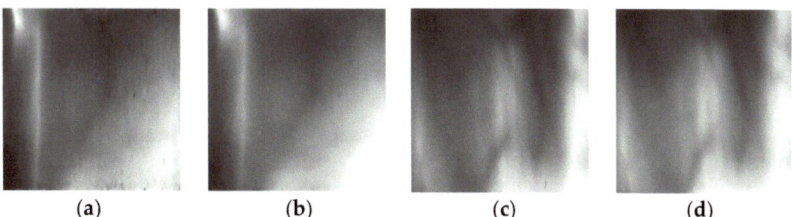

Figure 14. Examples of incorrect spoof detection by the proposed method. (**a**) and (**c**) are examples of real images from the ISPR and Idiap databases, respectively, and (**b**) and (**d**) are corresponding examples of fake images. In the proposed method, (**b**) and (**d**) are incorrectly identified as real images.

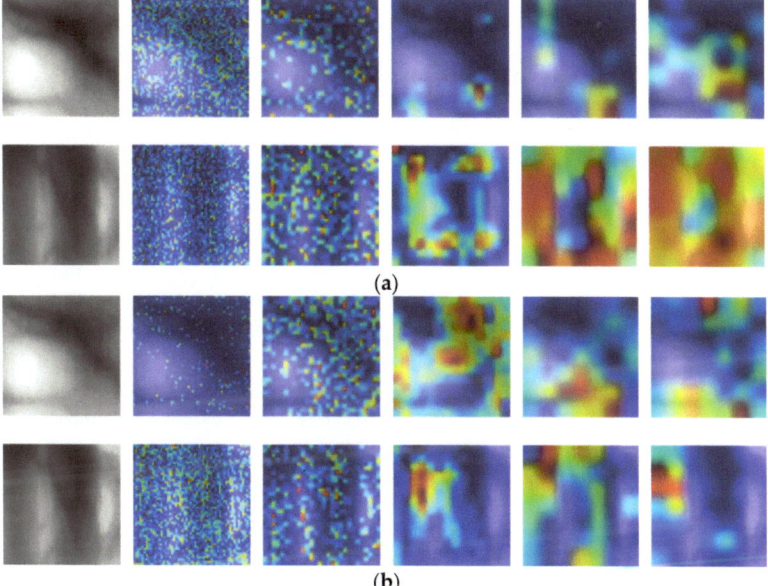

Figure 15. Grad-CAM images. (**a**) shows Grad-CAM images for real images, while (**b**) shows Grad-CAM images for fake images generated from the real images in (**a**). In both (**a**,**b**), the first row is from the ISPR database, and the second row is from the Idiap database. Each row starts with the input image on the far left, followed by Grad-CAM images acquired from the first ConvNeXt Block, second ConvNeXt Block, third ConvNeXt Block, fourth ConvNeXt Block, and LKA attention of Table 4, respectively.

6. Conclusions

In this study, we proposed a DCS-GAN capable of generating fake finger-vein images for training spoof detectors, aiming to mitigate the increasing risks of data spoofing, a negative impact of deep learning-based image generation models, in finger-vein recognition systems. The fake images generated by the DCS-GAN showed an improved spoof attack performance compared to existing spoof attack image generators. Additionally, our proposed enhanced ConvNeXt-Small spoof detector displayed a lower spoof detection error rate than the SOTA methods and effectively extracted significant features, which were confirmed based on Grad-CAM images.

To improve the spoof detection performance of the proposed method, we introduced fractal dimension estimation to analyze the complexity and irregularity of class activation maps from real and fake finger-vein images, enabling the generation of more realistic and sophisticated fake finger-vein images. However, as mentioned in the discussion section, our DCS-GAN aimed to preserve fingerprint residues in fake finger-vein images. However, the loss of these residues in some images made spoof detection easier. Additionally, camera noise contributed to incorrect spoof detection by our enhanced ConvNeXt-Small spoof detector in certain cases.

The proposed spoof detection method can work effectively between the image acquisition module and recognition part in existing finger-vein recognition systems in order to enhance their security level. An alternative usage would be to additionally train existing spoof detectors with the fake finger-vein images generated by our method, thus enhancing the accuracies of spoof detectors. Nevertheless, as illustrated in Table 20, the processing speed of our spoof detector was 10.29 fps on a Jetson TX2 board with limited computing resources. This may be deemed inadequate for real-time application in real-world scenarios.

Therefore, our future work would reduce the processing overhead of our spoof detection model by employing a knowledge distillation method, while improving its performance by considering fake images generated from various generative models, such as diffusion and variational autoencoders. Furthermore, we would apply our method to other biometric data such as palm-vein and hand dorsal-vein images, and explore multimodalities that are robust to external influences and capable of handling global information.

Author Contributions: Methodology, Writing—original draft, S.G.K.; Conceptualization, J.S.H.; Investigation, J.S.K.; Supervision, Writing—review and editing, K.R.P. All authors have read and agreed to the published version of the manuscript.

Funding: This research was supported in part by the Ministry of Science and ICT (MSIT), Korea, under the Information Technology Research Center (ITRC) support program (IITP-2024-2020-0-01789), supervised by the Institute for Information & Communications Technology Planning & Evaluation (IITP).

Data Availability Statement: The proposed DCS-GAN, enhanced ConvNeXt-Small and fake finger-vein images are publicly available via the Github site (https://github.com/SeungguKim98/Finger-Vein-Spoof-Attack-Detection, accessed on 26 July 2024).

Conflicts of Interest: The authors declare no conflicts of interest.

References

1. Nguyen, D.T.; Yoon, H.S.; Pham, T.D.; Park, K.R. Spoof detection for finger-vein recognition system using NIR camera. *Sensors* **2017**, *17*, 2261. [CrossRef] [PubMed]
2. Neves, J.C.; Tolosana, R.; Vera-Rodriguez, R.; Lopes, V.; Proença, H.; Fierrez, J. GANprintR: Improved fakes and evaluation of the state of the art in face manipulation detection. *IEEE J. Sel. Top. Signal Process.* **2020**, *14*, 1038–1048. [CrossRef]
3. Kim, S.G.; Choi, J.; Hong, J.S.; Park, K.R. Spoof detection based on score fusion using ensemble networks robust against adversarial attacks of fake finger-vein images. *J. King Saud Univ.-Comput. Inf. Sci.* **2022**, *34*, 9343–9362. [CrossRef]
4. DCS-GAN. Available online: https://github.com/SeungguKim98/Finger-Vein-Spoof-Attack-Detection (accessed on 26 July 2024).
5. Nguyen, D.T.; Park, Y.H.; Shin, K.Y.; Kwon, S.Y.; Lee, H.C.; Park, K.R. Fake finger-vein image detection based on Fourier and wavelet transforms. *Digit. Signal Process.* **2013**, *23*, 1401–1413. [CrossRef]
6. Tome, P.; Vanoni, M.; Marcel, S. On the vulnerability of finger vein recognition to spoofing. In Proceedings of the International Conference on the Biometrics Special Interest Group, Darmstadt, Germany, 10–12 September 2014; pp. 1–10.
7. Singh, J.M.; Venkatesh, S.; Raja, K.B.; Ramachandra, R.; Busch, C. Detecting finger-vein presentation attacks using 3D shape & diffuse reflectance decomposition. In Proceedings of the international conference on Signal-Image Technology & Internet-Based Systems, Sorrento, Italy, 26–29 November 2019; pp. 8–14. [CrossRef]
8. Ramachandra, R.; Raja, K.B.; Venkatesh, S.K.; Busch, C. Design and development of low-cost sensor to capture ventral and dorsal finger-vein for biometric authentication. *IEEE Sens. J.* **2019**, *19*, 6102–6111. [CrossRef]
9. Raghavendra, R.; Busch, C. Presentation attack detection algorithms for finger vein biometrics: A comprehensive study. In Proceedings of the International Conference on Signal Image Technology & Internet Based Systems, Bangkok, Thailand, 23–27 November 2015; pp. 628–632. [CrossRef]

10. Krishnan, A.; Thomas, T.; Nayar, G.R.; Sasilekha Mohan, S. Liveness detection in finger vein imaging device using plethysmographic signals. In Proceedings of the Intelligent Human Computer Interaction, Allahabad, India, 7–9 December 2018; pp. 251–260. [CrossRef]
11. Schuiki, J.; Prommegger, B.; Uhl, A. Confronting a variety of finger vein recognition algorithms with wax presentation attack artefacts. In Proceedings of the IEEE International Workshop on Biometrics and Forensics, Rome, Italy, 6–7 May 2021; pp. 1–6. [CrossRef]
12. Yang, H.; Fang, P.; Hao, Z. A GAN -based method for generating finger vein dataset. In Proceedings of the International Conference on Algorithms, Computing and Artificial Intelligence, Sanya, China, 24–26 December 2020; pp. 1–6. [CrossRef]
13. Zhang, J.; Lu, Z.; Li, M.; Wu, H. GAN-based image augmentation for finger-vein biometric recognition. *IEEE Access* **2019**, *7*, 183118–183132. [CrossRef]
14. Ciano, G.; Andreini, P.; Mazzierli, T.; Bianchini, M.; Scarselli, F. A multi-stage GAN for multi-organ chest X-ray image generation and segmentation. *Mathematics* **2021**, *9*, 2896. [CrossRef]
15. Wang, L.; Guo, D.; Wang, G.; Zhang, S. Annotation-efficient learning for medical image segmentation based on noisy pseudo labels and adversarial learning. *IEEE Trans. Med. Imaging* **2020**, *40*, 2795–2807. [CrossRef] [PubMed]
16. Choi, J.; Hong, J.S.; Kim, S.G.; Park, C.; Nam, S.H.; Park, K.R. RMOBF-Net: Network for the restoration of motion and optical blurred finger-vein images for improving recognition accuracy. *Mathematics* **2022**, *10*, 3948. [CrossRef]
17. Hong, J.S.; Choi, J.; Kim, S.G.; Owais, M.; Park, K.R. INF-GAN: Generative adversarial network for illumination normalization of finger-vein images. *Mathematics* **2021**, *9*, 2613. [CrossRef]
18. Zhu, J.-Y.; Park, T.; Isola, P.; Efros, A.A. Unpaired image-to-image translation using cycle-consistent adversarial networks. In Proceedings of the IEEE International Conference on Computer Vision, Venice, Italy, 22–29 October 2017; pp. 2242–2251. [CrossRef]
19. Tirunagari, S.; Poh, N.; Bober, M.; Windridge, D. Windowed DMD as a microtexture descriptor for finger vein counter-spoofing in biometrics. In Proceedings of the IEEE International Workshop on Information Forensics and Security, Rome, Italy, 16–19 November 2015; pp. 1–6. [CrossRef]
20. Kocher, D.; Schwarz, S.; Uhl, A. Empirical evaluation of LBP-extension features for finger vein spoofing detection. In Proceedings of the International Conference of the Biometrics Special Interest Group, Darmstadt, Germany, 21–23 September 2016; pp. 1–5. [CrossRef]
21. Bok, J.Y.; Suh, K.H.; Lee, E.C. Detecting fake finger-vein data using remote photoplethysmography. *Electronics* **2019**, *8*, 1016. [CrossRef]
22. Simonyan, K.; Zisserman, A. Very deep convolutional networks for large-scale image recognition. *arXiv* **2014**, arXiv:1409.1556; pp. 1–14, 1–14. [CrossRef]
23. Krizhevsky, A.; Sutskever, I.; Hinton, G.E. ImageNet classification with deep convolutional neural networks. In Proceedings of the 26th Annual Conference on Neural Information Processing Systems, Lake Tahoe, NV, USA, 3–6 December 2012; pp. 84–90. [CrossRef]
24. Shaheed, K.; Mao, A.; Qureshi, I.; Abbas, Q.; Kumar, M.; Zhang, X. Finger-vein presentation attack detection using depthwise separable convolution neural network. *Expert Syst. Appl.* **2022**, *198*, 116786. [CrossRef]
25. Chollet, F. Xception: Deep learning with depthwise separable convolutions. In Proceedings of the IEEE Conference on Computer Vision and Pattern Recognition, Honolulu, HI, USA, 21–26 July 2017; pp. 1251–1258. [CrossRef]
26. Huang, G.; Liu, Z.; Van Der Maaten, L.; Weinberger, K.Q. Densely connected convolutional networks. In Proceedings of the IEEE Conference on Computer Vision and Pattern Recognition, Honolulu, HI, USA, 21–26 July 2017; pp. 2261–2269. [CrossRef]
27. Sengupta, S.; Kanazawa, A.; Castillo, C.D.; Jacobs, D.W. SfSNet: Learning shape, reflectance and illuminance of faces in the wild. In Proceedings of the IEEE Conference on Computer Vision and Pattern Recognition, Salt Lake City, UT, USA, 18–23 June 2017; pp. 6296–6305. [CrossRef]
28. Kang, B.J.; Park, K.R. Multimodal biometric method based on vein and geometry of a single finger. *IET Comput. Vision* **2010**, *4*, 209–217. [CrossRef]
29. Park, T.; Efros, A.A.; Zhang, R.; Zhu, J.-Y. Contrastive learning for unpaired image-to-image translation. In Proceedings of the European Conference on Computer Vision, Glasgow, UK, 23–28 August 2020; pp. 319–345. [CrossRef]
30. Vaswani, A.; Shazeer, N.; Parmar, N.; Uszkoreit, J.; Jones, L.; Gomez, A.; Polosukhin, I. Attention is all you need. In Proceedings of the Conference on Neural Information Processing Systems, Long Beach, CA, USA, 4–9 December 2017; pp. 1–11. [CrossRef]
31. Foret, P.; Kleiner, A.; Mobahi, H.; Neyshabur, B. Sharpness-aware minimization for efficiently improving generalization. In Proceedings of the International Conference on Learning Representations, Addis Ababa, Ethiopia, 26 April–1 May 2022; pp. 7360–7371. [CrossRef]
32. Kingma, D.P. Adam: A method for stochastic optimization. *arXiv* **2014**, arXiv:1412.6980. [CrossRef]
33. Zou, D.; Cao, Y.; Li, Y.; Gu, Q. Understanding the generalization of Adam in learning neural networks with proper regularization. *arXiv* **2021**, arXiv:2108.11371. [CrossRef]
34. Mao, X.; Li, Q.; Xie, H.; Lau, R.Y.; Wang, Z.; Paul Smolley, S. Least squares generative adversarial networks. In Proceedings of the IEEE International Conference on Computer Vision, Venice, Italy, 22–29 October 2017; pp. 2813–2821. [CrossRef]
35. Johnson, J.; Alahi, A.; Fei-Fei, L. Perceptual losses for real-time style transfer and super-resolution. In Proceedings of the European Conference on Computer Vision, Amsterdam, The Netherlands, 11–14 October 2016; pp. 694–711. [CrossRef]

36. Liu, Z.; Mao, H.; Wu, C.-Y.; Feichtenhofer, C.; Darrell, T.; Xie, S. A convnet for the 2020s. In Proceedings of the IEEE Conference on Computer Vision and Pattern Recognition, New Orleans, LA, USA, 18–24 June 2022; pp. 11976–11986. [CrossRef]
37. Guo, M.-H.; Lu, C.-Z.; Liu, Z.-N.; Cheng, M.-M.; Hu, S.-M. Visual attention network. *Comput. Vis. Media* **2023**, *9*, 733–752. [CrossRef]
38. Brouty, X.; Garcin, M. Fractal properties; information theory, and market efficiency. *Chaos Solitons Fractals* **2024**, *180*, 114543. [CrossRef]
39. Yin, J. Dynamical fractal: Theory and case study. *Chaos Solitons Fractals* **2023**, *176*, 114190. [CrossRef]
40. Crownover, R.M. *Introduction to Fractals and Chaos*, 1st ed.; Jones & Bartlett Publisher: Burlington, MA, USA, 1995.
41. Tome, P.; Raghavendra, R.; Busch, C.; Tirunagari, S.; Poh, N.; Shekar, B.; Gragnaniello, D.; Sansone, C.; Verdoliva, L.; Marcel, S. The 1st competition on counter measures to finger vein spoofing attacks. In Proceedings of the International Conference on Biometrics, Phuket, Thailand, 19–22 May 2015; pp. 513–518. [CrossRef]
42. NVIDIA GeForce RTX 3060. Available online: https://www.nvidia.com/en-us/geforce/graphics-cards/30-series/rtx-3060-3060ti/ (accessed on 25 June 2024).
43. Heusel, M.; Ramsauer, H.; Unterthiner, T.; Nessler, B.; Hochreiter, S. Gans trained by a two time-scale update rule converge to a local Nash equilibrium. In Proceedings of the International Conference on Neural Information Processing Systems, Long Beach, CA, USA, 4–9 December 2017; pp. 6629–6640. [CrossRef]
44. Arjovsky, M.; Chintala, S.; Bottou, L. Wasserstein generative adversarial networks. In Proceedings of the International Conference on Machine Learning, Sydney, Australia, 7–9 August 2017; pp. 214–223. [CrossRef]
45. *ISO/IEC JTC1 SC37*; Biometrics. ISO/IEC WD 30107–3: Information Technology—Presentation Attack Detection-Part 3: Testing and Reporting and Classification of Attacks. International Organization for Standardization: Geneva, Switzerland, 2014.
46. Szegedy, C.; Vanhoucke, V.; Ioffe, S.; Shlens, J.; Wojna, Z. Rethinking the inception architecture for computer vision. In Proceedings of the IEEE Conference on Computer Vision and Pattern Recognition, Las Vegas, NV, USA, 27–30 June 2016; pp. 2818–2826. [CrossRef]
47. Isola, P.; Zhu, J.-Y.; Zhou, T.; Efros, A.A. Image-to-image translation with conditional adversarial networks. In Proceedings of the IEEE Conference on Computer Vision and Pattern Recognition, Honolulu, HI, USA, 21–26 July 2017; pp. 5967–5976. [CrossRef]
48. Wang, T.-C.; Liu, M.-Y.; Zhu, J.-Y.; Tao, A.; Kautz, J.; Catanzaro, B. Catanzaro, High-resolution image synthesis and semantic manipulation with conditional GANs. In Proceedings of the IEEE Conference on Computer Vision and Pattern Recognition, Salt Lake City, UT, USA, 18–23 June 2018; pp. 8798–8807. [CrossRef]
49. Muhammad, M.B.; Yeasin, M. Eigen-cam: Class activation map using principal components. In Proceedings of the International Joint Conference on Neural Networks, Glasgow, UK, 19–24 July 2020; pp. 1–7. [CrossRef]
50. Face Anti-spoofing Challenge. Available online: https://sites.google.com/view/face-anti-spoofing-challenge/ (accessed on 26 February 2024).
51. Tu, Z.; Talebi, H.; Zhang, H.; Yang, F.; Milanfar, P.; Bovik, A.; Li, Y. Maxvit: Multi-axis vision transformer. In Proceedings of the European Conference on Computer Vision, Tel Aviv, Israel, 23–27 October 2022; pp. 459–479. [CrossRef]
52. Jetson TX2 Module. Available online: https://developer.nvidia.com/embedded/jetson-tx2 (accessed on 23 July 2024).
53. Selvaraju, R.R.; Cogswell, M.; Das, A.; Vedantam, R.; Parikh, D.; Batra, D. Grad-CAM: Visual explanations from deep networks via gradient-based localization. In Proceedings of the IEEE International Conference on Computer Vision, Venice, Italy, 22–29 October 2017; pp. 618–626. [CrossRef]

Disclaimer/Publisher's Note: The statements, opinions and data contained in all publications are solely those of the individual author(s) and contributor(s) and not of MDPI and/or the editor(s). MDPI and/or the editor(s) disclaim responsibility for any injury to people or property resulting from any ideas, methods, instructions or products referred to in the content.

Article

RGB-D Camera and Fractal-Geometry-Based Maximum Diameter Estimation Method of Apples for Robot Intelligent Selective Graded Harvesting

Bin Yan [1,2,3,*] and Xiameng Li [4]

1 College of Automation and Information Engineering, Xi'an University of Technology, Xi'an 710048, China
2 College of Mechanical and Electronic Engineering, Northwest A&F University, Xianyang 712100, China
3 Shaanxi Key Laboratory of Complex System Control and Intelligent Information Processing, Xi'an 710048, China
4 Faculty of Liberal Arts, Northwest University, Xi'an 710127, China
* Correspondence: yanbin@nwafu.edu.cn

Abstract: Realizing the integration of intelligent fruit picking and grading for apple harvesting robots is an inevitable requirement for the future development of smart agriculture and precision agriculture. Therefore, an apple maximum diameter estimation model based on RGB-D camera fusion depth information was proposed in the study. Firstly, the maximum diameter parameters of Red Fuji apples were collected, and the results were statistically analyzed. Then, based on the Intel RealSense D435 RGB-D depth camera and LabelImg software, the depth information of apples and the two-dimensional size information of fruit images were obtained. Furthermore, the relationship between fruit depth information, two-dimensional size information of fruit images, and the maximum diameter of apples was explored. Based on Origin software, multiple regression analysis and nonlinear surface fitting were used to analyze the correlation between fruit depth, diagonal length of fruit bounding rectangle, and maximum diameter. A model for estimating the maximum diameter of apples was constructed. Finally, the constructed maximum diameter estimation model was experimentally validated and evaluated for imitation apples in the laboratory and fruits on the Red Fuji fruit trees in modern apple orchards. The experimental results showed that the average maximum relative error of the constructed model in the laboratory imitation apple validation set was ±4.1%, the correlation coefficient (R^2) of the estimated model was 0.98613, and the root mean square error (RMSE) was 3.21 mm. The average maximum diameter estimation relative error on the modern orchard Red Fuji apple validation set was ±3.77%, the correlation coefficient (R^2) of the estimation model was 0.84, and the root mean square error (RMSE) was 3.95 mm. The proposed model can provide theoretical basis and technical support for the selective apple-picking operation of intelligent robots based on apple size grading.

Keywords: fractal geometry; harvesting robot; apple; nonlinear surface fitting; multivariate regression analysis

1. Introduction

Nowadays, apple picking still mainly relies on manpower [1–5], which not only requires high labor and time requirements but also poses significant safety risks when picking apples from high places. With the rapid development of machine vision, robotics technology, and artificial intelligence technology [6–15], apple-picking robots are gradually becoming a new direction to replace traditional manual picking in order to reduce labor costs [16–18]. Therefore, exploring and optimizing the key technologies of apple-picking robots in depth to achieve efficient and automated picking operations is of great significance for ensuring efficient apple harvesting and promoting the intelligent development of agricultural production. Among them, intelligent perception of fruit information on apple

trees [19–23] is one of the core technologies of harvesting robots. On the other hand, the current apple-picking operation and the fruit-grading operation based on apple size after harvesting are based on two disjointed processes. In order to improve the efficiency of apple harvesting grading, the picking robot can intelligently detect the maximum diameter of apples on the fruit tree online and then selectively and accurately pick the fruits based on the diameter size, in order to achieve the integration of "intelligent apple picking and grading". This is an inevitable requirement for the future development trend of smart agriculture and precision agriculture, with important strategic significance and practical value.

The financial benefits of robot intelligent selective graded harvesting for apple fruits contains the following: (1) Improving picking and grading efficiency: The apple-picking robot adopts intelligent operation, unmanned driving, autonomous pathfinding, and autonomous path planning, which can operate continuously and greatly improve picking and grading efficiency. On the other hand, robots can accurately identify, pick, and grade apples based on their size characteristics, avoiding waste and errors in manual picking and grading. (2) Reducing labor costs: Traditional apple-picking and grading methods require a large amount of human resources, while robot picking and grading technology can replace some manual labor and reduce the labor intensity of farmers. On the other hand, robot harvesting and grading can reduce losses caused by human factors and ensure the quality of fruits. In addition, robot picking avoids the damage that may be caused to apples due to improper operation during manual picking and grading, improving the quality and commodity rate of fruits. (3) The adoption of advanced robot picking and grading technology can enhance the modernization level and market competitiveness of orchards, bringing more business opportunities and development space for orchards. These helps orchards achieve sustainable development, bring long-term economic returns, and increase market share in apple sales.

Up until now, scholars have conducted research on apple size estimation [24–29], but most of the research is focused on assembly line operations such as fruit quality detection, grading, and packaging under structured and environmentally controlled conditions. The growth environment of fruits on apple trees is unstructured, and the distance and angle between the camera and the fruits on the tree vary. Therefore, the above algorithm cannot directly estimate the size of fruits on apple trees.

On the other hand, Zeze Fan et al. [30] obtained the mapping relationship between the width and height values of the apple detection box and the actual physical size of the fruit based on size measurement, conversion models, and parameters of the Sony ICLE-6000 camera. Based on this mapping relationship, they used artificial intelligence algorithms to obtain the fruit detection box and obtain the diameter prediction information of the apple. However, the experimental verification of the apple diameter estimation model is based on setting the angle between the camera and the apple target to $0°$ and keeping the distance between the camera and the apple fixed at 3 m. In reality, the RGB-D depth camera installed on the apple-picking robot obtains a wider field of view, and the apples are not only distributed in the central area of the camera's field of view. Therefore, the angle between the fruit and the camera will not be a fixed value of $0°$, and due to the presence of the apple crown, the depth distance between each apple and the camera will vary and is not fixed. Therefore, it is not possible to directly apply this model to picking robots for real-time estimation of apple diameter on fruit trees in orchard environments. Shenglian Lu et al. [31] used two apple image capture modes and combined the YOLOv4 convolutional neural network model [32] to detect the position of fruits in two-dimensional images. They estimated the length and diameter of apples on fruit trees using artificial apple reference points. However, due to the fact that this method requires the use of a reference object (an artificial apple model with a size of 90 mm × 80 mm) placed in the camera's field of view to estimate the actual length and diameter of the fruit based on the size of the imitation apple, it is not suitable for robots that need to perform dynamic picking operations in apple orchards.

The research content of this article is related to intelligent agricultural robots; therefore, it is relevant to the research on multi-agent and non-linear systems in this context. Reference [33] proposed a performance-based neural network consensus control method for time-varying non-linear MAS with strict feedback to ensure that the synchronization error quickly converges to a tight error set when all system states are subject to full state constraints. A self-adaptive PI event-triggered control method was proposed in [34] for a class of multiple-input multiple-output (MIMO) nonlinear systems with uncertain input delay. Through the proposed method, MIMO nonlinear systems can dynamically handle input delays of different durations while still maintaining excellent tracking performance. The estimation of the maximum diameter of fruits for apple-picking robots requires precise measurement of the maximum diameter of fruits in an unstructured orchard environment, that is, under constrained conditions (various natural environments in the orchard), with a small margin of error.

Up until now, there have been no reports on the research of real-time estimation of apple diameter size on fruit trees in actual orchard operation scenarios providing technical support for robot "intelligent apple picking and grading fusion". Therefore, this study utilized the Intel RealSense D435 RGB-D depth camera and LabelImg software, based on multiple regression analysis and nonlinear surface fitting methods, to explore the relationship between fruit depth information, two-dimensional size information of fruit images, and the maximum diameter of apples. Furthermore, the correlation between fruit depth, diagonal length of fruit bounding rectangle, and maximum diameter was analyzed. Finally, a model for estimating the maximum diameter of apples based on RGB-D camera fused depth information was proposed. The proposed model can provide theoretical basis and technical support for the selective apple-picking operation of intelligent robots based on apple size grading.

2. Acquisition and Analysis of Maximum Diameter Data for Apples

2.1. Measurement Method for Maximum Diameter of Fruit

According to the differences in fruit tree planting layout, apple orchards are divided into two categories: traditional and modern standardized (or standard). The traditional apple orchard has significant characteristics, with staggered branches between fruit trees, as well as narrow and closed space between rows, which restricts the smooth operation of mechanical work in the orchard. For modern standardized apple orchards (as shown in Figure 1), the dwarf rootstock dense planting cultivation mode dominates. This mode, with its low crown, convenient management, low labor demand, superior ventilation and light transmission performance, uniform fruit coloring, superior quality, and ease of intelligent agricultural machinery operation, has become an effective way to achieve orchard standardization, scale, and intelligent management. This model is widely used in advanced countries for apple production worldwide and is also a core development direction in the modernization process of the apple industry. Among them, compared with other cultivation modes such as "V-shaped", "Y-shaped", and "wall-shaped", the spindle-shaped cultivation mode, as the mainstream type of dwarf rootstock dense planting mode, is highly favored due to its multiple fruiting branches and strong fruit-bearing capacity, and it has become the mainstream choice in modern standard orchard construction. Therefore, the spindle-shaped apple trees in the standardized orchard at the Apple Experimental Station of Northwest A&F University in Baishui County of Shaanxi Province were used as the research object in the study.

Figure 1. Spindle-shaped apple trees in a modern orchard.

The LF01 digital vernier caliper (measurement accuracy: 0.01 mm) produced by Quzhou Gangtuo Tools Co., Ltd. (Quzhou, China), was used to measure and record the true maximum diameter of the fruit on the spindle-shaped apple tree in the modern orchard located at the Baishui Apple Test Station of Northwest A&F University. The measurement process is shown in Figure 2. Among them, multiple measurements of the maximum equatorial circle diameter were taken for each fruit, and the measured maximum cross-sectional diameter data were recorded as the maximum cross-sectional diameter value of the apple.

Figure 2. Measuring the maximum diameter of the apple.

2.2. Measurement Results and Statistical Analysis of Maximum Diameter of Apples

Based on the maximum diameter value of Red Fuji apples measured using a vernier caliper in the previous section, we drew a distribution chart of the data, as shown in Figure 3. As shown in the figure below, the distribution range of the maximum diameter of apples was 50–100 mm, with the concentrated distribution range of the maximum diameter of fruits being 70–100 mm.

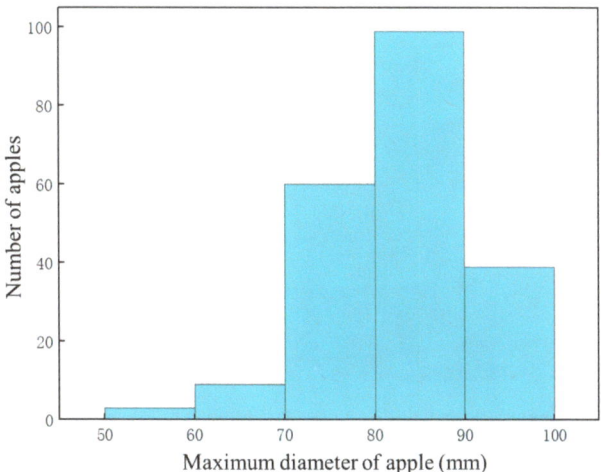

Figure 3. Maximum diameter distribution of fruit on apple trees in a modern orchard.

3. Calculation of Apple Depth Information and Two-Dimensional Image Size

3.1. Apple Depth Information Acquisition Based on RGB-D Camera

The Intel Realsense D435 camera (Intel Corporation, Santa Clara, CA, USA) imaging belongs to structured light-based 3D vision, and its depth measurement is based on the principle of optical triangulation, similar to laser detection. The difference is that the projection light (structured light) used in structured light 3D vision technology is an encoded light source, and the near-infrared signal emitter projects light with certain structural characteristics onto the surface of the object to be tested. The near-infrared images are received by the left and right near-infrared cameras, which can achieve real-time acquisition of depth images of the entire visual range scene and thus obtain information such as brightness, distance mapping, and 3D coordinates of the target object within the visual range. The module composition of the D435 camera and the assembly of the camera on the apple-picking robot are shown in Figure 4, and the schematic diagram of the structured light 3D vision principle is shown in Figure 5.

Figure 4. Module composition of the Intel Realsense D435 camera and its assembly on the apple-picking robot.

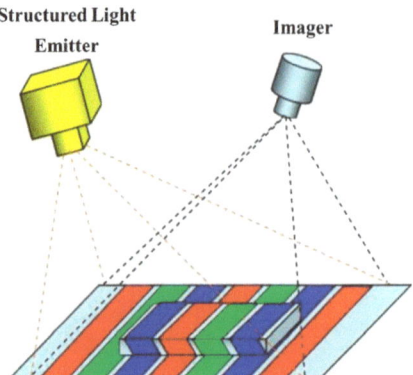

Figure 5. Schematic diagram of structured light 3D vision principle.

In the modern standard apple orchard of the Baishui Apple Experimental Station at Northwest A&F University, an apple two-dimensional image and depth data acquisition experimental platform was built. The main equipment includes a laptop (Lenovo Legion Y7000P, Intel (R) Core (TM) i7-9750H CPU, 2.6 GHz, 16 GB internal storage), Intel Realsense D435 depth camera, digital vernier caliper, etc. For different apple trees, fruit images and depth data were collected at different distances from the apple trees. The experimental scenario is shown in Figure 6.

Figure 6. Acquisition of two-dimensional image and depth information of apples.

Before capturing the image and recording data, we measured the light intensity of the environment at that time utilizing the digital luminometer (Model: TES-1332A), and the light intensities of high light and low light environments were 1.119×10^5 lux and 1.85×10^4 lux, respectively.

The acquisition of an apple's depth information is mainly based on the Intel Realsense D435 depth camera. Due to the inconsistency in size between the near-infrared images captured by the depth camera and the RGB color images, the first step is to match and align the RGB images captured by D435 with the near-infrared images. This was implemented using the Python (version 3.8) programming language, and the main steps are as follows:

(1) Configure the pipeline for streaming transmission to obtain the depth scale of the depth sensor.

(2) Create alignment objects and set the flow type for aligning depth frames, then perform the alignment operation between depth frames and color frames.
(3) Obtain the internal parameters of the aligned frames and color frames, and after verifying that the two frames are valid, obtain the aligned and matched color image frames and depth image frames.

After matching and aligning the RGB images obtained by the depth camera with the near-infrared images, RGB and depth pseudo-color images of the fruit were collected at different positions from the apple tree. At the same time, the depth information of all pixels in the image was automatically extracted and stored in an Excel (version 2016) spreadsheet. The collected RGB color images of apples and their corresponding depth pseudo-color images are shown in Figure 7a and Figure 7b, respectively (The symbol in the lower right corner of Figure 7 is the symbol of the input method software when taking a screenshot of the computer).

(a)

(b)

Figure 7. Apple RGB image (**a**) and corresponding apple depth pseudo-color image (**b**) collected.

The pseudocode that computes the depth information is shown as follows:

```
//Initialize depth camera
initialize_depth_camera()
//Configure camera parameters such as resolution, frame rate, etc.
set_camera_configuration(
stream_type: DEPTH,
resolution_width: 640,
resolution_height: 480,
frame_rate: 30
)
//Activate camera capture
start_camera_capture()
//Define a function to obtain depth information of a certain location
function get_depth_at_position(x, y):
//Waiting for the camera to capture the next frame
frame = wait_for_next_frame()
//Check if the frame has been successfully obtained
if frame is null:
raise_error("Failed to retrieve frame")
//Extract depth data from frames
depth_data = extract_depth_data(frame)
//Check if the depth data is valid
if depth_data is invalid:
raise_error("Invalid depth data")
//Get the depth value of the specified location
depth_value = depth_data[y][x]
//Convert depth values from one unit to another as needed
depth_value_in_meters = depth_value / 1000
return depth_value_in_meters
//Call a function to obtain depth information for a specific location
try:
x_position = 320
y_position = 240
depth_at_specific_position = get_depth_at_position(x_position, y_position)
except error as e:
print("Error retrieving depth information: " + e)
```

LabelImg (Version 1.8.1) is a visual image calibration tool software. In this study, the tool was used to read the collected apple images, and the cursor was manually moved to the centroid position of the target apple. LabelImg can automatically display the two-dimensional coordinate values of the pixel point in real time on the interface, as shown in Figure 8. The non-English term in Figure 8 are belonged to the storage path of the image in the computer.

Figure 8. Obtaining the two-dimensional centroid position of an apple based on LabelImg software.

After reading the center coordinates of the two-dimensional image of the target apple, the depth values at the corresponding coordinate points were obtained from the Excel file that stored the depth data of all pixel points in the image. The depth value distribution of all experimental apples was statistically analyzed as shown in Figure 9. It can be seen from the figure that the depth value distribution range of the obtained apples was 40–240 cm, with the main depth value distribution in the range of 80–200 cm.

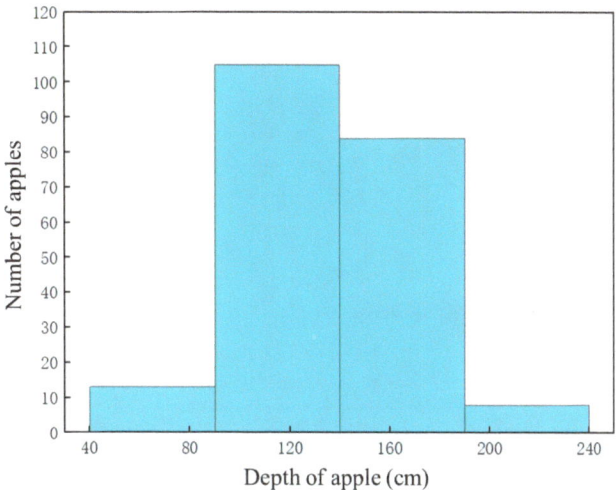

Figure 9. Depth distribution of apples.

3.2. Calculation of Two-Dimensional Size of Apples in Images

The LabelImg tool was utilized to read the collected 2D RGB image of the apple, and the software's built-in manual annotation function was used to draw the minimum bounding rectangle of the target apple. The software can automatically display the length and width dimensions of the rectangle (as shown in Figure 10). The non-English term in Figure 10 are belonged to the storage path of the image in the computer.

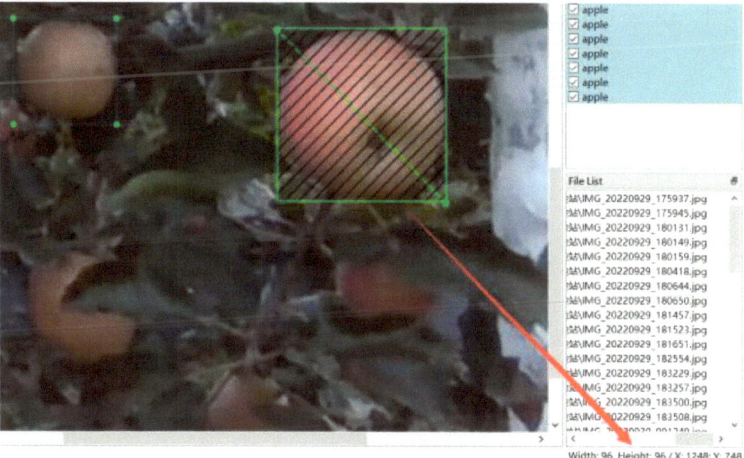

Figure 10. Obtaining the size of the circumscribed rectangle of an apple based on LabelImg software.

Due to the close positive correlation between the diagonal length of the bounding rectangle of an apple image and its length and width dimensions, the diagonal length of the bounding rectangle of an apple image (in pixels) was used to characterize the two-dimensional size of the fruit image. The diagonal length distribution of the bounding rectangle of apples collected in the orchard experiment is shown in Figure 11. It can be seen from the figure that the distribution range of the length of the bounding rectangle of apples was 40–160 pixels (px).

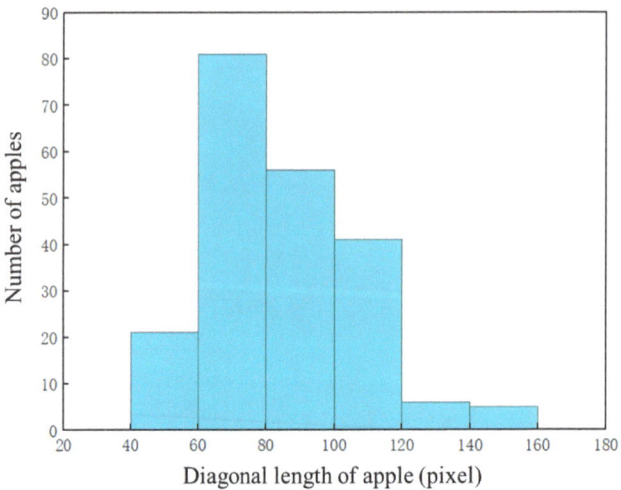

Figure 11. Diagonal length distribution of apple circumscribed rectangle.

4. Construction of the Maximum Diameter Estimation Model for Apples

4.1. Multivariate Regression Analysis of the Estimation Model

Based on the Intel Realsense D435 RGB-D depth camera, this study explored the relationship between fruit depth information, two-dimensional size information, and maximum diameter on apple trees. Furthermore, a fruit maximum diameter estimation model for selective apple picking by picking robots was proposed. Through multiple regression analysis and nonlinear surface fitting methods, the correlation between fruit depth, two-dimensional size, and maximum diameter was analyzed, and a multiple regression model containing the above parameter variables was established.

Binary quadratic polynomials can be used to fit three-dimensional surface models, and the normalized mathematical expression is as follows:

$$z = c_{20}x^2 + c_{10}x + c_{02}y^2 + c_{01}y + c_{11}xy + c_{00} \qquad (1)$$

In the formula, x, y, and z represent data obtained through actual measurement, and c_{20}, c_{10}, c_{02}, c_{01}, c_{11}, and c_{00} are the undetermined coefficients of the three-dimensional surface model expression. The expression for the sum of squared errors of this surface model is as follows:

$$Q(c_{20}, c_{10}, c_{02}, c_{01}, c_{11}, c_{00}) = \sum_{i=1}^{n}\left[z_i - \left(c_{20}x_i^2 + c_{10}x_i + c_{02}y_i^2 + c_{01}y_i + c_{11}x_iy_i + c_{00}\right)\right]^2 \qquad (2)$$

In the equation, (x_i, y_i, z_i) represents the measured and sampled data, where $i = 1, 2, \ldots, n$.

The principle for solving the undetermined coefficient terms in the above binary quadratic polynomial is to minimize the sum of squared errors of the three-dimensional surface model. According to the knowledge of calculus, this problem is transformed into solving the extremum of a six variable function $Q(c_{20}, c_{10}, c_{02}, c_{01}, c_{11}, c_{00})$, and solving the following equations (Equation (3)) simultaneously can obtain the values of the coefficients of each undetermined term of the fitted three-dimensional surface model.

$$\begin{array}{ccc} \frac{\partial Q}{\partial c_{20}}=0 & \frac{\partial Q}{\partial c_{02}}=0 & \frac{\partial Q}{\partial c_{11}}=0 \\ \frac{\partial Q}{\partial c_{10}}=0 & \frac{\partial Q}{\partial c_{01}}=0 & \frac{\partial Q}{\partial c_{00}}=0 \end{array} \qquad (3)$$

Based on the fitting theory of the three-dimensional surface model mentioned above, non-linear surface fitting was used to analyze the correlation between the dependent variable (maximum diameter of the apple) and the independent variables (fruit depth information, two-dimensional size information). The dependent variables of the maximum diameter estimation model for apples were fitted to the general form of a quadratic polynomial model, and the equation was expressed as follows:

$$z = ax^2 + bx + cy^2 + dy + exy + f \qquad (4)$$

In the formula, z is the estimated maximum diameter of the apple (dependent variable, unit: mm), y is the depth information of the fruit (unit: cm), x is the minimum diagonal length of the bounding rectangle of the apple (unit: pixel), f is the intercept, b and d are linear coefficients, a and c are quadratic coefficients, and e is the interaction coefficient.

4.2. Nonlinear Surface Fitting

The three-dimensional spatial distribution map of the maximum diameter, diagonal length of the bounding rectangle, and depth parameters of Red Fuji apples collected from the standard orchard at the Baishui Apple Experimental Station of Northwest A&F University for constructing the maximum diameter estimation model is shown in Figure 12.

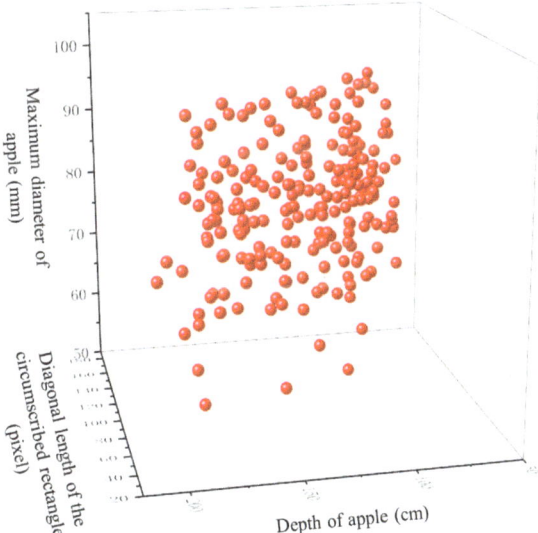

Figure 12. Three-dimensional distribution of the parameters of the maximum diameter, diagonal length of the circumscribed rectangle, and the depth of apples.

Origin is a scientific drawing and data analysis software developed by OriginLab corporation that runs on the Microsoft Windows operating system. Origin supports the drawing of various 2D/3D graphics, including powerful data analysis functions such as statistics, signal processing, curve fitting, and peak analysis. This study conducted multiple regression nonlinear surface fitting analysis on the measured maximum diameter, fruit depth information, and minimum external rectangle diagonal length parameter data of apples using Origin (version 2021) software. The nonlinear surface fitting function setting interface in Origin software is shown in Figure 13. The non-English term and symbol * in the software interface in Figure 13 are prompts for parameter settings, function selection, and other operation buttons for the non-linear surface fitting function.

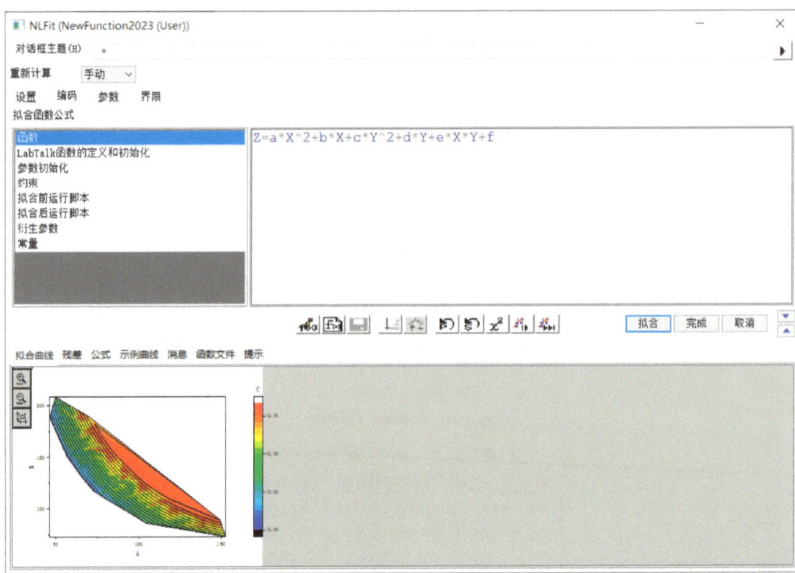

Figure 13. Origin software-based model nonlinear surface fitting setting interface.

The least squares method is a widely used nonlinear surface fitting algorithm in practical applications that determines the optimal fitting surface by minimizing the sum of squared distances between data points and the fitting surface. In this study, the fitting of the estimation model was performed using the Levenberg–Marquardt algorithm (LMA) and nonlinear least squares method for nonlinear 3D surface fitting. The multiple regression based on the Origin2021 execution estimation model resulted in a final fitting state of 'successful'. The coefficient of determination (R^2) reflects the proportion of the total variation of the dependent variable that can be explained by the independent variable through the regression relationship. The higher the value, the better the model. The key fitting parameter results of the constructed maximum transverse diameter estimation model for apples are shown in Table 1. It can be seen that R^2 was 0.80889, indicating that the model had good fitting correlation, and the correlation between variables was high. The model fitting result was good.

Table 1. Fitting results of the estimate model.

Estimating Model Fitting Parameters/Indicators	Parameter Values
Equation	$z = ax^2 + bx + cy^2 + dy + exy + f$
Reduced Chi-Sqr	13.49046
R^2 (COD)	0.80889
Adjusted R^2	0.80421
Freedom	204
Fitting state	Success (100)

The evaluation analysis of the coefficient terms of the multiple regression equation for the maximum diameter estimation model of fruits obtained by nonlinear surface fitting is shown in Table 2. As shown in the table below, the correlation between the coefficients of the estimated model was above 95%, indicating a good fitting effect of the model.

Table 2. Evaluation and analysis of coefficient terms of the multiple regression equation.

Estimate Model Coefficients	Parameter Values	Standard Deviation	t Value	Probability > |t|	Correlation
a	−0.00372	0.00184	−2.02229	0.04445	0.99975
b	1.22207	0.67377	1.8138	0.07118	0.99998
c	−0.00112	9.95579×10^{-4}	−1.12579	0.26158	0.99986
d	0.62816	0.49219	1.27627	0.20331	0.99999
e	0.00241	0.00273	0.88122	0.37924	0.99993
f	−82.58015	61.00251	−1.35372	0.17732	0.99998

The results of the multiple regression analysis of variance for the estimation model are shown in Table 3 below:

Table 3. Variance analysis of multiple regression of the estimate model.

Analysis Indicators	DF	Sum of Squares	Mean Square	F Value	Probability > F
Regression	5	11,648.65712	2329.73142	172.69474	2.82079×10^{-71}
Residual	204	2752.05373	13.49046	-	-
Uncorrected overall	210	1,448,389.83	-	-	-
Corrected overall	209	14,400.71085	-	-	-

The expression of the maximum diameter estimation model for apples based on multiple regression and nonlinear surface fitting is as follows:

$$z = -0.00372x^2 + 1.22207x - 0.00112y^2 + 0.62816x + 0.00241xy - 82.58015 \quad (5)$$

Among them, z is the estimated maximum diameter of the apple, y is the depth of the fruit, and x is the minimum diagonal length of the bounding rectangle of the apple.

Based on the actual maximum diameter, depth, and diagonal length of the bounding rectangle of modern orchard apples, the nonlinear surface fitting results of the apple maximum diameter estimation model is shown in the 3D figure below (Figure 14). Among them, the red small spheres represent each apple data point, and it can be clearly seen that the fitting surface covered the red small sphere data points well, indicating a good fitting effect.

On the other hand, the Intel Realsense D435 depth camera was utilized to collect apple image data in the study. The D435 camera is equipped with the OV2740 RGB sensor, which has a pixel size (the actual size represented by a single pixel in the length and width directions) of 1.4 μm × 1.4 μm. Due to the small differences in the size of individual pixels among different depth cameras, the maximum diameter estimation model for fruits needs to be applied to other depth cameras by multiplying the diagonal length of the minimum bounding rectangle of the obtained apple by a scaling factor k and then substituting it into the expression of the estimation model. Based on the pixel size of the D435 camera, the mathematical expression for the scaling factor k is shown in Equation (6), where k_0 is the pixel size of the camera used, measured in micrometers (μm).

$$k = \frac{k_0}{1.4} \quad (6)$$

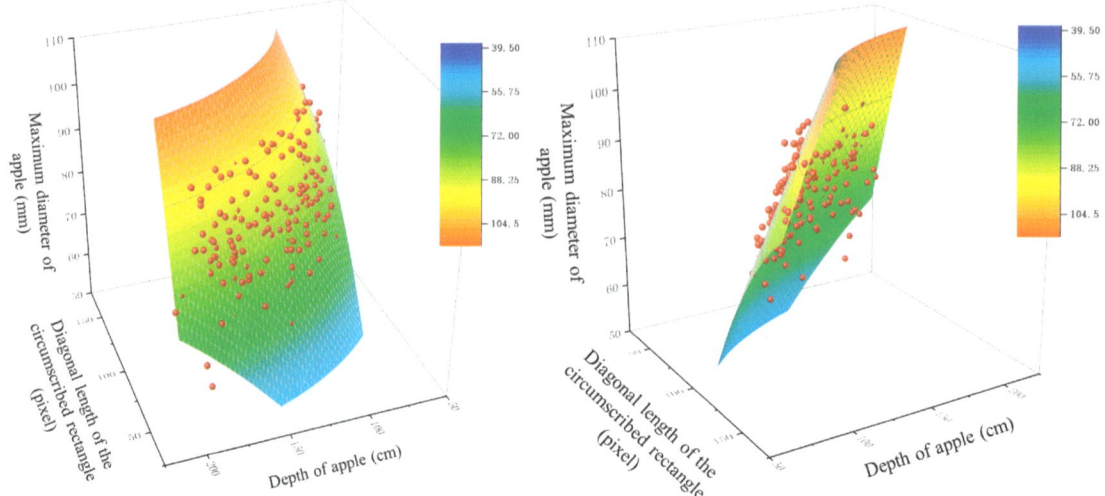

Figure 14. The 3D schematic diagram of the apple maximum diameter estimate model.

Correspondingly, the expression of the maximum diameter estimation model for apples is shown in Equation (7) below:

$$z = -0.00372(kx)^2 + 1.22207kx - 0.00112y^2 + 0.62816kx + 0.00241kxy - 82.58015 \quad (7)$$

5. Estimation Experiment and Result Analysis of Maximum Diameter of Apples

5.1. Estimation and Verification of the Maximum Diameter of Imitation Apples

Obtaining the maximum diameter parameter of imitation apples: Measurement of the maximum diameter parameter of imitation apples was conducted in the laboratory at the fully mechanized apple research base of the Ministry of Agriculture and Rural Affairs. The LF01 digital vernier caliper (measurement accuracy: 0.01 mm) produced by Quzhou Gangtuo Tools Co., Ltd., was utilized to measure the maximum equatorial circle diameter of each imitation fruit multiple times. We recorded the maximum cross-sectional diameter data obtained as the maximum cross-sectional diameter value of the imitation apple. The measurement operation is shown in Figure 15.

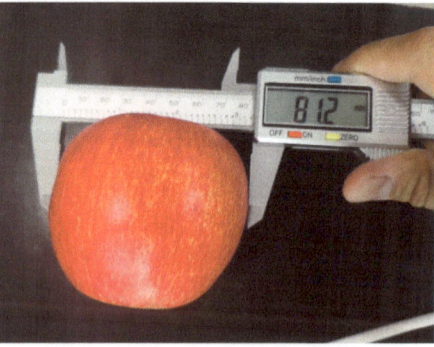

Figure 15. Measuring the maximum diameter of the imitation apple.

The measurement results and data distribution statistics of the maximum diameter of imitation apples are shown in Figure 16. It can be seen from the figure that the distribution range of the maximum diameter of imitation apples was 30–105 mm.

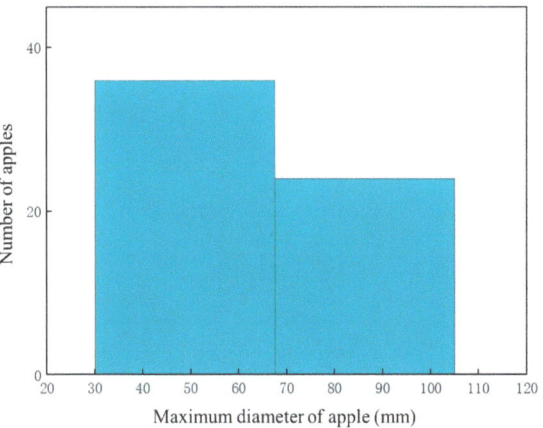

Figure 16. The maximum diameter distribution of imitation apples.

Imitation apples of different sizes in random positions were hung on the apple fruit hanging device in order to simulate the growth posture of real apples on fruit trees more realistically. We placed the fruit hanging device at different distances and positions within the field of view of the RealSense D435 camera to collect RGB and depth images of apples in order to obtain information on apples of different sizes at different distances from the camera, making the collected data more comprehensive and better verifying the maximum diameter estimation model obtained. The scenario diagram of the imitation apple validation test for the maximum diameter estimation model of apples conducted in the laboratory is shown in Figure 17.

Figure 17. Validation test situations for maximum diameter estimation of imitation apples in the laboratory.

Imitation apples of different sizes in the validation set were placed at different depths, positions, and directions facing the camera plane. Based on the D435 camera to capture RGB images of apples and combined with the image data captured by the near-infrared camera, the corresponding depth information of apples was obtained and stored. An example of using the D435 camera to capture RGB images of apples and pseudo-color images containing depth information is shown in Figure 18.

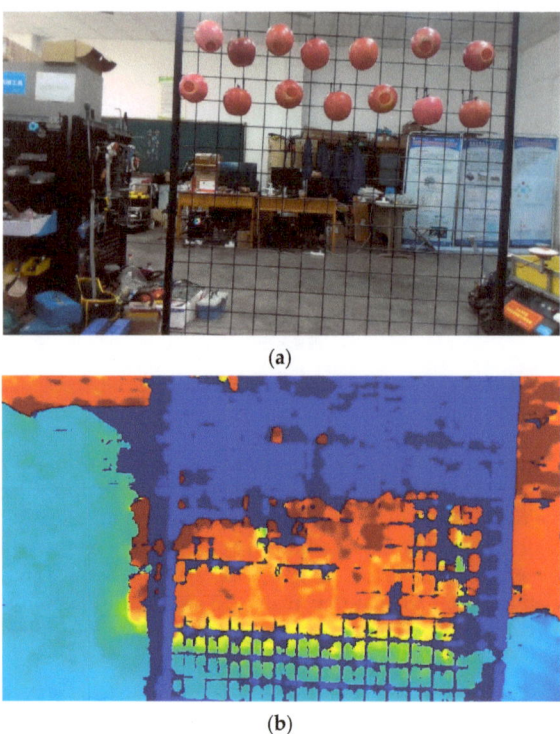

Figure 18. Obtaining the RGB image (**a**) and corresponding pseudo-color image (**b**) containing depth information of apples based on the D435 camera.

The imitation apple depth information collected through the above operation was statistically analyzed, and the distribution of depth values is shown in Figure 19. From the figure, it can be seen that the depth distribution range of the imitation apples in the validation set was 50–300 cm.

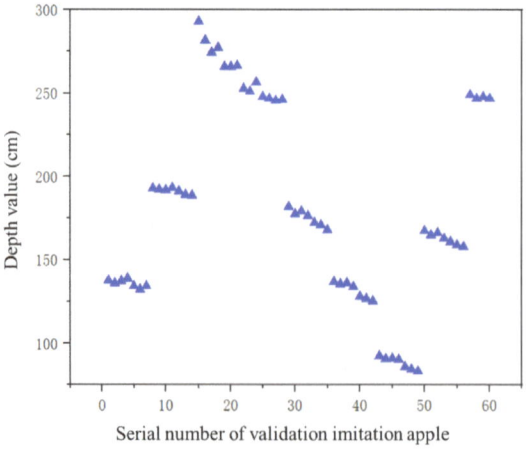

Figure 19. Depth value distribution of the validation of imitation apples.

Based on LabelImg software, we manually selected and obtained the length and width information of the bounding rectangle of each corresponding apple in the two-dimensional image (as shown in Figure 20), and then we calculated the diagonal length of the rectangle based on the Pythagorean theorem. The non-English term in Figure 20 are belonged to the storage path of the image in the computer.

Figure 20. Obtaining the size of the external rectangle of an imitation apple based on LabelImg software.

The diagonal length distribution of the external rectangle in the imitation apple image is shown in Figure 21. From the figure, it can be seen that the diagonal length distribution range of the external rectangular box was 0–200 pixels.

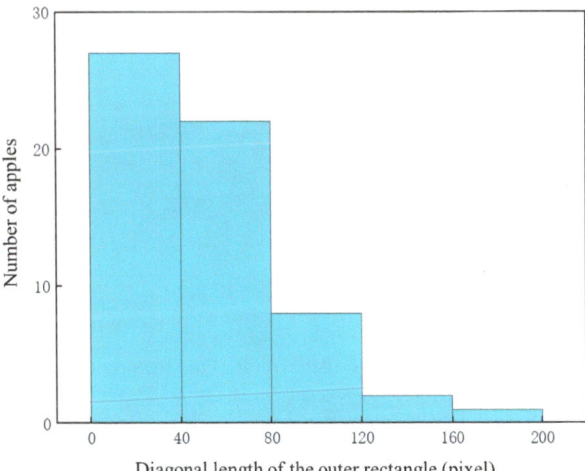

Figure 21. Diagonal length distribution of the outer rectangle of imitation apple images.

Verification results and analysis of the estimation model for imitation apples: Based on the constructed apple maximum diameter estimation model that integrates fruit depth information, the accuracy of the model was evaluated using experimental verification methods. The maximum diameter estimation results of 60 validation sets of imitation apples were compared with their actual measured values, as shown in Figure 22. It can be seen that there was a high degree of agreement between the two, which proves that the obtained maximum diameter estimation model is relatively accurate.

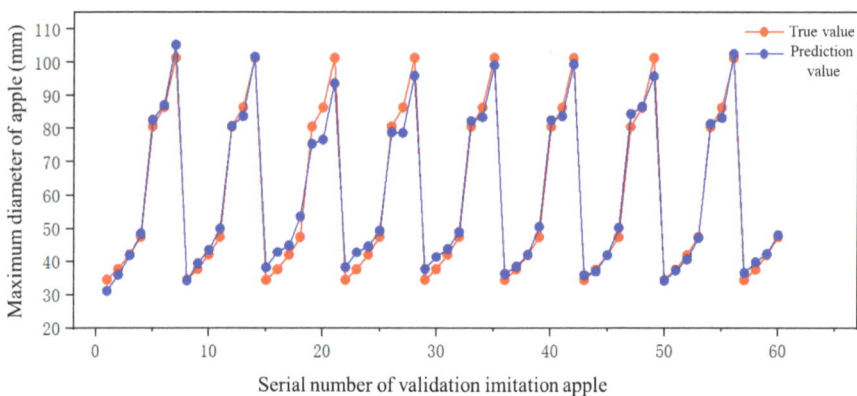

Figure 22. Validation results of the maximum outer diameter estimation model of imitation apples.

Root mean squared error (RMSE) is an evaluation metric used to measure the deviation between predicted and actual data values. The smaller the RMSE value, the more accurate the predicted results are. To measure the difference between the predicted value and the actual measurement value of the maximum diameter of the validation set apple using the fruit maximum diameter estimation model, the maximum diameter estimation relative error ($REE_{Max\_Diameter}$), average estimation relative error ($MREE_{Max\_Diameter}$), and root mean square error (RMSE) indicators are defined, which include variables such as the maximum diameter estimation value ($E_{Max\_Diameter}$), the maximum diameter actual value ($T_{Max\_Diameter}$), and the number of apples (Num_{apple}). The calculation formulas are defined as follows:

$$REE_{Max\_Diameter} = \frac{E_{Max\_Diameter} - T_{Max\_Diameter}}{T_{Max\_Diameter}} \times 100\% \quad (8)$$

$$MREE_{Max\_Diameter} = \pm \frac{\sum |E_{Max\_Diameter} - T_{Max\_Diameter}|}{\sum T_{Max\_Diameter}} \times 100\% \quad (9)$$

$$RMSE = \sqrt{\frac{\sum (E_{Max\_Diameter} - T_{Max\_Diameter})^2}{Num_{apple}}} \quad (10)$$

The relative error distribution of the maximum diameter estimation for all validation sets of imitation apples is shown in Figure 23, with an average relative error of ±4.1% for the maximum diameter estimation.

The linear correlation fitting results between the maximum diameter estimation model of the imitation apple validation set and the actual measured values is shown in Figure 24, where R^2 was 0.98613 and root mean square error (RMSE) was 3.21 mm.

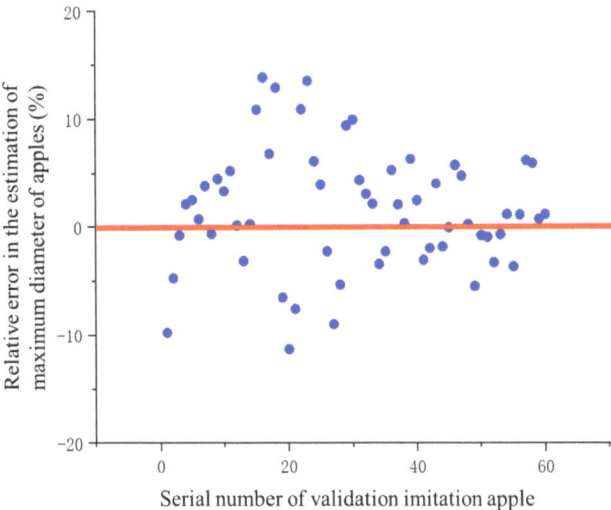

Figure 23. Distribution of the relative error in the estimation of the maximum diameter of apples in the validation set.

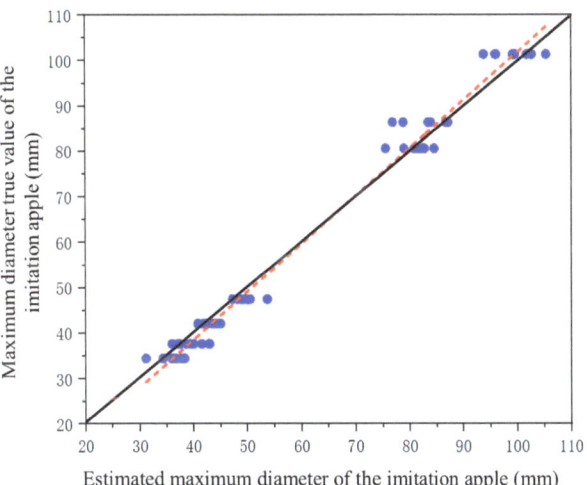

Figure 24. Linear correlation fitting results between the estimated maximum diameter and the true value of the imitation apple in the validation set.

5.2. Estimation and Verification of the Maximum Diameter of Fruits on Modern Apple Orchard Trees

Image acquisition was conducted on fruit trees located in the modern apple orchard at the Baishui Apple Experimental Station of Northwest A&F University. A total of 110 randomly selected fruits of Red Fuji apple trees under spindle-shaped cultivation mode were selected as the orchard apple validation set for the maximum diameter estimation model of apples.

The LF01 digital vernier caliper (measurement accuracy: 0.01 mm) was utilized to accurately measure and record the true maximum transverse diameter parameter value of the fruit on the apple tree. Based on the D435 depth camera installed on the apple-picking robot, two-dimensional RGB images of fruits were obtained at different distances from apple trees for different apple trees. Combined with the data collected by the near-infrared camera, the corresponding depth information of the apples was obtained and stored. The experimental scene is shown in Figure 25.

Figure 25. Verification situation of the test for estimating the maximum diameter of fruit on apple trees.

The actual measurement results of the maximum diameter of the validation set fruits on apple trees is shown in Figure 26. According to the analysis of the figure, the true maximum diameter distribution range of apples was 50–110 mm, with a concentrated distribution range of 70–110 mm.

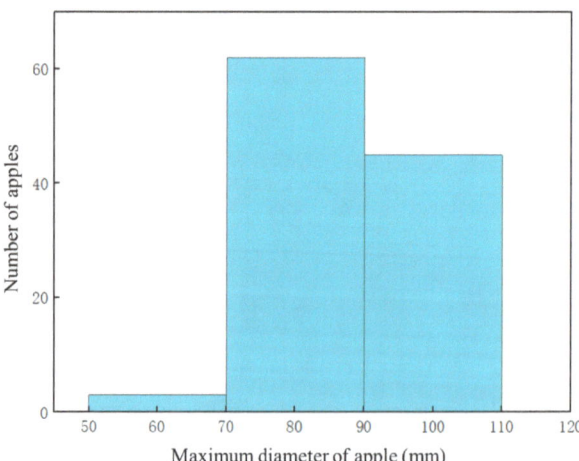

Figure 26. The maximum diameter distribution of fruit of the validation set on apple trees.

Based on LabelImg software and the collected RGB images, the length and width information of the bounding rectangle box of each corresponding validation set fruit two-dimensional image on apple trees was obtained. Then, based on the Pythagorean theorem, the diagonal length of the apple bounding rectangle box was calculated. The length calculation result is shown in Figure 27. As shown in the figure, the diagonal length of the fruit was mainly distributed between 40 and 140 pixels.

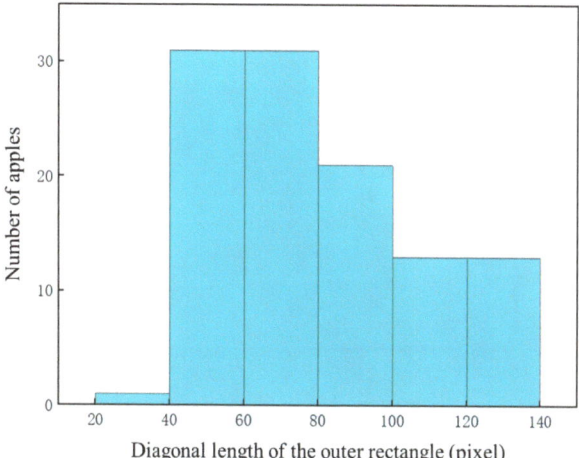

Figure 27. Distribution of the length of fruit outer rectangle diagonal on apple trees.

After obtaining the center position coordinates of the two-dimensional images of the validation set of apples on the fruit trees, the depth values corresponding to the centroid position of the fruit were extracted from the image data containing depth information collected by the D435 camera. The distribution statistics of the depth values of the validation set of apples in the orchard are shown in Figure 28. It can be seen from the following figure that the distribution range of the obtained apple depth values was 80–240 cm.

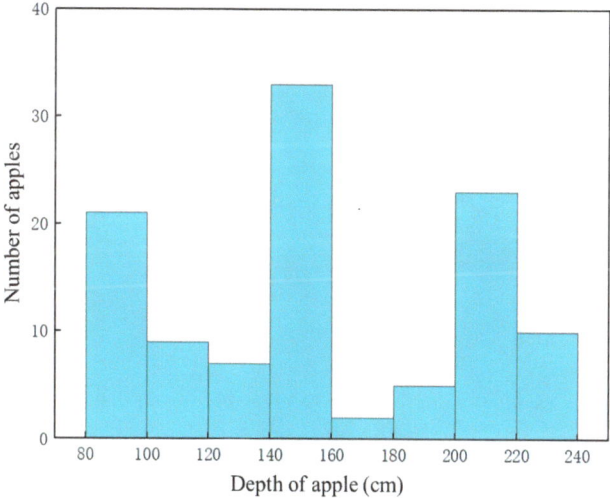

Figure 28. Distribution of fruit depth information on apple trees.

Based on the constructed model for estimating the maximum diameter of apples, its accuracy was evaluated through experimental verification. The comparison between the estimated maximum diameter of 110 validation set fruits on Red Fuji apple trees using the constructed model and their actual measurement values is shown in Figure 29.

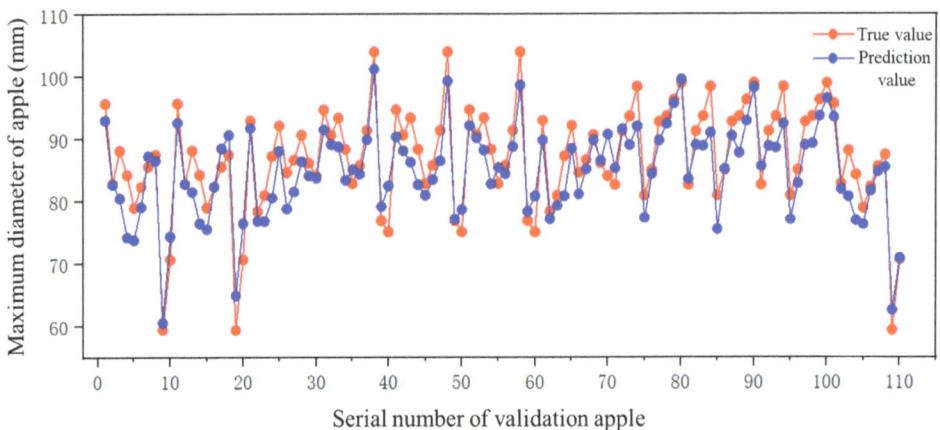

Figure 29. Validation results of the maximum diameter estimation model of apples.

Further analysis and evaluation were conducted on the validation results of the maximum diameter estimation model for fruit estimation on apple trees. The relative error of the maximum diameter estimation for all obtained validation set fruits on fruit trees was calculated, and its distribution statistics are shown in Figure 30. It can be seen that the relative estimation error of the model for the vast majority of apples was within ±10%, with an average maximum diameter estimation relative error of ±3.77%.

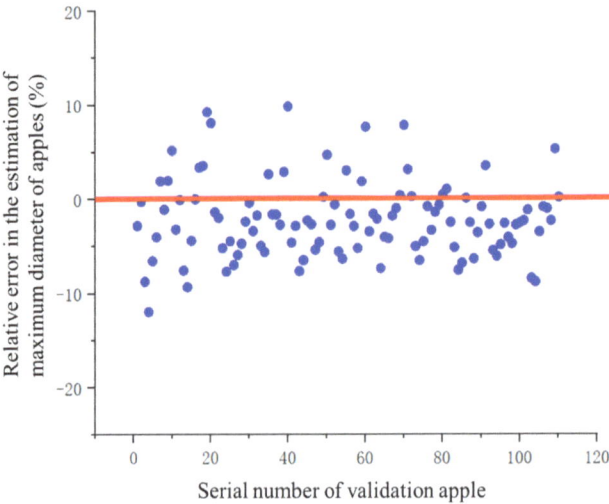

Figure 30. Error distribution of the estimated value of the maximum diameter of validation set apples.

The linear correlation between the estimated value and the true value of the maximum transverse diameter estimation model for the validation set fruits on apple trees is shown in Figure 31. Among them, R^2 was 0.84, root mean square error (RMSE) was 3.95 mm, indicating a good fitting degree, and overall indicating that the constructed model for estimating the maximum transverse diameter of apples based on RGB-D camera fusion depth information is relatively accurate, satisfying the requirements of selective grading and picking of fruits on apple trees by harvesting robots.

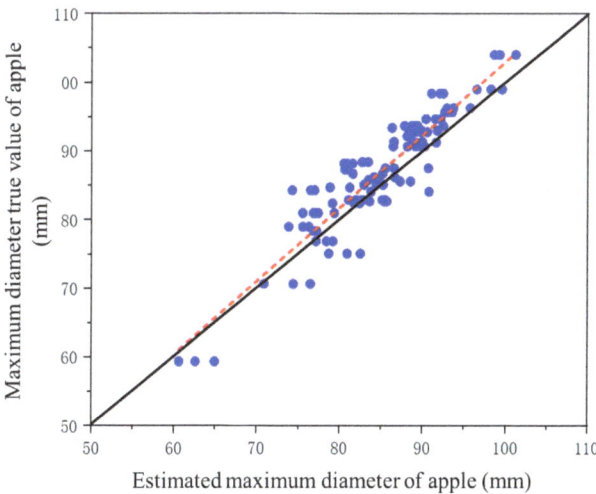

Figure 31. The linear correlation fitting results between the estimated value and true value of the maximum diameter of validation set apples in the modern orchard.

The process of estimating the maximum diameter of fruits on apple trees mainly includes the following steps: Obtaining apple images based on a depth camera, detecting the length and width of the bounding rectangle of the apple, calculating the diagonal length of the rectangle, obtaining the depth value of the center position of the rectangle based on the depth camera, inputting the diagonal length and depth value into the fruit maximum diameter calculation model, and obtaining the maximum diameter of the fruit. The flowchart, which shows the overall methodological approach, is shown as follows in Figure 32:

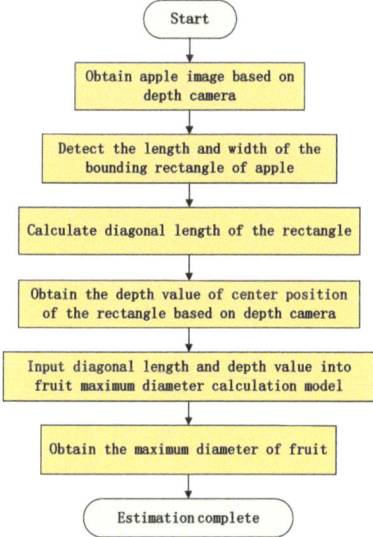

Figure 32. The flowchart of the overall methodological approach.

Based on the proposed maximum lateral diameter estimation model for apples, it is embedded into the YOLOv5 apple target recognition and localization algorithm to achieve real-time estimation of the maximum lateral diameter while detecting and locating apple targets. The real-time estimation effect of the picking robot on the maximum transverse diameter of the apple target is shown in the following Figure 33 (the maximum transverse diameter estimation value of the corresponding fruit is displayed above the detection box).

 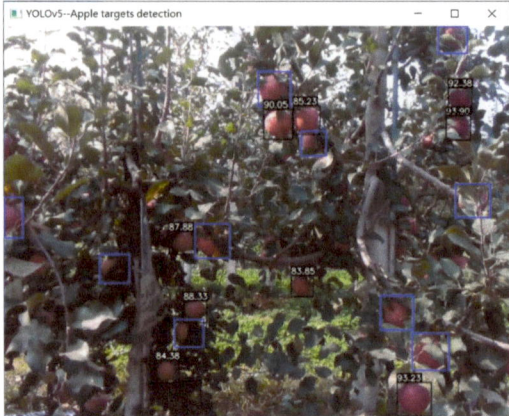

Figure 33. Real-time estimation of the maximum diameter of apple targets.

6. Conclusions

In response to the inability of existing algorithms for estimating the external dimensions of apples to provide theoretical and algorithmic support for robots to selectively pick and grade apples based on their size, a method for estimating the diameter of apples on fruit trees for the actual working scenario of picking robots in orchards was proposed in this study, in order to support in the integration of "intelligent picking and grading" of apple targets on fruit trees.

The maximum transverse diameter parameter of Red Fuji apples was collected from the fruits of modern apple orchards, and the results were statistically analyzed. The depth information of apples on fruit trees and the diagonal length parameter of the bounding rectangle of the fruit were obtained based on the D435 depth camera and LabelImg software. Based on Origin software, multiple regression analysis and nonlinear surface fitting methods were used to explore the relationship between fruit depth, diagonal length of the bounding rectangle, and maximum transverse diameter. A model for estimating the maximum transverse diameter of apples based on multiple regression and nonlinear surface fitting was constructed. Finally, maximum diameter estimation experiments were conducted to verify and evaluate the constructed model for imitation apples and fruits on the Red Fuji fruit tree in modern apple orchards at the Apple Full Mechanization Research Base and the Baishui Apple Test Station of Northwest A&F University. The experimental results show that the average maximum relative error of the constructed model in the laboratory imitation apple validation set was ±4.1%, the correlation coefficient (R^2) of the estimated model was 0.98613, and the root mean square error (RMSE) was 3.21 mm. The average maximum diameter estimation relative error on the modern orchard Red Fuji fruit validation set in the apple testing station was ±3.77%, the correlation coefficient (R^2) of the estimation model was 0.84, and the root mean square error (RMSE) was 3.95 mm. The proposed model can provide a theoretical algorithm basis and technical support for the selective apple-picking work of intelligent robots based on apple size grading.

7. Discussion and Future Work

According to the actual test results of the proposed fruit maximum diameter estimation model in apple orchards, it can be seen that the accuracy of the model can basically meet the requirements of fruit selective grading and picking for apple-picking robots based on the maximum diameter of the fruit. However, the estimation error of fruit diameter in the experimental results shows that there is still significant room for improvement in the accuracy of the model. Therefore, further work needs to collect more apple data of different fruit diameter sizes, expand the dataset used for estimating model modeling, and obtain a more accurate estimation model. On the other hand, the apple variety targeted in this study is the widely planted Red Fuji apple, so the effectiveness of the proposed fruit diameter estimation model in estimating the maximum diameter of other apple varieties is unknown. The excellent universality of the estimation model is necessary for the future development of smart agriculture. Therefore, in later research work, it is necessary to include data from multiple commonly planted apple varieties in the original dataset for modeling a universal estimation model of the maximum diameter of various apple fruits.

In addition, the night picking operation of apple-picking robots is also a development direction for smart agriculture and precision agriculture. Therefore, in later research, it is necessary to collect depth image data of apples at night and then conduct estimation experiments on the maximum diameter of apple fruits at night to verify and optimize the maximum diameter estimation model of apples, ultimately achieving the day/night selective picking operation of apple-picking robots.

Author Contributions: All authors contributed to this manuscript. B.Y. contributed to the development of the algorithm, obtaining data, programming, and writing. B.Y. also performed the experiments, analyzed the results, and contributed to funding acquisition. X.L. contributed to the original draft preparation. All authors have read and agreed to the published version of the manuscript.

Funding: This work was financially supported by the National Natural Science Foundation of China (NSFC) (Grant No. 62406244), the National Natural Science Foundation of China (NSFC) (Grant No. 62473311), and the Doctoral Research Project of Xi'an University of Technology (Grant No. 103-451123011).

Data Availability Statement: The original contributions presented in the study are included in the article, and further inquiries can be directed to the corresponding author.

Acknowledgments: We sincerely thank the editors and reviewers for their detailed comments and efforts toward improving our study.

Conflicts of Interest: The authors declare no conflicts of interest.

References

1. Yan, B.; Fan, P.; Wang, M.; Shi, S.; Lei, X.; Yang, F. Real-time apple picking pattern recognition for picking robot based on improved YOLOv5m. *Trans. CSAM* **2022**, *53*, 28–38+59. [CrossRef]
2. Yan, B.; Fan, P.; Lei, X.; Liu, Z.; Yang, F. A Real-Time Apple Targets Detection Method for Picking Robot Based on Improved YOLOv5. *Remote Sens.* **2021**, *13*, 1619. [CrossRef]
3. Gao, F.; Fu, L.; Zhang, X.; Majeed, Y.; Li, R.; Karkee, M.; Zhang, Q. Multi-class fruit-on-plant detection for apple in SNAP system using Faster R-CNN. *Comput. Electron. Agric.* **2020**, *176*, 105634. [CrossRef]
4. Kang, H.; Zhou, H.; Chen, C. Visual Perception and Modeling for Autonomous Apple Harvesting. *IEEE Access* **2020**, *8*, 62151–62163. [CrossRef]
5. Yang, F.; Lei, X.; Liu, Z.; Fan, P.; Yan, B. Fast Recognition Method for Multiple Apple Targets in Dense Scenes Based on CenterNet. *Trans. CSAM* **2022**, *53*, 265–273. [CrossRef]
6. Ma, H.; Li, Y.; Zhang, X.; Li, Y.; Li, Z.; Zhang, R.; Zhao, Q.; Hao, R. Target Detection for Coloring and Ripening Potted Dwarf Apple Fruits Based on Improved YOLOv7-RSES. *Appl. Sci.* **2024**, *14*, 4523. [CrossRef]
7. Liu, J.; Zhao, G.; Liu, S.; Liu, Y.; Yang, H.; Sun, J.; Yan, Y.; Fan, G.; Wang, J.; Zhang, H. New Progress in Intelligent Picking: Online Detection of Apple Maturity and Fruit Diameter Based on Machine Vision. *Agronomy* **2024**, *14*, 721. [CrossRef]
8. Sekharamantry, P.K.; Melgani, F.; Malacarne, J.; Ricci, R.; de Almeida Silva, R.; Marcato Junior, J. A Seamless Deep Learning Approach for Apple Detection, Depth Estimation, and Tracking Using YOLO Models Enhanced by Multi-Head Attention Mechanism. *Computers* **2024**, *13*, 83. [CrossRef]
9. Gao, F.; Wu, Z.; Suo, R.; Zhou, Z.; Li, R.; Fu, L.; Zhang, Z. Apple detection and counting using real-time video based on deep learning and object tracking. *Trans. CSAE* **2021**, *37*, 217–224. [CrossRef]
10. Zhang, Z.; Jia, W.; Shao, W.; Hou, S.; Ze, J.; Zheng, Y. Green Apple Detection Based on Optimized FCOS in Orchards. *Spectrosc. Spectr. Anal.* **2022**, *42*, 647–653. [CrossRef]
11. Sun, J.; Qian, L.; Zhu, W.; Zhou, X.; Dai, C.; Wu, X. Apple detection in complex orchard environment based on improved RetinaNet. *Trans. CSAE* **2022**, *38*, 314–322. [CrossRef]

12. Wang, Z.; Wang, J.; Wang, X.; Shi, J.; Bai, X.; Zhao, Y. Lightweight Real-time Apple Detection Method Based on Improved YOLO v4. *Trans. CSAM* **2022**, *53*, 294–302.
13. Hu, G.; Zhou, J.; Chen, C.; Li, C.; Sun, L.; Chen, Y.; Zhang, S.; Chen, J. Fusion of the lightweight network and visual attention mechanism to detect apples in orchard environment. *Trans. CSAE* **2022**, *38*, 131–142. [CrossRef]
14. Ye, R.; Gao, Q.; Qian, Y.; Sun, J.; Li, T. Improved YOLOv8 and SAHI Model for the Collaborative Detection of Small Targets at the Micro Scale: A Case Study of Pest Detection in Tea. *Agronomy* **2024**, *14*, 1034. [CrossRef]
15. Yang, S.; Yao, J.; Teng, G. Corn Leaf Spot Disease Recognition Based on Improved YOLOv8. *Agriculture* **2024**, *14*, 666. [CrossRef]
16. Yan, B.; Li, X.; Yan, W. Deep Learning-Based Biomimetic Identification Method for Mask Wearing Standardization. *Biomimetics* **2024**, *9*, 563. [CrossRef]
17. Yan, B.; Quan, J.; Yan, W. Three-Dimensional Obstacle Avoidance Harvesting Path Planning Method for Apple-Harvesting Robot Based on Improved Ant Colony Algorithm. *Agriculture* **2024**, *14*, 1336. [CrossRef]
18. Yan, B.; Liu, Y.; Yan, W. A Novel Fusion Perception Algorithm of Tree Branch/Trunk and Apple for Harvesting Robot Based on Improved YOLOv8s. *Agronomy* **2024**, *14*, 1895. [CrossRef]
19. Kang, H.; Chen, C. Fruit detection, segmentation and 3D visualisation of environments in apple orchards. *Comput. Electron. Agric.* **2020**, *171*, 105302. [CrossRef]
20. Fu, L.; Majeed, Y.; Zhang, X.; Karkee, M.; Zhang, Q. Faster R-CNN-based apple detection in dense-foliage fruiting-wall trees using RGB and depth features for robotic harvesting. *Biosyst. Eng.* **2020**, *197*, 245–256. [CrossRef]
21. Long, Y.; Li, N.; Gao, Y.; He, M.; Song, H. Apple fruit detection under natural condition using improved FCOS network. *Trans. CSAE* **2021**, *37*, 307–313. [CrossRef]
22. Song, H.; Jiang, M.; Wang, Y.; Song, L. Efficient detection method for young apples based on the fusion of convolutional neural network and visual attention mechanism. *Trans. CSAE* **2021**, *37*, 297–303. [CrossRef]
23. Song, H.; Ma, B.; Shang, Y.; Wen, Y.; Zhang, S. Detection of Young Apple Fruits Based on YOLO v7-ECA Model. *Trans. CSAM* **2023**, *54*, 233–242. [CrossRef]
24. Sofu, M.; Er, O.; Kayacan, M.; Cetişli, B. Design of an automatic apple sorting system using machine vision. *Comput. Electron. Agric.* **2016**, *127*, 395–405. [CrossRef]
25. Vakilian, K.A.; Massah, J. An apple grading system according to european fruit quality standards using gabor filter and artificial neural networks. *Sci. Study Res. Chem. Chem. Eng.* **2016**, *17*, 75–81.
26. Li, L.; Peng, Y.; Li, Y. Design and experiment on grading system for online non-destructive detection of internal and external quality of apple. *Trans. CSAE* **2018**, *34*, 267–275. [CrossRef]
27. Zhang, Q.; Gu, B.; Ji, C.; Fang, H.; Guo, J.; Shen, W. Design and experiment of an online grading system for apple. *J. South China Agric. Univ.* **2017**, *38*, 117–124. [CrossRef]
28. Li, J.; Zhang, D.; Liu, B. Design of Conveyer and Turnover Mechanism of Apple Grader. *Trans. CSAM* **2009**, *40*, 158–161+157.
29. Hu, G.; Zhang, E.; Zhou, J.; Zhao, J.; Gao, Z.; Sugirbay, A.; Jin, H.; Zhang, S.; Chen, J. Infield Apple Detection and Grading Based on Multi-Feature Fusion. *Horticulturae* **2021**, *7*, 276. [CrossRef]
30. Fan, Z.; Liu, Q.; Chai, J.; Yang, X.; Li, H. Apple detection and grading based on color and fruit-diameter. *Comput. Eng. Sci.* **2020**, *42*, 1599–1607. [CrossRef]
31. Lu, S.; Chen, W.; Zhang, X.; Karkee, M. Canopy-attention-YOLOv4-based immature/mature apple fruit detection on dense-foliage tree architectures for early crop load estimation. *Comput. Electron. Agric.* **2022**, *193*, 106696. [CrossRef]
32. Yu, J.; Zhang, X.; Wu, T.; Pan, H.; Zhang, W. A Face Detection and Standardized Mask-Wearing Recognition Algorithm. *Sensors* **2023**, *23*, 4612. [CrossRef] [PubMed]
33. Long, S.; Huang, W.; Wang, J.; Liu, J.; Gu, Y.; Wang, Z. A Fixed-Time Consensus Control with Prescribed Performance for Multi-Agent Systems Under Full-State Constraints. *IEEE Trans. Autom. Sci. Eng.* **2024**, 1–10. [CrossRef]
34. Wang, J.; Wu, Y.; Chen, C.L.P.; Liu, Z.; Wu, W. Adaptive PI event-triggered control for MIMO nonlinear systems with input delay. *Inf. Sci.* **2024**, *677*, 120817. [CrossRef]

Disclaimer/Publisher's Note: The statements, opinions and data contained in all publications are solely those of the individual author(s) and contributor(s) and not of MDPI and/or the editor(s). MDPI and/or the editor(s) disclaim responsibility for any injury to people or property resulting from any ideas, methods, instructions or products referred to in the content.

MDPI AG
Grosspeteranlage 5
4052 Basel
Switzerland
Tel.: +41 61 683 77 34

Fractal and Fractional Editorial Office
E-mail: fractalfract@mdpi.com
www.mdpi.com/journal/fractalfract

Disclaimer/Publisher's Note: The title and front matter of this reprint are at the discretion of the Guest Editors. The publisher is not responsible for their content or any associated concerns. The statements, opinions and data contained in all individual articles are solely those of the individual Editors and contributors and not of MDPI. MDPI disclaims responsibility for any injury to people or property resulting from any ideas, methods, instructions or products referred to in the content.

www.ingramcontent.com/pod-product-compliance
Lightning Source LLC
LaVergne TN
LVHW072317090526
838202LV00019B/2299